Germany

Germany

A COMPANION TO GERMAN STUDIES

edited by Malcolm Pasley

METHUEN & CO LTD

11 NEW FETTER LANE · LONDON EC4

First published in 1972
by Methuen & Co Ltd
11 New Fetter Lane London EC4P 4EE
© *1972 by Methuen & Co Ltd*
Printed in Great Britain
by Richard Clay (The Chaucer Press) Ltd
Bungay Suffolk

SBN 416 15260 0/32

Contents

Maps

Tables

Preface

The present volume, like its predecessor edited by Jethro Bithell, aims to provide a survey of the main fields of German studies in such a way that they can illuminate one another. The contributors have borne in mind the requirements both of the student and of the general reader who takes a serious interest in Germany. Each chapter may be regarded either as a starting-point for further study, or as supplying background information for those whose chief interest lies in an adjoining field. In this last respect I hope that the book may help to work, not against specialization, but against a blinkered approach to the separate aspects of German studies.

This edition of *Germany* differs somewhat in scope and shape from the earlier one. The most important additions are the chapters on present-day institutions and on the history of the language. More space than before has been allotted to German philosophy, in particular to the profoundly influential thinkers in the early part of the last century. In the sections on German history, which take pride of place, the fullest treatment is accorded to the events since Bismarck's time which have directly shaped the Germany of today. The chapters on German literature are now shorter, and set themselves a rather different aim: they are designed to bring out the essential pattern of literary development by means of continuous accounts which concentrate on the major authors. The remaining space has been given to the story of German music, which is so closely linked to the story of German thought and literature.

Each contributor speaks for himself, and no attempt has been made to secure a uniform approach. But some community of attitude will be discernible all the same. During the forty years since the first German *Companion* appeared the assumptions brought by British scholars to German studies have changed a great deal, and that change is reflected here. It does not, I think, involve any lessening of the will for a sympathetic understanding of Germany and of her achievements, but it does mean a far greater hesitation in accepting Germany's interpretation of herself, and in particular a far more wary and critical attitude towards the German Romantic movement and all that it implied.

Magdalen College   Malcolm Pasley
  Oxford
March 1971

1 The German Language

L. P. JOHNSON

The word 'German' does not imply a connection merely with the political area which we call 'Germany', though this is one of its uses. Used as a noun it indicates a person belonging either by birth or by adoption to the nation inhabiting Germany, but as a linguistic term it designates not only the language of the fifty-eight million inhabitants of the German Federal Republic and the sixteen million inhabitants of the German Democratic Republic, but also the language of those who use the same tongue without belonging to either of the political units mentioned. Just as a citizen of the USA stranded in a foreign country might inquire of a native whether he could speak 'English', so too might an Austrian ask if he knew 'German' (*Deutsch*).[1] Outside the boundaries of the two German Republics German is spoken, in one form or another, by the vast majority of the seven million inhabitants of Austria, by a substantial majority, some four million, of the population of Switzerland, and by the people of Liechtenstein. German dialects are spoken also in parts of Alsace and Lorraine, in Luxembourg, and in parts of Belgium, for example near Eupen. This is the result of the gradual fixing of the political boundaries between Germany and its western neighbours after centuries of oscillation. In Alsace-Lorraine, when dialect is dropped, speakers revert to French as the standard language, whereas in Luxembourg French or German is the official standard language. Similarly on the southern border of German-speaking territory, south of the Alps in Italy, German is spoken, particularly in the South Tyrol which became Italian only after the First World

---

[1] 'German' and *Deutsch* are almost exactly equivalent. The English word 'Dutch' which is cognate with *Deutsch* used also to have the same sense, but from roughly the sixteenth century onwards it came to be restricted to the Netherlanders except in the contrasting pair 'Low Dutch' (Netherlanders) and 'High Dutch' (Germans), where the older sense survived a little longer. The relation between German and Dutch will be touched on later.

War. Here the linguistic future is very uncertain. In the east under the present political dispensation German has been, or is being, ousted by Slav languages from the former German provinces of East and West Prussia, Pomerania and Silesia, which are now under Polish or Russian administration. Likewise former German-speaking enclaves now to the east of the Iron Curtain, notably in Baltic and Balkan countries and in Russia, some of them dating back to the Middle Ages, were for the most part eliminated during the last war or immediately after it. Where pockets have survived, their days must be assumed to be numbered.

The converse has been the case with the one non-Germanic language spoken in Germany. In the area of Upper and Lower Lusatia, roughly south and south-east of Berlin, there are remnants of the Slavonic-speaking peoples, who once were much more extensive and whose settlements reached as far west as the Elbe. This surviving Slavonic language, which is spoken largely in rural communities, for instance in the Spreewald, is called Sorbian or, more commonly in Germany, Wendish (*Wendisch*). From the later Middle Ages onwards Sorbian was on the wane, while during the National Socialist period its demise was hastened by the hostile policy of the Government. Now, however, the position has been reversed completely. Since 1945 the powers in control in East Germany have striven actively to reinforce the position of Sorbian. The Sorbs have their own educational administration, their own primary and secondary schools and a grammar school in Bautzen, whereas before 1945 Sorbian had been banned as an educational medium.

The only other non-German languages spoken in Germany are Frisian and Danish, though in this case both are, of course, Germanic languages.[1] Frisian, another minority language which is very much on the wane, was once used along an extensive strip of the North Sea coast of (modern) Holland and Germany, as well as on the neighbouring islands. This area has contracted slowly but considerably since the Middle Ages. Frisian flourishes best in its West Frisian form, which has developed a written language, but since West Frisian is a language of Holland, it falls outside our immediate concern. The two forms of Frisian spoken in Germany proper are East Frisian and North Frisian. East Frisian is in a very parlous position. It has vanished from the coastal

---

[1] The distinction between 'German' and 'Germanic' (often called 'Teutonic') will be returned to. For the moment suffice it to say that 'Germanic' is a term which includes Icelandic, Norwegian, Danish, Swedish, Frisian, English, Dutch and German, and their common ancestor or ancestors.

strip and from the adjacent East Frisian Islands and only survives in part of Saterland, in a remote moorland area west of Oldenburg, where it is yielding increasingly to the influence of the Low German dialect which surrounds it.[1] North Frisian, which would appear to be an off-shoot of East Frisian, is used on the more northerly North Frisian Islands, and in a small adjoining area of the mainland. It varies greatly from island to island and between the islands and the mainland. In the past North Frisian has been exposed to considerable interference from Danish, while similar pressure was and is exerted by Low German. It was mentioned that Danish is spoken in Germany, and it is equally true that German is spoken in Denmark. In each case the area involved is just to the south, or just to the north of the political frontier drawn after the plebiscites of 1920. Whereas the German-speakers in the Danish region of South Jutland (North Slesvig) are a substantial minority, the Danish-speakers on German soil are a smaller, less closely knit group.

It is either extremely easy or extremely hard to define the linguistic boundary between German and Dutch.[2] It is easy if we refer merely to the standard or written language. In this case we may imagine the people living along each side of the political frontier as standing with their backs to each other, the Dutch gazing west towards Amsterdam and the Hague, the Germans with their glance fixed on the east and south-east, for these are the directions from which each group draws its linguistic inspiration for purposes of government, education, litera-ture and culture in general. In other words, at this level of language the political frontier is the linguistic boundary, with standard Dutch on one side and standard German on the other. On the other hand, when we turn to everyday discourse, to the level of dialect, or even to the slightly less parochial, though still regionally restricted, level of collo-quial language, we find that the Dutch and the Germans turn to face each other, or at least are capable of facing in all directions. The only language boundaries between Holland and Germany at dialect level are the very minor ones which constitute the limits of single linguistic features and which represent the shadings in a continuous language spectrum from Germany into Holland. The north-east provinces of

[1] The significance of the terms Low and High German is dealt with on pp. 16f.
[2] There is a tendency nowadays to refer to 'Dutch' more pedantically, perhaps more properly though certainly less elegantly, as 'Netherlandic' or 'Nether-landish', terms which include the Germanic language of Belgium, more tradition-ally called 'Flemish'.

Holland (with the exception of the Frisian parts) speak Low Saxon dialect which is also the dialect of North Germany, while the south-west provinces speak what is essentially Low Franconian dialect (from which the Dutch standard has developed), which is also heard in the German areas on the lower Rhine and which forms part of a spectrum merging into the dialects spoken further up the Rhine.

It has been noted several times above that the boundaries between German and a neighbouring language and between Germany and a neighbouring country do not concur. None the less, here as every-where else, there would appear to be a tendency for the language border to fall in with the political one, and this not merely where government policy is directed more or less intentionally and with greater or lesser force against the minority language, such as in Alsace, South Tyrol, or the former German provinces of Pomerania, Silesia and East and West Prussia, but also in the Danish–German districts, where there is, by and large, peaceful coexistence. In short, the tendency for linguistic frontiers to follow political ones is as much a testimony to the closeness of intercourse and intensity of communication in a modern state and to the effectiveness of the media through which they are achieved as to the dictatorial pressure of a central administration.

Unlike several other European languages German is not very im-portant outside Europe, except perhaps as a language of scholarship. This is because Germany was late in entering the race for overseas colonies, and after 1918 lost what colonies she had. In consequence German is not the national language of any overseas state. There are, however, substantial groups of German-speakers in South and North America, in the latter notably in Pennsylvania and Chicago. Here again it would seem merely a matter of time before the national language of the majority submerges the minority language completely.

Germanic and German

As a preliminary to an account of the growth of German it is necessary to clarify certain terms relating to the language and the people. In German we have the following terms at our disposal: *Germanisch* and *Germanen*; *Deutsch* and *Deutsche*. It is not easy to find convenient equivalents in English for these terms. *Deutsch* and *Deutsche* are easily rendered as 'German' and 'Germans' and *Germanisch* as 'Germanic', but *Germanen* presents problems, since it lacks a precise single-word equivalent in English. It is a collective term referring to the peoples who speak the modern Germanic languages, Swedes, Danes, Norwegians, Icelanders, English, Frisians, Dutch and Germans, and to the ancestors of these peoples. 'Germanic', too, is a collective term signifying the older and the modern languages of these peoples and the languages of other Germanic peoples who have vanished from history. *Germanen* are frequently called 'Teutons' in works in English, but this is not altogether satisfactory, partly because the *Teutones*, the tribe whose Latin name gives rise to the form 'Teuton', and whose meteoric descent on the classical world towards the end of the second century B.C. caused astonishment and dismay among the Romans, may have been a Celtic not a Germanic tribe, but chiefly because the use of 'Teuton' puts English out of step with other European languages.[1] Another solution is to call the *Germanen* simply 'Germans', but to refer to the whole group by this name would seem to afford an excessive prominence to those sections who did in fact become 'Germans'. Moreover, to call both *Germanen* and *Deutsche* 'Germans' is a possible source of confusion. For these reasons, on the following pages *Germanen* will be referred to inelegantly as 'Germanic peoples', or, when this proves too cumbersome in a particular context, by their Latin name 'Germani'.

Germanic is, of course, more than a collective term in that it implies things about ancestry, suggesting that all the Germanic languages derive from the same source. This source may have been one parent language or several related parent languages in close contact with one another, the parent language (or languages) being called Primitive Germanic or Proto-Germanic. The latter term tends to stress the re-constructed, postulated nature of the parent language which is no-where attested, though some of our earliest records are assumed to be in a language not far removed from it. The notion of 'contact' is extremely important, since it stresses the human element, language as a means of communication between people. Languages do not exist apart from people, though intense concern with the growth of language, largely in the wake of nineteenth-century biological discoveries such as the theory of evolution, leads us easily to attribute bio-characteristics to the language itself. Not only is it necessary to resist the temptation of endowing the language with biological features, but we must also refrain from transferring assumptions about the genetic relations between languages to their speakers. Speakers of the same language

[1] There is a chance that the word 'German', the etymology of which has never been elucidated satisfactorily, is also of Celtic origin.

may come from different stock, while people of the same stock may speak different languages, if 'stock' has any meaning in view of the long prehistory of man's comings and goings, about which we know as good as nothing. Germanic peoples means above all people who spoke Germanic language(s) as their natural means of communication, and this is their common badge rather than the colour of their hair or eyes, the breadth of their skulls, or for that matter the size of their shoes. Needless to say, the various groups who make up the Germanic peoples have more in common than just their basically similar, though at various stages diverging or converging, languages. They would seem to have shared a common, polytheistic religion, evolved from that of their (Indo-European) ancestors; their tribal organization was similar, despite greater sophistication in some groups than in others, as was their culture in general. It must be realized that the closer the contact between two peoples the more similar their languages are likely to become, a principle which applies whether they are fundamentally different languages or merely dialects or offshoots of the same language. This linguistic levelling may be complete and one group may adopt the language of the other in its entirety, though rarely without the abandoned language exerting some modifying influence on the adopted one, or complete levelling may be achieved by a unified blend of the two languages, or the levelling may remain incomplete with one or both languages adopting individual features from the other. As examples of complete levelling of different languages, where one of two peoples gives up its own language entirely, we could take the adoption of Latin by the conquered Celts in Gaul, or of its descendant by the conquering, romanized Franks in 'France'. Most modern standard languages, for instance English, would serve as examples of eclectic blends with features culled from various dialects, and the internationalization of vocabulary to be found in modern European languages, itself a result of cultural contact, would illustrate adoption of individual features from various languages. Not all features which Germanic languages share need, therefore, go back to the common ancestor(s). They could be innovations of one group transferred through contact to others.

The Germanic languages are themselves members of a large group of languages found throughout Europe and in parts of Asia. This group is called Indo-European, or in German *Indogermanisch*. It includes Latin and the Romance languages, Greek, Celtic, Slavonic, Persian, Indic and several other groups of languages as well as Germanic. All the problems of contact and ancestry which have been hinted at above in connection with Germanic arise on a larger scale and for even more distant periods with regard to Indo-European. This leads us, however, into areas too remote from the German language itself.

Our knowledge of the early periods of the Germanic peoples and languages is fragmentary and has to be patched together from various sources: for the earliest times we are dependent upon prehistory and archaeology, and since the Germani were illiterate we have no knowledge of their language other than reconstructions; later we can learn something from classical Greek and Latin authors, who begin to mention the Germani from the last centuries B.C. onwards and whose accounts are often based on the account of the journey of Pytheas of Marseilles, who sailed to Thule and the amber countries around the middle of the fourth century B.C. Though not always reliable, these accounts offer valuable material which may corroborate archaeological evidence, while their recording of Germanic names of persons, places and gods together with the odd word furnishes us with our first glimpses of Germanic language; we learn more and more of the Germani as they come into closer contact with the Roman Empire, and our knowledge of their language increases with their first epigraphs written in runic alphabets, dating from roughly the third century A.D.[1] The first truly continuous literary monument in a Germanic language is the Gothic translation of the Bible by the Visigothic Bishop Wulfila (310–83).

Although it is often difficult to correlate the cultures revealed by archaeology with linguistic groups, it seems fairly clear that certain cultures which are recognizable archaeologically near the end of the Neolithic and the beginning of the Bronze Age (c. 1800 B.C.) do represent the Germanic peoples who have by this time become a separate and moderately unified entity. They are to be found in southern Scandinavia, the Danish peninsula and northern Germany around the Elbe. Their culture is seen as a merging of two cultures, which are characterized on the one hand by megalithic tombs which are collective graves and by pottery decorated with deeply incised lines or punctate designs, and on the other hand by single-burial in cists, by pottery with patterns produced by impressed cord, and by stone battle-axes, often

[1] Runic inscriptions are found from Britain to the western Soviet Union and from the Alps to Scandinavia. Though the genesis of the runic alphabets is not completely clear, they would seem to have been derived from the Greek alphabet, perhaps via Etruscan agency.

buried with their owner. Throughout the Bronze Age and the early centuries of the Iron Age the Germanic peoples appear to have been relatively static. They expanded their territory gradually eastwards along the Baltic coast of modern Germany and Poland, westwards along the North Sea coast and southwards into the North German plain. This expansion was at the expense of Celts and other peoples. Around the middle of the first millennium B.C. the movement becomes more agitated, possibly as a result of a shortage of land caused by a growing population, the slow sinking of the northern coastline and a deterioration of the climate, detectable by means of geological studies and pollen analysis and apparently beginning *c.* 1000 B.C.

It is only when the movements of the Germanic peoples bring them into immediate contact with the Roman world that any knowledge of their groupings and tribal organization becomes possible. Classical authors, notably Julius Caesar, Livy and Tacitus for the earlier period of Latino-Germanic contact, record several hundred names of Germanic tribes, not all of which are identifiable, or reconcilable with each other, or with the evidence of archaeology, or with the traditions of the Germanic peoples themselves. These traditions, although they become known to us very late after centuries of oral transmission, are often substantiated by archaeological and linguistic evidence. An instance of their credibility is the Gothic tradition, reported by Jordanes (551), that the Goths came from Scandinavia to the Baltic coast of Germany in three ships. Archaeology and comparative Germanic philology show that there is considerable justification for this 'legend' as far as the points of departure and arrival of the migration are concerned, and while we must undoubtedly accord some elasticity to the number of vessels involved, it is perhaps worth remembering that in English 'one or two' can mean 'five'. Though some of the hundreds of tribes of Germani named in classical authors are certainly spurious there must also have been many tribes, especially in the Scandinavian north, of whom the Romans knew nothing. We must imagine the tribes as living in very small communities, which could, however, form themselves into larger groups for special purposes, for instance defence or migration. Defeat or the successful accomplishment of its aim could then lead to the dissolution of the alliance and to regrouping, such political and military organization being very fluid. On occasion a large grouping might prove more permanent, particularly, it seems, when the tribes forming the group had some tradition of being related through descent from common ancestors, or shared a religious cult, or when the political alliance was held together by a particularly powerful leader, who was sometimes raised to kingship.

It is undoubtedly the great migrations of the early centuries of the Christian era which are responsible for the tribal groupings we see, as the Germani emerge from the historical mist of the Germania and begin to throw themselves against the frontiers of the Empire. Tacitus has it for instance that there were three main groups, and modern archaeologists follow him to the extent that they can recognize certain cultural groups which are larger than any individual tribes can have been. The view which would seem to command most support is that for the period around the beginning of the Christian era archaeologists are able to detect five distinct Germanic cultural groups: the *North Sea Germani*, on the North Sea coast of Germany, from whom the Saxons, Angles, Chauci and Frisians emerge; the *Weser–Rhine Germani* who are found roughly between these rivers, and who form the basis of the later Franks and Hessians; the *Elbe Germani*, on both banks of the middle Elbe and reaching south towards Bohemia, who included the Langobards, Quadi, Hermunduri (probably the basis of the Thuringians), Suevi, Alemanni (itself probably a collective term representing an alliance of several tribes of the Elbe Germani) and Marcomanni among others, and from whom it is assumed, for largely linguistic reasons, that somehow or other the later tribal group of the Bavarians was constituted; the *East Germani* (or *Oder–Vistula Germani*), at this time settled on the Baltic coast east of the Oder and extending beyond the Vistula, and consisting of the Goths, Vandals, Burgundians, Gepids and others; the *North Germani* in Scandinavia, who were ancestors of the modern Scandinavians. These five groups were probably each composed of separate tribes who were linked by alliances and common religious beliefs and practices such as we have envisaged above. It is possible that the cultural ties between them were strengthened by their coming together to celebrate religious festivals, or to undertake or renew oaths of political loyalty, or both. The first three groups are those which are known traditionally as West Germanic.

It is impossible for us here to follow the fates of all these peoples, so except for the following brief and fragmentary account of the great migrations only those peoples who were to form the 'Germans' will be dealt with. The most restless and, in terms of establishing themselves as national entities, the least successful Germanic peoples were the East Germani, since everywhere the powerful kingdoms they carved out for themselves by the force of their arms have vanished, and the peoples themselves together with their languages have been absorbed by others. By the second century A.D. conditions on the lower Vistula appear to have become so overcrowded that the Goths left the region and moved away south-east until in the second half of the century they had formed a powerful state in southern Russia stretching ultimately to the Black Sea. In their wake there lay a chain of other East Germanic states stretching back towards the Baltic, the settlements of the Gepids, Vandals and Burgundians. Early in the third century the development of the two Gothic tribes of the Ostrogoths and Visigoths (East and West Goths) was completed. Whereas the Visigoths remained relatively static during the succeeding century, the Ostrogoths occupied a vast area of the Russian steppe, so that their land stretched from the Black Sea back to the Baltic. But expansion eastwards proved the undoing of the Ostrogoths, for in so doing they encroached upon the territory of the eastern, nomadic people of the Huns, whose reaction was an explosive counterthrust which destroyed the armies of Ostrogoths, Visigoths and Vandals, bringing the Huns in three years (by 375) to the Danubian frontier of the Roman Empire. Both Gothic tribes and part of the Vandals sought refuge within the Empire and were granted it. Glad to have a buffer against the Huns, the Romans settled these East Germani along the Danube. It was in the second half of the fourth century that the Goths and Vandals, and other Germanic peoples settled near them, became converted to Christianity, and it was during this period that the Visigothic Bishop Wulfila produced his translation of the Bible, a feat for which he had not only to manufacture or borrow from Greek much of his vocabulary but also, according to early sources, devise his own alphabet. From now on the fate of the Goths is linked intimately with the fall of the Western Roman Empire. The growing use of Germanic and Hunnish mercenaries made the Empire, which was largely without cavalry, increasingly dependent upon them, and gradually their generals acquired considerable political power. It remains for us to trace, very briefly, the career of the Goths to its end and to allow this career to typify the fate of the other East Germani.

Soon after their settlement in the Empire on the lower Danube the Visigoths revolted against their 'protectors'. A series of ineffectual victories in battle and of resounding defeats in diplomacy led to their being resettled in north-west Greece, whence they made an unsuccessful attack on Italy and were defeated by the Vandal general, Stilicho. From here they proceeded to Spain in 414, attacking and destroying the states which had been founded there by a coalition of the Suevi, of the part of the Vandals which had not been settled in the Empire, and of others. In 417 the Visigoths withdrew to south-west France, where with Roman acquiescence they founded a kingdom, which they had extended to cover most of Spain and south-west France by the time of the final disintegration of the Western Empire in the last decades of the fifth century. Here they remained until they were engulfed by the tide of Islam in 711. As a national entity they vanished, being absorbed into the subsequent population of Spain, and leaving as traces of their language only loan-words in Spanish such as *hato* ('herd'), *ropa* ('clothing'), or proper names like *Alfonso*, *Fernando*, and also place-names.

The lot of the Ostrogoths was not to be very different. Towards the end of the fifth century the Eastern Empire was having trouble with its Ostrogothic federates, so the Government in Constantinople thought to kill two birds with one stone by sending off the Ostrogothic army led by Theodoric (the Great) to conquer the kingdom of Italy. Italy was ruled by the barbarian general Odoacer, who, nominally, owed allegiance to the Eastern Empire. By 493 Theodoric had achieved victory and made himself ruler of an enlarged Italian kingdom. The period from then until Theodoric's death in 526 represents the highest point of Gothic power, with Spain, much of France, Italy and part of the Balkans under their control. The Vandals, too, who had by now crossed to North Africa, ruled considerable areas including Corsica, Sardinia, the Balearic Isles and a coastal strip of Tunisia and Tripolitania, the latter somewhat reduced by Berber attacks. The emperor Justinian, determined to reconquer the Western Empire, inflicted a crushing defeat on the Vandals in 533, then turned to attack the Ostrogoths in Italy. Despite early setbacks the latter managed to hold out until their final defeat in 563. They, too, vanish from history, merging into the people of Italy and leaving a few linguistic relics such as *fiasco* ('bottle') and, appropriately, *bega* ('quarrel'), or place-names ending in *-engo*, for example Marengo in Northern Italy. There is some difficulty in distinguishing the Ostrogothic contribution to Italian, since the influence of the Ostrogoths is largely overlaid by that of the West Germanic people of the Langobards who followed them as rulers of most of Italy, and the remnants of whose Germanic language are not always distinguishable from those of Gothic. To round off this account of the Goths the Crimean Goths deserve mention. In the second half of the third century Goths had settled in the southern Crimea. They did not flee to the Empire with the other Goths and it must be assumed that they were forced to submit to Hunnish suzerainty. Though mixed with other peoples these Goths remained in the Crimea and retained their identity until relatively recent times. In 1560-2 Busbecq, an imperial ambassador to the Sultan, was able to write down eighty-six words of Gothic which he had collected in the Crimea and which he found akin to his native Flemish. It is thought that Crimean Gothic did not die out entirely until the eighteenth century.

If the Migrations of the Peoples (*Völkerwanderung*) began, as was mentioned, chiefly by reason of the shortage of land, it must be clear that their subsequent course was not always determined purely by this economic factor. Much of the bewildering coming and going, grouping and regrouping, was the product of a chain reaction, in which a people in motion would collide with a static people, setting them in motion and so on like balls in a game of snooker. The most extreme case we have seen is that of the Ostrogoths apparently setting the Huns in motion, an action which had the most profound consequences throughout central Europe from the last quarter of the fourth century to the last quarter of the fifth, since the mere fear of the Huns was often sufficient to cause a tribe to migrate. The tribes constituting the North Sea Germani, the Elbe Germani and the Weser–Rhine Germani whom I shall refer to henceforth collectively as West Germani had also been on the move. But though the bulk of the Elbe Germani had spread to southern Germany and Austria by the early fifth century, on the whole the movements of the West Germani, except where some of them threw in their lot with the East Germani, were not the long-range lightning thrusts which led Goths and Vandals from Scandinavia to the Baltic coast, to the Black Sea, to Greece, to Italy, to Spain and to North Africa. The close contact which the West Germani maintained with traditional Germanic territory may explain why they were mostly able to preserve their national identity, while the East Germani were submerged in the numerically superior, non-Germanic peoples around them. At first the West Germani built up against the Roman frontier, formed by the Rhine, the *Limes* (a system of fortifications running generally south-east from near the confluence of the Rhine and Moselle to the Danube near Regensburg) and the Danube, until the middle of the third century when the pent-up forces burst the obstacle in their path, Franks crossing the Rhine and Alemanni breaking through the *Limes* and driving a wedge into Roman territory as far as the upper reaches of the Rhine, which became the frontier until it was crossed early in the fifth century. At this time the following Germanic peoples were arrayed along both banks of the Rhine (proceeding from the sea to Lake Constance): Frisians, Franks, Burgundians (an East Germanic people with a kingdom on the middle Rhine) and Alemanni. In the rear of the Franks were Saxons and behind the Alemanni, Thuringians.

By 450 the Huns under Attila had swamped all these tribes, except the Frisians and part of the Franks. The Burgundians, apparently singled out for the typical fate of the East Germani, were almost annihilated, their remnants being accepted as federates and settled near Lake Geneva by the Romans, who, distrustful of Burgundian power, may perhaps have engineered the Hunnish attack. The catastrophe is commemorated, with modification, in the *Nibelungenlied*. Attila advanced into Gaul and reached as far west as Orléans, but he was met by an army of Franks, Romans and others at Campus Mauriacus in 451. The outcome is not altogether clear, but the Huns withdrew. Attila died in Hungary in 453, and during the following dissent among his sons the hitherto subjugated East Germanic Gepids led a revolt which in the battle of Nedao (454) finally broke the power of the Huns in western and central Europe.

After the withdrawal of the Huns, whose attack on Gaul had helped complete the break-up of the Western Empire, the Frisians, Franks, Alemanni, Saxons and Thuringians re-emerge, as do the Burgundians who made themselves masters of a large belt of land stretching from Switzerland to the Mediterranean between the kingdom of Italy and the Visigothic kingdom in Spain and south-west France. A new territorial unit is the kingdom of Soissons in the north-west of France on both banks of the Seine. It represents the last vestige of Gaul in Roman hands. The four centuries from 470 on see a gradual expansion, not without checks, of the Franks, who gradually conquer their neighbours on all sides, but since this growth of the Frankish kingdom represents really the beginning of German, it will be dealt with in the following section. There remain, however, one or two points to be made for the sake of tidiness. An important migration not yet mentioned was that of Saxons, Angles and Jutes from northern Germany and the Danish peninsula to Britain.[1] This move takes place from *c.* 450 onwards. Another important event concerning West Germanic people is the appearance in Bohemia towards the end of the fifth century of a new tribal grouping, the Bavarians. So far the ingredients of the grouping have not been analysed with any certainty.

[1] The precise composition and geographical origin of the settlers in Britain is not known and is hotly contested.

Finally, since we have reached the period when a small number of literary monuments in Germanic languages is available and when the amount of material to be culled from classical authors is fairly large, it would seem to be the point to mention some of the features which distinguish the Germanic languages from the other Indo-European tongues and probably, therefore, from the parent language. Germanic has some features which, while we assume them not to have been present in the parent language, are none the less shared by one, or perhaps even two or three other groups, particularly by Celtic and Italic. This would seem to point to close neighbourly proximity at various stages. But the two features of the Germanic languages to be mentioned here belong to Germanic alone. The first, and perhaps most far-reaching of all, is the fixing of the stress-accent of words on the root syllable, usually the first syllable. This contrasts with Indo-European, for which we assume on the basis of its descendants that word accent could move from syllable to syllable, similar to the alternation which we see in English words derived from Greek, for example *phótograph*, *photógrapher*, *photográphic*. This fixing of stress early in the word in Germanic led to a shortening, weakening, or loss of the sounds of unstressed syllables occurring towards the end of words. Since these were often inflectional endings, other means of expressing the syntactical relation between words had to be found, for example prepositions to express case-relationships, pronouns, auxiliaries and adverbs to make clear the subject of the verb and to indicate niceties of tense and the like, and a growing reliance upon, and consequent rigidity of, word-order as a syntactical element.[1] Another marked difference between Germanic and the other Indo-European languages is the Germanic Soundshift, a series of changes in the consonantal pattern of Germanic which is responsible for the differences between the sounds represented by bold-type letters in the following pairs of words: Latin **p**iscis, German **F**isch; Latin **t**res, English **th**ree; Latin **c**entum, German **H**undert; Latin **d**ecem, English **t**en; Latin a**g**er, German A**ck**er.

[1] Although it is likely that the erosion of inflectional endings caused the introduction of analytic forms of expression, it is not inconceivable that a tendency towards an analytic mode of expression led to a lack of differentiation in inflectional endings, a 'carelessness' of pronunciation which was tolerable because the inflections were becoming redundant.

The Beginnings of German

The modern national languages of Europe have come, or are coming, into being as a result of the emergence of the European nations, if we take as our working definition of national language something like 'the (relatively) unified form of speech, and, where appropriate, its written representation, used as the medium of communication within an area which constitutes a political unity'. Unless the area is so small that there is virtually no variation of speech within it, the political unification will precede the linguistic, which may lag behind by several centuries, or indeed never be achieved fully. If, as has been suggested, a unified standard language is the product of a national state, then first credit must go to the Franks for laying the foundations of that political and, eventually, linguistic unit which is called 'German'. Clovis, the Merovingian King of the Franks (481–511), began the process by uniting the Franks and by conquering the Alemanni who became his subjects in 505. Even more important, as things turned out, was Clovis's baptism together with that of 3,000 of his Frankish followers into the Catholic faith in 496. This move won him the support of the Catholic Gallo-Roman bishops in the large areas of Gaul which the Franks had wrested from the (Arian) Visigoths and from the kingdom of Soissons. Since these bishops were skilled in diplomacy and administration, a legacy of the great days of Rome, their support proved an important factor in Clovis's consolidation and extension of his already enlarged kingdom. Although after Clovis's death his territory was divided amongst his four sons, the Merovingians knowing no right of primogeniture and the Carolingians only a partial form of it, the expansion of Frankish territory continued, Thuringia being conquered in 531, Burgundy in 534, and in 555 the Bavarians, by then in an area corresponding roughly with modern Bavaria, accepted Frankish overlordship, though only losing their independent dukedom finally to Charlemagne in 788.

By 558 all Frankish territory was reunited under the rule of one man, the only surviving son of Clovis, and the following centuries were to see frequent repetition of such division and reunification of Frankish possessions. With Charlemagne's final defeat of the Frisians and, after extensive campaigns, of the Saxons in 804 all those Germanic tribal groupings, who were to form the ingredients of that mixture we call 'German', namely Bavarians, Alemanni, Thuringians, Franks, Saxons and Frisians, had been united under the suzerainty of the Franks. The territory occupied by this blending of tribes was to vary, contracting in some areas, expanding in others, and there were to be setbacks as well as advances, centrifugal and centripetal waves of political development succeeding each other, but with the latter predominating. The process of political unification in Germany has been very retarded in comparison with, say, France or England. As an illustration of this one need only recollect that as late as 1918 there were four separate kings in Germany. It seems typical of Germany's political fate that in the place of the one Germany which existed between the two World Wars there are now two German Republics. But for the moment it is the beginnings of German we must look at, and in order to do this further explanation of terms is necessary.

Usually when the term 'German' (*Deutsch*) is used of the language, it means 'High German' (*Hochdeutsch*), which contrasts with 'Low German' (*Niederdeutsch*). The original significance of these terms is easily appreciated, if one looks at a physical map of Germany. The flat northern plains are the region where 'Low' German is spoken, while the higher regions of central and southern Germany are the home of 'High' German. Usually in speaking of German one is referring to the standard language of Germany, and since this has derived most of its features from the German spoken in High (i.e. 'upland') Germany, 'German' alone has come to signify predominantly 'High German'. Occasionally, though it is not a practice to be recommended, German-speakers will use *Hochdeutsch* not as a contrast with *Niederdeutsch* but rather as a contrast with *Dialekt* or *Mundart* (both meaning 'dialect'), even where the dialect is itself a High German dialect. This usage is favoured by situations in which the dialect *is* Low German, so that the term contrasting with Low German, which has no pretensions to being a standard language and is considered *only* as a dialect, may be interpreted as meaning either 'High (not Low) German', or 'standard (not dialect) German'. The fact that standard German is High German is perhaps not the only factor conducive to *Hochdeutsch* being used as a term for the standard. It may well be that notions of social strata have also played a role, *Hochdeutsch* being understood as 'high'-class, the refined language of the educated 'upper' class, who do not normally speak dialect.

The most striking characteristic of High German is the Second Soundshift, or High German Soundshift, a series of changes in the consonantal system, which marks High German off from the other Germanic languages and from Low German. It is the Second Soundshift which is responsible for the differences between the sounds in bold type in the following pairs of cognate English and German words: *pound, **Pfund**; open, **offen**; **ten, zehn; eat, essen; make, machen**.[1] These changes began in southern German and spread northwards with ever-decreasing effect until they died out altogether, thus forming the border between High German and Low German. This border is not static, and with the growing prestige and importance of the (High German) standard language the boundary of Low German is being pushed steadily northward. It would be wrong, however, to think of this simply as an advance on a broad front. Towns with their greater mobility of population and more intensive and extensive intercourse with other areas tend to become High-German-speaking before more rural districts, and these High German islands then radiate High German forms out into the surrounding districts.[2] Once the town's hinterland has been covered completely, the result will look like a general advance of the particular linguistic feature or features. Not all features which are described above as High German extend over the whole area of High German, and since different features have different boundaries, it is to some extent arbitrary which individual feature is chosen as the criterion for distinguishing between High and Low German. The most that one can ask for is that a striking feature should be chosen, and that it should be supported as nearly as possible by other features. The present border separating High and Low German, which is usually represented on dialect maps by drawing a line between the High German area which says *mache* (first person singular of the verb 'to make') and the Low German which says *make*, begins at the Romance border not far from Eupen and runs near Aachen, Linnich, Benrath, Siegen, Kassel, Nord-hausen, Wittenberg, Lübben, Frankfurt an der Oder, Birnbaum an der Warthe. It is referred to usually as the Benrath Line, after the place where it crosses the Rhine. When one realizes, however, that nowadays Benrath is a busy suburb of Düsseldorf, it becomes obvious that such isoglosses, as lines indicating the geographical limits of linguistic forms are called, have real validity only for relatively static rural communities.

High German is further divided into two types: Upper German (*Oberdeutsch*) in the south, and Central German (*Mitteldeutsch*) in

[1] The sounds in question are to be pronounced much as the spelling suggests; *ch* is roughly as in Scottish 'loch'; *z* like *ts* in English 'bats'.
[2] This process of infiltration rather than frontal advance is, of course, characteristic of the spread of modern standard languages at the expense of dialect, whether the dialect be High German, Low German, or Northumbrian.

central Germany. The distinguishing features are, for instance, Upper German *Apfel*, Central German *Appel* ('apple'); Upper German diminutives which use a suffix containing an *l*, e.g. *Mädel* ('girl') as opposed to Central German which uses a *ch* element, e.g. *Mädchen*.[1] Thus, proceeding from north to south, we have three linguistic belts of Low German, Central German and Upper German, the two latter constituting High German. Since it will be necessary to refer quite frequently to some of the dialects which make up these three main sub-divisions, it would seem appropriate to list here the principal German dialects, mentioning roughly the areas in which they are to be found. The names of some of the larger centres within a dialect area are given, but merely as aids to identification, since the dialects are rarely heard in the main towns. No account has been taken here of whether those dialects in areas now under Slav administration still survive.

I. *Low German*

    1. Low Franconian – on the lower Rhine, akin to Dutch but not identical with it.

    2. Low Saxon – found in parts of Holland and in northern Germany from the Dutch border to East Prussia; several sub-types, e.g. Westphalian, Holsteinisch, Pomeranian, Low Prussian, etc. Often called colloquially *Plattdeutsch*.

II. *High German*

  A. Central German

    1. Central Franconian – on both banks of the Rhine from the L.G. border to a line crossing the Rhine south of Coblenz; divided into Ripuarian (around Cologne) and Moselle Franconian (Trier, Coblenz).

    2. Rhenish Franconian – also on both banks of the Rhine; extends from southern border of C. Franconian to just south of Mannheim; main centres Mainz, Frankfurt.

---

[1] *Mitteldeutsch* is as often as not translated into English as 'Middle German', but here *Mittel* will be translated as 'central' when it is a geographical term and as 'middle' when it has a chronological sense, thus avoiding confusion and utilizing the greater richness in synonyms which so often distinguishes English from German. From here on the following abbreviations will be used: L.G. – Low German; H.G. – High German; U.G. – Upper German; C.G. – Central German. These will be modified by means of E. – East; W. – West; O. – Old; M. – Middle; N. – New; thus E.C.G. – East Central German, M.H.G. – Middle High German, etc. Note, however, that E.N.H.G. is used for Early New High German. The significance of those terms not already discussed will be explained as they arise.

3. Thuringian – starting just west of the Werra and running east until it meets and almost merges into Upper Saxon, west of Merseburg; bounded in the south-west by the Thüringer Wald which is roughly the border with East Franconian; centres Erfurt, Weimar.

4. Upper Saxon – stretching from Thuringian eastwards until it encounters Silesian, east and north-east of Dresden; centres Meissen, Leipzig, Dresden; this area did not become German-speaking until the late Middle Ages.

5. Silesian – running east from Upper Saxon to the Slavonic border; like the Upper Saxon area not German-speaking until the late Middle Ages; centres Bautzen, Breslau.

B. Upper German

1. East Franconian – south-east of Rhenish Franconian; bounded in east roughly by the Thüringer Wald, Frankenwald and Fränkische Alb; centres Bamberg and Würzburg. (East Franconian is sometimes classified with the other High Franconian dialects as Central German.)

2. Alemannic – in Baden, Württemberg, Alsace and Switzerland; Alsatian, Swabian and Swiss are forms of Alemannic; the eastern boundary with Bavarian is the Lech.

3. Bavarian – in Bavaria and Austria, extending south into Alps to border with Italian and east to border with Czechoslovak, Hungarian and Yugoslav.

Finally in this review of terminology it is necessary to say something about chronology. Languages do not fall naturally into periods, yet to comprehend long vistas of time like those presented by the history of a language, the human mind seems to require sub-divisions and patterns in order to reduce the material to manageable proportions. It appears most appropriate in a survey of this kind to stick to the most widely accepted divisions, while acknowledging that the criteria upon which they are based are drawn from heterogeneous spheres, historical, linguistic, literary, social, etc., and that such divisions may be more hallowed by usage than sacred by sense:

Old High German 750–1050 (from the beginning of records of High German to the period when the vowels of unstressed, or weakly stressed, syllables, formerly *a, i, o, u,* begin to appear commonly as uniform M.H.G. *e*).

Middle High German 1050–1350 (the terminal date is very arbitrary, but it is chosen because it is around this time that a number of phonetic and morphological features found in modern standard German have spread over a considerable area of German-speaking territory).

Early New High German 1350–1600 (1600 is chosen since it is in the seventeenth century that an important force in the development of a German standard language begins really to make itself felt. This force is the work of normative grammarians and linguistic theorists, who reveal a growing interest in, and concern with, language on a practical and theoretical level.).

New High German 1600 to date.

It was mentioned above that German began with the uniting of Germanic tribes under the suzerainty of the Franks, and it will have been noted that the names of the medieval and modern German dialects are derived largely from the names of these tribes. This must not be taken to mean that the speakers of the modern dialects are necessarily the descendants of the respective tribes whose names they bear, nor that all differences in the modern dialects go back to differences in the speech habits of the earlier tribes. Medieval and post-medieval political, social, economic and ecclesiastical territories and groupings have been responsible for the area covered by many linguistic features and for the boundaries now observable between them. Yet it is most unlikely that some of the differences in modern usage do not go back to the usage of the various tribes who came to be 'Germans'. Moreover, Alemanni, Bavarians, Franks, Thuringians, Saxons and Frisians have all contributed something to the amalgam which is modern German, even though the contribution varies greatly from tribe to tribe. Some, for instance the Frisians, whose language cannot be considered as German, have contributed perhaps nothing more than a number of items in the German lexicon, while the Upper Germans have provided, amongst other things, much of the consonantal structure of the language.

What we mean by High German must, by definition, have come into being after the Second Soundshift, which in U.G. is thought to have begun probably in the sixth or seventh century. The reasons for these changes in the consonantal system are not clear, but it *is* clear that such changes can take place in two basically different ways: firstly as a more or less 'spontaneous' change in the mode of articulation within a speech-community; secondly as an imitation, conscious or unconscious, of the speech habits of another community, often as a conscious or unconscious desire to conform, because of the military, political, economic or cultural prestige of the community which is emulated. It appears that the Second Soundshift took place, either in Bavarian or Alemannic, as a spontaneous change of our first type. On the other hand, the spread of the shift northwards, which can be observed from O.H.G. times onwards, with ever-decreasing effect as it passes through the Franconian dialects, until it peters out altogether on the L.G. border, is an imitative change of our second type.[1] Such currents must be viewed as indicative of political and cultural trends in the early O.H.G. period, and there is also evidence of later linguistic currents, notably in the development of certain vowels, which flow in the opposite direction from Franconian into Upper German. This is further evidence of the inferential kind which linguistic history can provide about more general historical developments and movements.

The Franks found themselves at the head of a number of Germanic tribes, and it became the task of the Frankish kings to fuse these tribes into a nation, to give them some consciousness of a larger unit than the tribe, to awaken in them the notion of being 'Germans' and not Saxons, Bavarians or Thuringians. Needless to say, the task was not fulfilled for centuries. At the time there was no term 'German' or its equivalent, and the creation and propagation of the word *deutsch* or its etymon would seem to have had a powerful and peculiar role to play in the fashioning of the German nation and language. The word *deutsch* comes from an adjective **theudisk*, derived by means of the suffix **-isk* (English *-ish*, German *-isch*) from a Germanic noun **theudō*, meaning a 'people', or 'folk'.[2] The noun, which is now defunct in German, appears as O.H.G. *diot*, M.H.G. *diet* ('people'), and still exists in Middle English as *thede* ('people, nation, or the country or region occupied by a people'). Theoretically the adjective, which must have meant originally 'of the people, appertaining to the people, popular', could have been found in any Germanic language or dialect in which noun and suffix existed, but the semantic development from an adjective to a proper name is not comprehensible under just any circum-

---

[1] There is conjecture about the change being imitative even in U.G., but since this concerns early periods prior to written records of German, it is for the moment highly speculative.

[2] Forms which are merely postulated, which are reconstructions based on surviving reflexes of the words or forms, are marked with an asterisk.

stances. It seems that the West Franks had developed quite early a term to indicate the Romance-speaking population of the Gallo-Roman areas they had conquered. This term *walhisk* (N.H.G. *welsch*) is probably derived from the name of the Celtic tribe of the Volcae, and it appears to have signified 'foreign, appertaining to the others, not of us', cf. Old English *wealh* ('foreigner, stranger'). The term which contrasted with it in the early period was *frenkisg* ('Frankish') and this was applied to the Germanic-speaking Franks who constituted the upper classes of feudal society. Gradually, however, Franks in the old imperial territory of Gaul became romanized, in their way of life, their economy, their social structure, and some of them in their language. Around the turn of the sixth and seventh centuries, even in north-east Gaul where the Germanic population was in the majority, it is assumed that much of the Frankish population was bilingual. At the same time the term *frenkisg* was slowly becoming a political umbrella term embracing those who owed allegiance to the Merovingian kings, whether Romance-speaking or Germanic-speaking, whether of Gallo-Roman or of Frankish descent. Thus the old contrast *walhisk*:*frenkisg* was no longer adequate for expressing the somewhat blurred distinction between Romance-speaking 'foreigners' and Germanic-speaking Franks. It seems that under these circumstances the term *theudisk* (probably in the West Franconian form *theodisk*) meaning 'of the people, of our own people, native not foreign', and referring primarily to the main badge of their nationhood, namely their language, came into being, or at least came to be used regularly and with the precise sense which set it on its way to becoming a name, and ended its status as a sporadic nonce-word.

This word *theudisk*, signifying nationality and language, was to be an important tool of the Carolingian kings and their successors in their attempts to weld together the disparate elements of their people. One form which the welding took was to collect, preserve and transmit what could be salvaged of classical culture, to introduce similar political institutions and practices among the Saxons, Bavarians, etc., and to convert the various peoples, by force if necessary, to a Christianity backed by a highly organized and standardized ecclesiastical administration. Now the Carolingians possessed a term enabling them to express the kinship of their subjects, a kinship based on the common, Germanic origin of them and their languages, and on their political allegiance. At the same time it excluded Germanic-speakers such as the Danes or Anglo-Saxons, who did not belong politically, and this despite the fact that the language of the non-German Anglo-Saxons, for instance, had a good deal more in common with the language of the German Saxons than the language of the latter had with that of the German Bavarians. It is not until the second half of the eighth century that *deutsch* appears in written records, and then only in Latin guise as *theodiscus*. (This is linguistic confirmation of the supposition that the term first sprang up in its new sense on the western border between German and Romance, since *eo* for *eu* is assumed to have existed in such phonetic environments only in West Franconian.) With the exception of a few slightly earlier glosses, Notker of St Gallen, writing around 1000, is the first to provide us with an example of our word used in German, though only in set expressions like *in diutiscun* ('in German'). Only in the late eleventh and early twelfth centuries does the word *diutsch*, or its reflexes, become reasonably common, by which time it is applied to the people and the land as well as the language. It is not, however, until relatively late, in the fifteenth century, that the compound *Deutschland* is found frequently. It is preceded by adjectival expressions such as *diutschiu lant* ('German lands', plural). A century after the death of Charlemagne in 814 his Reich no longer represented a unity, but the concept of that larger political body expressed by the word *deutsch* had come into being, and term and concept remained alive until such time as they could become, almost completely, a reality.[1]

The Old High German Period

It is a commonplace among linguistic historians that the history of a nation is to be found in the history of its language, but like most commonplaces it contains much that is uncommon and much that is misplaced. Not all important events leave their mark on the language and not all the marks made on the language are made by matters of great importance. Naturally our commonplace is not meant to indicate in a simple-minded fashion that if one reads old texts, one finds information about ancient matters. The implication is that a historical

---

[1] It would be disingenuous to pretend that the view put forward above of the development of the word *deutsch* was not hotly contested, nor that it was not fraught with difficulties. The relation between *theodiscus* and Latin expressions such as *vulgariter*, *vulgari lingua*, meaning 'in the vernacular', the reason why *diutisk* appears so much later than *theodiscus* and whether *theodiscus* can mean 'Germanic' as well as 'German' are only some of the unresolved questions.

study of language will provide us inferentially with evidence of earlier attitudes, modes of thought, events, etc., and that some of this evidence would be unobtainable by other methods. For instance, to take only the case of linguistic borrowing, examination of the etymology of the German words *Reich* ('empire') and *Amt* ('office, official position') reveals that the phonetic form of these words is explicable only if we assume them to have been borrowed at an early date from Celtic into Germanic. This provides indirect evidence of a period of close contact between the Celts and Germani, during which it seems reasonable to infer that in matters of government and tribal organization the Celts were the superior people. Similarly an examination of Germanic borrowings from the Romans reveals close contact and a willingness to learn useful skills, arts, trades, etc., from the more civilized people – hence *Fenster* (Latin *fenestra*, 'window'), *Mauer* (*murus*, 'wall'), *Straße* ([*via*] *strata*, 'metalled (road)'), *Wein* (*vinum*, 'wine'), *Pfirsich* (*persicum*, 'peach'), *Kaiser* ((*Julius*) *Caesar*) – and teaches us much about the relative cultural levels of the two peoples.

There are, however, momentous occurrences which have produced no lasting linguistic results of this kind, and it is as well to realize on the other hand that linguistic borrowing is not always evidence of profound contact or real linguistic need. It may be a luxury as often as a necessity and people may use foreign terms for the same reason that they drink foreign beverages or buy foreign cars, namely for the cachet (*exempli gratia*!) connected with them and not because they are thirsty or unable to procure native products. An eminent German has remarked, 'Man bedient sich des Fremdwortes um sich en parlant von der Kanaille zu distinguieren', and this desire to speak in a manner which marks one as a person of refinement and discrimination, and which distinguishes one from the rabble, is a powerful motive in much linguistic borrowing or imitation.

Our earliest written records of O.H.G. date from around the middle of the eighth century and are for the most part glosses to Latin texts, translations of the Lord's Prayer, Catechism and Creed, baptismal vows or other texts which are of particular value in giving instruction in the Christian faith, or in expounding the working of the church or monastic institutions. Frequently the translations are nothing more than literal, interlinear versions of the Latin text and it is only later that more ambitious renderings are encountered. The sheer fact of the emergence of written texts in O.H.G. is in itself part of the cultural and linguistic history of the O.H.G. period. Seen in a purely German context, that is restricting oneself to German areas and German language, the so-called 'Carolingian Renaissance' is a naissance rather than a renaissance. Under the earlier Carolingian kings and their scholarly advisers – some of them imported from England – German was turned for the first time on a scale of any magnitude into a written medium. It was refashioned into a language capable of expressing Latin culture and above all it was made a vehicle of Christian teaching, to be used in planting faith in the heathen and in cultivating it in those in whom it had already taken rapid but shallow root. It would be more accurate to say that under the early Carolingian kings and their scholars this process was begun, since its completion required centuries.

The somewhat primitive, clumsy, and at times downright inept efforts of these early writers of German, largely monks and churchmen, should not blind us to the importance of their undertaking, to the energy which they devoted to it, or to the difficulty of their task. Although there must have been 'higher' levels of German amongst the educated and the noble, most matters of administration, education and culture were dealt with in Latin. Essentially the language of a nation of illiterate warriors and farmers was to be adapted to express all the interests, abstractions and niceties which Latin could handle, and needless to say this could only be effected under the tutelage of Latin. This is not to deny that at this time and even much earlier the Germanic languages were capable of literature of the highest order, but Germanic literature was by nature oral literature, and although the sparse relics of O.H.G. literature in the Germanic tradition are of a higher level of artistry than anything achieved at that time under Latin influence, they and their language could not serve the new requirements and be used unadulterated to convey Christian faith, Christian theology and Latin culture. We have already mentioned certain results of the contact between Romans and Germani, usually occurring in areas of the Roman Empire in which Germani were settled, or through German mercenaries being enlisted into the Roman armies. Whereas this earlier contact as revealed in linguistic borrowings had been largely practical and concrete, the later confrontation between German and Latin yields predominantly abstracts, concerned for the most part with Christian and ecclesiastical matters, or with learning and education. An exception to this principle is the large number of words expressing concrete objects connected with church buildings or equipment necessary for religious rites and the like, or with numerous activities arising from the monastic way of life. Leaving aside the question of specific missions

B

undertaken to christianize the Germans, the Christian borrowings fall into two groups, an earlier group from Latin into Germanic, which may be described as pre-Frankish, since the borrowing took place before the Frankish incursions into the Empire, and a later group from Gallo-Romance into Frankish. The two groups may be distinguished on the basis of their geographical distribution, for instance whether the borrowing occurred early enough for the word to have been carried to England by the Anglo-Saxon invaders and thus recorded in O.E., and linguistically on the basis of sound changes within Germanic and Romance. The earlier group, like the pre-Christian borrowings, has undergone the Second Soundshift, whereas the words belonging to the second group are untouched by this change, except for a limited number of analogical developments, but often they show evidence that they are derived from Romance forms which themselves are later developments of Latin. For instance words like O.H.G. *kiricha* ('church') from late Greek *kurikón*, or *biscof* ('bishop') from Romance **piscopu* represent the first type, while O.H.G. *priestar* ('priest') from Romance *prēstre* from Lat. *presbyter*, or O.H.G. *altāri* ('altar') from Lat. *altare* are of the second kind.

Though German had to be re-tailored to express Latin culture and learning, we must admit that in some ways the garment which emerged was a strait-jacket as often as a cloak or stola. That is, the results were scarcely elegant, frequently constricting and largely crude, yet they did guide the patient, for his own good of course, along the lines necessary for learning, civilization and, ultimately, salvation. In consequence, with a few exceptions O.H.G. texts may be regarded as monuments to industry and zeal, as documents embodying fascinating linguistic, theological or historical evidence, but rarely as objects rich in literary or aesthetic appeal.

The metaphor of a strait-jacket was used and nowhere is this more applicable than in the process of turning O.H.G. into a written language. Any system of representing a language by means of written symbols must not contain too many symbols, if it is to be workable. Thus in comparison with the variety of the spoken language the written is always a simplification, a reduction and a limitation. A crude comparison which springs to mind is that a written language is akin to a keyboard instrument, which can make only as many sounds as there are keys, while a spoken language is like a stringed instrument which can produce an almost infinite variety of sounds even between C and C sharp. If this constricting effect is observable even where the orthographic system is devised especially for the language in question, how much tighter is the strait-jacket when the system has been devised for an alien language and is then to be superimposed on another. This is the position in O.H.G., where the Latin alphabet was used as the means of writing down German.

Sometimes adaptation of the Latin alphabet sufficed, for instance O.H.G. possessed a sound similar to modern English *w*, for which the Latin alphabet could offer no ready-made symbol. Consequently *uu*, which has since fused into the symbol *w*, was employed. In other cases, however, particularly for the consonants of O.H.G. where the Latin alphabet proved most inadequate, less happy solutions were arrived at. The Latin symbol *z* was used to represent two fundamentally different O.H.G. sounds: on the one hand a fricative which was written as *z* or *zz*, for example O.H.G. *faz* ('vat or barrel'), *ezzan* ('to eat'), on the other an affricate sound as in O.H.G. *sizzen* ('to sit'), *zehan* ('ten').[1] If we miss a one-to-one relationship between symbol and sound when seen from the point of view of the symbol, this is much more so when we turn the question round and ask how a given sound was represented orthographically in O.H.G. At once we are faced with a bewildering multiplicity of orthographic practice. There are three principal reasons for this: writing systems were being devised simultaneously in different places, usually the scriptoria of monasteries, which were often not in close contact with each other; O.H.G. consisted of a series of dialects with no norm; far-reaching changes in the sound structure of the language were taking place, or at least spreading geographically, at roughly the same time that the orthographic systems were being devised. It will be necessary to examine these points briefly.

The writings which have survived from the O.H.G. period stem from a relatively small number of centres, islands of literacy in German, which do not cover all German-speaking areas. Whole regions, for instance Thuringia, are simply not represented by O.H.G. texts. There was no such thing as a single literary centre which enjoyed the status of a cultural capital. The centres which did exist were largely monasteries, St Gallen, Reichenau, Murbach, Weissenburg, Freising, Fulda, to mention some of the most important. In each the orthographic practice as it came into being was either a communal effort or was

---

[1] The fricative is pronounced like English *ss* in 'missing'; the affricate has no real equivalent in English in initial position, but it could be represented by *ts*, as for instance in 'cats'. The affricate in O.H.G. must have sounded like its N.H.G. equivalent in *sitzen* or *zehn*.

the achievement of one or two leading scholars. It is tempting to interpret the documents issuing from these scriptoria as records of the dialect of the area in which the monastery was situated, but this can be demonstrably false. It is, as often as not, the language of the monks or the leading figures working in the monastery, and these came frequently from far afield, from the opposite end of Germany, from England. Accordingly changes in personnel could lead to changes in orthographic practice.

In this respect the example of the abbey of Fulda is illuminating. It was founded in 744 by the Anglo-Saxon Boniface, but Bavarian monks were involved in the foundation and the earliest documents issuing from Fulda, for instance the so-called *Vocabularius Sancti Galli*, show strong traces of Bavarian, although the abbey was situated in territory that according to the testimony of later periods must have been Rhenish Franconian. In the first half of the ninth century East Franconian features become prominent in the O.H.G. translation of Tatian's *Diatessaron*, presumably the result of an influx of East Franconian monks, or of one powerful personality from that region. Not until the manuscript of the *Merseburg Charms* from around the end of the ninth century do Rhenish Franconian features come to the fore.

The tendency for every scriptorium to begin afresh to invent its own orthography is responsible for the considerable variety referred to above in the way a given sound is indicated. It is not, of course, impossible that the works coming from a monastery do approximate, in so far as primitive, inadequate and uncertain orthography would permit, to the dialect of the region from which they stem. It is merely that *all* variation is not attributable to the existence of dialects and the absence of a norm. Actual sound-changes taking place to various degrees in various regions at various times during the nascent period of German orthography, for instance the northerly spread of the High German Soundshift, or the spread of vowel changes from Rhenish Franconian, or the occurrence and gradual orthographic indication of *i*-mutation (*Umlaut*), all serve to diversify an already variegated picture. It is unlikely that the mobile higher nobility and clerics and perhaps the court officials around Charlemagne did not have a form of speech which was distinct from that of the more static lower classes. Such a higher form of speech may well have meant a levelling and reduction of dialect differences, but no norm developed from it, nor are any real signs of levelling visible in the written language. The unifying religious and political forces were as yet too weak, and the disruptive, regional, 'tribal' forces too powerful.

We have seen something of how O.H.G. became a written language, but so far only a few hints have been given as to how it was made capable of expressing the Christian and cultural ideas found in the Latin texts with which so many O.H.G. scribes, translators and scholars were concerned. The impression may have been given that this took place simply by borrowing Latin words, but this is incomplete, though it may not be incorrect. Vocabulary can be 'borrowed' in more ways than one. In addition to merely taking over the foreign word as a so-called 'loan-word', sometimes with an adaptation of its sounds or a substitution of the nearest equivalents possessed by the receiving language, the coveted word may be dismembered, each limb rendered by its literal equivalent, and the parts reassembled, thus producing a completely new word consisting only of native elements, yet sired by a foreign model. The product is a so-called 'loan-translation'. Attempts are made sometimes to distinguish between more or less exact imitations of the original, but this seems superfluous, and if a distinction is required, the case can be met by speaking of 'literal' or 'free' loan-translations. The third main possibility is that, instead of the two kinds of bodily borrowing considered hitherto, a 'marriage of true minds' takes place, wherein by a process akin to metempsychosis the spirit, the sense, of a foreign word is transferred to a native host-word, which thus acquires a new meaning in addition to its own. Sometimes this new meaning may be so powerful that the original one suffers partial atrophy, or even complete demise. Examples of this method of borrowing foreign vocabulary are commonly termed 'loan-extensions' ('of meaning' being understood).

German abounds in loan-translations of all periods; *Fußball* is modelled on English 'football' and replaces the latter which for some time after the introduction of the game into Germany was used as a loan-word in German; *Wolkenkratzer* is an example of a free loan-translation, since it means literally 'cloudscraper' though it is used to render 'skyscraper'. It may have been felt that there was something too hyperbolic about the jocular American term, if done literally into German as *Himmelkratzer*, or perhaps the latter might have been ambiguous, since *Himmel* means 'heaven' as well as 'sky'. Examples of O.H.G. loan-translations are provided by *armaherzi* (modified in N.H.G. to *barmherzig*) modelled exactly on Latin *misericors* which means literally 'having a heart for the poor', or by *lutzilmuati* based on Latin *pusil-*

lanimis, each meaning literally 'of small spirit'. Loan-extension is found in the two words *Gott* ('God') and *Geist* ('spirit, ghost'). Originally the Germanic term which is the etymon of *Gott* appears to have indicated supernatural beings, whose precise nature it is difficult to grasp, partly because the earlier writers in Germanic languages tend to be Christian and somewhat reticent about pagan matters, and partly because these beings were after all supernatural. At all events O.H.G. *got* was seized upon to render Latin *deus* and was invested with the meaning of the latter, while the original sense, though not all the force, of *got* was gradually lost. A certain grammatical influence was also exerted in that the Germanic word was originally neuter, but came to be masculine under the influence of *deus*. Similarly the word *Geist* was associated in Germanic with the supernatural and religious sphere. Its meaning may have been something like 'religious ecstasy or frenzy', but under Christian influence it was used to express Latin *spiritus* which itself had already undergone similar interference from Greek *pneuma*. In the expression the 'Holy Ghost' a rival attempt to render *spiritus* by *atum* ('breath') was at first successful, but later succumbed to *Geist*.

Apart from vocabulary the lasting effects of Latin were slight. Except for those works which are very dependent upon their Latin original, so dependent sometimes as to be merely interlinear versions such as can hardly be said to have any syntax of their own, Latin did not make a great mark on O.H.G. syntax. Its precise impact is of course difficult to discern in the absence of any large corpus of non-Christian texts, unexposed to Latin influence, particularly since many constructions could have been arrived at with or without Latin influence. In this latter respect it is worth citing the circumlocutions developed in O.H.G. to express the perfect, pluperfect and future tenses. Germanic had possessed only two tenses: first, a present which expressed all present senses and also the future, this being largely the position in modern everyday German, and, second, a 'past' tense which served to express all kinds of temporal priority, whether imperfect, preterite, perfect or pluperfect. There is little doubt that the desire for new tense-forms was provoked by Latin models; translators must have found it frustrating, if not humiliating, to render the range of four past tenses mentioned above by only one O.H.G. form. But there is considerable doubt as to whether the solutions adopted, infinitive plus modal-verbs 'shall' or 'will', etc., for the future, past participle plus tenses of 'to have' or 'to be' for the perfect and pluperfect, were based on Latin models or not. Vulgar Latin had long possessed periphrastic tenses formed in ways similar to the O.H.G. ones, but formal dependence of the O.H.G. periphrases on Latin models has not been proved, and we must allow for the possibility of polygenesis.

As the O.H.G. period progresses so does mastery of the written language, until by the time of Notker of St Gallen, around 1000, a considerable measure of sophistication has been reached in the treatment of theological and philosophical matters in O.H.G. We still miss any tendency towards linguistic standardization, for which the political circumstances were, if anything, less propitious than at the time of Charlemagne, and the spheres in which O.H.G. as opposed to Latin are employed are still restricted. But German is now a language with a tradition of writing behind it and it has taken its first steps on the path to becoming one of the written languages of Western European civilization, a process in which the dependency upon Latin language was only a few degrees lower than the dependency upon Latin culture.

The Middle High German Period

The tendency described above continued in the E.M.H.G. period in a fashion more unbroken than might be suggested by beginning this paragraph with a new heading. As stated already, the process of dividing languages into periods has only limited validity and even when one has settled on one's somewhat arbitrary linguistic criteria, it must be realized that changes happen neither overnight, nor in all regions at the same time. Nevertheless the reduction of unstressed or weakly stressed vowels to a uniform *e* (as in English unstressed 'the') which was chosen to demarcate O.H.G. from M.H.G. is largely carried out by 1050 and may be seen if we compare the inflection of an O.H.G. noun *tag* ('day') and the present tense of the verb *neman* ('to take') with their M.H.G. counterparts:

	Singular			Plural	
	O.H.G.	M.H.G.		O.H.G.	M.H.G.
Nom./acc.	*tag*	*tac*		*tagā*	*tage*
Gen.	*tages*	*tages*		*tago*	*tage*
Dat.	*tage*	*tage*		*tagum*	*tagen*
ich	*nimu*	*nime*	*wir*	*nemamēs*	*nemen*
du	*nimis(t)*	*nimest*	*ir*	*nemet*	*nemet*
er	*nimit*	*nimet*	*si(e)*	*nemant*	*nement*

While the refashioning of German as a language of learning and religion proceeded during the M.H.G. period, German was exposed to a new and equally momentous foreign influence from roughly 1150 onwards. This was the flourishing in twelfth-century France and Norman England of that colourful, splendid, aristocratic culture which we associate with the terms 'courtly' and 'chivalrous'. It found expression in clothes, customs, music, literature, architecture, manners and attitudes such as that towards love, and as the fashion for things French in these spheres swept Germany, so did the Old French words for these. Again we find loan-words, such as *palas* (O.F. *palais*, 'palace'), *curteis* (from *courtois*, 'courtly'), *fín* (from *fin*, 'fine'); or loan-translations such as *hövesch* ('courtly') (*hof* plus the adjective suffix *-esch*, modelled on O.F. *court-ois*), *dörperíe* modelled on O.F. *vilenie*, both meaning 'boorishness, rustic behaviour' (an interesting combination of a loan-translation and a loan-word, since the *vilain* is translated as *dörper*, literally a 'villager', while the French suffix itself is borrowed); or loan-extensions such as *süeze* ('sweet') which was used originally to refer only to the physical sense of taste, but under the influence of O.F. *douz* came to be used in a transferred, figurative sense, while *vriunt* ('friend') followed O.F. *ami* in developing a specialized auxiliary meaning of 'beloved, sweetheart'. Thus the expression *mín süeze vriundín* goes a long way towards characterizing the linguistic and cultural relationship between Germany and France at the time.

Once more the foreign influence tended to be restricted to vocabulary unless we count as syntactical influence the use of the second person plural pronoun *ir* instead of the singular *dū* as a mark of respect, conforming with the French practice of using *vos*. This might, however, be seen merely as lexical borrowing with morphological or syntactical repercussions. O.F. did provide M.H.G. with a few suffixes, some of which have proved important in modern German. We have already seen the ending *-ie*, which appears in N.H.G. as *-ie* or *-ei*, e.g. *Melodie*, *Phantasie* (older *Melodei* and *Phantasei*) or *Abtei*, *Bäckerei*, but even more important was the verb ending *-ieren*, which is by far the most productive suffix for forming verbs from foreign words in N.H.G.[1] It still shows something of its foreign origin in that contrary to most verbs those in *-ieren* are stressed on the ending, e.g. *studíeren* 'to study', while their past participles do not have the prefix *ge-* attached as do

---

[1] The origin of this ending has not been explained completely. It is assumed that the *-ier* stems from the O. French verb suffix, but that it has been influenced by the nominal suffix *-ier*. The German infinitive ending is then added to give *-ieren*.

other German verbs. In M.H.G. *ge-* is in fact usual with the past participles of these verbs. At first the ending is borrowed like the suffix *-īe* as part of whole words, e.g. *tjostieren* ('to joust'), but later it is attached to native stems such as *halbieren* ('to halve').

These borrowings from O.F. are the property of a restricted social class of the aristocracy, chiefly knightly though also clerical. Such vocabulary might be seen as the social badge of that caste and this is reflected in its concern largely with the military, artistic and social interests of the knights. With the decline in importance of the knights and the way of courtly life in the later Middle Ages much of this O.F. vocabulary vanished, though those items which had gained wider currency, extending themselves beyond knightly circles or beyond purely chivalric interests, survive, for instance modern German *klar*, *Tanz*, *Preis*. Contact between French and German knights came about in various ways. The Crusades proved a fruitful, if at times hostile, meeting-place; German noblemen sometimes held lands in fief from high members of the French aristocracy; French tutors were favoured for German youths and many of the latter undertook educational visits to France; literary influence was considerable, much of classical M.H.G. literature (i.e. around 1200) consisting in translations and adaptations of O.F. literature; finally trade proved a powerful contact, with luxury articles and their names flowing from France into Germany, as do Parisian *haute couture* and French cuisine nowadays.

Oddly enough the routes followed by trade and traffic are responsible for the guise in which many O.F. words appear in M.H.G. Because of geography and the nature of the terrain in medieval times the most passable routes from France to Germany were either down the Moselle or via the Low Countries. Exposed as they were to immediate French influence, Flanders, Hainaut and Brabant adopted courtly culture and habits rather earlier than other German-speaking regions, and soon the knights of these areas had gained the highest prestige amongst German knights who looked up to them as examples worthy of imitation. Thus many M.H.G. borrowings from O.F. come via M.L.G., and the route can be recognized either because the borrowing is based on a northern French dialect form, usually Picardian, or because the word occurs in M.H.G. in a L.G. guise, or because it is found in a form which can be explained only as a hyper-correction of a L.G. word. Picardian influence may be seen in M.H.G. *kastelan* ('lord of a castle') which must derive from a Picardian form with *c-* and not from O.F. which would have *ch-*; L.G. forms are shown in the words *dörper* ('rustic') or *wāpen*, 'weapon', 'coat-of-arms', or as an exclamation 'to arms!', since here H.G. would have shifted the *p* to *dörfære* or *wâfen*;[1] a word like M.H.G. *schâch* is a typical hyper-correct form, for if it had been borrowed directly from O.F., it would have appeared as *(e)schac* since M.H.G. did not lack the sound *k*, but as it stands it must be explained as a word which in crossing dialect boundaries (isophones) was treated as if it was a native word and 'corrected' so as to conform with the *ich/ik* contrast. The L.G. words constitute a social and linguistic fashion of the time, namely *daz vlæmen mit der rede* ('to affect a Flemish mode of speech'). Whereas the free use of O.F. terms may have been rather like speaking Oxford English – though with no connotation yet of this being a standard – to speak with a Flemish accent would seem to have been a case of 'putting on the Ritz'.

The question as to the precise sphere of usage of these O.F. terms arises. Were they purely literary, or had they wider application? If we examine M.H.G. courtly romances in which the loans from O.F. are most numerous, we discover that where the M.H.G. text is a translation or adaptation of a French original all the loan-words present in the translation are not necessarily to be found in the original. Of those that occur in both works many will not be found in the M.H.G. version at a point which corresponds to that position in the original. This would seem to indicate that there was a stock of O.F. words which existed in M.H.G. and which poets drew upon independently of their model. Such a reservoir can be imagined to have existed only in the spoken, colloquial language of the court, but we must distinguish probably between two kinds of loan-words; on the one hand a stratum of rather special, exotic words which led only a literary existence and usually were inspired by the poet's immediate model, and on the other hand a stratum which enjoyed wider usage and constituted a genuine active part of M.H.G. courtly language. Needless to say, earlier spoken German is virtually something without a trace and only on the rarest occasions has anything approaching it survived.[2]

---

[1] In modern German the H.G. *Waffen* has replaced the L.G. form except in the most chivalric of its functions, i.e. in the heraldic term *Wappen(schild)* ('escutcheon').

[2] An exception is provided by the so-called *Altdeutsche Gespräche* which appear to be a kind of handbook of useful phrases for a foreign traveller in tenth-century Germany. The expressions include the kind of requests one would be likely to make at inns, and there is the odd remark which can be intended only for taxi-drivers who have tried to cheat one. The phrases would seem to have been written down as they were heard, since they contain numerous elisions and

For a long time argument raged as to whether the M.H.G. period saw any development of a standard form of language, and since this sketch of the history of German is interested primarily in the growth of the modern standard, the question of such a development in M.H.G. times must be touched upon. Literary texts of the classical M.H.G. period do appear to show a certain amount of levelling of dialect discrepancies, which appear less extreme around 1200 than fifty years earlier or a hundred years later. This levelling is of a negative and of a positive kind. Negative, in the sense that extreme dialect features appear to be avoided, presumably not because there was a preferred standard form, but rather because the writer, or speaker, had gradually become aware through contact with speakers from other areas that some speech habit of his was unique to his own region and therefore, in a wider courtly context, parochial. The nature of the imperial court, at once collective and peripatetic, would serve to engender and emphasize such self-consciousness. The levelling was positive in the sense that poets adopted actively the forms of regions other than their own.

The diphthongization of the M.H.G. long monophthongs *î, û, iu* (although written as a digraph in fact a monophthong akin to the *ü* in N.H.G. *grün*) to *ei, au, eu* respectively, a hallmark of N.H.G., would appear to have begun in Bavarian at least as early as the twelfth century, yet literary texts of Bavarian provenance dating from around 1200 show few signs of this change; conversely Alemannic dialects have preserved the long vowels of O.H.G., where they occurred in unstressed syllables or inflectional endings, as differentiated vowels down to modern times (though as short vowels), instead of reducing them all to *e*, yet classical M.H.G. literary texts of Alemannic origin show the usual reduction to *e*. It is only when non-literary texts in German, deeds, documents, inventories, etc., become common in the second half of the thirteenth century that the differentiated vowels of Alemannic texts, as heard for instance in modern Swiss, reappear. Thus we see Bavarian poets clinging to an archaic form, when the spoken language of the area must already have introduced diphthongs, and we see the contrary example of Alemannic poets introducing the uniform *e* in unstressed syllables where even seven centuries later the spoken

---

assimilations such as we hear in modern spoken language, and for this reason the *Gespräche* are of considerable interest. Unfortunately their reliability is suspect, since amongst other things the language shows a Romance-speaker's propensity for dropping *h*'s such as would do credit to a true-blood cockney.

language has differentiated vowels. Perhaps the most extreme example of negative levelling is to be seen in Heinrich von Veldeke who appears to have taken increasing steps to avoid rhymes which, although pure in his native Low Franconian dialect, would prove inadequate if transliterated into H.G. and would thus reflect upon his skill as a poet. He shows a similar tendency to avoid parochial vocabulary. The most extreme case of positive levelling must be those L.G. poets who chose to write, with varying degrees of accuracy and success, in H.G., while between the two extremes we can descry countless examples of give and take between the main dialect areas, sometimes with the lure of convenient rhymes in mind.

The French vocabulary in itself must have represented a certain measure of lexical levelling, since two fundamentally different dialectal items could be replaced by one French word. Moreover, on a phonological level, the pronunciation of a given French word in various German dialects may well have been more similar, being presumably an approximation to the French pronunciation, than that of one native word in several dialects which had been subject to divergent phonological development for centuries. If there is any region which appears slightly to have pride of place in this courtly literary language it is N. Alemannic/Swabian, and this is evidence perhaps of the importance of the region from which the Hohenstaufen emperors stemmed.

The impression may have been given that the courtly literary language was the only form of written German during the M.H.G. period, but this is not the case. As the thirteenth century progresses we find more and more business and legal documents written in German at the expense of Latin, a development which accelerates as towns and their citizens gradually acquire an importance as centres of administration and commerce equal to that of the courts and the aristocracy. The written language of their chanceries also grows in importance, but since its full linguistic significance does not make itself felt until the E.N.H.G. period, that question will be deferred until the next section. Sermons, religious tracts and edifying homilies have also survived from the M.H.G. period, and these constitute yet a further stratum of written M.H.G. It is customary to single out the German mystics of the thirteenth and fourteenth centuries, for example Meister Eckhart (*c.* 1260–1327), or Johannes Tauler (*c.* 1300–61), as being of special linguistic importance, particularly in the creation of numerous abstracts ending in -*ung* and -*heit*, both of which derivative suffixes play an important role in N.H.G. An examination of the vocabulary of eleventh-century religious poetry shows, however, that many of the terms which are associated with later mystics must have existed already, and it seems that the mystics are to be credited with the proliferation, propagation and popularization of such formations rather than with their invention.

The M.H.G. literary language did not last beyond the middle of the fourteenth century and was on the wane even earlier. The koine of an exclusive class expressing its aristocratic interests did not provide the basis for a national standard language and could not survive the decrease in relative importance of its knightly exponents.

Early New High German

Once again the watershed chosen to distinguish between M.H.G. and E.N.H.G. turns out to be not a neat mountain ridge but rather an undulating table-land rising and falling and sloping haphazardly in various directions. The phonological features usually selected for this distinction are three in number: firstly the diphthongization of the M.H.G. long vowels *î, û, iu* to *ei, au, eu* respectively, e.g. *mîn:mein* ('my'), *hûs:Haus* ('house'), *diutsch:deutsch*; secondly, the development of the dipthongs *ie, uo, üe* to the long monophthongs *ie* (written the same as in M.H.G., but pronounced as a long monophthong), *u, ü,* e.g. M.H.G. *lieb:*N.H.G. *lieb* ('dear'), *guot:gut* ('good'), *güete:Güte* ('goodness'); thirdly, the lengthening of all short vowels in stressed syllables ending in a vowel (so-called 'open syllables'), e.g. M.H.G. *geben* ('to give'; the *e* pronounced as in English 'get'):N.H.G. *geben* (the *e* somewhat like the vowel in northern English 'pane'). These three phonetic changes began in different parts of Germany and at different times.

The first begins no later than in the early twelfth century in the S.E. of German-speaking territory, notably Carinthia, and has spread to most of Germany by the sixteenth century, though even nowadays this development has not taken place in several dialects, notably in L.G. and in S.W. German, for instance in Swiss. Monophthongization of *ie, uo, üe,* on the other hand, begins in the eleventh century in Central German and spreads through Franconian and also into East Central German from which it finds its way into the N.H.G. standard. Lastly, there is evidence of lengthening in open syllables in O.H.G. times, but the process reaches its climax in the thirteenth and fourteenth centuries. It begins in the N.W. and reaches Upper German slightly later than Central German. This change, too, did not take place in some Alemannic areas. It is, in fact, not always easy to determine whether lengthening has occurred in a specific text or not, since it is not usually indicated orthographically. Where it is indicated the most usual means is to double the vowel, e.g. M.H.G. *sal*:N.H.G. *Saal* ('hall'), or to write an *h* after the vowel, M.H.G. *wern*:N.H.G. *wehren* ('to defend'). Since a double consonant following the vowel meant that the syllable was closed (i.e. that it ended in a consonant, the syllables being divided as follows *bit-ten*), lengthening did not take place in such environments and the vowel remained short. Thus double consonants came to be associated with short vowels. If, therefore, for any reason a vowel in an open syllable was not lengthened, as was frequently the case when this vowel was followed by *m* or *t*, the following consonant tended to be doubled – a purely orthographical device – to indicate the shortness of the vowel, e.g. M.H.G. *himel*:N.H.G. *Himmel* ('sky'), *gate*:*Gatte* ('husband'). Occasional forms such as *Saal*, or *wehren*, with their lengthening indicated, or even forms such as *Himmel* and *Gatte* where shortness of vowel is shown emphatically, are probably evidence that all vowels in open syllables have been lengthened in the dialect of the scribe in question, provided, of course, that it cannot be shown by other means that the *aa*, or *eh*, *mm* or *tt*, etc., are not merely phonetically meaningless graphemes introduced from another area, or derived from the scribe's model.

It has been intimated that the changes discussed above do not take place at the same time and that in some regions they do not occur at all. Though it may seem an odd method of distinguishing between one period of a language and the next to choose changes which have not taken place in considerable areas of that language, there is a justification for this and the reason is not far to seek. The three changes under discussion, diphthongization, monophthongization and lengthening are all features of the N.H.G. standard language, therefore the early N.H.G. period is considered as beginning once these three changes are present in combination in substantial areas of German-speaking territory. This hindsight from the point of view of the modern standard will characterize our remarks more and more from now on, since the remainder of our account will concern itself largely with the growth, spread and victory of that form of German which has come to be accepted as the national standard. The gestation and birth of this standard was a more protracted process in Germany than, say, in France or England because of the incredibly fragmented political nature and particularist outlook of late medieval Germany, a situation which became more and more pronounced as the emperor's importance waned and that of the individual territorial rulers grew.

During the E.N.H.G. period German continued to increase its range of usage, at the expense of Latin. Various factors brought this about, amongst them the increased need for correspondence caused by the growth of trade and commerce, the merchants being rarely trained in Latin, and the inability of smaller centres, whether towns or seats of the lower aristocracy, to afford trained 'clerics' or 'clerks' who were skilled in Latin. The period is marked in general by an increase in the importance of the middle classes and of the towns and their inhabitants. Between the middle of the thirteenth and the middle of the fourteenth century most towns go over to German as the language of their official documents. But of all the influences on German in the period under discussion the three most powerful are undoubtedly the invention of printing, the emergence of Luther, and the shift in the centre of gravity of German-speaking territory due to its expansion in an easterly direction.

Let us begin with the latter. The eastern boundary of German territory had been subject to violent fluctuation from the earliest times onwards. On the whole it is idle to argue whether the territories in the east were originally Slav or German(ic), since it is not clear how far back 'originally' lies and since we know little about the very earliest times, many peoples having vanished from the area or even from history, and since problems arise in equating 'Germanic' and 'German'. For instance, moderate surprise might be expressed if nowadays large numbers of Anglo-Saxons decided to leave England and return 'home' to northern Germany and the Danish peninsula. Allowing for the fluctuations mentioned above, the north-eastern boundary of Germany might be considered as being formed by the rivers Elbe and Saale until the beginning of the twelfth century. From this time onwards more and more German territories were founded east of this line and consigned to dukes, margraves and ecclesiastical princes, since colonization and conquest were compounded with christianization and missionary zeal. Territories gained in this manner were amongst others the marches of Meissen and Lusatia, also Mecklenburg and Silesia. Bohemia had been incorporated into the Reich since the tenth century and subsequently further expansion took place in the south-east. In the first half of the thirteenth century the Teutonic Order of Knights conquered and later christianized the heathen Prussians whose territory became part of the Reich and whose non-Germanic, Baltic language finally died out in the seventeenth century. These eastern territories were settled by Germans from the north of Germany, from the Moselle and Lower Rhine, from Upper Franconia and Thuringia, areas in which a shortage of land was making itself felt.

As a result of this expansion of the east we find that territories which had formerly been on the periphery of German-speaking territory now occupied a much more central position. The importance of this factor will be discussed later. Moreover, the colonists who settled in East Central Germany stemmed from areas with L.G., Central German and Upper German dialects and it would not be surprising if a speech form developed among them which showed characteristics drawn from each of these dialect areas. In fact, written documents from East Central Germany, whether literary texts or those issuing from the more important chanceries, do begin to show a mixture of Upper German and Central German features which can, but need not, be explained as a blend of the language of Upper German and Central German settlers, and which appear as characteristics of the N.H.G. standard language. It is difficult to find evidence about the extent to which a spoken language ever existed which was a blend of the speech habits of the Upper German and Central German settlers. The written evidence which we have may indicate that such a blend existed and that it provided the basis for the East Central German written language, but although this view is likely to be correct, it is possible that a written language may have grown up as a compromise between the written languages of Upper Germany and Central Germany.

If one were attempting in the abstract to forecast what kind of standard written language, if any, late medieval Germany would develop, one might well forecast a compromise between central and southern forms such as one finds (though not, of course, precise details) without taking cognizance of the mixed population of East Central Germany. The extent of German territory from north to south was considerable, and in the normal nature of things if we have a series of dialects which we will call A, B, C, D, E running from north to south and situated relative to each other as the order of letters suggests, then it is likely that neighbouring dialects, for instance A and B, or even possibly A and C, will be mutually comprehensible, but that A and D, or B and E, will not. A view of this kind in respect of English is expressed around 1387: 'Þerfore it is þat Mercii, þat beeþ men of myddel Engelond, as it were parteners of þe endes, vnderstondeþ bettre þe side langages, norþerne

and souþerne, þan norþerne and souþerne vnderstondeþ eiþer oþer.'[1]
In such a situation it is likely that if a standard language grows up which
is acceptable and intelligible throughout all the dialect areas, it will be
based on one of the central dialects, probably modified by its neighbours. The central dialects have the advantage that they are intelligible
to neighbours on both sides. This applies, of course, only if all other
things are equal. But in Germany all things were not equal, since the
political and economic importance of Central Germany, particularly
East Central Germany with her powerful territorial groupings, was to
grow, while that of the north was later to decline as Hanseatic trade
receded in the fifteenth century. The balance of power between the
three linguistic regions of Germany was further upset by Luther and
the Reformation. Here again, Low German in particular suffered,
since in accepting the reformed religion it opened the floodgates to the
High German language in which it was couched. A tentative Low
German standard, based largely on the scriptorial practice of Lübeck,
had grown up in connection with the Hanse, but this collapsed in the
face of its H.G. rival which came, as indicated already, with the
Reformation. In contrast to the abortive attempt, if 'attempt' does not
imply too conscious a process, to establish a Low German written
standard, the nascent written standard in the Netherlands survived any
threat offered by H.G. and became the basis of the modern Dutch
standard. That unlike L.G. it was able to do this is due to various
factors including its extremely peripheral geographical position,
looked at from the Reich, and to a feeling of self-reliance and
separatism which found recognition finally in the granting of political independence to the Netherlands in the Peace of Westphalia
(1648).

The rivalry between Upper German and Central German was a more
complicated and protracted affair than that between High German and
Low German. Broadly speaking, in the fifteenth century the Upper
German written language, based on Bavarian–Austrian usage, and the
East Central German written language were equally powerful rivals.
The growing power and prestige of Central Germany was in some
measure symbolized by the fact that under the Luxembourg emperors
the imperial chancery was sited at Prague (1347 onwards). On the
other hand, in the fifteenth century under Habsburg emperors it was
moved to Vienna. It might be wondered why the documents issuing

[1] From John de Trevisa's translation of Ranulf Higden's *Polychronicon*, ed. C.
Babington, Vol. II (London, 1869), p. 163.

from chanceries with their formulaic flourishes and dry-as-dust contents should be of any importance in the development of the German standard. Their influence was indeed restricted in its sphere, but far-reaching within this sphere. Chanceries tended to develop their own practice with regard to morphology and orthography, chiefly the latter. It made for administrative tidiness to have a consistent orthographic and grammatical practice within one's chancery, and reliable rules of thumb, no matter how arbitrary, presumably increased productivity by eliminating soul-searching pauses and time-consuming discussion on the part of the clerks. As in the monasteries of O.H.G. times the practice varied from chancery to chancery and was often the work of one or two leading figures. Gradually, as more and more chanceries went over to German for an increasing range of uses, we see lesser chanceries adopting the practice of the great ones. The consistency within a chancery is only partial, and the influence of one chancery upon another is often only relative. None the less in many forms of written German the fourteenth and fifteenth centuries form a melting-pot in which contrasts between regional variants of written German are partially reduced and in which written forms of German move away somewhat from the dialect of the area from which they stem. It is difficult for us nowadays to grasp the importance of the limited measure of consistency which the chanceries introduced, since we take 'accuracy', 'correctness' and 'consistency' of spelling and grammar for granted, while in the centuries under discussion such concepts barely existed, even for the literate. A glance at contemporary letters, or letters written in Elizabethan England, in which writers spell proper names – even their own – in several different ways within the same letter, gives some insight into the totally different approach to language and writing which prevailed in earlier times. The limited tonal range and restricted vocabulary of chancery language had to be broadened and the degree of consistency had to be raised before there could be anything like the modern written standard. Luther and printing went a considerable way towards supplying these needs.

The immediate effect of printing, which was first practised as we know it by Gutenberg in Mainz around the middle of the fifteenth century, was to increase astronomically the number of people who could afford reading matter. But from our point of view it was just as important that for the first time identical copies of the same text could be produced, and the psychological effect of this must have been considerable. The result was that printers took more and more care to arrive at a consistent and 'correct' orthographic practice, and in order to achieve as widespread sales as possible in other parts of Germany they or their readers often modified their practice and approximated it to that of other important areas. In this way the regional variations among the printers tended to diminish during the sixteenth century, for again this was a tendency rather than a completed process. There is perhaps an inclination to overstress the printers' desire to find a form of language which would be intelligible over as wide an area as possible. Regional orthography does not necessarily produce unintelligibility, and even in a sphere where this might be expected, namely vocabulary, things may not have been so difficult as scholars imagine. The fact that the Basle printer Adam Petri attached a glossary to his 1522 edition of Luther's New Testament, in order to explain a number of Luther's words to his Alemannic readers, might have as much to do with a desire to boost sales of his own particular (pirate) edition as with any real difficulties of comprehension. That some of Luther's vocabulary was not *used* in Basle can be demonstrated, that it was not *understood* is more difficult to show. It is common to talk of printers' 'dialects', but this term can be misleading, since the printers' language tended to build on the regional variants of the written language which we have already mentioned, and these themselves were already removed from the regional dialects proper. It is common to distinguish five types of printers' language in Central Germany and Upper Germany, excluding Switzerland. They are in Central Germany the Upper Saxon (main centres Wittenberg and Leipzig) and the Central Rhenish (Mainz and Frankfurt), and in Upper Germany the Upper Rhenish (Strasbourg) and the Bavaro-Swabian (Augsburg). The language of the Nürnberg and Bamberg printers is seen as forming a transition between Upper German and Central German types.

The third major factor mentioned was the figure of Martin Luther (1483–1546), around whose role in the shaping of the N.H.G. standard a controversy has raged which has been almost as long and only slightly less acrimonious than the Reformation itself, and which has ranged in its assessment of Luther from naming him the 'creator of the N.H.G. language' to denying that he had any importance at all. Since it can be shown, and since Luther himself declared, that he did not invent his own form of language, and since, as has been often repeated, roughly one-third of all German writings appearing between 1518 and 1522 bore Luther's name, while between 1534 and 1584 Lufft's press in Wittenberg alone produced some 100,000 copies of Luther's translation of the Bible, each of these extreme viewpoints may be dismissed as exaggerated.

It is important that Luther was born and attended school and university on both sides of the Low German/Central German linguistic border, in Mansfeld, Magdeburg, Eisenach, Erfurt and Wittenberg, but always in close proximity to it. His own usage, therefore, was essentially Central German with a limited admixture of Low German, chiefly in his lexicon. In a much-quoted passage from his *Tischreden* (chapter 70) Luther himself claims to follow the usage of the Saxon chancery, adding that this linguistic form is employed by all territorial rulers in Germany. On this latter point he is sanguine, though also perhaps prophetic, and in any case Luther's usage changes with time and in some respects moves away from the more pronounced East Central German forms with which he begins and which are perhaps derived from the Saxon chancery of the Wettin rulers. It is customary to distinguish three periods in Luther's writings, seen from a purely linguistic, or rather orthographic, point of view, though it is not entirely clear what is to be attributed to Luther and what to the printer or his reader, since the latter were notoriously cavalier in their treatment of authors' texts.[1] In the first period down to 1524 we find considerable inconsistency and apparently little attention paid to orthographic practice. For the most part the practice of the East Central German scribes and printers is followed, for instance mutated and unmutated *o* and *u* appear undiscriminated as simply *o* and *u*, and there is a tendency to proliferate consonants unnecessarily, such as in *Czeytten* for *Zeiten*. The second period, extending to 1532, is characterized by greater orthographic tidiness and consistency and by a movement away from more 'extreme' Central German forms, and towards the written variant of Upper German, known as *das gemeine Deutsch*, which had gained prestige as a result of the interest shown in it by the Habsburg Maximilian I (emperor 1493–1519) and his Chancellor Niklas Ziegler; East Central German forms such as *gottis*, *tagis*, yield to *gottes*, *tages*, the prefix *vor-* to *ver-*, *ader*, *ab* to *oder*, *ob*, mutated *u* and *o* tend to be indicated, and the superfluous accumulations of consonants are simplified. In the third period after 1532 few noteworthy innovations take place, though the tidying-up process continues. Throughout Luther's career we notice a move in the direction of beginning nouns with capital letters, at first only proper names, but by 1540 it extends to

[1] The division is useful, but the choice of dates somewhat arbitrary. Here we follow Walter Henzen, *Schriftsprache und Mundarten*, 2nd edn. (Bern, 1954), p. 96.

eighty per cent of all nouns. This move like the others mentioned above agrees with the N.H.G. standard. Usually where Luther did not move in the direction of Upper German, his practice again agrees with the N.H.G. standard, for instance (Luther's form first, the Upper German form second): *Name, Nam; gebrannt, gbrannt; Bein, Bain; gut, gût; Verdammnis, Verdammnus; die Luft, der Luft*. Occasionally, however, Luther retains some Central German forms where they do not agree with the subsequent N.H.G. standard, for instance *treib* as the preterite singular of *treiben* where N.H.G. has *trieb*.

The question must be posed, even if it cannot be answered, how this correspondence in the majority of cases between Luther's practice and that of the modern standard comes about. Was Luther himself responsible for it? It is to be noted that whereas at times Luther follows East Central German practice without the N.H.G. standard doing the same, it does not seem that he ever adopts an Upper German form without the modern standard concurring. Presumably this is because Luther as a Central German would be inclined to fall easily into 'extreme' Central German, whereas the Upper German forms which he adopts were less restricted regionally and less parochial than his native ones, and were probably acquired as part of a standardizing tendency, as features of a written language developing between Upper German and Central German and deriving from and penetrating into both language areas. There is evidence that in the late fifteenth and early sixteenth centuries the language of the printers of Augsburg and of those of Central Germany were approaching each other. Moreover, this was a process in which each linguistic area gave and each took, so that gradually a koine grew up between them, though of course a koine with here a more Upper German and there a more Central German flavour. Thus Luther did not 'create' his own form of German, nor was he necessarily responsible for the individual selection of Central German and Upper German features which we find in it, but it seems rather that he launched himself into a current which he diverted only at certain points, either voluntarily or involuntarily. Does this reduce Luther from a bold swimmer in the flow of the German language to an impotent drifter, content to splash a little from time to time?

Belittlers of Luther's role in the history of German have stressed constantly that he was 'no philologist'. This might seem a surprising statement about someone who was a Greek and Latin scholar, who was able to translate the whole of the New Testament into German in a space of some eleven months, moreover from Erasmus's Greek text

(1516) when his predecessors had had to make do with Latin versions, who wrote a treatise on his aims and methods in translating, and who was interested enough in the sociological and etymological aspects of language to republish a book on thieves' speech with a glossary of their language and to furnish it with a preface in which he draws attention to the Hebrew origins of much of thieves' cant.[1] In addition, Luther was well aware of regional variation in German, both from corresponding with people in all parts of Germany and from travelling on foot through considerable areas of the country. All in all this adds up to a strong claim to being considered a 'philologist', but of course Luther was no philologist, if by this term we mean a normative grammarian whose express aim it is to regularize language and reduce regional differences. Luther's aim was to spread his message and God's word, and his linguistic importance springs from the success with which he did this. Whether or not he invented his own form of language, he propagated it, and his achievement as a stylist served to carry the form of his language to all German-speaking areas. Luther's message was of burning interest to all, supporters and enemies alike, and his style was calculated to bring it home with force and clarity. He tells us that he learnt how to write German by listening to the common people, and the directness, raciness, often verging on vulgarity, and strength which he derived from such everyday speech was the vitalizing spark which the language of the chancery and much of the stilted literary language of his day required and which supplied it with the wider range of registers it needed. A further important influence on Luther's style, chiefly in the field of syntax, were the writings of late medieval religious writers and mystics in East Central Germany. These two factors consolidated the East Central German basis of Luther's language.

A form of written German closely akin to Luther's was to form the basis of the N.H.G. standard, and Luther's use of it would seem to have been the weight which tilted the balance in favour of this modified form of East Central German. Opposition to Luther and his language was violent, especially in those areas such as Switzerland where local patriotism was involved, or in the Bavaro-Austrian area where local patriotism combined with religious antipathy. Yet even the Catholic Bible translations which appeared in the wake of Luther's, notably that of Johann Eck (1537), were nothing more than slightly altered versions of Luther's text, as Luther himself was not slow to point out.

[1] *Von der falschen Betler buberey, mit einer Vorrede Martini Luther* (Wittenberg, 1528). Earlier editions had appeared as the *Liber vagatorum*.

These plagiarized publications under Catholic names enabled the language of Luther's Bible to work as a kind of linguistic fifth-column, infiltrating areas where resistance to the name of Luther might have been more strong and protracted. As it was, the final victory of East Central German as found in Luther was to require centuries, and during those centuries matters were sufficiently undecided for events to have prevented this victory. That they did not was due in considerable measure to Luther and those of his followers and admirers who in the second half of the sixteenth century and throughout the seventeenth century championed East Central German and cited Luther as its most glorious exponent, even though the East Central German which they championed had developed away from the language of Luther.

The New High German Period

The sixteenth century had provided a written form of German which had power and appeal enough to serve as a model for the N.H.G. standard. In Germany, as in other western European countries, the written language led the way in the process of standardization. Such standard languages are notoriously eclectic, drawing now on one area, now on another, and a complete description of how modern German has come to be the way it is would require a detailed study of every sound, every inflexional form, every word and every syntactical pattern of the modern standard and of the history of each item. Needless to say much of this evidence is no longer discoverable and what is discoverable would amount to an astronomical number of details, many of which could not perhaps be synthesized and reduced to general principles.

The relative rigidity and strictness of the modern standard is recognized, but what is not always recognized is that the nature of the model which is to be observed has been arrived at by a chain of minute decisions, the reasons for which vary from foreseeable general principles (e.g. H.G. sounds as opposed to L.G. sounds) to the usage of one person and to bizarre individual events, so much so that the development of the modern standard becomes almost a random process of selection when viewed as a totality. One example will have to suffice to demonstrate this. The modern German verb meaning 'to print' is *drucken*. This is an U.G. form of the verb *drücken* ('to press'), it being characteristic of U.G. not to mutate the vowel before -*ck*- (cf. Austrian *Innsbruck* with North German *Osnabrück*). Presumably the U.G. variant of the verb 'to press' became accepted throughout Germany, because printing first developed on a large scale in U.G. areas and the U.G. *drucken* spread to other regions as the technical term together with the printing techniques themselves. Thus the reason why modern German has *drucken* as well as *drücken* would have to be sought in a complicated history of where Gutenberg was born and was active, where his pupils and emulators stemmed from, what economic, political and personal reasons led to printing flourishing first in Upper Germany and so on. And all this to explain only one item of the modern lexicon!

It is extremely difficult to write the history of the N.H.G. standard for a variety of reasons, the first of which is the complexity mentioned above. The paucity of evidence from the earlier periods enables, indeed forces us to make generalizations which would be inadmissible for the later period. As we approach modern times the amount of written evidence swells alarmingly as more and more is set down on paper and as German extends its sphere of usage to the law, to the natural sciences and to learning in general. Although Paracelsus had lectured in German at the University of Basle in 1526 this was an isolated occurrence and was not repeated until Christian Thomasius used German for his lectures at Leipzig in 1687. Similarly it was not until 1681 in Germany that the number of books (that is titles, not copies) published in German exceeded the number in Latin. Because of the mass of material as we approach modern German, histories of the language are often in danger of collapsing into histories of literature which deal with the language of the various literary movements and which tend to concentrate on their characteristic vocabulary. This may seem merely a rearrangement of the literary works themselves in such a way that their content is repeated, but now in the alphabetical order of the words, or according to some semantic principle, and the disappointment one feels is at once justified and mistaken. Presumably what the inveterate historian of language is seeking is some account of linguistic change and development, and if he misses it, this is for two reasons.

The first is because of what we might call 'the parallactic fallacy'. Just as the posts of a fence seem to draw closer together as the fence recedes in the distance, so too spans of time seem shorter at greater remove. In seeking developments, say, since 1800, comparable to the High German Soundshift or N.H.G. diphthongization we forget that these changes required perhaps four or five centuries. The second reason why our searcher for change may feel cheated is that perhaps there has been less change than there used to be. The dominance of the written language in an age of a literate majority, together with the influence of the language of mass media such as radio or television, whose language is often based on the written standard, may act as a considerable check on linguistic development. It is largely accepted that the spoken language, particularly at a colloquial or dialect level, changes more rapidly than the written language which is, for instance, notoriously backward in indicating orthographically changes in pronunciation. It has been a growing tendency in Germany since the seventeenth century to speak as one writes, and in this way the inertia of orthography acts as a brake on changes in pronunciation. The exception which proves the rule is English, where pronunciation in the standard changes more rapidly than in German, presumably because English orthography, based as it is on Middle English pronunciation, is by now too unphonetic and removed from modern pronunciation to halt sound changes.[1] In fact, we have perhaps no analogue for describing linguistic development in modern times, since the modern supremacy of the written word is unmatched in earlier periods and the mass media were unthought of. These considerations were necessary to explain the nature and the brevity of the following account of N.H.G., but they have led us away from the seventeenth century to which we must return.

The ingredient which the seventeenth century was to add to the development of the modern standard was the work of normative grammarians. Although in some ways the emergence of the modern standard may be seen as a process akin to natural selection, the degree of consistency and regularity demanded by it and the level of compulsion exercised by it is unthinkable without the pronouncements of grammarians, and these grammarians were supplied in the first instance by the seventeenth century which has been called the age of the 'Poesie-philologen' and of the 'Philologiepoeten'.[2] An active interest in the German language was indeed alive amongst poets and grammarians

[1] This must not be taken to mean that English orthography has no effect at all on English pronunciation. Through the phenomenon known as 'spelling pronunciation', for instance, sounds which had long vanished and which would have been forgotten, had they not been retained by an archaic orthography, are revived when readers begin to pronounce the obsolete symbols. Probable examples are the *t* in 'often' which is heard nowadays, the first *d* in 'Wednesday' and sometimes, as an individual variant, even the *r* in 'iron'.

[2] Friedrich Gundolf, 'Justus Georg Schottel' in *Deutschkundliches, Friedrich Panzer zum 60, Geburtstag überreicht* (Heidelberg, 1930), pp. 70 ff.

alike and both groups were characterized by what Gundolf calls 'Wortbesessenheit' (i.e. they were 'possessed by words'). Their common aim, to regulate the German language, was motivated by patriotism, since it was felt that in order to have the prestige of Latin or French, German had to be reducible to rules. As in eighteenth-century England this desire for rules and regularity was usually combined with demands for elegance, since to set up a standard of correct usage was to refine the language and remove inelegant dross. Only when German had achieved regularity could it hold up its head amongst other cultured European languages. Though the patriotism may have been misdirected, it was not entirely misplaced, since as a result of the language mixing of the Thirty Years War and later of the supreme prestige of France and *Le Roi Soleil*, Germany had been swamped with foreign clothes, weapons, customs and words, largely French, though also Italian and Spanish, and at some levels of 'polite' conversation German was in danger of being ousted completely by French. The type of borrowing, the scale of it and the level of society which favoured it show similarity with the borrowing from O.F. in the twelfth and thirteenth centuries. The word which describes this trait, *das Alamodewesen* (literally 'fashionable doings', meaning 'imitation of French language and fashion') at once expresses it and characterizes it by means of its hybrid Franco-German nature.

One hesitates to speak of nationalism in seventeenth-century Germany, since its myriad small territories with their conflicting claims meant that the only pegs for nationalism were the outworn memory of the Holy Roman Empire, and the common German tongue. Instead it is better to speak of resurgent patriotism, and nowhere did this patriotism find more vigorous expression than in the so-called *Sprachgesellschaften* ('language societies'). This term is a misnomer in so far as the renovation of the language defiled by admixture was only one, and not necessarily the most important, aim of the *Sprachgesellschaften*. Their goal was the restoration of German customs, the preservation of German virtues, and encouragement of courtesy and excellence wherever it might be found. The first of the *Sprachgesellschaften* and the most famous of them was the Fruchtbringende Gesellschaft, founded in 1617 by Prince Ludwig of Anhalt-Köthen. It numbered amongst its members Opitz, Logau, Gryphius, and Schottel. The linguistic influence of the *Sprachgesellschaften* was directed largely at ridding German of foreign words and expressions and at compiling a German grammar.

Rooting out the foreign word became amongst some a pastime akin to witch-hunting, with the saving grace that its excesses tended towards grotesqueries rather than atrocities. Inadequate account was taken of how old or well-established the foreign word was, and occasionally – again the similarity with the witch-hunt is obvious – harmless native words were seized upon, mangled and banished, above all by Philipp von Zesen and usually with little effect. At best Zesen coined or helped popularize some useful terms, at worst he enriched the pages of German humour and seemed to be more loved by his contemporaries for the latter than the former. While they ridiculed his substitution of *Tageleuchter* ('illuminator of the day') and *Gesichtserker* (literally 'balcony or bow-window of the face') for the innocent native *Sonne* ('sun') and *Nase* ('nose'), we can at least appreciate the usefulness of *Mundart* for *Dialekt*, of *Tagebuch* for *Journal* ('a daily account') or *Trauerspiel* for *Tragödie*.

The compiling of grammars in German had begun in the sixteenth century though the works are sometimes nothing more than books of rhetoric, instructing in the art of writing polished German. Perhaps the most important, certainly the most prophetic of the sixteenth-century grammars was that of Johannes Clajus, *Grammatica Germanicae linguae ex bibliis Lutheri Germanicis et aliis eius libris collecta* (1578). As the title indicates, it was based on and championed Luther's German, though from the second edition onwards Luther's name was omitted from the title, presumably in order to placate opposition and increase sales in Catholic areas. This work went through eleven editions, the last in 1720! One of the first influential 'grammars' of the seventeenth century was Martin Opitz's *Buch von der deutschen Poeterei* (1624), which was in fact a prosody and not a grammar, but which touched none the less on important grammatical points, for instance the status of the unstressed *e* in prefixes like *ge-* or *be-* or in endings, for example *Name, sollte*, where these impinged upon questions of metre or rhyme. With regard to unstressed *e* Opitz rejected the syncope and apocope met in U.G. writers, and his ruling coincides to a considerable extent with the usage of the N.H.G. standard. Opitz's influence did not extend far beyond the group of Silesian poets, but these were an influential group in terms of the growth of written German.

The grammarian *par excellence* of the seventeenth century was, however, Justus Georg Schottel(ius) (1612–76) whose *Ausführliche Arbeit von der Teutschen Haubt Sprache* (1663) is at once the most massive, thorough, perceptive, dogmatic and infuriating grammatical work of its century. In Schottel the main principles to which normative grammarians of the time appealed emerge more clearly than in other writers. It is the aim of such a regulator of language to remove doubt and where necessary choose and recognize one of two or more usages as 'correct', condemning the others as wrong. Like a policeman's, a normative grammarian's 'lot is not a happy one'. Not only does our grammarian lack the sanctions to enforce his decisions and punish wrong-doers, but his position is dangerously exposed, since he has frequently to choose as 'correct' one usage and reject as 'wrong' another where the two usages are merely regional variants. Each usage exists, so the decision to reject one must be arbitrary whichever way it falls. It is here that the criteria adopted are crucial, since the decision may be arbitrary and reasonable, or arbitrary and unreasonable.

The history of the gender of *See* ('sea' or 'lake') supplies a good example of an arbitrary but reasonable decision. *See* appears to have been a masculine originally in Germanic, but it appears also as a feminine in O.E. and later in L.G. Gradually the feminine creeps into H.G. The dictionaries are at variance about the situation in M.H.G., some asserting that the masculine was used for 'sea' or 'lake', whereas the feminine was used only for 'sea', while others maintain that masculine and feminine were used indiscriminately in both meanings. Certainly by E.N.H.G. times the indiscriminate use of both genders is prevalent and is continued until the eighteenth century. Gradually, however, the distinction which is observed in the modern standard appears, namely that *der See* is used to mean 'lake' and *die See* to mean 'sea'. This distinction is first found in 1542 in a work by the Pomeranian Thomas Kantzow who recounts that amongst his fellow countrymen the Baltic is called 'die sehe in feminino genere, und ein ander stehende waszer, den sehe in masculino genere'.[1] Either this distinction was later obliterated or it was not as rigidly or widely observed in Kantzow's own time as he would have us believe, since it is not until the nineteenth century that it is truly prevalent, and even then occasional derailments take place, though with decreasing frequency. The modern practice was described as arbitrary, because it is arbitrary to forbid an Upper German to say *der See* for the 'sea' or to forbid a Low German to say *die See* for a 'lake', when numerous examples from previous centuries

---

[1] Thomas Kantzow, *Pomerania, aus dessen Handschrift herausgegeben von H. G. L. Kosegarten* (Greifswald, 1816–17), Vol. II, p. 397. See also *Trübners Deutsches Wörterbuch* under the lemma *See*.

could be adduced for each of these practices. It is simply a case of eliminating regional doublets. Yet it is a reasonable decision, since the North Germans were those who of all German peoples had most to do with the sea and matters concerned with it, therefore it is arbitrary but reasonable to enforce their gender for the sea, and, if a one-to-one solution is to be reached, to enforce the Upper German masculine gender for a lake. Vice versa the decision would have been no more arbitrary but infinitely more unreasonable. Many solutions were less happy and it is one further feature of the unhappy lot of a normative grammarian that, whereas it can always be demonstrated subsequently that his decisions were wrong and were not followed, it can never be proved, when his decisions coincide with the practice adopted by the standard language, that his opinion had the slightest influence. At best he can be credited with perspicacity.

During the seventeenth century and for most of the eighteenth century the main principles appealed to by grammarians were analogy, etymology and usage. Analogy speaks for itself – what is applicable and well established in one instance must be appropriate and correct in all similar instances. The decision as to what constituted similar instances proved, however, no small problem. The etymological approach might better be termed the historical approach, and it operated in two ways: the first was the assumption that in cases of doubt what could be shown to be earlier or older was to be considered correct; the second was that etymological analysis, assisted by examination of the earliest evidence available, would enable the grammarian to make his pronouncement. The appeal to usage was seductively simple, but raised the thorny question of whose usage was to be considered authoritative – the usage of a certain region, the usage of writers, the speech of a certain class or what? In the majority of cases the answer was 'the usage of Meissen', but this was a vague answer since it would not be made clear whether the speech of Meissen or the writers of Meissen were meant and since the claims of Meissen would often be coupled with an appeal to the authority of Luther or the Saxon chancery, both of which were by now different from the Misnian spoken language of the time.

Though Schottel's was hardly a typical solution and although he was aware only at times of the true issues involved, it is worth looking at his answer to the question posed above. Analogy and etymology both played a fundamental role in Schottel's grammatical scheme, but it is with usage that we will begin. Schottel was violently opposed to the appeal to usage as a criterion, in so far as the usage was that of a particular area, notably Meissen. By birth Schottel was a Low German who presumably had learnt High German almost as a foreign language. Schottel challenged and poured scorn on the claims of the inhabitants of Meissen that theirs was the correct German and that their own ears were the arbiters of linguistic propriety. The process of learning H.G. artificially may have opened his eyes to the eclectic nature of a standard language, or there may perhaps have been a less praiseworthy sentiment of antipathy to those who spoke E.C.G. 'naturally'. One faces the same doubts in evaluating Schottel's position as one does in assessing Dr Johnson's lonely scepticism towards Ossian. In each case was it insight or xenophobia?

For Schottel *the* German language was not that of one region but was to be discovered in the language of learned, cultured and refined writers from all regions. Where they were in conflict the grammarian was to seek the *Grundrichtigkeit* ('basic correctness', one might say 'grammatical nature') of the language, and analogy was the means for doing this. Where analogy failed Schottel resorted to etymological analysis, and this led him to the conclusion that there were three kinds of elements in German: roots or stems, principal endings (i.e. derivative suffixes) and occasional endings (i.e. inflexional endings). Every syllable must fall into one of these categories and what could not be accounted for in this way was a excrescence and, being superfluous, was to be discarded. The final -*e* of words like *Speise* or *Name* was thus rejected, though not, of course, of *Güte* or *Röte*, for here Schottel could recognize the -*e* as a derivative suffix. The dogmatic assertion that the imperative was the root form of the verb, though allowance was made for mutation of the root-vowel, led Schottel to brand as incorrect the -*e* of the imperative of weak verbs. The imperative was the root form, therefore *gib* and *nimm* were correct and by analogy one must say *red* or *mach* and not *rede* or *mache*, thereby failing to allow for any distinction between strong and weak verbs.

Schottel's model is regulated written usage, and the spoken language must follow it. His attitude towards the dialects is extremely derogatory, but he does recognize that the vocabulary of standard German (*die Hochteutsche Sprache*) is something which has flowed together from all the dialects, and he was in favour of compiling a German dictionary which would include dialect words. Above all else he was quick to recognize the outstanding features of German – for instance his admiration for the language's ability to form compounds and derivatives – and he showed more insight into the history of German than his contemporaries, some of whom used 'linguistic history' merely to show that German possessed more of the root-words used in the Garden of Eden than Latin or Greek and that it was therefore at least as old and probably more venerable than these languages. In his search for the correct German Schottel, like many of his contemporaries, was involved in a confidence trick of which he was the victim as well as the perpetrator, for the entity which they were seeking was something which their search was in fact creating, or helping to create.

Schottel must stand for the other grammarians of his century though others are worthy of examination, for instance Wolfgang Ratke (Ratichius) whose works were not published in his day, but whose efforts to have German introduced as a medium of instruction and as a subject in the curriculum of German schools were influential. The advance of the language of Meissen or Upper Saxony (the two were not clearly distinguished) continues through the seventeenth century and into the eighteenth century and is reinforced by the fact that during this period most writers of any stature came from the centre or north of Germany. The seventeenth and eighteenth centuries introduced a new dimension into the writing of German, namely the appeal to authority. Gradually the notion arose of turning to the expert in cases of doubt, and the centuries in question, as well as fostering this notion, supplied the authorities without whose rulings the regularity of the modern standard could never have been reached.

The concept of authority at once suggests Gottsched (1700–66), whose *Grundlegung einer Deutschen Sprachkunst* (1748 and numerous reprints down to 1776) played an important role in the second and third quarters of the eighteenth century. The work is a rhetoric, a guide to cultivated German, rather than a systematic grammar, in which capacity it leaves much to be desired. As for Gottsched's basic principles, it is difficult to know whether to place him in the camp of those who saw the developing German norm as an eclectic language drawn from the best writers, or in the camp which championed Upper Saxon. He subscribes to the view that the best German is to be found in no particular province but rather in the usage of people of learning, of the best writers, and of the courts. Yet in practice he comes down heavily in favour of Upper Saxon, since almost all the writers he cites come from East Central Germany or northern Germany, and since in arguing the case for following the language of the court he states that if a country has more than one court, as do Italy and Germany for example, then the language of the greatest court which is near the centre of the country is to be chosen and this leads him 'inevitably' to Dresden and Upper Saxon.

Though the note of dogma which often creeps into Gottsched aroused the ire and opposition of the Swiss and of other South German writers, the cause of the E.C.G. variety of standard German, itself the product of blending and compromise, was as good as won. It still needed champions who would use it rather than preach it and in the writers of the Enlightenment and the classical period it was used with a clarity, eloquence and elegance which put paid to the chances of its rivals. What Luther did for the language of the 'Sechsische cantzley', Lessing, Goethe and even the Swabian Schiller did for its partially transmuted 'Upper Saxon' offspring. The removal of inconsistency and uncertainty was, and is, a gradual process, and the impression must not be given that by the second half of the eighteenth century all had been achieved. Yet investigations of uncertainty about the gender of nouns, for instance, have shown that between the first and second halves of the eighteenth century there was a marked reduction in the number of cases of doubt. The great authority of the end of the eighteenth century and author of the first truly satisfactory German dictionary, Johann Christoph Adelung (1732–1806) followed Gottsched in championing Upper Saxon, but he does show more discrimination than most of his predecessors in that he distinguishes between the language of the upper classes in that region, which he claims as his real model, and the dialect of Upper Saxony, which he denies exemplary status.

By early in the nineteenth century German has attained a considerable measure of grammatical regularity and unity, and it may not be chance that at roughly the same time the German 'peoples' were being bonded more closely together as a nation as a by-product of the Napoleonic wars. This unity embraced as yet only orthography and morphology, and pronunciation, of which more will be said later, remained largely untouched. In the field of vocabulary we note an influx of loan-words (sometimes loan-translations or loan-extensions) from English. Many of these are connected with men's fashions, or with products for which England was well known, or with sport. One important group of English imports is concerned with political procedures and machinery, words like *Speaker*, *Jungfernrede* (a loan-translation of 'maiden-speech') or *Adresse* (a loan-extension based on English 'address' when used in the sense of a 'speech') came into German in conjunction with the growing parliamentarian movement, the word

Parlament having been used in the sense of English 'parliament' towards the end of the seventeenth century. From the nineteenth century onwards we may observe a growing internationalism of vocabulary in German as in other European languages, and this trend continues and increases in the twentieth century despite occasional checks such as the (largely successful) attempts to Germanize the vocabulary of the German Post Office and Railways and the less permanent but more widespread onslaughts on foreign words during the National Socialist period. None the less, although attempts to check the internationalization of vocabulary have not met with much success, the result is that most Germans employ foreign words, but are more conscience-stricken about it than their English counterparts, and a peculiar offshoot of this is that most monolingual German dictionaries do not include foreign words.

Official steps in regulating the German language culminated in an 'orthographical conference' called by the Governments of the German Reich, of Switzerland and of Austria in Berlin in 1901. Its recommendations, which are the basis of modern German orthography, were published in 1903 and were accepted by most Government authorities and prescribed for German schools in 1907. The system devised has considerable anomalies in it and is by no means completely phonetic, but in this respect it is a marked advance on French or English orthography. Similar attempts to regulate the pronunciation of German led to the publication in 1898 of Theodor Siebs's *Deutsche Bühnenaussprache* (literally 'stage-pronunciation'). This has proved influential, though because of its own preferences, less acceptable in some areas than others. It has no real official backing, and standardization of pronunciation has been much slower than that of orthography, which is in the nature of things easier to regulate.

A few tendencies in the development of modern German may be mentioned briefly at this point. The clearly defined declensional classes of nouns had been subject to erosion from O.H.G. times onwards. The weakened articulation of unstressed vowels accelerated this process, and gradually a change of principle becomes apparent. Inflexional endings no longer indicate, no longer need to indicate, the case of nouns, and this function is taken over by the articles which become more and more frequent, until they are virtually indispensable. The instrumental case died out more or less during the O.H.G. period and the N.H.G. period has seen the virtual end of any formal indication of the dative singular of nouns by means of endings. The *-e* of masculine

c

and neuter nouns in the dative singular is restricted now to mono-syllabic words, where its presence or absence tends to be dictated by prosodic considerations. If used on polysyllabic words the effect is archaic or stylized. Moreover, the range of uses of the dative, as also of the genitive, has narrowed considerably since M.H.G. times, the use of the dative alone being replaced by prepositions (usually with the dative), or where the dative was governed by a verb, it is often re-placed by the accusative. Except for the use of the genitive -s with animates in order to indicate possession, the genitive case hardly exists in spoken German, which is perhaps coming near to the position seen in English. The tendency to give up formal indication of the case of a noun is, however, counterbalanced by a growing desire to indi-cate its number and to emphasize by formal means such as mutation of the stem-vowel or the use of endings the difference between sin-gular and plural. If one thinks of nouns written out in paradigms in the fashion common in grammars with the singular on the left and the plural on the right, then one might say naïvely that in N.H.G. the old horizontal distinctions between cases have been given up in favour of the vertical distinction of number. Another grammatical category which is very much on the wane is the subjunctive. Its wide range of uses in M.H.G. has shrunk to a few remnants, some of them virtually fossilized. Finally changes may be noticed in the strictness with which rules of German word-order, chiefly the final position of the verb in subordinate clauses, are observed. The tendency towards the order subject–verb–object even in subordinate clauses might be due in part to English influence, or it might be due to a change in fashion. Both in German and in English we appear to be in an age where style is tending towards the racy and colloquial. At such a level of speech the verb was rarely placed with deliberation at the end of the subordinate clause in German, and the change in word-order in the standard may be a result of this new style.

The modern German language is more regionalized than, say, English. This is to be seen in its lexicon when quite common objects and activities are expressed differently in different areas, even at the 'highest' level of spoken or written language, for example for 'chim-ney', *Schornstein, Rauchfang, Kamin*; for 'bread-roll', *Brötchen, Semmel, Rundstück*; 'to ring (a doorbell)', *klingeln, läuten, schellen*. In each case the list of synonyms given is by no means exhaustive. To find contrasts of this kind in English, one must resort to much more specialized levels of the language of trades and crafts or to rural language. Similarly in terms of pronunciation few or no Germans actually follow the recommended *Bühnenaussprache*. Instead we find that people of all social classes use the regional colloquial languages (*Umgangssprachen*) and thus betray the area they stem from. These colloquial languages are a kind of compromise between the standard and the dialects of the region. Seen from the point of view of the dialects they are a convergent, from the point of view of the standard a divergent form of language. The socially higher classes of society use these regional colloquial languages in their everyday intercourse and turn to *Bühnenaussprache* and the standard only on more formal occasions. The lower classes use dialect in their everyday intercourse and turn to the regional colloquial language on more formal occasions, or when they wish to make themselves understood by people from other areas. There are, of course, no hard and fast demarcation lines between dialect, colloquial and standard language, but instead we have a continuous spectrum. The amount of success with which the standard or the regional variant is realized fluctuates from individual to individual. Needless to say this regionally divided nature of German is the aftermath of the political separatism of earlier centuries. As for the modern separatism between East and West, although linguistic differences between the two zones are often stressed, they belong largely to the sphere of vocabulary, which is notoriously mercurial and ephemeral. It is doubtful whether any lasting or deep-seated language difference will result from the political separation of East and West, especially when we take into account the mass media and the general tendency towards internationalism in language.

It is a subjective and dangerous undertaking to try to characterize a language, but perhaps it is not totally out of place to mention finally one or two features of German which strike an English-speaker. The strongest acoustic impression which it makes is one of force and energy; distinctions between long and short vowels are marked, consonants are articulated strongly, and stressed syllables are given much more weight than in English. The grammatical structure of German with its three genders and numerous case-endings when compared with other Germanic languages seems very archaic – no value-judgement intended! Though there is a danger that because of the ease with which they are manufactured, words are produced which are virtually meaningless, none the less in its ability to produce derivatives by means of suffixes and prefixes and in its ability to compound words German has an instrument of great utility and expressiveness.

Bibliography

This is intended as a list of further reading and not as an acknowledgement of indebtedness which is wider and deeper than could be acknowledged. All the works are in English with the exception of Bach's which was included for its broad treatment and for its excellent, up-to-date bibliographical information.

BACH, A. *Geschichte der deutschen Sprache.* 8th edn. Heidelberg, 1965.

BLACKALL, E. A. *The Emergence of German as a Literary Language 1700–1775.* Cambridge, 1959.

COLLINSON, W. E. *The German Language Today, its Patterns and Historical Background.* 3rd edn. London, 1968.

KELLER, R. E. *German Dialects. Phonology and Morphology, with selected texts.* Manchester, 1961.

KUFNER, H. L. *The Grammatical Structures of English and German.* Second impression. Chicago, 1963.

LOCKWOOD, W. B. *An Informal History of the German Language.* Cambridge, 1965.

MOULTON, W. G. *The Sounds of English and German.* Second impression. Chicago, 1963.

PRIEBSCH, R., and COLLINSON, W. E. *The German Language,* 6th edn. London, 1966.

2 German Political, Legal and Cultural Institutions

W. H. BRUFORD

Political Institutions

THE FEDERAL REPUBLIC (WEST GERMANY)

The Basic Law

The larger, western half of Germany today, covering some 96,000 square miles, almost the area of the United Kingdom, calls itself the Bundesrepublik Deutschland and is governed in accordance with a written constitution, its *Grundgesetz* or Basic Law. This, like the constitution of the Weimar Republic before it, did not come into existence by a slow process of growth, but in a few months, as the direct result of military defeat. It was drafted in 1948–9 by a Parlamentarischer Rat or Constituent Assembly which was not, like the Weimar National Assembly, elected directly by the whole people, but indirectly by the already existing Landtage of the eleven *Länder* making up the British, American and French zones of occupation. The three Western occupying powers had authorized the summoning of the Assembly at their London Conference in the spring of 1948, when the French had at last agreed to the merging of their zone with the other two, and the Conference had laid down some important principles for the guidance of the Assembly. It was 'to draw up a democratic constitution which will establish for the participating states a governmental structure of federal type which is best suited to the eventual re-establishment of German unity at present disrupted and which will protect the rights of participating states, provide adequate central authority and contain guarantees of individual rights and freedom.'

The Assembly of sixty-five members was made up of delegations from each *Land* of a size corresponding to its population, and in each delegation the representation of the political parties fairly reflected the composition of the Landtag concerned. Dr Konrad Adenauer was elected Chairman at the first meeting, on 1 September 1948. It took the Assembly nearly six months to reach agreement on a final version of their draft and three more to satisfy the Allies. Meanwhile the attempted Russian blockade of Berlin had been defeated by the Allied airlift. Although the Occupation Statute of May 1949, which reserved rights of control to the occupying powers in certain contingencies, continued in force until 1954, the Federal Republic had by then possessed virtually full sovereignty for three years.

It is obvious that in West Germany only those Germans could hope to play a constructive part in politics who were willing to give parliamentary democracy a trial and to stamp out everything which in any way recalled National Socialist methods and ideas, while in East Germany a professed adherence to Communism was equally necessary to anyone who entered public life. It was no accident also that everywhere the *Land* boundaries were drawn in such a way as to break up the old Prussian provinces, and further that while in West Germany the deeply rooted love of a federal form of state, with its emphasis on regional loyalties, was warmly welcomed by the Military Governments, especially by the French, East Germany retained a centralized system of government, only parliamentary in appearance, but in reality dominated by a single-party machine under strict Soviet control. At the same time old regional loyalties were discouraged here by the splitting up of the existing five *Länder* with their historic names, Brandenburg, Mecklenburg, Saxony, Anhalt, Thuringia, into fourteen characterless *Bezirke* constructed round big towns. It was with similar totalitarian aims in view that Hitler's co-ordination policy had robbed the *Länder* constituting the Weimar Republic of their autonomy. In West Germany, therefore, the return to federalism was for democratic Germans in itself a symbolic rejection of Hitlerism, while at the same time it suited the policy of the Western Allies in their fear of a resurgent Germany.

The question of the future reunification of Germany was from the beginning a fundamental issue not only for the Germans themselves but for both sides in the Cold War which soon developed out of disagreements between Russia and her former allies. To the United States, Great Britain and France after her liberation, the Russian schemes for a reunited Germany always seemed to aim solely at extending Communism to the Rhine. When this policy proved impossible to realize, the Russians apparently came to see the best safeguard against the re-emergence of a strong, nationalistic Germany, their principal and entirely natural fear, in the whittling away of formerly German territory in the east and the division of the remainder into two halves under antagonistic forms of government. The Federal Republic, following the London Conference's directive, committed itself to opposing this policy in the preamble to its new constitution, the aim of which is described as the giving of 'a new order to political life for a transitional period'. West Germany, the preamble concludes, 'has also acted on behalf of those Germans to whom participation was denied. The entire people is called upon to achieve by free self-determination the unity and freedom of Germany.'

The Basic Law, like the Weimar Constitution of 1919, is clearly very largely the work of learned constitutional lawyers like Theodor Eschenburg, men familiar with the theory of parliamentary government in all its forms and intent on combining in their draft the democratic features best suited to West Germany's particular historical situation. Much reminds us of British practice but much also of the American constitution, influenced by Montesquieu and in particular by his idea of the separation of powers. Inherited German ways of thinking about the state are also to be traced, together with much that is the product of bitter German experience. Textbook ideas adopted in the Weimar Constitution, like the popular initiative and referendum on the Swiss model, have for instance been reconsidered in the light of history, for in Eschenburg's view, 'almost the only use made of the popular initiative and referendum in the Weimar Republic was as a means of attacking the constitution'.[1] Awareness of mistakes made earlier through inexperience, and determination to avoid at all costs the return of any form of dictatorship, are evident at many other points.

To emphasize its rejection of Nazism, the Basic Law begins with a revised and expanded version of the Weimar Constitution's formulation of the basic rights of Germans as men and citizens. In the Weimar Constitution, this statement had followed a description of the political structure and functions of the Reich, under the heading: 'Basic rights *and duties* of Germans.' Now, the first article of all proclaims in Kantian tones that the dignity of man is inviolable, and that the German *Volk* looks upon 'human right as the basis of every community, and of peace and justice in the world'. Unfortunately it proved impossible for the *Bund* in practice to recruit its higher civil service without appointing many men whose experience had all been gained under an authoritarian regime, though their administrative ability might be unquestioned, many men who, though their administrative ability might be unquestioned, had gained all their experience under an authoritarian regime,

[1] T. Eschenburg, *Staat und Gesellschaft in Deutschland* (Munich, 1963), p. 273.

especially as the *Länder* had already taken their choice of the possible candidates. The more radical press has often criticized apparent departures of the Federal Government from its excellent principles, and independent observers have criticized Dr Adenauer's admission of men with doubtful records to high office, and a fairly general tendency of the authorities to exercise indirect pressure on editors and journalists.[1] It cannot, however, be seriously maintained that the Federal Republic's declaration of human rights has been a mere piece of pious rhetoric, like corresponding clauses in the Stalin Constitution of the Soviet Union (1936), or the Constitution of the German Democratic Republic (1949). In accepting these articles, the Federal Republic was setting itself a goal which it knew from recent experience to be hard to attain, though liberal thought in Germany had aspired to it for more than a century. A declaration of basic rights had been a prominent feature of the draft constitution of the 1848 liberals, and the National Assembly in the Paulskirche in its idealism had spent more time discussing ethical questions of this kind than practical steps to secure power. Another historical link with Weimar and the liberal tradition in the Basic Law is the choice of the colours black-red-gold for the federal flag, colours associated first with the *Burschenschaften* in their struggle for German unity and political freedom, and then with the 1848 liberals, before being adopted by the Weimar National Assembly instead of the black-white-red of imperial Germany, the colours to which the National Socialists reverted.

Sections 2 to 8 of the Basic Law deal with the structure and functions of the Federation and its relation to the *Länder* of which it is composed. It was in the Weimar Constitution again, we may note, that the separate German states had first been called *Länder*. The political organization of the Federation as a democratic state is based like that of the Weimar Republic on the principle that 'all state authority emanates from the people', and not from the will of any Kaiser or Führer. The people exercises this authority by means of the ballot-box and through 'separate legislative, executive and judicial organs' – here is the doctrine of the separation of powers. The people's elected representatives make the laws, in accordance with the procedures laid down in the Constitution, and the executive and the judiciary are bound by the law.

[1] M. Balfour, *West Germany* (London, 1968), p. 223; Karl Otmar von Aretin in his article, 'Die Bewährungsprobe der Bundesrepublik' in *Die neue Rundschau* (1968), e.g. p. 376.

The Bundestag and the system of legislation

The legislature or parliament of the Federal Republic consists of two chambers. The first chamber, the Bundestag, is directly elected by universal suffrage for a period of four years – all German citizens over twenty-one years of age, men and women, have the right to vote – but bills passed by the Bundestag must be submitted to the Bundesrat, the second chamber, which consists of representatives drawn from the governments of the *Länder*. The *Länder* have either three, four or five votes each in the Bundesrat, according to their size, and these must be cast as a block vote of the *Land* by members present.

The idea of a two-chamber parliament goes back, like so much else, to the 1849 Constitution, with its Staatenhaus and Volkshaus. In the Constitution of the Reich in 1871 provision is made for a Bundesrat and a Reichstag, in the Weimar Constitution for a Reichsrat and Reichstag, but the relationship between the two houses, and between each of them and the Government, has varied greatly. In the Federal Republic, the head of the Government or Prime Minister, called Bundeskanzler, is elected in a rather elaborate way by the Bundestag alone. Immediately after a general election, a candidate is nominated by the Bundespräsident, naturally on the advice of the party leaders after negotiations among themselves. He is declared elected if, in a secret ballot, he receives an absolute majority of votes, i.e. is approved by more than half of the full membership of the Bundestag. If the requisite majority is not obtained, any member of the Bundestag may be put up as candidate within the next fourteen days, or one after another, until one obtains an absolute majority. If no one succeeds in doing this, a third election is held, for which a relative majority (a majority of the members present and voting) is enough, but the successful candidate must be approved by the Bundespräsident within seven days. If the Bundespräsident exercises his veto, he must dissolve the Bundestag, and the whole process begins again with a new general election. This way of choosing a Prime Minister seems very odd to us because we are used to a two-party system without proportional representation, under which a general election normally gives one or other of the main parties a clear majority, and the leader of this party, who has played a big part in the election, automatically becomes Prime Minister. All parties will have indicated clearly in their election literature and speeches their general lines of policy and the chief measures they will introduce if successful in the election. Parliament merely registers in effect the choice of the electorate, made largely on the basis of the party programmes.

What happens in practice in West Germany between the general election and the initiation of the procedure outlined above is that the newly elected parliamentary parties (called *Fraktionen*), if large enough to be admitted under the Rules of Procedure of the Bundestag, i.e. at least fifteen strong, have to hold discussions to explore the various possibilities that may exist of forming a coalition government, because no single party is likely to have an absolute majority in the Bundestag. They must negotiate about a common programme and a mutually satisfactory sharing out of the ministerial portfolios. This is done in private, and so far the details of the bargaining involved in the hatching-out of party alliances have always been kept secret. If and when an agreement has been reached, each party nominates its choice for the ministerial posts allotted to it. The Bundeskanzler elect must naturally have his say, but he himself is not necessarily the first to be chosen, and his hands are always to some extent tied when it comes to cabinet making. The meetings of the *Fraktionen* continue to be of great importance during the whole life of the Bundestag. Each elects a number of working groups to prepare party policy and keep it up to date in the main fields of legislation (economic affairs, foreign policy, defence, etc.), and their findings are periodically reported to the *Fraktion* in full session. Party discipline is normally fairly strict, especially, by long tradition, in the Social Democratic Party. It is for instance a recognized rule that the signature of a party chairman on a communication to the Government commits the whole *Fraktion*.

When the Bundeskanzler has been duly elected, the score or so of Ministers proposed by him are appointed by the Bundespräsident. They are responsible only to the Bundeskanzler and cannot be individually dismissed by the Bundestag, though they may be summoned before it or the Bundesrat to explain their actions, and questioned with varying degrees of formality as a normal procedure. The Bundeskanzler and his Government can only be made to resign by the passing of a so-called 'constructive vote of no confidence' by the Bundestag. This means a vote, proposed initially by at least a quarter of the membership of the assembly, and carried by an absolute majority in a secret ballot, for the election of a new Bundeskanzler, supported by a workable coalition. One name after another may be brought forward under these conditions until one is successful, failing which result there must be a general election. The aim of this novel procedure (taken over from the constitution of Baden-Württemberg, and originally an American suggestion) is to prevent the recurrence of what happened several times in the Weimar Republic, the combination of extremes, themselves quite unable to agree on a policy, against a moderate Chancellor.

The Bundespräsident, who plays an essential role in the formal initiation of a new Government, is elected for five years at a time, so that a presidential election will rarely be due in the same year as a general election. The Bundespräsident is elected by a special Bundesversammlung, made up of the whole Bundestag, together with an equal number of representatives from the diets of the *Länder*. In the Weimar Republic, the President had been elected for seven years by a national plebiscite, a method which certainly seems consistent with the principle that all authority emanates from the people, but had provided a demagogue with a disastrous opportunity in 1934, in the view of the Parlamentarischer Rat. The President has lost some of the power he had under the earlier system, in particular the power to suspend vital 'basic rights' as Hitler did. He is now much more like a constitutional monarch, and it is important that he should be above reproach, as was seen in 1968 in the controversy about President Lübke's past. As a further safeguard, the new constitution provides that no amendment of the Basic Law affecting either article 1 (the dignity and inalienable rights of man) or article 20 (the Republic as a constitutional democracy) is admissible, and that any amendment whatever of the Basic Law requires a two-thirds majority of all members of the Bundestag and of all votes in the Bundesrat. Moreover, a special organ has been created, rather similar to the Supreme Court in the United States, with the function of watching over the constitution. It is called the Bundesverfassungsgericht and is made up of two senates or courts, each of eight judges, who may not be members of the legislature or executive of either the *Bund* or any of the *Länder*. The only profession they may combine with their work on the Court is that of teaching law at a German university. They are elected for eight years, half of them by the Bundestag and half by the Bundesrat, and three members of each senate must have had some years of experience on one of the six highest judicial bodies in the Federation. A system of government guided by a new written constitution, and not by tradition and precedent, will always throw up problems that are only to be solved by an authoritative interpretation of the bearing on a new situation of the principles of the constitution. The judges have to decide, for example, by a majority vote, when a ruling is requested by a court of justice, by the government of the *Bund* or any *Land*, or by at least one-third of the Bundestag, whether a particular law is or is not compatible with the constitution, or how far the duties and competence of particular bodies or individuals go. On an appeal from the Bundestag or Bundesrat, the Court can even dismiss the Bundespräsident himself, if it finds that he has deliberately contravened the Basic Law or any federal law. For activities not in conformity with the constitution it can also, for instance, dismiss a newspaper editor, or suspend individual deputies and even whole parties. It was in this way that the neo-Nazi Sozialistische Reichspartei was banned in 1951, and the Communist Party in 1956.

From what has been said so far it is already clear that the parliamentary democracy of the Federal Republic is in many important respects very different from our own, partly because its makers had to take account of difficulties and dangers peculiar to the Germany of a particular time. More differences emerge if we consider the Federal Diet and Government in more detail and ask how the Diet is elected, how it goes about its principal business of legislation and exercises control over the executive, and how effectively the Prime Minister and his cabinet carry out their task of governing the country.

In size the Federal Diet is comparable with the House of Commons, but there are characteristic differences between the meeting-places of the two assemblies. The present Diet, elected in 1969, has 486 deputies from West Germany, and in addition twenty-two non-voting representatives from West Berlin. It meets in the Bundeshaus, a large building beside the Rhine in Bonn, originally a Teachers' Training College but greatly enlarged, so that it can provide not only a large hall for plenary sessions of the Bundestag but also a smaller one for the Bundesrat, together with committee rooms, lobbies, a library and other public rooms, and good deal of office space for deputies. The Plenary Hall, a square chamber in a simple, functional style, rather like a modern university *Aula*, with side galleries for the diplomatic corps and the press, and one at the back for the public, is so large, some forty yards wide, that everyone must speak through a microphone to be heard. Every deputy sits at his own desk and though any of them can put a question by using one of the microphones scattered over the body of the hall, without going up to the rostrum used for all formal speeches, there is not 'the facility for quick informal interruptions and interchanges' on which Churchill insisted when the House of Commons was rebuilt. In England the traditional narrow, oblong chamber is badly overcrowded when the House is full, but on normal days it does not look half-empty like the Federal Diet, the Government can sit facing the official Opposition front bench and exchange thrust and parry with it, and members can easily make themselves heard, singly or collectively, from their seats. English visitors usually find the Bundestag debates dull and formal, but they do not see the many committees at work, where proceedings are evidently much livelier.

In plenary sessions the President of the Bundestag, corresponding to the Speaker of the House of Commons, sits with a secretary at each elbow on a raised dais against the back wall of the chamber, under a huge Federal Eagle. There are rows of desks on his right for the Federal Government, our front bench, and on his left for Bundesrat members, who may attend any session of the Bundestag. These all face the body of the chamber where the deputies, as in most Continental parliaments, sit in a series of curved rows. As in the French National Assembly – the use of Left and Right in a political sense came of course from France at the time of the Revolution – the party furthest to the left in policy, the Social Democratic Party, sits row behind row in the segment on the President's left, the phalanx of the combined Christian Democratic and Christian Socialist Union sits in the centre and the Free Democratic Party on the President's right. The leaders of each party sit in the front row. Members of the Government, who are almost invariably also deputies of the Bundestag, though the constitution does not require this, normally sit on the dais, but they retain their reserved seats with their party in the body of the hall and occupy them when a vote is being taken. This is usually done by a show of hands. Occasionally on important issues the vote is by *Hammelsprung*, or what we call a division. The deputies leave the chamber and re-enter by one of three doors, marked 'Aye', 'No' or 'Abstention'. The name of this procedure has been traditional since Bismarckian days and may have begun as a joke about the House of Commons, with its party chiefs like 'bell-wethers' leading their flocks into divisions. In the lobby of the old Reichstag there was a picture of the blind Polyphemus counting his sheep as they passed between his legs. A third form of voting is by roll-call when, on demand by a sufficient number of deputies (at least fifty), a register is kept of how each member voted.

The three parties mentioned (counting CDU/CSU as one party) are all that have been represented in the Bundestag since the fourth election (1961). The Christlich-Demokratische Union (CDU), which in Bavaria calls itself the Christlich-Soziale Union (CSU), is a recent party, unlike any existing before 1945. Its primary aim is to unite Protestant and Catholic voters (*Union*) in a Christian party with a broad popular appeal. 'Only Christian faith', says a CDU statement of 1961, 'could hope to provide the energy required to stand up to brute force and dictatorship, to attack and in the end to conquer them.' The conquest was achieved, of course, with a good deal of foreign assistance, but it is true that the most determined resistance to Hitler had come from the Confessional Church and the Catholic hierarchy, and, as Michael Balfour says, 'many of the institutions and ideas which characterize Western Germany today owe their form to survivors of the resistance or to like-minded people who preferred for various reasons to avoid implication in resistance'.[1] There were the beginnings of a CDU party in all four zones soon after 1945, seeking a political expression for religious feeling in reaction against Nazism, but the federal party was not constituted until 1950, after the first federal election. The Bavarian CSU remained separate, but joined forces with the CDU in the Bundestag. The CDU/CSU appeals particularly to the comfortably placed, middle-class family man and his wife, whether the man is employer or employee, professional man or civil servant, if he believes in free enterprise and well-tried, middle-of-the-road policies based on traditional Christian principles. Erhard's highly successful economic policy and Adenauer's skill in maintaining good relations with both the United States and France won for the party very solid and faithful backing, and its fairly generous social legislation and sound republicanism have extended its appeal to people of all classes.

The Sozialdemokratische Partei Deutschlands (SPD) is over a hundred years old. It was suspended by the National Socialists and refounded in 1945. At first it continued on its traditional Marxist lines, though strongly opposed to Communism, but it never enjoyed anything like the same support from the trade unions as the Labour Party does in England. The Deutscher Gewerkschaftsbund is politically neutral and contributes nothing directly to the party's funds. As West German prosperity grew, the liberal strain which had long been evident in Social Democratic thinking became more pronounced, and the SPD's 'Godesberg Programme' of 1959 proclaimed the party's departure from the idea of the class struggle and from Marxist ideology. Like the CDU, the SPD now claims to be a party for all, a *Volkspartei*, and welcomes members from all classes and of all creeds, having shed the official atheism as well as the opposition to patriotism which had

[1] M. Balfour, op. cit., p. 126.

made it a bogy for all respectable people before 1914. 'The SPD is an association of people who come from various backgrounds of belief and thought. Their agreement is based on common moral values and political aims,' says the Godesberg Programme. This move to the Right has made the SPD more like the non-trade-union section of the British Labour Party than ever before. It appeals to white-collar workers and intellectuals as well as to its traditional supporters, but for the young in particular it has lost its distinctive character and become too staid and respectable. No one was greatly surprised when in 1966 the party entered into a coalition with the CDU/CSU. Willy Brandt's sustained and largely successful attempts, first as Foreign Minister of the coalition and after 1969 as Chancellor, to establish better relations with Russia and her satellites, particularly with Poland and East Germany, without weakening the Federation's ties with France and the United States, won for him personally high international prestige (Nobel Peace Prize, 1971), though the effect on the popularity of his party at home remained difficult to assess.

The Freie Demokratische Partei (FDP) arose through the fusion of various liberal groups formed after 1945 and became a federal party in 1948, after a conference of these groups at Heppenheim. Its first chairman was Theodor Heuss, who was elected the first Bundespräsident in 1949. The policy of this party is hard to define, but it is certainly not radical, though in Baden-Württemberg at least something survives among its members of the spirit of 1848. The main aim of the parliamentary party would appear to have been to ensure that its support was needed by the CDU/CSU for the formation of a Government. Between 1966 and 1969 the coalition of the major parties deprived it of its former influence, but after the 1969 election it was only the support of its twenty deputies which gave Chancellor Willy Brandt his precarious majority of two.

This very important clause in the present electoral law directs that the 'second votes' cast for a party on the *Landesliste*, as explained below, shall only be taken into consideration if it gains at least five per cent of the total number of 'second votes', or alternatively has gained three constituencies on the 'first votes' cast for it. The effect of this proviso is to eliminate small parties and to level out the votes obtained by the larger ones. In 1949, in addition to the parties mentioned above, there were seven others (holding 80 seats) in the Bundestag, in 1953 only three others (with 44 seats), in 1957 one other (with 17 seats), and in 1961 none. But in 1961 the weakest party, the FDP, though it gained no seats by direct suffrage ('first vote'), had 12·8 per cent of the 'second votes'. It therefore got over the hurdle of the 'five per cent clause' and was allotted 67 seats, which it owed entirely to the effect of the element of proportional representation in the electoral system. The other two parties, having received more seats by direct voting, obtained correspondingly few additional seats on the second votes, the CDU/CSU, for the same reason, gaining fewer in this way than the SPD.

Proportional representation in one form or another goes back a hundred years in German history, to the beginnings of the German Empire in 1871, when a system very like the one to which General de Gaulle reverted in the Fifth Republic, an election in two stages, was introduced. The Reichstag then, and down to the end of the empire in 1918, was divided into many parties, but even if it had been more united, it would have had no power to control policy, because Bismarck was responsible only to the emperor. The Weimar Constitution carried proportional representation to its theoretical limit, so that the extreme variety of political opinion in the country was faithfully reflected in the Reichstag. The voice of the people was certainly heard, and the executive was now responsible to the legislature, but the result was democratic government at its weakest and ultimately a dictatorship. Though the Bonn Constituent Assembly was well aware of this danger, it also attached great importance to the protection of minorities and the softening of political conflicts after a period of violent upheavals, and it decided to retain something very like the Weimar system of proportional representation, adapted to the new federal form of state, and combined as in the Weimar Republic with a simple majority system which gave half of the deputies constituencies of their own to look after.

The Federal Republic is divided into 248 constituencies, areas with a population of between one and two hundred thousand in most cases, much smaller, therefore, than those of Weimar days. In a general election, every elector is invited to cast two votes at one visit to the polling booth, both registered on the one voting paper, the first for a person, the second for a party. The first is to elect by the simple majority system one of the candidates in the contest for the constituency in which the elector lives, and the second to secure for all parties proportional representation in the complete Bundestag. As far as the first vote is concerned, the procedure is just like that in a British parliamentary election, except that as well as the party of each candidate his occupation and address are also stated opposite his name on the voting paper. The voter may of course support the candidate of his choice on personal or on party grounds, and the result often turns on a very small majority. The second votes are given for one party list among several, each containing the names of perhaps ten or twelve candidates belonging to that party, though only the first five names appear on the voting paper. Identical lists drawn up for the whole *Land* (in the Weimar Republic it had been the Reich) are used in every constituency in that *Land*. The voter puts his second cross against one of the lists, not necessarily (though no doubt usually) supporting the party of the individual to whom he has given his first vote.

The first votes are counted in the constituencies, and half the membership of the Bundestag is thereby decided, but so far only rough justice has been done in giving to each party a degree of representation proportionate to the total number of votes cast for it. Elaborate calculations have now to be made in two stages, the first to settle the relative claims to representation of all parties, excluding any which do not satisfy the five per cent clause, and the second to decide how the additional mandates (i.e. seats in the Bundestag) thus allotted to each party, over and above the constituency seats it has won, shall be spread out over the various *Landeslisten*. Since 1957 the calculations have been based on the total number of 'second votes' given to each party in the whole *Bund*, not as formerly in each separate *Land*. The proportion of the 486 places that is due to each party is worked out by the 'maximum number' method invented by the Belgian d'Hondt in 1882.[1] The same method is used in the second stage of the calculations to determine how many names, if any, shall be taken from each of the *Landeslisten* of every party concerned, to make up the total number of Bundestag seats allotted to it. If a party has done well in the constituencies in a

---

[1] A simplified example of the use of the d'Hondt method in a three-seat constituency:

Parties A, B and C gain (in thousands) 100, 80 and 30 respectively. These numbers are divided by 1, 2, 3, etc., in turn, and the quotients are arranged in descending order as follows:

A 100 ÷ 1 = 100 (seat 1 to A)
B   80 ÷ 1 = 80 (seat 2 to B)
A 100 ÷ 2 = 50 (seat 3 to A)
(B   80 ÷ 2 = 40
C   30 ÷ 1 = 30)

So A wins two seats, B one and C none.

In Germany, as explained above, the calculation is made for the whole *Bund*, not for the *Land* or for the single constituency.

particular *Land*, it will not gain as many additional seats in this way as the rival parties, because the number of seats already won on the first votes is subtracted from the total number due to it. Names are then taken from its *Landesliste*, beginning at the top, to make up the difference. In Hamburg, for instance, in 1965 (Hamburg, like Bremen and West Berlin, has the status of a *Land*) all eight constituency seats were won on the first vote by the SPD, but the party gained only one more after the proportional representation calculations, whereas the CDU, with no seats on the first votes, gained seven, because the proportion of second votes given to it was high, even in Hamburg.

Though there was a natural reaction towards proportional representation after Hitler's dictatorship, there have always been critics of the system on practical grounds, and in recent years they have made themselves heard to some effect in the Bundestag itself. Already in 1931 one critic had written: 'The more accurate we try to make the reflection of existing trends of opinion in the nation and their relative numerical strength, by the use of proportional representation methods in elections, the more empty of content and devoid of influence the people's will becomes with regard to what elections are there for.'[1] Under the present system, a West German voter helps to elect through his second vote a candidate whom he may never have seen and about whom he knows very little. Men whose judgement or influence are valued by the party, though they may not be the kind of people to face up to or succeed in the rough and tumble of a local election, can be put on a *Landesliste*, along with potential Ministers, who are always at the top, and women candidates, whose sex is still a handicap for them, though there was in fact a higher proportion of women in the 1965 Bundestag than in the House of Commons. Under the multi-party system encouraged by proportional representation, a party cannot usually commit itself to a clear programme of legislation, so the elector has to choose among several sets of vaguely defined policies, not even knowing with any certainty who will head the key Ministries or even, perhaps, who will be Prime Minister if his party is successful. It is only after the election, when the relative strength of the parties is known, that the process of bargaining can begin which will lead to the formation of a Government. For the same reason the inter-party struggle in elections is seldom an all-out battle because, as coalitions are the rule, parties must avoid antagonizing possible future allies.

The electoral law passed by the first Bundestag has subsequently been

[1] Erich Kaufmann, quoted by Eschenburg, op. cit., p. 209.

revised more than once, and for years there has been a persistent agita-tion for the curtailment or elimination of the provisions for propor-tional representation, in the hope of bringing about something like the two-party system of government, with an official Opposition assured of a real chance of coming to power. As early as 1960 there was even talk of making the seating arrangements in the Bundestag more like those in the House of Commons, but nothing has come of this so far. It is the CDU which has chiefly favoured reform, with the osten-sible aim of increasing the stability of the Government. Early in 1968 a committee of professors headed by Theodor Eschenburg reported in favour of a simple majority system of voting for general elections, arguing that the main function of an election is to decide which party shall rule. Until this time the other large party, the SPD, had not been happy about such proposals, because opinion polls seemed to have shown repeatedly that while about 30 per cent of the voters in the Federation as a whole are convinced socialists, about 20 per cent are unshakeably Catholic and another 20 per cent equally firmly *bürgerlich*, i.e. anti-socialist. The floating vote is apparently much smaller in proportion than in Great Britain, and the SPD feared that the CDU might enjoy a permanent advantage from the change to a simple majority vote. Many in the SPD had, however, been as much alarmed as the CDU at the successes in *Land* elections of the NPD, the new party of the extreme Right, which might come into the Bundestag in strength at the next general election given the continuance of proportional representation, but not on a simple majority vote. In spite of these fears, the SPD did not in the end accept the report of a commission of its own, also early in 1968, advocating a voting system in which there would be only a small element of proportional repre-sentation, confined to each single constituency.

According to the constitution, it is the Federal Chancellor who determines and is responsible for general policy in the cabinet. Adenauer spoke of the 'lonely decisions' he often had to make, when he found himself unable to accept the majority view and, conscious of his sole responsibility to the Bundestag, had to take it upon himself to adopt a policy opposed by most of his colleagues. A Bundeskanzler remains bound by the pacts made between his party and the others before the formation of the Government, but these are necessarily in general terms, and many factors combine to give him a position of great authority, one so great that Dr Adenauer, for example, seemed to many critics to reduce his Ministers to puppets. Ministers are, however, perhaps more masters in their own departments than their British counterparts, being individually, not collectively, responsible for them, and under Dr Erhard at least some seem to have asserted themselves very successfully. They had no junior Ministers to relieve their burden until 1967, when the first seven 'Parliamentary State Secretaries' were appointed to the Chancellor and six Ministers. With these and about twenty-two cabinet posts to distribute, the West German Government seems to have far less power of patronage than our own. The Chancellor is assisted also by a Deputy, nominated by him from amongst his Ministers, and by a considerable staff of civil servants in the Chancellor's office.

The organization of the business of legislation has many interesting new features. Most bills are introduced by the Government, though the Bundesrat and the ordinary members of the Bundestag also possess the power of initiative. Bills are normally drafted by a Ministry and submitted in draft for comment to other Ministries concerned, which will always include the Ministry of Finance. Outside organizations especially affected, those both of employers and employed in a particular industry for instance, are also fully consulted. The technical drafting is checked by the Ministry of Justice before the bill is brought before the whole cabinet. If they give their approval, perhaps after minor amendments, the bill is passed to the Bundesrat, who have three weeks to express their views. Only when it has been returned by them does the Government pass it on, with its own observations on the Bundesrat's comments, to the Bundestag, whose officials fix a date for the first reading. Meanwhile the draft goes to the parliamentary parties and their committees of experts.

A bill is read before the full Bundestag three times, as in Great Britain. At the first reading there is usually no debate, unless matters of great political importance are involved, and the text is forwarded to one or more of the Bundestag's Standing Committees, described below, for detailed discussion. If several are concerned, one of them is made responsible for presenting the final report of the committees, in the form of amendments to the draft with reasoned comment, and a particular member of this Reporting Committee is appointed Reporter on the measure. The committees sit in private and their proceedings are quite informal. Each has an experienced civil servant in attendance, to keep the minutes and help the chairman with advice, and they may summon Ministers and experts of all kinds before them for questioning. The detailed discussion in committee even of a fairly non-controversial measure, such as one about soldiers' allowances, may come up as one item of business at a dozen meetings of various bodies, extending over six months. The Reporter's systematic summary of the chief comments made in the discussions is finally sent in to the Bundestag by the Reporting Committee, with the original text of the bill and any amendments that are now suggested. At its second reading in the Bundestag, the bill is introduced by the Reporter, and debated first in general and then clause by clause. If it is passed without further amendment, the third reading follows immediately, but if amendments are carried, they must be approved by the Reporting Committee first.

Bills of certain types, mainly those in which the financial or administrative interests of particular *Länder* are involved, cannot become law at all unless they are passed by the Bundesrat, but all bills are submitted again to the Bundesrat for comment after their third reading in the Bundestag. If the Bundesrat raises objections, the services of a permanent Committee of Mediation (*Vermittlungsausschuß*) are called upon, with a view to reaching a compromise. If its findings are rejected by the Bundesrat, and the bill is one of the rather rare type mentioned above, that is the end of the matter and the bill must be abandoned. The normal bill can, however, be finally passed by the Bundestag in spite of an objection raised by the Bundesrat after the mediation attempt, but only if the requisite 'qualified majority' is forthcoming. An objection passed only by a simple majority in the Bundesrat can be overcome by the votes of a majority of the members (i.e. 244 ayes) in the Bundestag, but one passed by a two-thirds majority above needs a motion supported by two-thirds of those present and voting, with a minimum again of 244 ayes, to be negatived below. In a period of twelve years, only three bills were thrown out by a Bundesrat objection in this way. When a bill has been finally passed by the Bundestag, the Government sends it to the Bundespräsident for his formal signature before it becomes law.

The constitution of the Federal Republic was specially designed to provide a much stronger executive than existed in the ill-fated Weimar Republic, and up till now its provisions have worked well. The legislature, the Bundestag, has however a reasonable amount of control over the Government, though the machinery for this purpose is quite different from what is familiar to us in Great Britain. There is, for instance, nothing quite like the daily Questions period which is so essential a feature with us. There is a *Fragestunde* now at the beginning of every plenary session of the Bundestag (formerly only at least once a month), and here a deputy who has given three days' notice in writing may put a question orally to the Government, to be answered by a Minister, his Parliamentary State Secretary, if he has one, or otherwise the Secretary of State at the head of his departmental staff, a 'political' civil servant, who may be changed with a change of Minister. Supplementary questions are allowed, but no discussion. If on some issue a group of at least thirty deputies are seriously disturbed they may sign a *Große Anfrage*, and then the Minister's reply is followed by a debate. This is what is traditionally known in European parliaments as an *Interpellation*, a very frequent occurrence even in Bismarck's day. When the SPD was in opposition, it was able to use this device to harass the Government, but when there is a Grand Coalition, as between 1966 and 1969, members of the parties represented in it are chary of embarrassing their Ministers. On smaller points of administration or disturbing occurrences like a railway accident, a *Kleine Anfrage* may be put by means of a party motion supported by a prescribed number, and this is answered in writing.

It is through their regular activity on various Standing Committees rather than through questions that deputies make their weight felt. Such committees are found in varying forms in many European legislatures as well as in the United States, and they have been advocated by many recent critics of our parliamentary system. There are now normally 23 Standing Committees of the Bundestag, each having a permanent chairman. Their size ranges from 31 members for seven of the most important, e.g. those for Foreign Affairs, Economic Affairs, the Budget, Defence, Food Production, down to 13 for the five smallest, e.g. Election Questions, the Post, Penal Reform, Refugees, and in between come six with 27 members, for Finance, Home Affairs, Petitions, Town and Country Planning and Housing, Labour, Social Policy, and five of 21 members, for Science and Cultural Affairs, Public Health, Family and Youth Questions, Transport, Legal Affairs. In its composition each committee reflects the balance of the parliamentary parties. The committees discuss and report on draft bills, as described above, and any motions referred to them by the plenary body, taking the place of our *ad hoc* committees for particular bills.

The Budget Committee is of course of quite exceptional importance for the close check it keeps on Government expenditure. For every Government department extraordinarily detailed estimates are submitted annually. Every party has its budget experts and often specialists for particular departments. Each department's estimates are first studied in detail by a member of the Budget Committee familiar with that department's work, so that he may be in a position to lead the discussion of this item by the committee. Even so, it is hard to imagine how the Budget Committee can cope efficiently with an annual *Bundeshaushaltsplan* running to over 2,000 printed pages, but the mere fact that all departments may expect a close scrutiny both of recent expenditure, compared with the earlier estimates, and of plans for the coming year, and this both in the Bundestag and in the Bundesrat, with its Finance Committee of Treasury experts from the *Länder*, must have a sobering effect. A further safeguard is provided by the Bundesrechnungshof, a federal court of accountants, whose members have the same sort of independence as judges. Their main duty is constructive criticism of *Bund* expenditure, and the Bundestag must carefully consider their report before accepting any department's accounts.

Regional and local government in West Germany
The democratic pattern extends down through the *Länder* to the basic administrative units, the *Gemeinden* or communes, which may be villages, towns or cities. Each successive subdivision of the Federation down the scale has its own degree of legal competence and authority, exercised by a democratically elected assembly over a range of public affairs clearly defined in the Basic Law. This states in article 28 that all the *Länder* and all their administrative subdivisions must conform to the pattern of democratic government laid down for the Federation. Many *Länder* had their own constitutions before the Basic Law was agreed upon. All except Bavaria have single-chamber parliaments elected on the basis of proportional representation, as is also the Lower House in Bavaria. The relative strength of the parties and the complexion of the government differs from *Land* to *Land*.

Article 73 of the Basic Law gives a list of eleven matters on which the Bundestag has exclusive rights of legislation. They include foreign affairs, defence, military service; citizenship in the Federation; passports, immigration and emigration, extradition; currency questions, the issue of banknotes and coins, weights and measures; customs, commercial and navigational agreements, the regulation of exchanges of goods and payments with foreign countries; federal railways and air-services; post and telecommunications. Article 74 contains a list about twice as long of matters in which *Bund* and *Länder* have concurrent legislative rights, i.e. things concerning which they must collaborate in legislation, the *Länder* having the right to legislate if the

Bund does not do so. Examples are: civil and criminal law and procedure; registration of births, deaths and marriages; the law of association and assembly; economic legislation; public welfare; scientific
research. On certain matters, e.g. public services, the press, the cinema,
the *Bund* reserves the right to determine the general framework within
which the *Länder* may legislate. In this way, for example, the general
qualifications to be required of higher civil servants in the states are
prescribed, but details such as the age of retirement are not and may vary
from state to state. It was of crucial importance for *Bund* and *Länder*
to agree about their respective rights in the sphere of finance, and a
whole section of the Basic Law, articles 105–15, is devoted to this
subject. West Germans have to pay taxes both to the *Bund* and to the
Länder, some kinds of tax to one and some to the other, according to
the scheme laid down in articles 105–7. The *Bund*, for example, levies
and retains all customs duties, but the *Länder* collect and retain motor-
licence fees. The yield of the most important taxes, income tax and
corporation tax, is divided between *Bund* and *Länder*, in a proportion
determined from time to time by agreement, roughly one-third going
at present to the one and two-thirds to the others. There is provision
for financial equalization between the richer and the poorer states.

No attempt was made in the Basic Law to give a list of matters in
which the *Länder* have full control, but article 70 states that they have
power to legislate on all matters which are not, in the above-mentioned
articles 73 and 74, on exclusive and concurrent legislative powers,
reserved for the *Bund*. In practice, the chief fields left wholly to the
Länder are first cultural and religious affairs, which include education
at all stages and broadcasting (radio and television), and secondly the
control of the police. In the very large number of matters in which the
Bund has full or partial control, it is the *Länder*, acting through the
Landkreise and *Gemeinden*, which are responsible for the detailed administration of federal laws. In the maintenance of order, their control
of the police is subject to the overriding authority of the *Bund* in
grave emergencies.

Through Freiherr vom Stein's reforms of 1808, municipal government in Prussia had been made much more democratic than that of the
State, and all German towns came gradually to be influenced by this
example. It seems clear, however, that although voluntary public
service played an important part in the great development of the towns,
their outstanding efficiency and enterprise since Bismarck's day had
been due at least as much to the work of carefully chosen expert officials.

It is not surprising to find, therefore, that when left to themselves, most of the West German *Länder* came back to something very like this old and well-tried system of municipal administration, though there are differences from *Land* to *Land* in certain features.

It was the *Länder* which, after the establishment of the Federation, drew up the final constitutions of the local authorities, the *Gemeinden*, each *Land* separately for its own area, though all were directed by the Basic Law, as we saw, to give local authorities all possible autonomy in managing their own affairs. In every *Land* there are elective assemblies on three levels, for the *Land*, the *Landkreise* and the *Gemeinden*. The *Landkreise* may be thought of as something like our counties, and their elected councils (*Kreistage*) are responsible for matters concerning a whole group of *Gemeinden* in common, such as roadmaking and local railways, secondary education and youth services, hospital and public welfare services and control of the policing of the area, carried out by the *Land* police force. (Every *Land* has its own police force, and in some *Länder* the *Gemeinden* have one too, but the *Bund* has no police of its own. There is however a body of *Bereitschaftspolizei*, armed riot police, 10,000 strong, to which the *Länder* all contribute contingents.) The *Kreistag* elects a chairman, the Landrat, who in South Germany also acts as chief executive officer, but in the former British zone has an Oberkreisdirektor in charge of his executive committee, just as in the *Stadtgemeinden* of that area the elected Bürgermeister is backed by an appointed Stadtdirektor. This duplication of offices may be seen as a survival of an innovation introduced by the British Military Government, with their own home system in mind, of a political (elected) mayor assisted by a non-political (appointed) town-clerk, but this arrangement has probably been modified by memories of the efficient Prussian towns we have mentioned, where an appointed mayor acted as a kind of City Manager. The problem which is still found so difficult, of combining democracy with efficiency, is no longer solved mainly at the cost of the former, as in this earlier system, when the central Government was always passing instructions down to the mayors through the Regierungspräsidenten and Landräte.

In every *Land* there is a whole hierarchy of *Land* officials, quite distinct from the local government officers employed by the elective assemblies below the Landtag, namely the *Kreistage* and the *Stadträte* or *Gemeindevertretungen*. Their function is to administer the laws passed by the *Bund* and the *Land*, and to see that the actions of the lower assemblies and their agents conform to these laws. The difference is like that in Great Britain between civil servants and municipal or county officials. At the head of the *Land* civil service is the Landesinnenminister, a member of the *Landesregierung* under its Ministerpräsident. The larger *Länder* are divided for civil service purposes into a number of *Regierungsbezirke* or governmental districts – we may think of them as provinces – and these again into the *Landkreise* already mentioned, each made up of a number of *Gemeinden*. The head official of each *Regierungsbezirk* is the Regierungspräsident. The larger *Länder* have between three and eight *Regierungsbezirke*, according to their size. In the smaller *Länder*, the *Landesregierung* deals directly with the *Landkreise* and *Gemeinden*.

Finally we come to the *Gemeinden*, which are by no means all of one size. The smallest are the plain *Gemeinden*, which may be small towns, or villages with the country round them. Then there is the *Stadtgemeinde*, the average town, and the more important *Kreisfreie Stadt* or *Stadtkreis*, a town with a certain minimum population, which is deemed to be capable of exercising, together with the functions of a *Gemeinde*, all those normally belonging to a *Kreis*, having its own secondary schools, hospitals and so on. The elected assembly of every *Gemeinde* is presided over by the Bürgermeister, one of its own members, not a paid official as formerly in Prussia. But in some *Länder*, as mentioned above, the Bürgermeister of even a medium-sized town has a paid Stadtdirektor, with some paid and some voluntary *Beigeordnete*, to relieve him of executive duties, while in others he himself acts as chairman of the executive committee, and in others again he is even more firmly in charge of everything, the *Beigeordnete* being merely his technical assistants. In general there is abundant scope for voluntary work and civic spirit is strong, but the *Gemeinden* often complain that too little is left to their initiative. Certainly in many of their duties, schoolbuilding for instance, they have to follow exactly the directions of the *Landesregierung*, and the *Länder* can run the *Gemeinden* on a much tighter rein than the *Bund* does the *Länder*.

The principal departments of *Gemeinde* activity are housing and public services, the schools, cultural matters and public welfare. The rapidly rising standard of living is most clearly visible perhaps at this level, with the continual improvement of housing, lighting, water, gas and electricity supply and educational and cultural facilities required by a growing and more demanding population. For the local schools the *Gemeinde* provides buildings, equipment and the cost of administration and material upkeep, but not teachers' salaries, which fall on the *Land*. The towns take their responsibility seriously in the provision of cultural facilities of many kinds, ranging from parks and playing fields to public libraries and *Volkshochschulen*, museums, exhibitions, civic theatres and orchestras, a fine tradition which goes right back to the Age of Goethe and the activities of the little state capitals of that day, soon imitated by the larger towns generally.

THE GERMAN DEMOCRATIC REPUBLIC

Origins

The smaller, eastern half of Germany, with an area of 41,700 square miles, calls itself the Deutsche Demokratische Republik, though West German officialdom prefers to call it still the Soviet Zone of Occupation or Middle Germany, a name which implies non-recognition of the Oder–Neisse Line, the border between East Germany and Poland, as the definitive eastern boundary of Germany. The Soviet Military Government in its zone, like its allies in theirs, had assumed supreme authority from the end of the war and treated its part of Germany as a conquered enemy country, making the fullest use of the common policy of preventing Germany from ever again becoming a threat to world peace. This treatment involved the wholesale dismantling of industrial undertakings and their removal to Russia, as a contribution towards the rebuilding of her devastated towns. As late as April 1947, at the Foreign Ministers' Conference in Moscow, Mr Molotov advocated the setting-up of a German unitary state, to be governed according to the Weimar Constitution, but he could not agree to the economic unification desired by the United States and Great Britain, which had merged their two zones in their economic control arrangements since the beginning of the year, and begun to abandon the policy of restricting German production. In June 1947 it was agreed that Marshall Aid should be extended to West Germany, but in December of that year, at the London Conference of Foreign Ministers, Russia was still demanding reparations out of current German production. Three months later the Soviet representatives left the Allied Control Council, and soon the blockade of Berlin began. It seems clear that Russia had aimed at producing economic chaos in Germany, which would lead, it was hoped, to the spread of Communism in West Germany and the eventual establishment of a single satellite state in Germany under Soviet control. When this plan failed, the Soviets resisted any move towards reunification, but developed their own zone into a possible nucleus of a future Communist Germany.

The first move towards the establishment of an East German state was the organizing, ostensibly by the Sozialistiche Einheitspartei Deutschlands (SED) of a Deutscher Volkskongress für Einheit und gerechten Frieden in December 1947, while the London Conference mentioned above was in session, for the purpose of putting forward demands at this Conference in the name of all Germany. The SED had been created in April 1946 by the forcible amalgamation of the East German Social Democratic and Communist parties on the basis of a policy of sovietization in the zone, and support of the Soviet attitude towards German reunification at that time. A second Volkskongress met in March 1948 to set up a Deutscher Volksrat, whose task it should be to draw up a constitution. The Volksrat consisted of hand-picked delegates from 'parties and mass-organizations'. It appointed a committee, consisting entirely of SED members, which got to work speedily and produced a draft constitution, published on 22 October 1948, ahead of the Bonn Parlamentarischer Rat, and this draft was approved on 19 March 1949 by the Volksrat, after being discussed all over the zone, we are told, at no less than 9,000 meetings of various kinds. As a result of suggestions made at these meetings, over a third of the 144 articles in the draft were amended by the Volksrat. Some trouble was evidently taken to create a democratic image in the public mind for the new state, which was named the Deutsche Demokratische Republik, but the first actual election took the form of a plebiscite in May 1949, which was strongly reminiscent of National Socialist 'elections'. Voters were asked to say either 'yes' or 'no' to a list of candidates put forward by the 'Block of anti-fascist parties and mass-organizations'. In spite of intensive propaganda, only 61·8 per cent in the zone voted 'yes' (in East Berlin only 51·7 per cent). The assembly of 1,523 delegates thus elected was the third Volkskongress, which immediately confirmed the Constitution and nominated 330 delegates to form the new Deutscher Volksrat, which did not meet for some months yet, so that responsibility for splitting Germany might seem to lie with the West, for in August 1949 the first general election was held in West Germany, and in September it was proclaimed a Federal Republic. In October the Volksrat met, and on one day, 7 October 1949, it made itself into the provisional Volkskammer of the DDR, declared the Constitution valid, and set up a provisional executive of Ministers and a second chamber (the Länderkammer) to represent the existing *Länder* in the Soviet Zone.

System of government
Not only the origins but the whole history of the German Democratic
Republic make it impossible for outsiders to regard the state as democratic in the Western sense, for in reality it has gradually been completely bolshevized. From the second election on, the 'yes' figures have
always been little short of 100 per cent, because increasing pressure
has been exerted on the voters and the recalcitrant have been struck off
the roll. A democracy without genuinely free elections is for most of
us obviously a sham. What can be learnt about the real nature of the
DDR political institutions confirms this judgement. The Volkskammer
only meets once a month for a few hours to approve unanimously,
very like Hitler's Reichstag, measures already decided upon by the
Government. The so-called *Blockpolitik* practised since 1945 allows of
no coalitions and requires resolutions to be passed unanimously in order
to be valid. According to the Constitution, the 433 members of the
Volkskammer are elected for four years at a time by secret ballot, with
proportional representation, and the franchise has been extended to all
men and women over eighteen. The Chamber cannot be dissolved
until its time is up. It is supposed to play an important part in legislation and to exercise a close control over the Government, for instance
through its sixteen Select Committees, but in reality these do no parliamentary work and several of them have never met. As the five *Länder*
of East Germany were replaced in July 1952 by fourteen purely
administrative districts (*Bezirke*) named after large towns, the Länderkammer, corresponding to the West German Bundesrat, was also
abolished.

East Germany is really ruled, always with due regard to Soviet
approval, by two bodies to which there are parallels in Soviet Russia
and in all the satellite states, the Staatsrat and the central committee
of the SED, the Politbüro. On the death of the first President, Wilhelm
Pieck, in 1960, the office was abolished, and a Staatsrat of 24 members
was created with Walter Ulbricht, the First Secretary of the SED, as
its Chairman. The Staatsrat is elected for four years at a time by the
Volkskammer and is in theory a kind of executive committee which
acts for the Volkskammer between the infrequent meetings of that
body. As the effective Government, it determines policy in accordance
with the resolutions of the highest organs of the SED, so that the constitutional Ministerrat or cabinet is reduced to the status of a committee
of civil servants, the permanent heads of departments. Only the Chairman and Secretary of the Staatsrat do full-time service, and thus enjoy

a higher standing than the rest. Ulbricht, as Chairman of the Staatsrat and First Secretary of the Party, was till his semi-retirement in 1971 as all-powerful as Stalin or Khrushchev, but of course with this difference, that he and his Government had always been wholly dependent on the military power of a foreign state, Russia. Even after Russian recognition of the German Democratic Republic as an independent state in October 1949 the Army of Occupation remained, and since 1955, when the Warsaw Pact was concluded as the counterpart of NATO, the Russian forces on East German soil have been regarded as representing the one, just as those of the Western Allies in the Federal Republic do the other.

The SED in the German Democratic Republic corresponds in ideology, aims and organization to the Communist Party in Soviet Russia, and has so far apparently accepted guidance from Moscow without demur. For nearly a year after the war the Russians tolerated four parties in East Germany, the CDU, which in West Germany became the largest party, as described above, the LDP (Liberal-Demokratische Partei), corresponding to the FDP in West Germany, the SPD or Social Democrats and the KPD or Communists. In April 1946 the last two parties were made to amalgamate, the CDU was suppressed (as was the Communist Party in the Federal Republic) and many of its members were arrested, while the small LDP evaporated. From 1948 onwards the SED was more and more closely assimilated to the Soviet Communist Party, with its Marxist–Leninist ideology as interpreted by Stalin. The tightening of the party's organization was accompanied by repeated purges, and the country's institutions were gradually reshaped to serve the purposes of what the party regarded as a genuinely socialist society. The accepted Stalinist doctrine was, of course, very soon made a compulsory subject at all schools and universities, one most important for success in any career. It is not enough, however, for the ambitious to know the right textbooks and make the proper obeisances. After going through the appropriate youth organizations, they must also serve an apprenticeship for at least a year as *Kandidaten*, in addition to passing a formal examination, in order to gain admission to ordinary party membership. Even then all is not plain sailing, because the central party line is often in dispute – this was a special difficulty in the 1950s, because of the internal party struggle in Russia – and there is a never-ending heresy-hunt for deviationists. By 1963, just under 10 per cent of the population were members of the SED. Its strictly hierarchical organization is on the usual lines. As in

Russia, the large Central Committee seldom meets and the Politbüro, its executive committee of fourteen, is all-important. Ulbricht, First Secretary of the SED since 1950 and a faithful Stalinist, remained in office even after the repudiation of Stalinism in Russia. The Politbüro, in which all policy is originated, has four main divisions: Bureau for Industry and Building, Ideology Committee, Agitation Committee and Agricultural Bureau. They are served by the usual elaborate bureaucratic apparatus, including a Staatlicher Sicherheitsdienst or Secret Police. The intermediate party organization in each of the fourteen *Bezirke* of the Republic, and in East Berlin, is on similar lines to that of the Politbüro, and the pattern is repeated in the *Kreise* of each *Bezirk*, the twenty-four *Stadtkreise* and so on, down to the small town and village branches, and others for the army, the railways, for factories and offices and even for *Wohngebiete*, blocks of ten to twelve thousand people in their homes.

Mass organizations

As will be seen later, post-war Communism believes the 'super-structure' of culture to have a most important political function, but only, of course, if it is carefully controlled by the party. It is a theory familiar from National Socialist totalitarianism, but now it is still more strictly and consistently put into practice. The SED undertakes to control not only politics, agriculture, trade and industry, but also education and all cultural activities, in fact the whole life of citizens of all ages, at work and at play. The Germans have long had a liking for *Vereine*, associations for all kinds of leisure activities in particular. The majority of *Vereine* in the DDR have been incorporated in the officially fostered Mass Organizations, and the rest are closely watched by the police. The chief of the Mass Organizations are the FDGB (Freier Deutscher Gewerkschaftsbund), the anything but free association of trade unions, and the FDJ (Freie Deutsche Jugend), the only youth organization which is allowed, for young people of both sexes between fourteen and eighteen, with a junior branch, the Junge Pioniere, children between ten and fourteen. For women there is the not very popular DFD (Demokratischer Frauenbund Deutschlands), and for workers on the land the VdgB (Vereinigung der gegenseitigen Bauernhilfe) which is now, after the carrying-through of collectiviza-tion, concerned with cultivating correct socialist attitudes and organiz-ing village social life, but was formerly much more important as the only channel through which free peasants could obtain credits, tools, artificial manures and so forth. There is a Deutscher Kulturbund, which organizes lectures, discussions, readings by authors, concerts, exhibitions and competitions in the arts, more in the interests of the public (and of course sound doctrine) than of the writers, artists, composers, etc., who have their own separate professional associations. Finally there is the DTSB (Deutscher Turn- und Sportbund), an elaborate, State-supported organization which exists not so much to encourage people to play games themselves as to pick out, stimulate and support sports-men who seem likely to bring credit to the DDR in international competitions. Uwe Johnson's novel *Das dritte Buch über Achim* is a study of the political, social and ideological cross-currents in which a racing cyclist becomes involved, as his successes make him into a national symbol.

A NOTE ON BERLIN

The city of Berlin, the former capital of a united Germany, is in its present divided state an epitome of the institutional differences between East and West Germany with which this chapter is concerned, but it is only possible here to draw attention to the special position occupied by Berlin in the political and cultural life of Germany today, a position so obviously vulnerable that its indefinite continuance seems highly un-likely. The Russian blockade of West Berlin in 1948–9 and the spirited response of the inhabitants during the Allied airlift, the quickly sup-pressed revolt of East Berlin and Soviet Zone workers on 17 June 1953, and the building of first a barrier and then a wall between East and West Berlin from 13 August 1961: these are the central episodes in the long Cold War up till now. For sixteen years Berlin could serve as a bridge between East and West Germany, but the formerly good communications were then cut and traffic between the two halves of the city remains severely restricted even after some improvements in 1972.

Berlin still has a population of $3\frac{1}{4}$ millions (a million fewer than in 1939), of whom just over a million live in East Berlin, but a third of West Berlin's inhabitants are old-age pensioners, many refugees from the East. West Berlin, like Hamburg and Bremen, is a city with the status of a Federal *Land*, but according to the Four-Power agreements of 1944 and 1945, it is not a part of the Federal Republic, though it belongs to its currency and economic area and conducts its legal and financial affairs as a unit in the Federal system. For historical reasons and with a view to later reunification the *Bund* supports it with grants and loans, without which it could not balance its budget. All laws passed in Bonn have since 1952 been valid in West Berlin without further debate in detail, though they are subject to the reserve powers of control of the three Western powers. East Berlin is, contrary to the Four-Power agreements, incorporated in the German Democratic Republic as one of its *Bezirke*, and is its capital and the seat of its Government. West Berlin, as a great centre of industry, has shared in the economic miracle, built splendidly over its ruins and maintained its cultural pre-eminence. East Berlin, like the rest of East Germany, has recovered much more slowly, but it has its Staatsoper and five other theatres, the Berliner Ensemble and Komische Oper, both very good, to West Berlin's three State theatres and full dozen of private theatres.

Law and Justice

THE HISTORICAL BACKGROUND

In West Germany, law and the administration of justice are probably as humane and enlightened as anywhere in Europe, but like German political institutions they have a long and chequered history behind them, and uniformity was naturally achieved very late. Local law in its infinite variety was gradually supplemented in the course of the Middle Ages by Roman law, and the resulting combination came to be known as *Gemeines Recht*, law common to the whole empire. This ill-defined system prevailed in the central portion of Germany, excluding Austrian and Prussian lands, until 1900. The first codification, a logical amalgamation of Roman and native law, was initiated by Frederick the Great and carried through by 1794, but this *Allgemeines Landrecht* could be imposed only on Prussia's own scattered provinces. The French took their *Code Civil* of 1804 to the German territories they occupied, and it remained in force in the Rhineland, for instance, all through the nineteenth century, as did also the *Badisches Landrecht* derived from it. Austria had her own civil code from 1811 and Saxony from 1863, so until the *Bürgerliches Gesetzbuch* of the German Reich came into force on the first day of the present century, there were no fewer than five different systems of civil law surviving side by side in Germany and Austria, a typical illustration, parallel to the diversity of weights and measures and of coinages, of the difficulty experienced by the Germans in achieving nationhood. There was a similar diversity in criminal codes down to 1871, when a *Reichsstrafgesetzbuch* was approved by the new Reichstag, after Bismarck had had the clauses

D

abolishing the death penalty removed. Before this a number of states had been led by the growth of humanitarian feeling to do away with capital punishment, though often only temporarily, as for example in Austria between 1787 and 1796, but otherwise medieval ideas of trial and punishment still left many traces until they were gradually displaced by the principles embodied in Napoleon's *Code d'instruction criminelle*. This French revision of English criminal procedure substituted for inquisitions in private, and the protracted study of written protocols and comments, the now generally accepted practice of trial by jury, in open court, where all the essential evidence is brought forward by word of mouth. The *Reichsstrafprozessordnung* of 1877 still governs present-day criminal procedure in both halves of Germany.

Under the succession of regimes since the end of the First World War there have naturally been many changes, especially in criminal law and procedure. The Weimar Republic aimed, as in its Constitution, at correcting what it saw as defects in the existing system of law by a liberalization in tune with modern thought, a reform of the divorce laws, special treatment for juvenile offenders, an understanding use of psychiatric evidence and so on, but its more ambitious plans were never realized. The National Socialists reversed much of this and tried, like all totalitarian governments, to make law and justice serve their narrow political aims, where they did not openly replace the rule of law by the Gestapo's terrorization of all opponents of the party and its policies. The existing law was often a hindrance to Hitler because the courts, in spite of severe pressure on judges and the indoctrination of law students, could not easily bring themselves to go against the principles of law and justice, and new laws could not keep pace with the party's erratic changes of direction. After ten years, however,

a leading official in the Reich Ministry of Justice could state that the necessary basic changes of personnel in the leading positions of the administration of the law had been made, and that soldiers held all the important positions in this field. He pointed out that the main object was 'to revolutionize the corps of judges', adding the strangely naïve remark that 'the regeneration of the judges was more important than the regeneration of the law'. The 'regenerate' soldier-judge shares, by training and Party membership, the outlook and approach of the Gestapo.[1]

[1] E. K. Bramstedt, *Dictatorship and Political Police* (London, 1945), p. 163.

How far this regeneration had gone by 1944 can be seen from a Swiss journalist's description of the proceedings at the infamous Volksgerichtshof in Berlin, during the trial of a middle-aged woman for defeatism. She had been denounced by her maid for screaming, in her own home, a remark hostile to the Führer, on hearing of the death of her daughter in an air-raid.

> The speech by the defending counsel lasted exactly three and a half minutes. It began with good wishes for a long life to the Führer and for a German victory. It concluded with praise of German jurisprudence. In between counsel pointed out that, although the accused deserved severe punishment, it should be taken into account that her husband and her sons had served Germany. Counsel seemed to be very timid, and weighed every word before he uttered it. He was right to do so. How many barristers had put themselves into the dock because they had dared to bring out points, however harmless, in favour of their clients! After half an hour the trial was concluded: on account of her defeatist attitude, her insult to the Führer, her abuse of the German people and her words against the state, Frau Z. was sentenced to death by the axe.[1]

THE FEDERAL REPUBLIC

Civil courts

This is the kind of memory from the immediate past which those responsible for the reform of justice in the Federal Republic had in mind as a warning example. They returned naturally to the Weimar model, and in the favourable atmosphere of the last twenty years, their humanization of the law and judicial procedure has already achieved much better results than were possible in the earlier republic. 'Recoil from calamity and horror,' writes an English observer who has recently studied the West German courts at first hand,

> recoil, also and naturally, from insupportable guilt, is taking the form of deeds. There *is* the new regard for life – it would be hard for a Bismarck today to reintroduce the death penalty – there is the respect of man for man, the tending of liberty and the decencies and the due process of law, and with it goes a love, an almost avid love, of normality and all its trimmings.[2]

[1] Ibid., p. 249.
[2] Sybille Bedford, *The Faces of Justice* (London, 1961), p. 152.

The West German system of courts and the whole organization of justice remind one more of France than of England, though France had in some respects, as was mentioned, followed English precedents in the *Code d'instruction criminelle*. As in France and England, the legal procedure in civil cases, in which one citizen sues another, e.g. for an unpaid debt, an inheritance or for a breach of contract, is different from that followed in criminal cases, in which someone is charged by the authorities with a criminal offence, though both types of case may be tried by the same courts and judges.

Minor civil actions, about a petty complaint perhaps, or a claim for a few hundred marks, are heard in the first instance by a single judge in a so-called *Amtsgericht*, with someone in attendance, probably a young *Referendar* (see below), to keep the minutes (*Protokoll*). Plaintiff and defendant may or may not be represented by counsel, as they choose, but at all courts above this level counsel are required. These local courts, something like a magistrate's court, are very numerous. There are 177 of them in the largest *Land*, North Rhine–Westphalia, 16 in the smallest, Saarland, and 9 in West Berlin, each with a staff of judges. Next in the scale comes the *Landgericht*, something like a county court, which hears appeals from the *Amtsgericht*, and is also a court of first instance for cases where fairly high sums are at stake, at least a few thousands of marks, as well as for matrimonial cases. Here in each court-room there is, instead of a single judge, a *Kammer* or group of three judges. Appeal may be made from judgements of this court to the *Oberlandesgericht*, sitting in *Senaten* of three judges, and there is the possibility of a further review of the case (*Revision*) – but only on points of law, not of fact, and only if the claim exceeds 15,000 DM – by the Bundesgerichtshof at Karlsruhe (the seat of all the chief federal courts), sitting in senates of five judges. Actions for alleged *Beleidigung* (slander) and similar minor disputes have to be submitted first to an unpaid arbitrator (*Schiedsmann*), and in the *Amtsgericht* too the judge often attempts a reconciliation of the parties or a compromise. Apart from the regular civil courts there are many with specialized functions: *Verwaltungsgerichte* to hear complaints against Government departments, etc.; *Finanzgerichte* to hear tax appeals; *Arbeitsgerichte* for labour disputes; *Sozialgerichte* for social insurance complaints; and several others, including of course *Jugendgerichte*, juvenile courts. These special courts occupy well over 2,000 judges.

Criminal courts

Criminal offences are graded in the *Strafgesetzbuch* according to the penalties prescribed for them there. Minor offences, called *Übertretungen*, are those, such as drunkenness or disorderly behaviour, punishable by a fine of up to 150 DM or a short period of detention (*Haft*). Medium offences like theft or embezzlement, called *Vergehen*, are those punishable by a fine exceeding 150 DM or imprisonment (*Gefängnis*) for up to five years. Serious offences, like forgery or murder, called *Verbrechen*, are those punishable by a more formidable type of imprisonment (*Zuchthaus*) for over five years. It is a *Land* official called a *Staatsanwalt* who, when his department, the *Staatsanwaltschaft*, has been informed by the police or by a private person about a suspected offence, first asks the police to find out by preliminary inquiries whether there is a *prima facie* case and, if there is, organizes a thorough investigation, the *Ermittlungsverfahren*, before any arrest is made. The warrant for an arrest must be issued by a judge, and arrested persons must be immediately informed of the nature of the charge and be brought before a judge within 24 hours. There is no bail as we know it; the judge decides whether or not to hold the suspect in custody. Usually the *Staatsanwalt* requests a *Voruntersuchung*, or fact-finding inquiry by a judge of the *Amtsgericht*, at which the judge, sitting alone except for a clerk, hears witnesses, not in the presence of the suspect, and questions the suspect himself, who is not compelled to answer, and is allowed legal aid. The *Hauptverfahren* or public trial follows, if there still seem to be good grounds for it, perhaps after further investigation of doubtful points.

The criminal court of first instance is the *Amtsgericht*, with a single judge, for *Übertretungen* and lesser *Vergehen* (penalty up to six months), but a rather more serious *Vergehen* or minor *Verbrechen* (penalty up to two years) goes before a *Schöffengericht*, consisting of an *Amtsgericht* judge and two laymen called *Schöffen*. These are chosen from a list of people of good repute and some standing, as their function is more that of assessors than of jurymen in the British sense. They sit on the bench with the judge, who gives no summing up. After the hearing they all retire and make up their minds together, both as to the verdict and, if they find the accused guilty, about the sentence, following a fixed procedure intended to give the lay members of the court their full share of influence. A simple majority vote is enough for any decision, and the judge, who of course presides throughout, has no casting vote. When he returns to court with the *Schöffen* he must give reasons for their common decision even if he has been outvoted. This is trial by jury with a difference, and many in Germany are beginning to be doubtful about giving quite so much weight to the judgement of the common man, especially in view of the absence of British rules about contempt of court, by the publication of comment beforehand in the press, or on radio or television. If the verdict is 'not guilty', however, that is not the end of the matter, as in England, because both prosecution and defence have the right of appeal. Appeals from the *Amtsgericht* are heard by the *Kleine Strafkammer* of the *Landgericht*, consisting of a judge and two *Schöffen*, and appeals from the *Schöffengericht* by the *Große Strafkammer* of the *Landgericht*, with three judges and two *Schöffen*. There is a further appeal from either of these courts to the *Oberlandesgericht*, with its senates of three judges.

For *Vergehen* and *Verbrechen* punishable with more than two years' imprisonment (except those *Verbrechen* causing loss of life) the court of first instance is the already mentioned *Große Strafkammer* of the *Landgericht*. Very serious *Verbrechen* resulting in a death (murder, infanticide, manslaughter) are tried by the *Schwurgericht* of the *Landgericht*, with three judges and six *Geschworene*. The lay members here too play a similar part to the *Schöffen* in the *Schöffengericht* in deciding with the judges both verdict and sentence, and as they are again in a majority of two to one, the same kind of criticism has been heard about this court as about the other. Applications for review (*Revision*), on legal grounds only, of judgements of the *Große Strafkammer* as court of first instance, or of the *Schwurgericht*, are heard by the *Bundesgerichtshof*, with its senates of five judges. It is an anomaly, critics say, that for a petty thief, tried first by the *Amtsgericht*, three instances are available, but for a murderer only two, the second not concerned at all with matters of fact.

The study and practice of the law

In West Germany, as in continental Europe generally, trained lawyers play a much bigger part in the administration of justice than in England, because all the minor cases which in England come before lay magistrates, Justices of the Peace, of whom there are many thousands, are heard by professional judges, whose status is quite different from that of an English judge because they are so numerous, and so much concerned with comparatively unimportant conflicts and offences. They are not, as with us, former barristers with long experience of the courts. Barristers as such are in fact unknown in Germany, where a

Rechtsanwalt may both be active as what we should call a solicitor and defend clients in court. All lawyers have the same course of legal training and must pass the same examinations. After at least three and a half years of university study comes the first State examination, after passing which the young lawyer spends two and a half years as a *Referendar* or apprentice lawyer, gaining experience according to a prescribed programme in various types of court, as well as in *Staatsanwaltschaften*, private law offices and civil service departments. If he then passes his second State examination, he is eligible for employment as a *Richter*, a *Staatsanwalt* or in private practice as a *Rechtsanwalt* or a *Notar* (a notary, chiefly concerned with drawing up or attesting important legal documents), though before becoming fully fledged he must put in two or three years more as *Gerichtsassessor* or *Notarassessor*. As *Referendar* he has had some experience of all kinds of legal work, but after the second State examination he must make his choice and stick to it, as there is no free movement between the various branches of the profession. A very large number at this stage enter a non-legal branch of the civil service, or the legal side of big business, banking, trade-union or employers' organizations, later perhaps to go into politics. The study of the law seems to lead in Germany more often to a safe career than in England, without as good a prospect of glittering prizes for a small minority. There are nearly 10,000 *Richter* in the Federal Republic's regular courts, of course in many grades with different duties. There are over 600 in West Berlin alone, whereas judges in England number in all about 150, including county court judges and stipendiary magistrates. The present reform movement aims at greatly reducing the number of *Richter*, in particular by empowering laymen, something like our Justices of the Peace, to deal with minor offenders in the first instance.[1]

As was pointed out above, trial by jury and the observation of what German jurists call the principles of *Öffentlichkeit* and *Mündlichkeit* were only gradually introduced into Germany in the nineteenth century, and it is clear from our brief description of the West German system of courts that in spite of fundamental agreement on principles there are considerable differences in practice between West German legal procedures and our own. Eye-witness accounts of actual trials bring out many more. In England, for instance, the judge plays a rather passive role before his summing-up, embodying with the help of

[1] H. Domcke, *Die Rechtsordnung* (Geschichte und Staat 112) (Munich, 1965), p. 153.

ancient symbolism the majesty of the law. He digests the evidence as it is given and sees to it that everyone plays fair according to the fixed rules, especially the rules of evidence, designed to eliminate anything that might prejudice the jury against the accused and make it difficult for them to reach their verdict purely on the strength of the evidence before them. In Germany, as in France, it is the judge who does most of the questioning. He first examines the accused *Zur Person*, asking him about his personal circumstances and history, especially about any previous convictions, knowledge of which is carefully concealed from a British jury until they have given their verdict. In spite of German insistence that their trial procedure is 'accusatorial', not 'inquisitorial', i.e. that accuser and judge are different persons, and that it is not the judge's business to elicit the truth from the accused and witnesses – the *Staatsanwalt* has done this already to the best of his ability – but to give judgement on the evidence produced, there is for English ears an inquisitorial flavour still about certain features. After the hearing *Zur Person* the indictment is read, and the accused is invited by the judge to give his own version of what happened, as the first stage of the hearing *Zur Sache*. There is no real cross-examination by counsel either of the accused or of witnesses, though questions may be put with the judge's permission. At the beginning of the third stage in the trial, the *Beweisaufnahme*, the witnesses, who are kept under supervision in a separate room, are brought in together to hear a little formal address from the presiding judge – who is addressed simply as *Herr Vorsitzender* – about the seriousness of the occasion and the penalties for false statements on oath, but the oath is administered, again collectively, only at the close, when all have been heard singly and questioned by the judge and, with his permission, by the defending counsel and the *Staatsanwalt*. The judge has before him the full record of what the *Untersuchungsrichter* has heard the accused and the witnesses say at his *Voruntersuchung*, and the results of all the inquiries of the *Staatsanwalt*, which have lasted perhaps for weeks or months or, in a capital offence, possibly years. This long delay 'is inherent in the mechanism and spirit of the criminal prosecution in even a vestigial inquisitorial system, as that system with its predilection for packaged guilt must rely on a lengthy, cautious preliminary investigation conducted by a semi-administrative judiciary, without any positive regard for the passage of time'.[1] In earlier days, great weight was laid on the extortion of a confession, and hair-raising tales are told about the means employed

[1] Sybille Bedford, op. cit., p. 128.

to this end even in the mid-nineteenth century, not to speak of Gestapo inquisitions. There is no indication that oppressive methods are used now. They 'do not seem to go with the present climate of West German legal administration.'[1] Following many criticisms of the frequency and length of detentions of suspects for investigation, a reform of 1964 reduced the maximum period except in very special circumstances to six months.[2] The normal German view is still that the Staatsanwalt is much to be preferred to prosecuting counsel or the Public Prosecutor in England, just because he makes it his business to establish if possible the objective truth, bringing out equally every point in favour of the accused as well as everything against him, while the prosecution in England leaves it to the defence to discover what favourable evidence it can. Ralf Dahrendorf makes the interesting suggestion that there is something in the role of the Staatsanwalt to which there are significant parallels in other social institutions in Germany. 'Wherever opposing interests meet in German society, there is a tendency to seek authoritative and substantive rather than tentative and formal solutions.'[3] In court, anyhow, there is not the tension between prosecution and defence counsel which in England, in theory at least, keeps both sides on their toes, and has obvious analogies with the spirit of competitive enterprise. The two civil servants, the judge and the Staatsanwalt, especially the latter, play the big roles. Defence counsel, a private practitioner, seems to be there chiefly to beg for clemency, not to help in establishing the truth. Another difference we notice is that the ritual element, so prominent in England, is reduced to a minimum. Heinrich Böll, whose novel Ende einer Dienstfahrt (1966) is set in an Amtsgericht in 1965 and follows every stage of a trial, describes the atmosphere among onlookers in this local court as like that at a performance by amateurs of a classical play, 'a kind of good-natured excitement'. 'When the judge and Staatsanwalt entered', he writes, 'and the public present rose to their feet while the two went to their places, one could see in the way they stood up and sat down again that easy casualness to be observed in monastic communities, where the ritual has become a friendly gesture among familiar associates.' A German judge wears a black gown but of course no wig. His biretta normally lies on the table, but he dons it as he enters the court and again at the close when explaining the court's verdict in a kind of summing-up, and pronouncing

---

[1] Sybille Bedford, op. cit., p. 132.
[2] H. Domcke, op. cit., p. 110.
[3] 'Conflict and Liberty', in British Journal of Sociology, vol. XIV, p. 199.

sentence. After the *Beweisaufnahme*, the *Staatsanwalt* and counsel for the defence have both concluded their final addresses by stating what sentence they consider just, and after pronouncing sentence the judge asks first the accused and then the *Staatsanwalt* whether they accept the judgement. The accused has a week, if he chooses, in which to make up his mind and meanwhile, if he has not hitherto been kept in custody, is free to go home. If he decides to appeal, he remains at liberty until the higher court's decision is made known. The very full use that is made of the right to appeal is a great burden on the courts.

THE GERMAN DEMOCRATIC REPUBLIC

The Communist view of law

East and West Germany, in spite of their common legal inheritance before 1945, which is reflected in the fact that both still use as the basis of their law the *Bürgerliches Gesetzbuch* and the *Strafgesetzbuch*, differently revised, have already diverged to such an extent that West German courts, when dealing with people who have at an earlier stage appeared in civil or criminal cases before East German judges, feel themselves to be faced with something foreign and increasingly unacceptable in the judgements pronounced in these cases. This is because East German law and justice have inevitably become more and more completely assimilated to the Communist political system and its ideology. In all states which make Soviet Russia their model, law has an all-important political function to perform. It is not a restraining influence on those who hold political power, a guarantee of individual freedom built into the constitution, as in a *Rechtsstaat*. There is no insistence that judges must be completely independent of politics, as unbiased as humanly possible and absolutely correct in their observance of the forms and procedures devised to ensure their impartiality. They must, on the contrary, be committed to Communism and eager to promote it. In orthodox Marxist theory, law and the whole 'superstructure' of culture were held to reflect passively the social and economic 'basis' of life, but for the modern activist, convinced of the supreme importance of the role of the party as *avant-garde* and of its unique insight in political and economic affairs, 'the superstructure was created by the basis expressly for the purpose of serving it', as Stalin said in 1945.[1] In the Deutsche Demokratische Republik we find, therefore,

[1] Quoted in E.-W. Böckenförde, *Die Rechtsauffassung im kommunistischen Staat* (Munich, 1967), p. 29. See also Marion Gräfin Dönhoff in *Reise in ein fernes Land*, 10th edn. (Hamburg, 1968), pp. 48 f.

instead of the eternal vigilance which Western democrats have always held to be the price of individual freedom, and which seemed to West Germans particularly necessary after their experience of Nazism, a single party holding on to power with Russian help, but claiming in everything the authority of the *Volk*, and making the law, and culture generally, into a tool for the more and more complete 'socialization' of the country.

'*The democratization of justice*'

The basic rights clauses taken over from the Weimar Constitution are to be understood, as we have seen, only in a Pickwickian sense, or as a reward to be claimed when the perfect socialism has been established, but the citizen's duty to the State is meanwhile to be strictly observed. There is no *Verfassungsgericht* to challenge any contravention of the basic law, and the separation of powers is very imperfectly observed. In the process of legislation the executive is vastly more important than the nominal legislature, the Volkskammer, and Government decrees are just as valid as laws. There is therefore no insistence on the independence of the judiciary. The highest judges have always been nominated by the Staatsrat and appointed by the Volkskammer, and since 1960 judges of the *Kreisgerichte* and *Bezirksgerichte* (which correspond roughly to the *Amtsgerichte* and *Landgerichte* of West Germany) have been appointed by the assemblies of the *Kreise* and *Bezirke* respectively on the nomination of the Department of Justice. All appointments are for four years at a time and all courts have to report progress (in socialization, etc.) annually to the local assembly which appointed their members. The most urgent problem for the Government in relation to justice has been from the beginning that of 'democratization', which meant in particular the replacement of the old personnel by men and women in sympathy with the regime. For centuries the students of law at German universities had considered themselves a social élite, because of both their origins and their expectations, and the higher reaches of the judiciary, like the higher civil servants – all lawyers by training – were traditionally conservative and even feudal in their politics. Twenty-five years of social democracy followed by national socialism had of course left their mark, but the upper-class consciousness was very hard to eradicate. In the first years after 1945 there were many gaps to fill because of the wholesale dismissal by the Military Government of notorious Nazis in the profession. The so-called *Volksrichter* appointed to meet this temporary need were intelligent and ideologically sound working men and women, at least twenty-three years old, with some years of experience in a trade behind them. They were given short courses of training in law and party doctrine, at first only for six months, and for the rest left to learn from practice under supervision. Later correspondence courses in law as in other subjects were started at the universities, which enabled many of them to take the regular law examinations, and eventually all were required to pass the State examination by 1960 to retain their posts. Meanwhile the teaching of law was reformed, in several stages. Now it lasts five years, including a year of practical experience sandwiched in, in two halves, between the years of study. The early part of the course is general and common to all law students, laying great stress on Marxist economics and politics, and at the beginning of the fourth year, after an intermediate State examination, the student is directed towards a career either as a *Justizjurist*, i.e. a *Richter*, *Staatsanwalt* or private *Rechtsanwalt* – this last a profession only tolerated if a lawyer joins a sort of State-supervised guild or corporation – or as a *Wirtschaftsjurist*, in the service of the now almost entirely State-controlled industry and commerce or one of the many planning committees in the DDR. The specialized courses for the one type are held at the universities of East Berlin and Leipzig, and for the other at Jena and Halle. The reform of legal training has evidently been most thorough, and the democratization has in one sense at least been carried very far if it is true, as we are told, that 75 per cent of East German lawyers are now of working-class origin, and 30 per cent are women. It should be added that since 1963 only persons who have qualified in a trade and exercised it for two years may be admitted as students of law.

To suit the new social and economic conditions whole sections of the *Bürgerliches Gesetzbuch* have been eliminated, e.g. those concerned with (capitalistic) agriculture, transport, labour relations, and replaced by new legislation. New divorce laws were introduced by decree in 1955 which anticipated some of the 1970 reforms in Great Britain. The criterion is the extent to which the marriage has broken down, from the point of view of man and wife and from that of a socialist society; the question of guilt does not arise. Alimony is granted for two years at most, and only in certain cases. The *Strafgesetzbuch* has been revised by important new additions. New criminal offences include propaganda and agitation dangerous to the State, sabotage and inducement to flee from the country. The death penalty may still be imposed for serious crimes. The gravity of an offence is assessed largely according to its effect on society, and the aim of criminal law is described as the attempt 'to support the struggle of the mass of the people for peace, the victory of socialism and the national rebirth of Germany by the prosecution of particular offenders – and in general to overcome criminality as a social phenomenon'.

East Germany, it will be seen, like other Communist countries, does not make the clear distinction between legal and moral guilt which is familiar in the West, and the law is expected not only to regulate the external behaviour of the citizen but also to alter his attitudes, his *Gesinnung*, particularly his attitude towards the State and society. What is considered essential is that he should consider himself personally involved in both. 'The bourgeois idea of being free *from* state and society, i.e. of being legally entitled either to do a certain thing or to leave it undone, as a man personally decides, gives way to the socialist idea of being free *for* society, i.e. for realizing his personality in and through society.'[1] The Marxist–Leninist view of the relationship between the individual and society, as expounded in East Germany, sounds extraordinarily like the arguments put forward by German apologists during the First World War in reply to Allied propaganda about a war for democracy. Ernst Troeltsch, for instance, explaining the German idea of freedom in 1916, claimed that freedom meant for a German 'free, conscious, dutiful service performed by him for the greater whole, for his state and nation . . . This freedom consists of duties rather than rights, or at least of rights which are at the same time duties.'[2] That was three revolutions ago, but the German nation to whom the earlier remarks were addressed had two things in common with the people in East Germany today, that it was ruled by a highly autocratic Government, and that the intellectuals in it took readily to a sort of 'political mysticism' (Troeltsch) deeply rooted in German intellectual history, above all in the philosophy of Hegel. In West Germany, perhaps we can see a remnant of the same tradition in the persistent hankering after authoritarian solutions of social and political problems criticized by liberals like Ralf Dahrendorf, and even in the feeling expressed by many of the 'students in revolt' that the society they live in offers them no idea to live for.

[1] E.-W. Böckenförde, op. cit., p. 47.
[2] See my essay, 'British and German ideas of freedom', *German Life and Letters*, N.S. vol. I, p. 79.

Cultural Institutions – Education

The schools in their historical background

Germany's extremely rapid progress from the middle of the nineteenth century on, not only in science and scholarship but also in trade
and industry, would have been impossible but for the far-seeing
reform of the educational system initiated in Prussia after 1806 and
gradually imitated elsewhere, but owing to continuing political disunity, the co-ordination of elementary, secondary and university
education was still very imperfect even in 1871, and the whole system
reflected the social inequalities of the time, particularly in the gulf that
still lay between elementary and secondary education. Secondary
education had been at least partially adapted to current needs. By the
1880s there were three types of secondary school, the old *Gymnasium*,
where Latin and Greek were all-important, the more recent *Oberreal-
schule*, where language study was subordinated to mathematics and
science, and the *Realgymnasium*, where the study of one or two modern
languages could be combined with Latin. The full course at any of
these schools, only completed by a minority of pupils, lasted nine
years, after a three-year preparatory course, usually in the same school.
For boys intended from the outset for industry and commerce, a
course three years shorter, which could be completed by the age of
fifteen, was provided at the *Mittel-* or *Realschule*, leading to the *Mittlere
Matura*, a kind of Lower Leaving Certificate. It was not until 1901,
after a long campaign conducted by the moderns against the traditionalists, that the full *Matura* gained at one of the two more modern
types of secondary school was recognized as qualifying for entrance to
a university, as opposed to a *Technische Hochschule*. Technical schools
and colleges in the greatest variety had by now a very long development behind them in Germany, some going back well into the eighteenth century. They played a most important role in that 'application
of a trained intelligence to practical affairs' which, according to W. H.
Dawson, was a root cause of imperial Germany's rapid economic
progress, and they flourished not only in Prussia. Saxony, Hamburg
and one or two other states made attendance at a technical continuation
school for about six hours in the evenings compulsory for boys leaving
the *Volksschule* at fourteen, long before Prussia, namely soon after 1890.
Technische Hochschulen of university rank existed in many centres,

along with similar institutions for the most advanced study of music, art, architecture, etc. Much of this vocational training had been organized and financed by private enterprise, by industrial and commercial organizations continuing the age-old traditions of the craft guilds.

The outlines of this nineteenth-century educational structure are still clearly visible in the present West German system, and to some extent in that of East Germany too. In general, the Federal Republic has consciously aimed at a return to the educational aims of the Weimar Republic rather than a thoroughgoing attempt at reform, the first necessity being to eliminate as far as possible the results of the National Socialist reaction against Weimar ideals, while carrying on the urgent tasks presented since the end of the war by every new day. Educational thought in the earlier republic had been radical and forward-looking as in law and politics, inspired by advanced European and American thought but not forgetful of the older German idealism. The first innovation, introduced after much controversy in 1920, had been to abolish preparatory departments in secondary schools, and to make attendance compulsory for the first four years of school life at a uniform type of elementary school, the *Grundschule*. There were socialistic ideas about the abolition of privilege behind this, but also the sensible practical aim of linking up the hitherto entirely distinct systems of elementary and secondary education by providing them with a common basis. The four upper classes of the elementary school gave further general education and some vocational training to those who stayed on there, and this latter was carried further by compulsory attendance until the age of eighteen at a *Berufsschule*, usually once a week. Office workers would attend a commercial *Berufsschule*, and others the one most useful for their occupation. Two new types of post-elementary school were introduced, a shortened secondary school, the *Deutsche Oberschule*, in which the German language and German culture, instead of foreign languages, were made central in a humanistic course, and a school meant to provide a full secondary education for pupils who had missed their first chance of beginning it immediately after the four years of the *Grundschule*. They could enter this *Aufbauschule* two years later, at about sixteen, and complete the course up to the *Matura* in seven years. At least something was done to give country children an equal chance with town children by providing some boarding facilities at these schools. The normal three types of secondary school continued to have nine classes, following four of elementary education now instead of three, making thirteen years in all.

The National Socialists, with their frenzied nationalism and their racialist obsessions, made drastic changes which have had little permanent effect except to produce a violent reaction since the end of the war. Their most important change at the time was the centralization of control in all educational matters in the hands of the first Reich Minister of Education and Science, instead of leaving education as a *Land* affair in charge of the *Kultusminister* in each. Along with this went a reversal of the Weimar spirit, which had been democratic, conciliatory and humanistic, to policies reflecting the fanatical ideologies of the party and the power struggles within it. The main changes in the structure of the service were attempts at simplification. The result was that after the *Grundschule* there were only three types of school left, the classical *Gymnasium*, the *Oberschule*, where the emphasis was on science rather than languages, and the *Aufbauschule*, a shortened *Oberschule*. The first two had only eight classes instead of the traditional nine, making twelve years in all and leaving a year free for *Arbeitsdienst*, etc.

The restoration of a federal system of government in West Germany made necessary in the first place a number of decisions about the proposed division of functions between the *Bund* and the *Länder*, with the result now embodied in the Basic Law. School and university affairs are now subject only to the legislation of the *Länder*, as we have seen, and the ultimate authority in each of them is its government, and in particular its *Kultusminister* and his department. But the high degree of co-ordination that is obviously necessary in a closely knit union of states has been secured since 1949 by the regular meetings, at intervals of six or eight weeks, of the Permanent Conference of *Kultusminister*, with a staff of permanent officials in its secretariat, constantly in touch with all the Ministries concerned. Local traditions can be maintained, in the matter of confessional schools, for example, so that Catholic areas have for the most part separate schools for Catholics, while in other parts inter-confessional classes are favoured in all subjects but religion. At the same time there is a high measure of uniformity in all *Länder* as to types of school provided, normal standards and curricula, length of school holidays, teachers' salaries and conditions of service, and so on. Many reforms have been carried through in the separate *Länder* on an agreed basis, frequently following suggestions first put forward by an unofficial advisory committee of educationists from many

Länder, which has met regularly since 1953, the Deutscher Ausschuss für Erziehungs- und Bildungswesen.

The *Grundschule* is still the basic elementary school for all, for the first four years after a child's sixth birthday. Private elementary schools are only allowed under very special conditions, and secondary schools are still not allowed to have preparatory divisions of their own, though private schools are permitted under certain conditions after the elementary stage. All this is laid down in the Basic Law itself (article 7). About three-quarters of all pupils stay on in the *Volksschule* after the age of ten and remain for four, or in many cases now five, years in its *Oberstufe*. After that, attendance at a *Berufsschule* is compulsory for three years, or until the age of eighteen is reached. *Volksschulen* are mixed schools, and no fees are charged.

At ten, the remaining quarter of the *Grundschule* pupils go on either to the *Mittelschule*, which they normally leave at sixteen with the *Mittlere Matura*, or to a *Höhere Schule*. If they are late developers, or have changed their minds, they may still qualify for entering a university or technical *Hochschule* by staying on at the *Mittelschule* for three more years, in the *Aufbaustufe*, and gaining the full *Matura*. There are also *Abendgymnasien* where determined young people employed in the daytime may, in two to six years of hard work, also bridge the gap, but most university students have entered at ten one of the three types of *Höhere Schule* and obtained their *Matura* at about nineteen. Only 25 to 30 per cent of the entrants, however, get so far, for many are content with the *Mittlere Matura* gained at sixteen. The three types of secondary school are essentially the same as in the Weimar Republic or the Reich before that, but now they are all called *Gymnasium*, and the *Altsprachliches*, *Neusprachliches* and *Mathematisch-naturwissenschaftliches Gymnasium* all again have nine classes after the four-year *Grundschule*, so that the minimum age at which a pupil is ready for the university or *Technische Hochschule* is nineteen years. One *Land* after another has abolished school fees in all secondary schools as well as in primary education, and many supply books and stationery free also. The only fee-paying schools left are private schools, of which there are a considerable number, attended by about 12 per cent of the post-primary school population. The Basic Law requires that they shall be of at least as high a quality as the State schools and shall not 'promote a segregation of the pupils according to the means of the parents', which presumably means in practice that they must make it possible, by the award of scholarships, for able pupils whose parents cannot afford high fees to be accepted. Many of these schools are at least in part boarding-schools and some, like Salem, the school founded by Prince Max of Baden after the First World War, have a high reputation. Especially since Weimar Republic days educational reformers like Hermann Lietz have frequently started experimental schools, *Landerziehungsheime* and so on, which have usually had financial problems but have done much to break down the rigidity which has long been a defect of German education. Since the Reformation there have been groups of good boarding-schools in two German states. The Swabian *Klosterschulen*, designed to prepare boys for theological study at the Tübinger Stift and the Protestant ministry, produced Hegel, Hölderlin, Schelling, Mörike and a long succession of scholars, poets, philosophers and theologians, and they still survive, sometimes in picturesque and venerable old buildings, as in Maulbronn. The corresponding set of schools in Saxony, the *Fürstenschulen* like Meissen and Schul-Pforta, the one Lessing's school and the other Nietzsche's, are now inaccessible to West Germans and probably completely transformed. An attempt to continue the tradition of these schools is being made at Meinerzhagen (Westphalia) by the *Land* North Rhine-Westphalia.

The universities

Of all German institutions, the universities have probably in their time been most admired and copied by foreign countries. They are still numerous, active and larger than ever, but it seems unlikely that the West German universities can continue much longer without subjecting themselves to a long-delayed overhaul. The East German universities have by degrees, in the last twenty years, been thoroughly and apparently quite effectively adapted to the function required of them in a Communist society. Their severest critics are of course academic circles in West Germany, but to outsiders and in the last few years to the great mass of their own students, the West German universities have seemed more and more open to criticism themselves as organs of a free society.

The tradition generally regarded as specifically German, of the university as primarily a centre for research, began when the Prussian Government called in Wilhelm von Humboldt to reform the Prussian educational system, the defects of which were seen to be one cause of Prussia's total collapse in the 1806 campaign against France. As in the parallel series of administrative and military reforms, the Government agreed to far-reaching changes, and all concerned worked, under the shock of the Jena defeat, with feverish energy. It was thus possible to follow the advice of radical thinkers like Fichte, Schelling and Schleiermacher and encourage creative scholarship, instead of making the further provision for vocational training and the dissemination of useful knowledge that moderate opinion had long desired. In some ways it was a surprising triumph of the Romantic belief in *Geist* over Enlightened common sense. To many then and later, the Greek and Latin which Humboldt made staple fare at the reformed grammar school, the *Gymnasium*, was useless knowledge, but for him, the friend of Goethe and Schiller and apostle of *Bildung*, the classics were the key to the good life. He wanted every *Gymnasiast* and student to have the chance of being 'a Greek in spirit, in spite of the misfortune of being born a German'.

The new Prussian University of Berlin, planned and admirably staffed by Humboldt in his short term of office, and opened in 1810, determined the pattern of university development in the whole of Germany from that time on. All present-day discussions of university problems between foreign and German academics come round to the question of how far any proposed changes will favour a return to the Humboldt ideal, still fully accepted by the Germans, and summed up in the phrases *Freiheit der Forschung, Einheit von Forschung und Lehre* and *Lehr- und Lernfreiheit*. The university teacher is there, in the traditional German view, not to hand out basic information, which it is the business of the schools to impart – the curriculum of the *Gymnasium* was extended by Humboldt to include almost all that had formerly been taught by university Faculties of Arts – but to teach the student how to learn for himself, and in his turn to extend the bounds of learning. This is the spirit of *Wissenschaft* (meaning both 'scholarship' and 'science'), and the German university in its heyday used to find out whether or not a pupil had been filled with it by making him write a dissertation and submit himself to an oral examination in the general field of his subject, with which one or more *Nebenfächer* might be regarded as connected for the purpose of general culture. 'If the knife is once sharpened, all kinds of things can be cut with it,' Herder had said, and Fichte elaborated on the idea – which was later brilliantly argued by J. H. Newman in his *Idea of a University*. Innumerable foreign students have gratefully acknowledged their debt to some German professor who has fired their interest and guided their first steps in research. Many have spread the German idea of a university in their own country, with important results in the United States and central and northern Europe in particular. The seminar method of studying a topic, by getting a small group of students to compare their ideas on various aspects of it, under supervision, and the extraordinarily fruitful development from this, the study of a vast scientific problem, usually in the natural sciences, by team work, a professor selecting the field of research and breaking it up into separate research subjects, each capable of being tackled under his supervision as a doctoral thesis by a young member of his seminar, these are generally acknowledged to be invaluable ideas which the world owes to German scholarship, not to speak of the enormous contributions to knowledge which have been the fruit of these methods.

Great original discoveries are seldom made by scholars compelled to seek results of immediate practical value, or limited by any accepted ideas in, say, politics or religion. The scholar's untrammelled freedom to work on the problems in his subject which seem most interesting to him is what is meant by *Freiheit der Forschung*, and it was a great achievement to get this claim accepted even in theory in Berlin in 1810, after the recent experiences of so many scholars in small autocratic states, of Fichte in Weimar, for instance, fifteen years earlier. The boldness of German theology soon knew no bounds, but politics remained a dangerous subject for a very long time. Max Weber wrote as late as 1908 about the 'Michels case' – the refusal of *Habilitation* in a Prussian university to a socialist – 'We have freedom in science and scholarship in Germany – but only for those who are considered socially respectable in their opinions about Church and State.' *Einheit von Forschung und Lehre* means that to be a good teacher a scholar must be actively engaged in research, and vice versa. The two activities are naturally complementary to each other. This again is an unexceptionable doctrine, at least in theory, for in practice there is room for great variations between individuals following it. It is *Lehr- und Lernfreiheit* which gives rise to the greatest extremes of interpretation and consequently to the hottest controversy. The demand for *Lehrfreiheit* goes further than that for *Freiheit der Forschung*, for it implies that a teacher must be free not only to research in socially or politically dangerous subjects and publish the results in learned periodicals perhaps, but also to express unpopular ideas, or views objectionable to the ruling class, openly in his lectures. But what those who appeal to the principle more commonly have in mind is the right to lecture not just on topics of direct use to their students in examinations, because they are central to the subject, but on the most abstruse themes on its very verge which happen to be research interests of their own. It is implied that the content of the departmental subject is not defined in any sort of syllabus. It is only on this condition that *Lernfreiheit* too, in one of its meanings, is possible. A student should be free, it is claimed, to wander if he chooses in search of stimulating teaching from one German university to another without being penalized, as he would be if the one subject had a precise syllabus, varying from place to place. But *Lernfreiheit* means in the first place that a student must be free to attend any lectures he chooses in any order. It is for him to discover his real interests in this way and, having decided on his subjects of study, to find out for himself which teachers and which lectures are most helpful to him, in one university or several in turn.

It is only when we ask ourselves what familiar British features are missing in a German university that we realize how fundamental the differences between the two systems are. (1) There is no selection of students for admission to a West German university. Anyone with the full *Matura* can claim admission as a right. (2) In West Germany there are no elaborately planned courses of undergraduate studies, with a syllabus for each stage and an orderly progression from the elementary to the advanced aspects of a subject. In most subjects (medicine and law are now exceptions, and technical training has always been by stages) there are no intermediate examinations, either terminal or annual, indeed no final examination conducted by the university in arts or pure science, except for the small proportion of students who attempt the doctorate of philosophy. Again it is different in *Technische Hochschulen*, where the *Diplom-Ingenieur* examination is the normal goal. The great majority attend lectures and seminars until they think they are ready to pass the State examination for their profession, though for this there is a prescribed minimum number of terms of study. (3) As there are no real 'courses', in arts subjects at least, there is little or no systematic provision of lectures to assist the orderly study of a subject, there are no advisers of studies, though some are now promised, and no essay-work and discussion classes, involving frequent contacts between students and staff. Seminars, in spite of grading, are now so overcrowded that there is little real discussion and only a favoured few are able to read papers. In earlier days, when numbers were small, it could be claimed that lectures and seminars, even if idiosyncratic in their subjects, could serve as an introduction to the aims and methods of scholarship, and encourage good students to become intellectually independent. Able foreign graduates, requiring mainly intellectual stimulus and library facilities, may still benefit from the system, but the ordinary German student, with numbers as high as they are now, finds the sink-or-swim method of instruction ineffective and frustrating. To counter-act over-specialization, most West German universities introduced soon after the war lectures by leading professors which were intended to be scholarly but of general interest, so that scientists might hear about the humanities, for instance, and arts students about science, but by the mid-fifties it was already clear that even the enthusiasts who had started this *Studium Generale* had been discouraged by the lack of response.

The critics of the German universities see other defects which will not be remedied by a return to the Humboldt ideal, because they are the result of social developments in Germany since Humboldt's day. Weimar humanism itself was essentially aristocratic in spirit, and the new Prussian educational system had the effect, which for long aroused no protest, of perpetuating class distinctions by making higher edu-cation almost inaccessible to boys from poorer homes, because the classical *Gymnasium*, which was closed to a working-man's son unless he was quite exceptionally lucky, was until the beginning of the present century, as we saw, the only type of school which qualified its pupils for university entrance. The elementary school pupil went into manual work and did his military service in the ranks, but a *Gymnasiast* had if at all possible to pass the *Einjährige Prüfung* before his service, leaving the army as a Lieutenant of the Reserve, to enter a profession, or at least obtain a white-collar job in business. In spite of political democratiza-tion and many educational reforms, statistics show that there is still great inequality of educational opportunity in West Germany. Workers' children – and girls generally – have a comparatively poor chance of getting into a university.[1] This is of course a defect which East Germany has been at great pains to correct.

Another strikingly undemocratic feature of the traditional German university which still survives on both sides of the Iron Curtain is the excessive power and authority enjoyed by the *Ordentlicher Professor*. For British ideas, there are far too few teachers of other rank sharing the work of the department with the full professor, and far too many crucial decisions that are left, under the traditional system, to him alone. He is of course correspondingly better placed as to salary and perquisites. Now that he no longer receives lecture fees, a German professor's salary is much higher than that of his colleagues in this

[1] R. Dahrendorf, *Gesellschaft und Demokratie in Deutschland* (Munich, 1965), p. 88, for details.

country, but there is no hierarchy of readers, senior lecturers, lecturers, etc., with reasonable salaries, while the *Ordinarius* is very unwilling to give up any of his privileges and he is in a position to obstruct reform. Students who wish to work for the doctorate under his direction are entirely at his mercy. After doing satisfactory papers in perhaps a series of seminars, they must obtain his approval of their subject of research, which will almost certainly have to be one which fits in with his own work and distinctive methods. No external examiner will be called in to help in assessing the merits of the dissertation when finished. If after gaining his doctorate a man aims at a university career, he will have to spend two or three years more on a further piece of research for his *Habilitation*, his recognition as a qualified university teacher, and this too in most cases will have to be recommended to the faculty by the same *Ordinarius* under whom he gained his doctorate. Deviation from his sacrosanct method will seldom gain approval, so that originality is in some respects hampered by the system. When admitted as a *Dozent*, the young scholar earns so small a salary that it became increasingly difficult after the war to attract suitable men and women to an academic career. Through the sanctioning of many new chairs and other appointments in recent years, the staff position has been greatly improved, but if the universities continue to expand at the present rate, it is generally thought that there are serious staffing problems ahead.[1]

If any breach is eventually made in the system it will not come about, so Professor Kurt Sontheimer declared in his comment on the Berlin students' revolt in February 1968, through any organized protest from the non-professorial staff, for they, including the *Ausserordentliche Professoren* (Associate Professors), are too conscious of their dependence on the full professors. The struggle is rather, he believes, between these real masters of the university and the organized students. The students have been demanding too much and cannot expect to have a say in all university business, in examinations, appointments, finance for instance, but the professors should not abuse the power they have through their official position. 'This authoritarian attitude in intellectual matters', Sontheimer wrote, 'still comes too naturally to many of us.'[2]

[1] M. Balfour, op. cit., pp. 255–64, surveys these difficulties clearly.
[2] *Die Zeit*, 15 March 1968.

THE GERMAN DEMOCRATIC REPUBLIC
The schools

For obvious historical reasons educational institutions in East Germany bear a close resemblance to those of West Germany in their formal structure, but the Weimar Republic system has been much more extensively reshaped in the east and filled with an entirely different spirit. The East Germans claim that it is for the first time genuinely democratic, and in certain respects, particularly in the new opportunities opened up to the children of poorer parents, this seems to be true, but it is also clear that the system has been brought closer and closer with each change to the Soviet model. The Soviet Military Administration began this process immediately after the occupation, and in 1946 promulgated a 'law for the democratization of German schools', issued with identical texts in each of the five *Länder* into which the zone was then still divided. In contrast to the West German system, East German education is completely centralized, as it was under Hitler, and made into one of the most effective instruments for furthering the policy of another totalitarian regime. As was explained with regard to law, the 'superstructure' of culture is no longer regarded as merely reflecting the social and economic 'basis', but as a most important tool in the hands of the ruling élite, the party, for the creation of a socialist society. There is hardly any limit in this view, which is like that of the early Enlightenment, to what education can do. It not only imparts the lessons, especially the technical knowledge and skill, which are essential for modern life, but it also remoulds the whole nature of man, until he feels himself committed to the central aim of making socialism a reality.

Complete control from the centre of power, no fumbling experiments, no private schools, for instance – they are expressly forbidden in the Constitution – and a much nearer approach than in West Germany to a single-track school system: these are the outstanding features of elementary and secondary education. Not just a four-year *Grundschule*, then, but an eight-year *Volksschule* was in 1946 made compulsory for all children in East Germany. For those who leave school at fourteen, compulsory attendance at a *Berufsschule* follows as in West Germany and earlier in the Weimar Republic. In the 1946 plan, the *Mittelschule* was dropped, but the three traditional types of *Höhere Schule* were retained, for classics, modern languages and mathematics plus science, each with only four classes after the eight of the *Volksschule*. The Russian language was made a compulsory subject for all, beginning in the fifth class of the *Volksschule*. Then in 1953 a kind of Middle School was restored by adding two classes to the *Volksschule*, as a further option for children of fourteen. By reforms gradually introduced between 1955 and 1965, the school-leaving age was in effect raised to sixteen, because the 'Ten-class School' was made compulsory for all, under the name of (*Zehnklassige Polytechnische*) *Oberschule*. So, at least in theory, no East German child will in future have merely an elementary education, with its proletarian taint. All will attend the *Oberschule* for ten years, and many proceed to one of the three types of secondary school, now called *Erweiterte Oberschule*, for four years more, though how it is possible adequately to staff these schools is a mystery, in view of the fact that West Germany, with much greater resources, is desperately short of teachers.

It will be seen that the total school course leading up to the university is a year shorter than in West Germany, and that all but the last four years of it have been spent in something like a comprehensive school added on to an elementary school. There is a marked bias throughout towards science and technology rather than the humanities, and boys and girls from the age of twelve are made aware of the practical applications of their school knowledge by the weekly 'day of instruction in socialist production', i.e. a day spent with their class in a factory. For the great majority who leave school at sixteen, there are available not only the part-time *Berufsschule* but full-time technical schools leading to university education, although only to further study in the narrow field of technology – mechanical engineering, electro-technology or whatever it may be – in which they have specialized, not to general university study. Political indoctrination has to be accepted at every level, and advancement from one level to the next only follows for those who seem to be completely co-operative. The efficient dissemination and exploitation of technological expertise has a century of tradition behind it, as we have seen. In East Germany, hitherto unused talent among the mass of the people must have been made productive, as earlier in Russia, and this is probably one of the main causes of East Germany's outstanding success in recent years in industry and commerce, relatively to the other Soviet satellites.

The universities
The universities in East Germany have since 1933 been subjected to two successive totalitarian regimes. As key institutions of a Communist

state they have been completely refashioned since 1945 in accordance with the Marxist–Leninist ideas of the single party, the SED, which slavishly follows the Soviet model in everything. The reforms have been carried through in three stages, always under central direction, at first along with the schools under the *Ministerium für Volksbildung*, which worked through the corresponding ministries of the separate *Länder* until 1952, when the *Länder* were abolished. No definite move towards university reform was announced until 1951, when a special Secretary of State for the Universities was appointed, whose department in the next few years carried through preparations for a 'socialistic university' by tightening the control of the party and introducing many features based on Soviet practice. The process has been one of peculiar difficulty because of the flight of so many university teachers to West Germany and the priority given for some years to the democratization of the schools. The final details of the new structure were not worked out until 1958 at a special university conference of the SED.

The function of universities and technical colleges, in the view of the party, is to continue the indoctrination of the young begun in the schools, and to provide the civil service, the professions, industry and commerce, as well as educational and cultural institutions of all kinds, with able, well-trained and politically reliable leaders. *Forschung* and *Lehre* remain inseparable in the new theory, but to them is added *Erziehung*, which means at this stage compulsory classes in the 'elements of social science', i.e. Marxism, and the vigilant conditioning of students and staff by two party groups, the university branches of the SED and of the Freie Deutsche Jugend. The compulsory military training on one afternoon a week is no doubt brought under the same head. The announcement of the new aims set off a further wave of emigration to West Germany, both of students and staff, many of whom had been induced to stay so long only by being better paid than their colleagues over the border. The building of the Berlin wall (August 1961) finally stopped the flow.

We have seen how the East German school system is designed to give a chance of higher education to all children capable of it. Naturally the way to the university or *Technische Hochschule* is also left open as far as possible to young people who go to work after leaving the *Oberschule*. They can, if able and determined, gain a school-leaving certificate by study at a *Fachschule* after two years in a trade, or by private study helped by evening classes or correspondence courses organized by the universities. The *Fachschulen* are trade schools for advanced vocational training in any of more than a score of occupations, from engineering, mining, agriculture, etc., to nursing, art and music. There were 220 of them, some giving only one-year courses, in 1963, with 140,000 pupils. Most of the students attend for one to three years, to gain a diploma varying with the length of the course, as *Meister*, *Techniker* or *Ingenieur*, but there are over forty *Fachhochschulen* of university rank. As in the schools, there seems to be a deliberate emphasis in this whole scheme on practical work, as is made obvious in the requirement that students of all faculties must learn a *Beruf* before they can be admitted to a university or *Hochschule*, if necessary spending a *praktisches Jahr* under direction from a university after passing their School Leaving Examination, though it is becoming normal to qualify in this respect at school. There are other restrictions and priorities which make admittance to a university by no means automatic, as in West Germany, for holders of the equivalent of our GCE. Many who are not admitted, or for some other reason cannot attend classes, study as external students, under supervision in a university correspondence course. In 1963 there were 78,000 internal or 'direct' students, to about 30,000 engaged in *Fernstudium*.

As in Russia, there has been a drastic over-correction of the injustice which in most countries, and notably in Germany, has been done to working-class children in the provision of opportunities for higher education. In the allocation of university places, so high a priority has been given to workers' and peasants' children that they were stated to make up 59 per cent of full-time university students in 1963.[1] For the middle-class child, flight to West Germany was for long the obvious answer, if at all possible, to being refused a university education. Since 1959 those responsible for admissions to particular branches of study or training have been guided above all by the calculations of the current national plan about the numbers of trained personnel likely to be required in that branch in the near future. After completion of their studies, students are directed into employment according to national needs, with very little freedom of choice at any stage, so that *Lernfreiheit* is very limited, both because of this element of compulsion and from the nature of the new university teaching.

In the appointment of university staff, the last word is with the *Staatssekretariat*, and for younger scholars at least, faithfulness to the

[1] Figures from the official *Handbuch der DDR*, p. 686, which puts the share of the 'intelligentsia' at 15 per cent, of employees at 19 per cent, and of the rest of the population at 7 per cent.

party is often more important than scholarly competence. Older men, being difficult to replace, have frequently been allowed to continue in office if they were tactful and kept clear of political issues, even if they have never been through the doctrinal mill, but, being under constant surveillance, they never feel secure. Exactly as in Nazi times, scholarly publications regularly introduce respectful references to party ideology, with quotations now from Marx, Engels or Lenin instead of from *Mein Kampf*. The sacred principle is not objectivity, a bourgeois illusion, but avowed partisanship for the one permitted party.

Some Other Cultural Institutions in West and East Germany

Cultural institutions in Germany as a whole suffered much more severely from the effects of the Second World War than from the First, after which there was within a year or two a remarkable outburst of activity in music, literature, the theatre, painting and all the arts. After 1945, the total collapse of the regime, the occupation of the whole country by the Allies, the mass movements of refugees, the material damage done by bombing and so on brought civilized life for a time almost to a standstill. Denazification involved the cultural as well as the political élite and made necessary the temporary suppression, pending reform, of innumerable social institutions. Even when the currency reform (1948) made something better than a hand-to-mouth existence possible, talent was attracted rather to technical and industrial occupations than to the arts and sciences. But in spite of all this, the need experienced by large numbers from the beginning for the civilized things of life led first to privately organized concerts and entertainments on improvised or hastily repaired stages, and so gradually, as prosperity returned, to the reconstruction, especially in the West, of a set of cultural institutions as advanced as any in the world.

It was characteristic that even in the first months after the war people thronged to concerts all over the country, for music is still *the* German art, and the love of it goes much deeper than political differences. Yet these inevitably affect the forms in which this love finds expression, and the same is true of literature and all the arts. The differences between East and West began through the influence of the occupying forces, and the continued contacts, in the one half of Germany with Russia, and in the other with the United States and Western Europe.

So in music, for instance, West Germany has shown much greater readiness to follow the modern trends in composition which Schoenberg had done so much to initiate, just as in painting and architecture the interest in abstract forms, regarded as depraved by the Nazis, has quite displaced naturalism and the historical styles. But the traditional German passion for music and devotion to its native masters lives on in both halves of the country, and in both of them the necessary institutions have been built up again, dozens of orchestras and thousands of choirs, constantly fed by a whole system of State or civic *Hochschulen*, academies, conservatories, institutes and schools of music. The birthplace of baroque music lies now to the east of the demarcation line, and the old traditions are lovingly cultivated by the still excellent Gewandhaus orchestra and the choir of the Thomaskirche, Bach's resting-place, in Leipzig, and by the Philharmonie and the choir of the Kreuzkirche in Dresden. The old State Opera maintains high standards in East Berlin, but the Berlin Philharmonic Orchestra has emigrated to West Berlin, from where it frequently goes on tour throughout the world. Many other leading symphony and chamber orchestras and string quartets in West Germany, and the conductors and virtuosos connected with them, are also part of the world celebrity concert system, not always to the advantage of their home audiences, and all these and many more are of course familiar to millions at home and abroad through radio and television transmissions and gramophone records, so that it can safely be said that German music has never been so widely appreciated as today. From our side of the divide we naturally hear much about West German music and culture generally, and almost nothing about what corresponds to them in East Germany, but we should not underrate the opportunities enjoyed by East Germans of travel and cultural contacts in the satellite states, and in the vast expanse of Russia and even China.

German music owed its development for centuries to the Church, first the Catholic and after Luther also the Lutheran Church. The *Reformierte*, like Calvinists everywhere, banned the organ and instrumental music, but the Lutherans used all the resources of art for the praise of God, and this tradition, raised to sublime heights by Bach, is no doubt the chief source of the very widespread love of music in Germany. Something like our 'Bach Choirs' for laymen have flourished in Germany for more than two centuries, supplemented by all kinds of choral societies, amateur orchestras, quartets of friends and relations and so on, all making music for the love of it. If there are, as we are told, still some 15,000 lay choirs in West Germany and 5,000 in East Germany too, the tradition must be very much alive in spite of all temptations to passivity. From the eighteenth century on, instrumental music owed most to the patronage of the courts, especially ecclesiastical courts like Salzburg or Bonn, with the imperial court at Vienna where, by a tradition centuries old, the public appearances of the monarch and his court were linked with the celebration of the feasts of the Church, with fine music as an essential part of the requisite pomp. No other court could rival Vienna in the number of its music-lovers and its attraction for the professional musician, but all courts provided patronage in some degree and followed Vienna in cultivating the delightful luxury of opera, if only in the form of modest *Singspiele*. That is why every town of any importance in Germany must still subsidize opera, even if the civic theatre has to accommodate spoken drama and perhaps some ballet as well. First the capitals of the old Germany's numerous states were given their opera houses and sub-sidized repertory theatres by the princes for the entertainment of their courts, then more and more ordinary citizens came to share the taste for such things, and other towns did not want to be left behind. A good theatre with an international repertoire of drama and opera came to be regarded from early in the nineteenth century as no less necessary to a self-respecting community than an art gallery, a museum or a public park. So the extraordinarily wide distribution of such theatres, a feature which never fails to astonish visitors from countries like England and the United States, where the theatre is commercialized and com-paratively little developed outside the metropolis, is a direct conse-quence of German particularism. An attachment to these old cultural institutions is as much a part of the German social inheritance as the traditionally submissive attitude of the Germans towards established authority, which comes from the same source. Thomas Mann in 1917 rightly picked out *Bildung* and *Gehorsam* as the distinguishing features of the German inheritance.

Political passivity has given way in a great many West Germans since the last war, as we have seen, to democratic ways of thinking, and it would be surprising if recent social and political changes had not also affected cultural institutions. So we find that while in England, France and Italy, for example, repertory theatres very much on the German model have been the ideal striven for by reformers, as a correc-tive to the star system, in a commercialized theatre with *ad hoc* com-panies in the capital and touring companies in the provinces, the movement in Germany has been distinctly in the opposite direction, though without any tendency towards the abandonment of subsidies from the *Bund*, the *Länder* and the great cities, which support about 20, 18 and 80 theatres respectively in some seventy centres, or any diminution of the concern for actors' status and social security which has always been one of the main aims of endowed theatres with a relatively permanent staff. All actors engaged at a theatre in the Federal Republic or West Berlin are now entitled, for instance, to old-age pensions.

What has happened in recent years is an extension of the 'guest' system which was common even in Goethe's day, as a way of introducing a new face for a time into a perhaps over-familiar group of court actors by inviting a distinguished stranger to appear in some of his best roles. The practice is now carried so far that a civic theatre, instead of a frequently varied succession of plays, may present one play, or just two or three, for several weeks at a time, with 'guests' in the chief roles. One reason for this is that it has proved very difficult to get together anything like the old ensembles, the companies accustomed to playing together in repertory, when once they had been broken up on the closing down of German theatres in 1944. Another factor is that audiences are bigger than ever and can be found for longer runs of the same play than before the war. This has come about through growing prosperity and the continued activity of the Volksbühne and similar subsidized 'audience associations' in selling reduced price tickets, while the *Abonnement* or season ticket habit persists unchanged. In spite of the competition of broadcasting and the cinema, the latter an art which has lost ground recently as elsewhere, the living theatre seems as well patronized as ever even without the old variety.

Since Goethe and Schiller's time and even earlier, subsidized theatres in Germany have aimed not only at entertaining their audiences but also at educating their feelings. This was one reason for the passion for the theatre among the educated middle class in the later eighteenth century and for the consequent spread of the national theatre movement, from which in time the State and civic theatres of the following century resulted. Performances of serious drama, of not only the German but world classics, which are very frequent in most subsidized theatres, come near to being rites of an aesthetic religion, so conscious did Germany become through the writings of its classical-Romantic age of the blessings of *Kultur*. The present wide range of the concept may be seen from the contents of the monthly *Deutsche Kulturnachrichten* distributed abroad by the Inter Nationes organization in Bad Godesberg.

A typical number discusses 'Musik; Oper, Ballett; Bildende Kunst; Literatur; Theater; Film, Foto, Fernsehen; Hochschulleben; Religiöses Leben; Erziehung'. Often individual German towns publish a weekly pamphlet under some such title as: *Die Kulturwoche in* . . ., advertising current programmes in the theatre, concerts, films, art exhibitions, etc. A corresponding publication in England makes no mention of culture, and usually gives more attention to light entertainment and sport. Germans, however, are not self-conscious in speaking about their national *Kultur*, of which they are rightly proud. In the new Reich after 1871, Germany's new wealth and power came to be widely regarded as the natural and long overdue recognition of her cultural achievements, which for some seemed fully to justify further self-assertion, political and military, at the cost of her neighbours, a view which naturally turned the word *Kultur* into a portent for her opponents in 1914.

Many of Germany's most distinctive cultural institutions began like the theatre as little luxuries of petty princes, who all made Versailles their model. Even if some of them had no taste themselves for music, art or learning, there were always people around them who had, and theatres, picture galleries, museums, libraries, etc., gave new opportunities to actors, musicians, artists and scholars and became growing points for new creative work. At a later stage, cultural institutions came to be supported from public funds and imitated in towns which had never been state capitals. That is why German culture is still many-centred, and why its institutions are usually still readily supported by the free vote of democratic bodies. Considerations of prestige play a part in this, at all levels, but real appreciation and understanding at least of music, opera and the theatre are probably widespread.

German literature and thought are discussed in other chapters of this book, and there is only space here for a few notes on the effect of the present division of Germany on some cultural institutions not yet mentioned, and on the mass media. Until the war, when the treasures of the Prussian State Library had to be removed to places of safety in disused mines, etc., both east and west of the post-war line of division, it was easily the best library for scholarly purposes in German-speaking lands. It had started as the Königliche Bibliothek in the time of Frederick the Great and grown with the expansion of Berlin as capital of the Reich and seat of its highest-ranking university. Nearly half of its scattered stocks, including the best manuscripts, were picked up by the Russians and are back in what is now called the Deutsche Staatsbibliothek in East Berlin, and the rest, found by the American forces, are now at Marburg and will be transferred in due course to a new Staatsbibliothek now being built in West Berlin by Hans Scharoun. As a copyright library for all new German publications, the publishers' organization, Börsenverein deutscher Buchhändler, founded the Deutsche Bücherei in Leipzig in 1912 and with its resources published a classified weekly list of new books and half-yearly bibliographies based on them. Since 1945 the leading Leipzig publishers have established separate branches of their firms in West Berlin, Frankfurt-am-Main and other West German towns, and the Börsenverein has set up a second copyright library in Frankfurt, which produces a second current bibliography, largely overlapping the Leipzig one, but more reliable for West German publications, as the other is for East German ones. A similar story of wasteful, but at present unavoidable duplication has to be told of academies of science, literature and art, national research institutes, learned societies, organizations for the support of scientific and humanistic research, historical and literary archives, and so on.[1]

As was to be expected, however, the cultural institutions which most clearly reflect the transformation of Germany brought about by the last war and its aftermath are the so-called mass media, the daily and weekly press, sound broadcasting and television, the last a virtually new creation, though to be exact Berlin had put out a television programme, the first in the world, for an hour or so on three evenings a week from 1935 to 1943. Before 1914, because of German particularism, the country had about 4,000 newspapers, nearly all more or less regional and many just stereotyped variants, with different local news, of a regional *Stammzeitung*. Under National Socialism numbers rapidly fell, for political reasons, and the *Völkische Beobachter* became the first national newspaper. The year 1945 brought a completely new start. A few papers appeared in every zone, produced by the press officers of the army of occupation at first, then by selected German journalists under licence, following a strictly democratic 're-education' line in West Germany and a Communist one over the border. When controls were removed in 1949 in West Germany, many licensed papers continued and even the new papers avoided political controversy, except with their brother Germans in East Germany. A non-committal tone seemed to fit in with the prevailing feeling of exhaustion, of

[1] Details in H. Arntz (ed.), *Deutschland Heute*, 7th edn. (Bonn, 1965), pp. 769–77, 804–22, 854–9.

E

longing for 'a holiday from history'. In 1964 there were 550 *Stamm-zeitungen* in the *Bund*, with 750 *Nebenausgaben* or partial variants, a number that was steadily declining in favour of new picture papers with tabloid news. These are greatly inferior to the traditional German newspaper, with its good foreign news service, theatre and concert notices, reviews, etc. – features still prominent in the best papers, especially the weeklies, with modest circulations, as the following list shows:

Four dailies of high quality are: *Die Welt*, Hamburg (274,000); *Frankfurter Allgemeine Zeitung* (269,000); *Süddeutsche Zeitung*, Munich (225,000); *Stuttgarter Zeitung* (155,000). More popular are: *Westdeutsche Allgemeine Zeitung*, Essen (444,000), and other family newspapers like the *Hamburger Morgenpost* (344,000), *Ruhr-Nachrichten*, Dortmund (330,000), *Hamburger Abendblatt* (323,000) and the West Berlin *B.Z.* (320,000). All these call themselves independent. The German Daily Mirror is the Hamburg *Bild* (4,193,000). Only the illustrated broadcasting weekly, *Hör Zu*, approaches such a circulation (3,858,000), but several other illustrated weeklies sell between one and two million copies. The notorious *Der Spiegel* (540,000) leads the more serious weeklies, with the liberal *Die Zeit* (193,000) far behind. Both appear in Hamburg. *Die neue Rundschau*, quarterly, and *Merkur*, monthly, are excellent general periodicals for cultivated readers.

The East German press is extremely monotonous because it is wholly given up to agitation and propaganda, and is produced, still under licence, by the SED, the mass organizations, or parties in the approved Block, always under the close supervision of the Press Office of the Prime Minister. Two papers only are not described as licensed, the *Berliner Zeitung* and the *B.Z. am Abend*, but the firm responsible for them is owned by the SED. There are 38 dailies, some with circulations up to six millions, because whole occupational groups can be compelled to subscribe. The SED party press, with *Neues Deutschland* at its head, makes up 60 per cent of the total, and there is very little but party news and views in them all. It is a criminal offence to sell papers from the West.

There is an exactly similar contrast between the broadcasting systems in the two halves of Germany as in their press. Broadcasting was treated like education and other cultural institutions in the Basic Law, and made a matter for *Land* legislation. There is one broadcasting company in each *Land* in the former American and French zones, six in all, and two in the former British zone, Norddeutscher Rundfunk (Hamburg) and Westdeutscher Rundfunk (Cologne), which have developed out of the stations set up by the occupying forces. West Berlin was later given its own station, Freies Berlin. The *Bund* has since 1960 financed the Deutsche Welle (Cologne) to transmit on short wave to foreign countries, and the committee which co-ordinates the separate services, ARD (Arbeitsgemeinschaft der Rundfunkanstalten Deutschlands), controls Deutschlandfunk (West Berlin), with its transmissions aimed particularly at East Germany, where 400 transmitters try to jam all West German stations. The regional authorities are all public corporations with elected boards of governors. It is a rather complicated and untidy system, in which the largest company has twenty times as many listeners as the smallest, and a correspondingly higher income from the same basic licence fee, but has to make itself heard over a much wider area. The radio organization coped with its problems well enough to be entrusted with the television service too, the nine *Sender* being combined for this purpose into Deutsches Fernsehen. All nine have their own studios and contribute to a common programme according to their resources, also transmitting a short regional programme and half an hour's advertising a day to their own local area. The service is financed in the main by the special licence fee collected, like the radio fee, by the Post Office. The first television transmission was on Christmas Day 1952. Since 1963 a second programme has been provided from Mainz by Zweites Deutsches Fernsehen, a public corporation founded by the *Länder*, partly dependent on advertising, though this is limited to one-tenth of the transmission time. An attempt to set up an independent television authority in 1961 failed only because of a ruling of the Bundesverfassungsgericht, which feared an excessive influence of private individuals, the newspaper proprietors backing the proposal, on public opinion.

East German radio and television services are, of course, centrally controlled and fully exploited for purposes of 'agitation and propaganda'. One of their five radio programmes, *Deutschlandsender*, is addressed to 'all Germans', i.e. especially to West Germany. Television began, after long experiments, in 1956, and care has been taken to encourage its reception particularly in country districts, where the press is less active than in the towns. The Intervision net links Russia and her satellites in their television services, as a counterpart to Eurovision on the other side of the demarcation-line. In 1964 there were two and a half million television sets in East Germany, to eight million in the Federal Republic.

In the cultural institutions of both West and East Germany there is much, as we have seen, which has deep roots in the German past, but still more which is directly linked with the recent political, economic and social development of the country, so different in its two halves and so profoundly influenced by the world outside. In its first twenty years the Federal Republic has achieved a prosperity which is ascribed indeed, by economists, at least as much to favourable external circumstances as to German efforts, but which has greatly helped the acceptance of democracy, just as its collapse in the Weimar Republic was largely due to the 1929 world slump. There had been changes brought about by National Socialism and the war in the structure of German society, Eugen Kogon points out, which removed or transformed three social groups hostile to democracy: the great landowners, the officer corps and the élite of finance and industry, formerly strictly authoritarian all three. Then after the war 'every German question of importance was internationalized (or Europeanized) when it arose'.[1] The extremism of the Left has been filtered off into East Germany, and the formerly internal conflict now separates the two Germanies. The security of Europe and the world depends upon confining it to peaceful means of expression.

In general, it is agreed, West Germany observes the forms of democracy 'with an almost avid love of normality and all its trimmings', but occasionally disturbing features appear – in recent years the handling of student unrest, for example – which remind one of an observation made by Theodor Adorno in 1959: 'Democracy has not been assimilated to the point that the individual really identifies himself with it as his own cause and has an awareness of being an active participant in political processes. Democracy is felt to be one system among many . . . It is assessed according to its success or lack of success.'[2]

Ralf Dahrendorf has made a good attempt to balance the claims made by each side in turn that it alone is democratic. In some ways East Germany, he thinks, has a more 'modern' society, in the sense that the ideas of the French Revolution about the equality of all citizens have been pushed to their logical limit, but the citizens are equal as quasi-slaves, as 'abhängige Genossen', not as 'mündige Staatsbürger'. If they are born poor, they have greater social security and better opportunities of education than they would have had as West Germans, he thinks, who sometimes cannot make full use of the political rights

---

[1] In *The Road to Dictatorship* (London, 1964), p. 161.
[2] See W. Stahl, *Education for Democracy in West Germany* (New York, 1962), p. 91.

which are theirs by law, but in East Germany are possessed by none. In West Germany people with opposing views about education, the law, the army, as well as economic and political opponents, will listen to each other and rely on argument to a greater extent than ever before, but there are still clear traces of the old 'authoritarian aversion to social conflicts' and hankering after decisions by some omniscient authority. On the inescapable subject of a possible future reunification, Ralf Dahrendorf does not see the differences he has brought out between East and West Germany as an insurmountable obstacle in the long run.[1]

The conflicting images of the two Germanies in the mind of the foreign observer are no doubt largely due to the cultural diplomacy actively practised by both, and a family resemblance might soon be more evident if a political *rapprochement* were desired by the master powers. Even as things are, cultural rivalry has not made West Germany incapable of being stimulated from across the border, as the vogue of Brecht and techniques suggested by him has clearly shown. This is partly to be explained by the slowness of creative talent to emerge again after the war, the absence of any new writer with gifts at all comparable with Brecht's. For the same reason, the smaller nations which share the German language, German Switzerland and Austria, which have unfortunately had to be disregarded in our survey, have provided much of the best work in the German drama and novel, while performances of foreign plays and translations of foreign novels have continued to testify to the 'panoramic ability' of the Germans. Perhaps one may be allowed finally to record a personal impression, which may later prove to have been mistaken, that the attraction of Germany's best brains towards political and economic problems, very noticeable after 1945, as we saw, has continued, and that the old German tendency towards the inward life is now far less marked, so that in the cultural sphere the institutional machinery is more impressive than most of the native work produced. It seems indeed as if what Oswald Spengler wanted to see after the First World War is happening now at last, and that 'young men are turning to engineering instead of to poetry, to politics instead of the theory of knowledge', realizing that our age is one not of genuine *Kultur*, but of what Spengler called *Zivilisation*.

[1] R. Dahrendorf, op. cit., pp. 449 ff., 468 ff.

Bibliography

GENERAL

ARNTZ, H. (ed.). *Deutschland Heute*. Presse- und Informationsamt der Bundes-
regierung. 2nd edn. Bonn, 1965.
— *Tatsachen über Deutschland*. 6th edn. Bonn, 1963.
CALMANN, J. (ed.). *Western Europe, a Handbook*. London, 1967.
Handbuch der DDR. Institut für Zeitgeschichte. Berlin, 1964.

POLITICAL INSTITUTIONS

ARETIN, K. A. VON. 'Die Bewährungsprobe der Bundesrepublik'. *Die neue Rund-
schau*, 1968, pp. 373–92.
BALFOUR, M. *West Germany*. London, 1968.
DAHRENDORF, R. *Gesellschaft und Demokratie in Deutschland*. Munich, 1965.
— 'Conflict and Liberty'. *British Journal of Sociology*, vol. XIV.
DAWSON, W. H. *The Evolution of Modern Germany*. London, 1908.
— *Germany at Home*. London, 1908.
ESCHENBURG, T. *Staat und Gesellschaft in Deutschland*. Munich, 1963.
ESCHENBURG, T., et al. *The Road to Dictatorship*. London, 1964.
KING-HALL, S., and ULLMANN, R. K. *German Parliaments*. London, 1954.
KITZINGER, U. *German Electoral Politics*. Oxford, 1960.
SCHOLZ, P. *Die deutsche Demokratie* (mit Text des Grundgesetzes). Geschichte und
Staat, Nos. 101–2. 2nd edn. Munich, 1965.
TOWER, C. *Germany of Today*. London, 1913.

DÖNHOFF, LEONHARDT, SOMMER. *Reise in ein fernes Land*. 10th edn. Hamburg,
1968.
Handbuch der DDR. Institut für Zeitgeschichte. Berlin, 1964.
SBZ von A bis Z. Bundesministerium für gesamtdeutsche Fragen. 10th edn. Bonn,
1966. Articles: Gesetzgebung, Ministerrat, Regierung und Verwaltung, SED,
Staatsrat, Verfassung, Volkskammer, etc.

Berlin in Brief. Press and Information Office of *Land* Berlin. Berlin, 1967.
WINDSOR, P. 'German Disunity'. In Calmann (ed.), *Western Europe*, pp. 276–88.
— *City on Leave, Berlin, 1945–62*. London, 1963.

LAW AND JUSTICE

BRAMSTEDT, E. K. *Dictatorship and Political Police*. London, 1945.
SCHWERIN, C. VON *Deutsche Rechtsgeschichte*. Grundriss der Geschichtswissen-
schaft. 2nd edn. Leipzig and Berlin, 1915.

BEDFORD, SYBILLE. *The Faces of Justice*. London, 1961.
DOMCKE, H. *Die Rechtsordnung*. Geschichte und Staat, No. 112. Munich, 1965.

BÖCKENFÖRDE, E.-W. *Die Rechtsauffassung im kommunistischen Staat*. Munich, 1967.
SBZ von A bis Z. Articles: Rechtsstudium, Rechtswesen, Richter, Strafpolitik, Strafverfahren, Strafvollzug, etc.

EDUCATION

BUSCH, A. *Die Geschichte des Privatdozenten*. Stuttgart, 1959.
PAULSEN, F. *Das deutsche Bildungswesen in seiner geschichtlichen Entwicklung*. 4th edn. Leipzig and Berlin, 1920.
SAMUEL, R. H., and THOMAS, R. HINTON. *Education and Society in Modern Germany*. London, 1949.

ARNTZ, H. (ed.). *Deutschland Heute*, pp. 769–822.
BALFOUR, M. *West Germany*, pp. 255–64.
HILKER, F. *Die Schulen in Deutschland*. Bundesrepublik und West-Berlin. 3rd edn. Bad Nauheim, 1963.
HUEBER, T. *The Schools of West Germany*. New York, 1963.
RELLER, T. L., and MORPHET, E. L. *Comparative Educational Administration*. Section 'Germany' by P. S. Bodelman. Englewood Cliffs, N.J., 1962.
STAHL, W. (ed.). *Education for Democracy in West Germany*. New York, 1961.

SBZ von A bis Z. Articles: Erziehungs- und Bildungswesen, Hochschulen, Schule, etc.

OTHER CULTURAL INSTITUTIONS

ARNTZ, H. (ed.). *Deutschland Heute*, pp. 823–924.
BAUER, H. *Die Presse und die öffentliche Meinung*. Geschichte und Staat, No. 106. Munich, 1965.
SBZ von A bis Z. Articles: Fernsehen, Parteipresse, Presse, Rundfunk, etc.

3 German History 911-1618

BARRIE DOBSON

'A mortal disease has befallen the German realm: if it is not speedily treated with a healing antidote, death will inexorably ensue. Men will seek for the realm in Germany and will not find it.' Nicholas of Cusa's gloomy prophecy, made as early as 1433, has proved accurate in a way rather different from that he intended. Ever since the emergence of a new historical awareness in the fifteenth century the antinomy between the concept and the reality of medieval Germany has presented successive generations of European historians with their most intractable as well as most exhilarating problem. The central paradox in the history of Germany is the absence, until the creation of the Hohenzollern Reich in 1871, of any political unit named Germany. The consequent ambiguities in nomenclature accurately reflect the confused political realities of the German situation.[1] German history had begun, and thereafter continued, under the aegis of particularism: the history of the whole is inevitably less meaningful if more dramatic than the history of its constituent parts. For this reason alone the story of medieval

[1] Alone among the states of modern Europe, the name and concept of Germany derives not from an older tribal or territorial name but from the mother tongue of its inhabitants. Because the latter nearly all spoke a 'language of the people' (*theodisca lingua* or *diutischiu liute*), markedly different from that of the western sections of Charlemagne's empire, their territories gradually became known as the *Diutischin land* or *Deutschland*. In Latin, owing to their confusion with the Teutones who had broken into the orbit of the Roman world at the end of the second century B.C., the German-speaking peoples of the tenth and eleventh centuries were often called the *Teutonici*. Although the expression *regnum Teutonicorum* had accordingly been coined before 920, it failed to gain an official status. Between that date and the end of the fifteenth century the successive rulers of medieval Germany bore titles – *rex Francorum Orientalium, rex Romanorum* and (after their coronation at Rome) *Romanorum Imperator Augustus* – which had little or no relevance to the geographical bases of their authority. Only after 1486 did it become customary to describe the area of the Reich north of the Alps as the 'German section of the Roman Empire' (*Römisches Reich deutscher Nation*).

and sixteenth-century Germany is almost always discussed, and not only by German historians, in terms of frustrated opportunity and tragic waste. Admittedly the German Reich presents an extreme case of a classic medieval dilemma – the inherent dualism within the Augustinian conception of a heavenly as well as terrestrial 'city', the conflict between universalist aims and practical possibilities. On the other hand the fabric of medieval German society was a good deal less unique than is often claimed: it would be difficult to prove that conditions at the local level were either more disorderly or less prosperous than in other areas of Europe. Germany was not alone in being little more than a geographical expression, nor was it alone in being brought to a somewhat reluctant birth from the ruins of the Carolingian Empire. The Germany of 1618 was no doubt in part the product of the circumstances of 911; but between these two dates the general course of its development was always complex and never predetermined.

The Rise of an Empire 911–1056

The death in September 911 of the eighteen-year-old Louis the Child without a male heir not only brought the Carolingian dynasty of East Frankish kings to an end but forced upon his subjects an embarrassing yet fateful decision. Two months later the tribal hosts of Saxony and Franconia assembled at Forchheim south of the river Main and elected as his successor Conrad, Duke of the Franks. Conrad I was soon recognized by the magnates of Swabia and Bavaria who thus joined the Franks and Saxons in choosing as their overlord a non-Carolingian 'German' king rather than the West Frankish Charles the Simple. So in 911 the leaders and spokesmen of four of the five great German stem (*Stamm*) duchies – the Lotharingians alone looked westwards and did homage to Charles – had decided not only that the monarchy was worthy of preservation but that it was a dignity most fittingly held by a magnate whose own interests lay east rather than west of the Rhine and who could therefore help to wage successful defensive war on their behalf. In their attempt to find a war-lord or *Kriegsherr* who would protect them against the inroads of the Danes, Slavs and, above all, the Magyars or Hungarians, the aristocracy of 911 had inadvertently brought to birth not only the medieval German monarchy but also the tantalizing possibility of an autonomous and distinctive German Reich. No one realized it at the time, but the history of Germany, as opposed to the history of the German peoples, had begun.

The year 911 is therefore justifiably famous as 'the birth year of German history', the date at which the German tribes broke the already very fragile ties which bound them to the rest of the Carolingian Empire. Admittedly such a severance, although not its precise form, had been latent in the history of the East Frankish territories during the previous century. Between 720 and 800 Charles Martel and his grandson Charlemagne had been more successful in subjecting the Alemanni (Swabians), Thuringians, Bavarians and Saxons to Frankish military domination than in overcoming the separatist loyalties and institutions of these German tribes. The German-speaking areas of the Carolingian Empire were already showing marked centrifugal tendencies before Charlemagne's own death in 814. The frenzied attempts of Charlemagne's successors in the ninth century to preserve some semblance of the imperial tradition, if not of imperial unity, had the paradoxical effect of forcing these tendencies into two very different directions. At one level the late Carolingian emperors came to terms with German particularism by acknowledging the powers of the local war leaders, especially on the Slav frontier: the families which dominated the political life of the German duchies in the late ninth century were themselves the descendants of Carolingian administrators, counts (*Grafen*) and margraves (*Markgrafen*) who owed their status to the authority originally conferred on them by the emperors. By appointing, to take the most famous example, the Saxon dynasty of Liudolfinger as *duces orientalium Saxonum*, the official military commanders of the East Saxon frontier, the Carolingians seemed to be preparing the way for the complete fragmentation of their state. On the other hand, Charlemagne's heirs inevitably thought of their 'empire' as a patrimony rather than a state; and the extremely crude territorial arrangements which they adopted in order to satisfy the acquisitive instincts of their small family circle gradually began to introduce the concept of a political entity smaller than the empire itself but much larger than the county or duchy. Thus in 843, 'Charles went to meet his two brothers at Verdun, and there they divided the kingdoms between them. Louis obtained everything beyond the Rhine as well as the cities and districts of Speyer, Worms and Mainz on this side of the river.' In many ways this famous tripartite partition of the Carolingian Empire between Charlemagne's three grandsons created more problems than it solved: in the event the new 'middle kingdom' of the emperor Lothar collapsed as the result of dynastic accident and the refusal of the kings of both the East and West Franks to accept the loss of the Carolingian heart-land. But the fragile kingship of Louis the German east of the Rhine survived, if only because it was never exposed to a direct challenge. Louis and his heirs continued to think primarily in terms of a *renovatio imperii Francorum* but their inability to achieve this end became more and more apparent, particularly after the failure of Charles the Fat's attempt between 880 and 887 to maintain under his rule all the various territories that had been separated by the treaty of Verdun. In many ways the legacy bequeathed by the later Carolingians to the future German kingdom in 911 was therefore the *damnosa hereditas* of boundless but ill-defined ambitions based on inadequate resources; but they had preserved the tradition of a separate East Frankish king as an indefatigable war-lord. It was this tradition and not the consciousness of any German unity that proved decisive in 911.

If the German monarchy was born out of a sense of urgent military need, the social structure of the German-speaking lands was itself organized for a state of almost perpetual war. The primary fact in the history of early tenth-century Germany was the domination of political and social life by a small military aristocracy. In 911 the nobility not only monopolized the important offices of the church but controlled what little urban and commercial activity, still largely confined to the Rhine valley, existed in Germany. More significantly still, they had already subjected to their authority the great mass of the German population. By a mysterious and almost completely unrecorded process, the descendants of the once free members of the German tribes had been converted into a dependent peasantry, tied to their own land and the estates they cultivated for their lords. As in contemporary England, the heirs of freemen who had sought protection by commending themselves to their local lords became increasingly difficult to distinguish from the numerous class of emancipated slaves. Subjected to the crude but rigorous seigniorial justice of their landlords, German peasants had ceased to play an active and independent role in political and public life by the end of the ninth century. The obscure primitive institutions of the Germanic tribes, like early German law and custom itself, displayed remarkable powers of survival: but they had now been adapted to subserve the needs of a small warrior élite. Such a development is more fundamental to the history of early medieval Germany than the famous controversy as to the exact nature and viability of the five great German stem duchies. At first sight the existence in 911 of these duchies of Franconia, Saxony, Bavaria, Swabia and Lotharingia, the hereditary power of whose rulers had expanded dramatically during the previous generation, seemed to threaten the nascent German monarchy with death in infancy. Historians have constantly expressed surprise that the East Frankish kingdom avoided the fate that befell the Lotharingian middle kingdom of breaking apart into a series of small *regna*. But the authority of the dukes was itself completely dependent on the consent and co-operation of their nobles, large clan dynasties who combined a genuine loyalty to their tribal traditions and dialects with an obsessive desire to satisfy the territorial ambitions of themselves and their kindred at the expense of one another. It was in the interests of these magnates to have a ruler in addition to their duke, a king who could conduct successful war on the frontiers and dispense a modicum of rough justice within Germany itself. Accordingly at Hohenaltheim in northern Swabia a large assembly of nobles and prelates gathered in 916 'to strengthen the king'. Only Conrad I's military weaknesses prevented him from exploiting the real opportunities of his admittedly short reign (911–18).

On Conrad's death the determination of the Frankish and Saxon magnates to secure at all costs an effective warrior for their king led them to meet at Fritzlar where they chose the Liudolfing Duke of Saxony. This election of Henry, later called 'the Fowler', the first of the five Saxon kings of Germany (919–36), was difficult to justify on any but military grounds; and during the early part of his reign it might have seemed an unsuccessful gamble. Only with considerable difficulty did Henry I eventually secure the recognition of his kingship by the Swabians and the formidable Duke Arnulf of Bavaria. Gradually Henry's two greatest assets, his wealthy Liudolfing estates clustered around the Harz mountains and his command of the Saxon *exercitus*, one of the most formidable fighting-forces of the age, enabled him to dominate his rivals. The nine years' truce he bought from the Magyars in 924 or 926 gave him a breathing space in which to reorganize his aristocratic cavalry army and to establish a series of garrisoned fortresses capable of defending his eastern frontier. Meanwhile the insecurity and dynastic misfortunes of the West Frankish kings allowed Henry to gain control over Lotharingia in 925. The acquisition of suzerain rights over this most famous and wealthy part of the old Carolingian Empire proved a permanent gain: it immediately enhanced the prestige of Henry the Fowler and gave genuine substance to his successors' claims to ascendancy over all other European rulers. More specifically, the inability of the last Carolingian and first Capetian kings of France to challenge the German monarchy's authority in the old 'middle kingdom' provided the essential *sine qua non* for the emergence of a genuinely powerful kingship in central Europe. Secure in the west, the Saxon dynasty could now afford to indulge its hereditary and natural taste for an active policy in the east.

Territorial expansion at the expense of Germany's eastern neighbours was in fact to prove the mainspring of the rapid rise of the Saxon kings to hegemony and imperial status. The point was appreciated by their famous historian, Widukind of Corvey, who eulogized Henry the Fowler on the grounds that 'he left to his son a great and spacious Reich, not bequeathed to him by his forefathers but acquired by himself and given to him by God alone'. After Henry's death in 936, his son Otto I (king 936–73) continued and extended the *Drang nach Osten* which proved such a dominant theme in subsequent German history. Understandably enough it was the Saxon kings' unprecedented success in withstanding and then crushing the menace of the Magyar marauding raids that most attracted the admiration of their subjects. At Riade in 933 Henry I had routed a Hungarian onslaught on Saxony and Thuringia, and within a few years Saxony was permanently free from the danger of a new invasion. During the 940s and 950s it was the Bavarians who bore the brunt of Magyar attacks; but in 955 Otto himself put a final end to the dangers of Hungarian raids at a battle by the river Lech near Augsburg. It is difficult to overestimate the contribution of Otto's hard-fought victory to the cause of German kingship: according to Widukind, Otto's troops, by no means exclusively Saxon but drawn from all the German duchies, immediately acclaimed him as their *imperator*; and Otto himself exploited his military success so successfully that seven years later he was crowned emperor at Rome in 962. In theory at least, the German kings were henceforward lords of Rome and masters of the West.

Almost as significant was the political effect of the destruction of the Hungarian army in stabilizing the previously chaotic territorial position in south-eastern Germany. At last freed from the dangers of external aggression, the Carolingian marches to the east of Bavaria rapidly developed into the territorial principalities of the Ostmark (Austria), Steiermark (Styria) and the duchy (after 976) of Carinthia. On the north-eastern frontier of Germany, however, the situation remained much more fluid. During the middle years of the tenth century it seemed possible that Saxon expansionist policy against the Slavs, exemplified by Henry the Fowler's capture of 'Brennabor' (the later Brandenburg) in 928, might result in the speedy replacement of the Elbe by the Oder as Germany's eastern frontier. Otto I and the margraves of his East Saxon marks continued to raid the neighbouring Slav population in search of plunder and, more especially, slaves. Otto's foundation of the bishoprics of Brandenburg and Havelberg in 948 was followed by the erection of the great missionary arch-bishopric of Magdeburg in subsequent decades as part of a grand design to secure permanent political control over the heathen Slav tribes east of the Elbe. In this objective, however, Otto and his Saxon bishops and margraves were to fail almost completely. Their military occupation of the Slav lands, based on the garrisoning of fortified strongholds or burgwards, was unaccompanied by any genuine cultural penetration of the area. The net effect of Ottonian aggression was to increase rather than diminish the Slavs' hostility towards both Christianity and its representatives, those *Niemsti* (still the word for Germans in the Slav languages) whose speech they could rarely under-stand. In 983 a great anti-German rising of the Slavs east of the Elbe destroyed most of the political and ecclesiastical gains of the previous fifty years. German colonization of the area had to be postponed until the twelfth century when there at last emerged a surplus population of Germans in the west who could dominate or replace the native Slavs in the east. By that time, however, German expansion across the Elbe could no longer be directed centrally by the king.

Towards the end of his reign the multifarious obligations of his kingship were in any case distracting Otto I from his eastern policy, the original *raison d'être* of his dynasty. Only endless journeys back-wards and forwards across the German duchies could preserve the king's authority and his right to do justice on the local nobility. As early as 938, and again in 953, dissident sections of the Saxon nobility co-operated in serious revolts which threatened the collapse of effective royal power in Germany. The ingenious and ruthless measures adopted by Otto to preserve his ascendancy against such serious challenges were decisive in converting the hitherto loose federation of German duchies into a more intelligible political unit. He deliberately and suc-cessfully stressed the Frankish origins of his kingly authority, apparently dressing in the Frankish *tunica stricta* at his crown-wearings, observing Frankish law where it ran, and retaining the Franconian dukedom in his own hands after the death of Eberhard, Conrad I's brother, in 939. Taking all possible advantage of his rivals' dynastic troubles, Otto was able to intrude members of his own family clan into several of the German stem duchies and gradually introduce the concept that their dukedoms should be held from him as fiefs. The same policy was adopted towards the German counts who increasingly received their most extensive military and judicial privileges directly from the king himself. There was little however that Otto I and his successors could do to halt the irreversible extension of the hereditary principle: by the middle of the tenth century the German aristocracy had generally converted their offices as well as their estates into a hereditary patrimony which they were quite prepared to defend against king as well as duke. What saved the monarchy from early disaster was Otto's exploitation of the opportunities presented by the organization of the Christian Church in Germany.

Unlike his father, Henry the Fowler, who had refused anointment and coronation at the hands of the archbishop of Mainz in 919, Otto I deliberately cultivated a close and fateful alliance with the prelates of his realm. As appointments to the thirty-five or so dioceses in tenth-century Germany were almost always in royal hands, and as he was largely successful in freeing his bishops from any subservience to other magnates, Otto's ecclesiastical allies provided him and his successors with a political weapon of the greatest importance. Otto I began the policy, greatly extended under his successors, of undermining the secular authority of dukes and counts by endowing bishoprics and abbeys with estates and their appurtenant jurisdictional rights. The Ottonians positively encouraged the prelates to adopt a territorial approach towards their offices, a development which was certainly successful in for ever preventing the rise of a well-integrated major principality in western Germany. Otto I left no more lasting legacy to his successors, though it is difficult not to believe that he would have enjoyed the close support of his prelates without benefit of this alienation of demesne and other lands. Such support he certainly enjoyed, and the Ottonian Reich owed what strength it possessed to the mutual co-operation between king and bishops. The Ottonian prelates, almost all of noble birth, inevitably dominated the administrative and cultural as well as the religious activities of the kingdom. The bellicosity of the German bishops, their readiness to take up arms on behalf of their king, was soon proverbial throughout Europe. More indispensable still was the ecclesiastics' monopoly of literacy and learning. Individual bishops not only acted as the king's envoys and diplomats but were closely involved in the work of his peripatetic chancery, largely staffed by clerks of the royal chapel which was for long the only central organ of government. The influential role played by Otto I's youngest

brother, St Bruno (925–65), is the most famous example of the possibilities open to the great churchmen of the tenth century. Allegedly
educated by Byzantine tutors, St Bruno of Saxony became abbot of
the monasteries of Lorsch near Worms and Corvey on the Weser
while still an adolescent. In 953 he was appointed archbishop of
Cologne, an office he used in conjunction with his dukedom of
Lotharingia to extend Ottonian power throughout the Rhineland. At
an even earlier date Bruno had presided over the royal chancery and
made his elder brother's court, where he 'restored the long-ruined
fabric of the seven liberal arts', the centre of what artistic and intellectual life Germany enjoyed. The impressive new churches built by
Bruno in Cologne, only fragments of which now survive, appear to
have established a genuinely distinctive Ottonian architectural style.
Similarly it was under the patronage of the royal court that Widukind
of Corvey was encouraged to write the *Res gestae Saxonicae* in which
he demonstrated the antiquity and eulogized the achievements of the
Saxon race. At about the same time, Roswitha, a remarkably learned
nun of the wealthy Abbey of Gandersheim in Saxony, was writing a
Latin epic in praise of Otto I. Even the king himself learnt to read
some Latin, although he reputedly – like Barbarossa two centuries
later – was rarely confident enough to speak it. The most spectacular
achievements of the Saxon schools of architecture and illumination
are undeniably unique; but the detailed progress of this Ottonian
'renaissance' was sometimes deliberately reminiscent of developments
at the court of Charlemagne before and after 800.

In other ways too it seems clear that the forces inducing Otto I
towards the acceptance of the imperial crown at Rome were broadly
similar to those which had led to the creation of the Carolingian Empire
in 800. Like Charlemagne, Otto I was a successful war-lord under
pressure from his clerks to convert his lordship into an imperial
authority which would not only enhance the prestige of all his servants
as well as himself but provide a terrestrial mirror for the ideological
aspirations of his age. The concept of empire was initially so mysterious and alien to Otto that his approach to the central fact of an
imperial coronation was hesitant and devious. It was indeed the prosaic
demands of internal German politics that first compelled him to
intervene in Italy. Otto's first venture south of the Alps, during which
he received the Lombard crown at Pavia, took place in 951 and was
forced upon him by the need to counter the Italian ambitions of his
brother, Henry, Duke of Bavaria, and his son, Liudolf, Duke of Swabia.

It was, of course, inevitable that the wealth of the old Lombardic kingdom of northern Italy, unprotected by either a natural frontier (for the Alps were certainly not that) or any major political power, should attract the attention and greed of the German aristocracy; but Otto I realized both the dangers and the opportunities of the situation remarkably quickly and was almost completely successful in establishing the tradition that henceforward Italian expeditions were to be composed of forces drawn from the entire Reich and led by the German king. Otto's determination, shared by his successors for at least the next three centuries, to retain control over the lucrative political and financial profits of northern Italy led him by a logical development to enter Rome and accept imperial coronation on 2 February 962 at the hands of Pope John XII. Whatever Otto's precise motives, his revival of the Roman Empire inevitably revolutionized the nature of German kingship. The endless and often futile controversy as to whether the imperial ideal proved the cultural salvation or political damnation of the medieval German 'state' has at least the virtue of stressing that Otto's coronation in 962 genuinely altered the course of German history. No doubt the exact meaning and significance of the imperial title changed from generation to generation; but Otto himself would have appreciated and shared the sentiments ascribed by Otto of Freising to Frederick Barbarossa, his most famous successor: 'I am the lawful master. Let him who would wrest the club from the hands of Hercules come and do so if he can ... The hand of the Franks, who are also called Germans (*Francorum sive Teutonicorum*), has not yet lost its vigour.'

The practical consequences of the restoration of the imperial office revealed themselves immediately after 962. Although Otto I adopted an essentially conservative attitude towards his new authority and was buried, appropriately enough, in his own new East Saxon city of Magdeburg, the fact remains that ten out of the last twelve years of his life were spent in Italy. By the end of his short reign, Otto II, who had succeeded his father at the age of eighteen in 973, was genuinely obsessed with the desire to make a reality out of his imperial position in Rome and southern as well as northern Italy. In 982 his army suffered a disastrous defeat when ambushed by the Saracens between the Calabrian mountains and the sea; and in the following year he died in Rome while preparing a massive invasion of Moslem Sicily. Otto II's wife, the Byzantine princess Theophano, who acted as regent during the early part of Otto III's reign (983–1002), had an even greater in-

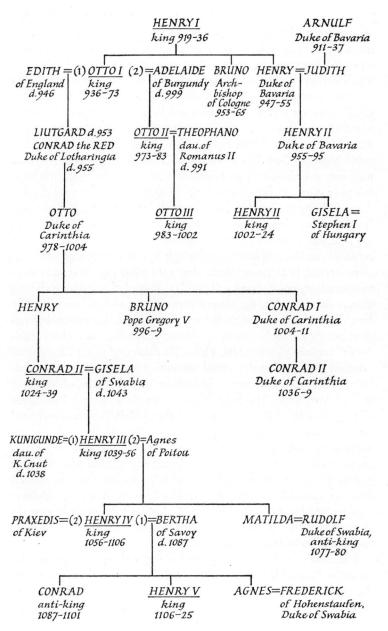

TABLE I The Saxon and Franconian Dynasties

fluence on her son than her husband. In 996, and when still only sixteen, Otto III crossed the Alps to secure his imperial coronation at Rome. The following six years of close co-operation and visionary scheming between the young Otto and the remarkable Gerbert of Aurillac (Pope Sylvester II, 999–1003) are deservedly famous as the most extraordinary episode in the history of the medieval empire. But Otto's *renovatio imperii Romanorum* had little relevance for Germany, a land which Otto valued merely as a source of military assistance and the spiritual energy which only Aachen, Charlemagne's burial-place, could provide. Otto III's early and childless death gave the German magnates a welcome opportunity to elect as his successor the considerably more prosaic Henry, Duke of Bavaria, the last male descendant of Henry the Fowler. Even Henry II (1002–24) was not immune from the attractions of his new Mediterranean sphere of interest. In 1014 he was crowned emperor by Pope Benedict VIII and in 1021 actually found himself marching through Apulia in command of a large German host. In Germany itself, Henry II's reign appears to have been comparatively tranquil and successful, a tribute less to his own abilities than to the strength of the alliance between king and prelates originally forged by Otto I. Although distorted memories of his personal asceticism and the favour he displayed towards reforming monks later resulted in his canonization (1146), Henry II's patronage of the Church was carefully calculated on the central assumption that (to use his own adaptation of St Luke's text) 'unto whomsoever much is given, of him shall much be required'. The most famous example is Henry's foundation of the bishopric of Bamberg in 1007: the cathedral there, consecrated by Pope Benedict VIII himself in 1020, was designed not only to convert the Slavs of the upper Main valley but also to provide the king's chapel with a training ground for talented ecclesiastical administrators and to drive a wedge of royal political influence into the geographical heart of central Germany. Significantly enough, it was the German bishops, notably Archbishop Aribo of Mainz, who apparently took the decisive initiatives during the disputed election that followed the death without heirs of Henry II in 1024.

It is usually argued that the accession to the throne of a Franconian count as Conrad II (1024–39) involved little change in royal policy. Certainly the new so-called Salian dynasty immediately took possession of the still vast territorial resources enjoyed by its Saxon predecessors. Conrad II's obsessive interest in his newly acquired estates brought him into rapid conflict with the East Saxon nobles and induced him to build his famous imperial palace at Goslar in the Harz mountains. Despite their use of Goslar as a military headquarters and of the mechanism of the royal *iter*, the solemn and ritualistic journey through the German lands, Conrad and his successors were inevitably associated with western Germany. Their authority was based on an alliance with the great prelates of the Rhineland, an alliance whose most appropriate as well as most striking visible memorial is the early Romanesque cathedral at Trier, rebuilt by Archbishop Poppo (1017–47) on Roman foundations. All four of the Salian kings lie buried within the even larger cathedral of Speyer, but they failed – like every German monarch – to provide their realm with an effective central power-base, the nucleus of a political capital. The effectiveness of sacerdotal kingship still depended upon the careful selection and patronage of the *capellani* of the court chapel, those able and often highly born clerks who undertook the written work of government in the absence of any other administrative machinery.

The fundamental financial and administrative weaknesses of the early Salian monarchy were in fact long concealed by the sophisticated court patronage and adroit ruthlessness of Conrad and his son Henry III (sole king 1039–56). Both kings emasculated the political power of the old stem duchies by bestowing vacant dukedoms on themselves and their kindred: Henry III was himself Duke of Swabia and Bavaria as well as Franconia. Conrad and Henry were, however, careful not to disturb the increasingly possessive attitude of the German nobles towards their own inheritances. According to Wipo, his chaplain and biographer, Conrad II 'disposed his vassals well towards himself in that he did not suffer the ancient benefices [*beneficia*] of parents to be taken away from any of their progeny'. In return Conrad was able to force through amidst much opposition the hereditary principle in the interest of his own house: in 1028 his eldest son, the future Henry III, was elected and crowned king by the Archbishop of Cologne. In the last resort, however, the control of Conrad II and Henry III over their nobility seems to have depended, somewhat dangerously, on their ability to demonstrate their ascendancy outside the frontiers of the German-speaking lands. For many years they were remarkably successful in establishing a very real degree of hegemony throughout western Europe. In 1032 Conrad II secured the crown of Burgundy, an acquisition which advanced the influence of the ruler of the German Reich to the river Rhône and brought him considerable prestige if little power or profit. More remarkable still was the short-term success

Germany in t[

MECKLENBURG
MARCH

BALTIC
SEA

DANZIG

POMERANIA

HAVELBERG

H MARCH

ANDENBURG

MAGDEBURG

RSTADT

MARCH

HALLE

BURG

MERSEBURG

UMARCH

ZEITZ

RT

EITZ MARCH

GNESEN

Vistula

Oder

Warthe

POLAND

MARCH OF LUSATIA

MISNIAN MARCH

MEISSEN

BAUTZEN

Eger

HHEIM

ARIAN

RDGAU

ADT

SING

AVARIA

PRAGUE

PILSEN

BOHEMIA

Moldau

REGENSBURG

PASSAU

TRAUN
GAU

SALZBURG

BAV. EAST MARCH

Danube

MELK

KREMS

MORAVIA

OLMUTZ

Morava

HUNGARY

enner Pass

IXEN

CARINTHIA

GURK

MARCH
OF
CARNIOLA

MARCH OF
STYRIA

OF

VERONA

German Archbishoprics and
Bishoprics underlined

0   50   100 MILES

0   80   160 KM

eventh Century

of Conrad II and Henry III in imposing their authority (after a series of brilliantly conducted expeditions) upon the magnates of Poland, Hungary and Bohemia, three newly formed and still inchoate territorial states whose recent emergence had revolutionized the political situation east of Germany since the days of Otto I.

But nowhere were the achievements of the mid-eleventh-century German monarchy more dazzling than in Italy. Despite some views to the contrary, Conrad II certainly appreciated the spiritual as well as material rewards to be gained by intervention south of the Alps. In his own and probably sincere words, 'Although we are bound to consider the interest of our commonwealth, we are not ignorant of our greater obligation to care for the state of the churches of God with even more diligence.' More remarkably, Henry III not only publicized the pontifical nature of his office and the theocratic conception of the empire, but was able to put these ideals into practice. A few days before his coronation as emperor on Christmas Day 1046 Henry presided over the synod of Sutri which deposed two of the three rival claimants to the papacy and prepared the way for the election as Pope Clement II of Henry's nominee, Suidger, Bishop of Bamberg. During the last ten years of Henry's life, a succession of German bishops followed Clement on to the papal throne, the majority of whom were dedicated, most notably his second cousin, Bruno of Toul (Pope Leo IX, 1048–54), to the cause of radical Church reform. There are few, if any, more ironical periods in the history of the German monarchy. At the very time that contemporaries began to speculate on the possibility that the papacy might become an imperial benefice, the foundations of royal authority in Germany itself were being rapidly eroded. For a few years in the middle of the eleventh century the view that 'The Rhine, by a turn of the wheel of fortune, now governs the Tiber' had become substance: after Henry III's early death in 1056 such a belief was rarely the product of anything more substantial than a piece of ingenious wishful thinking. The Ottonian Reich, by any standards the most successful as well as most unexpected political creation of post-Carolingian Europe, was about to disintegrate beyond repair.

The Decline of the Empire 1056–1250

For the chronicler Adam of Bremen, writing twenty years later, it was the succession in 1056 of 'a woman [Henry III's widow, Agnes of

Poitou] and a boy to the conduct of the realm which led to the ruin of the empire'. Certainly any explanation of the great political and ecclesiastical crisis experienced throughout Germany during the fifty-year reign of Henry IV (1056–1106) which ignores the damaging effect of the king's long minority and subsequent emotional instability can never be completely adequate. Nevertheless it is difficult to believe that this crisis could have been long avoided. The conversion of the papacy from a passive source of spiritual influence into a dynamic and energizing institution obviously presented a direct challenge to both the pretensions and the resources of the German kings and emperors. Such a challenge could only have been survived by a ruler much more securely based within Germany or Italy than were the last Salian kings or indeed the Hohenstaufen dynasty which succeeded them. In the period before 1056 the concept of a quasi-sacerdotal war-lord had often proved invincible; but during the following 200 years this Ottonian legacy proved to be no substitute for the more commonplace administrative skills displayed by the kings and governments of France and England. Moreover, the German monarchs of the eleventh to thirteenth centuries suffered from the need to dissipate their energies and resources over too wide a variety of fields, an obvious feature of their position but one which ought to be stressed because it is so easy to forget. More specifically, the sheer size of the German lands and the nature of the geographical barriers within them (notably the wide, unbridgeable rivers which flow from south to north) had been positive assets to the early Saxon warrior kings, but were quite the reverse during an age when the integrity of other West European states depended increasingly on the rapid dispatch of written instructions. How far the cause of 'German' intellectual and artistic life suffered from the resulting political divisionism is a more open question. The impressive architectural feats, speculative inquiry and literary experiments of late Salian and Hohenstaufen Germany lay heavily under French influence, but, if anything, to a rather slighter extent than was the case in Angevin and Plantagenet England.

The new era was introduced by the revolutionary Church reform movement of the middle and late eleventh century, a phenomenon best interpreted not in terms of morality but as a strenuous and ultimately successful attempt by the clergy of western Europe to achieve recognition of their distinctive and privileged status in society. The main objectives of the reformers – clerical celibacy, the abolition of simony, and freedom from secular control – were all deliberately aimed at emphasizing the gulf that existed between clerk and layman. Such a programme threatened to destroy the basis of political power in Germany, where (to a much larger extent than anywhere else in Europe) the ruler's authority derived from his proprietary rights over the Church and his freedom to appoint bishops. Two other factors converted an inevitably dangerous situation into one of open war. The private territorial ambitions of the major German prelates, best exemplified by the disruptive activities of Archbishops Anno of Cologne and Adalbert of Hamburg-Bremen during the minority of Henry IV (1056–66), destroyed their absolute loyalty to the policies of the crown. Meanwhile the emergence of a radical ecclesiastical intelligentsia, capable of articulating its criticisms of contemporary society in a quite unprecedented way, provided successive popes with a brilliant propaganda literature to accompany their heightened sense of self-confidence. The impending confrontation between papacy and empire was precipitated by the accession as Pope Gregory VII (1073–85) of the extremist Hildebrand, an Italian whose primary loyalties in this world lay with the city of Rome. By his determination to enforce his authority over the aristocratic German bishops, many of whom he summoned to Rome and suspended from their offices, Gregory showed himself prepared (in their own words of 1076) 'to scatter, with raging madness, the flames of discord through all the churches of the empire'. For his part Henry IV never had the slightest intention of observing the new papal decree (of February 1075) forbidding all lay investiture of bishops and abbots with their benefices. But the vehemence with which he reacted to Gregory's intransigence, however understandable, was politically ill advised at a period when his own position within Germany was extremely vulnerable. Henry's personal misfortunes, during many years of bewildering vicissitudes, gave Gregory the opportunity not only to put into practice his theoretical claim to depose the German king but to receive his penitent submission at the North Italian castle of Canossa in January 1077. Whether or not, as is often argued, Gregory's absolution of Henry at Canossa represented a short-term tactical victory for the latter, the position of the German kings and emperors could never be the same again. Despite the impressive efforts by Henry IV and his successors to combat the papacy's pretensions with its own ideological weapons, the German monarchy's claims to a unique, supernatural status were henceforward under permanent challenge. More dangerously, Gregory's denunciations of his adversary provided a legal as well as spiritual justification for rebellion against royal authority within Germany itself. After Canossa, and especially after Henry's second excommunication and formal dethronement by Gregory VII in 1080, the German nobles were faced with the exhilarating prospect of a political system in which the replacement of an unsatisfactory ruler by one of themselves was a practical possibility.

Aristocratic disaffection with the government of the Reich was not of course a new phenomenon; but the savage thoroughness with which so many German magnates pursued their vendettas against Henry IV has no real precedent. Henry IV's opponents sometimes resorted to violent action in order to recoup their own family fortunes, weakened as ever by the practice of partible inheritance. Meanwhile the king's attempts to secure adequate resources for himself aroused even more opposition. By looking for support from the petty nobility of south-western Germany and the class of unfree knights known as *ministeriales*, the king not only aroused the caste prejudices of the established noble dynasties but also weakened the all-important concept of general military obligation to the crown which had hitherto provided the German aristocracy with a *raison d'être* for loyalty to the crown. Conrad II and Henry III had already appreciated the advantages of employing loyal and reliable *ministeriales* to administer their estates and form the nucleus of their fighting forces. But after he came of age in 1066, Henry IV used his own Swabian knights and officials to organize and garrison a formidable new territorial complex which he planned to erect as a permanent centre of royal power in southern Saxony and Thuringia. Such aggression inside the territories of the Reich precipitated a major Saxon revolt in 1073, led by Count Otto of Nordheim and incorporating peasants as well as nobles within its ranks. Only the reluctant support of the South German princes, antagonized by the atrocities reportedly committed by the Eastphalian peasant rebels, allowed Henry to subdue this Saxon tribal revolt in 1075. But the leaders of South German aristocratic opinion, Rudolf of Rheinfelden, Duke of Swabia, Berchtold of Zähringen, Duke of Carinthia, and Welf IV, the new Duke of Bavaria, had already contemplated the deposition of their monarch in their own interests. Gregory VII's onslaught on Henry IV gave them their opportunity, and at Forchheim in March 1077 Duke Rudolf of Swabia was chosen king and subsequently crowned at Mainz.[1] Forchheim, like Canossa, bequeathed an unfortunate and enduring legacy to the future of the German

[1] Rudolph of Swabia was Henry IV's brother-in-law; see Genealogical Table I, p. 139.

monarchy. According to his anonymous biographer it was only when Henry IV died in 1106 and 'exchanged the turbulent for the celestial kingdom' that his reign ceased to be a cause for lamentation. The long series of civil wars which followed the election of Duke Rudolf of Swabia as anti-king in 1077 had a permanently damaging effect on the assets of the German monarchy. Paradoxically Henry's remarkable resilience, which enabled him to outlive both Rudolf and his successor Hermann of Luxemburg (anti-king 1081–8), wrecked the stability of German politics and society much more effectively than would have done his early death. With the intermittent support of most of the Franconian and Swabian prelates and magnates, Henry was able to hold his South German and Saxon adversaries at bay but not destroy them. After securing the imperial crown at Rome by force in 1084, Henry was irrevocably committed to sustaining a series of antipopes and hence denied the opportunity to participate in the greatest European movement of his reign, the First Crusade preached by Pope Urban II in 1095. Within Germany his military needs compelled him to alienate much of his demesne land by enfeoffing large numbers of *ministeriales* with his own hereditary estates. As an excommunicate, he notoriously failed in his primary obligation to protect the Church and, more seriously still, could not prevent the concentration of political power into the hands of a few great magnate families.

By general agreement the late eleventh and early twelfth centuries were the decisive period in the transformation of the previously loosely knit aristocratic clans (*Großfamilien*) into smaller, more durable and more closely integrated dynasties. Thus the Ascanian family (the first margraves of Brandenburg after 1134), the Ludowings (who became landgraves of Thuringia before dying out in 1247), the Wettins (who gradually acquired power in Meissen and Lusatia and survived as lords of Saxony from 1423 to 1918) and the Wittelsbachs (whose careers as rulers of Bavaria also lasted until 1918) all first rose to real prominence in this turbulent period. The prevalence of civil conflict placed a premium upon the possession of a local power base, the timber (and later stone) castle which was soon adopted by lay magnates throughout Germany. The financial profits to be gained from the advocacy (*advocatus*), a hereditary office peculiar to Germany which carried extensive rights of jurisdiction over a monastery's estates, similarly furthered the creation of geographically consolidated patrimonies. The territorial ambitions of these new dynasts, probably more cultivated and certainly in a much closer relationship with local prelates than their predecessors, encouraged them to adopt a more coherent as well as more aggressive policy towards the government of the Reich as a whole. Moreover, the authority of the magnate within his own lands often depended on his ability to extract, either by fear or favour, the necessary legal sanctions from the person of the German king. In particular, and in the case of the most ambitious noble dynasties, the royal conferment of an official title (as duke, margrave, landgrave or *comes palatinus*) was the essential precondition for permanent success. It was only after his father-in-law, Henry IV, had granted him the duchy of Swabia in 1079 that Frederick of Hohenstaufen (whose family name derived, characteristically enough, from the castle he built in the Swabian Jura) secured the fortunes of the most famous of German princely houses. Within a few years royal favour and marriage to a king's daughter transformed an obscure petty noble family into the most formidable power in South-West Germany. Similarly it was as dukes of Bavaria that the descendants of Welf IV (duke 1070–7, 1096–1101) established themselves as the Hohenstaufen's greatest rivals. The Zähringers too, a family which dominated the area between the upper Rhine and the Alps until its extinction in 1218, based their *Hausmacht* upon the personal dukedom originally conferred upon them as a gesture of reconciliation by Henry IV in 1097. For Hohenstaufens, Welfs and Zähringers, the friendship or hostility of the reigning German king was a matter of much more vital concern than it had been for their predecessors; and by a logical development the very choice of monarch became, what it remained for more than 300 years, a matter for the most acute dynastic rivalry.

The dangers which the ambitions of these great aristocratic families presented to the German crown were fully appreciated by the last of the Salian kings, Henry V (1106–25), whose ruthless attempt to replace his father by force in the year before he died was probably designed to prevent the complete erosion of royal authority before it was too late. However, Henry V's own campaigns to maintain the prerogatives of his crown were only a modified success, for he found himself trapped in the same historical context as his father. Since the rising of the 1070s relations between the Salian dynasty and the Saxons had almost degenerated into a blood-feud; and Henry V was unable to make any impression on that 'hard people, harsh in wars and as rashly inclined to arms as bold', now ably united and led by his hereditary enemy Lothar of Supplinburg, who succeeded the Billungs as Duke of Saxony in 1106. Henry found it almost as difficult to retreat from the entrenched position taken up by the German monarchy in the face of continued papal opposition. Although his turbulent coronation in St Peter's, Rome, at the hands of Pope Paschal II in February 1111 did something to revenge Canossa, the new emperor was unable to reassert his legal rights in northern Italy. In 1118 a faction of the Roman nobility persuaded Henry to set up his own imperial pope: the contest between empire and papacy, now increasingly centred upon the legalistic question of lay investiture, seemed as far from solution as ever. Although the German Church suffered more acutely from the investiture contest than any other group, the bishops themselves (notably Henry V's great enemy, Adalbert, Archbishop of Mainz from 1111 to 1137) were too deeply involved in political intrigue to exert the influence for compromise displayed by their French and English counterparts in similar situations. Significantly it was the German magnates who eventually forced the hands of both Henry V and Archbishop Adalbert and induced them to negotiate the famous Concordat of Worms, formally approved by nine ecclesiastical and nine lay princes in 1122.

At Worms Henry abandoned the canonical investiture by ring and staff, but Pope Calixtus II conceded that a German prelate could be elected in the royal presence, after which and before his consecration 'he shall receive the *regalia* from you by the sceptre and perform the services he owes you by law on account of them'. Despite the fact that Henry V had preserved his ability to influence the election of German (but not Italian) prelates, contemporaries regarded the Concordat of Worms as a major victory for the papacy. They were almost certainly correct to do so: the surrender of lay investiture was inevitably much more damaging to the theocratic ideals of the German crown and empire than was the similar concession made by the much less pretentious Anglo-Norman monarchy sixteen years earlier. Henceforward the bishops and abbots of the Reich, holding only their temporalities from the king, were increasingly assimilated to the other feudatories of the realm. Like their lay counterparts, the German prelates now found it more advantageous to exploit rather than augment the powers of the crown. The remarkable monastic revival in late eleventh- and early twelfth-century Germany similarly fostered the growth of ecclesiastical immunities independent of royal control. The extensive if heterogeneous collection of monasteries founded or reformed during the last decades of the eleventh century under the influence of Hirsau, an abbey on the north-east slopes of the Black

Forest, were more subject to pope or local lay advocate than to either bishop or king. Nor did the German kings derive much material benefit from the more coherent Cistercian movement which swept across the Rhine from the abbey of Morimund, one of Citeaux's original four daughter-houses, during the fifty years which followed that monastery's foundation in 1115. The most famous name in the history of German monasticism is that of Norbert of Xanten (*c.* 1080–1134) who founded, after a characteristically nomadic life in the Rhineland and northern France, the Premonstratensian or White Canons, an order which received recognition from Pope Honorius II in 1126, the year in which Norbert was appointed Archbishop of Magdeburg. Although Norbert co-operated with the German monarchy in the organization of missionary activity across the Slav frontier, there is no doubt that he regarded the papacy rather than the empire as his ultimate source of authority: he successfully used all his considerable influence to prevent a revival of the investiture contest and was rewarded by the pope's concession of metropolitan jurisdiction over the whole of Poland. Even in the case of Norbert, appointed imperial chancellor for Italy shortly before his death, the German prelate's sense of complete identification with the purposes of the Reich had weakened to an alarming degree.

The failure of Henry V to subdue either the particularist interests of the German bishops or the dynastic aggression of the lay magnates became abundantly clear when he died without heirs three years after the Concordat of Worms. The stormy election proceedings at Mainz in August 1125 resulted in the choice as ruler of Duke Lothar of Supplinburg (king 1125–37) in preference to either of Henry's two Hohenstaufen nephews, Frederick, Duke of Swabia from 1105 to 1147, and his younger brother Conrad. According to Archbishop Adalbert, his chief advocate, the fact that Lothar had no hereditary claim to the throne whatsoever was a positive advantage, an argument accepted by magnates for whom the right to elect a monarch was naturally regarded as a safeguard to their own dynastic ambitions. The rejection of royal blood-right in 1125 – at a time when the hereditary principle was becoming increasingly entrenched in the rest of Europe and indeed within German aristocratic society itself – undoubtedly created a more or less continuous atmosphere of political insecurity inside the Reich. It immediately raised the complex and controversial issues of the heritability of crown land and the extent to which it could be distinguished from the private property of the ruling dynasty. Lothar's attempts to deprive Frederick of Swabia of part of the Salian lands he had inherited from Henry V immediately led to civil war. Despite the new king's own considerable landed wealth and political ability, he could only force the Hohenstaufen brothers into submission (1134) by allying himself with the head of the Welf family, Henry the Proud, Duke of Bavaria (1126–39), to whom he married his only daughter and heiress. Henceforward dynastic competition between Welf or Guelf and Hohenstaufen dominated German politics.[1] Fear of Henry the Proud's overwhelming power – for by 1138 he had secured most of his aunt Matilda's allodial lands in northern Italy and Tuscany as well as the dukedom of Saxony – led to his rejection as royal successor to his father-in-law when the latter died in December 1137. The new king, Conrad III (1138–52), the younger of the two Hohenstaufen brothers who had opposed Lothar's election twelve years earlier, devoted most of his energies to depriving the Welfs of their ascendancy in Germany. The death of Henry the Proud in 1139 enabled this first Hohenstaufen monarch to retain his throne but only at the cost of recognizing Henry's thirteen-year-old son, Henry the Lion, as Duke of Saxony in 1142. By the end of the Conrad III's reign ten years later, Germany was again plunged in civil war. Both Lothar and Conrad had appreciated the need to emancipate the German monarchy from its embroilment in internal dynastic conflict by identifying themselves with ideals outside the frontiers of the Reich. But Lothar's successive interventions in Italian and papal politics were unaccompanied by any successful exploitation of his financial rights south of the Alps and positively damaged his prestige by allowing his adversaries to disparage him as 'homo papae'. Conrad III was compelled by circumstances to postpone his descent into Italy until it proved too late: he was the first of the German kings since Henry the Fowler never to be crowned emperor at Rome. By taking the cross at the hands of St Bernard of Clairvaux in the cathedral church of Speyer, Conrad did, however, try to associate the German monarchy with the most prestigious movement of the age. But the failure of the Second Crusade of 1147–9 and Conrad's own long absence from his realm weakened his position within Germany without securing any compensations in the form of military or religious glory. It was left to Conrad's nephew and successor, Frederick Barbarossa, to find a purpose for the monarchy and arrest the decline in royal fortunes so noticeable to contemporaries.

The long and celebrated reign of Frederick I (1152–90), nicknamed

[1] See opposite, Genealogical Table II, p. 153.

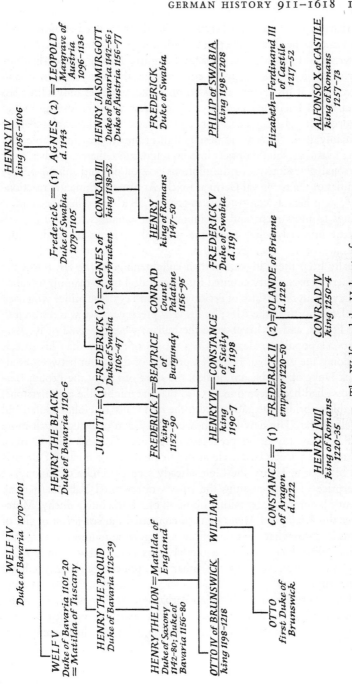

TABLE II The Welfs and the Hohenstaufen

Barbarossa by the Italians because of his short-cropped auburn beard, illustrates to perfection the political advantages which accrue to a ruler determined to stand upon his official dignity. The air of rock-like imperturbability with which the emperor met the many challenges and adversities of his career impressed his contemporaries only a little less than it has fascinated posterity. By contrast with the more obvious inadequacies of his predecessors and successors, Barbarossa's qualities certainly make him an imposing figure; and it was inevitable that later historians should project into his reign, more than any other, their personal obsessions as to the glorious possibilities and missed opportunities of the medieval German Reich. At times a 'romantic reactionary', at others a 'constructive statesman', Barbarossa has been most things to most men; and the innumerable attempts to deduce a coherent imperial policy from the political decisions he made under pressure or the rhetorical phraseology of his chancery clerks have usually been more ingenious than enlightening. In the last resort the emperor's personality counted for a good deal more than his so-called policy: as his uncle Otto of Freising noted in 1157, 'the prince won back the lands north of the Alps; by his very presence peace was restored to the Franks, and by his absence the Italians were deprived of it'. Barbarossa's popularity depended less on his originality than his success in doing the expected. Himself a product of the union between Frederick Duke of Swabia and Judith, the sister of Henry the Proud, Barbarossa had been elected in 1152 so that 'he might, like a cornerstone, be able to bridge the gap between the two walls' of Hohenstaufen and Welf power. The new king showed every sign of being much more willing than any of his predecessors to come to terms with German aristocratic particularism. He at once conferred the duchy of Bavaria on his cousin, Henry the Lion, already securely Duke of Saxony, at the price of compensating the latter's dispossessed Babenberg rival, Henry Jasomirgott, by raising his mark of Austria into a duchy. Moreover the *Privilegium Minus* of 1156 converted the *beneficium* or fief of Austria into what was in effect a largely autonomous perpetual principality, henceforward a model to be emulated – with varying degrees of success – by the other lay princes of later medieval Germany.

For the greater part of his reign Barbarossa's regime within Germany was therefore based on the concession of extensive privileges to the magnates and above all to Henry the Lion, who was allowed complete freedom to organize his conquests in Mecklenburg, Holstein and Pomerania. The extent to which the king sacrificed the spirit and at times the letter of his royal prerogatives was concealed by the deliberately impressive ceremonial grandeurs of his kingship. It is debatable how far Barbarossa's famous peace ordinances (*Landfrieden*) of 1152, 1158 and 1186 actually succeeded in eliminating the private feud within his realm, but they undoubtedly exalted his own reputation as 'the inexorable Frederick'. Thanks to the ceaseless and adroit propaganda of the highly cultivated clerks in his entourage, perhaps more influenced by the reading of Roman literature than the rediscovery of Roman law at Bologna, Barbarossa's court was always imposing, if often out of touch with German social realities: it is no coincidence that the greatest figures in the 'Hohenstaufen vernacular renaissance', Walther von der Vogelweide, Gottfried von Strassburg and the author of the *Nibelungenlied*, flourished in the generation after Barbarossa's death and wrote for audiences well removed from the royal presence. The appearance of an articulate lay element in the entourage of the ruler seems to have been a later development in Germany than elsewhere in western Europe: Frederick II's administration of the Reich, such as it was, still depended on the *capella regis*, the court chapel, he had inherited from his Ottonian and Salian predecessors. Barbarossa's high-sounding and artificial imperialism had, however, few dangerous implications for the German aristocracy: their own prestige, like that of the prelates, was in fact enhanced by being subjects of a king who regarded 'the free crown of our empire as a benefice [*beneficium*] held from God alone'. For his part Barbarossa was careful not to offend the territorial susceptibilities of his greatest lay subjects. When, after his defeat at the battle of Legnano in 1176, Frederick finally turned against Henry the Lion, he did so in response to the wishes of North German nobles and prelates rather than because he had long plotted the destruction of his most formidable over-mighty subject. Moreover the 'fall' of Henry the Lion in 1180, a complicated process by which the Saxon duke was tried under folk and then feudal law, outlawed, deprived of his imperial fiefs and forced into an English exile, benefited the princes of the Reich much more than its emperor. The resulting settlement altered the tenurial map of Germany by enfeoffing the Archbishop of Cologne with the western part of Saxony (Westphalia) and establishing the Wittelsbachs as dukes of Bavaria, from which the duchy of Styria was henceforward independent. After 1180 it was clear that the old stem duchies of the Ottonian Reich, and above all Saxony itself, had finally disintegrated and been replaced by the much smaller hereditary principalities of nobles prepared to hold their lands as fiefs from the crown in return for legal security and the recognition of their special status as 'princes of the empire'.

Compared with his role in accelerating this fundamental transformation of the German political scene, Barbarossa's other achievements seem less significant if more spectacular. Much has been made of Frederick I's determination to counterbalance the centrifugal tendencies within the Reich by consolidating his own demesne lands and creating a Hohenstaufen 'state' within the empire. Certainly Barbarossa increased his sources of revenue fairly steadily until towards the end of his reign; and his second marriage to the heiress of Upper Burgundy in 1156 confirmed his personal attachment to his inherited interests in south-western Germany. But there is little evidence that the extremely heterogeneous Hohenstaufen lands were exploited much more effectively, or were less liable to partition among relatives, than those of other German princes. Barbarossa himself had no doubt that only in Italy could he hope to gain the resources he required. The five expeditions he led south of the Alps between 1154 and 1177 in his long and eventually unsuccessful struggle for supremacy over the Lombard communes undoubtedly caught the imagination of contemporaries; and it is a tribute to the effectiveness of Hohenstaufen propaganda that the harsh realities of this aggressive policy in northern Italy have so often been concealed. Barbarossa's attempt to revive direct imperial control in Lombardy was aimed at the financial exploitation of the communes in the interests of himself, his *ministeriales* and his allies among the German prelates, men like Rainald of Dassel and Philip of Heinsberg, successively archchancellors of Italy as well as archbishops of Cologne. By providing an outlet for the military zeal and territorial appetites of his subjects, Barbarossa's involvement in Italian affairs buttressed his position within Germany at the inevitable price of antagonizing the Roman popes. Although the support of the German bishops allowed the emperor to hold his own during the prolonged schism of the papacy (1159–77), the suspicions and passions aroused at this time were to influence European politics for at least the next century. Barbarossa was compelled to come to terms with the Lombard communes in 1177 after his defeat at Legnano, but his interest then shifted further south towards Tuscany, the Romagna and Spoleto where they presented a yet more explicit threat to the territorial position of the papacy. Even more alarming was the marriage celebrated at Milan in 1186 between Henry, Barbarossa's son and designated successor, and Constance, the heiress (after 1189) of the Norman kingdom of Sicily. When the emperor died on the Third Crusade in 1190 his dynasty had become in fact as well as theory a European rather than a specifically German power.

The sixty years that elapsed between Barbarossa's death and that of his grandson, Frederick II, in 1250 were therefore dominated by the famous contest between empire and papacy for ascendancy in Italy, a struggle of only limited relevance to the course of political development in Germany. Throughout this conflict, the greatest weakness of the popes was their inability to raise a substantial or reliable army of their own and their consequent dependence on a series of unstable allies. The Hohenstaufens on the other hand were at the mercy of genealogical fortune and the willingness of their German and Italian subjects to respect the existing forms of government. Thus Henry VI (1190–7) made good his authority in northern Germany and Sicily against considerable opposition only to die prematurely in Messina at the age of thirty-two. As his son Frederick (elected king of the Romans in the previous year) was only three years old, a succession dispute was almost inevitable, even without benefit of papal intervention. To escape the perils of a long minority, a large assembly of magnates and prelates elected Philip of Swabia, Henry VI's younger brother, as king in March 1198; but three months later the Welf faction and their supporters in the Rhineland seized the opportunity of setting up as rival king Otto of Brunswick, the younger son of Henry the Lion. The long civil war between Otto IV and Philip of Swabia did not even come to an end with the latter's assassination in 1208. Pope Innocent III ruthlessly exploited, at times to his own disadvantage, the political and constitutional weaknesses of the German electoral system. The issue was only resolved after the young Frederick II's arrival in Germany to claim his father's crown in 1212 and the subsequent defeat of Otto of Brunswick by the forces of the Capetian monarchy at the battle of Bouvines in 1214. King Philip Augustus's gesture in sending to Frederick the captured gold eagle of the imperial standard was an event symbolic of a genuine revolution in the power structure of western Europe. Capetian France was now on the eve of its greatest age: the success of Philip Augustus in dramatically extending the geographical area of the French royal demesne stands in sharp contrast to the alienation of German regal rights and lands forced upon Otto of Brunswick and Philip of Swabia during the same period.

The central thread throughout the extraordinary career of Frederick II (king 1212–50) was his resolution not to divide his inheritance but to retain for himself the crowns of both Germany and Sicily. Frederick spent less than ten years of his long life north of the Alps and there is little doubt of his personal preference for his native Sicily, 'the apple of his eyes' and 'garden of his delights', rather than the 'stern seas and mountains of Germany'. It is equally clear that Frederick valued his still considerable German resources, both in men and money, chiefly as a means of furthering his Mediterranean and Italian ambitions. Nevertheless it would be quite wrong to regard the last of the great Hohenstaufen emperors as an insignificant figure in the history of Germany. Paradoxically Frederick's almost perpetual absence from the scene helped him to appreciate the political realities of the German Reich and even to develop a new constitutional role for its ruler. The famous privileges of 1220 (*privilegium in favorem principum ecclesiasticorum*) and 1231 (*statutum in favorem principum*), by which the prelates and lay princes were protected against the expansionist activities of imperial or urban officials, surrendered few prerogatives that Frederick II had any power to enforce and did little more than recognize the *status quo*. The German princes were already *domini terrae* and any attempt by the ruler of the Reich at direct competition with his more powerful subjects was almost inevitably bound to end in disaster of the sort that befell Frederick's own son, King Henry VII, in 1235. On the other hand the very fragmentation of the German political map made the services of an impartial judge and arbiter more desirable than ever before. In the great peace legislation or *Landfriede* he promulgated at Mainz in 1235 (the first imperial law in the German language) Frederick seized the opportunity of associating the empire with the principles of the public peace. Despite the difficulties of converting legislative theory into executive practice, the Reich had been provided with a *raison d'être* more convincing to German opinion than its claims to world supremacy. It was partly for this reason that Frederick retained the loyalty of most of his German subjects during his last bitter struggle with the papacy for control in Italy. Despite the intrigues of successive popes and the election of two ineffective anti-kings, Henry Raspe, Landgrave of Thuringia (1246–47), and William, Count of Holland (1247–56), the Hohenstaufens were still the most formidable power in Germany when Frederick died in 1250. Only dynastic misfortune, less the death of Frederick himself than that of his son Conrad in Italy four years later, forced the German prelates and princes to accept the bleak prospect of a Reich without a generally accepted ruler. The extinction of the Hohenstaufen line was a genuine catastrophe, and not for the dynasty alone.

The Later Middle Ages 1250–1493

At the time of Frederick II's death in 1250, the political misfortunes and impending annihilation of the Hohenstaufen dynasty stood in marked contrast to the social and economic prosperity of their Reich. From at least the early twelfth century the gradually accelerating extension of arable agriculture at the expense of the forests and marshes of southern and western Germany had raised the living standards of the majority of landlords and led to the acquisition of a greater degree of personal freedom by most peasants. Although direct, as opposed to circumstantial, evidence of demographic growth in this period is almost completely lacking, it seems certain that a dramatic rise in the number of Germans provided the foundation for such expansion. The ability of western Germany to produce a surplus population able and willing to settle in the Slav lands across the Elbe was, in any case, the basis for perhaps the most sensational development in medieval German history, the colonization of the north-east. As early as 1108 the advantages of settlement in Slav territory had been well publicized: 'The country is excellent, rich in meat, honey, poultry and flour: therefore come you hither, Saxons and Franconians, men from Lorraine and Flanders, for here you can obtain the double advantage of deeds for the salvation of your souls and settlement on the best land.' But it was in the 150 years after the middle of the twelfth century that wave after wave of colonists swept across the river barriers to found innumerable new settlements in the economically backward areas of what is now eastern Germany. It has been estimated that in Silesia alone approximately 1,200 villages were founded between 1200 and 1350. Intensive competition for immigrant labour between both German and Slav landlords helped to secure the best possible conditions for the settlers – personal freedom, subjection to only a few days' labour services a year, the right to migrate from one village to another and a quite remarkable degree of independence from the workings of seigniorial justice. The initial impact of the colonists' technical skills and implements, particularly the iron felling axe and the heavy wheeled plough, was consolidated by systematic organization of agricultural practice and village life. Wherever conditions permitted (and of course regional variation was infinite) the settlers introduced three-course rotation of the best-quality corn crops within the context of a carefully planned and sited village in which the individual peasant holding or *Hufen* was normally the basic unit. A great increase of corn production had probably accompanied the colonizing movement from the start and became clearly apparent in the 1250s, a decade in which corn from Brandenburg and areas further east is known to have appeared on the Flemish and English markets. By this date Lübeck (founded in the reign of Conrad III) and Danzig (created by West German merchants a generation later) had already emerged as the two pivots of the profitable Baltic trade and enjoyed a commercial supremacy they retained throughout the later Middle Ages.

It seems very probable that it was during the middle years of the thirteenth century that most other medieval German towns attained their first maturity as economic and social units. In the wake of increased agricultural activity, the German cities had developed genuinely urban functions as well as a heightened sense of communal *esprit de corps* within the ranks of their more prosperous inhabitants. By 1250 the burgesses of the older towns had largely emancipated themselves from control by the agents of their episcopal overlords and established in their place civic officials responsible to a common council or *Stadtrat*. They were consequently able to resist absorption into the territory of the local prince and enjoyed a high degree of constitutional autonomy. How much political influence such burgesses exerted outside the walls of their towns was a more variable matter. Although the later Middle Ages are proverbially the golden age of the German cities, the latter did not dominate either the society or the political life of the Reich as a whole. By Italian or even Flemish standards, German towns although numerous (perhaps 3,000 in all) were relatively small: as late as 1474 the population of Leipzig was apparently less than 4,000 while Basle contained fewer than 10,000 inhabitants when it joined the Swiss Confederation in 1501. Only a dozen or so German urban centres ever exceeded this figure at any point in the later Middle Ages, the most notable examples being Cologne (always the largest German town, with a population fluctuating around 30,000), Lübeck and the South German cities of Nürnberg, Ulm and Augsburg. Nor did the German towns form a politically coherent group within the Reich. They fell into two main categories, partly overlaid by the legal distinction between 'imperial' and 'free' cities. The older towns along the Rhine (Constance, Basle, Strasbourg, Speyer, Worms, Mainz and Cologne), Danube

(Regensburg, Passau) and their tributaries were usually of Roman origin: in their struggle for independence they aspired to the status of *Reichsstädte*, partly on Schiller's principle that 'they want to have the emperor as their lord, wishing to have no lord at all'. Conditioned to adopt a positive attitude towards the policy and the personality of the German king, the patrician class which governed such cities was prepared – if only in times of crisis – to appreciate the advantages of mutual self-help. The foundation of the Rhenish league of towns (*Rheinischer Bund*) in 1254 established a precedent for the series of similar short-lived military alliances which characterized the political life of southern and western Germany in the later Middle Ages. Although these town leagues undoubtedly helped to prevent or delay the emergence of integrated territorial states in their vicinity, their role was essentially defensive and they had no new political solution to offer. The same was even more true of the newer German towns founded under princely patronage on the 'colonial' lands settled in the twelfth and thirteenth centuries. From Freiburg-im-Breisgau to Riga in the far north-east innumerable foundations of this type were made, but only when they attracted the business attentions of the German merchant or *locator* could they hope to develop into centres of commercial activity. The most famous example is the chain of towns stretching along the south coast of the Baltic from Lübeck to Reval which formed the breeding-ground of the famous Hanseatic League. But the North German Hanse towns, always dominated by Lübeck, the only *Reichsstadt* on the Baltic, deliberately and consistently refused to erect a coherent political organization upon the framework of their common economic interests. During the century which followed its triumph over Waldemar IV of Denmark at the peace of Stralsund in 1370, the Hanseatic League was the most formidable international power in the Baltic but failed to exert any sustained influence upon the internal affairs of Germany itself.

The rise of the German towns in the thirteenth century had therefore increased the social and cultural potentialities of the Reich at the cost of complicating rather than simplifying its political structure. In other ways too, economic expansion and the eastwards extension of the German frontier added new complexities to the age-old contradictions within the kingdom. Although western and southern Germany continued to be the centre of German political tradition and precedent, power itself had begun to gravitate towards the east. The rapid fragmentation of the Hohenstaufen demesnes in Swabia that followed

Frederick II's death ruined any prospect of a major principality in the west at exactly the time when the establishment of viable political principalities within the old Slav lands had become a practical possibility. The most dramatic development of all was the erection of an autonomous state in the extreme north-east by the knights of the Teutonic Order. Within a few years of being invited (in 1226) by the Polish duke Conrad of Masovia to settle in the district of Kulm, the Grand Master of the Teutonic Order, Hermann von Salza, had subjugated the whole region between the rivers Vistula and Memel. In 1237 the Order absorbed the Livonian territories of the Brothers of the Sword, a previous army of occupation founded at Riga in 1202 by its first bishop, Albert von Buxhoven, the last of the great conquering and missionary prelates of medieval Germany. Under its long succession of Grand Masters, settled at Marienburg from 1309, Prussia provided a unique example of a centrally administered state in which a large population of small landowners normally held their estates directly from the ruler. Although the other principalities along the new east German frontier were more conventional in being dominated by a powerful landed aristocracy, they too were both larger and more coherent than those in western Germany and so gave their princes an infinitely greater opportunity for successful financial exploitation. Thus in the north of Germany the Ascanian dynasty, descendants of Albert the Bear, the first margrave of Brandenburg, had gradually established their overlordship over a wide tract of territory stretching from the Altmark west of the Elbe to the Polish frontier well east of the Oder. By the middle of the fourteenth century the powers and prestige of the elector of Brandenburg had become one of the major prizes in dynastic politics, held by the Wittelsbachs from 1324, the Luxemburg family from 1373 and finally (after 1415) by the Hohenzollerns. Further south the expansionary activities around the middle Elbe of the Wettin margraves of Meissen resulted in their succession to the title of elector of Saxony (1423) and offered a similar target for the territorial aspirations of the princes of the Reich. The extension of German influence and interest in eastern Europe rapidly led to a situation in which not only Meissen-Thuringia and Brandenburg but the duchies of Austria, Styria and Silesia – and eventually the three great non-Germanic kingdoms of Poland, Bohemia and Hungary – attracted more covetous attention and strenuous effort on the part of the great dynasties than the royal crown itself.

In such circumstances the exact future of the German monarchy was inevitably an even more open question than in previous centuries. The extinction of the Hohenstaufens, the last royal dynasty fully committed to the ideal of imperial supremacy in Europe and the preservation of a dynastic connection with Italy, shifted emphasis away from the crown to the other wielders of political power north of the Alps. Henceforward the nearest German equivalent to the late medieval English, French or Aragonese kingdoms was not the Reich but the individual territorial principalities of which Austria, Bavaria, the new electorate of Saxony, the Palatinate, Brandenburg, Brunswick, Hesse and Württemberg, although all exposed to the constant possibility of family partition, eventually proved to be the most formidable. For this reason, and despite later Habsburg propaganda, the so-called 'Great Interregnum' of the empire (1254-73) which followed the death of Frederick II's twenty-six-year-old son, Conrad IV, made little practical difference to the well-being of the political classes of the Reich. At first sight the most obvious deduction to be drawn from the long and inconclusive contest between the two rival kings, Richard of Cornwall (1257-72) and Alfonso of Castile (1257-73), might seem to be that Germany could survive without a monarchy at all: Richard's precarious authority in the north-west was completely dependent upon the personal fortune he was able to bring with him on his four visits to the Rhineland, while Alfonso of Castile never came to Germany at all.

Yet both monarchy and empire did survive the interregnum, a period during which political centrifugalism made the German prelates and magnates gradually more rather than less interested in maintaining the consolatory ideal of a supra-territorial Reich. Such an ideal had to be personified in the form of a single ruler, but there was no *a priori* theoretical reason why the *Romanorum rex semper Augustus* (from the late eleventh to the sixteenth centuries the invariable title of the monarch between his German and Roman coronations) should need to be the most powerful German magnate or even a German-speaking prince at all. These reservations found expression in the immediate aftermath of the Hohenstaufen catastrophe when there emerged into the open an embryonic college of seven imperial electors (the three Rhenish archbishops of Mainz, Cologne and Trier; the Count Palatine of the Rhine; the Margrave of Brandenburg; the Duke of Saxony; and the Duke of Bavaria, later replaced by the King of Bohemia) specifically aimed at ensuring the continuity of the monarchical institution with the least possible risk of disturbance and civil war. In many ways the much maligned electoral princes of the later Middle

Ages handled their extremely difficult task surprisingly well; but they too were continuously subjected to the dynastic pressures which shaped German political life. Baldwin, Archbishop of Trier from 1307 to 1354, a prelate whose political skills dominated German public life during the first half of the fourteenth century, was the guiding genius behind the rise of the Luxemburg dynasty to which he himself belonged. In retrospect it seems obvious that the electors, and the aristocratic interests which they represented, wished to have the best of both worlds: they preserved the crown but not the resources through which that crown's authority could be at all effective in securing the civil peace they genuinely desired. Thanks to genealogical chance and the ever-changing balance of political power within Germany, they could delay, but in the last resort not prevent, the only practicable if unfortunate solution to the Reich's central constitutional problem – the emergence of a powerful and long-lived dynasty which would make the royal and imperial crown hereditary within its own house and subservient to its own sectional interests.

The coronation at Aachen on 24 October 1273 of Rudolf, Count of Habsburg, as king of the Romans should therefore be regarded as the event which heralded rather than achieved a new era in the history of the Reich. In Goethe's words: 'Of Charles the Great we had various legends; but the historically interesting began for us with Rudolf of Habsburg.' Certainly the unexpected success of a Hohenzollern, Frederick III, Burgrave of Nürnberg, in persuading the electors of 1273 to confer the royal title on the elderly and relatively unknown Count Rudolf was the turning-point in the history of the Habsburg dynasty itself. During the preceding two centuries the descendants of the Alsatian bishop Werner of Strasbourg, who built the Habichtsburg ('the castle of the hawk') on the right bank of the Aare early in the eleventh century, had slowly and erratically established their power in Alsace, the Aargau and central Switzerland. But nothing in the early history of the dynasty prepared contemporaries for the extraordinary skill and ruthlessness with which Count Rudolf IV, who succeeded his father as head of the senior Habsburg line in 1240, satisfied his enormous appetite for territorial acquisition. 'Lord God, sit tight in heaven', remarked the Bishop of Basle in 1273 on receiving the news of the election to the German kingship, 'or this Rudolf will usurp your seat.' The electors themselves were soon to be startled and dismayed at the skill with which Rudolf exploited the resources of the kingdom in the interests of his family. The new king's greatest achievement was un-

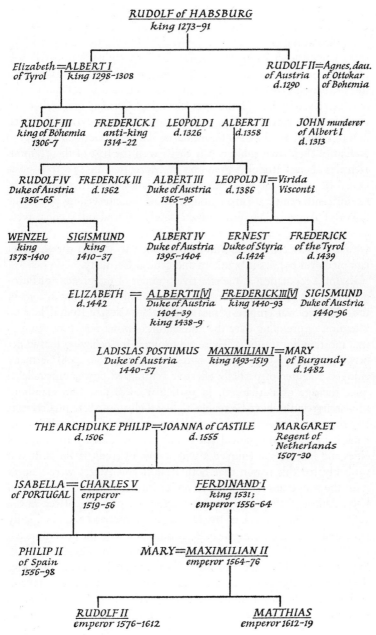

RUDOLF of HABSBURG
king 1273–91

Elizabeth=ALBERT I
of Tyrol *king 1298–1308*

RUDOLF II=Agnes, dau.
of Austria of Ottokar
d.1290   of Bohemia

RUDOLF III
king of Bohemia
1306–7

FREDERICK I
anti-king
1314–22

LEOPOLD I
d.1326

ALBERT II
d.1358

JOHN *murderer*
of Albert I
d.1313

RUDOLF IV
Duke of Austria
1356–65

FREDERICK III
d.1362

ALBERT III
Duke of Austria
1365–95

LEOPOLD II=Virida
d.1386   Visconti

WENZEL
king
1378–1400

SIGISMUND
king
1410–37

ALBERT IV
Duke of Austria
1395–1404

ERNEST
Duke of Styria
d.1424

FREDERICK
of the Tyrol
d.1439

ELIZABETH = ALBERT II [V]
d.1442   *Duke of Austria*
1404–39
king 1438–9

FREDERICK III [V]
king 1440–93

SIGISMUND
Duke of Austria
1440–96

LADISLAS POSTUMUS
Duke of Austria
1440–57

MAXIMILIAN I=MARY
king 1493–1519   of Burgundy
d.1482

THE ARCHDUKE PHILIP=JOANNA of CASTILE
d.1506   *d.1555*

MARGARET
Regent of
Netherlands
1507–30

ISABELLA=CHARLES V
of PORTUGAL *emperor*
1519–56

FERDINAND I
king 1531;
emperor 1556–64

PHILIP II
of Spain
1556–98

MARY=MAXIMILIAN II
emperor 1564–76

RUDOLF II
emperor 1576–1612

MATTHIAS
emperor 1612–19

TABLE III The Habsburg Dynasty

doubtedly his relentless campaign against Ottokar, the Slav king of Bohemia and ruler of Austria, Styria, Carinthia and Carniola. Ottokar was killed at the great battle of the Marchfeld (August 1278) and four years later Rudolf formally invested his sons with the imperial fiefs of Austria, Styria and Carniola. Habsburg lordship of Austria, which survived until November 1918, was henceforward to remain one of the few fixed points in the ever-changing German political scene. However, the partition of their dominions between various co-heirs, family dissension and the opposition of the other German princes as well as of their own subjects (the Swiss won the first of their famous victories against Rudolf's grandson at Morgarten in 1315) all post-poned the rise of the Habsburgs to ascendancy in Germany until the late fifteenth century. Throughout most of the intervening period the dukes of Austria, their power increasingly centred on Vienna, were at least potentially the most formidable of German dynasties, a family whose very existence and ambitions tended to dictate the shape of late medieval politics in southern and central Germany.

Rudolf's reputation as the effective founder of the greatest of Euro-pean dynasties is therefore beyond question: his role in the history of the late medieval empire is more debatable. Clearly Rudolf had no intention of presiding over the liquidation of what may now seem to us a moribund institution. There are grounds for believing that under his kingship (1273–91) and that of his son Albert I (1298–1308) Germany enjoyed a degree of partially effective centralized power unparalleled since the age of Barbarossa. In particular these first two Habsburg monarchs seem to have been able, unlike their immediate predecessors and successors, to exploit their rule over the Reich in financial terms. Rudolf increased the annual tax (*stura*) paid to him by the imperial cities and like his son enjoyed a wide range of credit facilities. It was probably for this reason that both Rudolf and Albert were able to resist the dangerous temptation to revive imperial interests in northern Italy. Although they paid the inevitable price of being placed in the valley of negligent rulers by Dante, both monarchs undoubtedly benefited from this indifference. By comparison with the governmental revolutions carried out by their western contemporaries Edward I of England and Philip the Fair of France, the achievements of Kings Rudolf and Albert may seem miserably inadequate; but it is difficult to believe that they could have done much more. Both monarchs realized that the future of royal authority in Germany lay in the establishment of hereditary succession to the throne. Despite desperate attempts to secure the electors' consent to make the empire *de facto* if not *de jure* hereditary in their own house, the early Habsburgs failed in this critical objective. The 'poor count' Adolf of Nassau (1292–8), Henry VII of Luxemburg (1308–13) and the Wittelsbach Louis IV of Bavaria (1314–47) were all elected to prevent Habsburg candidates from securing permanent control over the empire. This was the issue which dominated internal German politics from the accession of Rudolf I in 1273 until the battle of Mühldorf in 1322 when Louis the Bavarian finally captured his rival Frederick of Austria, Rudolf's grandson.

Where the Habsburgs had failed it was hardly likely that their competitors could succeed. Although able and ambitious kings, Adolf of Nassau, Henry of Luxemburg and Louis the Bavarian were trapped by the circumstances of their election and their own poverty. They had no choice but to act as stepfathers to the empire, for the simple reason that only by the exploitation of the crown's powers in the interests of their dynastic power, their *Hausmacht*, could they hope to survive at all. According to one contemporary chronicler, there was barely eleven pounds in the chamber of Louis the Bavarian when he set forth on the critical Mühldorf campaign. Financial pressures and the need to find a justification for the empire in the post-Hohenstaufen world urged the early fourteenth-century kings into adopting aggressive attitudes which they lacked the resources to maintain. Henry of Luxemburg's flamboyant attempt to revive imperial power in Italy came to a sudden end when he died of malaria (1313) in the year after his coronation as king of the Lombards in Milan and emperor in Rome. The prospects of financial gain, particularly by the conferment of imperial vicariates on local Italian *signoria*, also tempted Louis the Bavarian to undertake the *Romerzug* in 1327–9. Although most famous as the last of the great contests between empire and papacy, Louis's failure to profit from this Italian venture was due less to the antagonism of the Holy See (resident at Avignon from 1309 to 1377) than the weaknesses of his own position in Germany. The small but expensive force of 4,000 hired retainers which Louis led to Rome stood in sharp and feeble contrast to the levies once raised by the Hohenstaufens on similar occasions. Louis wisely withdrew and a few years later made an anti-French alliance with Edward III of England (itself foreshadowed by Adolf of Nassau's relationship with Edward I between 1294 and 1298) which allowed the German king to pose as a champion of his people against the aggressive activities of the French monarchy in western

Germany while enjoying the benefits of an English pension. It was at the height of a wave of anti-French feeling in 1338 that six of the German electors met at Rense on the Rhine and declared that any prince who had been duly elected king held his dignity directly from God and should be free to exercise his imperial functions without the need for any further ceremony or confirmation. Although the Declaration of Rense protected the German monarch from future papal interference, its other result was to weaken his position by enhancing the already extensive corporate powers of the princes. Eight years later, and again at Rense, Charles of Moravia, Henry VII's grandson, was formally elected king of the Romans by five of the seven electors. After the death of Louis the Bavarian while hunting near Munich in the autumn of 1347, Luxemburg succeeded Wittelsbach as ruler of the Reich.

According to the Emperor Maximilian, Germany never suffered a more 'pernicious plague' (*pestilentior pestis*) than the long and apparently successful reign of Charles IV (1346–78). Although such criticism from a Habsburg is not without its irony, it is easy to appreciate the grounds for Maximilian's complaint. The scintillating careers of successive members of the Luxemburg family between Henry VII's election as king of the Romans in 1308 and the Emperor Sigismund's death without children in 1437 provides the extreme case of the exploitation of surviving royal prerogatives within Germany in the interests of dynastic ambition. Not surprisingly, the Luxemburg king Charles IV and his sons Wenzel and Sigismund are among the most controversial rulers in the history of the German monarchy. Despite several recent attempts to portray Charles IV as an altruistic statesman whose 'legalization of anarchy' was the recognition of necessity, it is hard to avoid the conclusion that he was more than usually detached from the problems of his German-speaking subjects and indeed from the problems of the Reich itself. Charles, born and christened Wenzel at Prague in 1316, was himself the eldest son of John of Luxemburg, whose primary loyalties were always to the court of France, and Elizabeth, heiress of the native Czech kings of Bohemia. Throughout the long period during which the Luxemburgs ruled Bohemia, that kingdom inevitably attracted most of their attention. Charles's own affection for his birthplace redeems the otherwise arid pages of the autobiography of his early years: on his return there in 1333 as his father's representative he had 'found that kingdom desolate, not a castle free that was not pledged, so I had nowhere to lodge except in houses in cities like any other citizen'. The remainder of Charles IV's life was primarily devoted to the establishment of a strong Bohemian state. At Prague itself, and under strong French influence, the king built a new and largely Czech-inhabited quarter of the city as well as the famous Charles Bridge and the neighbouring castle of Karlstein: the cathedral of St Vitus was rebuilt by French masons in Gothic splendours appropriate to the new metropolitan status it acquired after its severance from the see of Mainz in 1344. Charles's rapid success in developing a cultural and social capital at Prague had an incalculable effect in stimulating the rulers of other central European principalities to do likewise: Prague university, for example, the first university founded north of the Alps and east of the Rhine (1348), was quickly imitated in Poland (Cracow, 1364) and Austria (Vienna, 1365). Much more transitory was Charles IV's achievement in increasing the geographical extent of Luxemburg territorial possessions. Thanks to his own matrimonial good fortune (he had four wives) and the family difficulties of his Wittelsbach and Habsburg rivals, he was able to add to his inherited lands (Luxemburg, Bohemia, Moravia and Görlitz) part of the Upper Palatinate, the margraveship of Lusatia, the duchy of Silesia, the electorate of Brandenburg and even the prospect of a reversionary interest to the whole of the Habsburg territories. No dynasty in the history of medieval Germany was potentially more formidable than the Luxemburgs in the 1370s. Yet Charles's deliberate and systematic partitioning of his inheritance between his closest relatives shortly before he died in 1378 proves that in the last resort he too was incapable of rising above the patrimonial policies of his age.

Charles IV's attitude towards his position as king and emperor was equally traditional. Far from being a revolutionary document, the famous Golden Bull, enacted before the princes of the realm at Nürnberg in January 1356, was essentially a conservative measure. Its detailed regulations for the conduct of future elections to the monarchy by the seven electoral princes were securely based on the generally accepted conventions of the previous two generations. The most radical or idealistic clauses of the Bull, like that requiring a knowledge of Latin, Italian and Slavonic on the part of the lay electors and another proposing regular annual meetings between king and electors, were never observed in practice. Much of the Golden Bull was already at odds with political reality in 1356; in particular the electoral preponderance accorded to the lay and ecclesiastical princes of the Rhineland fossilized past history. But perhaps the astonishing success of the Golden Bull in providing generally accepted rules for the continuity of the Reich until 1806 was due to its very anomalies. It made a powerful and emotional appeal for the preservation of an imperial and electoral mystique while being sufficiently imprecise to allow the operations of dynastic intrigue within the framework of the electoral procedure it formalized. Certainly the Golden Bull did not prevent Charles IV himself from having his eldest son Wenzel elected king during his own lifetime. In other ways too Charles showed himself adroit at manipulating traditional royal privileges to his own family interest. Committed to the ideal of co-operation with the papacy, Charles led two peaceful expeditions into Italy (1354–5; 1368–9), from both of which he returned with considerable profit as well as prestige. Within Germany itself, the emperor's readiness to sacrifice regalian rights for financial rewards which he then used to extend his hereditary dominions aroused the opposition of the *Reichsstädte*, many of whom feared permanent mediatization to a local lord. Charles's real order of priorities emerged most blatantly in 1373 when he bought the succession to the Brandenburg electorate for some 500,000 florins, an enormous sum raised at the expense of the imperial cities, which he taxed and pledged more ruthlessly than any of his predecessors.

The extent to which Charles IV's ascendancy in the Reich had been a personal *tour de force*, dependent on stable political conditions within Europe, became clearly apparent during the reign of his eldest son Wenzel (1378–1400). The latter had the misfortune to succeed his father within a few weeks of the outbreak of the Great Schism in the papacy, whose disruptive effects both within and without Germany he proved unable to arrest. Personally disinclined to make extensive travels across the territories of the Reich in the manner of his father (who even visited Lübeck in 1375), Wenzel attempted to delegate the responsibility of maintaining public peace within the Reich to a series of leagues: paradoxically these constitutional experiments, although a good deal more realistic than the Golden Bull, had the unfortunate effect of publicly exposing the antagonisms (between west and east, towns and princes) always latent within German society. However it was the erosion of Wenzel's influence and resources within Bohemia itself that formed the essential prelude to his fall. After a long series of violent quarrels with the Bohemian clergy and nobility, led by his younger brother Sigismund and his cousin Jobst, Margrave of Moravia and Elector of Brandenburg, Wenzel was deposed by the Rhenish electors at Rense in August 1400 on the specific grounds that he had neglected the *Landfrieden* and failed to resolve the schism. By any standards the subsequent election of Rupert, Count Palatine of the Rhine, was an anachronistic and futile gesture, soon regretted by his Rhenish electors themselves. Politically and financially bankrupt for most of his ten-year reign, Rupert died in 1410 and the throne reverted to the house of Luxemburg. Family dissension in the east and political chaos in the west led to a disputed election and the appearance of no less than three Luxemburg competitors for the crown. Wenzel's increasing inertia – he lived on until 1419 – and Jobst of Moravia's providential death in 1411 ensured the triumph of Sigismund, the last Luxemburg king of the Romans (1410–37) and emperor after 1433.

During the generation which separated Sigismund's succession to the throne from his father's death in 1378 the powers of the monarchy had become increasingly irrelevant to the main tendencies of German political life. This decline was not unnoticed by contemporaries, who from the first decade of the fifteenth century increasingly lamented the fact that (in the words of a Heidelberg professor in 1408) 'Every nobleman, however modest his standing, is king in his own territory; every city exercises royal power within its own walls'. In an increasingly literate and articulate society, the paradoxes within the Reich's political structure were henceforward the subject for melancholy prognostication or over-ingenious plans for reform, not least in Sigismund's own circle. Sigismund was himself fully conscious of the weaknesses of his position in Germany even if these were at first disguised by his personal energy and charm, his prestige as king of Hungary from 1387 to 1437, and his role in summoning the Council of Constance and helping to end the papal schism. Above all the threat of social as well as religious sedition presented by the Hussite movement, although it delayed Sigismund's recognition as king of Bohemia until the year before his death, united the conservative forces within Germany, both princes and towns, in defence of a very vulnerable *status quo*. Nevertheless the inability of successive German expeditions to crush Czech religious and political separatism demonstrated, like nothing in the previous history of the Reich, the gulf that now existed between the king and his nominal kingdom. During their monarch's frequent absences, the electoral princes arrogated regalian power to themselves and arranged special meetings or *Kurvereine*, thus laying bare the political duality which now lay beneath the formal constitution of the Reich. Sigismund was compelled to acknowledge that 'the electors were themselves the law' and it is doubtful whether he exercised any real control at all outside his hereditary lands during the last years of his life. Like his successors, Sigismund did, however, retain the ability to dispose of imperial fiefs as he wished: none of his actions in Germany had a more permanent effect than his investiture of his ally, Frederick of Hohenzollern, Burgrave of Nürnberg, with the electorate of Brandenburg in 1415 and his conferment of the dignity of elector of Saxony upon the Wettin margrave of Meissen. By contrast with Hohenzollern and Wettin dynastic good fortune, Sigismund's own vast family inheritance barely survived his own death in 1437: as he was without sons he left his dominions – Luxemburg, Bohemia, Moravia, Silesia and Hungary – to his Habsburg son-in-law, Albert of Austria, who died in 1439 after a reign of less than two years.

The replacement of the Luxemburg by the Habsburg dynasty as nominal lords of the Reich was generally welcomed by all sections of public opinion in Germany, inevitably unaware of its far-reaching consequences. Albert II himself died of dysentery acquired while leading a small Hungarian army against the Turks, an event symbolic of the growing conviction that the German monarch's primary obligation should henceforward be the defence of his kingdom against Ottoman aggression even at the expense of his role in preserving the peace within Germany itself. This was the motive predominant in the minds of the electors when they chose Frederick of Styria, the eldest Habsburg prince, as king of the Romans in 1440. In the event, they received the worst of both possible solutions. Throughout his long reign of fifty-three years Frederick III failed to preserve stability on Germany's eastern frontier, where the three kingdoms of Bohemia, Hungary and Poland reacted violently away from German influence. By comparison with his rivals, George Podiebrad of Bohemia (1458–71), Matthias Corvinus of Hungary (1458–90) and, above all, Casimir IV of Poland (1447–92), Frederick was little more than a petty princeling: in 1485 he was expelled by Corvinus from Vienna itself and compelled to wander poverty-stricken through southern Germany. The humiliation was all the more galling in that Frederick had deliberately withdrawn himself from the affairs of the Reich: after an initial period in which he allowed himself to be guided by his experienced chancellor, Kaspar Schlick, Frederick abandoned Germany in 1444 and was not seen there again for twenty-seven years. For Philippe de Commynes, Frederick III was 'the most niggardly man that ever lived', a famous comment which points to the fundamental reason for the emperor's failure to do more than survive. Frederick was almost continuously in serious debt – to such an extent that in 1473 he found it difficult to leave the city of

Augsburg because of his debts to the local tradesmen there. Contemporaries noted that his 1452 expedition to Italy – Frederick was the last emperor to be crowned in Rome – was blatantly conducted as a business enterprise. Never had imperial ideal and reality been so at odds with one another, and even Frederick's closest political ally, the Elector of Brandenburg, joined with his colleagues in 1461 to assert that the Reich 'has not been provided with proper institutions as would be necessary, no general peace has been kept, and the courts and law are in disarray'. Paradoxically Frederick's indifference to the problem of actually exercising rule within his empire made him more rather than less determined not to surrender any of his regalian rights. The possibility of a much-debated imperial reform by which monarchical theory might be assimilated to federal practice was consequently postponed until after Frederick's death in 1493, by which time the consolidation of the German territorial principalities as autonomous units in their own right had progressed so far that constitutional reform of the Reich proved almost impossible. There are notoriously many lost opportunities in the history of Germany; but the opportunities lost during the reign of Frederick III were perhaps the greatest of them all.

Political Diversity and Religious Reform 1493–1608

The 'Holy Roman Empire of the German nation' to which Maximilian I quietly succeeded on the death of his father in 1493 was a Reich under territorial pressure. Germany's long and almost unique immunity from external aggression, an immunity which had done so much to condition its political development during the previous five centuries, showed obvious signs of coming to an end. To the east German influence was in manifest retreat. Since their defeat by the Poles at the battle of Tannenberg (1410) the possessions of the Teutonic Knights had been rapidly eroded; in 1466 they were compelled to accept a position of feudal dependence on Poland, to whose king they surrendered the whole of West Prussia including Danzig. At the other end of the Baltic the Estates of Holstein accepted the rule of the Danish king (1460). Much more complicated was the process by which the Valois kings of France and more especially the Valois dukes of Burgundy had gradually advanced their authority east of the Meuse and Rhône. The disintegration of the Burgundian 'state' on the death of its last duke, Charles the Bold, in 1477 benefited the French monarchy rather than the Reich. Above all it benefited the Habsburg dynasty itself: the marriage in 1479

Germany at the Tin

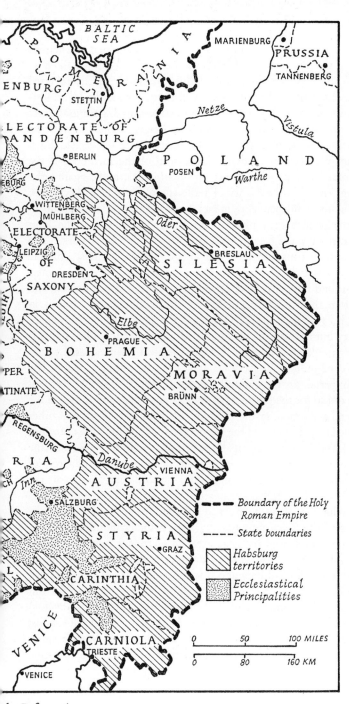

the Reformation.

of Maximilian to Mary of Burgundy, Charles's daughter and heiress, established the future emperor and his successors for centuries to come as the main residuary legatees of Valois Burgundy. Henceforward their possession of the Low Countries provinces made the Habsburgs the paramount power in Germany; but there was no disguising the fact that the inhabitants of the Netherlands no longer retained any strong sense of loyalty or obligation to the purposes of the Reich. Such alienation was even more dramatically true of the members of the Swiss Confederation, whose long and confused struggle against the Habsburgs ended in the Treaty of Basle (1499) by which Maximilian recognized their independence in fact if not in theory. For Maximilian himself the greatest if still most distant danger was inevitably the 'long shadow cast over the face of the earth' by the Ottoman Turks. The most important consequence of the Turks' capture of Constantinople in 1453 was that it allowed the Ottoman Sultans to organize their empire around a fixed capital. During the years which followed, and long before their shattering defeat at the battle of the Mohacs in 1526, it became increasingly clear that the Hungarians alone could only delay but not halt the inexorable Moslem advance. The German-speaking population of central Europe was now itself exposed to the likelihood of military aggression; and when Maximilian proposed a general imperial tax, the Common penny, at the Worms Reichstag of 1495, he did so for the purpose of 'maintaining peace and justice in the empire and withstanding the enemies of Christ, the Turks and other foes of the Holy Empire and the German nation'. Neither the notorious failure of the German principalities to unite their forces against the Turks, nor the fact that in the event Habsburg Vienna became a frontier rather than a conquered town, should conceal the reality of the danger.

This reduction of authority and influence along and outside the perimeter of the Reich undoubtedly reflects the economic and social contraction experienced by large areas of Germany towards the end of the Middle Ages. The agricultural expansion of the twelfth and thirteenth centuries had long ago reached its limits and been followed by a period of serious recession. The most startling evidence for this decline is the large number of 'lost' or deserted villages (*Wustungen*) which stretched in a broad band from Alsace and Württemberg east across Hesse, Thuringia and the Harz mountains to Mecklenburg, Pomerania and East Prussia. Although depopulation was most startling in the new colonial lands of eastern Germany (240 of the known 363

Wendish villages in Anhalt disappeared during the two centuries after 1300), it was not confined there. The Black Forest and Austrian Alps were more densely peopled in 1300 than in 1600 or indeed even today. There can be no doubt that this decrease in the acreage of land under the plough – sometimes estimated at 25 per cent for late medieval Germany as a whole – was closely linked to an absolute fall in the total German population. Much more controversial is the exact chronology of this demographic decline. As early as 1337 the *Landbuch* of the district of the New Mark in eastern Brandenburg contained the names of eighty completely deserted villages. The first outbreak of the bubonic plague or Black Death which swept through most of Germany (although apparently not Bohemia) during the summers of 1348, 1349 and 1350 therefore accelerated tendencies already at work rather than inaugurated a completely new era of economic contraction. Moreover it seems likely that in most parts of Germany the agrarian crisis was past its worst by the end of the fifteenth century: after that date indications of recovery and renewed prosperity become increasingly frequent. Nevertheless the agricultural depression had un-undoubtedly transformed the German social scene, sometimes out of recognition. The large numbers of small and medium-sized towns whose fortunes depended directly on the marketing functions they provided for the surrounding hinterlands had found it extremely difficult to retain their political independence once their prosperity declined; the most famous example is the successful campaign waged by the fifteenth-century Hohenzollern electors to deprive the Brandenburg towns of their urban self-government. Even more significant for the future was the impact of the economic recession on the farming policy of land-lords in eastern Germany. Both before and (more obviously) after 1500 the latter gradually increased the size of their demesnes, at first com-pelled and later preferring to rely on the profits of corn exporting rather than money rents from tenant land; their subsequent demands for heavy labour services led by a series of logical steps to the intro-duction of serfdom and the subjugation of a previously tenurially free peasantry. In western and southern Germany, however, as in con-temporary England, the agrarian depression eventually weakened seigniorial ties and often furthered the cause of personal freedom. The sporadic rising of German peasants in the Black Forest, Württemberg, the Tyrol and western Saxony during the sixty years before the Peasants' War of 1524–5 remain extremely mysterious phenomena; but they should certainly be interpreted as the work of farmers (*Bauern*) fully conscious of their legal rights rather than as a movement rooted in social despair. Otherwise few convincing generalizations seem possible. The Germany of 1500 was more economically diversified than ever before, and certain areas, notably those engaged in silver mining, were enjoying veritable boom conditions. In 1523 Charles V estimated the number of people engaged in mining and metallurgy throughout his empire at about 100,000. Mining concessions from the Habsburgs lay behind the wealth of the Augsburg banking houses: although neither as original nor as securely based as those of the Italian merchants they are sometimes alleged to have replaced, the financial operations of the Fuggers were already legendary by the year of Maximilian's death in 1519.

To contemporary observers, however, it was the political rather than economic divisions within the Reich which distinguished Germany from the rest of Europe. In Machiavelli's words: 'Of the power of Germany none can doubt, for it abounds in men, riches and arms ... but it is such as cannot be used.' From Maximilian's reign to the outbreak of the Thirty Years War the territorial map of Germany presented a kaleidoscopic mosaic of perhaps 300 semi-autonomous principalities. After the imperial diet or Reichstag had been reorganized at the end of the fifteenth century it was assumed that it should represent about 30 lay princes, 140 counts and lords, 120 prelates and 85 cities as well as the emperor and the other six electors. All in all the most remarkable feature of German political history in the sixteenth century was the survival and indeed strengthening of these internal divisions. The fortunes of a particular principality still depended directly on the dynastic ambitions and ability of its ruler; and no greater disaster could befall a territory than a succession dispute, a long minority or the death of its prince without an obvious heir. The governmental consolidation of individual German territories was therefore a gradual and erratic process, certainly not complete in Maximilian's reign although by that time already under way. Like the Reich itself, each territorial principality was normally the prey to a wide variety of entrenched and vested interests; and the most successful ruler was likely to be the prince who co-operated with these interests rather than he who tried to subjugate his subjects by force and acts of arbitrary will. The normal instrument for such co-operation was the Landtag, a central assembly of representatives from the most important estates within the principality. The estates of late fifteenth- and sixteenth-century Germany, like the parliamentary commons in England, were of especial value to the ruler as instruments for securing assent to taxa-tion. In some cases they were able to halt the advance of princely authority and even take decisive political initiatives on their own account: a celebrated, but quite exceptional, instance is that of the estates of Württemberg which in 1498 carried through a revolution by deposing their duke for his alleged bad governance. Elsewhere, however, the estates usually remained instruments of princely govern-ment rather than platforms for political opposition: on balance, and despite inevitable struggles with their ruler over financial matters, they helped to promote rather than delay the movement towards greater territorial cohesion within the principality. The same trend was furthered by such developments as the creation of a supreme law court, the gradual extension of effective governmental supervision over local administration, and increasing control – long before the Reforma-tion – over the Church. By 1500 the emergence of a class of professional bureaucrats, now often trained in Roman law and ready to advance their careers by moving from one principality to another, reflected the new situation. So too did the dramatic growth of the number of German universities. On the model of Charles IV's foundation at Prague, every ambitious lay prince began to contemplate the establish-ment of a university which would have the dual advantage of en-hancing his own prestige and ensuring a supply of educated adminis-trators: by the eve of the Reformation there were almost twenty uni-versities east of the Rhine, perhaps the most notable being Vienna (1365) which served the Habsburg dominions in the south-east, Heidelberg (1386) in the Palatinate, Leipzig (1409) in Meissen, Tübingen (1477) in Württemberg, Erfurt (1379) in central Germany, and Wittenberg (1502) in the electorate of Saxony. By comparison with the older univer-sities of Italy, France and England, those in later medieval Germany were controlled by a privileged élite of endowed professors who co-operated with the local secular authorities and so reflected the political regionalism of the Reich. Luther owed his life to the fact that, whatever his personal feelings towards his most famous subject (they never met), the Elector Frederick the Wise of Saxony was not prepared to sacrifice the most distinguished professor of his own university of Wittenberg. In the last resort the prince's determination to maintain his affinity and look after his own was perhaps the single biggest obstacle to a greater degree of unity within the Reich.

The paradox of Maximilian I's reign (1493–1519) was that this steadily continuing fragmentation of the Reich into more autonomous and self-sufficient principalities was accompanied by an increasing dis-inclination to accept the inevitable. Old problems were given a new dimension by an outspoken stream of critical comment. For many reasons – of which the most obvious are the extension of literacy and the impact of the printing press after John Gutenberg of Mainz pro-duced the first book printed with movable type in about 1455 – the protagonists within the German scene became increasingly articulate. Thus the effect of the Italian Renaissance on scholars and artists north of the Alps was to make them more rather than less conscious of their national distinctiveness. The first attempt to write a history of Germany, the *Epitome Rerum Germanicarum* by Jacob Wimpheling (1450–1528), is among the most chauvinistic books ever written; and in his 'Martyrdom of the Ten Thousand Christians', commissioned by the Elector Frederick the Wise in 1508, Dürer – not long returned from Italy – portrays himself proudly carrying a banner with the words 'Albertus Dürer alemanus'. Contemporaries shared the young Goethe's later view that the early sixteenth century was the first period in which 'Germany could take pride in having a native art of her own'. They were also impressed by the new style and panache with which Maximilian publicized what were essentially traditional dynastic policies. In his eloquent attempts to persuade the Reichstag and the leading princes of the need for a strong monarchy, free to impose common taxation and maintain a standing army, Maximilian deliberately courted patriotic and anti-French sentiment within Germany. So too did his constitutional opponents who were understandably nervous of Habs-burg *Hausmacht* and put forward an alternative programme of im-perial reform based on the principles of aristocratic federalism. The leader of opposition to Maximilian was Berthold of Henneberg, Archbishop of Mainz and chairman of the electoral college, perhaps the only prince in the history of the Reich who had an absolutely clear conception of how its constitution might be radically remodelled. For Berthold it was as imperative to protect the empire against the territorial ambitions of its ruler as those of its leading subjects. He therefore planned to establish a series of bureaucratic departments of state, including a permanent executive council (the *Reichsregiment*) and an independent high court of justice or *Reichskammergericht*, in which the electors would take the lead as councillors of the crown. Between the Diets of Worms (1495) and Augsburg (1500) this political reform movement was at its zenith, and some of Berthold's institutional reforms survived until the extinction of the Holy Roman Empire in

1806. At a more fundamental level, however, the reforming programmes of both the electors and Maximilian were foredoomed to failure. The most formidable German princes, like the Hohenzollern electors of Brandenburg, the Wittelsbach dukes of Bavaria and the Wettin dukes and electors of Saxony, had already passed the point at which they would accept the amount of central control envisaged by either Berthold or the emperor. Nothing reveals the bankruptcy of imperial reform more clearly than the squalid manœuvres which preceded the election (June 1519) of Maximilian's grandson as his successor. The accession of Charles V, heir to Aragon and Castile as well as the Burgundian dominions, marks both the greatest triumph of Habsburg diplomacy and the failure of the Reich to emancipate itself from its medieval past.

According to his chancellor Gattinara, Charles's coronation at Aachen in October 1520 'has set you on the way towards a world monarchy, towards the uniting of all Christendom under a single head'. Three years earlier Martin Luther had fastened his famous ninety-five theses to the door of the castle chapel at Wittenberg; and the reign of Charles V (1519–56) is inevitably remembered as a period decisive not for the restoration but the permanent collapse of religious unity within the Reich. It must never be forgotten that the Reformation in Germany began as an academic heresy and that Luther's theological revolt had intellectual roots quite independent of his own emotional difficulties and the social tensions of his age. The very fact that Luther was not a representative German figure made the impact of his remarkable mind and energy all the more startling and incalculable. On the other hand the almost instantaneous success with which he catalysed so many aspirations and frustrations within the Reich caused him to become a German hero long before his evolution as a religious leader was complete. 'We Germans cannot attend St Peter's. Better that it should never be built than that our parish churches should be despoiled' was the defiant note sounded by the 1519 *Theses*; it struck an immediate response from contemporaries as distinguished and as different from each other as Albrecht Dürer and Ulrich von Hutten, imperial knight (*Reichsritter*), poet and political visionary. Obviously Luther owed much of his appeal as well as his own intellectual buoyancy to the skill with which he applied the new techniques of humanist scholarship to the traditional obsessions of German religious life in the preceding century. He addressed an audience long accustomed to the *devotio moderna* and the belief that it was more essential to cultivate the still small voice of individual conscience than listen to the official pronouncements of the Church. Similarly Luther's doctrine of the priesthood of all true believers, already formulated by 1520, was to some extent foreshadowed by the fifteenth-century popularity of *The Imitation of Christ*, that guide and manual to an intensely personal devotion. Like his famous contemporary, Erasmus of Rotterdam, Luther exploited the latest methods of communication and reached an even wider audience: he published at the rate of about a piece a fortnight throughout most of his career. It was in his two famous works of 1520, *The Babylonish Captivity of the Church* and *The Liberty of a Christian Man*, both printed in German, that Luther demolished the need for the whole external apparatus of the Church. His translated Bible, of which the first edition of the New Testament appeared in 1522 and a completed edition of the whole in 1534, was the first version in German from an original text. Luther was triumphantly successful in his self-confessed endeavour 'to make Moses so German that no one would suspect he was a Jew'. His Bible rapidly became the central document in the evolution of German language and literature as well as the single greatest spiritual and intellectual influence on the progress of the Lutheran Reformation.

Luther's amazing success in persuading an astonishingly large section of the German population to break with the ideals and institutions of the Roman Church can never be altogether easy to explain. From the outset political factors – the fragmentation of ecclesiastical as well as secular authority within Germany, the protection afforded Luther by the Elector of Saxony, the accession of an inexperienced if well-meaning emperor distracted by his struggles with the Valois and the Turks – played their part. Luther himself was under no illusions as to the importance of support by the princes: as early as 1520 his *Address to the Christian Nobility of the German Nation* (*An den Christlichen Adel deutscher Nation*) announced the alliance between 'throne and altar' which was to dictate the future course of the German Reformation. The political anomalies within the Reich gave Charles V full legal authority to put Luther under the imperial ban after his appearance at the Diet of Worms in 1521 but then deprived the emperor of the sanctions necessary to apply the spiritual and temporal swords in practice. The result was inevitable: Luther, his fellow professor Melanchthon and their allies in Wittenberg were compelled to organize an alternative Church order. Within a few months of the death of Frederick the Wise (1525) and his replacement by the more amenable

Elector John, the Lutheran Church of Saxony provided a sophisticated and efficient model for the German state Churches of the future. The willingness of other princes to follow this lead was greatly encouraged by their knowledge that the ensuing dissolution of monasteries and secularization of church property would add to their own material profit. At the same time the speedy and savage suppression of the Peasants' War of 1524–5 and the annihilation of Thomas Müntzer's radical theocracy in Thuringia convinced the lay aristocracy – quite correctly – that religious reformation could be separated from political sedition. By 1525 Luther, who went on record with his own hostility *Against the murdering, thieving hordes of the peasants*, had almost become a respectable figure. In that year Albrecht von Hohenzollern, Grand Master of the Teutonic Knights, dissolved his order, secularized its lords and became the first German duke of Prussia. A few months later the able if unpredictable Landgrave Philip of Hesse officially adopted Lutheran forms of Christian worship, soon to be followed by the Duke of Schleswig and Brunswick, the Margrave of Brandenburg-Ansbach and the Count of Mansfield. It is easy but dangerous to be too cynical at the expense of the opportunism which underlay some of these princely conversions; for territorial rulers were undoubtedly under considerable pressure to make radical religious reforms from the most articulate and intelligent of their subjects. Despite the catastrophes of 1524–5 the German Reformation remained a genuinely fervent popular, and especially bourgeois, movement for many years to come. Within Luther's own lifetime virtually all the major German cities except Cologne, Munich and Regensburg succumbed to Lutheran influence. At no time of course did the leaders of religious change consider that they had opted out of the political structure of the Reich: the famous Confession of Augsburg presented to Charles V in the summer of 1530 was prepared by Melanchthon on behalf of the northern Protestant princes in an attempt to secure doctrinal reconciliation within Germany. However, the failure of so studiously moderate a document to receive anything but criticism from the Catholic theologians at Augsburg revealed the extent of religious differences: in Luther's words to Melanchthon, 'Agreement on doctrine is plainly impossible, unless the pope will abolish his popedom'.

The effect of the fiasco at Augsburg was therefore to stimulate the Protestant forces to new and impressive feats of organization. After the appearance of the *editio princeps* in the spring of 1531, the Confession of Augsburg itself became an authoritative religious document, even now – in its later versions – the chief standard of faith in the Lutheran churches. In the same year an alliance was concluded in the town hall of Schmalkalden, a town on the borders of Hesse and Saxony, between eleven cities and eight princes of the empire who undertook to assist one another if they were attacked 'on account of the Word of God and the doctrines of the Gospel'. In some ways the League of Schmalkalden marks the climax of the great late medieval tradition of mutual self-help by German territorial states with common interests: when Philip of Hesse and his colleagues restored the Protestant Duke Ulrich to Württemberg in 1534 they were imitating the behaviour of the then moribund Swabian League which had originally driven Ulrich into exile fifteen years previously. But, of course, because of its close doctrinal ties, its common spokesman on religious matters (Luther lived on until 1546) and its sense of living under constant threat, the Schmalkaldic League presented a more formidable challenge to imperial authority and unity than any of its medieval predecessors. Henceforward, although Charles V was naturally reluctant to face the fact, the cause of religious unity in Germany could only be promoted by political and, in the last resort, military action. During the 1530s the Protestant Reformation in Germany consequently became a much more obviously political phenomenon than in the previous decade, less spontaneous and more closely controlled by the princes. The continued territorial expansion of Lutheranism, especially in northern Germany, was accompanied by a rapid rise in the self-confidence and prestige of the Schmalkaldic League. Its leaders, John Frederick, Elector of Saxony (1532–47), and Philip, Landgrave of Hesse (1509–67), did not hesitate to rebuff Henry VIII of England when he sought co-operation with the League in 1539. In the immediate aftermath of the Augsburg Diet it is just possible, if unlikely, that Charles V might have been able to extirpate heresy and suppress the dissident princes by force. When he returned to Germany early in 1540 after a nine years' absence he had no alternative but to promote, yet again and for the last time, a policy of religious reunion by peaceful negotiation. The intricate manoeuvres which resulted in the abortive Diet of Regensburg in 1541 testified, like the proceedings at Augsburg ten years earlier, to a general desire for conciliation as well as to the reluctance of both sides to make the necessary sacrifices in the cause of religious or imperial unity. Even Charles V was at last convinced that the political and religious schism could now only be ended by war. The years between 1541 and 1555 were to be dominated by the emperor's grand design to break the Schmalkaldic League.

Circumscribed as ever by the hostility of the Valois to the west and the Ottomans to the east, Charles V's campaign to restore order within Germany began with his successful conquest of the duchy of Cleves in the summer of 1543. Although this was only the emperor's third visit to Germany, he was not to leave again for twelve years, a period during which he made a sustained and determined attempt, perhaps unparalleled in the history of the empire, to grapple with the constitutional as well as religious problems of the German Reich. In the face of Charles's political skill, his ability to draw upon reserves of loyalty towards the crown, his manipulation of ambitious princes like Maurice, Duke of Saxony and, above all, his determination not to present himself as an implacable enemy of all Lutherans, the Schmalkadic League proved extremely fragile. After the imperial victory at Mühlberg in Saxony (April 1547), both John Frederick of Saxony and Philip of Hesse were in Charles's hands and the days of the Lutheran princes seemed numbered. The Lutheran religion, however, remained almost as secure as before and Charles was never able to enforce religious uniformity on his recalcitrant subjects. After 1548 a doctrinal compromise, the so-called Interim of Augsburg, that 'masterpiece of ambiguity' which conceded nothing of substance to the Protestants except clerical marriage and communion in both kinds, was spasmodically applied in parts of southern Germany; but in the northern cities and principalities the Interim was treated with contempt. At Wittenberg Melanchthon continued his reorganization of the Church in Saxony while Flacius Illyricus and others converted the city of Magdeburg into a violently anti-papal 'chancery of God and Christ'. The complete failure of Charles V to heal the religious schism was in fact inevitable; and the emperor himself placed greater hopes on a successful redefinition of his relationship to the princes. At the 'ironclad' Augsburg Diet of 1547–8, he proposed the establishment of a general imperial league, partially modelled on the now defunct Swabian League, whose major role would be the maintenance of peace and order throughout the Reich. This scheme was sabotaged by the dukes of Bavaria, long jealous of Habsburg predominance, while any hope that the princes would adopt a more respectful attitude to their emperor was shattered by the adventurist policy of the ambitious Maurice of Saxony. In uneasy alliance with the Lutheran powers of northern Germany and Henry II of France, Maurice invaded the Tyrol in

G

April 1552 and forced the now elderly and exhausted emperor to fly across the Alps to Carinthia. Charles V's valiant attempt to restore imperial authority throughout Germany had proved a failure. His own decision to withdraw from public life and the death of Maurice of Saxony at the battle of Sievershausen in 1553 left the way open for the achievement of a more permanent religious and political settlement.

The six months of arduous negotiations between Charles's younger brother Ferdinand (king of the Romans since 1531) and the diplomatic representatives of the German princes resulted in the Religious Peace of Augsburg (1555), perhaps the most successful as well as the most maligned compromise treaty in German history. An imperial diet, albeit in the absence of the emperor, at last recognized the existence of Lutherans (adherents to the Augsburg Confession) as well as Catholics within Germany, provided that in each territory individuals should henceforward observe the religion of their ruler. Although it was not actually used in the recess of the diet but employed by jurists of the next generation faced with the problems of working out the implications of the settlement, the famous phrase *cuius regio eius religio* not unfairly summarizes the result of the Peace of Augsburg. It would be anachronistic to imagine that the settlement could have been anything but a victory for territorialism rather than toleration. No one at Augsburg in 1555 could foresee that Geneva, only brought absolutely under John Calvin's authority in that very year, was soon to bring new disruptive forces to bear upon the German religious scene. By conceding to individual subjects the right to emigrate from their principalities on religious grounds and compelling certain cities to maintain parity between different confessions, Ferdinand and his opponents had in fact made a creditable attempt to come to grips with some of the anomalies inevitably created by the chaotic and revolutionary events of the previous forty years. Like all such compromises, the Peace of Augsburg failed to solve every problem; but there is no doubt that it created the conditions within Germany for a quite remarkable degree of peaceful religious coexistence. During the first part of his long career Johannes Kepler (1571–1630) of Weil der Stadt in Württemberg was able to practise his idiosyncratic variety of Lutheranism as well as his remarkable scientific skills in such apparently uncongenial places as Graz in Styria and the Habsburg court at Prague. Only at the very end of the century did the progress of the Counter Reformation in southern Germany and of Calvinism along the Rhine threaten to destroy rather than adjust the balance achieved by the

Peace of Augsburg. Above all the Reich's freedom from civil war in the late sixteenth century was due to the fact that the constitutional issue had already been decided in the reign of Charles V. Thanks to its association with the principles of the public peace, reorganized along more logical lines by the Executive Ordinance of 1555, the imperial structure was to survive; but Charles's Habsburg successors, the emperors Ferdinand I (1556–64), Maximilian II (1564–76) and Rudolf II (1576–1612), had neither the ability nor the will to assert direct authority outside their hereditary dominions in the east. Charles V, the last ruler of the Reich to receive imperial coronation and the first to make a voluntary abdication, deserves his reputation as the last of the medieval emperors.

The period between 1555 and the outbreak of the Thirty Years War in 1618, the so-called Confessional Age, therefore proved to be one of the most peaceful eras in the history of the Reich. Too often dismissed as a sombre prologue to the seventeenth-century German catastrophe, it was also – until the monetary crisis of 1619–23 – one of the most prosperous. Admittedly Germany's central geographical position within Europe deprived its merchants of the opportunities enjoyed by those with direct access to the Atlantic and Mediterranean: the progress of Dutch and English trade in the north speeded the decline of the Hanseatic League just as in the south and east the financiers of Italy and Poland overtook those of Augsburg and Nürnberg. But the familiar view that during the late sixteenth century the great majority of German cities were in a state of serious decay seems increasingly less justified: it was, for example, at precisely this time that Leipzig in Saxony became the centre of the international fur and book trades. Much more significant is the evidence for renewed economic activity in the German countryside. The growing demand of West European countries for corn imports led to a three- or fourfold rise in the price of cereals and the emergence of large and efficient arable farms throughout northern and eastern Germany. In the south and west a general rise in the standard of living provides the most convincing explanation for the waning of peasant discontent during the generations after the wars of 1524–5: the surviving records of duties levied by the estates of Upper Bavaria on the sale of alcoholic drinks suggest a fairly steady increase in the consumption of wine and beer between 1543 and 1608. Economic expansion was accompanied by a genuine cultural efflorescence throughout Germany and especially in the Protestant states of the north-west. At the beginning of the seventeenth century the reputation of the German university and the German scholar – whether mythical like Dr Faustus or real like the first *philosophus teutonicus*, Jakob Böhme – had reached unprecedented heights. It was a German prince, Duke Heinrich Julius of Brunswick, who established the first regular court theatre in Europe; and it was in western Germany that the English actors of Elizabeth's reign found perhaps their most appreciative audiences. Nor is there any parallel north of the Alps for the vast building programme undertaken by so many German princes, prelates and cities during the second half of the sixteenth century. Most famous of all was the palace of the Palatine electors at Heidelberg, the most appropriate extant memorial to the political realities of the Confessional Age and post-Reformation Germany. As so often in the past, the Reich's failure to achieve political unity affected its nominal subjects a good deal less than it has disturbed later historians; and by comparison with their contemporaries in Spain, France and even England, it is arguable that the Germans of the late sixteenth century were fortunate rather than the reverse to live within relatively small political units. The constitutional and social tensions within the Reich were as real and obvious as in the very different days of Barbarossa; but on the other hand the Thirty Years War was soon to demonstrate that they could not yet be resolved by force.[1]

Kings and Emperors of the Reich

I THE AGE OF THE SAXON AND FRANCONIAN DYNASTIES 911–1125

Conrad I (of Franconia), king of the East Franks 911–18

Henry I (of Saxony), king of the East Franks 919–36

Otto I (of Saxony), king of the East Franks 936; emperor 962–73

Otto II (of Saxony), co-emperor 967; sole king and emperor 973–83

Otto III (of Saxony), king under mother's regency 983; emperor 996–1002

Henry II (of Bavaria), king 1002; emperor 1014–24

Conrad II (of Franconia), king 1024; emperor 1027–39

Henry III (of Franconia), elected king 1028 (succeeded 1039); emperor 1046–56

[1] This chapter owes much to the generosity of Dr M. C. Cross, Mr K. J. Leyser and Professor G. R. Potter in providing advice and information. However, as the reader will already have discovered, the course of German history between 911 and 1618 is highly controversial: for the interpretations advanced here the author is alone responsible.

Henry IV (of Franconia), king 1056; emperor 1084–1106
Rudolf of Swabia, anti-king 1077–80
Hermann of Luxemburg, anti-king 1081–8
Conrad of Franconia, anti-king 1087–1100 (died 1101)
Henry V (of Franconia), elected king 1099; crowned king 1106; emperor 1111–25

II THE RISE AND FALL OF THE HOHENSTAUFEN DYNASTY 1125–1273

Lothar II (of Saxony), king of the Romans (i.e. Germany) 1125; emperor 1133–7
Conrad III (of Swabia), king of the Romans 1138–52
Henry (Conrad II's son), king of the Romans 1147–50
Frederick I (of Hohenstaufen), king of the Romans 1152; emperor 1155–90
Henry VI (of Hohenstaufen), king of the Romans 1169 (succeeded 1190); emperor 1191–7
Philip II (of Swabia), king of the Romans 1198–1208
Otto IV (of Brunswick), king of the Romans 1198; emperor 1209–18
Frederick II (of Hohenstaufen), king of the Romans 1212; emperor 1220–50
Henry [VII] (Frederick II's son), king of the Romans 1220–35 (died 1242)
Henry Raspe (of Thuringia), anti-king 1246–7
Conrad IV (of Hohenstaufen), king of the Romans 1237 (succeeded 1250); died 1254
William (of Holland), anti-king 1247–56
Richard (of Cornwall), king of the Romans 1257–72
Alfonso (of Castile), king of the Romans 1257–73 (died 1284)

III HABSBURGS, WITTELSBACHS AND LUXEMBURGS 1273–1437

Rudolf I (of Habsburg), king of the Romans 1273–91
Adolf (of Nassau), king of the Romans 1292–8
Albert I (of Habsburg), king of the Romans 1298–1308
Henry VII (of Luxemburg), king of the Romans 1308; emperor 1312–13
Louis IV (of Bavaria), king of the Romans 1314; emperor 1328–47
Frederick [III] (of Habsburg), anti-king 1314–22 (died 1330)

Charles IV (of Luxemburg), king of the Romans 1346; emperor
  1355–78
  Günther of Schwarzburg, anti-king 1349
Wenzel (of Luxemburg), king of the Romans 1376 (succeeded 1378);
  deposed 1400 (died 1419)
Rupert (of the Palatinate), king of the Romans 1400–10
  Jobst (of Moravia), anti-king 1410–11
Sigismund (of Luxemburg), king of the Romans 1410, emperor 1433–7

IV THE HOUSE OF HABSBURG 1438–1619

Albert II, king of the Romans 1438–9
Frederick III, king of the Romans 1440; emperor 1452–93
Maximilian I, king of the Romans 1486 (succeeded 1493); emperor
  elect 1508–19
Charles V, king of the Romans 1519; emperor 1520–56 (died 1558)
Ferdinand I, king of the Romans 1531; emperor elect 1556–64
Maximilian II, king of the Romans 1562; emperor elect 1564–76
Rudolf II, king of the Romans 1575; emperor elect 1576–1612
Matthias, king of Germany and emperor 1612–19

Bibliography

GENERAL SURVEYS

BARRACLOUGH, G. *The Origins of Modern Germany*, 2nd edn. Oxford, 1947.
BONJOUR, E., OFFLER, H. S., and POTTER, G. R. *A Short History of Switzerland*.
  Oxford, 1952.
BRYCE, J. *The Holy Roman Empire*. New edn. London, 1904.
CALMETTE, J. *Le Reich Allemand au Moyen Age*. Paris, 1951.
Cambridge Medieval History, Vols. I–VIII. Cambridge, 1911–36.
DOLLINGER, P. *La Hanse (XIIe–XVIIe siècles)*. Paris, 1964.
DVORNIK, F. *The Making of Central and Eastern Europe*. London, 1949.
FOLZ, R. *The Concept of Empire in Western Europe from the Fifth to the Fourteenth
  Century*. Trans. S. A. Ogilvie. London, 1969.
GEBHARDT, B. *Handbuch der Deutschen Geschichte, I: Frühzeit und Mittelalter*. 8th
  edn. by H. Grundmann. Stuttgart, 1954.
GIESEBRECHT, W. VON. *Geschichte der deutschen Kaiserzeit*. 5 vols. 3rd edn.
  Brunswick, 1863–80.
HALLER, J. *The Epochs of German History*. London, 1930.
HEER, F. *The Holy Roman Empire*. Trans. J. Sondheimer. London, 1968.
PLANITZ, H. *Die deutsche Stadt im Mittelalter von der Römerzeit bis zu den Zunft-
  kampfen*. Graz and Cologne, 1955.
RÖRIG, F. *The Medieval Town*. Trans. Don Bryant. London, 1967.
STEINBERG, S. H. *A Short History of Germany*. Cambridge, 1944.
THOMPSON, J. W. *Feudal Germany*. Chicago, 1928.

GERMAN HISTORY 911–1250

BARRACLOUGH, G. *Mediaeval Germany, 911–1250: Essays by German Historians,* translated with an Introduction. 2 vols. Oxford, 1938.

BOSL, K. *Die Reichsministerialität der Salier und Staufer.* 2 vols. Stuttgart, 1950–1.

BRUNDAGE, J. A. (ed. and trans.). *Chronicle of Henry of Livonia.* Madison, 1961.

GILLINGHAM, J. B. *The Kingdom of Germany in the High Middle Ages (900–1200).* Historical Association Pamphlet G. 77. London, 1971.

HOLTZMANN, R. *Geschichte der Sächsichsen Kaiserzeit.* Munich, 1943.

JOHNSON, E. N. *The Secular Activities of the German Episcopate, 919–1024.* Chicago, 1931.

KANTOROWICZ, E. *Frederick II, 1194–1250.* Trans. E. O. Lorimer. London, 1931.

KERN, F. *Kingship and Law in the Middle Ages.* Trans. S. B. Chrimes. Oxford, 1938.

LEEPER, A. W. A. *A History of Medieval Austria.* Oxford, 1941.

LEYSER, K. 'The Battle at the Lech, 955. A Study in Tenth-Century Warfare.' *History,* Vol. L (1965), pp. 1–25.

— 'The German Aristocracy from the Ninth to the early Twelfth Century. A Historical and Cultural Sketch.' *Past and Present,* No. 41 (1968), pp. 25–53.

— 'Henry I and the beginnings of the Saxon Empire.' *English Historical Review,* Vol. LXXXIII (1968), pp. 1–32.

MAYER, T. (ed.) *Kaisertum und Herzogsgewalt im Zeitalter Friedrichs I.* Leipzig, 1944.

MIEROW, C. C. (ed. and trans.). *The Two Cities by Otto Bishop of Freising.* Columbia, 1928.

MIEROW, C. C., and EMERY, R. (ed. and trans.). *The Deeds of Frederick Barbarossa by Otto of Freising.* Columbia, 1953.

MOMMSEN, T. E., and MORRISON, K. F. (trans.). *Imperial Lives and Letters of the Eleventh Century.* Ed. R. L. Benson. Columbia, 1962.

MUNZ, P. *Frederick Barbarossa. A Study in Medieval Politics.* London, 1969.

OTTO, E. *Friedrich Barbarossa.* Potsdam, 1943.

PACAUT, M. *Frédéric Barberousse.* Paris, 1967.

TSCHAN, F. J. (ed. and trans.). *Helmold of Bosau's Chronicle of the Slavs.* Columbia, 1935.

GERMAN HISTORY 1250–1618

ANDREAS, W. *Deutschland vor der Reformation.* 6th edn. Stuttgart, 1959.

ANGERMEIER, H. *Königtum und Landfriede im deutschen Spätmittelalter.* Munich, 1966.

BAINTON, R. H. *Here I Stand: A Life of Martin Luther.* London, 1950.

BAYLEY, C. C. *The Formation of the German College of Electors in the Mid-Thirteenth Century.* Toronto, 1949.

BRANDI, K. *The Emperor Charles V.* Trans. C. V. Wedgwood. London, 1939.

BRUNNER, O. *Land und Herrschaft.* 4th edn. Vienna and Wiesbaden, 1959.

CARSTEN, F. L. *The Origins of Prussia.* Oxford, 1954.

— *Princes and Parliaments in Germany from the Fifteenth to the Eighteenth Century.* Oxford, 1959.

CHRISMAN, M. U. *Strasbourg and the Reform.* Yale, 1967.

CLASEN, C. P. *The Palatinate in European History, 1559–1660.* Oxford, 1964.

COHN, H. J. *The Government of the Rhine Palatinate in the Fifteenth Century*. Oxford, 1965.

DICKENS, A. G. *Luther and the Reformation*. London, 1967.

GERLACH, H. *Der englische Bauernaufstand von 1381 und der deutsche Bauernkrieg: Ein Vergleich*. Meisenheim am Glan, 1969.

GERLICH, A. *Habsburg, Luxemburg, Wittelsbach im Kampf um die Deutsche Königskrone*. Wiesbaden, 1960.

HILLERBRAND, H. J. *The Reformation in its own Words*. London, 1964.

HOLBORN, H. *A History of Modern Germany: The Reformation*. London, 1965.

— *Ulrich von Hutten and the Reformation*. New Haven and Oxford, 1937.

JARRETT, B. *The Emperor Charles IV*. London, 1935.

LAU, F., and BIZER, E. *A History of the Reformation in Germany to 1555*. Trans. B. A. Hardy, London, 1969.

OFFLER, H. S. 'Aspects of Government in the Late Medieval Empire.' *Europe in the Late Middle Ages*. Ed. J. Hale, R. Highfield and B. Smalley. London, 1965.

— 'Empire and Papacy: the Last Struggle.' *Transactions of Royal Historical Society*, 5th series, Vol. VI (1956), pp. 21–47.

ROSSLER H. *Rudolf von Habsburg*. Munich, 1962.

RUPP, E. G. *Luther's Progress to the Diet of Worms*. London, 1951.

SETON WATSON, R. W. *Maximilian I, Holy Roman Emperor*. London, 1902.

SKALWERT G. *Reich and Reformation*. Berlin, 1967.

STENGEL, E. E. *Avignon und Rhens*. Weimar, 1930.

STRAUSS, G. *Nuremberg in the Sixteenth Century*. New York, 1969.

4 The Making of Modern Germany 1618–1870

AGATHA RAMM

The theme of this chapter is the transformation of the Holy Roman Empire, which exemplified in a rough and ready way a principle of justice, into a single political unit, which exemplified a principle of power. The Holy Roman Empire was a system of rights, which allowed the smallest unarmed ecclesiastical sovereignty to survive side by side with strong duchies of international standing. It accommodated within its jurisdiction states identified with the Lutheran, Calvinist and Catholic confessions, though by 1618 it was becoming increasingly difficult for them to maintain the balance of power among themselves which made this possible. The Thirty Years War (1618–48) sprang from the struggle to maintain the balance. In the context of the war the Habsburg monarchy made an early attempt to change the structure of rights into a unit of power.

The diets of the empire were the first scene of the struggle over the balance of power. Catholic princes tried to stop the attempt of Protestants to increase the number of their votes by further secularization of ecclesiastical territory. Protestant princes tried to stop Catholic attempts to extrude Protestant lay administrators of ecclesiastical territory from the diets altogether. Efforts to settle these questions by vote invariably failed. When Frederick IV of the Palatinate founded the Evangelical Union (1608) and Maximilian of Bavaria founded the Catholic League (1609) the conditions necessary for a settlement by force were created. Five years later the Truce of Xanten (1614), by assigning Cleves and Mark to the Protestant Elector of Brandenburg and Jülich and Berg to the Elector Palatine, caused an enlargement of Protestant power that was both intolerable to the Catholics and a defiance of the emperor.

Simultaneously within the complex of territories that constituted the personal dominions of the House of Habsburg (the duchies of Upper and Lower Austria, Carniola, Carinthia, Styria, the Tyrol, the Breisgau in Swabia and the kingdoms of Hungary and Bohemia) the causes of rebellion were being prepared. The rights of the Bohemian Protestants were embodied in the Letter of Majesty (1609) which the emperor Matthias had confirmed on his coronation in 1611. Before Matthias died (1619), power in Bohemia passed to Ferdinand of Styria, who was to become emperor as Ferdinand II. He had an ominous strength of character and rigid Catholic loyalties. Trouble began when a Protestant Assembly in Prague alleged infractions of the Letter of Majesty and petitioned the emperor for redress. Matthias rejected their appeal. The magnates, believing the rejection to be the work of the regents who governed in Bohemia pending Ferdinand of Styria's arrival, reconvened the Assembly, which met in a state of considerable ferment. A group headed by von Thurn determined to make the breach with the crown irreparable and planned the murder of two of the most hated regents. Martinitz and Slavata were hurled from an upper window of the council chamber. The Defenestration of Prague (23 May 1618) was the signal for the rebellion of the magnates with the Protestant community supposedly behind them.

Ferdinand of Styria organized the operations of an avenging imperial army and the invasion of Bohemia was in full swing when Matthias died. The magnates, aware that an imperial victory would mean the end of their 'liberties' as well as those of the Protestants, repudiated Ferdinand and elected Frederick V of the Palatinate (1610–23) king. Ferdinand, believing that the loss of Bohemia might entail the loss of Hungary and that he could not afford either, let alone both, resolved on the complete reduction of Bohemia. This was accomplished during the German war, the first of the four wars into which the Thirty Years War is traditionally divided. The victory of the White Hill (1620) enabled Ferdinand to wreak a terrible vengeance upon the Bohemian nobility, who had, after all, been ill-supported by the Protestant peasants. About half of Bohemia was taken from its existing owners and given or sold to new men. Constitutional changes followed (1627 and 1628). These gave the Habsburg monarchy hereditary rule over Bohemia and Moravia and endowed it with the right to legislate there, to appoint officials, to summon and dismiss the estates, to revise the judgements of the courts and to command the armed forces. Bohemia and Moravia were thus closely integrated into the Habsburg monarchy and governed thenceforward from the Bohemian chancery in Vienna. Religious changes also followed. The Catholic Church was declared to be the Church of the realm and its clergy to be the first estate. The decay of Protestantism was assured when Lutherans and Calvinists were expelled, emigrated or submitted to the Church. In the Austrian arch-duchies, too, Protestant communities disappeared and the power of the estates declined. Lusatia was transferred from Bohemia to Saxony. The combined effect of these penal, constitutional and religious measures was that Bohemia for two centuries lost its national Czech character and that the first step towards absolutism was taken in the hereditary Habs-burg dominions.

Another result of the German war was that 'a military society' grew up outside the civilian society which 'it was supposed to defend or even to purify'. In 1621–2 German territory bore the burden of no fewer than eight armies. A Spanish army occupied the Rhenish Palatinate to cut off German assistance from the Dutch with whom Philip IV had resumed war. Frederick V of the Palatinate had two English regiments and a few troops of his own stationed in or near Heidelberg, until they were destroyed by Tilly in September 1622. Ernst von Mansfeldt, who had been General of the Evangelical Union until it fell apart and had then entered Frederick's service, commanded an army in the Upper Palatinate between Saxony and Bavaria. After 1622 it moved into the Rhenish Palatinate, thence to Alsace and thence, by way of Holland, to East Friesland. Margrave George Frederick of Baden was a Calvinist idealist marching to the aid of Frederick until in 1622 he too was defeated at Wimpffen by Tilly. Christian of Brunswick, the Protestant administrator of the bishopric of Halberstadt, held together the fifth army by a mixture of romanticism and acquisitiveness. It operated in an area between Westphalia and Alsace, next in Holland and lastly in the Lower Saxon Circle, where in 1623 Tilly defeated it at Stadtlohn. The Catholic prince, Maximilian of Bavaria, commanded the biggest army in Germany. Its costs were very much greater than his own annual revenue could pay. Count Johannes Tsercleas von Tilly commanded an army raised in the name of the Catholic League and, by moving against each of the Protestant armies in turn, had brought the German war to an end in the Lower Saxon Circle in 1623. The eighth army was commanded by a young adventurer, Albrecht von Wallenstein. He had acquired great wealth by buying confiscated Bohemian lands and marrying a rich wife, and he employed it to recruit soldiers. By 1622 he was commandant of Prague and had acquired from the emperor the right to billet troops where he chose in Bohemia and Moravia. He continued to amass forces.

All these armies had a mercenary element; all were accompanied by women and children, servants and camp followers of all kinds; all these people required pay in cash, food for themselves and their horses, and general maintenance in fuel and shelter. Only those of Spain, Bavaria, Baden and the Palatinate had any State finance behind them. Forced contributions from the land where they were billeted and, when this was refused or fell into arrears, crime against the civilian population were the normal means of maintenance. Lines of nationality and even of religion became blurred; the overriding distinction was between the soldier mob, living by its own code, and the plundered and helpless civilian. It is true that all Germany did not suffer all the time. Brandenburg and Saxony were exceptions to the general rule of murder, suicide, starvation and epidemics. East, in Bohemia and Silesia, west, from Westphalia to Swabia by way of the Rhineland, respites from destruction and fear were few and short.

The second of the wars was the Danish. It lasted from 1626 to 1629. After Tilly had brought the German war to an end, desultory fighting had continued in the Lower Saxon Circle and spread northwards to the frontiers of Denmark. Her strong and grasping king, Christian IV, took his opportunity to come to the rescue of the Protestants and to gain spoil, as he hoped, in the form of secularized bishoprics. He was foiled in this by Tilly at the battles of Dessau Bridge and Lutter (1626).

Meanwhile the whole of Germany had fallen under the shadow of imperial troops, and the military foundation of Ferdinand's attempt to consolidate a German territorial state had been laid. Ferdinand had deprived Frederick V of the Palatinate (1621) and made Maximilian of Bavaria an elector (1623). These were already unprecedented assertions of the emperor's power. Tilly's successes seemed to put all Germany in his grasp. When in 1625 he accepted Wallenstein's offer to raise an army of 20,000 men for him, he seemed to have the means to close his grip. The outbreak of a peasants' revolt in Austria and Christian IV's intervention only delayed his doing so. Ferdinand appointed Wallenstein head of all his forces and gave him authority to exact contributions for them and for his own army. In 1627 he removed the limit upon the size of Wallenstein's personal army and allowed him to quarter it anywhere. He made him Duke of Mecklenburg and a Prince of the Empire. By 1628 Wallenstein exercised authority throughout north Germany, where his troops were dispersed, in the emperor's name. Ferdinand made him governor of the Oceanic (North) Sea and Baltic Sea.

Ferdinand sought to consolidate this military power by a political measure: the Edict of Restitution (March 1629). It proclaimed the restitution to the Catholic Church of all church property appropriated by German princes since 1552, as well as all archbishoprics, bishoprics and convents that were held immediately of the emperor and had become Protestant since 1555. The edict was executed at once in Württemberg and Brunswick. Subsequently individual free cities that had been subject to mixed Catholic and Protestant rule were one by one restored to exclusive Catholic control. They constituted oases of Catholic power scattered throughout north and south Germany, outliers to the blocks of power represented by the Catholic states. The Peace of Lübeck (7 June 1629) now brought the Danish war to an end. Ferdinand's intrusive hand was everywhere, but it carried reconciliation as well as power.

It was, however, reconciliation on his own terms. These Brandenburg and Saxony were not prepared to accept. They were significantly absent from the meeting of German electors which Ferdinand convened at Regensburg in the summer of 1630. Meanwhile, the successful resistance (1628) of the old fortified Baltic port of Stralsund to Wallenstein's authority had marked the turn of the tide for him. Ferdinand had dismissed Wallenstein and so retained, at least, the loyalty of Maximilian of Bavaria and asserted his control over the military force that had given him his unprecedented power. But general reconciliation still did not follow.

The Swedish war of 1630–2 is the third of the wars into which the Thirty Years War is traditionally divided. Gustavus Adolphus of Sweden had taken the chance of Wallenstein's failure at Stralsund to strike a blow for Protestantism, to implement his own strong interest in curbing imperial power in north Germany and to respond to the prodding of France with whom he signed the Alliance of Bärwelde. He won great victories and made a spectacular march from Peenemünde to Leipzig, from Leipzig to the Main and down the Main to the Rhine. Above all he rallied the Protestant princes and brought the hitherto unexploited resources of Brandenburg and Saxony into the service of the Protestant cause. His death at the battle of Lützen meant, however, that the fruits of this and earlier victories were ungarnered. Thus the Swedish war delayed, but did not prevent, the climax of Ferdinand's policy.

In January 1632, Ferdinand had been obliged by the exigencies of the Swedish war to recall Wallenstein and submit to his creating a colossal private army (40,000 men). The death of Tilly at seventy-three had, moreover, left Wallenstein the only great imperial general. Yet, in the end, Wallenstein's independence put the game into Ferdinand's hands. Axel Oxenstierna, who succeeded Gustavus Adolphus in the direction of Swedish policy in Germany, had united the Swabian, Franconian, Upper Rhine and Electoral Rhine Circles, under a Swedish directorate, in the Heilbronn Confederation (1633). This provoked the imperial forces into unexampled solidarity against him. Imperial loyalty was further consolidated under the provocation of Wallenstein's negotiations with the Elector of Saxony and other Protestant princes, conducted as if he had independent power. Wallenstein's officers disowned his treachery and murdered him. In February 1634 Ferdinand assumed the sole command of Wallenstein's great army. He became the rallying point for a certain mounting German sentiment among the princes, which expressed itself against both Swedes and French. In November 1634 Ferdinand signed with Saxony the Preliminaries of Peace which in May 1635 became the Peace of Prague.

This was the climax of Ferdinand's policy of German consolidation. The Heilbronn Confederation broke up. Ferdinand recovered the loyalty of the Protestant princes by withdrawing the Edict of Restitution and allowing ecclesiastical property to remain in the possession of those who held it on 12 November 1627. All Protestant administrators of one-time Catholic bishoprics were to be excluded from the diets and a Catholic restoration was to take place on knights' land and in the free imperial cities, irrespective of the date, 1627. Saxony retained Lusatia; Bavaria retained the Palatinate and the electoral title. The Treaty was open to all German princes, but Sweden and France might only sign if they restored the German land they held. It was decisive that George William of Brandenburg and John George of Saxony signed as well as Maximilian of Bavaria; for these three were now the most powerful rulers of Germany. All the German princes followed their lead except those of Baden and Württemberg, who were under the ban of the empire and so could not, and Hesse-Cassel. The Thirty Years War might now have ended; for nearly all the German princes had rallied to the emperor. When Ferdinand II died in 1637 he headed a league united against Sweden and France.

The war, in its last phase a French war, continued because Ferdinand had not been able to release the empire from the net of international antagonisms in which it was enmeshed. The German princes stopped short of giving him military support when further action against France or Sweden might lead to the strengthening of his international position. The emperor's new-won German power crumbled as he attempted to gain this. From 1621, when Spain occupied Jülich and the Palatinate, Austrian and Spanish policy had been particularly closely co-ordinated. The Spaniards in occupying the passes of the Valtelline served the Austrians in 1622. The Austrians in mitigating the disasters the Spaniards suffered at the hands of the Dutch and in sequestrating the duchy of Mantua (it lay astride Spanish Milan) served the Spaniards in 1626 and 1627. It was this close co-ordination that France found so provoking. It was not surprising that Cardinal Richelieu, the able First Minister of Louis XIII, used every opportunity to divide the two Habsburg allies, turning the Spaniards out of the Valtelline (1624), resisting the occupation of Mantua in the name of a French claimant and, in 1630, laying plans for intervention in the German fighting. He was baffled by Gustavus Adolphus's apparent ability to turn German events into a new current. After the Swedish king's death, renewed and even closer co-ordination of Spanish and Austrian military action by Philip IV's brother and Ferdinand II's son was partly responsible for the defeat of the Swedes at Nördlingen (1634) and the great position of the emperor in 1635. Bernhard of Saxe-Weimar, the Swedish commander, tried to hold out in Franconia, but was eventually driven into Alsace, and he took his army into the pay and service of France (1635).

Through Bernhard of Saxe-Weimar, Richelieu had a substantial thread of the German net in his hands. He used it to keep the Swedes from signing the Peace of Prague and then to draw together a tight group of anti-Habsburg interests. The Dutch (January 1635), the Italo-Swiss by alliance with Savoy, Mantua and Parma, and the only free German prince, the Landgrave of Hesse-Cassel, composed this group. France declared war upon Spain, occupied one after the other the Rhineland bridgeheads, declared war upon the empire and won a series of military successes in the southern Netherlands. Thus a German solution of the German problem was prevented. The German situation could have meant peace in 1635, but the European situation caused it to be delayed until 1648, even though peace negotiations began in 1640. The two Treaties of Münster and Osnabrück constituted the Peace of Westphalia made in 1648.

The Swedish war had already strengthened the impact of the outside world upon Germany. The French war made it decisive; for its outcome meant that the peace treaties established not pacification alone but positions of strength from which either the Bourbon or the Habsburg dynasty could renew the European conflict when it chose. France continued at war with Spain for another eleven years, until the Peace of the

Pyrenees in 1659, and the emperor continued to assist the king of Spain. Ferdinand III (1637–58) ceded to Louis XIII of France, by the Treaty of Münster, his rights and possessions in Upper and Lower Alsace. These were not easy to define and a satisfactory definition was not achieved by excluding from the cession 'the estates of the empire', that is the city and bishopric of Strasbourg, ten free cities of the empire and the lands of many counts and knights who were immediate vassals of the emperor. The French possession of the Lorraine bishoprics of Metz, Toul and Verdun was confirmed, but the fate of the duchy of Lorraine, which surrounded them, was not settled, since the duke remained at war with France and an ally of Spain. France, in addition, acquired the fortresses of Breisach and Philipsburg on the right bank of the Rhine. She was thus well placed both to divide the Spanish from the Austrian Habsburgs and to interfere in German affairs; whereas the empire was left insecure. The Treaty of Osnabrück recognized that the Dutch state was no longer, any more than the Swiss Confederation, part of the Holy Roman Empire. It pacified Sweden at Brandenburg's expense. The elector, it is true, received East Pomerania, but Stettin and the whole estuary of the Oder, West Pomerania and the island of Rügen went to Sweden. Sweden was also established in the land between the rivers Elbe and Weser and was able to control their estuaries because she acquired Bremen, Verden and the port of Wismar in Mecklenburg. These territories remained part of the empire and so Sweden became a member of it with a seat in the diet. It was lucky for Germany that Sweden was never able to exploit the stranglehold which she thus acquired on the political and economic life of north Germany.

The religious provisions of the Treaty of Osnabrück implied that a balance of power between the confessions had, in fact, been established. Calvinist rulers were admitted to the same right of determining the religion of their states as Lutherans and Catholics had enjoyed for more than a century. Special provisions assured the security of an established religion when a ruler changed his faith. The date for fixing the possession of ecclesiastical territories was put at 1 January 1624. It was favourable to the Protestants, since it disallowed the restitutions to the Catholic Church effected under the Edict of Restitution. They were favoured, too, by the provision allowing Protestant administrators of former Catholic sees to sit in the diet. Private persons were allowed to worship privately and to educate their children according to their own faith. Otherwise, whatever freedom of worship, public or private, had existed in 1624 was to be perpetuated until the reunion of the Church.

To strengthen the balance of power, the Treaty of Osnabrück regulated the deputation which prepared legislation for the diet and was fast superseding it in importance. It met in two colleges, one for the electors and one for the princes and free cities together; the agreement of both was necessary for a decision. The treaty provided that there should be an equal number of Protestants and Catholics in the princes' college. The diet of 1654 later gave the three Protestant electors a fourth vote, to be exercised by each in turn, to balance the four Catholic votes and assure the equilibrium in the electors' college. The next diet, which met in 1663, declared itself permanently in session. The rulers now ceased to attend, and the diet became a permanent congress of their representatives: diplomatists who made imperial business their profession. This was a sign that, though the achievement of a balance of religious forces had safeguarded the future of the empire, its authority continued to decline.

Apart from the restitutions of ecclesiastical territory, the Peace of Westphalia made other restitutions and amnesties. The eldest son of Frederick V, Karl Ludwig, was restored to the Rhenish Palatinate and a new electorate created for him and his heirs. The margravate of Baden, the landgravate of Hesse-Cassel and the duchy of Württemberg were all virtually restored to their position in 1618 or, for Baden, 1622. The bishopric of Osnabrück was to alternate between a Catholic bishop and a Protestant lay administrator from the House of Brunswick. Mecklenburg was restored and compensated with two bishoprics for the loss of Wismar to Sweden. Three states emerged clearly as those in whose hands the future of Germany lay. They were: Brandenburg, where the Great Elector, Frederick William (1640-88) gained the bishoprics of Kamin, Halberstadt and Minden, the archbishopric of Magdeburg, and East Pomerania; Saxony, where John George retained Lusatia; and Bavaria, where Maximilian retained the electoral dignity and the Upper Palatinate. All the German principalities gained a measure of emancipation from imperial control, but these three were strong enough to profit thereby. Austria remained, internationally, the greatest German power, but the Habsburg effort to reduce the princes to dependence and to create a single power unit in Germany had failed. Even in internal German affairs the authority of the emperor, once having been successfully challenged, now rapidly declined.

It is impossible to make a precise generalization about the economic effects of the war. It is clear that it caused serious economic setback. How serious this was is a matter of controversy for two reasons: parts of Germany were for long periods at peace (see above, p. 196); death and destruction bring into play a compensating mechanism, about which little is known except that the birth-rate is stimulated and production and town-dwelling are promoted. There was depopulation and there was for long a shortage of capital and consumer goods. On the other hand, the areas where fighting was worst became the town-dwelling areas of Germany, where demesne farming was rare and serfdom disappeared early.

Seventeenth-century absolutism in Germany was conspicuously realized, not in the empire, but in the absolute power of the German princes. Because of the special need, created by the destruction of the Thirty Years War, for social and economic policies of a restorative kind, and because most of the states were too small and poor to participate in European politics, the material well-being of his subjects became the most obvious concern of the abler German ruler.[1] The size of the armies, maintained during the war, had an irreversible effect upon the amount of taxation a ruler was able to levy and upon its permanence. Economic policy and permanent taxing stimulated administrative skills, and administrative skill increased a ruler's power. Thus in Germany, by the end of the seventeenth century, absolutism and enlightenment already went hand in hand, and the concept of the *métier du roi*, royal professionalism, was already familiar.

In the second half of the century, even more markedly than in the first, Germany was the fulcrum on which an international balance of power turned. To use a more precise metaphor, German history was henceforward polarized on Prussia in the north, where the Great Elector made a first-class international state, and on Austria in the south, where the cultivated and wise Leopold I (1658–1705) increased Austria's standing as an international force. Each was the centre of an international struggle and each used the struggle of which the other was the centre in his own alliance and war policy. The northern struggle was prompted by Charles X of Sweden, the southern by Louis XIV of France and Mahmud IV, Sultan of Turkey, with Küprülü his Grand Vizier. The outcome of these struggles meant that by 1715 a new European state system had been brought into existence. The share of the German states in creating the new political Europe deflected them from any substantial interest in strengthening or altering the German structure of state rights embodied in the Holy Roman Empire.

[1] The word *Wohlfahrtsstaat* was coined in Germany during the eighteenth century.

Some such interest was certainly shown before the new wars began. The active archbishop of Mainz, Elector John Philip (1647–73), who belonged to a powerful family in the habit of providing bishops and archbishops to the sees of south Germany, tried to make of the empire a real political federation. He was arch-chancellor of the empire and believed that Ferdinand II's attempt to convert it into a single monarchy was plain usurpation. John Philip brought together the three ecclesiastical electorates, the bishopric of Münster and the duchy of Jülich-Berg in the League of the Rhine (December 1654). The king of Sweden for Bremen and Verden, the three Dukes of Brunswick and the Landgrave of Hesse-Cassel signed in 1658 and the Great Elector in 1664. Saxony and Bavaria remained aloof, but a start seemed to have been made in realizing the federal ideal. It was an illusion. John Philip had tried to create a defensive system which the German princes might use either against France or against the emperor. Both France and the emperor, however, simply exploited the League for their own international purposes. France, where Mazarin had succeeded Richelieu, joined it in 1658. Leopold I gained its support to defeat the Turks, with whom he had renewed war in 1664, at St Gothard on the Raab.

Meanwhile in the north the international struggle had begun. The Great Elector was able to exploit Sweden's quarrel with Poland to make himself independent in East Prussia. He was the ally of Charles X in an invasion of Poland and by 1656 held East Prussia as a fief, no longer of Poland, but of Sweden. When Poland revived and sought to throw off Sweden's control, Frederick William continued at Charles's side. The battle of Warsaw, which they won together in 1656, is said to mark the beginning of the military history of the House of Hohenzollern. When Charles X left Poland to pursue his war with Denmark, Poland bribed Frederick William to change sides by recognizing him as *independent* ruler of East Prussia. Charles X, having settled with Denmark at Roskilde, turned back to Germany only to find Brandenburg and Poland united with the emperor against him. Thus he too was ready to oblige Frederick William. Sweden – in the Peace of Oliva, 1660 – recognized Frederick William's independence in East Prussia. Thus the arrangements were made which created the kingdom of Prussia, though the title of king was only assumed by Frederick William's son, Frederick I of Prussia (1688–1713).

Seven years after Oliva, the wars of Louis XIV opened the international struggle in the south. Louis XIV's first objective was to keep the two branches of the House of Habsburg apart. Philip IV of Spain, in order to preserve the tie, had married his second daughter, Margaret Theresa, to the Emperor Leopold. Louis, had, however, already gained the hand of the elder, Maria Theresa, for himself (1660). Philip could only safeguard the future by insisting that she should renounce her claim to the Spanish throne. Louis successfully hedged the renunciation about with conditions. When Philip died in 1665, Louis laid claim to at least one part of the Spanish inheritance. He asserted that the Spanish Netherlands 'devolved' by Brabant law upon the children of a daughter, born to a first marriage, to the exclusion of the sons of a second: that is, upon his wife to the exclusion of the new king of Spain. When his assertion was denied he invaded the Spanish Netherlands. The importance of the so-called War of Devolution (1667–8) for Germany was threefold. First, Leopold's failure to take the attack upon the Spanish Netherlands as an invasion of imperial territory was a formal recognition that the Flemish and Walloon Burgundian Circle was, as everyone already knew, no longer part of the empire. If in the future the empire was to become a German state, the point when it shed territory not ultimately included was important. Secondly, Louis XIV used the war to induce individual princes and, in 1668, the emperor himself to ally with him. Thus the war was important in hardening the net of international antagonisms in which the empire was more enmeshed than ever. Thirdly, the war – by the Peace of Aix-la-Chapelle (1668) – gave Louis a line of strong places, including Lille and Charleroi, along the Netherlands frontier, which were to enable him effectively to prevent in the future any military co-operation between the two branches of the House of Habsburg.

The Dutch were Louis's next victims in his ruthless march to ascendancy in Europe. He invaded the United Provinces in 1672, and the Dutch war lasted until the Peace of Nymegen in 1678. The emperor again tacitly disowned the Burgundian Circle, when the war spread there and the princes again disowned their German interests, though they might serve individual state interests, by making agreements with Louis. The chief significance of the war was, however, that it left behind it something like a patriotic German feeling against France. As a result of the war the empire shed yet another territory that was not ultimately to be part of the German state. This was Franche-Comté – the territory about Besançon, the old county of Burgundy. But the landmark in the creation of anti-French feeling was the incorporation of the ten imperial cities of Alsace into the French monarchy, despite the reservations of the Treaty of Münster. A lesser landmark was the devastation to which Louis subjected the Palatinate, where all the healing work of Karl Ludwig was destroyed. The war had been carried into the southern Netherlands and the Rhineland when the Great Elector and Charles II of Spain had joined the Dutch, and the devastation of the Palatinate had followed.

The Great Elector's French policy had, indeed, been tortuous. With the permission of his allies, he withdrew from the French war to meet a Swedish threat in the north. At the battle of Fehrbellin (18 June 1675) he won a great victory. This was another milestone in the military history of the Hohenzollern. But Louis compelled Frederick William – by the Peace of Saint-Germain-en-Laye (1679) – to restore to the Swedes the Pomeranian territory from which he had driven them. The latter's response was not to lament the injustice but, characteristically, to ally himself to Louis. Fortunately for him his German fellow sovereigns never knew how close his secret commitment to France was; luckily, he gave, in his promises, a cheque that Louis never had the chance to cash.

Meanwhile a third landmark in the growth of German feeling against France had been passed, when Louis crowned the incorporation of Alsace into France by the conquest of the free city of Strasbourg (September 1681). Between 1679 and 1681, Louis also consolidated his hold on the valley of the Moselle and on the land between the southern Moselle and the Rhine (the Saar valley). The decisions of special tribunals at Metz, Besançon and Breisach gave colour of legality to these *réunions*.

Much always depended upon a careful choice of priorities by the emperor and the German princes: in the west, they could temporize, buy off or fight France; in the east, they could temporize, buy off or fight the Ottoman Empire with its inchoate and complicated system of subordinate princes. They could not make the *same* choice among these possibilities in both west and east at once. In 1683 the Turks forced the choice of war upon the emperor and the German princes, so they had to temporize or buy off the hostility of the French in the west. A Polish incursion into the Ukraine was the beginning of a movement which shook the pieces in the intricate Turkish system out of place. It caused a Turkish war upon Poland and Russia and a chain of events through Transylvania and Hungary which gave the impulse for a new surge forward of Ottoman power in the Danube valley. In 1682 the Turks decided not to wait for the expiry of the twenty years' truce in 1684, but to attack in the campaigning season of 1683. A vast force, calculated at 100,000 at least, moved up the Danube valley and invested Vienna from July to September 1683.

A by-product of increasing German insecurity was another league not unlike the League of the Rhine of 1654. It too was exploited by the emperor. The Union was the work of George Frederick of Waldeck, the astute adviser of William of Orange. It began as a league between a number of authorities of the Wetterau – an area near the Main, the most fragmented of all Germany. By 1682 it included the Upper Rhine and Franconian Circles. Meanwhile William of Orange and Charles XI of Sweden had signed an Association for 'the defence of the empire' and the settlement of Europe on the basis of the treaties of 1648 and 1678–9. Leopold came to terms with both the Association and the Union. During the winter of 1680–1 he began to bring his standing army up to strength and to organize contributions from the Circles of the empire. Both Ernst August of Hanover and Max Emanuel of Bavaria undertook substantial military obligations. John Sobieski and the estates of Poland came forward in the spring of 1683. In July 1683 John George II of Saxony dispatched his not inconsiderable army to the battlefield on condition that Leopold bore the cost of its maintenance. In August the Great Elector was on the point of agreement with Leopold but after the relief of Vienna saw no reason to conclude. When Innocent XI, who gave financial aid, and Venice, who had been at war with Turkey since 1648, came to terms with Leopold (March 1684) the parties interested in the last of the crusades were assembled. Leopold had achieved a formidable coalition of actual fighting forces. But the enterprise on which he was engaged was only in the very broadest sense a German one. German interests were absorbed in grand European strategy.

The crusade lasted from 1683 to 1689. Great military reputations were made: those of Charles of Lorraine, Rüdiger von Starhemberg, John George of Saxony, John Sobieski, Leslie, Daun, Croy. War covered the Danube valley from Vienna to Budapest. The relief of Vienna by a European force (Sunday, 2 September 1683) was followed by the destruction of the Turkish army, on its retreat towards the Hungarian capital, and the capture of Eztergom in October 1683. This in turn was followed by a general offensive in 1684 and a thrust forward in the Mediterranean which penetrated into the Greek mainland. The outcome was the reconquest of Turkish Hungary. When the wars ended – by the Peace of Karlowitz in 1699 – Austria had acquired a new Hungarian empire, which she retained until 1918. The Habsburg monarchy was being turned into a Danube monarchy. It would be more difficult for this monarchy to transform the German structure of rights into a unit of power than it would have been for one weighted towards the west.

Yet it was characteristic of the European view of Leopold and his advisers that even during the crisis on the eastern frontier they had not lost touch with the west. When Louis XIV tried to exploit Austria's desperate need, Leopold dared to defy him. In 1682 Louis withdrew his forces from Luxemburg, which he had been blockading for several months, and threatened Leopold with his whole army. Under this threat he demanded that Leopold should recognize all his territorial acquisitions since 1678–9. Leopold steadily refused and Louis had to extend the time-limit of his ultimatum. Leopold still refused, though it was 23 August 1683 and during the siege of Vienna. It was the southern Netherlands which suffered. The Most Christian King dared not risk his reputation by invading the empire while the emperor stood at the head of a European coalition against the Turk. So he ravaged Flanders and Hainault with impunity and bombarded Luxemburg, which capitulated on 7 June 1684. Leopold then at last accepted – by the Truce of Regensburg, August 1684 – all Louis XIV's annexations, including Strasbourg and Luxemburg, in the Alsatian and Moselle areas. Louis built a wonderful defensive system, the strongest that France ever had along the best strategic frontier she ever had.

It was this frontier that foiled the activities of the next German league. This was the League of Augsburg. The impetus to the new coalition came from the Great Elector, who in March 1686 at last signed an alliance with the emperor. Thus stimulated, Leopold concluded in July 1686 the Augsburg alliance with Spain, Sweden, the Bavarian and the Franconian Circles and the Thuringian duchies, for the defence of Germany. Unlike the League of the Rhine and Waldeck's Union this was a European rather than a German combination from its inception: it was an outcome of Austria's increasingly supranational policy. Yet it nevertheless served the cause of German consolidation against France. This was more than ever necessary, since Louis was again attempting to dictate to the empire, interfering with the succession to the Palatinate and the election of the archbishop of Cologne. When Leopold refused yet again to be browbeaten, Louis invaded the four Rhenish electorates: Trier, Mainz, Cologne and the Palatinate. The emperor issued a manifesto (October 1688), said to be drafted by Leibniz, clearly proclaiming his intention to defend the established rights of the German princes. The princes of Brandenburg, Saxony, Hanover and Hesse-Cassel then signed yet another German league: the Magdeburg Union of October 1688. It was joined by William of Orange, now King of England, and the Duke of Savoy and so suffered the fate of all German leagues in becoming a European confederacy. The war of the League of Augsburg then followed: a war of sieges, ruthless devastation and the firing and demolition of cities. The very great defensive strength of France meant that she was not invaded, and that the battlefields, unless in Savoy or Flanders, were in Germany. The importance of the war for Germany was twofold. It deprived France of her footing, acquired in 1648, on the right bank of the Rhine, though it did not restore the conquests made by Louis since 1678 – Alsace was not to be 'recovered' until 1870. Secondly, the war further promoted German solidarity confusing it, as always, with European power politics and rooting it, as always, in anti-French feeling. The confusion with European politics was likely to continue; for the House of Saxony now provided the kings of Poland and that of Hanover was about to provide those of England.

At the end of the century, after the Peace of Ryswick (1697) and the Peace of Karlowitz (1699), Leopold seemed immensely strong. He embarked upon the serious pursuit of his claims to the Spanish inheritance, prefacing his endeavours by a treaty with William III in 1698. They shared the view that France must not have the whole inheritance and especially not the Spanish colonies. They were able to agree to promote the claims of a third candidate who had recently appeared. He was Joseph Ferdinand of Bavaria and had the advantages of not making the inheritance an immediate issue between Habsburg and Bourbon and of being liked in Spain, because he might be able to keep the bulk of the inheritance together. Leopold and Louis were to have compensation for surrendering their claims: the one, Milan, the other, Naples and Sicily. On Joseph Ferdinand's death, the work of European agreement had to be done over again. It failed, however. The second partition treaty was acceptable only to William III and Louis XIV or, as events proved, only to William III. Leopold's second son, the Archduke Charles, was assigned Spain, the Spanish Netherlands and Spanish America by the treaty of 1700, while the whole of her Italian territories, Milan as well as Naples and Sicily, were to go to Louis's grandson, Philip of Anjou. The treaty was unacceptable to both Leopold and Charles II of Spain and, when Charles II died on 1 November 1700, Louis set it aside and fought for the whole inheritance for his grandson, Philip of Anjou, the second son of the Dauphin, who was proclaimed king in Madrid in January 1701.

The war which followed was not at first a German war. Austria, her troops commanded by Prince Eugene of Savoy, fought the first campaign in Italy (1701). Even after the signature of the Grand Alliance and the empire's (as distinct from Austria's) declaration of war on France (1702), the fighting of German troops was still mainly in Italy. That there were German campaigns was the result of the astonishing policy of Max Emanuel of Bavaria. He tried at first to be on both sides at once. But he recognized Philip as king of Spain and he opened to French troops the fortresses of the Spanish Netherlands, of which he was Governor. By 1702 he was compelled to commit himself entirely to France. So he took Ulm, the key to the safety of Austria, and held it for France; for himself, he embarked on the conquest of the Tyrol. In 1703 a French army under Villiers invaded Swabia and marched to the Danube valley. In 1704 Louis concentrated upon reinforcing the Franco-Bavarian forces. Hence the Blenheim campaign of the Duke of Marlborough. The English victory of Blenheim, which bears in Germany the name of the second battle of Höchstadt, was fought on 13 August 1704 and ended the war in Germany. Both French and English withdrew and Bavaria was occupied and administered by Austria. Leopold died on 5 May 1705. The new emperor, Joseph I (1705–11), prepared his defences with energy and decision, but he only had to face one more French incursion – that into Swabia in 1707. He did nothing for his brother, Archduke Charles, who, under English protection, had been proclaimed king of Spain. He was more interested in gaining for Austria the Italian part of the Spanish inheritance. When Charles, in his turn, became emperor this had been done. Spain itself had become impossible for Charles to hold, since one ruler in both Spain and Austria was incompatible with the European balance of power. The Peace of Rastatt between Austria and France was signed on this basis in 1714, Charles renouncing Spain and gaining Milan, Naples and Sardinia, as well as the southern Netherlands.

Austria's place in the new European state system was distinctive. She was no longer merely a German power, but a great European power and a supranational state. She had, moreover, achieved a characteristically loose articulation. It is significant that she did not annex Bavaria. Max Emanuel was restored, and Austria did not add to her German territory. Had she done so, she would still have been a supranational state, but would have had a large instead of a small German base. She could have linked up her main possessions with her outlying lands in Swabia and stretched from the middle Danube to the upper Rhine. It is unlikely that had she done this she would have ultimately been driven out of Germany by Prussia in the way she was.

During the eighteenth century, when Charles VI (1711–40), Maria Theresa (1740–80) and for ten years (1780–90) Joseph II ruled, the Habsburg monarchy so organized its power as to preserve this loose articulation. The bond which held together the parts of the structure was the pragmatic (general) sanction. This was the sum total of the sanctions given by the several parts to a declaration which Charles VI had promulgated on 19 April 1713. It laid down the rule of succession for all his hereditary lands. On 6 December 1724 it was re-enacted with all the separate assents. It did not alter the relationship between the parts but was tantamount to an affirmation by them that they all wished to remain parts of one single whole.

The monarchy was aristocratic in its organization. On the landed estate – the community in which most men lived – the noble or gentle-man landowner was the source of all capital and enterprise, all relief in hard times, all justice and authority. Its economic activities included, besides farming, brewing and distilling, the manufacture of linen and woollen cloth, mining and metal founding. In Bohemia, Moravia and Silesia and to some extent in Hungary and Transylvania too, it included towns, the lords providing the town's magistrates, regulating its privileges, drawing a revenue from it and often maintaining in it both the inns and the shops. Only in the Austrian parts, where they were independent, did the towns prosper and produce something like the modern professional and business classes. The extensive repopulation of Hungary after its reconquest from the Turks – by 1787 its population had trebled – produced social diversification on the central plain, where free peasants settled, or landowners made no provision for peasant holdings, and sometimes imported their own wage-earning labour force. On the Transylvanian frontier there were peasants holding their land in return for military service. In the Tyrol and other mountainous parts of Austria there were free peasant proprietors. But the normal rule was the noble landowner on one side and the serf, land-holding labour force on the other – partners in a single producing unit. Given the shortage of labour, of capital and of consumer goods that lasted from the Thirty Years War until well into the eighteenth century, given the increasing frequency of a business attitude to his land on the part of the landowner, it is not surprising that serf oppression increased and capital investment by the landlord in peasant holdings and houses and in public utilities fell off. Nor is it surprising that the crown intervened to check serf oppression, since the taxation to which the estate was liable was not usually paid by the lord, but levied by him from his serfs.

The crown, then, normally had no direct contact with the peasants, only with the landowners. But the institutions through which it ruled the landowners were also staffed by them. The chancellor and coun-sellors of the Bohemian chancery, through which the crown ruled the Bohemian kingdom from Vienna, were noblemen, whether Czech or German. Similarly the Hungarian chancery, which sat in Vienna, the Hungarian treasury, which sat in Pressburg, the new *consilium regium locumtenentiale* set up by Charles VI, and the new supreme court at Pest which he also established, were staffed by lesser or greater nobles nominated by the emperor as king of Hungary. The same could be said of the court treasury (*Hofkammer*), court chancery, privy council or court war council (*Hofkriegsrat*) which dealt with the business common to all three parts of the monarchy, much Austrian business and some business of the Holy Roman Empire. This did not, of course, preclude work being sometimes actually done by meanly paid commoner deputies.

The crown's authority was most nearly absolute in the Bohemian kingdom; for, since the estates of Bohemia were parochial in outlook, since those of Moravia had been suppressed and those of Silesia were ineffective and ill attended, the landowners had no corporate organiza-tion. They could not, therefore, act as a brake on the crown. In Hun-gary, by contrast, not only was there a very large number of magnate and gentry landowning families – said to be 25,000 – but they were highly organized. They met in the diets of the ten counties to control local affairs, regulate the militia which they officered, and elect their representatives to the Lower House of the Central Hungarian Diet and other officials. The two houses of the diet (in the Upper House the magnates sat in person) had real power; for they legislated in all internal matters and appointed the Palatine who commanded in war. The Hungarian landowners were a bulwark of Hungarian independence. The position in the remaining parts of the Habsburg hereditary lands was somewhere between the Bohemian and Hungarian extremes. The estates – to which the landowners were alone summoned – had sub-stantial power and gave the aristocracy some corporate organization, which, however, it tended to use to create a partnership with the crown rather than to oppose it or control it.

The reforms of Maria Theresa showed no especially rational policy, but simply a growing administrative sophistication. Her statesmanship lay in her sensitive response to administrative needs. In 1742 she set up the *Haus- Hof- und Staatskanzlei* to deal with that business of the monarchy – principally foreign affairs – which concerned all three parts, leaving the old court chancery to deal with the internal business of the Austrian part. Thus began the development of institutions on a functional basis. In 1749 Maria Theresa carried this further. On 15 January an imperial rescript formulated the important principle of the separation of judicial from political administration. Then in May she abolished the existing Austrian and Bohemian court chanceries and set up two new functional institutions: the *erste Justizstelle*, the highest judicial authority for both Austria and Bohemia and the *Directorium in interno*, a department of internal affairs for Austria and Bohemia. Each of the two new institutions then began to carry out large-scale reorganization. In justice new codes of law were prepared. In internal affairs the new *Directorium* organized subordinate councils in the localities of Austria and Bohemia (known by a variety of names, e.g. *Gubernia*, deputations, representations) and began through them to take over business hitherto done by officials of the estates. Below these were the *Kreisämter* of Austria and Bohemia which answered for some things to the estates and for others to the officials of the crown, though they were always staffed by the crown's nominees. The increasing differentiation of business is reflected in the principal concerns of Maria Theresa's three greatest Ministers. Prince Kaunitz, who became State Chancellor in 1753, was especially concerned with foreign affairs, Count Rudolph Chotek with finance and Count Ludwig Haugwitz with internal affairs. Two further reforms, carried through between 1749 and 1753, set up the Staatsrat, an advisory council to assist in general policy and co-ordination (necessary when the business of other bodies became more specialized) and gave the financial administration an autonomy and professionalism it had not had before. Haugwitz planned a scheme of permanent taxation on all land, noble and non-noble, to maintain an army of 108,000 men, so that defence should be independent of annual grants made by the estates. When the execution of the plan was attempted in the following reign, the land survey it demanded proved in itself a stimulus to the development of administrative skills.

The difference between the radical and rational Joseph II (who ruled with his mother after the death of Francis of Lorraine in 1765) and the conservative, empirical and devout Maria Theresa was a difference of temperament and ability and not, in most respects, one of policy. The great measures of Joseph II were foreshadowed by actions of his mother and sprang from the same needs. The imperative need was for more revenue. The relief of the peasant from burdens imposed by his lord enabled him to bear more taxation imposed by the crown. So Maria Theresa, by edicts of 1767, 1771 and 1775, regulated labour services due from the serfs. That of 1767 for Hungary turned them into hereditary leasehold tenants there, able to leave the land. Joseph's edict of emancipation (1781) made the peasant a subject of the crown, instead of a chattel of his lord, from the same motive. It did not relieve him from labour services and dues and only applied to peasants with substantial holdings of their own. His second great measure, the toleration edict, also belongs to 1781. It removed all civil disabilities imposed upon non-Catholics and allowed them to worship in private according to the rites of their own faith. It did not declare a general freedom of religion. Its motive was, at least partially, economic, since the disabilities included many which obstructed, in Joseph's view, economic expansion. Its consequence was to end the close identification of the Austrian monarchy with the Roman Catholic religion that Ferdinand II had made so pronounced. To this Joseph was indifferent. The relationship between Church and State which henceforward prevailed is known as Josephism. But it had been foreshadowed by Maria Theresa, who set up machinery to enforce the regulations of the State on religious matters. She abolished clerical immunity from taxation, dissolved monasteries and made entry into the monastic life difficult. She profited from the abolition of the Jesuit order (1773) to lay the foundation of a State system of education. Joseph II, though he crowned a general continuation of this policy with a complete reorganization of dioceses and parishes, had the same aim as his mother. Both sought to weaken the link of the Church in Austria with the universal Church and to make it play a part in holding the monarchy together and bringing their citizenship home to the peasants of the villages. The third measure of 1781 was in preparation for the general land tax, instituted finally by the patent of 1789. By that date Joseph had carried through a census of the population and compiled a complete land register. A uniform land tax, levied as a percentage of gross yearly income from noble and peasant land alike, could then be established. It realized a principle, that each should pay according to his means, formulated by Joseph II, but it equally realized the plan set out by Haugwitz over thirty years earlier.

In one respect Joseph II made a clear departure in policy. He sought to end the loose articulation of his dominions and to impose a quite uncharacteristic cohesion upon them. He streamlined the administration by cutting out differences between the several parts of his dominions; he made German the one official language; he sought to mould Hungary into the system of *Kreisämter* and *Gubernia* and to make them generally as efficient and bureaucratically centralized as the later Napoleonic prefectorial system was to be; in 1784 he imposed a single protective tariff. This part of Joseph's policy did not work during his lifetime and did not survive him. Cohesion was advanced only in so far as much business formerly dealt with by committees of the estates was absorbed by the royal officials. But, by and large, the Austrian Empire emerged at the end of the eighteenth century as a loosely articulated, supranational empire in a Europe of centralized states. Its power to survive as a loosely knit group of nationalities depended upon the survival of the monarchical and aristocratic order.

In the eighteenth as in the seventeenth century the German states were polarized upon Austria in the south and Prussia in the north. Prussia had, however, developed in an opposite direction: towards close cohesion and bureaucratic organization. The power of the Junker landowner in his estate was as fundamental in Prussia as it was in the Habsburg monarchy. But demesne farming and serf owning, though prevalent, were not dominant in Cleves, Mark, Magdeburg, Halberstadt or even in the western part of Brandenburg. Moreover, from the time of the Great Elector the landowners had been excluded from the towns. These were governed by royal officials; they were differently taxed, paying an excise rather than a land tax; above all, they prospered and produced strong merchant and artisan classes. If noble land enjoyed a permanent protection, so that it could not be bought by peasant or burgher, the burgher was equally protected; for neither noble nor peasant might exercise the crafts and trade he monopolized. The peasant for his part could not be evicted by nobleman or burgher. Except in Prussia and, after 1740, in Silesia, the bureaucratic centralism of the kingdom rested upon a more varied society and a more even distribution of power and wealth than existed, as a rule, in the aristocratic Habsburg monarchy. Brandenburg-Prussia owed much of the broad basis of its strength to an absence of great personal fortunes, to the crown's policy of home colonization, which introduced men of moderate means, and to the even operation of the crown's interest in the material prosperity of its subjects.

Frederick William I (1713–40) began the process of internal centralization. The separate institutions which the Great Elector had erected in the localities and at the centre for the administration, severally, of the income from the royal domains and the income from taxation were in his reign united. Thus the line of subjection ran from the royal official (*Steuerrat*) in the towns, or from the landowner in the countryside up to the Chambers of War (for taxes) and Domains and from them up to the new board – the General Directory – in Berlin. The king dealt with the latter through his personal secretaries or *Kabinett*. He thus instituted the system of personal government through the *Kabinettsordern* of an anonymous cabinet, which Frederick the Great used so effectively. The men who staffed these bodies were officials and if some were also noblemen, this was incidental.

The army also became an effective instrument of centralization. Even if some two-thirds might still be recruited outside Prussia – especially 'die langen Kerle' for the Potsdam guard – by professional recruiting officers, supplied with much money but few scruples, a native military tradition came to predominate through the king's unremitted interest in and personal attention to his soldiers. When the army was recruited at home, the nobility for the first time became proud to serve the crown as its officers, and the tradition of the Prussian officers' corps with its exclusive social status had begun. Frederick William stimulated it by founding a corps of cadets for the education of young noblemen. The army thus drew the provinces together.

Moreover, because it was a constantly expanding force, its maintenance stimulated both economic and administrative centralization. After the establishment of the cantonal system in 1733, the towns had a part to play here. Every canton of 5,000 peasant or craftsman households was responsible for finding the recruits to keep the local regiment up to strength. The regiments were stationed in private billets in a number of garrison towns, where the local tradesmen were responsible for supplying the stores and equipment. The towns could not, therefore, remain under independent, easy-going, privileged oligarchies. The old elected town councils were abolished and replaced by paid officials, appointed for life. A typical town would be run by three burgomasters responsible respectively for justice, finance and police, assisted by some six councillors, a town clerk, a treasurer and a secretary. They were answerable to Berlin and directly controlled by the *Steuerrat*, who levied the excise, devised and helped to execute the mercantilist policy of the State and was always available to hear complaints and stimulate activity. The army was an instrument of economic centralization, because this mercantilist policy was geared to its needs. The encouragement of manufactures, the enticement of skilled immigrants, the prevention by high tariff duties of the import of corn, cloth or luxury goods and the export of raw materials for manufactures were all ways of keeping up production in order to keep up the yield of the excise, which maintained the army.

Frederick William was succeeded by Frederick the Great (1740-86) whose economic policy was one of his three principal means for increasing the power of his state. It was a policy of home colonization, land drainage and reclamation, the improvement of agricultural methods, the planting of new industries, the subvention of old, the founding of overseas trading companies and the Royal Bank and a policy of discriminatory tariffs. It was too much geared to the production of goods (cloth or armaments) needed by the army, too much dominated by family and State monopolies and too much confined by rigid class distinctions to be a policy creative of economic change. But it stimulated a conservative economy sufficiently to be of *political* importance: to increase effectively, that is, the power of the Prussian state.

His second principal instrument was his own immense energy. He was not an organizer as his father had been, but a man of action, courage and above all of grim toughness. He was the dynamo which generated the current that worked Frederick William's bureaucratic machine at a new pace. The fixed routine of each day enabled him to work tirelessly after five or six hours' sleep. He read his political letters before breakfast and before a midday dinner had answered these and scribbled or dictated enough to indicate how all the petitions, reports and other State documents, prepared and sorted by his *Kabinett* secretaries, should be dealt with. The rest of the day could be filled as the routine of the year prescribed. This routine allowed him to travel through his dominions in the summer and to inspect the army in the autumn. During these tours everything came under his eye and he was infinitely accessible. The machine was improved in so far as Frederick the Great added to the undifferentiated system of the General Directory functional Ministries – for trade (1742), for Silesia (1742), for military administration (1746), for the *régie* or new excise farmed by a French firm, for mining (1768), for forestry (1770) – like those for foreign affairs and justice that had begun to exist under Frederick William. But the power of Prussia under Frederick the Great depended upon him as much as upon the machine which he ran.

Finally, the third instrument for the extension of his power was the army, which he expanded, reorganized and above all used. He increased it from 72,000 to 195,000 men, thus more than doubling its size. It constituted 4 per cent of the population and required nearly two-thirds of his revenue for its upkeep. In financing the Seven Years War, he was helped by British subsidies, levies on Saxony and other occupied territories, but the bulk of the burden was borne by the increased war fund. Frederick was unwearied in building fortifications, improving the system of grain depots, drilling and inspecting troops and devising new ideas on training, tactics and strategy.

Frederick the Great's main concern was Prussian power. But he shared the rationalist philosophy of his age and applied it, with Cocceji's assistance, to the reform of justice and the recodification of Prussian law. The conservatism of the new codes was, however, marked: they retained, for example, the rigid legal barriers between class and class. Yet it was in relation to justice that Frederick – with the story of miller Arnold – lived long in popular legend. He did not end the system of patrimonial justice on the Junker estates, but he increased the security of all in their civil rights. If the Prussian world was a somewhat harsh, bureaucratic world of labour and service, it was also a law-abiding and upright world where everyone ultimately had his due.

The eighteenth, like the seventeenth, was for the German states a century of war. But war, with more tightly disciplined armies, no longer caused widespread destruction, famine and disease. It was used with a most precise economy as the instrument for the assertion of the power of the tightly knit bureaucratic Prussian kingdom against the loosely organized, hierarchical Habsburg monarchy. The battlefields were now in the north, centre and east. The Great Northern War (1700–21) had, indeed, been limited to north-east Germany. It arose from the ambitions of Charles XII of Sweden, but the future of both Saxony and Prussia was decided by it. The general settlement of Nystad left Augustus of Saxony just about as strong as he was when the war began. He retained both Poland and Saxony, though during the war he had been dispossessed of both. Hanover, by acquiring Bremen and Verden, grew significantly. But Prussia by acquiring most of Swedish Pomerania and Stettin made a more notable gain of strength. Prussia's activity during the war was all the more important because of the small part played in it by the Holy Roman Emperor.

Charles VI was indeed the first emperor of whom it may, with some

H

accuracy, be said that he had no German policy. He had a Turkish policy and considerably improved the monarchy's position in the east. The Peace of Passarowitz, 31 July 1718, gave Austria the Banat of Temesvar, the last part of the old Hungarian monarchy to be recovered, and also large parts of Serbia, including Belgrade and a strip of Wallachia. These last territories were lost in the reign of Joseph II, but their temporary possession, coupled with the decline of Ottoman greatness, gave the monarchy security on its south-eastern frontier.

Charles also had a maritime policy. He tried to develop the Mediterranean trade of Trieste as well as the overseas trade of Ostend in the recently acquired southern Netherlands. Despite efforts to use the alliance, first of England, Holland and France and then of Spain for this purpose, his maritime policy had failed by 1729 and alienated all these powers from him.

Charles further had an Italian policy. This had been so far successful as to enable him to exchange Sardinia for Sicily (1720). But after 1723 his policy was increasingly bedevilled by the desire to gain European acceptance of the pragmatic sanction. In 1725 he reversed the old system of alliance with England and Holland and allied with Spain, who accepted the pragmatic sanction. England, France, Holland and Prussia then coalesced in the alliance of Hanover. Charles's reply was an alliance with Russia, who also accepted the pragmatic sanction. This was too much for Prussia, who renewed friendship with Austria and gave her adhesion to the pragmatic sanction. In 1731 by the Treaty of Vienna (16 March) Charles surrendered both his maritime and Italian policies in order to recover the alliance of England and Holland and to gain their adhesion to the pragmatic sanction. In Italy Charles accepted the Spanish succession to Parma and Piacenza and their immediate occupation by Spanish troops. Two years later he was engaged in the War of Polish Succession. At stake, ultimately, were the security of the eastern frontier of the Austrian monarchy and the ascendancy of France in Europe. The immediate issue was whether the Polish throne should go to the French candidate, Stanislas Leszczinski, or the Austrian candidate, yet another Augustus of Saxony. The second Treaty of Vienna of 3 October 1735 settled Augustus's accession to Poland and made provision for Stanislas Leszczinski's taking the duchy of Lorraine, provided that it reverted to France on his death. The Duke of Lorraine, Francis Stephen, was to be married to Charles's heiress, his daughter, Maria Theresa, and to receive Tuscany, when the Medici line died out. The marriage was celebrated in 1736 and Francis acceded to Tuscany in

1737. The definitive peace signed on 8 November 1738 confirmed all these arrangements. Charles paid the price in Italy. Here he gave up Naples and Sicily to Spain and acquired the miniscule territories of Parma and Piacenza instead. The Treaty of Aix-la-Chapelle after the War of Austrian Succession in 1748 arranged for Parma and Piacenza to go to Philip of Spain. Thus in Charles's reign the Italian possessions of the Habsburgs, with Lombardy directly ruled and Tuscany under a Habsburg collateral, acquired the shape they continued to have until the mid-nineteenth century, except that they did not yet include Venice.

In 1740 Maria Theresa succeeded Charles VI, and Francis of Lorraine was elected Holy Roman Emperor. This partition of responsibility meant the strengthening of the tendency of the Austrian monarchy to dispense with a German policy. It is not surprising, then, that Frederick the Great's increasing power entitled him to claim what the Habsburgs discarded. He increased his territories with a ruthlessness which surpassed even that of Louis XIV. In 1740 he invaded Silesia. Uninformed opinion condemned his action as unchivalrous and vaguely dishonest. Informed opinion condemned it as an infraction of the pragmatic sanction and as such a threat to European security. Frederick had anticipated this view and had told the chief foreign courts that he did not dispute Maria Theresa's succession to the Habsburg lands, only to the four Jagendorf duchies in Silesia which belonged to the Hohenzollern. But the first Silesian War ended, after the victory of Mollwitz, with the truce of Klein Schnellendorf, October 1741, which left Frederick with the whole of Lower Silesia. Even he dared not deny that his next step was an infraction of the pragmatic sanction; for in 1742 he renewed the war as a member of a confederacy headed by France and pledged to support the succession of the Elector of Bavaria to the Austrian dominions and to the title of emperor.

Frederick no longer disguised his motives of self-interest: to establish decisively by some spectacular act the international standing of his state; to consolidate his territories so that the pattern of scattered small units might be replaced by the pattern of one large solid block with outliers; to increase his resources by the Silesian treasure house of minerals, corn and manufactures. His behaviour to his allies during the war established his reputation for unscrupulous self-interest. In July 1742, after the victory of Chotusitz, he deserted them, making peace for himself and Saxony in the Treaty of Berlin. But when the general war went too well for Austria, he rejoined the confederacy. The victory of Hohenfriedburg gave him all he wanted, so he signed the Peace of

Dresden (December 1745), deserted his allies a second time, clinched his reputation for ruthless militarism and gained all Silesia.

In 1756 Frederick the Great invaded Saxony. He felt himself strong enough to enter what became the Seven Years War on the thinnest of pretexts. He adopted the defence of preventive war, arguing that unless he attacked first, he would be attacked by a powerful European coalition. The only way to forestall Austria's attack was to threaten her Bohemian frontier; it was unfortunate that the way to Bohemia lay through Saxony. But the agreements between Austria and France that constituted the so-called diplomatic revolution only acquired an offensive character after Prussian diplomatic and military movements had begun. There is ample evidence that Frederick had long planned the conquest of Saxony – the next leaf of the artichoke – and by the disposition of troops he in fact made. After the great victories at Rossbach (November 1757) and Leuthen (December 1757) and the drawn battle of Zorndorf against Russia, Frederick negotiated for peace. His terms show his determination to acquire Saxon territory, if not the whole of Saxony; for he was prepared to offer Rhenish territory to France and East Prussia to Russia in order to gain it. The Peace of Hubertusberg in 1763 left this ambition unfulfilled. But the scale of the operations against Austria, France and Russia, and his success in pursuing the calculated aggression that had begun them, marked the emergence of Prussia 'as the keystone of the European balance of power'. She had displaced France as the rival of Austria.

Finally, calculated aggression brought Frederick West Prussia. In 1764 he signed an alliance with the Empress Catherine II of Russia. It contained a mutual guarantee of territories and promises of military assistance against common enemies, but its principal object was the establishment of a dependent of Catherine II, Stanislas Poniatowski, on the throne of Poland. When Poniatowski had been crowned and Russia's influence over Poland made secure, Catherine II had gained what she wanted. Frederick, however, was only at the beginning of his plans. He continued to develop them by provoking civil war in Poland and by undermining every effort Poniatowski made to reform or strengthen the monarchy. By 1768 Catherine was at war with Turkey and by 1769–70 Joseph II of Austria was negotiating reconciliation with Prussia. Frederick used this heaven-sent opportunity to make Russia feel her dependence upon Prussia's friendship and to induce her to pay his price for security in it. His price turned out to be a territorial distribution: West Prussia from Poland to Prussia, Polish territory on the Hungarian border to Austria and whatever Polish territory Russia cared to take in compensation. The first partition of Poland was carried through by the Treaties of 5 August 1772.

One last opportunity Frederick used. That was the war between Austria and Bavaria which arose when Austria contested the succession of Karl Theodor, who already ruled the Palatinate, Jülich and Berg, to the electorate of Bavaria. The Peace of Teschen (May 1779) which concluded it in Karl Theodor's favour brought him Ansbach and Bayreuth in Franconia. Austria had for some time now sought to reverse the decision of 1714 (see above, p. 209) and to exchange the Austrian Netherlands for Bavaria. It is not surprising that the equality with her that Prussia had established brought this ambition to a head; nor that, by negotiating the *Fürstenbund* in 1785, Frederick the Great foiled it. This league also marks the point at which Frederick annexed Austria's German mission to himself. There may have been something spurious in Frederick's claim to protect 'the liberties of Germany', but he made it in the intimacy of letters to his sister Wilhelmina, and no less a person than Mirabeau ascribed to him the right to do so. It was a real claim, if it meant that he would protect the princes of the empire against the emperor and had the effective power to do so. Frederick had used three wars to demonstrate that his power was greater in Germany than that of the Habsburgs. It became for the first time possible to speculate whether Prussia might not turn Austria out of Germany and herself create a single power unit out of the structure of rights that was the Holy Roman Empire.

The rise of Prussia was only the most striking phenomenon that accompanied Austria's becoming more of a Danubian monarchy. The emergence of 'the third Germany' – Saxony, Württemberg, Bavaria, the two Hessen, Hanover and Baden – was equally important though less conspicuous. The electorate of Saxony was a relatively compact territory with good natural resources at the junction of two trunk routes, the one from Hamburg to Austria, the other from the Rhineland to Poland. Its population was large; its characteristic community was the town rather than the landed estate; it was the leading industrial and commercial centre of Germany. Frederick Augustus III (1763–1827) was a good administrator, patient, punctilious and cool, who ruled by wisdom rather than rigid principle. Saxony prospered, because private and traditional enterprise was unhampered, and it became the home of the first German bourgeoisie in the Marxist sense. It was a Lutheran state whose royal house became Catholic, when it began to provide kings of Poland. Above all, it was a state with pretensions to equality with Prussia and Austria. Frederick Augustus had no particular policy towards Revolutionary France. He remained neutral when Prussia and Austria declared war on France in 1792; he supplied his contingent to the troops of the Upper Saxon Circle when the empire declared war in 1793, but kept his state free from war and its costs from 1796 to 1805. After Napoleon's victories there was, however, no room for neutrals. Frederick Augustus had provided Prussia with troops, when she made the Jena campaign, but saved his state and, indeed, enlarged it at Prussia's expense by joining the victorious Napoleon in time. From 1806 onwards Saxony was bound to France as a member of the Confederation of the Rhine, obliged to supply 20,000 men and a sub-sidy each year. It was, after Jena, for some time occupied and adminis-tered by French intendants. The last German battlefields (Leipzig, 1813) of the Napoleonic Wars were on Saxon territory. At the Peace of Vienna, Saxony lost territory to Prussia, but the kingdom of Saxony, as it had become in 1806, was not weaker than it had been in 1800 and it continued to develop unobtrusively. It continued to be politically conservative and economically progressive. The absolutism of its kings was limited only by the imperfect powers of the parliament set up in 1833. About the same time it became the home of the first German proletariat.

Hesse-Darmstadt, which also lay partly to the north of the Main, was ruled by a landgrave who practised, under the stimulus of danger from French attack, *Realpolitik* half a century before the word was invented. Ludwig X (1790–1830) was an optimistic, intelligent, self-confident man, whose mind had been moulded by the rationalist and progressive notions of the University of Leyden. Conscious of the defenceless condition of his territories, in 1790, he desperately offered troops, sought subsidies and tried to keep both revolutionary agents and French *émigrés* out. From 1793 to 1801 Hesse-Darmstadt was at war with France. The state was too far south to profit from the neutrality for north Germany, which Prussia had gained from France at Basle in 1795, and so remained at war until the Peace of Lunéville (1801). The astute Ludwig relied on his own resources and by skilful representation and lavish expenditure of money in Paris gained for himself promises of secularized ecclesiastical territory and free cities of the empire as com-pensation for what he lost on the left bank of the Rhine. These promises were made good in 1803 and 1806, and France recognized the sovereign independence of the Grand Duchy, as it became, of Hesse-Darmstadt.

Ludwig joined the Confederation of the Rhine and his troops fought on Napoleon's side at the battle of Leipzig, but he joined the last coalition against Napoleon and so gained recognition of his independence from the other European powers. Ludwig had inherited and acquired a complex of territories and stood in a variety of relationships to his old feudatories and new subjects. Under Napoleon's protection he annulled privileges, immunities and exemptions and proclaimed the unlimited power of the state. By 1815 Hesse-Darmstadt was a well-consolidated state of some considerable size. With the abolition of guild monopolies, the emancipation of serfs and the introduction of a parliamentary constitution, all before 1820, it was ready to take a leading part in the liberal national movement of the nineteenth century.

To the south of Hesse-Darmstadt lay the margravate of Baden-Durlach. It was even more directly threatened by France. Karl Friedrich (1746–1811) was an able man of strong character, who accepted, like Ludwig of Hesse-Darmstadt, the progressive ideas of his day. He was also singularly articulate and penetrating in writing of the problems of Germany. He tried to activate the empire and to induce the princes to combine in self-defence. He joined Austria and Prussia in declaring war upon Revolutionary France in 1792 and remained at war with her until 1796, when he signed a separate peace. Thenceforward, again like Ludwig, he negotiated independently in Paris to acquire territorial spoil. The treaty he signed with Napoleon in May 1802 assigned to Baden ecclesiastical land and imperial towns which with few exceptions were already surrounded by her territory and, in addition, the secularized bishoprics of Constance, Basle, Strasbourg and Speyer so far as they lay on the right bank of the Rhine. These were all incorporated in 1803 and further gains followed in 1806. Karl Friedrich joined the Confederation of the Rhine and gained from France recognition of his sovereign independence as Grand Duke. He paid the price in men and money. He had already fought on Napoleon's side during the war of the third coalition in 1805, and he and his successor, Karl Ludwig (1811–18), were on his side during the war of the fourth coalition and at the time of the battle of Leipzig. Karl Ludwig, like Ludwig of Hesse-Darmstadt, was, however, a member of the last coalition against France and so gained from the other European powers recognition of his independent sovereignty. Baden, again like Hesse-Darmstadt, acquired a parliamentary constitution (1818) and was by 1820 an up-to-date, well-consolidated state ready to play a forward part in the liberal national movement.

To the east of Baden lay the duchy of Württemberg: half Catholic and half Protestant. It was conscious, like Saxony, of a certain international standing and was almost comparable in size. Karl Eugen (1744–93) had lavished money upon an extravagant court, costly theatre, opera and ballet companies and orchestras, upon buildings, an academy of painting, a magnificent royal library and the Karlsschule. He had later abjured this patronage of pleasure and settled down to spend upon model farms and manufactures. When Revolutionary France repudiated feudal obligations and annexed the territory of German rulers, to whom Louis XVI stood in some feudal relationship, Karl Eugen was a considerable loser. He preferred to negotiate with successive regimes in France rather than depend upon the empire to protect his rights; he still remained neutral when the empire declared war on France in 1793. His death (24 October 1793) brought his younger brothers, Ludwig Eugen and Friedrich Eugen to power in turn. They brought Württemberg into the war and fought against France until 1796. Württemberg was at peace when Duke Friedrich succeeded (1797–1816), but he re-entered the war and fought it with unprecedented vigour. This did not prevent him from negotiating with Napoleon and he gained, by a treaty of 1802, an assignment of secularized ecclesiastical territory and imperial cities, which he duly annexed in 1803. Württemberg stands apart from all the other German states by the seriousness of its response to the French Revolution. Elsewhere the first heady enthusiasm, on the part mostly of writers and urban artisans, was followed by disengagement, but in Württemberg a serious movement developed (1794–8) to convert the already powerful estates into an elective parliament, if not to turn the duchy into a republic. Like Karl Friedrich of Baden, Duke Friedrich changed sides and fought for Napoleon against Austria in 1805. He made further acquisitions of territory and was recognized as an independent sovereign with the title of king when he joined the Confederation of the Rhine and signed a fresh alliance with Napoleon (1806). He, too, was on Napoleon's side during the war of the fourth coalition (1809) and at the time of the battle of Leipzig. But at the end he too was a member of the last coalition against Napoleon and so gained from the other European powers recognition of his independent sovereignty. For him, too, a parliamentary constitution (1819) completed the reorganization of his state that took place as a result of the Napoleonic wars. Württemberg was only slightly less affected by the liberal national movement than Baden.

The extensive dominions of Karl Theodor (1777-99) of Bavaria-Palatinate entitled him to be regarded as one of the most powerful of German rulers in the eighteenth century. He pursued a reforming policy and was associated with the Catholic enlightenment. But he was a cautious ruler, of average ability, who preferred to husband rather than use the resources of his complex state. He was always on the defensive against French and Prussian ambitions in the Rhineland and Austrian designs upon Bavaria. Many of the plans for resisting Revolutionary France inevitably turned upon him, but he was no Frederick the Great and did not rise to the occasion. Bavaria, nevertheless, supplied her contingents like Saxony, when the empire declared war against France. Karl Theodor lost his southern Rhineland territories, when the left bank of the Rhine was annexed by France (1795), and Berg in the north later became the core of the artificial state which Napoleon fashioned (1806) for Murat, husband to Napoleon's sister Caroline and known as Prince Joachim. By this time Max Joseph had already ruled in Bavaria for six years. Like Friedrich of Württemberg he had fought in the war of the second coalition against France with unusual energy; and like Friedrich, although somewhat earlier (1801), obtained promises of territory from Napoleon. Again like Friedrich he changed sides and by 1805 was an ally of Napoleon fighting against Austria and the third coalition. Most of the Bavarian annexations in 1803 and 1806 were of enclaves within existing dominions or enabled her to push her frontiers east. Max Joseph was recognized as king by Napoleon in 1806 and by the allies in 1813, for in 1812-13 he was still in step with Württemberg. Membership of the Confederation of the Rhine and the reorganization necessary to supply the insatiable Napoleon's demands for men and money stimulated thoroughgoing reform in Bavaria. It was the time of her greatest general, Field-Marshal Fürst von Wrede, and of her greatest statesman, Freiherr de Montgelas, who was Minister from 1799 to 1817. In 1818 she too acquired a parliamentary constitution, but she was not greatly affected by the liberal national movement.

It remains only to refer to the Thuringian duchies, to Hanover and Hesse-Cassel to complete the picture of the third Germany. There were some half-dozen tiny Thuringian duchies clustering in a bunch at the south-western tip of the kingdom of Saxony. Saxe-Gotha or Saxe-Coburg were often given as examples, when foreigners wished to scoff at the pretensions of the little German states. But Karl August of Saxe-Weimar (1775-1828) was taken seriously. Able, original and discerning, he appointed Goethe to his privy council and combined the patronage of all progressive ideas with the organization of an effective army and the expression of an articulate German patriotism. He joined Prussia and Austria in war upon France in 1792, but from 1795 until 1806 he was glad to remain neutral. He survived Napoleonic reorganization to be restored in 1815 and to endow his state with a parliamentary constitution in 1816. Landgrave Wilhelm of Hesse-Cassel (1785–1821) was active in supporting the attempt of Karl Friedrich of Baden to bring about an association of princes to defend Germany against Revolutionary France in 1789–92. He joined Prussia in war against her in 1792 and supplied troops to England and to the empire when they declared war in 1793; but he lapsed into neutrality under Prussia's protection from 1795 to 1805. He lost territory when France annexed the left bank of the Rhine and secured both territorial compensation and elevation to the status of elector in 1802–3. He was one of the few German princes who made the Jena campaign by the side of Prussia against Napoleon in 1806 and suffered accordingly. He was deposed and Hesse-Cassel became (with Hanover, Brunswick and the duchy of Westphalia, taken from Hesse-Darmstadt) part of the artificial state – the kingdom of Westphalia – which Napoleon created in 1806 for his brother Jerome. Elector Wilhelm was restored in 1815, but he did not provide his subjects with a parliament and his state had an unhappy history of internal conflict, until it was finally absorbed into Prussia in 1866. The fate of Hanover under the rule of George III of England was not dissimilar. In 1793 she took part in the war against France; she was nominally neutral from 1795 to 1805, under the protection of Prussia; sacrificed in the Napoleonic territorial reorganization of 1806, she disappeared from the map until 1815. She too had a history of internal conflict and ultimate absorption into Prussia.

The impact of the French Revolution and of the wars which followed stimulated, then, the emergence to importance and independence of the medium-sized states. At the same time they destroyed the Holy Roman Empire. The disappearance of this ancient structure of rights when confronted by a modern territorial state, such as Revolutionary France had become, was to be expected. Yet it went gradually and with difficulty by three stages. The first stage lasted from 1792 to 1799. The disturbance of territorial rights, when France annulled feudal obligations in 1789, and the presence of the French émigrés on German soil were the immediate causes of war in 1792. Important too were the miscalculations and ambitions of Frederick William II of Prussia and the unwisdom of a new young ruler (Francis II) in Austria in accepting the war which Emperor Leopold (1790–2) might have avoided. Deeper causes were the impulses of fear and idealism at work in France and the responses they provoked outside. Fighting spread in 1793, when the empire, Britain and Holland declared war upon France. The German victory of Longwy was won and the defeat at Valmy suffered on French soil, but by the end of 1793 the French were in possession of Mainz and a substantial part of the Rhineland. Thenceforward fighting between Germans and Frenchmen was wholly on German soil. The war of the first coalition ended, however, for north Germany when Prussia made the Peace of Basle in 1795; for some other German states in 1796, for Austria in 1797, with the Peace of Campo Formio, and for the empire as a whole in the abortive negotiation at the Congress of Rastatt (November 1797–April 1799). The results may be summarized. Peace in north Germany for ten years (1795–1805) was significant for art and letters. Austria lost the southern Netherlands, which she had ruled for just under a century, experienced a temporary change in Italian possessions, losing Lombardy and gaining Venice, and was more than ever a Danubian monarchy. All Germany west of the Rhine had been incorporated in France, some since 1793, some since 1795 and the rest by 1797, but its annexation was not definitively accepted by the empire with whom no peace was in fact achieved. The principle was accepted, before the Congress of Rastatt broke up, under the shadow of the murder of the French representatives, that ecclesiastical territory in south Germany should be secularized to provide compensation for those princes dispossessed west of the Rhine. It was the acceptance of this principle which entitled these years to be described as a stage in the disappearance of the Holy Roman Empire.

The second stage in the disappearance of the empire lasted from 1799 to 1803. The war of the second coalition engulfed the whole of Europe and was on a larger scale than any previous war. But the German campaigns, apart from Moreau's march through Bavaria (1800) and his victory over the Austrians at Hohenlinden, were relatively unimportant. The Peace of Lunéville (February 1801) brought the war of the second coalition to an end for both Austria and the empire. It was followed by negotiations at Regensburg about the application of the principle of secularization and compensation accepted at Rastatt. They were between the French and a deputation of the imperial diet (*Reichsdeputation*, see above, p. 201). The outcome was to confirm the French possession of Germany west of the Rhine; to sharpen the separation of the emperor from the empire, since far from protecting it against

France he joined in the competition for spoil; and to institute the territorial distribution and the mediatization[1] of imperial territory by the *Reichsdeputationshauptschluß* (25 February 1803), known as the Princes' Revolution. The chief beneficiaries, as we have seen, were the South German states.

The third stage in the disappearance of the empire lasted from 1803 to 1806. In May 1803, only a week after the *Reichsdeputation* had been dissolved, war had already been renewed between France and Britain, who was soon joined by Austria, and together they negotiated the third coalition. Between 1804 and 1806 the defencelessness of the German princes became so clear that all but Ludwig X of Hesse-Darmstadt among those in the south, as we have seen, sought the protection of France. Francis II had already on 14 August 1804 proclaimed himself Francis I of Austria and taken his dissociation from the Holy Roman Empire a step further. His defeat at Austerlitz (December 1805) was the signal for the signature of a number of treaties which made a general pacification and enabled Napoleon further to strengthen Hesse-Darmstadt, Baden, Württemberg and Bavaria. They then (1805-6) completed their consolidation by absorbing all the territory of former imperial counts and knights. This was called the Knights' Revolution. In north Germany Prussia at last broke her neutrality, was defeated in the disastrous Jena campaign and not rescued by Russia, who intervened ineffectively. The peace treaties of Erfurt and Tilsit enabled Napoleon to effect a territorial redistribution in north Germany and to create the satellite states of Westphalia, Berg and Frankfurt. The Emperor of the French, as Napoleon had become in 1804, next stepped into the place of the Holy Roman Emperor as head of the German princes. Sixteen states, including the four South German ones, joined the Confederation of the Rhine and thereby undertook to abjure the Holy Roman Empire and to accept Napoleon's protection. Saxony joined soon afterwards. Finally on 6 August 1806 Francis I issued the proclamation dissolving the Holy Roman Empire.

It remained to be determined what new order would evolve from all this destruction; for all that had so far been achieved was the independence and the strengthening of the medium-sized states of the third Germany. These had swallowed up nearly all the 300 pieces of the old mosaic and the number of German states had fallen to something over thirty. The alternatives lay between a further consolidation forced upon the governments from below on one side, and the creation of some new

[1] A technical term for the dissolving of one imperial territory in another.

bond between the much-strengthened governments on the other side. The first movement, though it had powerful men such as vom Stein among its leaders, never came to anything. The first spontaneous explosion of German patriotism (1808-9) was provoked by the rule of Napoleon's relatives and the trade war inaugurated by his continental system. The leaders of the risings against Napoleon looked for help to Austria, now under the reforming Minister, Philip Stadion. But the defeat of Wagram, the marriage of Marie Louise to Napoleon (1810) and the supersession of Stadion by Metternich put an end to their hopes. By 1813 the leaders of the German movement looked instead to Prussia, which had been reformed and reinvigorated by Stein, Hardenberg, Gneisenau and Scharnhorst. Stein got rid of the *Kabinettssystem* in the central government and restored the self-government of the towns. His emancipation edict will be discussed below. Hardenberg restored the finances. Gneisenau and Scharnhorst reformed the army.

Frederick William III (1797-1840) was pushed into the lead in 1813 by the Prussian nobility and generals, supported by the peasants, who were also the rank and file of the army, and the academic and merchant classes of Berlin. The *Tugendbund* canalized the devoted patriotism of the first group; the poet Ernst Moritz Arndt expressed that of the second; while the philosopher Johann Gottlieb Fichte, in his *Reden an die deutsche Nation*, rendered articulate the somewhat muddled idealism of the third. The retreat of the Napoleonic armies from Russia provided the occasion for Frederick William's revolt from Napoleon's control. Napoleon was defeated at the battle of Leipzig by a coalition of German princes under Prussia's leadership. His armies were swept back into France. Leipzig is rightly called the battle of the nations; for many European nations fought there and there were Germans on both sides.

The defeat of Napoleon transformed the situation and enabled the governments, and especially the Austrian government, or rather Metternich, to recover control. The initiative from below died away. Metternich manipulated both Castlereagh of Britain and Alexander of Russia so that, by yielding them what they were most interested in, he gained for himself freedom to reorganize Germany. The governments were in control of the situation when they stood together. Metternich had worked the miracle of bringing them together by securing the allies' recognition of the independent sovereignty of each of the four South German states and later of Saxony. The dissolution of the Napoleonic satellites and the release of the left bank of the Rhine from France, the restoration of some of the German states, the recovery of the

Germany

E A

DANZIG
(free city after 1918)

EAST

PRUSSIA

S   I   A

(P   o   s   e   n)

Warthe

Vistula

R   U   S   S   I   A

Oder

Vistula

Elbe

CRACOW

M I A)

U   S   T   R   I   A   N

U S T R I A)   (H U N G A R Y)

E   M   P   I   R   E

Danube

s

Palatinate by Bavaria and the creation of the Prussian Rhine Province, the redrawing of the Prussian-Saxon boundaries, the restoration of Polish Posen to Prussia and Polish Galicia to Austria – all this completed the new political map of Germany made at the Congress of Vienna in 1815.

The German states to the number of thirty-eight, later thirty-nine, constituted a league or diplomatic alliance, known as the Germanic Confederation. They were pledged not to make war upon each other and to render each other military assistance at need. In order to arrange this and other matters of common interest their diplomatic representatives met in a diet at Frankfurt. Austria was president of the new organization and Prussia was content to play the second part. Europe was still a society of governments and not of nations and into this society the new Germanic Confederation fitted well enough. It is true that the King of Holland, as Duke of Luxemburg, and the King of Denmark, as Duke of Holstein, were members of the Germanic Confederation, but it was nevertheless a more nearly all-German organization than the Holy Roman Empire, the political structure which it superseded.

The Germanic Confederation failed to correspond to the idea of the German nation which social changes that had happened during the wars had done much to stimulate. There grew up a cultural nationalism which was far in 1815 from having the force which it subsequently obtained. The prerequisites for this force did, however, already exist in 1815.

The idea of the State as composed of the common subjects of one prince was already yielding place to an idea of the State as the members of a single society. Whether the State was governed by a monarch or not, a sense of membership was one precondition of men's identification of it with the nation. This change in political assumptions is partly explained by the influence of the philosophers.

The fifty years from Kant to Hegel, roughly from 1780 to 1830, was the golden age of German political philosophy. Though ideas during this period spanned the whole range of liberal, conservative and 'state-power' thought, they had a single effect, in so far as they stimulated a new openmindedness towards the problems of government and a sense, among those whom they influenced, that they were themselves responsible for their own fate. Herder by the poetry and wisdom of his writing familiarized Germans with the notion of a peculiarly German contribution to the general stock of human civility and virtue, and taught them to think of this as made by themselves, not by their princes and governors. Kant was especially important in creating for Germans a notion of the State as a community of free, equal and self-dependent citizens. His influence stimulated the belief that men were free in society because they lived under the restraints of the law, which in turn was not imposed but grew out of the tension between the sociable and unsociable qualities in the individual. The rule of law implied a dynamism, since it was achieved only by the constant effort of all men in society. The monarch, whom Kant saw no reason to abolish, and his subjects were constantly involved in this effort of reasoning out what it was right to do and constantly acting upon the knowledge of right at which they thus arrived. Humboldt drew out and elaborated what was implicit in Kant's ideas, namely, the view that the function of the State should be limited to the enforcement of the law. He taught that the State should concern itself neither with morality, the motives of men's actions, nor their material well-being. In concrete terms, the liberals of the nineteenth century expressed the notion of membership and self-dependence, which they derived from Kant and Humboldt, in demands for elective parliaments, a free press, defence by a citizens' militia and trial by jury. Conservative thinkers such as Novalis, Adam Müller or Josef Görres endowed the religious ideal with new life. They attached more importance than the liberals to authority in the State, or rather to the monarch in whom its unity was expressed. But with them, too, monarchism was coupled with a notion of citizenship. The conservatives thought in terms of a society in which each man had his place in a hierarchical structure; they, too, postulated general participation or equal service to the State from each according to his position. The opposite interpretations to which Hegel was subjected are discussed in chapter 6. The only generalization that needs to be made here is that during his lifetime (d. 1831) his influence too stimulated the Germans' passion for political theorizing. This in turn increased their open-mindedness on political questions and their sense of self-dependence in solving them. This political vitality and this element of self-reliance in it help to explain the widespread commitment in the early nineteenth century to the aim of creating a German state that should correspond to the German nation, as its common way of life or its law, its common experience or its history had made it and as its common language marked it off to the outside world. Nor is it surprising that there should be widespread interest in political speculation in a land where many who had been petty sovereigns (as imperial counts or knights) were now subjects and politically dispossessed.

The emancipation of the serfs, and the enlargement of the political nation which resulted from it, was another prerequisite for the national movement. In the Rhineland, south-west Germany and in parts of Saxony, serf tenure, though it existed, was relatively unimportant. The feudal principle of many people with smaller or greater rights in the same piece of land was easily displaced here by the principles of absolute ownership and individual freedom. It happened either during the period of annexation to France, or, for the three Napoleonic creations of Westphalia, Berg and Frankfurt, during the period of government under the Napoleonic code. Elsewhere in western Germany as in Baden (by 1783) or Holstein (by 1800) or Württemberg serfdom simply died out. In Bavaria, where the landed estate rather than the town was the community in which most men lived, and serfdom had been more important, a series of edicts, the last of 1808, had the effect of abolishing serfdom and of gradually bringing feudal tenures to an end. Labour services continued to exist and Bavaria only became a land of peasant proprietors and rent-paying farmers during the first half of the nineteenth century. In Prussia Stein's emancipation edict of 1807 swept away, at one stroke, the prohibitions upon burghers of buying land, upon noblemen of engaging in trade and upon peasants of buying land traditionally owned by noblemen. It abolished the legal status of serfdom and many of the most personal services. It effected a revolution in the social basis of legal relationships. But it was not until 1850 that a workable system of compensation for the landowners enabled dependent tenures to be brought to an end. It is true that the lord's power (e.g. his judicial power) also survived in some estates in east Germany, which were exempted from the authority of the organs of local government, until 1918. But after Stein's edict of emancipation there were no longer large numbers of men in Prussia of whom it could be said that they belonged to other men and were not directly citizens of the State. In Austria, where labour services survived until 1848, there was not the same marked growth in free citizenship: it had begun earlier (under Joseph II) and was slower in being accomplished. Broadly speaking the abolition of all privileges and tax and legal immunities had accompanied the emancipation of the serfs. Before the law and the administration, all individuals became equal, either because this was one of the assets of French administration or, as in Hesse-Darmstadt, Württemberg and Bavaria, because this was the only way that these states could supply the ever-increasing numbers of men and amounts of money which Napoleon exacted from the members of the Confederation of the Rhine.

In addition to the vitality of political speculation and the growth in political equality, there was a third change. Land lost its primacy as a claim to political power. The Rhineland, much of north-west and south-west Germany and Saxony were town-dwelling and enjoyed a steady spell of prosperity during the late eighteenth century. There were big commercial and financial centres at Hamburg, Leipzig, Frankfurt-am-Main and bustling industrial towns, for example at Remschied, Solingen and Chemnitz. There were innumerable state capitals and watering-places that created good markets for consumer goods of all kinds. The economy of these areas was dislocated, but not depressed, by the French annexation, by incorporation into one of the new states, or by the French continental system. The consequence of continued prosperity was the cumulative increase in the wealth and self-confidence of the *Bürgertum* in these areas. Monied men, however, had often too much to lose to be the most active of the new classes, pressing forward into political power. Already in the eighteenth century the increasing complication and sophistication of administration coupled with the political fragmentation of Germany had worked to create an abnormally large class of officials. The bureaucracies of the princes tended to form a distinct social class cutting across state boundaries and detached from state loyalties. The fall in the number of German states did not cut down the number of officials; for the newly consolidated states had lively and even more sophisticated administrations. This class was more active than the monied men in pressing its claims to political power and it formed a most ready audience for the political thinkers. The most characteristically German, however, of the new claims to political power was that of the *Gelehrten*. The multiplication of states, by increasing the number of the universities, which were state institutions, and the freedom of movement from university to university had encouraged the emergence of this group as a social class. In the flowering period of German literature, philosophy and letters the *Gelehrte* came into his own. It is no accident that all those who took the lead in welcoming the French into Mainz and in seeking to set up a republic there in 1793 were connected with the university. Nor is it surprising that the nationalist movement of the early nineteenth century, with its intellectual roots, should have been fed by the academic workers in jurisprudence, history and philology. It seems natural too that the students of the universities should have provided volunteer corps for fighting the French in 1813 and that in the *Burschenschaften* of 1815–19 they should have foreshadowed the liberal national movement that came to a head in 1848.

Only in quite extraordinary times would the poor man diminish his family's livelihood by taking time from work for public causes. In Germany there were such times even before 1848. During the last years of the French occupation, just before and just after 1813, numbers of quite humble men had made an individual choice whether to act as unpaid agents of a voluntary intelligence service against the French or to take the easier course of protecting and serving them. At the very least, resentment at French exactions was a kind of political reaction. It was thus that an intellectual movement among the literate minority came to have a root in the nation among peasants and artisans. This root was as anti-French as the movement among the princes and landowners of the seventeenth century.

During the period of reconstruction and so-called reaction in Germany the influence of Metternich prevailed. From 1810 to 1848 he was the Minister successively of Francis I and Ferdinand I (1835–48) of Austria. His influence on Germany was immobilizing and not invigorating. The constitution of the Germanic Confederation, which was part of the Treaty of Vienna, contained certain articles of good promise for the future. These looked to the assimilation of the legal systems of the thirty-nine German states through the creation of a supreme court, the assimilation of their economic systems through a single tariff, and the common liberalizing of their internal governments by the setting up of state constitutions. Under Metternich's influence these articles were interpreted so as to prevent any of these things from happening. Decisions taken by the diet at Frankfurt and applied in the states by their separate governments were all restrictive. The Carlsbad decrees, planned at a meeting of princes guided by Metternich at Carlsbad and enacted by the diet in 1819, disciplined the universities and imposed a press censorship. They were renewed in 1824. The diet's decrees of 1832 shackled the state parliaments and banned political societies and public meetings. The decisions of the Vienna conferences of 1834 were not enacted by the diet but had a similar restrictive influence; for by reaffirming the absolute sovereignty of the princes of the several states they frustrated the efforts of the state parliaments to create a common German constitutionalism. It was not until the military articles of the federal constitution were developed under the guidance of Prussia after 1836 that anything that might be called federal life existed in the Germanic Federation. After that date there was at least a federal army, which was to act in Schleswig-Holstein in 1848 and again in 1864.

Yet, despite Metternich and especially after 1830, a vigorous parliamentary life developed in Hesse-Darmstadt, Baden and Württemberg. Even with their limited powers the parliaments in these states gave many men political experience and sometimes responsibility. It was these parliamentarians who were the spearhead of the liberal national movement. Heinrich von Gagern, the able president of the Frankfurt National Assembly in 1848, had led the opposition in the Hesse-Darmstadt parliament. Between 1830 and 1833 there were popular risings and the extension of parliamentary government to Hesse-Cassel, Hanover and Saxony. But it was the parliaments in the southern states which became the centre of the agitation for the reform of the Confederation. The demands crystallized into a call for a central German executive, a central German elective parliament and the creation of a single German economic and legal system. But actual demands were too varied for it to be proper to speak of a liberal national programme. Within the states demands ranged over the whole field of liberal ideals, but faith in full legislative power and financial control for elective parliaments and in a free press and in a free economy lay behind them all.

Metternich's influence was then restrictive in vain. Nor was he ultimately successful in subordinating German policy to the wider international needs of Austria. This was another aspect of his influence. Metternich worked with subtlety and much professional skill within the tradition of eighteenth-century *Kabinettspolitik* in which primacy was always accorded to foreign policy. Between 1826 and 1831 and again from 1834 to 1848 he virtually suspended policy for Germany. His successes in preserving Austria's alliance with Russia and Prussia and in safeguarding Austria's interests in the eastern question or her position in Italy were not appreciated in Germany.

Behind the immobile façade of Austrian primacy Prussia stepped forward to the actual economic, intellectual and eventually political leadership of Germany. One cause of her economic leadership was the good tradition of her officials in fostering the adoption of advanced industrial techniques by loans to individual firms or by themselves importing technicians or machines, and in promoting technological education and in spreading technical information. The most important cause was the relatively advanced economy of the Rhenish and Saxon territories, which she acquired in 1815. These were rich in coal and minerals, had good communications and possessed a labour force not unready to work in the new factories and, above all, had forward-looking, experienced business classes ready to finance new enterprises. The *Zollverein* was the outward sign of Prussia's economic leadership. This had many roots – not all of them Prussian – but the most important was the Prussian tariff of 1818. This like the Bavarian tariff of 1807 was a frontier tariff. The same duties were levied under it on the frontier all round the Prussian kingdom; there were no duties on, for example, entry into towns or at the frontiers of enclave territories. Nevertheless, in the enclave territories prices went up, because under the new system higher duties were levied on goods coming into Prussia for consumption in non-Prussian territory than on those for consumption in Prussia. Between 1819 and 1831, therefore, the nine states surrounded by Prussian territory negotiated agreements which allowed them to be treated for tariff purposes as part of Prussia. Meanwhile, all the other German states had been faced with their own tariff problems. Some dealt with these by creating tariff unions. Thus in 1828 Saxony, the Thuringian duchies and Hesse-Cassel made a mid-German union, while Bavaria and Württemberg made a South German one. Hesse-Darmstadt, having earlier failed to make a union around herself, gained in 1824 admission within the Prussian tariff system. In 1829 the Bavaro-Württemberg union negotiated an agreement with the Prussian–Hesse-Darmstadt system. The mid-German union found itself hemmed in and could not survive. By 1834 a fully constituted customs union, including all except three of the German states, was in operation. It adopted the Prussian tariff of 1818 and took its policy from Berlin. Austria was excluded.

Soon after 1830 – Goethe died in 1832 and Hegel in 1831 – Berlin began also to set the tone in thought and learning. Berlin, where the university had been founded in 1810, was responsible for a shift in the emphasis of German interest from classical Greece to ancient Rome, from philosophy to jurisprudence, from drama to history, from poetry to philology. The reputation of Berlin in historical studies began with Barthold Georg Niebuhr and Theodor Mommsen, who wrote on Rome, and reached its peak with Leopold von Ranke, who made a remarkable contribution to our knowledge of the medieval and modern history of all European countries. In jurisprudence, Savigny's teaching emphasized the single essentially German element in all the varied legal systems that had existed in Germany before 1800. The brothers Grimm, who also ended by working in Berlin, were among the greatest of those whose philological researches popularized a mass of German folklore and established the essential outlines of the history of language and the conventions for its study.

The force of the German national movement lay in the frontier states such as Holstein or Baden. Leaders such as F. C. Dahlmann, Karl Welcker and J. G. Droysen had, as young men, taught at Kiel University. Others such as Karl Mathy and F. D. Bassermann, who founded the *Deutsche Zeitung* in 1847, wrote and worked in Baden. Yet the nationalist movement was by the end of the forties focused on Prussia and it seemed that Prussia had only to rise to the occasion and to take over the political primacy in Germany for which Austria was proving inadequate. In 1840 Frederick William IV had come to the throne. A gifted king, though not one temperamentally fitted for the role thrust upon him, he began by abandoning the caution of Frederick William III and, by the plans he ventilated, made Prussia seem politically a progressive state. In 1847 he suddenly summoned the provincial estates of Prussia to meet in Berlin as a united diet. He seemed on the point of setting up the elective parliament, frequently promised by Frederick William III. He had, moreover, associated Prussia with German patriotism. In 1840 there was fear of a French attack on the Rhineland. Frederick William called for a strategic plan for the defence of Germany. When it was produced, it distributed the ten corps of the federal army under three commands. Frederick William embarked on tedious negotiations with the states for its acceptance, which he had brought to success by 1844. It was clear that Prussia was prepared to take the lead in Germany's defence if necessary. Finally Frederick William set in motion plans for federal reform. His Minister, von Radowitz, made a number of mild proposals in the federal diet. When revolution erupted in Vienna in March 1848 and on the afternoon when the demonstration that caused Metternich's fall assembled, he was engaged in discussions on reform with Radowitz. Since Prussia was the largest and most powerful of the German states, if Austria is not counted, the slightest encouragement served to induce liberals and nationalists to hope for Prussian leadership.

Several movements came to a head in 1848: the conservative reforming movement among the princes and their advisers; the liberal nationalist movement for reform within the states and for the creation in the wider Germany of a central executive and elective parliament and common legal and economic systems; and, on the far left, an armed popular movement with as yet very little articulate support and still fumbling after its revolutionary objectives.

Not *armed* revolution, but the elective assembly was characteristic of the year 1848. There were sitting in 1848 three elected assemblies: the National Assembly at Frankfurt from 18 May 1848; the National Assembly – confusingly so called since it was limited to the kingdom of Prussia – at Berlin from 22 May 1848; and the parliament at Vienna from 22 July 1848. These were not revolutionary assemblies; for their election had been organized by the established authorities, not by provisional governments, far less by leaders of insurrection. A self-convened committee of liberal nationalists – the Heidelberg Committee – had invited members of parliament, members of the Prussian elective town councils and well-known liberals from all over Germany to meet in a convention that became known as the *Vorparlament*. This devised the electoral law under which the governments in the several states organized elections for the Frankfurt Assembly. During March all the princes of the German states had committed themselves to promote the summoning of a national German parliament. It is true they had some-times done so under pressure from public meetings that also demanded and obtained liberal reform – a state parliament if one did not exist, relaxation of press censorship or a liberal ministry. But commitment to the ideal of a nationally united Germany was for one brief month none the less universal. During the summer, differences of opinion, reserves and, ultimately, withdrawal broke this solidarity. By June 1849 the Frankfurt Assembly had disappeared. A remnant had withdrawn to Stuttgart, where the soldiers of the King of Württemberg dispersed them. The Assembly had created a German *Centralgewalt* under a *Reichsverweser*, the Archduke John, with a small Ministry nominated by it. This it failed to sustain beyond some ten months. It had made the greatest invasion of the sovereign rights of the individual princes ever made, when it enacted the *Grundrechte* or basic liberties of all Germans. Though many of the states, in fact, assimilated their law to its articles, it had not been able to impose their adoption. It drew up and enacted, on 28 March 1849, a monarchical parliamentary constitution for a united Germany. It failed to compel the adoption of this constitution by all the states and met a refusal (3 April) when it offered the crown to Frederick William of Prussia. After the failure of the Frankfurt Assembly, real revolution with armed clashes – already foreshadowed in the Rhenish risings of September–October 1848 – broke out in, for example, Baden, and in Saxony in the spring of 1849.

Though the liberal national movement had focused upon Berlin, the events of 1848–9 still left Austria and Prussia equally possible as the creators of a united Germany. This equality was expressed in the alternatives of *kleindeutsch* or *großdeutsch*; for the discussion at Frankfurt had scarcely concealed the sharpness of the choice between a united Germany that should exclude even the German parts of the Austrian Empire (the *kleindeutsche* solution) and a united Germany that should include the whole of the Austrian Empire (the *großdeutsche* solution). The only occasions when the sharpness of the choice was concealed occurred when proposals were made which represented some stopping place between these extremes. By 1849, when the initiative from below had failed, power politics and government action seemed the only means to create a united Germany. In power, however, Austria surprisingly enough again had the advantage over Prussia.

By 1850 Austria had renewed her strength. In 1848 after the fall of Metternich in March, a series of short-lived ministries and outbreaks of revolutionary violence in May and again in October had carried the government gradually, perhaps not leftwards, but away from the right, while the revolt of the subject nationalities in Hungary and Bohemia had threatened to break up the monarchy altogether. The elective parliament, which abolished the peasants' labour services (*Robot*) and devised an elaborate and effective system of compensation for the land-lords that made possible at last the end of feudal tenures, did not finish drafting a constitution before the tide turned. In November 1848 Francis Joseph took the place of Ferdinand I; the strong and bold Prince Schwarzenberg (d. 1852) took control of the government; the subject nationalities were defeated by military victories – with Russia's help in Hungary; the elective parliament was dissolved and a new constitutional regime inaugurated from above. By 1850 the power of the Austrian monarchy was greater than it had been since 1814–15, because Schwarzenberg knew how to mobilize the latent economic and military strength of its great territories and to cause this to be felt behind its diplomacy. By 1851 the Germanic Confederation of 1815 was again working, while conferences of the German governments were meeting in Dresden to discuss its reform and the Austrian scheme of a single German tariff system to include the whole Austrian Empire and in-augurate the *Siebzigmillionen Reich*.

While Austria went from near break-up to new strength, Prussia went the reverse way. It is true that Prussia was the only state in which the army was called out to quell insurrection in March 1848. But Frederick William had sent the army back to barracks and proclaimed his faith in German unity – Prussia would be dissolved in Germany – and in liberal reform – a parliamentary constitution would be devised by an elected parliament. Prussia derived an accession of strength from this new-found amity between king and people, until it was seen that Frederick William did not mean to abide by the consequences of his professions. He acted against the liberal national movement in Schleswig-Holstein while he seemed to lead it in Berlin. His dismissal of the Berlin National Assembly, his enactment of a parliamentary constitution by decree (October) and his rejection of the crown of united Germany meant that Frederick William was pursuing the absolutist Prussian policy in which he really believed. His objectives were difficult to obtain, even though he had in Radowitz a man of great ability to devise for him the means to gain them. They were: loyal co-operation with the Emperor of Austria and the execution of the constitution enacted by the Frankfurt Assembly, shorn of its most leftist articles, through the governments of the states. He proposed, then, the creation of a united Germany by the initiative from above, by evading the choice between *kleindeutschen* and *großdeutschen* solutions and by preserving the Prussian *Zollverein*. To achieve this set of incompatibilities, Radowitz brought into being the Four – later Three – Kings' Alliance (the kings of Prussia, Hanover, Saxony and Bavaria), the Erfurt Parliament, elected and in session from March to April 1850, and the proposal of the *engere* and *weitere Bund*. This last was a scheme whereby a united Germany, *excluding* the Austrian Empire, with a single German *Centralgewalt* at its head and an elective parliament at its base, might exist within a wider federal system composed by all the governments *including* the Austrian Empire. All these arrangements and plans were defeated by the able diplomacy of Schwarzenberg, who entangled Prussia in an arrangement of his own – the Interim – to stave off acceptance or rejection of the Erfurt Union and the *engere* and *weitere Bund*. Then, when he was strong enough, he used an incident in Hesse-Cassel and the continuing Schleswig-Holstein question to force Prussia to abandon all her own initiatives and to accept the restoration of the Confederation of 1815 (*Punktation* of Olmütz, 1850). In 1851 Austria and Prussia were close allies and, in the alliance, to use Bismarck's metaphor, Austria was the rider and Prussia the horse. Schwarzenberg and his Minister of Commerce, von Bruck, were still trying to replace the *Zollverein* by the *Siebzigmillionen Reich*.

After the failure of the initiative from below and while Austria and Prussia contended for primacy, the position of the governments of the third Germany was especially important. None of the German governments had lost authority during the agitations of 1848 or the outbreaks of violence of 1849. The events in Bavaria – the abdication of Ludwig I, the accession of Maximilian II and the liberalizing of the government – had more the character of comic opera than political revolution. The governments of 1850, except for that of Hesse-Cassel, where the elector and his parliament continued to be at odds, were stronger, more liberal and administering laws and institutions more closely assimilated to each other than ever before. In plans for the reform of the Confederation, a directory composed of nominees of Bavaria, Saxony, Württemberg, Baden and Hanover, or some of them, now had strong champions. During the Crimean War, when Austria, under Buol, was preoccupied with the eastern question, Prussia was weak and the liberal national movement was still depressed after the defeat of 1848-9, the third Germany came into its own. Men such as von Beust, von der Pfordten or von Dalwigk, who controlled its policy, attained European reputations. In meetings together the states tried to devise a German policy that might be unaffected by Austrian ambitions in the Near East and Prussian fears of her Russian ally. They had, however, prejudiced the success of their bid for the leadership of Germany by failing to back Austria in her attempt to destroy the *Zollverein* and by consenting in 1854 to its renewal and consolidation, and so to the continuation of economic unification under Prussia's leadership.

The Austro-French war (1859), whose outcome was Austria's loss of Lombardy, was a turning-point. Prussia again became the hope of all those who wished for a German foreign policy. Frederick William IV had been displaced by the Prince Regent William (1858) who had inaugurated the so-called New Era. The liberal national movement had revived with the foundation of the *National Verein* (1859). Prussia was again strong and Austria weak.

The more open-minded Ministers whom Prince William appointed attempted to combine the reform of the army with a more liberal regime. This provoked a constitutional conflict which brought the New Era abruptly to an end. Prince William and his advisers were aware, as Frederick William IV had not been, of the new power which industrialization, railways and accelerated population growth had brought to Prussia. These economic changes had, indeed, only gained momentum at the end of the fifties, though they had begun much earlier.

It is no accident that this awareness should have led the Regent and his Ministers to propose changes in relation to the army. Prussia, whenever she sought to make latent strength actual strength, looked first to her army as the means to do so. She had done so under the Great Elector, under Frederick the Great, in 1813 and, most recently, when she had taken charge of the arrangements for the Confederation's army between 1836 and 1845. Moreover the traditional military conscription was in fact no longer effective. The size of the army, fixed in 1813, was too small to take all the men which the population growth made available. The proposed increase of expenditure on the army was to deal with this situation and to end the emphasis on a citizen army, which the arrangements of 1813 had also embodied. Nor was it an accident that these proposals should lead to a constitutional conflict; for the Prussian parliament had a liberal majority that cherished the emphasis on the militia and the short two-year term of service and believed that the control of the budget, with power to limit military expenditure, was the palladium of its liberties.

By 1862 deadlock had been reached. The king, as the Regent had become, believed that he must either abdicate or accept Bismarck, who was ready to rule without a budget, as his Minister. This moderate conservative but strong-willed man had come to the fore as a noisy monarchist in 1848, a rightist member of the Erfurt parliament in 1850 and then, as a cooler and wiser man, the very skilful representative of Prussia at Frankfurt after the revival of the Germanic Confederation. William had hesitated to use his abilities because of his notorious independence. He was a man conscious of the roots of power in *himself*. Yet the partnership that was established in 1862 between William I of Germany, as he became, and Bismarck was to last until 1888. It was the effective instrument for the making of a united Germany.

Bismarck created great power for himself. He identified himself with Prussia and created great power for Prussia in Germany. He was also to identify himself with Germany and to create great power for Germany in Europe. He understood the uses of power and harnessed the liberal national movement to its purposes. He began by shaping for Prussia a policy of self-assertion in support of the German movement in the duchies of Schleswig and Holstein. Here Danish and German nationalism confronted each other under the cloak of a complicated quarrel about constitutional arrangements and the succession to Denmark and the duchies. The last attempt (the March Patent of 1863) to settle the constitutional conflict had favoured Danish nationalism, since it tightened the ties between Denmark and Schleswig (with its mixed population) and loosened those between Schleswig and Holstein (with its German population). It provoked revolt in the duchies and the German liberal nationalists were ready to 'free' them and to support the claims of the Duke of Augustenburg to rule them as an independent state. To the diet of the Germanic Confederation, or the princes of Germany led by the third Germany, this too was an acceptable policy. Meanwhile the development of his foreign policy, especially his policy of opposing Denmark without committing himself to Augustenburg, created confidence in Bismarck in Prussia, and the liberal opposition, now formally organized as the Fortschrittspartei, lost its hold on the Prussian parliament. By 1866 Bismarck was master of the internal situation in Prussia and could manipulate it as he chose.

He was also master of an important section of the public throughout Germany. He attained this by offering an alternative to the liberal national movement, not by putting himself at the head of it. The alternative he offered was especially attractive to the prosperous business classes and, through them, to the urban lower middle class that prospered too when business was lively. He had less to say to the urban working man. But he and Ferdinand Lassalle, who founded the Allgemeiner Deutscher Arbeiterverein in 1863, respected each other, and those of the workers who were not indifferent supported Bismarck. The support of the rural right, Junker and peasant, in north Germany was assured to him by its respect for the crown and established authorities. He was never sure of Catholic support, but a Catholic political party was not organized until 1870. Only the South German particularists were irreconcilable. It was decisive, then, that he won the business classes, whom he attached by the reorganization of the Zollverein, a commerial treaty with France (1862) and the creation of a Customs Parliament (1868) elected by the votes of all German men over twenty-one.

Meanwhile he continued to handle the Schleswig-Holstein question as a piece of Prussian foreign policy, leaving the third Germany and the German nationalists high and dry. Thus it came about that Holstein was occupied in vain by the troops of the Germanic Confederation in the interest of the Augustenburg claimant who had established a provisional government there in December 1863; that Austria and Prussia signed a separate Punktation for joint action in January 1864; that these two declared war upon Denmark, invaded her and compelled her to accept their joint occupation of the duchies in October 1864. Disputes engineered between the Prussian and Austrian occupying authorities made the partition of responsibility achieved by the Convention of Gastein (Schleswig to Prussia and Holstein to Austria) in 1865 an acceptable compromise, until Austria was as ready as Prussia to use fresh disputes between the occupying authorities as pretext for an Austro-Prussian war. This would settle the contest for leadership in Germany that had been implicit in the logic of the German situation for over a century.

In 1863 Austria had made a last attempt to reform the Germanic Confederation on *großdeutschen* lines. She had invited the princes to meet in a *Fürstentag* and put her plan to them. Bismarck had induced King William to refuse this invitation and the *Fürstentag* had failed. Prussia had demonstrated her ability to defy Austria. The whole course of the Schleswig-Holstein question reinforced this demonstration. For the first time in a European question Prussia led and Austria was obliged to follow. Austria fought the war of June to July 1866 to recapture the position she had already lost.

The Seven Weeks War was a civil war between the forces of Austria, Saxony, Hanover, Bavaria, Württemberg, Baden, Hesse-Darmstadt, Hesse-Cassel and Nassau on one side and Prussia, supported by the minor German states and Italy, on the other. The issue was decided by the battle of Königgrätz and the consequences mostly formulated in the Peace Preliminaries of Nikolsburg (26 July 1866) which was the basis for the definitive Peace of Prague, 23 August 1866.

Austria assented to Prussia's annexation of Schleswig-Holstein, Hanover, Hesse-Cassel, Nassau and Frankfurt and so to the enormous territorial preponderance of Prussia in Germany. Prussia stretched from Mainz to Königsberg and from Kiel to Breslau. She herself lost no territory to Prussia, but she lost the last of her Italian territories, Venice, to the kingdom of Italy. After the war, in 1867, her reorganization as the dual monarchy of Austria-Hungary opened the last chapter in the history of the Habsburg Empire. She assented to the dissolution of the Germanic Confederation and the reorganization of north Germany as the North German Confederation. It could only be a question of time before the four South German states entered this; for they were now without any federative bond, though each was bound individually to Prussia by an offensive and defensive alliance. The constitution of 1867 was so contrived that it needed no change of substance to admit them. United Germany was created by the war of 1866, not by that of 1870.

No one would now maintain the simple proposition that Bismarck provoked the Franco-Prussian War of July 1870 to May 1871 in order to complete German unification, which France, had she not been defeated, would have resisted. Bismarck, as always, used an opportunity and did not create it. The offer by the Spanish provisional Government of the crown of Spain to the Catholic or Sigmaringen branch of the House of Hohenzollern was not inspired by him, though he knew of it from the time it was first considered. Even without war resulting, the acceptance had many advantages. At the least, it prevented a Wittelsbach candidacy; at the most, it would place the Hohenzollern dynasty in an unexampled position of strength; for with one hand on Romania, where Leopold's brother was king, and the other upon Spain it could exercise diplomatic pressure on the Continent wherever it chose. The responses of France to the several twists in the situation were such that from 12 July Bismarck actually did work for war. His publication of the Ems telegram – a shortened version of the king's report of an interview with the French ambassador – was the final incident which tipped the scale. The acceptance of the crown had been withdrawn; the French had unwisely asked for a guarantee that the candidacy would not be renewed; the ambassador had so handled his task that the Ems telegram made him seem to have been discourteously rebuffed by the king just as it made the king seem to have been discourteously accosted by the ambassador. Bismarck could work for war – it was declared on 15 July – because the military chances of victory were good and the chances of support from the South Germans were incontestable. The great advantage of war was that it brought into operation the treaties of offensive and defensive alliance signed with the four South German states in 1866–7. The further treaties signed by these states in November 1870 after the victory of Sedan and the capitulation of Napoleon III, meant that the German Confederation now included all Germany. The empire was proclaimed on 18 January 1871 at Versailles.

The Peace of Frankfurt of May 1871, with its provision for the annexation of Alsace-Lorraine to the German Reich, not to any one German state, symbolized the transformation of Germany into a single power unit under the domination of Prussia. But national emotion had not swept Germany into a war against France. The war was a piece of Prussian foreign policy. The ebullition of national feeling came in January 1871. National feeling, whose growth this chapter has traced, always had been rooted in feeling against the French. Yet, as this chapter has also shown, in so far as national consolidation depended upon the policy of the German governments, it depended upon Prussia's defeating Austria or being defeated by her.

Bibliography

GENERAL SURVEYS

The New Cambridge Modern History. The relevant chapters in Vols V to X. Cambridge, 1957–70.

HOLBORN, H. *A History of Modern Germany, 1648–1840*. London, 1965.

HOLBORN, H. *A History of Modern Germany, 1840–1945*. London, 1970.

WORKS ON SEPARATE TOPICS

CARSTEN, F. L. *The Origins of Modern Prussia*. Oxford, 1954.

CARSTEN, F. L. *Princes and Parliaments in Germany*. Oxford, 1959.

WEDGWOOD, C. V. *The Thirty Years War*. London, 1933.

CRAIG, G. *The Politics of the Prussian Army, 1640–1945*. Oxford, 1955.

STOYE, J. *The Siege of Vienna*. London, 1964.

HENDERSON, W. O. *Studies in the Economic Policy of Frederick the Great*. London, 1963.

GOOCH, G. P. *Frederick the Great*. London, 1947.

BERNEY, A. *Friedrich der Große*. Tübingen, 1934.

BRUFORD, W. H. *Germany in the Eighteenth Century*. Cambridge, 1935.

GOOCH, G. P. *Maria Theresa and other Studies*. London, 1951.

PADOVER, S. K. *The Revolutionary Emperor Joseph II*. London, 1938.

WANGERMANN, E. *From Joseph II to the Jacobin Trials*. Oxford, 1959. Second edn., 1969.

DROZ, J. *L'Allemagne et la Révolution française*. Paris, 1949; also published in German translation, Wiesbaden, 1955.

RAMM, A. *Germany, 1789–1919*. London, 1967.

PINSON, K. S. *Modern Germany*. New York, 1955.

HAMEROW, T. S. *Restoration, Revolution and Reaction, Germany, 1815–71*. Princeton, 1958.

VALENTIN, V. *1848. Chapters in German History*. London, 1940.

PFLANZE, O. *Bismarck and the Development of Germany, 1815–71*. Princeton, 1963.

RICHTER, W. *Bismarck*, London, 1964.

TAYLOR, A. J. P. *Bismarck, the Man and the Statesman*. London, 1955.

MACARTNEY, C. A. *The Habsburg Monarchy, 1790–1918*. London, 1969.

5 From Bismarck to the Present

P. G. J. PULZER

Bismarck's Empire

THE LIBERAL PHASE

On 18 January 1871, four months after the Prussian victory at Sedan, in the Hall of Mirrors at Versailles, William I of Prussia was crowned *Deutscher Kaiser*. For many Germans, the coronation symbolized a political coming-of-age. At last they, too, were citizens of that most modern of political forms, the European nation-state. What Englishmen and Frenchmen, Swedes and Spaniards had been able to take for granted for centuries, what even Italians had achieved in the preceding decade, Germans, too, could now claim as their own. This is certainly what the Parliament of the North German Confederation had in mind when it called on William 'durch die Annahme der deutschen Kaiserkrone das Einigungswerk zu weihen' ('to consecrate the work of unification by accepting the German imperial crown').

Yet beneath the euphoria of military triumph and the pride at political achievement there remained doubts and ambiguities. Both the structure and the public symbols of the new state left many dissatisfied. This was not merely because any major innovation falls short of what its most ardent supporters hoped for, while it heightens the regrets of those who are attached to the past. The out-and-out opponents of the new state were initially few. More seriously, it emerged in the long run that its out-and-out supporters were also few.

What sort of a Reich was this, and what sort of a Kaiser? The words conjured up memories of medieval universality. They would appeal – so Bismarck hoped in reviving them – to the traditionalists who feared the revolutionary implications of the doctrine of national self-determination. The new emperor accepted his crown not from popular acclaim, nor from a parliamentary resolution, but from the hands of the Grand Duke of Baden. He was *Deutscher Kaiser*, the emperor of a nation, not *Kaiser Deutschlands*, which would imply sovereignty over the other kings and princes of the German states. The empire itself was created by treaty. The south German states of Baden, Württemberg, Bavaria and Hesse-Darmstadt acceded individually to the North German Confederation; Bavaria only after a last-ditch stand in parliament by the anti-Prussian Patriotic Party.

Yet it needed considerable powers of self-deception to believe that the empire of 1871 was a revival of the one that had expired in 1806, or that William I was in any except the most nominal way the successor of Charles V or Frederick Barbarossa. It was a new state decked out with old names. The emperor declared war and peace. There was an imperial army, which included the troops of all states except – in time of peace only – those of Bavaria; there would, in time, be an imperial navy, too. There was an imperial bank with a monopoly of note issue; an imperial railway office and an imperial post office which governed communications, though here again the southern states retained some autonomy. Effective decisions in the major policy fields were therefore made in Berlin.

Yet to suggest that this was 'centralization' at the expense of local autonomy is to misread the symptoms. In many ways it was unclear whether the Reich was the nation-state that the Liberals had hoped for or the *ewiger Bund* (eternal confederation) of princes that the Constitution spoke of. The Reich lacked many of the elementary symbols of a unified people. The Constitution contained no ringing, emotive appeal to the populace: it had not been drawn up, as had that of the United States, 'to establish justice, insure domestic tranquility . . . promote the general welfare, and secure the blessings of liberty to ourselves and posterity'. There was no national holiday, like Bastille Day: 18 January was celebrated in Prussia only. There was, amazingly enough, no imperial flag: it was only in 1892 that the naval and mercantile black-white-and-red was promoted to this status. (Black and white were the Prussian colours, red the colour of the Hanseatic cities.) There was no national anthem: 'Deutschland, Deutschland über alles' – a revolutionary lyric set to Haydn's imperial anthem – was not adopted until 1922.

It was not the new central administration of the Reich that diminished the status of the individual states, it was the overwhelming preponderance of one state, Prussia, within this Reich. Two-thirds of the Reich's population lived in Prussia; the Prussian bureaucracy was larger than the imperial even in 1914, and the same was true of taxation revenue. Berlin was the capital of both Prussia and the Reich and it was inevitable that the imperial Ministries should be staffed mainly by Prussians. But what gave Prussia moral as well as material superiority within the new Germany was the way in which the country had been unified. The pious hope of the 1848 revolutionaries that Prussia might be merged in the new nation-state – *in Deutschland aufgehen* – was a mere memory. The Reich had been made by Prussia, and by Old Prussia at that. For the wars of the 1860s were as much a victory of the dynasty over parliament, of the army over the middle class, of autocracy over self-government, as of Prussia against Austria, Bavaria and France.

Thus Prussia emerged in 1871 with her political and social institutions, rooted in the agrarian economy of eastern Europe, not only intact but strengthened, crowned by a military and political triumph unequalled in half a century of European history. With that triumph vanished all hope of reforming a structure that had little in common with the urban, industrial developments transforming Germany. The Prussian Landtag continued to be elected by the three-class franchise of 1850. This meant that 84 per cent of the electorate returned only one-third of the deputies. In many constituencies east of the Elbe the local landowner, as the chief taxpayer, was the only elector in the first class and thus had a third of all the votes; in the city of Essen the head of the firm of Krupp enjoyed the same privilege.

Though the Prussian state bureaucracy in Berlin recruited many talented middle-class graduates and was quite liberal in character at any rate until the 1880s, the provincial administration – that of the twelve *Regierungsbezirke* – was predominantly conservative and aristocratic. Municipal government was even more oligarchic. East of the Elbe the Junker estate – the *Gutsbezirk* – remained an administrative unit with virtually no check on the arbitrary power of the proprietor. Only very minor reforms in local government were achieved before 1918.

Prussian influence on imperial policy was exerted through the Upper House of the imperial parliament, the Bundesrat, over which the emperor presided. In it sat the representatives of the federated governments: of the 58 seats Prussia held 17. This was not by itself an absolute majority, but many of the smaller states were so hopelessly dependent on Prussia, economically, militarily and geographically, that they could not dream of acting independently. Prussia could be outvoted only by a coalition of Bavaria, Württemberg, Baden, Saxony and Hesse – an improbable combination that would herald the break-up of the empire. Moreover, fourteen votes were sufficient to veto any change in the constitution, and Prussia could cast these without the aid of clients,

Given this Prussian preponderance, the Bundesrat never became the forum for great debates or momentous decisions.

Policy-making was in the hands of one man, who had led Prussia to victory against internal opponents and external rivals. There was only one imperial minister directly responsible to the monarch, the Chancellor, and Bismarck held this post from 1871 to 1890. The post was not necessarily tied to that of the Prussian premiership; for two years, indeed, Bismarck gave up the latter post, but the experiment did not work. The Chancellor, as an imperial servant, had no vote in the Bundestag. He could cast a vote only as a member of one of the states' delegations, and for this reason Bismarck always retained the post of Prussian Foreign Minister. To propose a policy which did not have the prior backing of Prussia was unthinkable. To govern Germany it was necessary to govern Prussia. 'Schneiden Sie mir die preußische Wurzel ab,' he told Parliament, 'und machen Sie mich allein zum Reichsminister, so glaube ich, ich bin so einflußlos, wie ein anderer.' ('Cut off my Prussian roots, and make me solely an imperial Minister, then I think I shall be as uninfluential as any other man.')

To make certain of the special relationship between himself and the emperor, Bismarck always opposed the creation of an imperial cabinet. As new government departments had to be created, their heads received the rank of State Secretary only. They were the Chancellor's subordinates, unlike the members of the Prussian cabinet who were, nominally the Prime Minister's equals. As long as Bismarck was Chancellor they were not allowed to meet in his absence, nor to correspond directly with the emperor.

Though Bismarck was anxious to preserve the personal link with the emperor and to maintain his ascendancy over Prussian affairs, he resisted an imperial cabinet chiefly in order to fight off parliamentary control. This threat to his authority came from the Lower House of the imperial parliament, the Reichstag. Like the Reichstag of the North German Federation and the Customs Parliament of 1868, it was elected by universal male suffrage and secret ballot. Bismarck had encouraged this move towards democratic participation, partly as a tactical move – to outflank the sectional preoccupations of the middle-class Liberals and the pro-Austrian state governments – partly because he was always anxious to widen the basis of his support. Given the still predominantly rural and small-town character of Germany in the 1860s, he calculated that a politically nationalist but socially conservative appeal would be victorious.

A parliament so elected could be useful as a servant, even as a partner, but it threatened to be more than this. It had, under the Constitution, the right to initiate legislation and to reject the Government's bills, both of which it occasionally exercised. It could reject the Budget (which it never did) and could address questions to the Chancellor which, however, he was not compelled to answer. What it could not do was to impose its wishes on the Government, or oblige its Ministers to resign after a vote of censure. The Reichstag was a representative institution, no more. Whether its members would remain content with this subordinate status depended on the party composition produced by elections.

The parties represented in the Reichstag of the 1870s and 1880s were of two types. There were those, on the one hand, which survived from the constitutional struggles and ideological debates of the previous decades. Though their spokesmen might claim to have 'the people' or 'the nation' behind them, they had a narrow organizational base. Conservative or Liberal, they were parties led by men of education and property, national or local notables who claimed the allegiance of their followers in the House or the constituencies through personal distinction or social status. Their organization was informal, paid-up membership small; they might even lack a constitution or an official programme.

Much the most powerful of these was the National Liberal Party which had, since 1867, accepted Bismarck's solution of the German question: the exclusion of Austria, the leadership of Prussia. Beyond a desire for national unity and civil liberties there was little to keep the party together. It represented in the main the industrial and professional middle classes, those with the greatest material and emotional attachment to a united Germany. It was strongest in the Protestant areas of the middle and smaller states: two-thirds of its deputies sat for constituencies outside the pre-1866 frontiers of Prussia. Its leader, Rudolf von Bennigsen, was, significantly, a Hanoverian, untouched by the bitter constitutional conflict of Prussia.

To their left was the irreconcilable hard-core remnant of the Fortschrittspartei, refusing to accept that might could be right, but with little to offer once might had been proved right. They retained much of their Prussian following, where memories of the *Konfliktszeit* died hard, and gained that of the South German democrats and of free-traders in the major commercial centres. They had distinguished leaders – the historian Theodor Mommsen, the pathologist Rudolf

Virchow – but were doomed to an oppositional role and could rarely influence policy decisively.

Like the Liberals, the Conservatives were divided. In Prussia, east of the Elbe, they were the party of the Junkers. Loyal to the dynasty and to the values of the Prussian state, they were embittered against Bismarck who had, in their eyes, sold out to the Liberals and the middle classes, destroying the old, reliable soldier-state in favour of the vague, fashionable slogans of nationalism. They were sure of their voice in the Prussian Landtag, but in the Reichstag they counted for very little: in 1874 they held only 22 seats out of 397. Other Conservatives, like many of the Liberals, decided to make their peace with the new order. They were men not exclusively tied to the soil: aristocrats, like Henckel von Donnersmarck or Hohenlohe-Ratibor, who had diversified into industry and finance, tycoons like von Kardorff who were all for the new, enlarged market that the Reich offered, but had no time for liberal questionings of the prerogatives of authority. This, the Freikonservative Partei, later known as the Reichspartei, supported Bismarck unconditionally: unlike the crustier Junkers they foresaw the Reich as 'die deutsche Weiterbildung der preußischen Monarchie' ('the German extension of the Prussian monarchy').

The individualist structure of all these parties meant that none of them stood for very clear-cut principles or interests. They might describe themselves as 'liberal' or 'conservative', or acquire labels like 'bourgeois' or 'aristocratic', yet the border-lines between them were uncertain. Personal taste, family tradition, regional peculiarity, electoral calculation: each or all of these might determine a man's allegiance. The National Liberals in particular divided into a right wing, increasingly national and decreasingly liberal, often indistinguishable from the Reichspartei, and a left wing that wanted to maintain a link with the Progressives.

No such ambiguities beset the newer parties, with their mass-memberships and their popular roots, the parties of the Catholics and the industrial workers. Initially the workers' party was much the weaker of the two. German industrialization was still only beginning in the 1860s, and Socialists were split into factions. The founder of the German Labour movement had been Ferdinand Lassalle, the son of a Jewish merchant from Silesia, a Byronic figure who was killed in a duel in 1864. He dominated his party by personality, not organization; after his death, the followers of Marx, led by August Bebel and Wilhelm Liebknecht, gained the upper hand. The Social Democratic Party, founded in 1875, was nominally a fusion of the two groups, but the organizational superiority and ideological toughness of the Marxists had its predictable effect. By 1878, when Bismarck turned the force of the law against the new party, it had half a million voters, ten per cent of the total.

The other mass party, the Catholic Zentrum, was the strangest of all the political formations of the Second Empire. The second half of the nineteenth century was throughout Europe a time when the political and intellectual influence of the Catholic Church was most strongly under attack, and when it began to organize its defence. Catholic parties of one kind or another arose in most European states with large Catholic electorates. In Germany, however, there were special circumstances, which had to do both with the make-up of the Catholic tradition and the manner of national unification.

The leading German Catholics of the Restoration period – the Rhenish ex-Jacobin Joseph Görres, who became Professor of History at Munich, or the convert Adam Müller who settled in Vienna – had been conservative Romantics, exalting traditional authority against the challenge of the Enlightenment and the Revolution. They preferred 'particularism', the multiplicity of small states, on the grounds of territorial legitimacy, combined with a loose confederation under the aegis of Catholic Austria. But this preference did not permit a uniform attitude towards Church–State relations. In Austria or Bavaria the unity of throne and altar could be taken for granted. But elsewhere, notably in Prussia, where Protestants predominated, constitutionalism was the best guarantee of Catholic rights.

Already in the Frankfurt Parliament of 1848–9 there had been a Catholic faction led by Wilhelm von Ketteler, the Bishop of Mainz, and the theologian Ignaz Döllinger; later, in the Prussian Landtag, there had been one to safeguard the parity of the two faiths under the Prussian administration. It was the defeat of Austria at Königgrätz that spelt the end of Catholic Greater Germany. 'Die Welt stinkt,' Hermann von Mallinckrodt recorded; and indeed any *kleindeutsch* solution put the Catholics in a minority. Prussianization filled them with dismay; the annexation of Schleswig-Holstein and Hanover seemed sacrilege. The constitutions of the North German Federation, and then of the Reich, with their mundane, commercial concerns, and their silence on fundamental rights, confirmed their worst fears.

Given their concern for a bill of rights, they might have been expected to find common ground with the Liberals. But the Liberals were secular, capitalist and, for the most part Prussophile; their dominance of German politics in the Reich's first decade determined the character of the Zentrum. It was founded in 1870, at first in Prussia only, to defend the federal principle, the rights of religion, the interests of traditional occupations – farmers, artisans, the old *Mittelstand*. Its leader was Ludwig Windthorst, a brilliant debater and tactician who had been a Minister of the last King of Hanover until 1866. Of course, not only Catholics wanted to defend these interests, and the founders of the party hoped it would be interconfessional. But the religious cleavage of Germany was too deep for that and it remained *de facto* a Catholic party. This was its weakness, but also its strength. It limited the Zentrum's size, but gave it internal cohesion and an obedient following. Through the parish priests it reached into every village. Through the social consciousness of Bishop Ketteler and Adolf Kolping, with his journeymen's associations – there are still *Kolpingvereine* and *Kolpingshäuser* throughout Germany – it reached deep into the working class. Like the Social Democrats, the Zentrum had a strict organization and a ready-made mass following. The Volksverein für das katholische Deutschland reached half a million members before the First World War.

The fox, says the Greek proverb, knows many things, the hedgehog knows one big thing. The Zentrum was a political hedgehog. Socially its following ranged from landowners to coal-miners, geographically it was strongest at the periphery – Silesia in the east, Bavaria in the south, the Rhineland in the west. It was heterogeneous in all except religion, and several times it threatened to fall apart. Indeed, in 1918 its more conservative Bavarian wing did split off. But it was never more hedgehog-like than in the years of Liberal supremacy, in the opening decade of the Reich.

From 1867 to 1878 the Liberals dominated the Reichstage; they built up a working relationship with Bismarck, and their leaders, the lawyers Eduard Lasker and Ludwig Bamberger, were virtually his parliamentary managers. From their very different standpoints they seemed, for the time being, to desire the same ends: Bismarck to assert the hegemony of Prussia as a great power in Central Europe, the Liberals to ensure not merely a German *Nationalstaat* but a German *Machtstaat* (a powerful state). Bismarck was no economist, but he realized that Germany's diplomatic credibility and military self-sufficiency rested on economic strength; the Liberals, speaking for industry and finance, saw in economic unity the road to wealth as well as to the fulfilment of their ideals.

Internal free trade had, after all, been the effective beginning of German unity. The economic union of the southern states with Prussia, through the *Zollparlament* of 1868, had preceded the constitution of the empire by three years. The industrial boom in Prussia since 1857, contrasting with the stagnation of Austria, was a major factor in Bismarck's success with the middle classes. One recent economic historian has justly described 1866 as the victory of the North German *Thaler* over the South German *Gulden*. If Bismarck opposed federalism because it circumscribed the influence of Prussia and inhibited his conduct of foreign policy, the Liberals saw that it ran counter to their economic ambitions. A centralized state, with a uniform administrative code in which contract counted for more than status, rationality for more than tradition, efficiency for more than maintenance of the social order – this, the ideal of the Napoleonic state – symbolized and guaranteed what they strove for.

Bismarck acquiesced. Pass laws, restricting freedom of movement, were abolished. Guild certificates, restricting the right to ply a trade, were abolished. The usury laws were repealed. Weights and measures were unified on the metric system. The *Reichsmark*, linked to a fixed gold value, became the sole currency. The formation of joint-stock companies, whose shares could be freely bought and sold on stock exchanges, was made easier. Import duties on raw and half-finished metals were abolished. Bismarck did more than acquiesce. He appointed Germany's leading advocate of free trade, Clemens Delbrück, as Secretary of the Chancellery, his own administrative assistant. He freely gave the middle class these economic concessions, so that he would not have to offer the constitutional ones that were the Progressives' *raison d'être* and that still retained a place even in the National Liberals' programme.

The second link in the alliance between Bismarck and the Liberals was the matter of Church–State relations. In one sense Germany was simply experiencing the anti-clerical offensive familiar in Italy and Spain, France and Belgium, Switzerland and Austria. The Church had isolated itself intellectually with the 1864 Syllabus of Errors, with its denunciations of liberalism, secularism and rationalism. The 1870 declaration of Papal Infallibility further provoked its enemies and embarrassed many of its friends. The implication in the declaration that the spiritual power had authority over the secular threatened the sovereignty of the new German state and sought to undermine the patriotism and loyalty of one-third of its citizens. However, the matter became troublesome to the Government only through the split in the German Catholic Church which resulted from the declaration, and the emergence of an anti-infallibilist group, the Old Catholics, led by two eminent lay scholars, Ignaz Döllinger and Johann Friedrich.

Initially it was a Prussian problem. The arrangement in force since 1840 had given both Protestant and Catholic Churches considerable internal freedom as well as a State subsidy. After the Old Catholic split, there was increasing evidence of victimization of dissident teachers, paid by the taxpayer but appointed by the Church. These isolated incidents brought out the latent hostility of the Church and Zentrum on the one hand, of Bismarck and the Liberals on the other. The Zentrum's attachment to the old, federal *großdeutsch* order turned them, in Bismarck's eyes, into *Reichsfeinde* (enemies of the empire), in the Liberals' eyes into traitors to the national idea. The Church, on the other hand, saw its worst fears of impending aggression by the State confirmed, fears which had been the *raison d'être* for the formation of the Zentrum.

Just as Bismarck pushed through the liberalization of the German economy by appointing a dedicated liberal, Delbrück, to supervise it, so he turned to an ideologically reliable official in his fight with the Church, and made Adalbert Falk Prussian *Kultusminister* in 1872. The 1840 compromise had evidently ceased to be workable. For Falk the supremacy of State over Church was an article of faith: 'Soll die Staatsregierung nicht imstande sein, dem . . . entbrennenden Kirchlichen Konflikt mit nachhaltiger Energie zu begegnen, dann wird es eines umfänglichen Eintretens der Gesetzgebung bedürfen,'[1] he wrote in one of his earliest memoranda to the Prussian Government.

And indeed appropriate legislation was not lacking. It began with laws giving the State the right to inspect schools and banning the Jesuit order from Prussia. It reached its climax with the so-called *Maigesetze* of May, 1873. These gave the State power over the education of priests, and removed much of the disciplinary powers of bishops. In the years that followed civil marriage was made compulsory, all religious orders except medical ones dissolved, and the constitutional guarantees of self-government to the churches rescinded.

Bismarck was an orthodox Lutheran; believing in the 'priesthood of all believers' he was naturally out of sympathy with the claims of Rome

---

[1] 'Should the state Government not be capable of countering the conflagration of the Church conflict with effective energy, then the extensive intervention of the legislature will become necessary.'

and the Catholic hierarchy. But his primary quarrel was not with the Church as an institution: it was with the *Reichsfeinde* who preached disloyalty, whether in parliament or from the pulpit, who persisted in Polish-language teaching in the eastern provinces, who encouraged separatism in newly annexed Alsace and Lorraine, who urged military intervention against Germany's ally, Italy, to liberate the Pope, and who sought the sympathy of the right wing, revanchist Government in France.

While these diplomatic considerations also appealed to the parliamentary liberals, the ideological impulse of the conflict mattered most to them. The mantle of Voltaire seemed to have fallen on their shoulders. It was the Progressive intellectual Virchow who declared that the contest 'mit jedem Tage mehr den Charakter eines großen Kulturkampfes der Menschheit annimmt' ('daily acquires more of the character of the great cultural conflict of the human race'). The *Kulturkampf* had profound and lasting effects on German public life. It gave German Catholicism the halo of martyrdom. The policy of passive resistance enjoined by the hierarchy led many priests, including two archbishops, to prison. Above all it strengthened the zeal of the laity. In the 1874 Reichstag elections the Zentrum vote doubled and the Liberals' hope of a secure base in the economically advanced and intellectually open region of the Rhineland – one of the strongholds of radicalism in 1848 – were dashed. German Catholicism was confirmed as a minority culture, at one remove from the main streams of national life – inward-looking, often backward-looking. German Catholics remained poorer, worse educated, and under-represented in the public service compared with their fellow citizens. There were virtually no Catholics in the highest ranks of business or finance. In the 1890s a Protestant boy stood twice as good a chance of going to university as a Catholic; as late as 1924, only 12 per cent of the highest-ranking civil servants were Catholics. These inequalities have not been entirely eliminated even in the second half of the twentieth century.

A rather more short-term consequence of the severity of the *Kulturkampf* was its effect on the Prussian Conservatives and the royal family. Many of the Junker class had strong anti-Catholic prejudices. But unlike the Liberals they did not care for the secularizing implications of the *Kulturkampf* and they had a powerful ally in the Empress Augusta who exerted strong influence on her husband in ecclesiastical matters. The Catholic Church was, in the last resort, a bulwark against paganism and materialism: when William I declared, 'Die Religion muß dem Volke erhalten werden' ('Religion must be preserved for the people'), he did not distinguish between denominations. The more his own class and the court were alienated from him, the more Bismarck had to lean on the Liberal Reichstag majority. The more dependent he was on them, the harder they might press for greater parliamentary powers. He had therefore to find a way of restoring relations with the Conservatives and, if possible, the Zentrum. He found it in economic policy.

The boom which had gathered pace in the 1860s continued into the 1870s. Germany, which in 1840 had lagged behind France and even Belgium in iron, steel and textile production, was now the leading industrial power on the Continent. The boom came to only a temporary halt with a bank crash in 1873; the psychological and political consequences of this crash were, however, profound. The idea of unfettered economic competition, of relying solely on the forces of supply and demand to bring prosperity and happiness, was both new and unpopular in Germany. The doctrines of what Disraeli had dubbed 'the school of Manchester' tended to atomize and subvert society. Conservatives disliked this because they were emotionally tied to a society based on land, crafts and hierarchy; but so did many Liberals because they saw individualism as the enemy of strong national feeling.

In the 1840s the economist Friedrich List had advocated protective tariffs and self-sufficiency for political as well as economic reasons – free trade was fit for philistine foreigners, Englishmen, Jews and the like. Connected with this attitude was a paternalistic social conscience, supported by both the bureaucracy and academic opinion. Thus Prussia, though hardly yet industrialized, prohibited factory labour for children under twelve in 1853, well in advance of any such measure in Britain. In 1872, when the boom was still unchecked, a group of Germany's leading economists and lawyers, including Gustav Schmoller, Lujo Brentano and Rudolf Gneist founded the Verein für Sozialpolitik (Association for Social Policy), to advocate 'das wohlerwogene Eingreifen des Staates zum Schutze der berechtigten Interessen aller Beteiligten' ('well-considered intervention by the State for the protection of the justified interests of all participants'). This group, nicknamed *Kathedersozialisten*, differed sharply from the proletarian socialists. They were neither democrats nor egalitarians. But in the short run they were more influential, with the churches, with some of the aristocracy, at the court, and with Bismarck. They demonstrated how foreign the ethos of cut-throat business competition was to the culture of Germany –

foreign, one might say, until domesticated by Ludwig Erhard and the post-1948 *Wirtschaftswunder*. They demonstrated what a temporary, though remarkable, deviation the speculation mania of 1867–73 was, that promoters' era, the *Gründerzeit*, whose name was soon to become an evil memory and term of abuse.

The chief impetus towards a new economic policy, however, was the crash of 1873, for it undermined the confidence of the entrepreneurs. They were disturbed by falling prices, by British competition, by the unrest that might follow unemployment. The conservatively inclined magnates of heavy industry, men like Stumm and Kardorff of the Reichspartei, became the chief spokesmen of the Zentralverein deutscher Industrieller, the first really effective industrial pressure group. However, 'industry' or 'business' are not homogeneous interests that can speak with a uniform voice. There remained plenty of business-men who did not like the new body and who, out of liberal principle, did not care for the proposed link with the State. To make sure of success, therefore, the protectionist lobby needed an ally. It found one in agriculture.

Farmers in general, and the big landlords in the east in particular, had felt pushed to one side during the rush to favour industry and com-merce. Quick profits seemed to be honoured more than slow cultiva-tion. But as long as Germany was a net exporter of grain, they had nothing to gain from protective tariffs. By 1876, under the pressure of urbanization, Germany was a net importer of wheat; and this change coincided with the flooding of Europe with cheap, high-grade prairie wheat following the completion of North American transcontinental railways. So, by 1876, the first agricultural protection society was founded to propagate 'Ideen und Grundsätze einer gemeinnützigen, auf christlichen Grundlagen beruhenden Volkswirtschaft' ('ideas and principles of a mutually beneficial economy, resting on Christian principles'). The association's leaders were, overwhelmingly, large land-owners from the east, although eighty per cent of Germany's farms belonged to peasants with family holdings. These peasants, mainly in the west and south, many of them dependent on cheap feeding stuffs for the poultry-, pig- and dairy-farming that was more profitable for them, had to be persuaded to make common cause with the Junkers. This was not too difficult. The small farmers had hitherto lacked political leadership; their resentments against towns, commerce and organized labour could easily be exploited, with a plentiful dose of the anti-Semitism that formed an integral part of agrarian propaganda.

A united conservative front of industry and agriculture was, there-fore, not easy to bring about. Each wing had to deal with dissidents in its own ranks and their demands were not all that compatible: manu-facturers did not love dear bread and farmers did not love dear machines. But it could agree on a minimum programme. It could demand the head of Delbrück, and Bismarck, who was anxious to keep his options open, obliged. That the alliance would, within three years, secure all its essential demands, was not, at this stage, to be foreseen. It was to come about through a conjunction of domestic and diplomatic, social and religious, economic and constitutional considerations; it was to have effects on the evolution of the empire far beyond the fiscal merits of this or that import duty.

Of the non-economic factors, three favoured the protectionists. The first was Bismarck's desire to reduce the political influence of the National Liberals. He first tried to achieve this by inviting the National Liberal leader, Bennigsen, whom he regarded as a moderate, into the Prussian cabinet; he might hope thereby to tempt Bennigsen into a less independent line. But Bennigsen refused to enter except as a party leader and in company with two party colleagues. That was in Decem-ber 1877. The negotiations were never completed because two months later Pope Pius IX died. Pius IX had been an ardent supporter of the Zentrum, refusing all requests to act as a mediator. As long as he lived any retreat from the *Kulturkampf* was all but impossible, and as long as the *Kulturkampf* lasted the National Liberals were indispensable. Now, with the election of a more conciliatory Leo XIII, a choice was possible.

In May and June there followed two attempts on the life of the emperor, the first by a subnormal adolescent, Hödel, the second, which injured William quite seriously, by an anarchist, Dr Karl Nobiling. The genuine public indignation which followed these acts of violence gave Bismarck a heaven-sent opportunity. After the Reichstag had turned down an ill-drafted bill to ban the Social Democratic Party, which was blamed – without evidence – for the assassination attempts, he dissolved the Reichstag although it was only a year since elections had taken place. Out of the electoral campaign, which was conducted against *Umsturz* (subversion) and in favour of *Ordnung* (order), there emerged a majority which from Bismarck's point of view was conservative, from the protectionists' point of view pro-tariff. Bismarck was no doubt genuinely frightened by the growth of Social Democracy and especially by the party's gains in 1877 – it was, after all, only a few years since the

Paris Commune which had been publicly acclaimed by August Bebel. But he also saw clearly that an illiberal proposal like this would embarrass and possibly split the National Liberals, for ever divided between patriotism and civil liberties. As for tariffs, Bismarck saw no particular virtue in them – he was, in matters of economic policy, an agnostic – and he did not cherish feather-bedding heavy industry. But he had a sincere emotional link with the land and could see the advantages of strengthening that conservative interest.

THE CONSERVATIVE PHASE

After the elections, the Conservative parties, for the first time since 1871, almost equalled the Liberal parties. The anti-Socialist law, which forbade Socialist meetings, gave the police arbitrary powers of search, arrest and banishment and even empowered the government to declare a state of siege, was quickly passed with the shame-faced assent of the National Liberals. The Zentrum voted against. They recognized another outsider when they saw one; they could not very well complain of discrimination and yet tolerate it against others. Official persecution, though it temporarily harmed the Socialists' electoral effort, merely strengthened their cohesion and determination. It also widened the gulf between themselves and the rest of society, and thus had the same effect on them as the *Kulturkampf* on the Catholics. The common experience of persecution also led to a curious political camaraderie between Socialists and Catholics, unbridgeable though the ideological gulf might seem. Their mass bases gave them resources which the other parties lacked; they alone survived the holocaust of 1918 intact and co-operated not only in founding but in governing the Weimar Republic. From 1919 to 1932 they headed, in coalition, the now democratized government of Prussia.

Having refused to follow Bismarck in persecuting the Labour movement, the Zentrum now prepared to join him on the tariff question. They favoured tariffs intrinsically, because they represented, in the main, economically vulnerable classes, but also because their social theory favoured State regulation of private competition. Above all, however, they saw tariff reform as a way of ending the *Kulturkampf*, indeed as a way of becoming part of the governmental majority.

The tariff bill was passed in 1879. It was a 'package', giving concessions to both industrialists and landowners. The National Liberals were divided on the first and opposed to the second. But what emphasized the ever-widening gulf between Bismarck and themselves was that the bulk of the new revenue was to go not to the imperial treasury but to the individual states. This accorded with the federalist tenets of the Zentrum; it ran directly counter to any Liberal doctrine that parliament must remain sovereign over an annual budget.

The tariff debate was the last straw for the left wing of the National Liberal Party. Led by Lasker and Bamberger they seceded in 1880 and later joined with the Progressive Party in a new Liberal body, the Deutschfreisinnige Partei. What remained of the National Liberals was a chauvinistic rump. In 1881 they held only 47 seats; seven years earlier it had been 155. The Bennigsen episode was unlikely to be repeated. In contrast, Bismarck had to be more respectful to the wishes of the Zentrum. Falk was dismissed from his Ministry, but the *Kulturkampf* laws were dismantled only slowly and never completely. Nevertheless, German politics had taken a crucial change of direction.

The protection campaign had never restricted itself to purely fiscal objectives. It was anti-liberal in every sense. Its spokesmen emphasized that they were out to break ' . . . die wesentlichen Errungenschaften des Jahres 1848 . . . Wir werden zum sogenannten Patrimonial- und Patriarchialstaat zurückkehren müssen.' (' . . . the essential achievements of the year 1848 . . . We shall have to return to the so-called patrimonial and patriarchal state.') They wanted 'eine wirtschaftliche Gesetzgebung, welche . . . den Sinn für Autorität im Volke wieder wachruft' ('an economic legislation that will reawaken the people's feeling for authority'). There is no doubt that the success of their agitation reversed the direction of German politics. In the first place the virtual disintegration of the National Liberals meant that the prospect of genuine parliamentary government in Germany became quite remote. Bismarck relieved himself of the prospect of control by a Liberal majority, and indeed by a majority formed by any one party, in the British style. Whether this was ever a strong threat must remain an open question. Not even in the southern states, where parliaments had a longer history, did any class have much experience of self-government; less still in Prussia. If the Prussian Liberals could achieve nothing during the *Konfliktszeit*, when William I was at one stage on the point of abdicating, what were the chances of their doing so during the seventies? German parliamentarians were often learned debaters, sometimes skilled negotiators, but they were not statesmen. Bismarck repeatedly taunted them with being skilled only at opposition: if the government were to call their bluff and resign, they could not possibly form a Ministry. The National Liberal historian Heinrich von Sybel, writing in the *Fortnightly Review*, explained the difference between British and German parliamentary conventions thus:

No-one in England would understand an Opposition which attacked a Ministry without wishing to occupy its place . . .

Even now the majority of electors regard the criticism and control of the Government as the most important part of a member's duty . . . A candidate who allowed it to be seen that he possessed both the power and the wish to become a minister would immediately forfeit the support of a large number of the constituencies . . .

When, in the year 1863, the Liberal Minister in Baden, Baron Roggenbach, sent in his resignation (in consequence of the rejection of an important Bill by a Liberal Chamber), and called on the Grand Duke to summon the leader of the Opposition to the Cabinet, the victorious party declared that they would submit to no such *unheard-of violence*, that it was the duty of Roggenbach to retain office, but to suit himself to the duties and wishes of the representative body. The English reader will see at once, that while the majority entertain sentiments like these, parliamentary government is not to be thought of, that it is impossible, in the midst of these parliamentary parties to form a school of practical statesmen.

A fragmented parliament, whose members spoke for rival interest groups, was much more convenient to Bismarck, and after 1879 the already strong trend in this direction was accelerated. The sociologist Max Weber once distinguished those politicians who live 'für die Politik' ('for politics') from those who live 'von der Politik' ('of politics'). The notables who still predominated in the 1870s gave way to the professional politicians: professional not in the sense that belonging to the Reichstag was a full-time occupation – its sessions were short and members were unpaid until 1906 – but in the sense that they were the salaried employees of party machines or economic lobbies. By 1912 nearly one member in four was a professional of this type.

With the decline of the National Liberal Party, and the withdrawal of its most distinguished leaders into opposition, the social and political ideals of the protectionists now became those of the government. The victorious alliance was not so much one of 'industry' and 'agriculture' – these categories were altogether too diverse internally – but of iron and rye. Thus the most traditionalist and paternalist sections of Germany's economic leaders became the most influential, and remained so until 1918. Therein lies the real significance of the tariff of 1879.

Its most immediate effects were to be seen in the reorganization of the civil service and the army. The lower ranks of the Prussian civil service were largely staffed by former army regulars, the provincial administrations headed by aristocrats. It was these two types of official who helped to give German bureaucrats their reputation for arrogance and pedantry. But the middle and higher ranks, both in Berlin and the provinces, were largely recruited from the liberal-minded bourgeoisie, deistic and enlightened, and had been so ever since the reforms of Stein at the beginning of the century. Of the National Liberal MPs in 1874, 51 – almost a third – were professional civil servants. (It was, and is, one of the curiosities of German public life that one can be politician and civil servant at the same time.)

The task of purging the civil service – and the judiciary – fell on Robert von Puttkamer, who had succeeded Falk as *Kultusminister* and became Prussian Minister of the Interior in 1881. Puttkamer was as orthodox in his conservatism as in his Lutheranism: '. . . Kann ich mich nie von dem Gedanken trennen,' he wrote to his father, 'daß Preußen doch der ganz besondere Liebling des lieben Gottes ist, der vielleicht noch große Dinge mit ihm vor hat.'[1] To sack ideologically unsuitable civil servants and magistrates was impossible, but their recruitment could be stopped and their promotion made difficult. By the mid-eighties it was possible to ban the actor Barnay from the royal theatres because he had addressed an 'oppositional' (i.e. liberal) meeting; by the mid-nineties the reintegration of the bureaucracy into the values and outlook of pre-liberal Prussia caused Hohenlohe, the Chancellor, to record:

> Wenn ich so unter den preußischen Exzellenzen sitze, wird mir der Gegensatz zwischen Nord- und Süddeutschland klar . . .
>
> Die Deutschen haben recht, wenn sie meine Anwesenheit in Berlin für eine Garantie der Einheit ansehen . . . so muß ich hier darin streben, Preußen beim Reich zu erhalten; denn alle diese Herren pfeifen auf das Reich und würden es lieber heute als morgen aufgeben.[2]

[1] 'I can never quite separate myself from the thought that Prussia is the Good Lord's quite special favourite, who perhaps still has great things in store for her.'
[2] 'When I sit among the Prussian excellencies, the contrast between North and South Germany becomes clear to me . . . The Germans are right, when they see my presence in Berlin as a guarantee of national unity . . . I have to endeavour

The consequence of this was that though Prussians did not monopolize the new imperial civil service, they could command its ethos. Non-Prussians who were suspected of liberalism or particularism found entry difficult. It is this that accounts for the sparsity of Catholics, and for the almost total absence of – at any rate unbaptized – Jews. In theory the civil service stood above party and served only the State. But since loyalty to the State was measured in largely partisan terms, this fiction became less and less easy to maintain.

The same pressures towards social and political conformity were felt in the army, for even the army had had its battle with the civilian spirit. Indeed, it was the proposal to disband the *Landwehr*, the civilian militia dating from the Wars of Liberation, that had sparked off the constitutional conflict. Much more than the civil service the army had always reflected the rural social structure of eastern Prussia: the landowner commanded, the peasant obeyed. To the maintenance of this order the *Landwehr* had always seemed an irrelevance and a disruption. As late as 1913 half the army officers above the rank of Colonel were aristocrats. Similarly some regiments, especially in the guards and the cavalry, remained almost entirely aristocratic. Nevertheless, as the army expanded and as technical complexity demanded higher educational requirements, a gradual *embourgeoisement* did take place. This happened particularly through the institution of the reserve officer, who was to replace the *Landwehr*. Many deplored this dilution. Count Alfred von Waldersee, who succeeded the elder Moltke as Chief of Staff, noted that:

> ... viele alte und sogar noch aktive Offiziere ihre Söhne für eine andere Laufbahn bestimmen. Söhne von kleinen Beamten, Kaufleuten usw. werden bald die Majorität des Infanterie-Offiziersersatzes bilden, in die Kavallerie drängen vielfach die Söhne schnell reich gewordener Industrieller und verderben die noch einfachen Sitten.[1]

But there were advantages in the arrangements, too. It was a way of binding the middle class, especially the socially ambitious, to the most

---

here to keep Prussia attached to the Reich, for all these gentlemen do not give a fig for the Reich and would sooner be rid of it today than tomorrow.'

[1] '... many old and even active officers decide on a different career for their sons. Sons of petty officials, shopkeepers and so on will soon form the majority of the new infantry officers, the sons of rapidly enriched industrialists push themselves into the cavalry and ruin the still simple way of life.'

conservative institution in the state, an idea popularized for instance, in Franz Adam Bayerlein's novel *Jena oder Sedan*. Moreover, since a reserve officer had to be acceptable to his regiment, his rank held more prestige than in the old *Landwehr* (which was raised by the municipality), and the social and political selection could be more stringent. A reserve officer, like a regular officer, was subject to regimental *Ehrengerichte*, and liable to fight duels, contrary though these might be to the civil legal code. A Jew was no more eligible for a reserve than a regular commission. A Social Democrat, too, lacked the 'moralische Qualitäten' (according to the Ministry of War, a bare six months before the outbreak of the First World War), even for *Einjahr-Freiwilligen* service – the special concession for the academically qualified. Liberals, too, might suffer: more than one scion of a distinguished family was asked to resign his reserve commission for voting the wrong way in parliament. But for every nonconformist who was victimized, there were ten *Manöveronkel* who were delighted with the entrée that their uniform gave into *altpreußisch* society. It was a further aspect, inseparable from the others, of the integration of the urban middle class into an order based on land and patriarchal authority.

While disarming potential Liberals by offering them social privileges, the army also succeeded in withdrawing further from parliamentary surveillance. Bismarck was opposed to 'militarism': he believed in the primacy of civilian authority and the army was always the instrument, never the master, of his policy. He vetoed the army's demand for a triumphal march through Vienna after Königgrätz; he insisted on the bombardment of Paris in the winter of 1870–1 against Moltke's advice; he resisted demands for greater annexations after the French defeat. But, as in 1862, he was prepared to defend the army against politicians other than himself. He knew, and the Liberals knew, that the supremacy of Parliament in Britain depended on the Mutiny Act of 1689, annually renewable. In 1874 he managed to get the military budget settled for seven years at a time. The periodic battles over this *Septennat* were invariably bitter, but the government always won them. In 1883, finally, the position of Prussian War Minister – who was *de facto* Minister for the imperial army, and therefore had to face the criticisms of the Reichstag – was weakened. Personnel matters, which touched many of the army's most conspicuous privileges, and therefore evoked most parliamentary objections, were moved to the Military Cabinet which was answerable to the emperor only.

The impulses towards greater national and social solidarity were not exclusively repressive. Bismarck himself, and many of his new supporters, were, for instance, aware that the growth of revolutionary socialism stemmed from genuine social grievances. The social welfare measures – 'praktisches Christentum' according to the emperor – passed between 1883 and 1889 were intended to win workers back to piety and loyalty. Sickness insurance, accident insurance (with premiums payable only by employers) and finally old-age and dependants' pensions made Germany the world's most advanced Welfare State. The agitation of the Verein für Sozialpolitik was crowned with success, in a way which would not have happened had the *laissez-faire* Liberals continued to dominate the Reichstag.

The new domestic policy and the new balance of social forces saw a revival of illiberal ways of thought not merely in the narrowly political sphere but in the intellectual climate of the country. The career of Heinrich von Treitschke illustrates this. He had, in the 1860s, been a leading member of the Nationalverein and a leading opponent of Prussian absolutism – partly, but not solely, because he thought the Hohenzollerns would be both unwilling and unable to bring about national unification. Like many Liberals he made his peace with Bismarck; unlike some of these, he drifted into increasingly conservative, authoritarian and intolerant attitudes. As he did so, his audience, academic and lay, grew.

In 1873 he was appointed Professor of History at Berlin. In 1874 he began his series of lectures on *Politik*, which were for many students their chief introduction to the subject and which were filled with superficial and tasteless remarks about German and non-German national character. In 1879 he published the first volume of his *Deutsche Geschichte im 19. Jahrhundert*, a paean to a Prussia predestined to lead Germany. But he achieved more immediate impact with a series of articles in *Preußische Jahrbücher*, of which he was now editor, in which he emphasized the Christian character of the German State and railed against Jewish influence and especially Jewish immigration (whose extent he greatly exaggerated):

> Über unsere Ostgrenze . . . dringt Jahr für Jahr aus der unerschöpflichen polnischen Wiege eine Schar strebsamer hosenverkaufender Jünglinge herein, deren Kinder und Kindeskinder dereinst Deutschlands Börsen und Zeitungen beherrschen sollen . . .

Bis in die Kreise der höchsten Bildung hinaus . . . ertönt es heute wie von einem Munde: 'Die Juden sind unser Unglück!'[1]

Ever since the bank crash of 1873 there had been voices blaming the Jews for the evils of the day, but they remained largely unheard. 'Was *er* sagte,' Harry Bresslau wrote to Theodor Mommsen, 'war damit anständig gemacht.' ('What *he* said . . . was thereby made respectable.') Treitschke's outburst coincided with the political campaign of one of the court chaplains, Adolf Stöcker, who, appalled at the growing secularization of life in the capital and alarmed at the progress of Social Democracy, tried to found a Christlich-soziale Arbeiterpartei to convert the working class to monarchism and the middle class to social welfare. The working-class audience at which he aimed took no notice of him, but clerks and shopkeepers did respond to his anti-liberal tirades, and Stöcker soon spiced these with anti-Semitic slogans.

Treitschke's articles and Stöcker's speeches had a particular effect on student opinion. In 1881 delegates sympathetic to the new cause met on the Kyffhäuser mountain and founded the Verein deutscher Studenten, the first and most important right-wing student organization for many decades.

Max Weber, a student at Berlin in the 1880s, complained of the 'frenetischer Jubel' ('frenetic cheers') which greeted any anti-Semitic remark by Treitschke and the widespread anti-Semitic graffiti 'verschiedener Rohheitsqualität' ('of varying coarseness'). 'Das unglaublichste', he wrote to Hermann Baumgarten, 'ist jedoch die fabelhafte Unkenntnis in der Geschichte dieses Jahrhunderts bei meinen Altersgenossen . . . bis auf einige Schandtaten des Fortschritts und den Taten Bismarcks. Innere Politik gibt es in diesen Köpfen erst seit 1878.'[2]

The reaction against liberal principles at the end of the 1870s had many causes – humanitarian, aesthetic and religious. There was a widespread fear that liberalism would lead to moral decay and political subversion. Underlying all these, there was a desire to find a meaning in the new nation-state which went deeper than administrative formulae

---

[1] 'Year after year there pours over our eastern frontier . . . from the inexhaustible Polish cradle, a host of ambitious trouser-selling youths, whose children and children's children are one day to dominate Germany's stock exchanges and newspapers . . . Right into the most educated circles . . . we can hear, as if from one mouth, "The Jews are our misfortune."'

[2] 'The most incredible thing, however, is the fantastic ignorance of the history of this century among my contemporaries . . . apart from a few crimes by the Left and Bismarck's achievements. Inside their heads domestic politics began in 1878.'

and trading paragraphs; the hope that the sacrifices and victories of the sixties would lead to a new golden age of German prestige and influence; above all, the determination that no power, military or ideological, should threaten the newly achieved. In Germany, lacking natural frontiers and surrounded by old-established but wary powers, considerations of foreign policy could never be ignored during the domestic debate – certainly not by Bismarck, whether the subject was the *Kulturkampf* or tariffs. Germany was now a power, most of her influential citizens wanted her to be a *Machtstaat*. It was a new situation for Europe.

GERMANY AND THE WORLD

Few contemporaries missed the significance of the victory of Prussia over France in 1870. 'L'Europe a perdu une maîtresse et gagné un maître,' was a widely heard verdict. The harshness of the peace terms imposed on France – Alsace, Lorraine and an indemnity of five million gold francs – confirmed many fears that Europe was not at the end but at the beginning of a period of Prussian expansion. There were many witnesses to the bellicose, arrogant public mood of Germany in the wake of these victories. 'O wie wird sich die arme deutsche Nation irren,' wrote Jacob Burckhardt to his friend Friedrich Preen, 'wenn sie daheim das Gewehr in den Winkel stellen und den Künsten und dem Glück des Friedens obliegen will! da wird es heissen: vor allem weiter-exercirt!'[1] and Friedrich Nietzsche, appalled at the popular notion that German military superiority somehow implied German cultural superiority, warned, 'Ein großer Sieg ist eine große Gefahr' ('A great victory is a great danger'); it risked 'die Niederlage, ja Exstirpation, des deutschen Geistes zugunsten des "deutschen Reiches"' ('the defeat, even the extirpation, of the German spirit in favour of the "German Reich"').

Certainly Bismarck's successes had given the German public, and many men in high places, a taste for national self-assertion and quick, violent solutions. Bismarck himself did not share these predilections even though his 'blood and iron' rhetoric encouraged them. He had been concerned to secure the hegemony of Prussia in Central Europe and to this end he needed to displace, but not destroy, Austria, to reduce the power of France and to keep the goodwill of Russia. After

---

[1] 'Oh, how the poor German nation will be deceived, if it wants to stand the rifle in the corner at home, and give itself over to the arts and fortunes of peace! The call will be: carry on drilling!'

1871 he was concerned to maintain these achievements, with all the conservatism of the successful revolutionary, but the means to this end were now peace, not war. Threats to the Bismarckian order could come from two sources. The first was a desire for revenge by France, and for this reason he needed to keep France diplomatically isolated. In the first few years this was difficult. France had a right-wing, royalist government, well connected internationally; to break these connections was one of the purposes of the *Kulturkampf*. After 1877, when the republican ascendancy began in France, he needed to bother less about this danger. The other threat came from the Balkans where, ever since the Crimean War, Austria had been trying to sustain the decaying Turkish Empire while Russia tended to support the Turks' subject nationalities – mostly Christian and predominantly Slav – in the hope of profiting her own expansion towards Constantinople and the Mediterranean.

To keep the rival empires at peace Bismarck encouraged the formation, in 1872–3, of the Drei-Kaiser-Bündnis (Three Emperors' League), ostensibly with the common purpose of maintaining the monarchical political order. This was not entirely a smokescreen. The revolutions of 1848 had been a frightening experience, the Paris Commune of 1871 even more so. The First Working Men's International, founded by Marx in 1864, never amounted to very much, divided as it was by sectarian quarrels; but this is more obvious today than it was at the time. Even so, the main purpose of the Emperors' League was diplomatic, and in this it failed. Within a few years it was tested by both of the kinds of crisis that menaced Germany most, and found wanting.

The first test came from France. The speed of French economic recovery after the defeat worried Germany; the beginnings of military recovery even more. In 1875 Bismarck instigated a number of anti-French press articles, the most alarmist of which bore the headline 'Krieg in Sicht?' The effect of this was to rouse both Russia and Britain. Both states were convinced that a new Franco-German war would further weaken France, both feared that such an outcome would give Germany an intolerable preponderance in Europe. Both therefore warned Bismarck of their alarm.

This co-operation by Russia and Britain on behalf of France was ominous. It was a premonition of 1914. It lent substance to that 'nightmare of alliances' – *le cauchemar des coalitions* – from which Bismarck freely admitted that he suffered. It illustrated how easily Germany might have to face enemies on two fronts and how a situation which others saw as a reasonable counterweight to German hegemonial designs, Germans might be tempted to interpret as 'encirclement'.

The second crisis involved the Balkans. Its immediate cause were revolts by Bulgarians and Bosnian Serbs against Turkish rule. Bismarck very much hoped to stay out of this quarrel; it involved no interest 'welches auch nur die gesunden Knochen eines einzigen pommerschen Musketiers wert wäre'. But he could not stay out, for the interests of his allies were irreconcilable. Austria was determined to maintain the integrity of the Turkish Empire, partly to block Russia, partly because the triumph of national self-determination would necessarily undermine the multinational structure of the Habsburg monarchy. Russian policy was more ambiguous. There was a conservative faction which favoured good relations with Germany and therefore an unadventurous foreign policy. But there was also an increasingly powerful pan-Slav faction which favoured a course of intervention and liberation, and the more desperate the situation of the Balkan Slavs became in 1876–7, the more they had the ear of the Tsar. Accordingly, Russia declared war on, and defeated, Turkey. The peace, signed at San Stefano, was dictated by the Russian ambassador at Constantinople, Ignatiev, an extreme pan-Slav: it drastically reduced Turkish rule in Europe, created a large independent Bulgarian state with an outlet to the Aegean and omitted any compensation for Austria. This was not only contrary to a secret agreement between the Russian and Austrian Governments, it was offensive to the rest of Europe because it marked a serious shift in the balance of power. The new Bulgaria was seen as a potential satellite of Russia and to Disraeli, the British Prime Minister, as a particular threat to the route to India.

Only a European conference could settle these conflicts; the statesman most interested in preventing the other powers from coming to blows – or from forming an alliance which he could not control – but least interested in the geographical details was Bismarck. So the congress met in Berlin in 1878 under his presidency and this was in itself significant. The last conference to discuss the Near East had been held in Paris in 1856, after the Crimean War.

The Congress of Berlin could have only one outcome: to secure from Russia some disgorging of the gains of San Stefano. In addition Austria gained the right to occupy the former Turkish provinces of Bosnia and Herzegovina. Much as Bismarck tried to hold the balance between Russia and her antagonists, Russia inevitably saw him as an opponent and Austria as an ally. The new relationships seemed to be confirmed when the Dual Alliance was signed the next year between Austria and Germany. Though the terms were defensive (and secret), and though Bismarck saw it as much as a restraint on Austria as moral support for anti-Russian adventures, it demonstrated that Germany's fate was in the last resort more strongly tied to Austria. Bismarck himself had spelt this out to the Russians in 1876:

> Unser erstes Bedürfnis sei, die Freundschaft zwischen den großen Monarchien zu erhalten ... Wenn dies zu unserm Schmerze zwischen Rußland und Östreich nicht möglich sei, so könnten wir zwar ertragen, daß unsre Freunde gegeneinander Schlachten verlören oder gewönnen, aber nicht, daß einer von beiden so schwer verwundet oder geschädigt werde, daß seine Stellung als unabhängige und in Europa mitredende Großmacht gefährdet würde.[1]

It was Austria rather than Russia for which he feared such an extreme fate. It was to be avoided not only for balance-of-power reasons, but because the collapse of the Habsburg monarchy would reopen all those questions of Greater or Lesser Germany which he hoped had been settled once and for all in 1871.

The year 1879 was the beginning of the special relationship between Germany and Austria which lasted until 1918 and in which the weaker partner was increasingly able to blackmail the stronger. However, though Austria was from now on Germany's one reliable ally, this was not the situation Bismarck desired. He wanted reconciliation with Russia, though his agricultural tariffs made this even more difficult; he wanted to bring in Britain to bolster Austria's defences in the Balkans; he wanted to include Italy – a potential enemy of Austria and a potential friend of France – into his system. He wanted to ensure that Germany would always be '*à trois* in a Europe of five', and that he himself would remain, in the words of the French ambassador, 'arbitre suprême des destinées des trois Empires'.

Initially he seemed highly successful in mending the broken fences. In 1881 the Drei-Kaiser-Bündnis was revived, Russia having decided that isolation did not benefit her. In 1882 Italy joined Austria and

[1] 'Our first requirement is to maintain friendship among the great monarchies ... If, to our regret, this should not be possible between Russia and Austria, then we could tolerate our friends' losing or winning battles against each other, but not that one of them should be so severely injured or damaged as to endanger its status as an independent Great Power, with a voice in Europe.'

Germany, making the Dual a Triple Alliance, in return for help in her colonial and naval ambitions in the Mediterranean. But the new structure was fragile. France could not be kept permanently from re-asserting herself. Bismarck had encouraged her in colonial adventures as a distraction, but when these failed nationalist passions were diverted towards Europe again, fanned by a flamboyant, politically ambitious general, Georges Boulanger, who was made Minister for War in 1886 and who embarked on an electoral campaign devoted to 'revanche'.

For a time there was a distinct risk of war in the West. More signifi-cant, however, was the echo which Boulangism found in Russia. Pan-Slavism prospered in the 1880s. Alexander III, who became Tsar in 1881 and who was more autocratic and reactionary than his assassinated father, had some sympathy with the notion that Slavs had special spiritual and moral qualities that set them aside from others – especially from Teutons – and that Russia had a divinely appointed mission to lead the other Slav peoples. And many influential Russians continued to feel that Bismarck's behaviour at Berlin had been poor recompense for Russia's benevolence during his own wars against Austria and France. In Paris the crowds sang

Avec le Tsar, pour Dieu, France, pour la patrie,
Mort aux Prussiens, et vive Boulanger

and the pan-Slav press reciprocated with eulogies of France. It was un-likely that the Tsar would base his diplomacy on an unstable adventurer like Boulanger, who indeed disappeared from the scene in 1889, but the ice had been broken.

By 1887, Russia refused to renew the Drei-Kaiser-Bündnis and secured instead the bilateral agreement known as the Reinsurance Treaty, whose secret clauses bound Germany to stronger support of Russia than the merely defensive agreement of 1881. This promise was inconsistent with those to Austria in the Dual and Triple Alliances; it was inconsistent also with the terms of the 'Mediterranean Entente' which Bismarck now fathered, under the terms of which Italy and (at last) Britain were to help Austria in preventing Russian expansion. Bismarck was apparently determined to maintain at all costs the two cardinal principles of his foreign policy: to retain the friendship of Russia, and to ensure the survival of Austria. But the most immediate tangible benefit to him was in domestic politics. The bellicose noises of Boulanger and the coquetry of Russia ensured a tame parliamentary majority in the 1887 Reichstag election – the so-called *Kartell* of the

National Liberals and the two Conservative parties, which passed the septennial military budget without any fuss.

Whether these complex diplomatic schemes and the uncannily quiet domestic climate had any real chances of long-term survival was never put to the test. In 1888 the old emperor died; within ninety-nine days his son, Frederick III, already suffering from cancer when he ascended the throne, was also dead. The new emperor was William's grandson, William II. He was twenty-seven years old, a representative of a new generation which took Bismarck's achievements – German unity, and Germany's place as a power – for granted and was impatient for greater things. Bismarck had been born in 1815, the year of the Congress of Vienna; William II in 1861, the year before Bismarck became prime minister of Prussia. Their worlds were far apart.

The Wilhelmine Empire

ECONOMY AND SOCIETY

It became a cliché in the 1960s that while Germany had become an economic giant she remained a political dwarf. The observation could have been applied as well to the 1890s. The outsider, viewing Bismarck's diplomatic and military successes over the previous thirty years, might think that Germany had done very well for herself. In Germany itself, there was growing feeling that too little had been achieved; that the Second Empire was still a power of medium rank rather than of true world status; that Germany's influence in the world was not keeping pace with her economic expansion.

Maynard Keynes remarked after 1918 that the Reich had been founded not so much on blood and iron as coal and iron. Not only would Bismarck have found it much more difficult to win over middle-class opinion and the southern states without the Prussian economic dynamism of the 1860s, but industry, and especially heavy industry, forged ahead from 1867 onwards, profiting from political unity and only briefly impeded by the banking crash of 1873. It was therefore a stimulant as well as a sustainer of both entrepreneurial self-interest and national self-confidence. The figures alone show decisively that Germany had seized the economic leadership of Europe by the time of the First World War.

Between 1870 and 1913 the productive capacity of Germany increased eightfold, while that of Britain doubled and that of France tripled. Only the United States, among major producers, showed a faster rate of growth. By 1893 German steel production had overtaken British; by 1910 Germany's iron and steel exports exceeded Britain's. The metallurgical hegemony of Britain, already dented by America, was further reduced.

But the figures alone tell only half the story. The German economy in 1870, though prosperous and expanding, had not gone very far in assimilating and diffusing the technology of the industrial revolution, let alone in contributing to it. Mining engineering and textile knowhow came predominantly from Britain, chemical know-how predominantly from France and Belgium. Many industries were only on the threshold of mechanization; manufacture in one-man workshops, back-yards and even parlours, under contract to a *Verleger* (factor), was still usual. Many skilled artisans could still prefer the life of a *Wandergeselle*, carrying the tools of his trade in a knapsack, to that of a factory operative.

INDUSTRIAL DEVELOPMENT 1850–1913

	Germany	France	UK
Coal Production			
(*million metric tons*)			
1850	5·1	4·5	57·0
1871	29·4	13·3	118·0
1890	109·3	26·1	184·5
1913	191·5	40·8	292·0
Pig Iron Production			
(*million metric tons*)			
1850	0·2	0·4	2·2
1871	1·5	1·4	6·5
1890	4·7	2·0	8·0
1913	14·7	4·6	11·0
Steel Production			
(*million metric tons*)			
1850	—	—	—
1871	0·2	0·1	0·3
1890	2·2	0·6	3·6
1913	17·9	4·6	7·8

These Arcadian conditions did not last much longer. The depression of the seventies hit most severely the least capitalized and least efficient producers. From the eighties onwards, mechanization, size of unit and productivity commanded the direction and pace of industrial growth. This was particularly true of the two industries to which Germany made the greatest technical contributions, the chemical and the electrical.

A natural advantage – the extraordinarily rich deposit of potassium salts at Stassfurt, between Magdeburg and Halle – and an educational one – the high standard of scientific knowledge – enabled Germany, when the time came, to snatch the chemical lead from Britain and Belgium who had, in this as in every other field, started first. By the 1880s Badische Anilin at Ludwigshafen, Bayer at Leverkusen, AGFA in Berlin and Höchst near Frankfurt were giants by world standards. Their most spectacular success was in dyestuffs. By the turn of the century they provided 90 per cent of world exports.

But it was the electrical industry which saw the greatest of all achievements. Its founder was the technician-entrepreneur Werner von Siemens, who in 1867 invented the dynamo and in the 1870s was experimenting with electric traction. Resting on American as well as German inventiveness, Germany's electrical factories became leading producers of equipment for lighting, heating, generating and transmitting. They quickly concentrated themselves in two giant combines: Siemens-Schuckert and Emil Rathenau's Allgemeine Elektrizitäts-Gesellschaft (AEG). These two companies were paradigms of the way Germany had developed industrially: a belated start, a rapid rise based on technological excellence and rational organization, well-financed consolidation of production, and an emphasis on quality. As a reward the German electrical industry in 1913 provided a third of the world's output and more exports than Britain and the USA combined.

The years 1873–1914, then, were the years when Germany's industrial base was laid, when she turned from a predominantly rural country into a manufacturer second only to the USA. What happened to Germany in those years – 'industrialization' – is what has happened to most European states, and what most non-European states would like to happen to them. The process is easily recognizable and has certain standard features: the movement from country into town, the concentration of production in fewer and larger units, the manufacture for a market economy instead of for subsistence or local consumption, the tendency for society to divide into those who provide or manage the increasingly large capital needed for sophisticated plant, and those who provide labour in return for a wage or a salary. Yet it is equally evident that industrialization does not happen in a vacuum, that it can follow very different courses in Japan or Sweden, in Brazil or the United States. This is partly a function of *when* it happens: clearly a country which 'takes off' in the second half of the twentieth century does so rather differently from one which did so in the first half of the nineteenth. It is also a function of climate, natural resources and access to trade routes. But it is also very much a function of the existing structure of society, for this will determine how that society absorbs the industrializing process. Hence we cannot make any uniform deductions about the effects of what are outwardly similar technical developments. Hence we must look not only at, but beyond, the form that the industrial revolution took in Germany if we want to understand the particular cultural malaise and political frustrations that characterize the Wilhelmine Empire, if we want to explain the dissonance between the economic dynamism of the Reich and the stagnation of its social norms and political institutions.

There were, indeed, many explanations. There was, in the first place, the speed and thoroughness of the industrialization compared with that of France or the Anglo-Saxon countries. In Britain something like a century elapsed between the first large-scale application of steam-power to manufacture and the climacteric of industrial growth: the process took place in stages, one industry at a time. In Germany it took place in, at best, forty years and in those forty years it covered more ground. There was therefore less chance for mental adjustment to new conditions, for permeating society with the ideas of a new type of man.

Secondly, and even more importantly, Britain was already better prepared for the social impact of industrialization at the beginning of that process than was Germany. There were undeniably distinctions of class in eighteenth-century England, but these were not distinctions of caste. The dividing line between landed and commercial wealth was far from clear, and no bar to intermarriage. The ideas that social betterment was admirable, that the pursuit of financial gain was a public service and that the maximum competition for these gains should be encouraged were widely known and widely accepted, so that when prosperity grew under free trade and *laissez-faire* the empirical evidence served merely to reinforce the validity of these ideas. Thus the competitive spirit could be transferred from the economy to other spheres of life, bringing about a general tendency towards equality, not indeed of wealth or social station but of opportunity – in politics through the extension of the franchise, in the public service through replacing connection with examination, in education by dismantling the privileges of the Church of England. Above all, the distinctions between town and country were well on the way to breaking down, principally because by 1800 – or at the latest 1840 – little remained of the distinctively peasant class characteristic of continental Europe. The farmer, whether landowner, leaseholder or tenant, was an entrepreneur, sinking capital, buying machinery, employing labour like any other businessman.

German industrialization, in contrast, hit a society in which the stratifications of an older epoch were still firmly implanted, and in which the intellectual and literary resistance to the doctrines of Manchester were strong. It was, we have seen, no accident that the first phase of industrialization coincided with the wars of unification, and that these wars reinforced the position of the army, the landowners, the monarchy and the Prussian constitution – all of them forces hostile to the values of industrial society, all of them entrenched in institutions which one would otherwise have expected to give way to bourgeois onslaught. But not only did they not give way, they were confirmed in their primacy by the course of internal politics from 1878 onwards.

The willingness of so many of the makers of the industrial revolution to accommodate themselves to the pre-industrial social and political order sprang partly from fear of social unrest. But it sprang also from the effect of the industrialists and the middle classes of the experience of unification – the respect for the State, the worship of force and craving for social unity which it enhanced. The individualistic materialism preached by the economists and political scientists of capitalism in Britain and France seemed destructive of the social fabric. 'Nicht Frieden und Menschenglück haben wir unseren Nachfahren auf den Weg zu geben,' said Max Weber in his inaugural lecture in 1893, 'sondern die Erhaltung und Emporzüchtung unserer nationalen Art . . . die soziale Einigung unserer Nation, welche die moderne ökonomische Entwicklung sprengte.'[1] And Weber ranked as a modernizer.

Above all, the speed and technical thoroughness of the whole process left their mark. The German industrial revolution was the work of a very few men, who soon dominated the entire economy. There was no transitional period during which a large number of small and medium-sized factory-owners was characteristic of manufacturing industry; they existed, certainly, but their role was subordinate. Very quickly, the giant firm towered above them. In 1910 there were 50,000 joint-stock

---

[1] 'It is not peace and human happiness that we have to bequeath to our descendants, but the preservation and cultivation of our national peculiarity . . . the social unification of our nation that modern economic development has blasted asunder.'

companies in Britain, 5,000 in Germany. But the average capitalization of the German firms was three times that of the British. Krupp's of Essen employed nearly 70,000 men, the AEG of Berlin over 30,000. Not only was the capitalist class small, but many fewer Germans than Britons had a stake in industry through direct investment. After the speculative mania of the *Gründerzeit* (promoters' era) most Germans preferred to put their savings into banks and Government bonds, and it was from the banks that industry got the credit it needed for its expansion.

The rather privileged position which these captains of industry acquired explains why, although they were obviously motivated by a strong competitive impulse, they did not behave as though they were. They showed this in their attitudes towards their rivals, their employees and the State. Towards their employees many of them displayed the conscientious, autocratic paternalism of the Prussian State. Krupp provided housing estates and health services for his employees well before the end of the century; in return they were expected to place loyalty to the firm first; and many of them did, boasting of their often hereditary status as 'Kruppianer'. The most extraordinary of the Wilhelmine tycoons was Baron von Stumm von Halberg, the Saar coal and steel magnate, Conservative Reichstag member and personal friend of the emperor. He forbade his employees to belong to or recruit for the Social Democratic party, to belong to any trade union (even a Christian one) or to subscribe to any non-Conservative newspaper. They could not marry unless they were at least twenty-four years old, had personal savings and had submitted the bride for approval. Their children had to go to church.

This militant hostility to Socialist and even Liberal 'subversion' was strongest in heavy industry, which had indeed taken the initiative towards tariffs and alliance with the State in the 1870s. The iron, coal and steel firms now took the lead in fashioning a development which was by no means unique to Germany but which became dominant there as nowhere else: the 'cartel'. The cartel is not a merger of hitherto independent firms, nor is it a 'trust' of the American type, with its interlocking shareholdings. It is simply an association of manufacturers who come to a contractual agreement about the level of production and the scale of prices. As such it can acquire a monopolistic grip on a basic commodity. After the turn of the century the Rheinisch-West-fälisches Kohlensyndikat controlled almost the entire Ruhr coal and coke output and about half that of Germany. The two electrical giants,

Siemens and AEG, came to an effective price-fixing agreement. The most famous of all the cartels, I. G. Farben of the chemical industry, did not formally come into being until after the war.

The German cartel did not meet with the hostility that industrial concentration evoked in Anglo-Saxon countries. There were no 'trust-busting' campaigns; 'restraint of trade' was not a term of abuse. Most Englishmen and Americans, but few Germans, would have assumed the self-evident truth of Adam Smith's remark that 'people of the same trade seldom meet together, even for merriment or diversion, but the conversation ends in a conspiracy against the public'. It was not only the comfortable profits that they secured for their participants that made the cartels attractive. They expressed the German ideal of *Gemeinschaft* (community), as opposed to the materialistic, contractual *Gesellschaft* (society) favoured by the western nations. They represented the final stage of national economic unification, a triumph over the *Kleinstaaterei* (petty provincialism) of the individual firm. They also protected not only the owners but the employees against the extremes of world price and demand fluctuations, and were therefore welcomed not only by the *Kathedersozialisten* but by some trade-union leaders as well.

Yet the welcome which this dynamic but non-competitive capitalism got was symptomatic of the failure of Wilhelmine Germany to develop into a society fully attuned to the new industrial structure, of the strange schizophrenia which affected much of the middle class on the subject of modernity. On the one hand they were proud of Germany's achievements and indeed wanted more of them – objectives to which further industrial growth were essential. On the other hand their social and aesthetic ideals were predominantly pre-industrial and pre-capitalist, a tribute to the tenacity of the older social forces, but also to the failure of the new to capture the imagination.

Literary taste, and the place of the city in literature, are a good indicator of this. One looks in vain for a German Dickens or Arnold Bennett, a German Balzac or Flaubert. Certainly these novelists did not accept city life uncritically, but they accepted it, sometimes even rejoiced in it. The German literary hero, in contrast, was not (in Oswald Spengler's phrase) the *Asphaltmensch* (creature of the pavement) but the *Schollenmensch* (creature of the soil). The best-sellers of the day were works of rustic sentimentality: Gustav Freytag's *Soll und Haben* (*Debit and Credit*) Wilhelm Raabe's *Der Hungerpastor* (*The Poor Pastor*), Wilhelm von Polenz's *Der Büttnerbauer* (*The Farmer from Büttner*), C. F. Meyer's

Jürgen Jenatsch or Hermann Löns's *Der Wehrwolf*. More sinister, all these works, in contrast with the more lyrical ones of Berthold Auerbach or Annette von Droste-Hülshoff, mixed sentimentality with brutality. Either they extolled nature red in tooth and claw (Löns), or they made the peasant hero a covert or overt nationalist symbol, or they provided the Jew as a hate-object – Veitel Itzig in *Soll und Haben*, Moses Freudenstein in *Der Hungerpastor*, Samuel Harassowitz and Isidor Schönberger who drive Polenz's hero to suicide.

Equally popular, and of more direct political influence, was a work of non-fiction which first appeared anonymously in 1891; Julius Langbehn's *Rembrandt der Erzieher*. It was an appeal to youth, against the pomposities of *Stammtisch* politics, against the emptiness of 'official', academic art, against the fact-collecting of German scholarship. 'Der Professor', he wrote, 'ist die deutsche Nationalkrankheit.' ('The professor is Germany's national disease.') Much of what he denounced needed denouncing, not least the opulent vulgarity of the *nouveaux riches* of Berlin. He was not alone in speaking up for sensitive youth against their uncomprehending elders and it was a highly necessary advocacy. In Prussia alone, between 1883 and 1889, 110 schoolboys committed suicide. But Frank Wedekind, who wanted to emancipate the individual through frankness about sex and the emotions, and whose importance is now recognized in literary histories, broke too many of the taboos of the day; his works were execrated and their performance banned. Langbehn, on the other hand, prescribed old remedies for new complaints. The peasantry: 'Man muß demnach politisch wie geistig die Provinzen gegen die Hauptstadt aufbieten . . . Auf Bauerntum . . . wird sich das neue deutsche Kunstleben zu gründen haben.'[1] Social stratification: 'eine auf überlieferten geschichtlichen Zuständen beruhende und darum mit den gesunden Elementen der niederen Volksklasse einige Sozialaristokratie . . . Das Prinzip der korporativen Gliederung, welches jetzt allmählich wieder in Deutschland zur Herrschaft gelangt.'[2] Ethnic purity: '[Die] heutigen Deutschen . . . sollen Das sein, was sie von Uraltsher waren . . . Sie sind, waren und werden sein Arier.'[3] But he was a prophet, too. Dissatisfied with their present

[1] The provinces will have to be mobilized, politically as well as spiritually, against the capital . . . the new German art will have to base itself on the peasantry.'

[2] 'A social aristocracy resting on traditional historical conditions and therefore at one with the healthy elements of the lower classes . . . the principle of corporative organization which is now gradually returning to favour in Germany.'

[3] 'The Germans of today . . . ought to be that which they were from long ago . . . they are, were and will be Aryans.'

political leaders, Germans yearned for their 'heimlicher Kaiser' ('secret
emperor'), an artist-dictator: '[eine] cäsaristisch-künstlerische, gewaltige
und rein geistig dominierende Einzelindividualität' ('a caesaristic-
artistic individual, powerful and spiritually overwhelming').

By 1918 the book had sold 150,000 copies. It addressed the idealism
and touched the frustrations of middle-class youth. It became the bible
of the strangest of all the products of industrial Germany, the Youth
Movement. This began in 1897 among a group of schoolboys and
sympathetic teachers in the Berlin suburb of Steglitz. They, too,
wanted to turn their backs on the city, by hiking, climbing and
mountaineering. By 1913 they had thousands of followers, of whom
the best known were the Wandervögel troops. They encouraged
folksongs, madrigals and amateur dramatics. They avoided tobacco,
alcohol, elaborate, unhealthy clothing and all luxuries. And yet, as
Charles Péguy pointed out, 'Tout commence en mystique et finit par
politique.' In an Anglo-Saxon context these solemn devotees of raw
carrots, guitars and homespun clothes would most likely be pacifist,
internationalist, anti-authoritarian, scanning the latest Fabian pamphlet
or *New Republic* round the camp-fire. In the Wilhelmine context they
were inevitably nationalist and reactionary. To reject the effects of
urbanization and industrialization meant – unless one were a working-
class Marxist – rejecting the institutions and assumptions of industrial
society. The innocuous wanderings to the forests, castles and half-
timbered towns, the revivals of folk dances were a search for a past that
could heal the divisions of the present: the static, idealized past of
Sachs's Nürnberg or Goethe's Weimar. The more ambitious tours
abroad were often visits to scattered German-speaking minorities in the
Habsburg monarchy or the Russian Empire. This *völkisch* solidarity
applied equally to the movement's own composition: very few groups
accepted Jewish members. In sexual matters they took their cue from
Langbehn rather than from Wedekind: the flight from the city was a
flight from Babylonian erotic stimulations into the imagined purity of
asceticism. The youth movement was, at any rate before 1918, an overwhelmingly male phenomenon. And though they despised the politics
of State secretaries and Reichstag parties, they did so to show that they
were the true patriots. When the various youth organizations joined
together for a festival on the Hohe Meissner mountain, the date they
chose was the centenary of the *Völkerschlacht* at Leipzig – 11 October
1913. And they proclaimed their ideals in impeccably military language:

Wir wollen . . . weiter getrennt marschieren, aber in dem Bewußt-
sein, . . . daß wir Schulter an Schulter kämpfen.[1]

THE EMPEROR AND THE REGIME

The search for spiritual unity, whether in admiration of the past, or in
cultural nationalism, or in the disavowal of practical politics showed
how strong were the fissiparous trends in the lands that the Prussian
army had unified. What Germany lacked was, in Langbehn's phrase, an
'inneres Sedan' – some momentous event which would do for popular
loyalties what the defeat of Napoleon III had done for the State.

Wise political leadership could have contributed to the slow evolution of an unspoken consensus, yet it is precisely this that the Second
Empire lacked. Bismarck had certainly been a popular hero, but the
contempt in which he held public opinion and the brutality with which
he treated antagonists did little to lessen the distance between ruler and
subject, or to diminish the mixture of fatalism and cynicism with which
most citizens regarded authority.

Wilhelm II was equally ill qualified for coaxing his subjects into the
habits of mature citizenship, but for different reasons. He was, according to Professor Michael Balfour, 'the copybook condemnation of the
hereditary system': his intelligence, his conscientiousness, even his
geniality came out when, after his abdication, he lived in Holland for
twenty-two years as a country gentleman with archaeological tastes.
But when he became Emperor, at the age of twenty-seven, he felt more
inclined to give free rein to the qualities he had inherited from his
military grandfather and his Calvinist tutor, Georg Hinzpeter, than
those which he owed to his liberal father and his rather domineering,
enlightened mother (Queen Victoria's eldest daughter). His drive for
self-assertion, coupled with his evident immaturity, led him to that
stream of indiscretions and faulty judgements to which some observers
ascribed all the misfortunes of his thirty-year reign. He took a personal,
interfering interest in almost every subject from ship-design to theatrical productions. His love of military ceremonial verged on the pathological. Count Zedlitsch-Trützschler, a senior court official, noted in
1904, 'Momentan sind wir bei der 37. Uniformänderung seit der
Thronbesteigung.' ('At the moment we are witnessing the 37th altera-
tion of uniforms since the accession to the throne.') Helmuth von

[1] 'We want to continue to march in separate formations, but conscious . . . of
fighting shoulder to shoulder.'

Moltke, the Chief of the General Staff, complained of the uselessness of war-games in which the emperor always won. He poked the ribs of senior officers doing their physical exercises on his annual cruises. He slapped the Tsar of Bulgaria on the posterior at a public reception. He annotated official papers – intended for further circulation – with such marginalia as 'gemeiner Schuft' (common blackguard), 'elender Lügner' (miserable liar), 'Ochs' (ox), 'Esel' (ass) and 'Kamel' (camel). He sent his Ministers autographed portraits with messages such as 'Suprema lex regis voluntas' ('The will of the king is the highest law'). He publicly denounced the Social Democrats as 'vaterlandslose Gesellen' ('scoundrels without a fatherland') and the leader of the Zentrum as needing 'einen Tritt in den Arsch' ('a kick in the arse'). He surrounded himself at court with dubious personalities like the expatriate racialist theorist Houston Stewart Chamberlain, who had married Wagner's daughter, and the homosexually inclined spiritualist Philip von Eulenburg, whose companion, General Cuno von Moltke, referred to the emperor as 'das Liebchen'. In 1907 the journalist Maximilian Harden published a number of scandalous allegations (never conclusively proved) against these two in his periodical *Die Zukunft*, but to little effect; the next year the chief of the military cabinet, von Hülsen-Häseler, collapsed and died while entertaining the emperor dressed as a ballerina.

These episodes would have mattered less had they been restricted to Wilhelm's private life. But his refusal, indeed inability, to distinguish between the private and public spheres made him susceptible to intrigue and gossip and led him into disastrous errors of judgement. Yet it is difficult to accept his undoubted eccentricities as the alibi for the political mistakes of the Wilhelmine period, for no man, however powerful, can act alone, and Wilhelm acted within the admittedly ill-defined constitutional framework he had inherited. It was under Wilhelm that the question which his grandfather and Bismarck had always succeeded in smothering was increasingly, and publicly, asked: who governs in Berlin?

The unique, though by no means always smooth, relationship between emperor and Chancellor that prevailed until 1888 could not outlast these two men. It was not only the obvious incompatibilities of character that estranged the new emperor and the old Chancellor almost from the beginning. Bismarck had, after all, saved the old emperor's crown: his grandson owed him no such debt. The other kings and princes of Germany, by contrast, owed nothing to the new emperor: there was a distinct risk that under him lack of respect for the central authority might have a disintegrative effect.

In addition to all this, Bismarck and Wilhelm did not see eye to eye on several important policy issues. As Bismarck grew older, he grew more obstinate in his obsessions. This meant, in domestic policy, a growing fear of Social Democratic subversion, so that he began to toy with at any rate the possibility of a *coup d'état* against parliament, should it fail to meet his wishes. It meant in foreign policy an increasing dependence on the Russian connection, exemplified by the Reinsurance Treaty, despite growing signs of Russian dissatisfaction with this arrangement. Wilhelm, on the contrary, wanted to drop the repressive legislation against the Labour movement, not because he was a convinced democrat but because he saw himself as a *Volkskaiser*, a *roi des gueux*, with an understanding of the social question. He also wanted to break the Russian link which inhibited his expansionist ambitions and his desire for better relations with Britain. Given these incompatibilities, it was evident that anyone with a grievance against Bismarck would be tempted to insinuate himself with the emperor, who was soon surrounded by a very heterogeneous coalition. Some, like the alleged 'grey eminence' of the Foreign Office, Friedrich von Holstein, because they feared Bismarck was losing his grip and staking too much on Russia; some, like the arch-Conservative chief of the general staff, Alfred von Waldersee, because they hoped for high political office, others, like Eulenburg, because intrigue flattered their self-importance.

In the event Bismarck engineered his own downfall sooner than his enemies, or the emperor, might have wished. The compact parliamentary majority of the *Kartell* – Conservatives and National Liberals – which he had used to get through the septennial army estimates, disintegrated when he insisted on the renewal of the anti-Socialist legislation, which even the parties of the Right now viewed with increasing scepticism. The outcome of the 1890 elections, in which the *Kartell* parties were heavily defeated, left him without a majority unless he were to turn to the Zentrum whom the new emperor distrusted. This domestic defeat coincided with the need to renegotiate the Reinsurance Treaty, and this dual crisis culminated in the disastrous, final meeting between Wilhelm and Bismarck on 15 March. The emperor accused the Chancellor of constitutional improprieties, whereupon Bismarck quoted to Wilhelm a letter in which the Tsar called him 'un garçon mal élevé et de mauvaise foi' ('a badly brought-up boy of bad faith').

It was a bad card to play. It confirmed Wilhelm in the anti-Russian course on which he was determined to embark and which he emphasized in the public letter to his Chancellor that left Bismarck no choice but to resign. Yet, on the day he wrote that letter, a Russian delegation arrived in Berlin to discuss treaty renewal.

Bismarck left office, after twenty-eight years of continuous service, for the same reasons that he had entered upon it. He was determined to save the Prussian monarchy, if necessary against parliament, if necessary against the wishes of the monarch. Habituated to compliance from one whose nominal servant he was, he was incapable of accepting a view of the State's interests that differed from his own. The moment the monarch determined to press such a different view, his position became untenable, for he had – deliberately – refused to create those political institutions – party government, or an imperial cabinet – that would have given him a base for resisting.

So Bismarck's resignation opened the question: who governs? but did not settle it. The beginnings of an answer were suggested by the brief course of his successor's chancellorship. General Leo von Caprivi was an intelligent, honest, dignified public servant with no previous political experience. He wanted to stand above parties and above interests, unaware that there are no impartial, disinterested solutions to political questions. He discovered very quickly that there were interests and factions who were determined, and able, to interpose their veto the moment Government policy went against them. He negotiated trade treaties with eastern European states, in return for which he had to lower Germany's grain duties. This pleased industrial exporters and urban consumers, but it displeased the agrarian lobby. He attempted to reform local government in eastern Prussia, again at the expense of the landowners. He allowed Polish language instruction again, for the first time since the *Kulturkampf*, in Polish-populated Prussian areas. He signed a treaty with Britain, exchanging Zanzibar against Heligoland. Equally alarming were the parliamentary majorities on which Caprivi depended for some of his measures. The trade treaties got through only with the votes of the Social Democrats, the 1893 military budget only with the votes of the Poles, *Reichsfeinde* both of them.

It began to look as though everything that had been achieved since 1878 was once more in danger. The agrarians, already well organized, launched a counter-attack through the creation, in 1893, of the Bund der Landwirte (Agrarian League). Though its leadership was, as in the preceding bodies, aristocratic, it managed to recruit large numbers of peasant farmers from the western parts of the Reich. And though its immediate task was to drive Caprivi from office and reverse his tariff policy it soon became an important ideological pressure group on behalf of conservatism and nationalism, with a membership of nearly 300,000. It was wealthy, which the political parties were not. It endorsed or denounced parliamentary candidates according to their stand on individual issues. Its members sat not only in legislatures but in Ministries. It published national newspapers which spread its ideas beyond the immediate circle of paid-up members. In its agitational, demagogic practices it deliberately modelled itself on the Social Democrats and aimed at being their right-wing counterpart.

In the same year another important pressure group was founded in protest against Caprivi's policies: the Alldeutscher Verband (Pan-German League), inspired by men who were indignant at the loss of Zanzibar. It was more urban and middle-class in composition, but it too had ready access to the press and helped to undermine what was left of Caprivi's authority.

By 1892 he had become so frustrated at the need to cope with the internal politics of Prussia that he resigned the Prussian premiership (though remaining, like Bismarck, Prussian Foreign Minister). The immediate cause had been the emperor's refusal to support him over a schools bill. Two years later the emperor stabbed him in the back on an imperial matter: an anti-Socialist bill that the new Prussian Prime Minister Botho von Eulenburg had prepared and which Eulenburg had insisted should cover the whole Reich. Wilhelm publicly supported the bill, although its terms were unacceptable to Caprivi.

Faced with the enmity of both the Prussian Conservatives and the emperor, Caprivi could no longer remain in office. Under his successor, Chlodwig von Hohenlohe-Schillingfürst, the emperor's triumph over the chancellorship was consummated in circumstances more humiliating than any Caprivi had endured. The occasion this time was a bill to establish public hearings at courts martial, which had the unanimous support of Hohenlohe and the Prussian cabinet. The bill would not only remove a widely resented grievance but would make it easier to get supplementary military funds out of the Reichstag. The emperor, under pressure from the army, was bitterly opposed to the bill and refused to give his consent to it even after Hohenlohe had, in 1897, persuaded the Reichstag to part with the money by promising that the bill would be presented. Had Hohenlohe then resigned, the inexorable subordination of his office might have been halted. But he felt that to hang on was the lesser evil. He did, in fact, get the bill – or most of it – in 1898, but by then the damage had been done.

That Bismarck would have no successor was thus clear in the year before his death. But the episode of the canals bill demonstrated that even the emperor's authority could not prevail against the resistance of those who paraded their loyalty most loudly. The admittedly expensive project to extend Germany's canal network by linking the Rhine and Elbe systems had obvious economic advantages. It had the enthusiastic support of Wilhelm, who loved grandiose public works. It was less welcome to the Junkers. They did not care for the expenditure of public money for the benefit of industrialists; they feared that the canals would lure labour and raise wages in the eastern provinces; they calculated that the canals would facilitate food imports. Since the project was a purely Prussian one it had to be settled in the Prussian Landtag which the Conservatives dominated. It was defeated when first introduced in 1898, despite the emperor's support and despite the fact that many of the Conservative deputies were public officials and therefore subject to pressure. They were able to blackmail Wilhelm because, now that he had turned his back on his Ministers and on the parties of Reichstag, he could govern only through them. If he dissolved the Landtag to get his way he ran the risk of a Liberal majority in Prussia; and this reminder of 1862 he wanted even less than they wanted canals.

What this interlude, like the one over the courts martial, demonstrated is that in the twenty-year-old alliance between industry and Old Prussia, Old Prussia was the senior partner. In the country which dominated the production of the world's most advanced electrical and chemical goods, in which Gottlieb Daimler and Carl Friedrich Benz had just manufactured the world's first marketable automobile, the old aristocracy, dominating the land, the army and the bureaucracy, could achieve notable rearguard victories. It owed the ability to do so to the protective tariff, which not only ensured the income of agriculturists but stabilized their numbers. True, those employed in agriculture dropped from 42 to 34 per cent between 1882 and 1907, but this was still an enormous proportion in the light of the country's industrialization. In Britain the proportion was under 10 per cent.

Neither of Hohenlohe's peacetime successors, Bernhard von Bülow (1900–9) and Theodor von Bethmann-Hollweg (1909–17), was inclined to question the emperor's prerogatives; each, in his different way, tried instead to 'manage' him. If there was a challenge to the authority of the Government in the remaining years of peace it came, surprisingly, from the Reichstag, and this was attributable to the rapid rise of the Social Democratic Party. The party had emerged from the period of repression with its organization tightened and its morale fortified with martyrdom. In 1893 it polled a quarter of all votes, in 1903 over 30 per cent. In 1912 it became the largest party in the Reichstag, with over one-third of all votes.

Though its programme and its rhetoric proclaimed the strictest revolutionary Marxism and its opponents liked to paint it as the party of *Umsturz*, the SPD was in many ways ambiguous about violent change. Subterraneously it continued to provide a home to the Lassallean tradition of the German Labour movement, that of securing social reform by democratizing the State. The more the party secured a mass-basis – and by 1913 it had a million members and two and a half million in the Socialist trade unions – the more it became a part, even if an oppositional part, of the existing State structure. All the party's efforts to segregate the urban working class from contamination with bourgeois ideology – newspapers, sports clubs, evening classes, allotments – did indeed create a hermetic 'sub-culture' whose members shared a *Weltanschauung*, but they also made these members more content to live peaceably within that sub-culture. Moreover, the Bismarckian social security system, though it failed in its aim of changing the workers' partisan allegiance, almost certainly succeeded in softening their hostility to existing society.

Of those within the SPD who questioned the sterility of the orthodox programme the most important was Eduard Bernstein, the father of 'revisionism'. The evidence before his eyes suggested that capitalism was not about to collapse through its internal contradictions. He therefore wanted the party to face the fact that the working class could make considerable gains without revolution, especially if it sought allies among the peasants and the middle class, some of whom were worse exploited in Wilhelmine Germany than some of the workers. Accepting the existing state not only meant a painful intellectual readjustment which the majority of the party were unwilling to make, it also meant a revised attitude to German national defence – could the SPD under certain circumstances vote for the military budget? – and even to Germany's colonial ambitions – what good did it do German workers if Britain and France grabbed the best colonies?

Though the party continued to affirm its unaltered principles, its practice was frequently revisionist. Though opposed to militarism and above all to the Prussian-led army, it did not deny the principle of national defence, and conceded that defeat by Tsarist Russia would be a disaster to be avoided at all costs. The logical conclusion of this ambiguous stance was the SPD's vote for the war credits on 4 August 1914. In some of the southern states universal suffrage had been introduced for the state parliaments, thus – in contrast with Prussia – enabling Socialists to participate in the work of government in proportion to their electoral strength. They made electoral alliances with the Zentrum and Liberals, exactly as Bernstein had prescribed; they were becoming just another political party.

In the Reichstag the situation was not comparable. Yet the SPD's growing representation – 83 seats in 1903, 110 in 1912, out of 397 – was a symptom of the public mood to which the party could not fail to respond. Most Germans were patriotic, loyal to the monarchy, proud of their country's achievements, increasingly willing to accept the nationalist and imperialist slogans with which they were bombarded. At the same time – and this is the only plausible interpretation of the voting figures – they were less and less satisfied with their system of government. They resented the injustice of the Prussian franchise, the privileges of the military, the prerogatives of the bureaucracy, the indirect taxes which hit the poor proportionately more than the rich, above all the high price of food exacted by the agrarians.

As a result the Government found it increasingly difficult to patch up working majorities for getting its legislation through. The parties of the *Kartell*, the only really *reichstreu* ones, never again sufficed after 1890. Chancellors had therefore to include the Zentrum or the Progressives. In general Bülow and Bethmann-Hollweg preferred the Zentrum with its conservative outlook, and except for two years the *schwarzblau* bloc predominated. But the Zentrum exacted a high price for its collaboration and was unhappy about the Government's aggressive foreign policy. When, therefore, it went into opposition – as it did over a colonial scandal in 1907 – the Progressives had to be brought in. They were more amenable to nationalist policies but less so on economic and constitutional issues, and the short-lived alliance broke up in 1909, technically on a question of death-duties (against which the Conservatives rebelled), in fact out of an incident which epitomized political life in the Wilhelmine Empire.

On 28 October 1908, the *Daily Telegraph* published an interview with the emperor which contained a number of egregious indiscretions, on the follies of British foreign policy and his own misunderstood role as a friend of Britain. In the Reichstag Bülow admitted that he had approved of the interview, though without reading it, and agreed that the emperor's choice of words was unfortunate. But it was the emperor who reaped the constitutional benefit. Bülow's resignation merely accelerated the downgrading of the chancellorship, and the Reichstag, which had attempted to call the Government to account, went away empty-handed.

In the long run, however, the *Daily Telegraph* affair resulted in attempts to strengthen the rights of parliament. The stronger the Social Democrats became the more they could attempt to use the Reichstag as a 'control' on the executive. They automatically gained representation on the committees and after the swing to the Left in 1912 they secured, in collaboration with the Liberal parties, membership of the presidium of the House, and with it a say in business and procedure. Indeed, a Social Democrat, Phillip Scheidemann, was elected Vice-President of the Reichstag, only to resign rather than be presented at court. The same Reichstag also extended its right to ask questions and debate Government policy. It still could not enforce replies – it could not, after all, change the constitution unilaterally – but it could become a more vocal organ of critical opinion than before.

The limits of its powers were graphically illustrated by the Zabern incident of 1913. In this small Alsatian town (now known as Saverne) the local commander had arbitrarily arrested twenty-eight civilians and detained them. The Reichstag censured the Chancellor, who defended the military, with only 55 Conservative votes in support of the Government. No action followed this gesture, none could; but it demonstrated once more the gap between the sentiments of an urban, literate population and an insensitive, dynastic Government.

That these small revivals of parliamentary initiative could have led to the peaceful evolution of parliamentary sovereignty seems doubtful. The mere fact that a numerous Socialist party was needed to push them through made the Socialists' potential allies cautious, and no reform of the Reichstag could have achieved anything without the simultaneous democratization of Prussia. Nevertheless, the trend of public opinion was ominous to the country's rulers. Murmurs of a *coup d'état* were once more heard, but a more effective counter-move was to attack public opinion head on – to provide alternative attractions and other objectives for political enthusiasm, 'to export the social question' in Holstein's cynical phrase.

It would be foolish to attribute Germany's more expansionist policy after the fall of Bismarck solely to a well-hatched publicity stunt.

It accorded too closely with the personal inclinations of Wilhelm, and with the interests of industrialists and generals, for that to be true. It would have been pursued even if the Social Democrats had been feebler, or the cartoons in *Simplicissimus* less scabrous. But its utility as social cement was lost on no one. Johannes Miquel, a National Liberal who was Prussian Minister of Finance in the 1890s and who advocated a *Sammlung* (concentration) of industry, landowners and the monarchy, emphasized, in his proposals for the Government's 1898 election programme, how public opinion might be diverted from vexations like the Courts Martial Bill:

> . . . Die Kolonialpolitik würde uns nach außen wenden, das tut sie aber nur zu einem gewissen Grade. Man müsse daher auch andere Fragen der auswärtigen Politik in den Reichstag bringen . . . Unsere unleugbaren Erfolge würden einen guten Eindruck machen und dadurch die politischen Gegensätze gemildert werden.[1]

WELTPOLITIK

Bismarck had to the end thought of Germany as a European power. He had no objection to overseas colonies and he could see their commercial value, but he was content to leave their creation to private enterprise. He wanted to restrain France, control Austria and to be the partner of Russia. He had no desire at all to compete with Britain. Not merely Wilhelm but many public men of the next generation dissented from this view. The link with St Petersburg they regarded as an indignity, a restraint on Germany's freedom of movement. Austria was to be the chief ally in the incipient Teutonic–Slav confrontation. For Wilhelm, in addition, there was the personal ambition of a partnership with Britain to rule the waves and to immunize Russia.

The course of events in the 1890s was to show that the new policy had flaws far greater than the contradictions in the Bismarckian edifice. In the first place, it was not Germany but Russia which gained a free hand when the Reinsurance Treaty lapsed. The tentative approaches of the Boulanger period matured into official negotiations. The French navy visited Kronstadt in 1892; the Paris money market was prepared to supply the loans which Berlin now refused. In 1894 a formal defensive military alliance was signed between the two countries, reinforced

[1] 'Colonial policy would turn our minds outward, but it does so only to a certain extent. We must therefore bring other foreign policy issues before the Reichstag. . . . Our undeniable successes would create a good impression, and in this way partisan antagonisms would be moderated.'

in 1899 so as 'to maintain the balance of power'. This meant, in effect, a French promise to come to Russia's aid in the event of either German or Austrian attack, and a Russian promise, in the event of German aggression, to help recover Alsace-Lorraine, 'la réalisation de nos vœux et de nos espérances', as Delcassé, the French Foreign Minister, reported on his return.

The Germans could afford to be fatalistic about the Franco-Russian alliance as long as there was a prospect of British support. Germany could assert herself against Russia with Britain, or against Britain with Russia. That she succeeded in neither was the consequence, even if not the intention, of *Weltpolitik*, the policy of pursuing world-power status. This policy is particularly associated with two Ministers whom Wilhelm was able to appoint in 1897 after his defeat of Hohenlohe – Bernard von Bülow who became State Secretary for Foreign Affairs and Admiral Alfred von Tirpitz who became State Secretary for the Navy.

Bülow proclaimed the new aims in his first speech to the Reichstag: 'Wir wollen niemand in den Schatten stellen, aber wir verlangen auch unseren Platz an der Sonne . . .' ('We want to put no one in the shade, but we too demand our place in the sun . . .'). The trouble with this formulation was that more sunshine for Germany inevitably meant less for Britain. Britain, the world power *par excellence*, owed her position to her colonies and her navy. Neither the Kaiser nor his advisers wanted to overthrow the British Empire. They wanted to be its equals: 'Was für England gegolten hat, gilt auch für uns' ('What was considered right for England is right for us too'), wrote Hans Delbrück in the *Preußische Jahrbücher*. But it was precisely this that Britain could not permit. Britain's colonies were not mere blobs on the map, nor her battleships expensive toys, to be accumulated because they were fashionable status symbols. They were the substance of her political power and of her trading profit. Germany embarked on her policy of antagonizing Britain at a time when British opinion, both official and public, was predominantly pro-German. France was still her chief colonial rival, Russia the main threat to her eastern empire: the alliance between the two seemed to compound two traditional dangers. As late as 1898 Britain and France were on the verge of war when their respective patrols met at Fashoda in the Sudan, each laying claim to the head-waters of the Nile. In Britain, as in Germany, there was, under the influence of Darwinism, some support for a 'racial' basis to politics. In 1899 Joseph Chamberlain, the Colonial Secretary, called for 'a new Triple Alliance between the Teutonic race and the two great branches of the Anglo-Saxon race'. He made a specific offer of a defensive alliance to Germany, even offering to bypass Parliament. But Germany feared that such an alliance would tie her to British influence, and Britain was unwilling to make those concessions over colonies which would have satisfied Germany.

Chamberlain's offer came at a time when the atmosphere between Britain and Germany was already becoming clouded. Wilhelm had offended British public opinion in 1896 when he sent a message of congratulation to President Kruger of Transvaal (the 'Kruger Telegram') after the repulse of the British-inspired Jameson Raid. But the true dimensions of the German challenge outlined themselves in a project whose rationale was to oblige Britain to share her spoils – the building of a navy. 'England', in the words of Tirpitz's decisive memorandum of June 1897, 'ist der Gegner, gegen den wir am dringendsten ein gewißes Maß an Flottenmacht als politischer Machtfaktor haben müssen.'[1] The navy, in Tirpitz's eyes, was to be a lever with which Britain would be forced to respect Germany. No project was dearer to Wilhelm's heart: it satisfied his need (in Bismarck's phrase) 'jeden Tag Geburtstag [zu] feiern' ('to celebrate his birthday every day'); it convinced him that it made Germany the arbiter of her external relations ('England kommt uns nicht trotz, sondern wegen meiner kaiserlichen Marine' – 'England approaches us not in spite of, but because of my imperial navy'), it fed his moods of sulky petulance ('Ich kann und will John Bull nicht erlauben, mir das Tempo meiner Schiffsbauten vorzuschreiben' – 'I can and will not permit John Bull to prescribe the rate of my naval construction programme').

Yet the wishes of Wilhelm and Tirpitz did not suffice to produce a navy. Unlike the army, it was not an arm inherited from Prussia; in 1871 it hardly existed. No navy could be built without a Reichstag majority. It was to secure this that Tirpitz organized a vast campaign of publicity and persuasion. The Flottenverein, aimed at the general public, quickly outstripped the Social Democratic Party in members. Its journal, *Die Flotte*, was selling 300,000 copies within two years. Elite opinion was wooed by the *Flottenprofessoren*, distinguished academics who went on lecture tours. Their names included not only the predictable nationalist contingent but theologians like Adolf von Harnack, classicists like Ulrich von Wilamowitz-Möllendorf, medical

[1] 'England is the opponent against whom we need most urgently to have a certain measure of naval power as a factor of political power.'

men, chemists, biologists. Enthusiasm for the navy was the nearest that Wilhelmine Germany got to a loyalist mass movement, that elusive 'inneres Sedan' which would give her antique institutions popular foundations and meet the challenge of the Left on its own ground.

The idea of a navy was popular for all the reasons that made the army unpopular. The navy would be German, not Prussian. A navy had been one of the aims of the Frankfurt Parliament, the prospect of suitable naval bases one of the reasons why the Liberals were so enthusiastic for the annexation of Schleswig-Holstein in the 1860s. The navy was predominantly middle-class and recruited from northern and western Germany. A non-privileged, non-reactionary force of this kind would give even the normally anti-militarist Zentrum a chance to show its patriotism. So, partly thanks to the skill of Tirpitz's propaganda, partly thanks to the way battleships seemed to fill an emotional vacuum in the political life of Germany, the navy bill was passed. The Reichstag agreed to an expenditure of over 400 million marks (£18 million), to be further increased on four subsequent occasions, for a project whose purpose was at best ill defined and whose efficacy was at the least questionable.

In the decade before the outbreak of the First World War the naval building programme, in which Britain was determined – successfully – to maintain a lead, was the chief cause of deteriorating relations between the two countries. The failure of Chamberlain's negotiations in 1898, and the humiliations of the Boer War (1899–1902) which left Britain friendless, both contributed to Britain's emergence from isolation. The only alternative to the 'Teutonic' alliance was an association with France and Russia, and this came about, slowly and in stages.

The reconciliation with France was easier, if only because France was now willing to renounce claims to Egypt – disputed with Britain since the time of Napoleon – as the price of Britain's support against Germany. In 1904 the Entente Cordiale – not a treaty with contractual obligations, merely the beginning of a desire to collaborate – was signed between the two states. The architect of the Entente was Delcassé, the French Foreign Minister, in many ways the true heir of Bismarck. Like Bismarck he saw in Russia's friendship the key to the military dominance of Europe, like Bismarck he saw the need to be *à trois* among the five great powers of the Continent. He could secure this superiority only by ending the enmity between Britain and Russia, an ambition achieved in 1907 when these two states also signed an *entente*. The Triple Alliance of Germany, Austria and Italy, dating from 1882, was thus faced with a Triple Entente whose military and economic potential was at least its equal. The Entente was, however, an informal grouping with highly flexible relationships; what cemented it was the course of German policy in the years to 1914.

The Anglo-French side of the Entente was fortified by Germany's attempts to split it; the Anglo-Franco-Russian side by Germany's support of Austria and her infiltration of Turkey. Twice, in 1905 and 1911, Germany tried to challenge the Anglo-French 'share-out' of Morocco, one of the bases of the Entente. In 1905 Wilhelm, on a State visit to Tangier, declared his hope for an 'open door' Morocco, with equal chances for German trade, in itself a reasonable demand. The purpose of the speech was to demonstrate to France that she could not collude with Britain against Germany; in fact, the eleven-power conference at Algeciras in 1906, which met at Germany's instance, rejected her case. Five years later, when the German cruiser *Panther* dropped anchor off Agadir, again ostensibly to protect German interests, it was Britain who was more offended than France, for France was beginning to assume an essential role in British 'balance of power' calculations.

Having failed to frighten Britain with a navy, Germany tried to weaken Britain by attempting a reconciliation with Russia. Here again, the German Government failed and for the same basic reason: it seriously underestimated the suspicion it evoked by the impulsiveness and inconsistency of its actions. The project for a railway from Berlin to Baghdad – never completed – aroused Russia's fears; so did Germany's noisy support for Austria's annexation of Bosnia and Herzegovina, Turkish provinces she had occupied militarily in 1878; so did the sending of a German officer to supervise the training of the Turkish army.

Yet if Germany's often incomprehensible initiatives helped to escalate nationalism, aggressiveness and even hysteria among her antagonists, she was entitled in her turn to complain of some of these reactions. What, after all, was wrong with a place in the sun? Was imperialism a free for all, or was it not? Why did Britain view with such envy (Wilhelm's word) Germany's efforts to establish a new balance of power on a world-wide scale? Why the double standard which condemned Germany to her existing sphere of influence while apparently condoning Russia's drive on Constantinople, or French *revanche*, which revived after the second Moroccan crisis with the Lorrainer Raymond Poincaré becoming first Premier, then President?

It was this indignation that constituted Germany's genuine grievance about 'encirclement', and despair about this situation led her policy-makers to think more readily of war as the sole solution. 'Wenn wir aus dieser Affaire wieder eingezogenen Schwanze herausschleichen,' wrote Moltke, the Chief of Staff, at the time of Agadir, 'wenn wir uns nicht zu einer energischen Forderung aufraffen können, die wir bereit sind, mit dem Schwerte zu erzwingen, dann verzweifle ich an der Zukunft des Deutschen Reiches.'[1] Such outbursts do not prove that Germany plotted war, but they do suggest that her leaders were resigned to its inevitability – a fatalism that affected even such non-bellicose men as the Chancellor, Bethmann-Hollweg. The political fatalism was compounded by tactical inflexibility. Faced with the risk of a war on two fronts, once the Franco-Russian alliance was a reality, Moltke's predecessor, Schlieffen, had perfected a war plan which recognized only this one contingency. Since France was easier to knock out than Russia, the first blow must be struck westwards; since France was more vulnerable from the flank, Belgian neutrality must be violated. With Paris in German hands, Russia could be mopped up – provided she wished to fight on alone. The fatal element of this plan was that it deprived the Government of all freedom of manœuvre in a crisis. It was 'militarist' in the crudest sense, in subordinating foreign policy to strategy. It ran completely counter to the *aperçu* of the Prussian army's mentor, Clausewitz, that war should be seen only as an *instrument* of policy.

These political and military presuppositions were put to the test in the summer of 1914. The assassination of the Austrian heir-apparent, Franz Ferdinand, at Sarajevo in Bosnia on 28 June was a blow aimed at Austria, not Germany. But Austria's determination to hold Serbia, from where the assassin had crossed the frontier, responsible, required the support of her German ally. It was the need to maintain the ally's morale that explained, to a great extent, why the emperor, the general staff and, after some hesitation, the Foreign Office decided to give Austria the famous 'blank cheque' of 5 July: the assurance of Germany's 'volle Unterstützung in gewohnter Bündnistreue' ('full support in an ally's customary loyalty'). Those who issued the cheque knew that Russia might feel obliged to come to the aid of her protégé Serbia, if only to maintain her credit with the Slav nationalists of the Balkans, and that a war with Russia would certainly involve France and possibly

[1] 'If we once more creep out of this affair with our tail between our legs, if we cannot brace ourselves to an energetic claim that we are ready to enforce with the sword, then I despair of the future of the German Empire.'

Britain. But equally they hoped that Russia would stay out, thus localizing the conflict.

Austria, however, decided to draw fully on the generous account Berlin had opened. She sent an ultimatum in humiliating terms to Serbia and rejected a conciliatory reply. She declared war on 28 July, whereupon Russia made her mobilization – already secretly in train for some days – public. It was a partial mobilization only, directed, like the gunshots of Sarajevo, at Austria, not Germany. But the German Government refused to recognize the distinction, leading the Tsar to order total mobilization on 31 July. On 1 August Germany responded by declaring war against Russia, on 2 August against France; and a German attack on France, via Belgium, put an end to Britain's hesitations. The Entente had become an alliance.

Of all the scholarly debates which have raged in this century among historians, that concerning Germany's 'war guilt' in 1914 has been, and is, the most emotion-laden. Some Germans, soldiers, diplomats, above all the propagandists of the Pan-German League, wanted a war – to gain colonies, to unify the nation, to complete Germany's transition from a continental to a world power. Others, including those in the most responsible positions, failed to do what they might have done to prevent one, because they were convinced that Germany's case was just, or that war was inevitable, or that if it threatened it was for Germany to wage it at a time, and on terms, most favourable to herself. No one showed more clearly the constrictions of this self-spun web than the Hamlet-like Chancellor, when he wired to his ambassador in Vienna on 29 July:

Es handelt sich lediglich darum, einen Modus zu finden, der die Verwirklichung des von Österreich-Ungarns erstrebten Ziels... ermöglicht, ohne gleichzeitig einen Weltkrieg zu entfesseln, und wenn dieser schließlich nicht zu vermeiden ist, die Bedingungen, unter den er zu führen ist, für uns nach Tunlichkeit zu verbessern.[1]

---

[1] 'It is solely a question of finding a means of making the realization of Austria-Hungary's aims possible ... without at the same time unleashing a world war, and if this is in the end not to be avoided, to bring about the best possible conditions under which we may wage it.'

War and Revolution

UNITY UNDER SIEGE

'Ich kenne keine Parteien mehr, ich kenne nur Deutsche,'[1] the emperor proclaimed from the balcony of his palace on 4 August to the cheering multitude. Enthusiasm for the war was not restricted to Germany; it gripped the cities of every belligerent state, as if the war provided a release from peacetime tensions which were becoming unbearable, as if hostilities of class, religion and ideology could now be safely redirected against a unanimously hated foreigner. The impasse which German political development had reached in the years before 1914 made this release especially welcome, and it seemed to be as welcome to the opposition as to those who most feared subversion. The key to this apparent paradox is the dominant role of foreign policy in German public life, the so-called *Primat der Außenpolitik*.

Of course all states are concerned primarily to preserve their sovereignty and their security; but not all states are so placed that foreign relations are permanently at the centre of public debate. German statecraft has been especially indebted to the legacy of Leopold von Ranke (1795–1886), the father of scientific history, for whom history was the story of struggles between the powers, and for whom 'the supreme law of the state' was self-assertion: 'es legt ihm sogleich die Notwendigkeit auf, alle inneren Verhältnisse zu dem Zwecke einzurichten, sich zu behaupten' ('it imposes the necessity of ordering all internal relationships for the purpose of asserting itself'). This doctrine is welcome to conservatives everywhere, not just in Germany. It emphasizes authority, order and discipline, habits that conservatives value highly; it enables them to deny civil liberties or social reforms with the claim that these endanger the security of the state. For the same reason the doctrine is unwelcome to the Left. Imperialism, colonialism, militarism, 'power politics' appear as not merely undesirable in themselves, but as instruments of internal repression, alibis for authoritarianism. This explains much of the 'little Englandism' of British radicals, or the isolationism of midwestern Americans.

What made the debate on the sanctity of the state so lopsided in Germany was not so much the existence of a Right, wedded to the primacy of foreign policy, as the absence of a Left, willing to dispute it.

[1] 'I know no more parties, I know only Germans.'

Bismarck defeated the Liberals not least because they, too, wanted a *Machtstaat*. The Social Democrats, like the mid-century Liberals, affirmed the principle of national defence; they merely took exception to the Prussian–German army as its instrument. Like the Liberals half a century earlier, they were offered no choice in the matter. In trying to assert a primacy of domestic politics, Liberals and Socialists were therefore fighting with one hand tied. This explains the ease with which all parties and all sections of opinion – initially with only negligible exceptions – came together in a national truce, the *Burgfrieden*.

It was not merely the Government, the Conservatives, the Pan-Germans and those close to them who saw political advantage in the war. The alienated romantics of the youth movement saw in it Germany's spiritual regeneration and their members were among the most enthusiastic volunteers. 'Der Krieg hat dem Wandervogel recht gegeben,' wrote Hans Breuer, the compiler of their song-book, in a special preface, 'hat seine tiefe nationale Grundidee los von allem Beiwerk stark und licht in unsere Mitte gestellt. Wir müssen immer deutscher werden . . . Werdet Männer, festzustehen und Euren Platz auf der Erde zu behaupten!'[1] Many Liberals hoped that the war would at last make Germany into a true nation-state, in which middle-class values would predominate. The historian Friedrich Meinecke wrote,

Das industrielle Deutschland mit allen Massen, die es umfaßt, hat seinen Willen und seine Kraft gezeigt . . . Aber auch der konservative Agrarstaat, in dem die Eigenart des preußischen Staates ihren sozialen Halt fand, hat neue, große und unentbehrliche Leistung vorzuweisen . . .

Zugleich sind die unseligen Spannungen verringert, die zwischen den konservativen Gewalten Preußens und den liberalen Bedürfnissen des weiteren Deutschlands . . . bestanden . . .

Wenn unserem Heerwesen die volle Synthese von Volksheer und Berufsheer gelingt, so wird auch unserem Staatsleben die volle Synthese von preußischem Organismus und Reichsorganismus gelingen.[2]

[1] 'The war has proved the *Wandervogel* right; it has placed its fundamental national idea, stripped of all superfluities, in our midst, in all its strength and light. We must become more and more German. . . . Become men, to stand firm and assert your place on the earth.'
[2] 'Industrial Germany, with all the masses that it encompasses, has shown its will and its might. . . . But the conservative agrarian state, in which the peculiarity of

The revisionist Socialists equally saw their moderate, evolutionary programme justified: only by co-operating with the Government could they hope to gain recompense for the services of the working class in industry and the army. A week after the war credits had been voted Eduard David, the SPD member who had helped to draft his party's statement, recorded in his diary that the war would evoke a democratic as well as a nationalistic wave. 'Die preußische Wahlreform muß als Frucht gepflückt werden . . . Notwendigkeit für uns, zu positiver Mitarbeit auf dem Gebiete der Wehrforderungen.'[1]

One reason for this consensus was the almost universal belief that Germany was fighting a defensive war. The 'declaration of the 93', signed by Germany's leading intellectuals and ultimately numbering 4,000 subscribers, constituted an appeal to German and world opinion to exculpate Germany from aggressive intent. It was particularly important in maintaining the SPD's loyalty to the war effort, which was based on the assumption that the war was not an expansionist one. The case would have been more convincing had not many of the signatories of the declaration given their pens to the crudest hate-propaganda, combining xenophobia and self-satisfaction, in which the war appeared a crusade waged on behalf of superior German culture. Dissenters from this chorus were, initially, few. Albert Einstein was one. Hermann Hesse was another, but his pamphlet 'O Freunde, Nicht diese Töne', published in Switzerland, did not contain the sort of literary allusion then fashionable.

The consensus might well have survived had the German armies gained the quick, decisive victory which her military commanders expected. But the German breakthrough in Belgium and northern France was halted along the Marne in the second week of September, and though Paris came within the range of the heavy guns, this was the nearest the German army ever got to the French capital. From then on the opposing front lines in the west moved for little more than a few

---

the Prussian state found its social support, has also displayed new, great and indispensable achievements . . .

'At the same time the unfortunate tensions that existed between the conservative forces of Prussia and the liberal needs of wider Germany have diminished . . .

'If our army succeeds in bringing about the full synthesis of people's army and professional army, then in the life of our state the full synthesis of Prussian organism and Reich organism can also come about.'

[1] 'Prussian electoral reform must be picked as a fruit. . . . Necessity for us to collaborate positively in the field of mobilization.'

miles until the summer of 1918. Repeated attempts by both sides to break through – by the British on the Somme and at Ypres, by the French in Champagne, by the Germans at Verdun and in Artois – came to nothing. In three full years of war (1915 to 1917) the three armies lost eight million men, killed and wounded, three million of them Germans.

In contrast, Germany's campaign against Russia went brilliantly, thus doubly falsifying Schlieffen's anticipations. At the end of August 1914 the Germans routed the Russians at Tannenberg, just inside East Prussia; by the end of 1915 German armies had occupied most of Poland. As more powers entered the war, the tide turned even more strongly in Germany's favour. Turkey came in as an ally of the Central Powers, to be followed by Bulgaria. Aided by Bulgaria, Austro-German armies occupied most of Serbia in 1915 and most of Romania in 1916. Thus half-way through the war Germany had military control of an area stretching from the Baltic to the Persian Gulf and, more importantly, possession of major wheat and oil resources. Italy, on the other hand, having evaded her obligations to the Triple Alliance at the outbreak of war, joined the Entente Powers in 1915 in return for lavish promises of territorial gains. Though her declaration of war further stretched Austria's tenuous resources, she did badly, suffering the disaster of Caporetto in 1917.

All these successes sufficed to keep Germany going, but not to secure the final victory which both the Government and the general staff assumed was the one aim worth pursuing. The military impasse had its effects on domestic politics, but these were in an increasingly authoritarian direction. The democratization, which not only Liberals and Socialists but some right-wingers, such as Tirpitz, expected as a natural outgrowth of a 'people's war', did not come. In economic matters the centralized direction worked effectively. Walther Rathenau, son of the founder of the Allgemeine Elektrizitäts-Gesellschaft, became the virtual economic dictator of Germany, at the head of the *Kriegsrohstoffabteilung* (Department of Military Raw Materials). Hugo Stinnes on behalf of the industrialists and Karl Legien on behalf of the trade unions signed a formal agreement to pool their resources. Under General Wilhelm Groener and the banker Karl Helfferich, and with the unions' co-operation, complete conscription of labour was introduced. These measures involved a degree of planning, and of associating the major interests with the State, which is familiar enough in the 1960s, but which was not equalled by any of the other belligerents. In part, there were ideological reasons for this: Rathenau's *dirigisme* appealed to the social ideal of *Gemeinschaft* and remained an object of nostalgia long after it had been dismantled.

The parallel growth in political authoritarianism, however, was less popular. In Britain and France the unprecedented degree of Government control that the war required was personified by popular civilian politicians, Lloyd George and Clemenceau, who exercised fairly effective control over the military. Strategy was subordinated to war aims, and both strategy and war aims were open to discussion in Parliaments which could, if they wanted to, bring Governments down. In Germany, the power of the Chancellor declined, and was reduced to a shadow when, in 1916, the victors of Tannenberg, Hindenburg and Ludendorff, were appointed Chief of the General Staff and Quartermaster-General respectively. Of these two Ludendorff, obstinate and conspiratorial, obsessed with reactionary and racialist doctrines, soon became the real dictator of the country. He involved himself not only in the formulation of war aims and overall strategy, but also in domestic and constitutional questions.

Ludendorff was committed to a victory in which Germany would be able to dictate the terms of peace – a *Siegfrieden*. In this he was supported by the emperor, the army, by many politicians and intellectuals, as well as those who had directly material interests in German expansion – industrialists who coveted the resources of Belgium and France, land-owners who coveted the wheatlands of the east, merchants who longed to see British competition removed from Africa and the open seas. Many of the war aims which the German Government now officially accepted coincided closely with the schemes that Pan-Germans and other influential pressure groups had dreamed up before the war; this has led recent historians, notably Fritz Fischer in *Griff nach der Weltmacht*, to conclude that Germany went to war in 1914 with a programme of expansion specifically in mind. That must remain hypothetical. What is demonstrable is that the adoption of an ambitious programme of annexations made Germany deaf to any suggestions of a compromise peace – whether these came from President Wilson, the Pope, or private intermediaries.

One way of securing victory was to break the British naval blockade which was effectively cutting Germany off from overseas supplies. The one major engagement which the German navy fought with the British – the battle of Jutland in 1916 – failed in this objective. Though more British ships than German were sunk, the British could afford these losses more easily, and the German fleet stayed in port for the rest of the war. The only alternative to an open sea battle was unrestricted submarine warfare, a weapon guaranteed, according to Tirpitz, 'England auf die Knie zu zwingen' ('to force England to her knees'). Since this strategy involved sinking any ship making for a British port, including neutral (mainly American) merchant vessels, Bethmann-Hollweg resisted it on political grounds. By the spring of 1917, however, Ludendorff, who favoured it, prevailed, and the submarine campaign was launched. Since it coincided with a clumsy German intrigue in Mexico, which was uncovered by the British secret service and revealed to the American Government, its principal effect was to bring the United States into the war on the side of Britain and France. But since it also failed to force Britain to her knees, it brought about the most serious political crisis yet in Germany.

DISUNITY UNDER SIEGE

The *Burgfrieden* had rested on the assumption that the war was defensive and would end quickly. When neither of these assumptions was borne out, the old political divisions, between those who trusted the German State and those who did not, re-emerged. At first discontent was restricted to the Social Democrats; an anti-war group, dissenting from the majority line, formed itself into an independent party (USPD) in 1917. Though its core was the old Left, it united, in its leadership, the chief apostles of revisionism (Bernstein) and orthodoxy (Kautsky), as well as of revolution. By the summer of 1917 discontent had spread across a much wider spectrum of opinion. On 19 July the Socialist parties, the Progressives and the Zentrum supported a motion that 'Der Reichstag erstrebt einen Frieden der Verständigung und der dauernden Versöhnung der Völker' ('The Reichstag strives for a peace of mutual understanding and lasting reconciliation among the peoples').

This was the coalition of the old Bismarckian *Reichsfeinde*, only this time, thanks to the Left swing of the 1912 elections, they commanded a majority in the Reichstag. For the first time now they were prepared to use this majority to achieve a policy objective. They created a joint caucus – the *interfraktioneller Ausschuß* – with the short-term aim of bringing about a change of Government and the long-term one of imposing parliamentary control on the Chancellor. In their short-term objective they were anticipated by the High Command in a way that illustrated where the power in Germany really lay. Bethmann-Hollweg had done his best to keep the Social Democrats within the *Burgfrieden*, fearing social and political chaos if he failed to do so. This meant maintaining public ambiguity about war aims and moving cautiously towards domestic reforms. It was this inclination to 'appeasing' the Left, as well as his lukewarmness towards the U-boat campaign, that made him unacceptable to the military leaders. The last straw for them was a promise to democratize the Prussian electoral system, which Bethmann had wrung out of the emperor. Hindenburg and Ludendorff declared that they could no longer retain their commands if Bethmann remained in office. The blackmail worked and a new Chancellor – an obscure civil servant named Dr Georg Michaelis – was in office by the time the peace resolution was debated. Parliamentary government seemed further away than ever.

The dragging out of the war broke not only the political consensus but also the social pact. Deteriorating food and fuel supplies were the main reason for the unrest, which first became serious in the spring of 1917, but the revolutions in Russia were also influential. In March 1917 Tsarism was overthrown and a Liberal government took its place. But the Liberals were unable to reverse the military situation and delayed the eagerly expected land reform, so that they in turn were overthrown, in early November, by the Bolsheviks – the left wing of the Russian Social Democratic party – under Lenin. Fear of Tsarist tyranny had been a major factor in keeping the German workers loyal to the war effort; the removal of this threat made the continuation of the war seem all the more pointless.

But events in Russia also set an example in revolutionary technique. Lenin had seized power by gaining control of the workers' and soldiers' councils – the *soviets* – committees which had sprung up spontaneously to press the claims of the discontented. These councils made their appearance in Germany in January 1918, when, in the depth of the second 'turnip winter', strikes broke out which, in a few days, affected more than a million men. The councils arose out of dissatisfaction with the loyalist, official union leadership; they were led by unofficial shop-stewards (*revolutionäre Obleute*) who were to make their appearance again after the military collapse. Significantly, the strikers' demands were political as well as economic: democratic government and peace negotiations.

The Russian revolution, though it spurred on the opposition, also gave the Government respite. Lenin was determined to take Russia out of the war he had opposed all along, and in March 1918 Germany and Russia signed the peace of Brest-Litovsk. This was a *Siegfrieden* with a vengeance: Russia lost control of Poland, the Baltic provinces and the Ukraine. It would solve Germany's supply problems and release troops for the west, for a final offensive before the American build-up was under way. Accordingly, Ludendorff launched his greatest attack yet on 21 March. The Entente armies lost heavily and the Germans advanced up to forty miles, their greatest success since August 1914.

It was a Pyrrhic victory. The Allied line re-formed. By July there were a million Americans in France. The Ukrainian harvest did not collect itself: it took almost as many troops to occupy Russia as it had done to conquer her. On 8 August the Allied counter-stroke came. What some of his subordinates had for some time guessed dawned at last on Ludendorff – that the game was up. August 8, he acknowledged, was 'der schwarze Tag des deutschen Heeres in der Geschichte dieses Krieges' ('the blackest day of the German army in the history of this war'). He was determined now to make any political concessions necessary to save the German army from total destruction and to maintain, as far as possible, the territorial integrity of the Reich.

At a Crown Council on 29 September the generals explained to an astonished emperor that a cease-fire could no longer be delayed: Bulgaria had already left the war, and Turkey and Austria could hardly last much longer. The time had come, in the words of the imperial decree of the following day, to share the rights and duties of government with 'Männer, die vom Vertrauen des Volkes getragen sind' ('men borne on the confidence of the people'). The new people's Chancellor was Prince Max of Baden: his deputy and the State secretaries were drawn from the three parties of the Reichstag majority. It was a revolutionary change, but not a revolution. Parliamentary government, like unity, like universal franchise, came as a gift from above.

The task of the Baden Government was to seek an acceptable cease-fire. The best hope for this lay in a direct appeal to President Wilson whose programme, contained in the Fourteen Points of January 1918, was one of 'open covenants of peace, openly arrived at', to afford 'political independence and territorial integrity to great and small states alike'. The United States was not formally an ally of the Entente belligerents; she was not bound to recognize the generous promises of post-war gains that the Allied powers had made to each other, and there was no contractual bar to America's seeking a separate peace. But if America was not an ally of Britain and France by treaty, she was one in fact. Wilson insisted that all armistice negotiations must involve all belligerents, that the armistice must not be a cover for a German counter-offensive, that he would be prepared to negotiate with representatives of the people, but not with autocrats and militarists.

Thus the next stage of German democratization was commanded not from Potsdam but from Washington. The constitution of the Reich was amended to abolish the executive functions of the Bundesrat, to make the Chancellor and his Ministers subject to the confidence of the Reichstag, and to make the Reichstag alone competent in matters of war and peace. By 28 October the German Empire had become a parliamentary monarchy, whose monarch was a ceremonial figurehead. Ludendorff, recognizing a sinking ship when he saw one, asked to be relieved of his command.

Yet, as in September, the Reichstag parties were one step behind events. For the revolution from above, declaring that the old order was untenable, was a signal to the revolution from below. The overwhelming desire of the German populace was now for an end to the war; constitutional amendment was seen as a means, not an end. When, therefore, the order went out on 29 October for the German fleet to set sail, in order to retrieve its honour in a final battle, the crews refused to obey. By 4 November the mutineers were in command of every ship, they controlled the naval base at Kiel, they elected a 'council' and joined forces with the workers' council of the dockyard employees. The revolution spread to every major city. Workers' and soldiers' councils arose spontaneously, the revolutionary shop-stewards reappeared. Though the SPD and the USPD tried to gain control of the movement, they had not initiated it. To the left of them the Spartakus-Bund of Rosa Luxemburg and Karl Liebknecht had a revolutionary time-table of its own; but it, too, was overtaken. In Berlin, on 9 November, as a giant demonstration made for the royal palace, Philipp Scheidemann of the SPD proclaimed the German Republic. The emperor had already abdicated that morning and left for Holland; Scheidemann acted in order to forestall Liebknecht who was waiting to proclaim a Socialist Republic.

There was now a complete vacuum of political legitimacy. With the emperor's abdication Max von Baden regarded his mandate as completed, and handed his office to the Social Democrat, Friedrich Ebert. Ebert now formed a government of three SPD and three USPD members. The Berlin workers' and soldiers' council, meeting the next day, expressed its confidence in the Government, who now gained the title of *Volksbeauftragten* (people's commissars). It was a Government of

Socialists, but not a Socialist Government. The Spartacists and the *Obleute* were not represented in it. The armistice of 11 November solved its most pressing need; the question of public order, of disarming millions of soldiers who had taken the law into their own hands, of reassuring the Allies that 'Bolshevism' was not about to reign in Germany, remained. It was Wilhelm Groener, Ludendorff's successor, who suggested a solution. On 10 November he rang Ebert, confirmed 'daß das Heer sich seiner Regierung zur Verfügung stelle' ('that the army places itself at the disposal of his Government') and demanded, in return, the maintenance of discipline (i.e. the continued rights of officers) and the combating of Bolshevism. Ebert accepted. And so, with the war at an end, Germany had a cabinet responsible to a Reichstag elected in 1912; a congress of councils which claimed a monopoly of political sovereignty and whose executive (*Vollzugsrat*) set itself up as the watchdog of the cabinet; and a defeated but coherent army whose officers were in secret league with the chairman of the people's commissars.

THE REVOLUTION

Until the spring of 1919 the provisional Government rode out the revolutionary situation, basing itself uneasily on both the enthusiasm of the councils and the coercive power of the still intact army. Of the rival contenders for the succession to the empire the Social Democrats, who headed the Government, had the clearest notion of the political future they wanted. They wanted a democratic, parliamentary republic. Further details, such as the distribution of property, could be decided only by a properly elected constituent assembly, not by a caretaker administration of dubious legitimacy. They distrusted the councils, whom they regarded as at best agents of chaos, at worst a stepping stone to Bolshevism. They were not prepared to give up the semi-autocratic discipline they had evolved in the years of opposition, and the prestige of the party's name enabled them to retain the loyalty of the mass of the working class, many of whom would probably have preferred a more radical policy.

The SPD's coalition partners, the USPD, though not, in the main, opposed to parliamentary government, wanted to retain the councils as channels of Socialist enthusiasm and instruments of economic democracy. They regarded the tide of public opinion as a sufficient mandate for the abolition of capitalism. To the Left of them, the Spartacists, who in December renamed themselves the German

Communist Party, wanted the violent overthrow of the existing order, though without the dictatorship which Lenin had in the meantime imposed on Russia.

On the political Right the confusion was even worse. The liberal and conservative formations simply broke up in demoralization; only the Zentrum, with its secure confessional roots, survived. The army, the administration, the judiciary, men almost exclusively with a stake in the monarchical order, were prepared to support Ebert as the securest defence against Communism. They were delighted to let the civilian politicians reap the odium of the military collapse, the armistice, the disorder and the prospective peace terms. It was not long before Erzberger and Ebert were to become the 'November criminals' who had stabbed the nation in the back.

During December and January there was a race between the advocates of a national government by councils, and those who wanted the election of a constituent assembly. The national congress of councils was the first to meet. Its composition suggested the continued readiness of most workers to follow moderate leaders. The SPD were in a majority and neither Liebknecht nor Rosa Luxemburg secured election. The council congress was thus reduced to being an appendage of the Government, and this accentuated the split in the revolutionary forces: the minority saw itself without a constitutional voice, while the old imperial officials – civil and military – took their orders from Ebert only, who could thereby sidestep some of the more radical demands. Two incidents, in particular, served to radicalize the Left and, as it turned out, to seal its fate. In mid-December a mutinous naval division held the Social Democratic city commandant of Berlin hostage. Ebert, taking advantage of the 'hot line' to Groener, ordered the army to disarm the mutineers, which its officers were only too anxious to do. To the Left the ensuing bloodshed demonstrated the reactionary character of the Government, and the three USPD Ministers, under pressure from their own party, resigned. This clarified the dividing line between pro- and anti-Government Socialists, which the council congress had succeeded in blurring. On the one hand Ebert had a freer hand in the Government, on the other he had to reckon with growing opposition in the streets.

The bitterness of this confrontation was shown in the middle of January when the Government dismissed the extreme Left police chief of Berlin. For a time it looked as though the 'second revolution', the one that would replace bourgeois democracy with the rule of the proletariat, had broken out: by 6 January the centre of Berlin was largely in the hands of revolutionary workers. But the demonstration turned out to be one of spontaneous militancy, led by the shop-stewards, without a clear political aim. The leaders of the USPD and the new Communist Party both thought the rising ill timed, though the latter joined in out of loyalty. Ebert dealt with the rising as he had now become accustomed. The regular officers finished it off in a few days, capturing the leaders. On 15 January Liebknecht and Rosa Luxemburg were murdered in captivity.

With this event the possibility of subversion from the Left was, for the time being, quashed, the more so as elections to the constituent assembly four days later made the Social Democrats the largest party (SPD 39 per cent, USPD 8 per cent), but did not give the Left the absolute majority which they had rather unquestioningly assumed would be theirs. It opened, however, the possibility of subversion from the Right, and this came from the forces of law and order on which Ebert found himself obliged to rely.

Though Groener and his subordinates continued to offer conditional loyalty to the provisional Government, they were soon without men to command. As the defeated troops reached home they either formed themselves into revolutionary committees or simply disappeared. The officers were therefore obliged to recruit independently, and their natural sources were former regulars, middle-class students and anyone else with a taste for fighting and a grudge against the revolution. It was these units, collectively known as *Freikorps*, who were responsible for the deaths of Liebknecht and Luxemburg, who fought Polish insurgents in Silesia and the Bolsheviks in the Baltic states, and who increasingly took it upon themselves to put down political strikes.

The *Freikorps*' major opportunity came in Bavaria. Here, among a presumably inhospitable, largely rural and Catholic population, Kurt Eisner of the USPD had proclaimed a republic as early as 7 November, and secured the support of both wings of the Social Democratic Party. When he was assassinated in February 1919, the Munich workers' and soldiers' council established a Soviet Republic in which power soon passed to the Communist Party. A Communist Government in Munich was a threat that Berlin could not tolerate; the army – which meant the *Freikorps* – were sent to 'restore order', which they did, in a massacre lasting several days. Although a mild Social Democrat formally headed its Government after the army's intervention, Bavaria was the first part of Germany in which the Right regained power.

Elsewhere in Germany parliamentary democracy seemed to be growing stronger. The newly elected Constituent Assembly met in Weimar and legitimated Ebert in his office. A new coalition Government was formed, based on the strongest parties in the Assembly – the Social Democrats, the Zentrum and the Democrats, an enlarged successor party to the pre-war Progressives. Only the USPD and the decimated Right were in opposition. The wheel had turned full circle. The fighting in Berlin and Munich had dashed all prospect of red revolution; the elections had not given a mandate for Socialism. The Government looked much like the Government of Max of Baden. But the civil war between the two wings of the Labour movement saddled German democracy with a liability from which it did not recover. The SPD was blamed for the deaths of the heroes of the revolution, for losing nerve at the vital moment, for permitting the survival of imperial institutions, economic privilege and anti-democratic officials. What had gone wrong?

Not only the war but the years before had shown that the SPD was the party of democratic republicanism, not of the dictatorship of the proletariat. 'Wir können nicht sagen, wir haben die Revolution "gemacht",' one of the SPD leaders reflected in retrospect, 'aber wir sind nicht ihre Gegner gewesen . . . [Es] steht fest, daß Tag für Tag wir es gewesen sind, die der Arbeiterschaft Ziel und Richtung gegeben haben.'[1] Yet 'Ziel' and 'Richtung' were invariably in the direction of restraint. At any given moment there were excellent tactical reasons for this. The army officers were needed, first to bring home the troops, then to maintain order, then to protect the eastern frontiers against marauders. So they retained their command. The landowners were needed to see Germany through the hungry winter, especially since the Allied blockade had not yet been lifted. So they retained their estates. The industrialists were needed to keep production going, and there was a feeling that nationalized property would be more vulnerable to Allied reparation demands than private property. So the capitalists were not expropriated. Civil servants and judges held legally guaranteed posts. To replace them with 'politically reliable' officials would be arbitrary and would reduce the morale of those who remained in service. So democratically elected Governments had to rely on administrators who had been trained to serve an abstract, timeless authoritarian State – the

[1] 'We cannot say we "made" the revolution, but we were not its opponents. . . . What is certain is that it was we who, day by day, provided the working class with aims and direction.'

L

Obrigkeitsstaat – and who were intellectually and emotionally out of sympathy with republican methods. Having to cope with half a dozen emergencies at once, the Government was apt to congratulate itself on keeping civilized life going at all. The winter of 1918–19 was not the time to initiate grandiose reforms: a law establishing the eight-hour working day was its principal measure. Above all there was the fear that anything resembling 'Bolshevism' – a concept generously interpreted by the Liberal and Conservative statesmen who led the victorious powers – would bring Allied military intervention.

So, while these omissions were individually defensible, their combined effect was fatal to the republic's chances. When the revolutionary fervour subsided, the new Germany looked remarkably like the old. The emperor was gone, but the imperial institutions, run by men with imperial mentalities, remained. Perhaps the provisional Government could have recruited a republican militia to keep the wilder extremists in check; perhaps some socialization of industry or land redistribution need not have led to production crises. But the Social Democratic Ministers were not only extremely legalistic, observing the constitutional niceties which their enemies to the Left and Right ignored and despised, they also suffered from an inferiority complex. Condemned to opposition until 1918, largely self-educated and excluded from the higher reaches of society, they lacked – or thought they lacked – the ability to run the complex industrial and administrative machinery of Germany single-handedly. The example of Russia, where such an attempt had been made, was not encouraging.

The Weimar Republic

THE PEACE AND THE CONSTITUTION

On 31 July 1919 the Constituent Assembly in the National Theatre completed its work. Its five months' deliberations were devoted to two tasks, neither of which endeared it to its fellow countrymen. It accepted the terms of the Paris Peace Conference, and it drew up a democratic, republican constitution.

The peace demands of the Allied powers, which were submitted to the German delegation on 1 May, came as a great shock. Though there was no specific mention of President Wilson's Fourteen Points when the armistice was signed, politicians and public alike had expected the peace treaty to be couched in terms of Wilsonian reconciliation. At least one of Wilson's principles had already been breached: the discussions among the victors' delegations were held behind closed doors. 'Few negotiations in history', wrote one of the participants, Sir Harold Nicolson, 'have been so secret, or indeed so occult.' The outcome of these negotiations, though it watered down many of the original demands of France and even Britain, was essentially designed to protect French security.

Overseas Germany lost all her colonies. In the west she predictably lost Alsace-Lorraine to France; less predictably she lost the Saar coal basin to France for fifteen years. In the east the German city of Memel went to Lithuania, and the German city of Danzig was made Poland's main port, under League of Nations supervision. Danzig was joined to the rest of Poland by a 'corridor' which split East Prussia from the rest of Germany. Upper Silesia, industrially rich and with a 60 per cent Polish population, was also to go to Poland. The Republic of Austria, which contained most of the German-speaking citizens of the now defunct Habsburg Empire, was prohibited from joining the Reich, despite the expressed wish of the population to do so. Only on Upper Silesia did the Germans gain a concession. Supported by Lloyd George, the British Prime Minister, who wanted to prevent the creation of 'new Alsace-Lorraines' they secured a plebiscite, the outcome of which saved some of the province for Germany.

These territorial changes deprived Germany of 13 per cent of her pre-war population, 26 per cent of her coal resources, 75 per cent of her iron ore. But this was nothing compared with the direct economic deprivations which the treaty imposed. Germany forfeited most of her overseas investments and merchant fleet; most seriously Germany was to be required to make good all civilian damage caused to the Allied Governments and their citizens. The damage was interpreted to include war pensions, mainly so that Britain could benefit more from the payments. It was not calculated at a fixed sum, but at a level to be assessed later by a commission. The imposition was justified in article 231 of the treaty, the famous 'war guilt' clause, which held that the war had been 'imposed . . . by the aggression of Germany and her allies'.

In addition most of the German battle fleet was to be surrendered, and the instrument which Tirpitz had conceived to coerce Britain and which had seen the outbreak of the revolution, was scuttled at Scapa Flow on 22 June. The German army was reduced to 100,000 men. As a guarantee of the victors' security, their troops were to occupy the Rhineland for fifteen years, and even after their withdrawal the area was to remain unfortified,

When these conditions became known, the German Foreign Minister, Count Brockdorff-Rantzau, refused to sign, and the Chancellor, the Social Democrat Scheidemann, resigned in protest at its injustice. There were agonized debates in the National Assembly, though it was obvious from the start that any renegotiation was out of the question, and that rejection of the terms would bring unmitigated disaster. In the end, against the votes of the Right and some Government supporters, the Assembly bowed to the inevitable and on 28 June three Ministers of the new Government signed on Germany's behalf. The ceremony took place in the same hall at Versailles in which the Second Empire had been proclaimed.

With this vote and this signature another dangerous rift appeared in German public opinion. Dismay and indignation were widespread and genuine, and they were made worse by the 'war guilt' clause which the Allies had thought of less as a final historical judgement than as legalistic underpinning for the reparations demands. Outside Germany, the protests gained little sympathy, at any rate initially. The treaties which Germany had imposed on defeated Russia and Romania were infinitely harsher, and German war loans had been raised with the assurance from the banker Helfferich: 'Der Feind wird zahlen' ('The enemy will pay'). Britain, France and America had done nothing to Germany that Germany would not have done to them, given the chance. Dissenters from this view were at first the exception. Keynes argued in *The Economic Consequences of the Peace* that to impoverish Germany was to impoverish Europe. Some Liberals and Socialists argued that the Germans who were being punished were not the Germans who were guilty. But it was a decade or more before this attitude became widespread, and then to the benefit of German leaders whose sole thought was revenge.

Inside Germany the peace terms were seen as the logical consequence of the armistice: the 'November' criminals who had signed the first now compounded their treason. Those who had every reason to hate the new political order could use the peace terms to convince their public of one vast conspiracy of subversion. Germany, they claimed, had not been militarily defeated, but politically undermined. 'Was die Feinde in jahrelangem Ringen nicht geschafft haben, haben wir uns selbst angetan. Unseren kämpfenden Truppen haben wir den Dolch in den Rücken gestossen,'[1] wrote the Conservative *Kreuzzeitung*. The

---

[1] 'What the enemy, in years of struggle, did not achieve we have done to ourselves. We thrust a dagger into the back of our fighting troops.'

German army had died, according to one Nationalist spokesman, like Siegfried: 'und der Speer der von dem Hagen dem Siegfried von hinten in den Leib gestossen worden ist, ist von langer Zeit vorher geschmiedet worden.'[1] And so the *Dolchstoßlegende*, the myth of the stab in the back, was born. In part the republican politicians, the victims of this myth, weakened their own position. They could have admitted the war guilt of the imperial Government, while disclaiming responsibility for its acts. This might have cut no ice diplomatically, but it would have given them the initiative domestically. As it was, fearing that admissions of guilt would aggravate the Allies' conditions, they defended Germany's part in the 1914 crisis and thereby revealed themselves as the ineffectual guardians of an innocence they claimed to believe in.

The trouble with the treaty was that it was neither conciliatory nor Carthaginian. The democratization of German government had been one of the conditions of the armistice; now the leaders of German democracy were saddled with the odium of collecting dues which they thought unjustly and arbitrarily imposed. The revision of the 'Diktat von Versailles' became the declared objective of all parties: to outbid the moderate parties in revisionism was a heaven-sent weapon to those whose primary aim was to undermine parliamentary government.

The republican constitution, which the National Assembly had virtually drawn up by the time the treaty was signed, also served to intensify the divisions in public opinion. The document was a model of republican sanity. It confirmed the reforms of the autumn of 1918, making the Government answerable to parliament; it confirmed the electoral law for the Constituent Assembly which gave the vote to men and women over twenty for both the Reichstag and the state parliaments. Their votes were distributed to the parties by strict proportional representation.

On other points, involving traditional Reich institutions, there were clashes among the constitution-makers. The 1848 republican flag – black, red and gold, which is also the flag of the Federal Republic – won narrowly over the imperial colours. The Head of State, the *Reichspräsident*, was to be elected by universal suffrage, an *Ersatzkaiser* who was to stand out among the run-of-the-mill politicians, though Ebert himself was confirmed in his office as first Republican President by the Constituent Assembly. The President was also, under article 48, given

[1] ' . . . and the spear that was thrust by Hagen into Siegfried's body from the rear was forged a long time before.'

powers to rule by emergency decree. Above all, although there were strong arguments for abolishing the old Prussian state and unifying the republic's administration, traditionalism and vested political interests secured the survival of the old *Länder*, subject only to some boundary adjustments. The upheavals of the post-war months made many people unwilling to entrust a virtual monopoly of power to Berlin: in particular, the *Länder* managed to retain control of two important and controversial matters, public order and education.

Whatever prestige republicanism and parliamentary democracy might have enjoyed at the time of the empire's collapse – if only as a defence against revolution – had greatly diminished a year later. Social unrest and the weakening of authority made many people yearn for the certainties of imperial days. The men of Weimar were seen as the men of Versailles: the constitution and the treaty were both seen as embodying alien principles, imposed on Germany by the victorious West. There was an opposite disenchantment on the part of many of the workers who had hoped, if not for revolution, at least for radical reform and now saw, as a consequence of the maintenance of 'order', a social structure differing little from that of 1914 or 1890.

These disillusionments were mirrored in the first Reichstag elections of June 1920. The 'Weimar' coalition which had governed for over a year and held the political initiative since the 'Peace Resolution' lost its majority and never again regained it. The SPD lost nearly half its support, much of it to the USPD. The Catholic vote held steady, but the Conservative, Bavarian wing of the Zentrum, broke away to form an independent party, less willing to support the republic. The most disastrous losses were those of the Democrats, the party *par excellence* of parliamentary liberalism and the Weimar constitution. They lost three-fifths of their support; at their expense the Right swelled. The chief gainers were the Democrats' rivals, the People's Party (DVP), led by the ex-National Liberal Gustav Stresemann, whose loyalty to the republic was dubious; and the Nationalists (DNVP), reconstituted from old Conservatives and pan-Germanists who were frankly anti-republican and anti-democratic and who secured what had always eluded the old Junker-led Conservative Party, a firm urban base in the western parts of the country.

This shift from the political middle towards the extremes, and particularly towards the Right, was reflected in the colouring of the republic's later Governments. The USPD was too isolated to think of participating or to be asked to do so. So, *a fortiori*, were the Communists who inherited most of their voters after the USPD decided on self-dissolution in 1922. The Social Democrats withdrew from the cabinet in August 1920 and, except for two brief periods of office under non-Socialist Chancellors, did not return to power until they formed the Great Coalition in 1928. Defeated on the battlefield, defeated at the conference table, defeated at the polls, the republic embarked on its uncertain career.

SURVIVAL AND REVIVAL

For the first three years the new state led a hand-to-mouth existence, as it slowly established its legitimacy in the eyes of the population. The challenges came from extremist opponents of parliamentary republicanism, from the victor powers and from the constituent *Länder*.

Even before the elections there had been an attempt at a right-wing *coup d'état* which ought to have raised republican morale but, typically, failed to do so. The *putsch* was led by a former Prussian civil servant, Wolfgang Kapp, and the commander of the Berlin army district, General von Lüttwitz. The Government was obliged to retire to Stuttgart, but the *putsch* fizzled out. While many army officers and civil servants, and some politicians, such as Stresemann, and the DNVP sympathized with its aims, few were prepared to risk their political future on so half-baked an adventure. The *putsch* was defeated, firstly by a general strike, called by all the unions, which paralysed Berlin; secondly by the strange neutrality of the army. The army's clear duty was to support the legal Government: this, in the words of General von Seeckt to the Minister of Defence, it was not prepared to do.

> Truppe schießt nicht auf Truppe. Haben Sie, Herr Minister, etwa die Absicht, eine Schlacht vor dem Brandenburger Tor zu dulden zwischen Truppen, die eben erst Seite an Seite gegen den Feind gekämpft haben?[1]

How dependent the Government was on the army's benevolent neutrality was shown in the next few weeks. In some areas, particularly the Ruhr, the anti-Kapp strike movement began to assume revolutionary proportions. To dislodge the 'Red' militias from the industrial towns the army was needed and the army, in turn, needed the *Freikorps*,

---

[1] 'Troops do not fire on troops. Do you, Herr Minister, perhaps have the intention of tolerating a battle in front of the Brandenburg Gate among troops who have only just fought side by side against the enemy?'

who had but recently supported the Kapp–Lüttwitz adventure. The renewed threat from the Left expunged the discredit of the Right.

Nor did other acts of right-wing terrorism leave lasting impressions, however great the momentary indignation they evoked. In 1921 one of the leaders of the Zentrum, Matthias Erzberger, inspirer of the Reichstag Peace Resolution and a signatory of the armistice and the peace treaty, was murdered. A year later, the Foreign Minister, Walther Rathenau, especially vulnerable as a Jew, was murdered. In each case the assassins had belonged to the 'Erhardt brigade', implicated in the Kapp *putsch*. The assassination of Rathenau caused a very unfavourable impression abroad, and the Chancellor, Josef Wirth of the Zentrum, declared before the Reichstag: 'Da steht der Feind, wo Mephisto sein Gift in die Wunde eines Volkes träufelt . . . der Feind steht rechts.'[1]

Neither then nor later could any statesman convince the German people of this truth. The real Mephistopheles they saw in the vindictive Western powers who sought to enslave Germany, the baneful bond of blood between their demands and the pragmatic Weimar politicians who saw no alternative but an *Erfüllungspolitik*. The predominant mood of Germany was one of national resentment and anyone who articulated this mood, whatever his faults of style, could gain a more indulgent hearing than any *Verzichtspolitiker*. In this demagogic competition the anti-republican Right had a clear advantage, though some of the Left, in particular the Communists, were not far behind in equating Western policies with an imperialist rivalry for which all classes in Germany paid the bill.

The resentment was heightened by the reparations terms which the Allied commission presented in April 1921: a non-negotiable demand for 132 thousand million gold marks (just over 30,000 million dollars). Wirth, Rathenau and the Social Democrats who supported them decided that Germany should put the best possible face on the inevitable, and pursue a 'fulfilment' line, but such was the weakness of the German economy that even the first instalment of deliveries was not handed over in time. While opinion in Britain was swinging over to concessions towards Germany, a hard-line Government in France, under Raymond Poincaré, insisted on exacting the full quota. Following up an ultimatum, French and Belgian troops moved over the line of the Rhineland occupation zone in January 1923 and occupied the Ruhr

[1] 'There the enemy stands, where Mephisto drips his poison into a nation's wounds. . . . The enemy stands on the right.'

industrial area to enforce deliveries – an occupation which was to last ten months.

The principal cause of Germany's economic feebleness was the creeping inflation which the war had initiated and which had thereafter continued unabated. At the beginning of the reparations crisis a paper mark was worth only one-hundredth of a pre-war gold mark; and while those who owned fixed capital – industrial plant or land – could keep pace with the inflation and even benefit from it, the purchasing power of all classes was eroded and the Government's taxation plans lay in tatters. Anyone who had put his savings into fixed-interest bonds was faced with ruin. The fantastic spiral of inflation which left the mark, at the end, with two-thousand-millionths of its 1914 value, began in April 1923. But because there were some, including many industrialists, who profited from this cheapening of money, and because it made the computation of reparations even more chaotic, the Government took its time over ending it. It also tried to undermine the occupation by ordering a policy of 'passive resistance'. Since this amounted to no more than administrative non-co-operation, and since the objectives of the occupation could be largely achieved without the co-operation of the Germans, it was little more than a solemn farce.

Reparations and the Ruhr occupation were not the cause of the German inflation, though, by increasing the demand for paper money, they aggravated it. But many Germans, especially pauperized bourgeois Germans, saw a direct causal link; the dual experience embittered many who were already inclined to blame the republic for all their ills and made them even readier to listen to nationalist agitators.

During 1923 the republic was further weakened by a number of challenges to its authority which, though facilitated by the Ruhr–inflation crisis arose basically out of the structural weaknesses of the republic and the absence of a political consensus. One of the weaknesses was that the ideological diversity of the country became institutionalized in various *Land* governments, the parties acting much like new dynasties. In Prussia, which the constitution-makers had, on second thoughts, preserved intact, this was a source of strength to the regime. Here, thanks to universal suffrage, the Social Democrats and Zentrum now predominated, and for most of the republic's lifetime 'Weimar coalitions' headed the Prussian Government. Since Prussia had the responsibility for public order in Berlin, control of the Prussian police was a politically highly sensitive matter.

Elsewhere the vestiges of federalism were less helpful, least of all in Bavaria. Here the restoration of Right, which dated from the overthrow of the Munich Soviet Republic, was confirmed after the Kapp *putsch*, with the appointment of Gustav von Kahr, a high official with monarchist leanings, as Prime Minister. The traditional conservatism of Bavaria was accentuated by experience of the brief left-wing adventure. Officials, police officers and judges were overwhelmingly unfavourable to the republic. They protected the various armed bands – *Freikorps, Einwohnerwehr, Vaterländische Verbände* – which meted out indiscriminate political justice, and offered hospitality to those that were chased out of other parts of the country. When the chief of the Munich police, Ernst Poehner, was asked about these gangs, he replied that there were not enough of them. Wilhelm Frick and Josef Gürtner, later Hitler's Ministers of the Interior and of Justice, served on Poehner's staff.

One of the many nationalist groupings that flourished here was the Deutsche Arbeiterpartei, founded by a Munich railwayman, Anton Drexler, but soon under the dictatorial control of one of its early recruits, an out-of-work ex-serviceman with exceptional oratorical gifts, Adolf Hitler. His ability to organize, and above all to raise funds, made his party, renamed Nationalsozialistische Deutsche Arbeiterpartei ('Nazi'), one of the biggest of its kind, although still restricted to Bavaria. Another characteristic of the party was its strong-arm squad, the Schutz-Abteilung (SA) organized by a Bavarian regular officer, Major Ernst Roehm, from among his *Freikorps* companions. Its task was both to protect speakers at the party's meetings and to pick fights with opponents.

The first major clash between Bavaria and the Reich concerned these private armies. At the time when the Versailles Treaty came into effect, and the whole German army was supposed not to exceed 100,000 men, there were reckoned to be at least 420,000 armed irregulars in Bavaria alone. Only after the murder of Erzberger was it possible to enforce some disbandment.

A more serious act of insubordination occurred during the Ruhr crisis when, in August 1923, Gustav Stresemann formed a Government, including Social Democrats, to secure French withdrawal by abandoning passive resistance. In response to this left-wing challenge Kahr was appointed Government commissioner with dictatorial powers. More seriously, the Bavarian contingents of the army, under General von Lossow, pledged their support to him. Bavaria was therefore in virtual rebellion and there was talk of a march on Berlin. This seemed to Hitler to be the opportunity he had been waiting for, especially as he had secured respectability through the support of General Ludendorff. On 8 November he and some followers burst into a meeting in the Munich *Bürgerbräu*, addressed by Kahr, and persuaded the Bavarian dictator to engage in a joint *putsch*. The morning after, Kahr and Lossow thought better of it, and Hitler and Ludendorff marched on the Feldherrnhalle alone, where they were easily dispersed and arrested.

Apart from their hatred of democracy and internationalism Kahr and Hitler had little in common. The Bavarian Government was ultra-Conservative; it wanted a restoration of the monarchy and the old Reich. Hitler despised such men as has-beens. His ambition was to lead a mass movement which would establish an élitist dictatorship on racialist lines. The lesson he drew from the failure of his *putsch* was that he needed to act with, not against, the forces of order and property, and that he would have to wait until they needed him more than he needed them.

A different threat to Berlin came from the *Länder* of Saxony and Thuringia, where the Social Democrats decided to form coalitions with the Communists. Whether these two industrial states could have formed a viable base for a new wave of proletarian revolution is doubtful; in any case they did not get the opportunity. Since the existence of these Left governments was a pretext for Kahr's insubordination and intolerable to the army, a military expedition was authorized by presidential decree to overthrow them. Kahr and Ludendorff, however, got off scot-free, and even Hitler was sentenced to only five years' detention, of which he served eight months. Once more fear of the Left had put a premium on subversion from the Right.

Even before these revolts fizzled out the central Government had regained the initiative. A new unit of currency, the *Rentenmark*, was established, to be replaced the next year by a gold-based *Reichsmark*. Elections in France resulted in a Government of the Left, with the Radical Herriot as Prime Minister and the conciliatory Briand as Foreign Minister. This paved the way for a new relationship with the outside world. Its architect was Stresemann, who had ceased to be Chancellor but remained Foreign Minister until 1929.

The most immediate problem to be solved was that of reparations. To maintain regular payments Germany needed a stable economy and currency; to achieve these she needed a dollar loan. Both were ensured by the Dawes Plan, drawn up by an international committee under the American general, Charles Dawes. The demands that this committee made, though heavy, were realistic. In return for a loan of 800 million gold marks, which provided the backing for the new currency, Germany was to make guaranteed annual payments, the revenue for which was to come from bond issues and specially earmarked budget and railway surpluses. Half the governors of the new central bank would have to be foreigners. But the size of the loan was tempting enough to overcome nationalist objections: the Dawes Plan was accepted and the occupation of the Ruhr thereby ended.

Stresemann's longer-term ambition was to re-establish Germany's position in the international community and this again could be achieved only on terms acceptable to the West. Even before 1924 Germany had not been diplomatically isolated. The overwhelming priority which 'revision' had in the republic's foreign policy led its statesmen to seek the support of any other 'revisionist' power there might be. The chief candidate for any such partnership, however unlikely at first sight, was Soviet Russia. Lenin's peace policy in 1917 had been 'no annexations, no indemnities': Versailles was in clear contradiction to this formula and Russia did not hesitate to denounce the 'robber treaties'. Moreover the victorious powers had done all they could to undermine the Bolshevik regime, to the extent of sending expeditionary forces during the civil war which followed the revolution. The territorial resettlement of eastern Europe displeased Russia as much as Germany. Deprived of Russia as her eastern 'anchor', France encouraged the establishment of a large Poland, with whom she signed a treaty of alliance in 1921. France also did all she could to ensure generous frontiers for the succession states of the Habsburg Monarchy, Czechoslovakia, Romania and Yugoslavia, and these, known as the 'Little Entente' were also heavily dependent on French diplomatic patronage, thus forming a strong anti-revisionist bloc.

Thus the 1922 Treaty of Rapallo between Germany and Russia ought not to have created the shock and surprise in the rest of Europe which it did. It was not a military alliance, but Germany became the first 'capitalist' state to break the diplomatic quarantine of Russia, and both states ostentatiously agreed to waive any wartime claims on each other. The political colouring of the Soviet regime notwithstanding, Rapallo was welcomed by the German Right – by industry for the opportunities in trade that the treaty opened, by the army for the facilities which were secretly agreed for the production of arms and the training of men beyond the Versailles limits, by all for the added weight it gave to any defiance of the peace treaty.

Stresemann's 'turn to the West' was therefore more welcome to the republican parties than the opposition of Right and Left. The outcome of his initiative was the Locarno Treaties. Germany abandoned all revisionist claims in the west (which meant principally Alsace-Lorraine) and the security of the frontier was guaranteed by Britain and Italy as well as the neighbours involved. In return Germany was admitted to the League of Nations (also anathema to Communists and nationalists). But Stresemann also secured valuable concessions. Germany was exempted from taking part in any military operations that might be ordered by the League, and thus kept on good terms with Russia. A treaty dealing with Germany's eastern frontiers was much vaguer than the 'western' Locarno: it merely provided for arbitration in case of dispute and it was not signed by Britain, who had no desire to underwrite these French spheres of influence. Thus Stresemann gave away nothing in the east and did nothing to stop the secret rearmament of which he was well aware. What he did, and what the collapse of Poincaré's pound-of-flesh policies enabled him to do, was to make Germany a 'normal' member of the diplomatic community. As a sign of their reborn confidence in Germany the Western powers soon abandoned any effective control of German armaments and prematurely withdrew their last occupation troops from the right bank of the Rhine.

The era of Stresemann was the high noon of the Weimar Republic. Tempers dropped, political extremism subsided. In large part this was due to the return of prosperity. Between 1924 (admittedly a very bad year) and 1928 money wages doubled and the value of the currency was maintained. The standard of living was higher in 1928 than in 1913. Unemployment was generally below one million. German industry regained its technical and organizational lead. The Dawes loan, following the premium which the inflation had put on machines and bricks and mortar, encouraged modernization. The trend towards vast combines was accelerated. The four major chemical firms fused in the I.G. Farben, which in turn reached pricing and marketing agreements with its principal British and American equivalents. The six major steel concerns fused in the Vereinigte Stahlwerke. Though these developments helped German manufactures in the world's markets, they did not necessarily strengthen the republic politically.

Men like Dr Carl Duisberg of I.G. Farben, Albert Vögler of the steel combine and Alfred Hugenberg, the general manager of Krupp's, regarded the republic with distaste, if not hostility. They were certainly more powerful men than any Chancellor or President. Their stake was so vast, the patents they possessed often so vital strategically, that they considered themselves entitled to negotiate independently with the administration, with the army and with intelligence services – ambitions which the Third Reich was better able to satisfy than the Weimar Republic.

Nor can the republic's political leaders be said to have made the most of their opportunities during the mid-twenties. The notion that political parties should train men of ministerial calibre and accept responsibility for overall policy was understood by too few voters or politicians. The notion that 'administration' was good and 'politics' bad, that parties served, at best, as spokesmen for sectional interests, survived from the *Obrigkeitsstaat*. The republic's system of proportional representation perpetuated and accentuated party fragmentation, but did no cause it. The cause was the failure, during the empire, to associate parliamentary politicians with responsibility for the welfare of the State. The 1928 elections, which gave the republican parties the best results since 1919 and which resulted in a Socialist-led Grand Coalition, thus gave a misleading impression of republican strength. The 491 seats were shared among sixteen parties, only four of whom held over 50 seats. Many of the remainder represented only the narrowest regional and occupational interests, like the Wirtschaftspartei or the Bayerischer Bauernbund. Attempts to unite the various liberal trends in one middle-class republican party failed; political Catholicism remained divided; and the Social Democrats were unable to widen their appeal, or to slough off their reputation for mediocrity, pedantry and bureaucratism. Only eight of the twenty-one cabinets in the republic's lifetime rested on secure parliamentary majorities; the rest were 'tolerated' by parties not represented in the Government. Four out of twelve Chancellors, and a similar proportion of Cabinet Ministers, were 'non-party experts', drawn from outside the ranks of professional politics. During periods of crisis – in 1923 and after 1930 – the Reichstag abdicated altogether, leaving the Chancellor to govern by decree. In 1927 Edgar Jung, one of the most prominent conservative theorists, later Franz von Papen's secretary and murdered by the Nazis, wrote: 'Würde eine Rundfrage erlassen, nicht wer auf dem Boden der heutigen Republik stehe, sondern wer sie liebe, das Ergebnis wäre erschütternd.'[1] The

[1] 'If there were to be an opinion survey, not of those who support today's Republic, but of those who love it, the result would be devastating.'

truth of his observation had been illustrated two years earlier, in the presidential election held on the death of Ebert. Field-Marshal Hindenburg, nominated by the parties of the Right, defeated Wilhelm Marx of the Zentrum and the Communist Thälmann, by recruiting many who normally did not vote and some who normally voted for republican parties.

It was not merely industry which considered itself exempt from complete loyalty to the regime. The Churches, though they had little to complain of in their treatment by the State, remained lukewarm. The Protestant Churches looked back with nostalgia to the 'official' position they had enjoyed under the deposed monarchs, especially in Prussia; their clergy and laity were predominantly nationalist. Like the Catholic Church they recoiled from the greater 'permissiveness' in art, literature and private morals which seemed to flourish under the more liberal aegis of the republic. Catholicism was particularly conservative in Bavaria. The Archbishop of Munich, Cardinal Faulhaber, later consigned to a concentration camp by Hitler, refused to celebrate a requiem for the deceased President Ebert, who was not a practising Christian.

The civil service and judiciary continued largely to be staffed by men imbued with imperial principles, especially since little was done to reform the educational system. Though such men claimed to serve 'the State' rather than governments, their system of values led them to interpret this code in anti-democratic terms. This came out most clearly in the uneven measure which the courts dealt to acts of political violence or murder: those emanating from the Left, though less numerous, were dealt with much more harshly than those from the Right. Attempts by some governments, notably that of Prussia, to appoint men in sympathy with newer policies, were resented as political interference and merely alienated professional civil servants further from the republic.

That the army possessed all these characteristics in an extreme form is evident from the high-handed way in which it interpreted its duties whenever it might be needed. The new *Reichswehr* was largely the work of General Hans von Seeckt, who was its commander from 1920 to 1926. He turned the numerical restrictions of the Versailles treaty to his advantage, using it to recruit much more selectively than had been possible before the war. The proportion of aristocrats among officers was higher in the mid-twenties than in 1913; the non-commissioned ranks were filled with highly trained, politically 'reliable' men who could handle much larger numbers when this once more became possible. The army's solidarity and independence was well illustrated at the time of the Bavarian crisis in 1923. When Ebert asked Seeckt where the army stood, Seeckt replied, with pride as well as accuracy, 'Die Armee steht hinter mir' ('The army stands behind me').

It was symptomatic of this situation that the republic never gained the wholehearted support of the academic and intellectual community. Of writers in the front rank only Gerhart Hauptmann and Thomas Mann – the latter a late convert – were truly committed to it. *Der Zauberberg* must rank as a more moving and revealing epic than many longer-lasting or more successful regimes can claim to be remembered by. Distinguished scholars – the sociologist Max Weber, the theologian Ernst Troeltsch, the historian Friedrich Meinecke – rallied more out of common sense or duty than enthusiasm. They were 'Vernunftsrepub-likaner' ('republicans of the head'), but 'Herzensmonarchisten' ('mon-archists of the heart'). Others on the Left – dramatists like Ernst Toller and Bertolt Brecht, artists like George Grosz and Käthe Kollwitz – were too concerned to expose the hypocrisies of bourgeois society to be the republic's allies against their joint enemies.

To most Germans, articulate and inarticulate, the energy, the experi-mentation, the chaotic creativity which made Weimar culture the envy, and mecca, of so many foreigners, represented *Kulturbolshewismus*, the overturning of forms and values in a world in which too much had been overturned already. The predominant cry was in favour of what Hugo von Hofmannsthal, in a lecture delivered in 1927 at the Univer-sity of Munich, called 'eine konservative Revolution'. The denial of materialism and egalitarianism, the revival of hierarchy and national consciousness, the praise of tradition and rural civilization, separation from the economically and politically victorious West – these were the common themes of such otherwise divergent manifestoes as Count Hermann Keyserling's *Reisetagebuch eines Philosophen*, Oswald Spen-gler's *Untergang des Abendlandes* and Moeller van den Bruck's *Das dritte Reich*. Much more even than before 1914, youth listened to this romantic message, and flocked to the *Bünde*, some of them merely escapist, others aggressively reactionary, that made up the youth movement.

THE RISE OF HITLER

The stability of the Stresemann years rested on economic prosperity; this in turn depended on world trends, and particularly on trends in the USA, given the role of American loans in Germany's recovery. By the end of 1929 a distinct deterioration had set in. In October Stresemann died: his death removed not only the architect of Germany's diplomatic comeback but the one major representative of the conservative middle classes committed to the republic. In the same month began the collapse of share prices on the New York stock exchange, putting at risk the many short-term loans on deposit in Germany. Yet even before the autumn of 1929 there had been warnings that good times could not last. The decline in the German economy had begun in 1928, partly because the over-heated American boom neutralized the attractiveness of investment in Germany, which had been one of the features of the Dawes Plan. Indeed by the spring of 1929 it had become necessary to rephase Germany's reparations payments through the Young Plan.

Unlike the Dawes and any previous reparations settlement it named a total sum. Germany's remaining liability was put at 120,000 million marks ($28,800 million), to be repaid over fifty-nine years. This was a much lower annual rate than before and a much lower sum than the Allies had originally reckoned with; its political effect was nevertheless disastrous. By spelling out, for the first time, how much, and for how long, Germany would be indebted, it helped to rouse opinion against the treaties, and to revive agitation from the extreme Right. In the 1928 elections the right-wing opposition – both Nationalist and Nazi – had done badly. The intransigent wing of the Nationalists attributed this defeat to their participation in republican governments; their spokesman, Alfred Hugenberg, who had graduated from Krupp's to control of the Scherl newspaper combine and the Ufa film corporation, became party chairman.

The Young Plan gave him his opportunity to create a broadly based, nationalist, anti-republican political movement. He launched a petition to demand a referendum which would repudiate the Young Plan in particular, and the Treaty of Versailles in general. He did so in company with the ex-servicemen's organization Stahlhelm, which had strong links with the Nationalists; the Pan-German League; and Adolf Hitler. The petition gained four million signatures, the referendum just under six million votes – nothing like enough for success, but an extremely valuable publicity exercise. What was significant about Hugenberg's new alignment was that it drew in the Nazi party.

Since his release from prison in 1924, Hitler had ranked as little more than a sectarian fanatic. The party was low in funds and threatened by splits. The original programme, the 'unalterable' (*unabänderliche*) Twenty-Five Points had contained a strong dose of social radicalism and anti-capitalism, above all the 'breaking of interest slavery' (*Zerbrechung der Zinsknechtschaft*) which was the hobby-horse of the party's chief economist, Gottfried Feder. This dislike of modern industrial society, and the cash basis of social relationships in it, had deep roots in the romantic, anti-Semitic, *völkish* movement of the nineteenth century (see pp. 282–4).

Hitler shared its prejudices, but did not give the social part of the programme high priority. He himself was obsessed with a racial doctrine in which he saw the key to history, to economic life and to international relations. He formulated politics, in a way which had become popular by the turn of the century, by analogy with Darwinian biology, as a struggle for the survival of the fittest: 'Die Sünde wider Blut und Rasse ist die Erbsünde dieser Welt,' he wrote.

> Die völkische Weltanschauung glaubt keineswegs an eine Gleichheit der Rassen, sondern . . . fühlt sich verpflichtet, gemäß dem ewigen Wollen, das dieses Universum beherrscht, den Sieg des Besseren, Stärkeren zu fördern, die Unterlage des Schlechteren und Schwächeren zu fördern.[1]

There were, moreover, tactical reasons for playing down any threats to property rights in the party's manifesto, since Hitler had decided that he could come to power only by legal means, and only with the help of conservative Nationalists. The party's left wing was therefore either persuaded of the superiority of Hitler's tactics (Josef Goebbels, for example) or driven into the wilderness (Otto Strasser). So the offer of Hugenberg's embrace suited Hitler admirably. Each of the partners calculated he would gain from the connection; in the nature of things only one of them could be right.

As the world economic crisis grew worse, and the Great Coalition floundered more deeply, the enemies of the republic prospered. The Great Coalition, comprising all parties favourable to the republic, had been formed after the moderate parties' election victory in 1928. Yet beyond an attachment to parliamentary methods the Social Democrats, the Zentrum, the Democrats and the People's Party had little in common. On economic policy, on education, on Church–State relations they were divided. In countries accustomed to democratic stability,

[1] 'The sin against blood and race is the original sin in this world. . . . *Völkisch* ideology in no way acknowledges the equality of races, but . . . considers it its duty, in accordance with the eternal will that commands this world, to foster the victory of the better and the stronger, the defeat of the worse and the weaker.'

elections can be fought to decide between policies and governmental teams, taking for granted universal acceptance of the constitution. In Weimar Germany the choice was more often than not for or against the constitution, leaving it to multi-party coalitions to bargain about the issues which the election left unresolved. So, while the Government struggled to get the Young Plan through the Reichstag, and was dead-locked on the issue of social insurance contributions, production fell, interest rates – designed to attract the savings needed for reparations – remained high, and unemployment rose. Agriculture was, if anything, in a worse condition than industry. Technical backwardness and the fall in world food prices imposed intolerable debt burdens on many peasants. The enforced sales of family holdings led to first passive, then violent, resistance under the aegis of the *Landvolk* movement; it also gained an eager audience for the Nazi message of 'breaking interest slavery'.

Under the impact of the crisis the 1930 elections produced a result that made parliamentary institutions virtually unworkable. The Nazi party leapt from 12 to 107 seats. They, not the Nationalists, were the beneficiaries of Hugenberg's manœuvre. Splinter parties, concerned with pressing only the narrowest of sectional interests, went up from 51 to 72 seats. The only political forces which survived this holocaust were those with firm social roots dating from the empire – Catholicism and the working-class Left. But within the Zentrum, once the party of Wirth and Erzberger, power passed to authoritarian conservatives like Heinrich Brüning and Monsignor Kaas, disenchanted with parlia-mentary government. And within the working class the Communists, up from 54 to 77 seats, were gaining at the expense of the Social Democrats.

But it was Hitler who now carried the main challenge to 'the system', as he liked to call it. He had become, overnight, a figure of international importance. His antagonist, Heinrich Brüning, who had become Chancellor on the collapse of the Great Coalition, was a Catholic lawyer, a much-decorated war veteran, a confidant of President Hindenburg, whose views on 'strong government' he shared. He set himself the task of solving the reparations problem, and with it the worst of the financial crisis, by a combination of domestic austerity and diplomatic bargaining.

Brüning was in power for two and a quarter years. His cabinets lacked working majorities in the Reichstag; in the last cabinet 'non-party experts' outnumbered party politicians. The Reichstag became increasingly irrelevant. It met only 41 times in 1931 and 13 times in 1932. Brüning ruled by decrees issued under article 48 of the Weimar constitution. This article, giving the President special powers, was intended to cover special national emergencies: now it became the normal instrument for performing the function that the legislature was unable to fulfil. In its last two years the Weimar Republic was governed in the name of the *Ersatzkaiser* by a bureaucracy whose assumptions and values were those of the empire.

The measures Brüning took to remedy the crisis were courageous: in retrospect they can also be shown to have been disastrous. The main phobia of German public opinion – or at least of the conservative classes to whom Brüning, Hindenburg and the civil service were closest – was inflation. Brüning therefore determined to balance the budget, a difficult operation since falling production and falling incomes meant lower tax revenue. Most modern economists would prescribe a budget deficit for the situation Germany faced – lower taxes, higher Government expenditure, or both. Orthodoxy in 1930 demanded the opposite. The Government therefore raised taxes, reduced public investment and cut social benefits at a time of record unemployment and ordered reductions in wages and civil service salaries. It also decided against a devaluation of the overvalued gold-based *Reichsmark*, because this would have been interpreted as an attempt to sabotage the Young Plan.

Brüning was determined not to repeat the mistakes of 1923. He would retain Germany's credit-worthiness so as to maintain the inflow of foreign loans. He would try to end reparations by diplomacy, thus scoring a major political triumph and taking the wind out of the Nazis' sails. Neither calculation worked. Unlike the 1923 crisis, that of 1931 was world-wide. Apart from the French no one had any credit to invest in Germany, however worthy she might be of it. Minor palliatives, like the proposed customs union with Austria, which would also appeal to nationalist opinion, were vetoed by the victor powers. In July 1931 President Herbert Hoover of the USA proposed a general moratorium of all inter-allied war debts and reparations – one which, as it turned out, remained permanently in force; it was the end of reparations. But because the decision came unilaterally from America and not as a direct result of German lobbying, Brüning reaped little benefit from it.

Meanwhile the German people were becoming more acutely aware of the economic crisis. By the spring of 1932 there were over six million unemployed and almost everyone's standard of living had dropped. The only interest group to get special treatment from the national exchequer was agriculture, accustomed since the 1870s to public largesse. Large subsidies, under the name of *Osthilfe*, were earmarked to relieve the East Elbian landowners of debt and mortage burdens. Many of them simply used the money to enlarge their estates, among them the President's son, Oskar von Hindenburg. His implication in these scandals was of some political importance, given his growing ascendancy over his ageing father.

That social conflict and bitterness should grow, and political extremism and fragmentation flourish under such conditions was inevitable. The Nazi party went from strength to strength. Throughout 1931 it made further advances in a series of provincial elections. Its rough-house militia, the Sturm-Abteilungen (SA), numbered 170,000 by the end of 1931. Its members specialized in beating up Jews on their way to synagogue services, picking street-fights with their Communist opposite numbers, the *Rote Frontkämpfer*, and preventing the showing of *Im Westen Nichts Neues* (*All Quiet on the Western Front*), the celebrated anti-war film.

The bolder the Nazis became, the more they were sought as allies. At an anti-republican rally in Bad Harzburg in 1931 Hugenberg and Hitler were joined by the leaders of the Stahlhelm, the Reichslandbund (formerly the Agrarian League), the Pan-German League, numerous industrial and financial magnates and, most significantly of all, Hjalmar Schacht who, a year earlier, had still been President of the Reichsbank. All they had in common was hatred of the republic and an urge to get rid of Brüning; indeed, it was significant that so many 'Establishment' figures who might have sympathized with Brüning's style of government now regarded him as the source of current disasters.

But the Harzburg Front was an unequal alliance, growing more unequal every day. The conservatives knew they could get nowhere without Hitler, though they deluded themselves that they could dispose of him once his usefulness was over. Hitler, now committed to gaining power legally, needed them only as long as he felt he was short of a majority himself. In their vilification of the republic, in their demands for a total repudiation of Versailles, in their demagogy, frequently in their anti-Semitism, the older groups in no way lagged behind the Nazis. But however much they might always have hated the republic, they had co-operated with it when times were good. Too many of them were associated with monarchy and its taint of failure. Their public image was that of has-beens. The Nazis, on the other hand – and this they shared to some extent with the Communists – represented youth, novelty and dynamism. Two-thirds of the revolutionary parties' Reichstag deputies were under forty. They were unsullied by the failures of this, and any previous 'system'. What the Nazis could offer was what the other right-wing opponents of the republic lacked, a mass following. Hitler lost no opportunity of ingratiating himself with those who controlled influence or funds, culminating in his crucial address to the exclusive Industrie-Klub of Düsseldorf in January 1932, in which he pledged respect for private property. Equally the Nazis needed to maintain the radicalism of their mass constituency at full pitch, to the extent even of supporting strikes in places where the Communists were the chief rival, and of blackmailing their Junker patrons over the *Osthilfe* scandals.

The fragility of the Harzburg alliance was shown by the Presidential election of April 1932. Hindenburg had been elected in 1925 as the trump card of the Right. So far had fortunes changed that he was now, though semi-senile, the moderates' last hope against subversion. Against him the Stahlhelm put up one of their officials to represent the self-styled *nationale Opposition*, only to find themselves outflanked by Hitler's own intervention. Hindenburg was re-elected only in the second round, having failed to gain an absolute majority. He finally got 53 per cent of the vote, Hitler 37 per cent, the Communist Thälmann 10 per cent. Later the same month the Nazis plus Communists gained an absolute majority in Prussia, the last republican stronghold, though since the new Landtag was incapable of agreeing on a new government, the Social Democrat Otto Braun remained Prime Minister.

But the full extent of the old Right's disappearance as an electoral force was demonstrated in the Reichstag election of July, when the Nazis repeated their triumph of April and became the largest party. As in 1930 they made no headway against the Catholic parties, who indeed also increased their poll, and little against the Left, though further Communist advances reflected the alarming polarization of opinion. The forces which all but disappeared from public life were those of middle-class liberalism and moderate conservatism, of regional and occupational particularism. The Nazis had become their spokesman, as well as of many former non-voters now mobilized by the hysteria of crisis and extremism. For all their talk of change the Nazis were the articulators of fear, not hope. The areas in which they did best were almost exclusively those with an archaic social structure – Schleswig-

Holstein, East Prussia, Pomerania and Lower Silesia. With few exceptions they did badly in the big cities, in areas of heavy industry, in the Catholic south and west.

By this time Brüning was no longer Chancellor. Though Hindenburg owed his re-election to him more than anyone else, he dismissed him a month later, mainly at the instance of the agrarian caucus round his son, who feared that Brüning would insist on land reform in return for continued Osthilfe. Yet if Brüning's power base was narrow, that of his successors, Franz von Papen and General Kurt von Schleicher, was narrower still. One of Brüning's last acts, taken in concert with his defence minister General Groener, was to put a ban on the SA: it was this unwillingness on his part to come to terms with Nazism as an ally, however temporary, against the republic and the rise of Communism that exasperated men like Papen and Schleicher. By bringing Hitler's followers into broad alliance of patriots and loyalists they hoped to cure them of their excesses and use them to undo the shame, domestic and foreign, of 1918. For this reason Papen rescinded the SA ban and blamed the violence which inevitably ensued on the police authority, in this case the Prussian Government. Their alleged incapacity to keep order was his excuse for toppling Braun's administration, under article 48, thus removing the last republican hand from the levers of power.

Papen's coup suggested that the republic was now on its death-bed. The Social Democrats have been much criticized for not resisting it – if only symbolically, to save their honour. They were no doubt dispirited and defeatist by then, their followers demoralized by unemployment and tempted by the rival attractions of Communism. The brave days of the Kapp putsch, when a general strike could mobilize republicans of all shades, were a long way behind. The balance of violence had tipped against the republic.

If the republic was visibly dying, it was by no means certain who would succeed. Under Papen's Chancellorship the first steps were taken towards a reflation of the economy. More important in the short run, reparations, already suspended by Hoover's moratorium, were formally terminated. But it is difficult to govern a modern state without either a mass base or an overt dictatorship and Papen seemed unable to find the first and unwilling to embark on the second. While the modest improvements in conditions led to a sizeable decline in Nazi votes in a yet further Reichstag election in November – thus demonstrating that the Nazi bandwaggon was far from unstoppable – Papen himself had to give way to the one force capable of sustaining his type of authority.

Now began the fateful interlude of the last of the Weimar Chancellors, General Schleicher, who had himself hoisted Papen into office.

Schleicher's aim was the same as Papen's: a 'Konzentration der nationalen Kräfte' ('concentration of national forces'), in which Hitler was to play an allotted role. It was a scheme that also had Hindenburg's sympathy. The Nazis' electoral reverses made it even more attractive: they were still needed, but their bargaining power was reduced. Moreover Schleicher was impressed with the headway Nazi ideas were making among junior army officers – more and more Nazism seemed synonymous with national regeneration. In addition, Schleicher fancied himself as a social reformer: through the army he was to reconcile both the unions and the Nazi Left round Gregor Strasser. Yet he failed to overcome the distrust of the mass organizations, while mortgaging the confidence of industrialists and landowners. He was prepared to embroil the army in politics, but not to associate it with parties: there was no reason why he should succeed in clearing the hurdles which had tripped Papen and Brüning.

The impasse did not last long. Unable to gain the parliamentary support of any party, unable to persuade President Hindenburg to dissolve the Reichstag yet again and rule dictatorially through article 48, he vied with Papen in intriguing for Hitler's crucial support. The army was by this time convinced that only Hitler could restore political order; Ruhr industrialists were paying off the Nazi party's debts. The hardest bargainer was, in fact, Hitler, insisting, as he had done for months, that he would join no Government of which he was not the head. On 30 January 1933 his patience was rewarded.

Hitler's was not a Nazi cabinet. Of its eleven members only the Chancellor, Goering and Frick were Nazis. Five, including Hugenberg, were Nationalists; Papen was Vice-Chancellor; General von Blomberg represented the army's – and the President's – interests. Hitler's claim on Hindenburg rested on his parliamentary following, for the President was tired of minority Governments. To secure his majority Hitler demanded, and obtained, yet further elections, this time with himself in command of the State machine, the means of publicity and the forces of order.

Nothing contributed more to the atmosphere of panic that Hitler needed than the Reichstag Fire of 27 February. Its causes are obscure to this day. That it was a Communist plot, as the Nazis claimed, may be ruled out. The documents do not support it, and the four Communists arrested on charges of arson, including the later Secretary-General of the Communist International, Dimitrov, had to be acquitted in what was intended as a show trial. That it was a Nazi plot to discredit the Communists, once widely believed, is now also less likely. Marinus van der Lubbe, a Dutch labourer of anarchist leanings, whom the Nazis claimed to have apprehended in the burning building and who, alone of the accused, was found guilty and executed, was probably a 'loner' and not, as many were tempted to believe, a Nazi stooge. More important, the fire enabled Hitler to secure from Hindenburg his signature to the *Verordnung zum Schutz von Volk und Staat* (Decree for the Protection of the People and the State), which suspended freedom of the press and of assembly; permitted search and imprisonment without warrant, and interception of mail; and instituted the death penalty for acts of sabotage.

Five days later Hitler secured his last and greatest electoral triumph. In a record turn-out the Nazis won 44 per cent of the votes, but even now, despite mounting intimidation, they needed their Nationalist coalition partners for an absolute majority. This Reichstag had only one function to perform, to pass the *Gesetz zur Behebung der Not von Volk und Reich* (Law for the Alleviation of the People's and the Reich's Misery), known as the *Ermächtigungsgesetz* (Enabling Law), giving the Government sweeping powers and rendering parliament virtually superfluous. The Communist members of the Reichstag were by this time under arrest; the Zentrum leader, Monsignor Kaas, assured his party's support, partly in return for promises to respect the rights of the Church and Germany's federal structure, but also because even this once-democratic party feared Bolshevism more than Fascism, and had never been entirely free from the authoritarian patriotism that had periodically gripped the country since the beginnings of the unification movement. With only the Social Democrats against, the law passed without difficulty. 'Jetzt', wrote Goebbels in his diary, 'sind wir auch verfassungsmäßig die Herren des Reiches.' ('Now we are also the constitutional masters of the Reich.') It was a significant consideration. The Reichstag Fire decrees had given Hitler all the powers he needed. But, ever since the fiasco of the 1923 *putsch*, he had insisted on the legitimation of popular approval and constitutional propriety.

The Nazis were fond of referring to their seizure of power as a 'nationale Erhebung' ('national uprising'), or a 'nationales Erwachen' ('national awakening'), the culmination of an irresistible popular movement. Yet the events of 1930 to 1933 tell a different story. 1932 was a year of plebiscitary triumph, but also of political frustration; in

Goebbels's words, 'eine ewige Pechsträne'. 'Die Vergangenheit war schwer,' he wrote at the end of 1932, 'die Zukunft is dunkel und trübe; alle Aussichten und Hoffnungen vollends entschwunden.'[1] The Nazis triumphed because many of the slogans and symbols which they exploited – those of national solidarity, resentment at defeat, a yearning for strong government, a dislike of urban, industrial civilization, anti-Semitism – were the common ground of many Germans, inculcated by the experience of the nineteenth and twentieth centuries, strengthened by the educational system. They triumphed because they found in Hitler a matchless demagogue and ruthless tactician who outflanked and outmanœuvred all those who sought to offer solutions similar to his. They triumphed because parliamentary democracy in Germany was tarred as a foreign import and the product of defeat, because the leaders of the parliamentary parties, inexperienced in exercising their responsibilities, gave Germany neither stable nor effective government. They triumphed because the Depression brought many of the middle class to economic despair, and to a fear of a Bolshevik take-over. They triumphed above all because, in the crucial autumn and winter of 1932–3, many who feared or despised them nevertheless perceived them as a lesser evil or as a necessary ally against the republic that they, too, wished to kill – generals, landowners, industrialists, civil servants, academics, churchmen, men who a few years later were to join the Resistance, flee into exile or die in concentration camps. But for the moment they ignored the warning of that previous *Walpurgisnacht*:

Der ganze Strudel strebt nach oben;
Du glaubst zu schieben, und du wirst geschoben . . .

The Third Reich

CONSOLIDATION

A third empire, to crown the glory of its two predecessors, the Holy Roman and the Wilhelmine, an empire to last a thousand years – that is what Hitler promised not only to the German people but to himself. It is known to history for its unexampled tyranny and aggressiveness, but the apparatus for carrying out the ultimate fantasies of the Nazi programme was built up gradually and, at times, hesitantly. And the Nazis did have a programme. Some parts of it, like economic and social

[1] '. . . an eternal stream of bad luck. The past has been difficult, the future dark and sombre; all hopes and prospects completely vanished.'

reform or the ideological superstructure associated with the party's self-appointed philosopher, Alfred Rosenberg, were ballast, to be taken on or jettisoned as occasion demanded. Others were genuinely *unabänderlich*. The will to secure a monopoly of absolute power, to wield this power through a racially pure élite on the leadership principle, to undo the 1919 peace settlement and replace it with a 'New Order', in which the *Herrenvolk* would lord it over Slavs and Latins, reduced to helotry – this was the movement's *raison d'être* and its dynamic. Hitler never lost sight of these aims, first outlined in *Mein Kampf* and repeated in all subsequent records of his opinions right down to his political testament of April 1945. In his methods and his tactics he was, however, opportunist. He could be patient and flexible as well as impulsive; he preferred, if possible, to let his antagonist make a fatal mistake.

Throughout 1933 and 1934 he had to move cautiously – with enough terror to dispose of any threat to his rule and to satisfy the blood-lust of his followers, with enough circumspection to lull those whose help he needed inside and outside Germany. The first wave of terror came through the Nazis' control of the federal state governments, these being, under the constitution, the police authorities. Hermann Goering was appointed Prussian Minister of the Interior and set about creating the first concentration camps for the – entirely illegal – detention and ill-treatment of political opponents. He also recruited an 'auxiliary police', mainly from the two party militias, the SA and the SS, against whose assaults and robberies the regular forces of the law were powerless. Hitler used the Reichstag Fire decrees to turn out the elected governments of the states and give executive power to appointed governors, usually the *Gauleiter* (regional bosses) of the party. In Prussia the post went to Goering. The arrangement was temporary only. In 1934 the state governments were abolished altogether; for the remaining eleven years of Hitler's dictatorship Germany had the one and only truly centralized executive in her history.

The same process of *Gleichschaltung* (enforced integration) was applied, one by one, to all autonomous organizations of citizens. The first to suffer were the trade unions, whose buildings were seized, leaders arrested and members compulsorily recruited into the Deutsche Arbeitsfront under Robert Ley. Next to follow was the Social Democratic Party, first persecuted and then banned, much as the Communists had been after the Reichstag Fire. The remaining political parties took the hint, and dissolved themselves, though not before Hitler's coalition partners, the Nationalists, had suffered the indignity of occupation by storm-troopers. By the middle of July the Nazi party was the only political party in the country.

Hand in hand with terror and *Gleichschaltung* went conciliation, especially of the more conservative forces. By the beginning of August the 'auxiliary police' forces had been disbanded and some of the concentration camp detainees released. The first wave of civil service purges, directed against Jews and 'Marxists', was completed. The public burnings of 'decadent' books ceased. Acts of arbitrary injustice, excusable in the heat of the revolution, would arouse the suspicions of Hitler's allies if indefinitely escalated. The autonomy of industrial, commercial and agricultural interest groups was, like that of the trade unions, abolished, but the economic claims of these interests were not seriously damaged. Though the radicals in the Nazi party, representing small tradesmen and subsistence farmers, might rail against big business, landowners and chain stores, and demand reduced mortgage rates, nothing was done to satisfy them beyond a temporary campaign to boycott department stores. Schacht was back as President of the Reichsbank, firmly opposed to any sentimentality towards the inefficient. Moreover, Hitler was disinclined to antagonize industry and finance, whose expertise and goodwill he needed for his programme of rearmament and economic revival. The new head of the Reichsverband der deutschen Industrie was no less a representative of the old order than Gustav Krupp von Bohlen and Halbach.

Similarly Hitler had some success in mollifying the Churches. Of course the pagan, racial creed of Nazism, demanding total subordination to the wishes of the dictator, was in the last resort incompatible with Christianity and in private Hitler did not disguise his contempt for the Churches. Yet he bore in mind the fatal effect on German national unity of Bismarck's attempts to force the Catholic Church into submission, and was encouraged by the precedent of the Lateran Pacts of 1929, through which Mussolini had made his peace with the Vatican. German Catholic leaders had already shown, by their support for the Enabling Bill, that they were willing to meet the new regime half-way. In July 1933, shortly after the Zentrum's disbandment, the Vatican signed a concordat with Hitler's Government. In return for abstaining from politics, the Catholic Church gained generous guarantees for parochial and educational independence.

The Protestant Churches were, on the face of it, even easier to deal with. Unlike the Catholics, they had never reconciled themselves with the republic; unlike the Catholics they were quite heavily infiltrated with Nazi sympathizers. In particular, a sect known as the Deutsche Christen showed a strong *völkisch* ideology, including a dislike of the traditional Lutheran emphasis on the 'Jewish' Old Testament. Helped by heavy Nazi pressure, the Deutsche Christen got one of their leaders, the army chaplain Ludwig Müller, elected to the newly created post of *Reichsbischof* by a special synod.

Nazi domination of the Churches was never complete, however. The concordat notwithstanding, many party organs continued to harrass Catholic organizations and individuals, particularly youth leaders, and party members were encouraged to leave the Church. By the end of the year Cardinal Faulhaber was preaching his famous advent sermons against Nazi racialist doctrine. Among Protestants those who disapproved not only of the way Müller had been appointed but of other Government acts, such as the application of 'racial' tests to the clergy, grouped themselves round the former submarine hero, Pastor Martin Niemoeller, eventually to form the Bekennende Kirche, the Confessing Church. Though Hitler was forced to drop Müller after a time, the Confessing Church itself remained a small minority. The majority of churchmen were also German patriots, dazzled by Hitler's promise of national regeneration. The emphasis he put on a crusade against Bolshevism held many back from expressing their discontent too firmly.

The most important of the groups Hitler had to appease was the army. He did so early and spectacularly, two days before the passage of the Enabling Bill when, in the Memorial Church at Potsdam, in the presence of Hindenburg, the Crown Prince and a full complement of field-marshals he apostrophized 'die Vermählung zwischen den Symbolen der alten Größe und der jungen Kraft' ('the marriage between the symbols of ancient greatness and youthful strength'). But Hindenburg's crucial influence, and Blomberg's presence in the cabinet, were a constant reminder of how vulnerable he was to the army's displeasure. Moreover, he needed the generals as much as he needed the industrialists if his ambitions for Germany were not to remain dreams. The army, in turn, demanded a showdown with the radical wing of the Nazi party, which Hitler could not in the long run evade: a showdown not so much with the economic cranks as with the SA.

The SA, now numbering over half a million, represented the rowdy, plebeian, semi-criminal element of the Nazi movement. Borne along by envy and social resentment, they talked increasingly of a 'second revolution'. By this they meant the overthrow of the existing social dominance by the wealthy, the educated and the respectable and, more specifically, their ambition to replace the old, 'reactionary' army as the revolutionary fighting force of the Reich.

Throughout the autumn of 1933 and the spring of 1934 relations between party leadership and the SA chief of staff, Ernst Röhm, steadily worsened. At the beginning of June 1934 the SA were sent on a month's compulsory leave; on the night of 29–30 June the SA leaders were surprised in their homes or holiday resorts and summarily shot. Not only Röhm and his associates were the victims of this 'night of the long knives'; they included General Schleicher, Hitler's predecessor as Chancellor, Gregor Strasser who, unlike his brother Otto, had stayed inside the party, Edgar Jung, the conservative publicist and secretary of Vice-Chancellor Papen, and Gustav von Kahr, Bavarian Premier at the time of the beer-hall *putsch* of 1923.

Five weeks later President Hindenburg died and Hitler succeeded him as Head of State and Commander-in-Chief of the armed forces. The oath that the armed forces were expected to swear, however, was not to the holder of an office, but to an individual, 'dem Führer des Deutschen Reiches und Volkes, Adolf Hitler'. The army's triumph, apparently complete on 30 June, carried within it the seeds of danger.

With Hindenburg's death formal Nazi control of the Government was strengthened. Papen ceased to be Vice-Chancellor; Hugenberg had already resigned over the treatment of the Nationalist party. Indeed the cabinet now ceased to play any role in the decision-making process, as the Reichstag had already done. In a plebiscite on 19 August 1934 90 per cent of the voters predictably approved Hitler's new titles and powers. The purpose of the exercise was to stress the direct authority the *Volk* gave to the Führer, bypassing all other institutions. The last traces of the Weimar constitution had disappeared. Yet Germany was not yet a totalitarian state. The dominance of the party's arbitrary authority over the governmental apparatus and the everyday life of citizens was extended only gradually, more slowly and more dis-creetly between 1934 and 1938 than in the first eighteen months of Nazi rule. The country was still open to foreign diplomats and journalists and it was more desirable for them to see grand scenarios like that of the 1936 Berlin Olympics than street pogroms or brown-shirt hooligan-ism.

One of the first consequences of the purge of the SA was a rise in the status of the rival militia, the black-shirted Schutz-Staffeln (SS). They were intended to be a highly disciplined, politically reliable, racial élite, the advance guard of the Nazi revolution. Its leader, Heinrich Himmler, who believed, if anything, more fanatically than even Hitler in world dictatorship by Aryan supermen, advanced rapidly. Originally the SS had been subordinate to the SA, but even before Himmler laid claim to primacy by playing a crucial role in the ousting of Röhm he had set up his own security service (Sicherheitsdienst: SD) under Reinhard Heydrich. Even before the purge, Himmler had succeeded in getting himself appointed chief of political police in one after another of the federal states, thereby gaining control of the secret State police (Geheime Staats-Polizei: Gestapo) and dove-tailing his own SD into the State apparatus. By 1936 he was Reichsführer SS, and *Chef der deutschen Polizei* in the Ministry of the Interior. By aiming at police rather than military power he had succeeded where Röhm had predictably failed. He preferred to outflank rather than confront the army, securing the Waffen-SS as an armed unit, ultimately of major proportions, entirely independent of the regular military command.

Himmler's accumulation of powers suggests an inexorable trend towards a monolithic hierarchy of command and obedience. That would be a misleading picture of how the Third Reich was governed. Hitler was bored with office routine, indeed with system of any kind. New organizations were created *ad hoc* to deal with new situations, or in order to bypass objections or obstructions from an entrenched part of the machine. The organs of the State were more and more subordinated to the dictates and requirements of the party, but the two were never entirely fused. Instead there arose, beside the regular, established civil service, police and judiciary, parallel institutions with ill-defined prerogatives, their competences resting on secret, but legally enforcible *Führererlasse* (Führer decrees). Thus the SS was given direct control of the concentration camps of which there were, by 1938, six. Such arrangements led, of course, to endless demarcation disputes, but this, too, suited Hitler: it exhausted the energies of his subordinates in mutually destructive rivalries. Nor were these fragmentations of authority of any help to the ordinary citizen. Like Josef K., he knew only that there were regular and irregular forces of order; that he might have to answer to one, or the other, or both; that the boundaries between them were uncertain, constantly shifting and probably unknown even to the subordinate functionaries whom he would confront; that each had its own norms and *modus operandi* of which some might, and others might not, be discoverable in advance. For each activity, whether it was to do with his livelihood or his leisure, there was now only one, party-dominated organization of which membership tended increasingly to become compulsory; the Hitler Youth for children, the largest and possibly best known, was but one of many. In this way it was possible gradually to reduce the individual to that atomized anonymity without which the Nazi – or any similar – regime could not have achieved 'die Erfassung des ganzen Menschen' ('getting hold of the whole man').

It was equally necessary to deprive all remaining corporate organizations of their autonomy, especially the more conservative ones that had initially got off lightly. The universities offered little resistance, after Jewish and politically 'unreliable' teachers – some 1,200 in all – had been purged. The nationalist ultra-conservatism of the student body and the educated classes generally made accommodation with the Nazis relatively easy. That this subservience would cost Germany her world lead in many fields, from classical scholarship to nuclear physics, was more quickly appreciated outside than inside the country. The honeymoon with the Churches was, on the other hand, brief. The aggressive atheism of some of the Nazi leaders and the harrassments of the Churches' social work were bound to evoke protests. In March 1937 Pope Pius XI's encyclical *Mit nnenderbre Sorge* (*With Burning Sorrow*), largely drawn up by Faulhaber and listing the regime's many breaches of the concordat, was read from Catholic pulpits. A few months later a letter from Dr Otto Dibelius, a leading Protestant dignitary, protesting against interference in Church government, was published. Thereafter a stalemate ensued. Open resistance was restricted to a few individual churchmen, who were accordingly persecuted: Niemoeller, for instance, spent from 1938 to 1945 in a concentrtaion camp. But there were no further attempts at *Gleichschaltung*.

A relationship that could not be left ambiguous was that between the regime and the army. There were many causes of friction – social antagonism, the close links between the army and Prussian Lutheranism, the pace of rearmament and Hitler's foreign policy gambles. But basically Hitler was waiting for an opportunity to drive home the tactical advantage he had gained in the summer of 1934. That opportunity came in January 1938, when he secured the dismissal of the War Minister, Blomberg, and the chief of staff, Fritsch, on trumped-up morality charges. He followed this coup with the enforced retirement of sixteen high-ranking generals and a complete reorganization of the army command. A new High Command, the Oberkommando der Wehrmacht (OKW), was created, absorbing the old War Ministry and directly responsible to Hitler. The general staff, though not abolished, was largely superseded. Into this new post Hitler placed a political sycophant of no military distinction, Field Marshal Wilhelm Keitel. It was a blow from which the army never recovered. For almost three centuries it had been like a state within the state, exercising social privileges and political influence before which Governments had to bow. Now it was reduced to being one more cog in Hitler's expansionist machine. Where the Liberals of 1862 and the Socialists of 1919 had failed, the *böhmische Gefreite*[1] had succeeded.

The one section of the population which, in contrast with the Nazis' other victims, was persecuted with open and spectacular brutality was the Jews. Anti-Semitism had from the beginning been an integral part of the Nazi programme. It was one of many that they shared with the *völkisch* movement of the nineteenth century and the authoritarian antiliberalism of the more conventional nationalists. Jews were singled out as the leaders of commercialism and materialism, of Marxism and subversion, of cosmopolitanism and avant-gardism, of urban modernity as opposed to the traditional values and society of pre-industrial provincialism. Identified in this way, Jews became especially vulnerable after 1918 and even more during the world economic crisis. Though the great majority of German Jews wanted nothing more than to be solid, patriotic citizens, they found themselves cast as scapegoats not merely for the defeat of 1918, the failures of democracy and the degradations of capitalism, but for the German nation's failure to secure emotional solidarity. Unlike Communists, Catholics or Jehova's Witnesses, who were persecuted for what they did or thought, Jews were persecuted for what they were and could not help. A Jew could not be *gleichgeschaltet*, only *ausgeschaltet*.

The exclusion of Jews from public life began soon after the Nazi seizure of power by their expulsion from all State employment and by the boycott, largely organized by the SA, of Jewish shops, businesses, doctors and lawyers. This was followed in 1935 by the Nürnberg Laws – the *Reichsbürgergesetz* which deprived anyone with three or more Jewish grandparents of German citizenship, and the *Gesetz zum Schutze des deutschen Blutes und der deutschen Ehre* (Law of the Protection of German Blood and German Honour) which prohibited marriages, and indeed any sexual relations, between Jews and non-Jews. Gradually Jews were edged out of one profession after another; schools were segregated; access to universities made more difficult.

[1] Bohemian corporal – Hindenburg's way of referring to Hitler.

M

These pressures culminated in the pogrom of 9–10 November 1938, instigated in response to the murder of a German diplomat in Paris by a Jewish youth. Under direct orders from the party leadership the SA plundered Jewish shops and homes and set fire to synagogues. About 20,000 Jews were arbitrarily arrested and many ill-treated in concentration camps. A collective fine of 1,000 million marks was imposed on the Jewish community as 'atonement' for the murder. Following the *Reichskristallnacht* – so called after the broken panes of glass – the imposition of economic and social apartheid was speeded up. Increasingly Jews sought refuge in other countries; by the outbreak of the war half of them had emigrated.

For all the regime's difficulties in the first few years, there is no doubt that it had a solid basis of popular support. This was due not only to the terror, though its mixture of intimidation and cajoling certainly helped, nor exclusively to the work of the Propaganda Ministry under Josef Goebbels, though its intensity and technical skill far exceeded anything previously experienced. What mattered equally was that Hitler scored notable foreign policy and economic successes.

Hitler stood, and had always stood, for a repudiation of the Treaty of Versailles. So did many other Germans; what helped him to power was the belief that he would succeed where others had failed. The considerable concessions that Stresemann and Brüning had won did little to satisfy the widespread resentment at the treaty and Germany's status. The very first response of the other powers to Germany's new Government seemed to confirm Hitler's claims. On Mussolini's initiative a four-power pact was signed between Britain, France, Germany and Italy for the purpose of maintaining peace. Its propaganda value to Hitler lay in the fact that the other powers now frankly treated Germany as an equal, without reference to the treaties, the League or Locarno. Hitler exploited the new diplomatic equality by demanding military equality: in the autumn of 1933 he walked out of the world disarmament conference and left the League of Nations.

Yet he continued to speak of peace, and only of the satisfaction of Germany's just demands. As long as the victor powers persuaded themselves that his aims were limited, that he was no more than a revisionist, they were prepared to meet him half-way. In Britain both Government and public opinion were convinced that Germany did have just grievances and that these should be satisfied peaceably. Neither Britain nor France, still less America, wanted a repetition of the four-year slaughter of 1914–18. France had in any case adopted a purely defensive strategy, embodied in the fortifications of the Maginot Line, and could act effectively only with British agreement and help. All Governments shared the hope that what Hitler had ranted while in opposition would be modified by the realities of political power.

That was their biggest miscalculation. Hitler's aims were not limited and he was not just another revisionist. He despised the *Grenzpolitik* of the bourgeois nationalists: his was *Raumpolitik*, the reshaping of continents, not the shifting of frontier posts. He was not interested in restoring the frontiers of 1914. As far as he was concerned Bismarck had not unified the German nation: by excluding the ten million Germans of the Habsburg Monarchy (see p. 246), now living in Austria and Czechoslovakia, he had driven a wedge into it. Hitler came from the pan-German lower middle class of provincial Austria: he wanted the Germany of 1848, not of 1871. No wonder Ernst Niekisch dubbed him 'die Rache für Königgrätz' ('revenge for Königgrätz'). Hitler also disavowed the cardinal item in the conventional revisionist policy, alliance with Russia. The Bolsheviks he regarded as part of world Jewish conspiracy, Russians as *Untermenschen*. Instead he sought allies with whom he could share a cause. Fascist Italy was the obvious candidate, and for the benefit of this alliance the 300,000 oppressed Germans of the South Tyrol were exempted from his crusade of liberation.

Though Hitler's aims were unchanged, his time-table was flexible. He compensated for his breach with Russia with a non-aggression pact with Poland, though Poland, too, was an intended victim. But by drawing a former ally of France, and an important link in France's eastern European security belt, into his orbit, he struck a further blow at the Versailles system.

Hitler's first major success in 'liberating' Germans was the cheapest. The population of the Saar territory was, according to the treaty, due to vote on its future in 1935, after fifteen years of League administration and French economic dominance. That such a vote would favour reunion with Germany seemed highly probable; but the Nazis turned the plebiscite into a major propaganda feast, and the 90 per cent in favour of reunion, despite the strength of Catholicism and trade unionism, was undoubtedly a triumph.

By 1935 Hitler also felt ready to repudiate the military clauses of the Versailles Treaty and to announce conscription and full rearmament. The effect of these developments was to force Soviet Russia into seeking

Western allies. Russia joined the League of Nations, an act symbolizing a new commitment to collective security against revisionist aggressors, and signed pacts with France and Czechoslovakia, the most reliable of France's remaining eastern European outposts. As a counter-blow Hitler decided on a military reoccupation of the Rhineland, which Allied troops had vacated in 1930 but which was to remain, under the treaty, demilitarized. The operation was his boldest bluff yet. He had, as we now know, given orders for immediate withdrawal in the event of any French counter-move. But France was without a Government and unwilling to act without British support, and the British Government saw no reason to intervene as long as no international frontiers were violated. Indeed, Britain had already responded to Hitler's rearmament policy by signing a naval agreement which allowed for a greatly expanded German fleet, though maintaining British numerical superiority.

Hitler was also becoming more sure of Italy's support, as Mussolini's ambitions made him increasingly the natural ally of his fellow aggressor. The Italian invasion of Abyssinia in 1935, condemned by the League, and Italy's open support for the right-wing rebellion in Spain, under General Franco, against the Popular Front republican Government widened the gap between Italy and the Western powers, though neither Britain nor France had given up hope of using Italy to restrain, or mediate with, Germany. The only serious threat to the 'Rome–Berlin Axis', as it came to be known, was Hitler's intention towards Austria. The incorporation of Austria in Germany, and the consequent pressure on the frontier with the South Tyrol, were anathema to Mussolini, and when Austrian Nazis tried to force Hitler's hand in June 1934 by staging a coup, he was obliged to disavow them. But from 1936 onwards they renewed their pressure for an *Anschluß*, abetted and financed from Germany, and the survival of an independent Austrian state became ever more questionable. By the spring of 1938 the Austrian Chancellor, Schuschnigg, felt obliged to take pro-Nazi representatives into his Government, after a conference with Hitler at Berchtesgaden. Within a month they had ousted Schuschnigg and invited German military intervention. Hitler responded; Mussolini, appreciating that Britain and France would do nothing to stop an *Anschluß*, acquiesced in return for a guarantee of Italy's frontiers. So, paradoxically, the *Anschluß* strengthened the Axis.

The ease with which the *Anschluß* had been accomplished, and its apparent popularity in Austria, hastened the crisis caused by the agitation of the German minority in Czechoslovakia. The extremist Sudetendeutsche Partei, led by a physical training instructor, Konrad Henlein, had been scoring impressive election victories: though he claimed to want only autonomy, we now know that he was working, in collusion with the German Government, for the destruction of the Czechoslovak state. Since Czechoslovakia was the ally of France and Russia and had a strong army, the risks that Germany ran if Czechoslovakia and her allies were to resist German military intervention were enormous. But Hitler relied not on his armour but on his political instinct. Neither France nor Russia, least of all Britain, would embark on European war for 'a far-off people of whose affairs we know little', in the words of Neville Chamberlain, the British Prime Minister. Chamberlain therefore took the initiative in offering Hitler a compromise solution, the territorial cession of German-populated areas to the German state. Since the alternative seemed to be war, Chamberlain succeeded in persuading first the French Government, and then the hitherto determined Czech President, Beneš, to bow to his proposals. On 30 September the powers signed an agreement at Munich to dismember the Czechoslovak state, leaving only a defenceless and economically impoverished rump to fend for itself. Twice in one year the frontiers of the Reich had been extended. Within five years of taking office, Hitler had achieved what the professors of 1848 had failed to do, what Bismarck had striven to prevent, what the peace-makers of 1919 had forbidden.

These foreign policy successes would not have been possible without economic recovery; moreover, the economic improvement was probably the biggest single cause of the regime's popularity. Unemployment fell from six million in the winter of 1932 to 1·7 million in the summer of 1935. By the outbreak of the war there were seven million more jobs than in 1933. Real wages, i.e. the purchasing power of earnings, also rose, but more slowly. Possibly the regime claimed, and got, more credit than it deserved. The gradual recovery of the world economy reopened export markets, enabling Germany to pay for increased imports of raw materials. Some at least of the increased public works expenditure was 'in the pipeline' from earlier Governments. Moreover, this type of job-creation could have proceeded much faster, had not the Nazi Government, like its predecessors and successors, been obsessed with the dangers of inflation.

From 1934 onwards Schacht – not a Nazi himself – combined the Ministry of Economics with the presidency of the Reichsbank, thereby becoming the economic architect of the Third Reich. His ingenuity was concentrated on foreign trade: exchange controls, export subsidies and bilateral trade agreements with supplier countries, based on exchange rates tailored to each individual case. Many of these trade partners were in eastern and south-eastern Europe; their increasing dependence on German credit and markets gave Germany strategically vital political influence.

Until 1936 rearmament played little part in the economic upswing. In that year the second Four-Year Plan was announced: its purpose (not made public) was to equip Germany to wage war by 1940. The plenipotentiary of the Plan was Goering; Schacht disapproved of it, because he saw it as incompatible with his own policies of stimulating production for consumption and export. He therefore resigned as Minister, though he stayed on at the Reichsbank. The famous dilemma between guns and butter was never resolved. Rearmament certainly stimulated the economy, but the Plan fell short of its targets and Germany was, at the outbreak of the war, a long way from self-sufficiency in strategic materials.

Schacht's chief contribution was in the shape he gave to economic activity. The need to increase production and keep down prices led, necessarily, to policies that favoured large rather than small enterprises. The only legislative sop to the mystique of *Blut und Boden* (blood and soil) was the *Erbhofgesetz*, which prohibited the subdivision and, under certain circumstances, the sale of viable farmsteads under 300 acres (about a third of all agricultural holdings). In this way the Nazis hoped to build up the peasant aristocracy so dear to their hearts. In all other respects the move was away from the *völkisch* social utopia. By 1939 more Germans than ever lived in big cities and worked in large-scale industry. More women than ever were in employment instead of minding *Kinder, Kirche und Küche* (children, church and kitchen). The class struggles and interest group conflicts which characterize a pluralistic, liberal society and which the Nazis hoped to abolish were merely bureaucratized. The new, party-dominated economic organizations fought out their rivalries through the combativeness and mutual distrust of the various sections of the party leadership. Neither the economy nor society was thoroughly transformed. In so far as changes did take place, it was in the direction of modernization and occupational mobility: an acceleration of the trends under the empire and Weimar, an assimilation with the advanced industrial societies of the West. The propaganda of *Volksgemeinschaft* (national community), *schaffende*

Stände (creative classes), *Kraft durch Freude* (strength through joy) might disguise this fact, but could not alter it.

EXPANSION AND CATASTROPHE

The Munich agreement of September 1938 marked the climax of the Western powers' policy of appeasing Hitler. Each side publicly claimed that Munich would form the base of peace in Europe; each side took out insurance policies against the opposite happening. Both sides stepped up their rearmament programme, though the gap between them was not reduced. Up to and including Munich, appeasement seemed justified by the character of Germany's demands. The Rhineland, equal armaments, Austria, the Sudeten lands – each seemed a move to rectify a genuine injustice, to restore a balance that had been upset at Versailles. If Hitler meant what he said at Munich, that he had no further territorial demands, appeasement would remain justified; the permanent discredit of appeasement began in March 1939, when Hitler took advantage of growing internal difficulties in Czechoslovakia and sent his troops into Prague. What had remained of Bohemia and Moravia became a 'Reich protectorate'; Slovakia, to the east, became a puppet republic, nominally independent.

If Hitler did indeed have territorial demands beyond these, they would mostly probably be at the expense of Poland: perhaps merely to recover the port of Danzig, to seize back the industries of Upper Silesia, to abolish the 'corridor' to the sea that divided East Prussia from the rest of the Reich; perhaps, on the other hand, to turn Poland into another 'Reich protectorate'. The British Government responded to the occupation of Prague by offering a guarantee of independence to Poland, but without very clear ideas on how to implement it. The one military and diplomatic combination certain to deter Germany was a revived Triple Entente; yet the British Government was reluctant to involve itself in a close alliance with the Soviet Union, and Poland and Romania, the states most threatened by German expansion, refused to let Russian armies on to their territories, even in the event of war. Stalin thus became increasingly impatient with Western hesitations; suspecting the West of wishing to deflect Hitler's aggressiveness to the East, he moved first, hoping to deflect it in the opposite direction. Stalin's conclusions were welcome to Hitler, who had in no way changed his views on Communism or the racial inferiority of the Slavs, but who saw that with Russia neutralized a Western guarantee to Poland was worthless. On 23 August a Nazi–Soviet non-aggression pact was signed, with a secret clause recognizing Soviet rights in the Baltic states and the eastern half of a partitioned Poland.

The newly gained Soviet complaisance enabled Hitler to step up the pressure on Poland for the return of Danzig; the Poles, having concluded from Czech experience that concessions to Hitler were useless, refused to budge. So Danzig became the occasion for the outbreak of the Second World War. German troops crossed the frontier on 1 September; a British ultimatum, demanding a withdrawal, expired unanswered on 3 September. The French, restrained by the British for twenty years from acting against Germany, were now propelled by Chamberlain's initiative. The Western powers' declarations of war did not save Poland, but they showed that there was a limit to appeasement.

Hitler rightly calculated that Anglo-French entry into the war would make little difference to his short-term plans. Neither militarily nor economically nor politically was Germany ready for total war in 1939. Not only was the Four-Year Plan behind schedule, but all Germany's preparations were dominated by the need to avoid the type of conflict which had worn her down in 1914–18. This time Germany was to succeed in dealing the initial, shattering blow that had eluded her in August 1914, and her equipment – armour, motorized infantry, dive-bombers – was designed for the conduct of a lightning war, a *Blitzkrieg*. The defeat of Poland in just over two weeks was the first of many vindications of the new strategy.

The next six months saw the 'phoney war', an interval of little fighting as the antagonists faced each other across their fortifications on the Franco-German frontier. It was rival intentions towards Scandinavia that forced the deadlock. Each side suspected the other of planning an intervention there, especially as Russia, in an attempt to secure her command of the Baltic, had been waging war against Finland during the winter. In April 1940 Germany took the initiative by invading Denmark, which was occupied without difficulty, and Norway, the defence of which Britain had regarded as both necessary and possible, but which was also subjugated within a month. But it was on 10 May that *Blitzkrieg* came into its own, in the boldest and most devastating German offensive of the war, when her armies poured over her Western frontiers. They overran Holland and Belgium in less than a week, and entered Paris scarcely a month later. The French Government, which had fled to Bordeaux, faced the increasing inevitability of an armistice and a military surrender. This was finally signed on 22 June in the same railway coach in the same forest clearing at Compiègne as the armistice of 1918. By it Germany reannexed Alsace and Lorraine and occupied the whole of northern France and the Atlantic littoral. The rest of France retained nominal independence, with a Government headed by Marshal Pétain, centred on Vichy.

This transformation of the military balance left only Britain in the war against Germany. Towards Britain Hitler had no coherent policy: he did not regard the British, in contrast with the French, the Poles or the Russians, as hereditary opponents or racially inferior. He assumed that with the defeat of her continental allies Britain would want to seek an honourable peace, in return for the safeguarding of at any rate most of the empire. He had no plans for an immediate invasion, assuming that even if Britain did not negotiate, German air superiority would keep her militarily neutralized. In fact the German military successes had strengthened, not weakened, British commitment to continuing the war. The Norwegian fiasco had led to a change of Government: Winston Churchill, the chief opponent of appeasement of the thirties, replaced Chamberlain as Prime Minister. Thanks to Hitler's insistence on capturing Paris at the earliest moment, most of the British army, though short of weapons, was evacuated from Dunkirk. Moreover, Hitler's successes had gained him an ally. Three days before the fall of Paris Italy cautiously entered the war on Germany's side, and while she contributed nothing to the defeat of France she presented an immediate threat to British interests in the Mediterranean and the Suez Canal.

The British Government's decision to continue the war constituted the first major strategic frustration Hitler had suffered. Both sides were agreed that command of the air would decide whether Britain could survive as an independent power. During five weeks, from mid-August to mid-September, daily air battles raged over southern England; by the time the Battle of Britain was over – that is, by the time the German air offensive was called off – the Germans had lost 1,733 aircraft, the RAF 915. Plans for an invasion were indefinitely called off and the prospects for an immediate confrontation in the West faded. Instead the war moved south and east, in response to Mussolini's ambitions and Hitler's suspicions of Russia.

It soon emerged that Italian interests, far from complementing those of Germany, rivalled them, and Italian incompetence in pursuing them extended Germany's commitments. An Italian offensive into Egypt, aimed at the Suez Canal, was stopped well short of its target, and a British counter-offensive during the winter drove the Italians back several hundred miles. An Italian assault on Greece fared even worse, with the Greek army advancing into Italian-occupied Albania. But the chief reason for Germany's renewed interest in eastern Europe, after the stalemate on the English Channel, was rivalry with Russia for the domination of the Balkans. The right-wing Governments of Russia's neighbours were prepared in varying degrees to become Germany's vassals, with Hungary, one of the victims of the 1919 peace settlement, as Germany's most eligible ally. By the spring of 1941 plans for Hitler's most ambitious undertaking, Operation Barbarossa, were well advanced. The attack on Russia was scheduled for 15 May, in time to knock Russia out before the winter. It was Yugoslavia that upset the time-table. By the beginning of April Yugoslavia was the only Balkan state not under Axis military dominance; moreover, through Yugoslavia led the road to Greece, where Hitler had decided to bail out his Italian allies. The Yugoslav Government's military agreement with Germany at the end of March was, however, repudiated by a patriotic rebellion and Germany was obliged to impose her will by armed force. Once more *Blitzkrieg* tactics paid off: in less than a month German control of both Yugoslavia and Greece was secure. But the diversion meant the postponement of Barbarossa and the invasion of Russia did not take place until 22 June – the exact anniversary of Napoleon's attack.

In retrospect Hitler blamed Mussolini for upsetting his schedule, thus depriving him of victory over Russia in the summer of 1941. Yet Hitler failed for the same reason that Napoleon had failed – the vastness of the country, the fanatical patriotism of the population make it almost impossible to defeat Russia in conventional war. Although Stalin was – amazingly – taken by surprise by the German invasion, although the Soviet armies lost three million men in the first weeks of the war, although the German armour had advanced up to 400 miles by the end of July, the Germans failed to reach their objective. Leningrad was besieged, but not captured. The German thrust was halted a few miles short of Moscow. When the winter set in it was the Germans who were found to be unprepared, and for the first time since 1939 German armies were on the retreat.

Two days after the Russians began their successful winter offensive Germany gained a valuable new ally. As negotiations between Japan and the USA were breaking down, the Japanese launched a surprise air attack on America's main Pacific base at Pearl Harbor. Japan, whose Far Eastern ambitions equalled Germany's in Europe, had been drawing closer to Germany for some years and had become the formal ally of Germany and Italy in 1940; in Russia, Britain and ultimately America the two states had common enemies. Having repeated Napoleon's mistake in June, Hitler now repeated Ludendorff's and Wilhelm II's in December: he, too, declared war on America.

In the long run, this committed America to a degree of military intervention in Europe she might otherwise not have contemplated, but in the early months of 1942 Japan's spectacular victories further weakened Germany's enemies. The Japanese swept through Hong Kong, Malaya, Singapore, the Philippines and the Dutch East Indies (now Indonesia). They inflicted grievous losses on the British navy, and threatened Australia and India, whose armies had hitherto formed an important part of British strength in the Middle East. And with the coming of the spring the campaigning advantage in Russia passed once more to the Germans, who extended their domain still further, thrusting deep into the Caucasus and reaching the River Volga at Stalingrad. They were even able to come to the aid of the Italian armies in North Africa, and in a brilliant campaign Field Marshal Rommel advanced to within sixty miles of the Suez Canal. While Japan bestrode the Pacific and Indian oceans, Hitler was master of all continental Europe except Sweden, Switzerland, Spain and Portugal, and of most of North Africa. It was the apogee of the Third Reich.

It was not only militarily that Nazism realized its potential in the years 1938–43. Politically, too, the years of caution and compromise were now over. The accelerating momentum in foreign policy after the *Anschluß* was paralleled by radicalization domestically. The annexations increased the competences of the police and the party, and the opportunities for their specialized skills. The number of concentration camp inmates, relatively stable at 10,000 until 1938, rose to 25,000 in 1939 and 100,000 in 1940. The *Kristallnacht* symbolized an intensification of the regime's racialist drive, and this reversion to the aims and methods of the *Kampfzeit* also required an easing-out of those public servants, borrowed from the older élites, who still held positions of responsibility. Schacht finally went in 1938; von Neurath, the career diplomat, gave way at the Foreign Ministry to von Ribbentrop, the *arriviste* sycophant; the army purges ensured the subordination of the Prussian officer corps.

But it was the outbreak of the war that created the atmosphere in which the values of the party could flourish without hindrance. The link between war and the realization of the Nazis' most psychopathic aspirations was so close that war appears as the logical, inevitable and inescapable climax of their seizure of power. This was so not merely because Hitler was determined to overthrow the Versailles system: he was, but better political judgement, greater courage, more skilful diplomacy by his opponents could have stopped him in his path. Nor was it because under Nazism the pre-1914 pan-German dream of European hegemony was revived, with its promise of plunder and slave labour for industrialists and landowners: this explains the popularity of Hitler's course of action, not why he embarked on it in the first place. War was the apotheosis of the Nazis' pseudo-Darwinian belief that life was a struggle for the survival of the fittest, of their dedication to the *Führerprinzip* at all levels, of their insistence on the total mobilization, the total politicization, the total integration into the movement, of every aspect of social, economic, intellectual and private life. The growth of internal tyranny after the outbreak of war is therefore not to be explained merely by military exigencies; on the contrary, the purpose of the war was to bring about the Nazi utopia in all its plenitude.

German conquests in east and west provided the perfect cover for the private, even secret, accomplishment of some of the Nazi aims. The conquered territories did not, in the main, come under the responsibility of established Reich Ministries; even the military had limited prerogatives in them. The Reich commissars appointed to rule them were essentially party satraps, and the army, the civil government and the regular judiciary, only too anxious 'not to know' what was happening, did not resist this exclusion. War was particularly favourable for the implementation of the Nazis' racial policies, which the regime wanted to carry out in secrecy. Thus the 'euthanasia' programme, i.e. the killing of all those suffering from mental or congenital diseases, on which Hitler had decided as early as 1935, was deliberately postponed until the outbreak of war. The conquest of Poland was almost immediately followed by a secret Führer decree 'zur Festigung des deutschen Volkstums' ('for the consolidation of German national life'), which charged Himmler with the task of settling Germans in the occupied territories and deporting 'volksfremde Bevölkerungsteile' ('ethnically alien sectors of the population'). Above all, but for the war the regime could never have embarked on that enterprise which has given it its greatest notoriety, the 'final solution of the Jewish question'. Exactly when Hitler gave the order for the extermination of all European Jews cannot be established: it is assumed that (significantly) the instruction was oral only. The programme began in earnest in January 1942, after Himmler's deputy, Reinhard Heydrich, had presided over a conference in the Berlin suburb of Wannsee. The 'final solution', like the programme for the extermination of other racial 'undesirables', such as gypsies or homosexuals, was the direct responsibility of the SS and SD, thus further extending Himmler's empire of command and patronage.

Indeed, by 1942–3 the grip of the totalitarian machine, not only on occupied Europe but on the German civilian population, was complete. Every major department of government was now in the hands of a trusted party potentate. The Ministry of Justice went to Otto Thierack, who had won his spurs in the lynch-justice of the *Volksgerichtshöfe* of the thirties; Sauckel, a *Gauleiter*, was put in charge of labour mobilization; Albert Speer, no ideological fanatic, but a close personal associate of Hitler, gained overall control of the economy; Himmler reached the summit of his power by becoming Minister of the Interior in addition to his other posts. But if the victories of 1939–42 made the building of this edifice possible, the reversal of military fortunes made its maintenance even more essential. Goebbels's propaganda apparatus – in 1943 he became *Beauftragter für den totalen Kriegseinsatz* (Commissar for Total War-Effort) – Sauckel's role as national chargehand, Speer's production empire with its millions of slave labourers now came into their own. It was only with the failure of *Blitzkrieg* in Russia that 'total war', which Britain had been waging since 1940, became a necessity for Germany.

The military glory of the Third Reich was brief. As in 1941, so in 1942, the onset of winter enabled the Russian armies to go over to the offensive. Counter-attacking from Stalingrad, they surrounded and destroyed the German army besieging it. And this time the thaw did not give the Germans a respite. Their retreat, once begun, continued throughout the summer. The battle of Stalingrad was the military turning-point of the war. Almost simultaneously the British defeated Rommel's army at El Alamein, while Anglo-American landings in French North Africa threatened his rear. By May 1943 North Africa was clear of Axis troops. In July the Allies landed in Sicily; in September the Fascist Grand Council deposed Mussolini and Italy signed an armistice. While the Russians continued to bear the brunt of the land fighting against Germany, Britain and America stepped up their bombing offensive and, thanks to improved radar, ended the menace of German submarines to transatlantic convoys.

By the spring of 1944 enough men, materials and ships had been assembled for the eagerly awaited Allied assault on western Europe, one for which the Germans had prepared by building the *Westwall* along the Channel coast. On 6 June British, American and Canadian troops landed in Normandy. Two months later a smaller army landed along the Mediterranean coast of France. Aided by the increasingly powerful French Resistance they liberated Paris and Marseilles on the same day, 25 August. Neither in the east nor in the west was Allied progress easy: the Germans continued to resist strongly and to pursue even more energetically their genocidal frenzies. Indeed, nothing illustrates better the strange priorities of the Nazi regime than the way in which badly needed men and transport were commandeered to shunt more and more Jews into the gas-chambers of Auschwitz and Treblinka while decisive battles were being lost at the very gateways to central Europe.

Yet this determination could not disguise that it was no longer within the power of any German Government to determine the future of Germany. Meeting at Casablanca, at the height of the battle of Stalingrad, Churchill and Roosevelt announced their formula for ending the war: unconditional surrender by Germany. Stalin, though not present, endorsed it. Though Allied propaganda had always emphasized that Hitler and Nazism, not the German people, were the enemy, it was now obvious that the political reconstruction of Germany would have to follow the complete capitulation, not only of the German armies, but of the German state.

Initially the Allied powers were attracted by the notion of partitioning Germany into its older constituent units, particularly in order to weaken Prussia and end its grip on German policy-making. At their first meeting in Teheran, in November 1943, Churchill, Roosevelt and Stalin agreed on this principle. For a time the Western powers toyed with the even more radical proposal, elaborated by the US Secretary of the Treasury, Henry Mogenthau, of dismantling the greater part of German industry and restricting the German economy to agriculture. As victory drew nearer, the attractions of both agrarianization and dismemberment receded. It was obvious that the end of the war would leave a political vacuum in Germany which would initially be filled by the victorious powers themselves. Whichever of the victor states could wrest the greatest influence in the post-war disposal of Germany's economic and territorial resources had great prizes to hope for; the case for preserving these resources therefore grew stronger. Accordingly at their Yalta conference in February, 1945, the Big Three concentrated on more immediate problems, the demarcation lines between their zones of military occupation, with added provision for a fourth,

French, zone. That it was these zonal borders, and not the earlier schemes for resurrecting 'historic' units, which would determine the frontiers of the post-war German states was at that stage neither intended nor expected.

Though the Nazi Government was, outwardly at least, unaffected by the publication of these Allied plans, the prospects of ruinous defeat, and the now overwhelming evidence of the criminality of the regime, stirred the first organized attempts at resistance. Despite the bombing, the hunger and the mounting casualty toll at the front, a popular revolt was out of the question. Strikes of the kind that had broken out in 1917–18 were not to be contemplated: they would be immediately crushed. The most likely leaders of such a popular uprising, Socialists or trade unionists with roots in the pre-1933 Labour movement, had been effectively immobilized – they were either in exile, or in concentration camps, or, at best, living privately under surveillance. Probably the biggest success of Nazi propaganda was to inculcate in ordinary people an overwhelming fear and horror of Russia and Communism, cancelling out any war-weariness or other dissatisfaction. The only conspiracies likely to succeed would have to come from within groups that still held power or influence – the army, industry, the Churches, perhaps even party dissidents: in other words, not from anti-Nazis of the first hour, but from men who had turned, perhaps quite late in the day, from collaboration to disgust.

This was indeed the form which the one serious plot against Hitler took. Its leaders bore some of the proudest names in Prussian history – Moltke, Stauffenberg, Yorck von Wartenburg. They had links with the intelligence services and with senior generals. As their political figurehead they chose Carl Goerdeler, a former DNVP member and pre-war Mayor of Leipzig. Gradually – for what united them was hatred of the Third Reich's institutionalized violence – they became convinced that Hitler would have to be assassinated as a prerequisite for all other action; once he was out of the way, the rule of law could be established and the Allies approached for an armistice. But the bomb which they planted in Hitler's headquarters on 20 July 1944 failed to kill him. The conspirators were rounded up: those who did not commit suicide were subjected to tortures, to the obscene degradation of trial by the *Volksgerichtshof*, whose president heaped abuse at them, and finally to death by slow strangulation, suspended from meathooks, their agonies filmed for Hitler's delectation.

But if they had succeeded? That the Allies would have deviated, at that stage of the war, from their declared objective of unconditional surrender seems out of the question. They desired a free hand, and were within reach of it. A repetition of 1918, with another stab-in-the-back legend, was not inviting. To many on the Allied side the plotters appeared as nationalists and militarists who opposed Hitler only because he was losing the war. Their naïve proposals for Germany's post-war frontiers – those of 1914, plus Austria, the Sudetenland and South Tyrol – confirmed these suspicions.

The war lasted nine months longer. In January 1945 the Russians launched their final great offensive, crossing the River Oder; in March the Americans crossed the Rhine; on 25 April the two armies met at Torgau on the Elbe. Berlin, which Hitler had intended to leave for a last stand in the mountain fastnesses of Bavaria, was cut off and within reach of Russian artillery. Hitler had no choice but to make his final dispositions as even his closest associates began to go their own way. Goering tried to take over the reins of government from Bavaria, Himmler tried frantically to negotiate peace through Swedish intermediaries. Hitler expelled both from the party and empowered Grand Admiral Doenitz to head the Government. On 30 April he and his wife, Eva Braun, committed suicide in the *Führerbunker*, now a few hundred yards from the firing line. Goebbels followed his example. As military resistance wilted further, Doenitz sought a cease-fire from General Eisenhower. On 7 April 1945 the instrument of unconditional surrender, applying to all fronts, was signed at Reims, to come into force at midnight.

It was not merely the Third Reich which had ceased to exist. There was no German army any more. After the extinction of the shadowy Doenitz Government at the end of May, there was no political authority in Germany except that of the Allied military commanders. Given the destruction, the lack of even the most elementary means of subsistence, the uncontrolled westward stream of refugees, it is arguable that even ordered society had broken down. The theatrical analogy of the *Götterdämmerung*, so dear to the imagination of the Nazi leaders, had revolutionized Germany, as the upheavals of 1918 and 1933 had not even begun to do.

From Year Zero to Year One

For the first twelve months the overriding preoccupation of most Germans was to find a roof and secure the next meal. That active

German interest in the country's government was in any case unwelcome to the victors emerged from the directive that General Eisenhower received from the Allied Governments: 'No political activities of any kind shall be countenanced, unless authorized by you.' The Big Three, for their part, met for the last time in Potsdam, in July 1945, to elaborate a joint plan for the future of Germany. In contrast with the wartime discussions the emphasis was now on the unity of Germany. The occupation zones were not to be seen as instruments of dismemberment and the individual Allied commanders acted collectively as the Control Council. The long-term task of this Control Council was to draw up a peace treaty, for acceptance by an eventual 'government of Germany'. The Western Allies also agreed to the *de facto* annexation by Poland of all territories east of the rivers Oder and Neisse (East Prussia, Pomerania, most of Silesia and some of Brandenburg), while the area round Königsberg went to the Soviet Union. The final shape of Germany's frontiers, however, was to await the peace treaty. The Big Three also confirmed their reparations claim of 20,000 million dollars, already agreed at Yalta, to be collected by the Allies directly from their respective zones. Lastly they agreed on the 'orderly and humane' expulsion of all Germans from the Polish-occupied provinces and the Sudetenland.

There has been no peace treaty with Germany and none is in sight. Potsdam was the last act of Allied unity. Shortly thereafter the dropping of the first nuclear bombs on Hiroshima and Nagasaki ushered in that 'balance of terror' which has characterized the relationship of the two super-powers since 1945. Given their growing mutual distrust, and the suspicions that each harboured of the other's expansionist tendency, that joint administration of a unitary Germany to which they had put their signatures in Potsdam remained and remains a mirage. It was therefore inter-Allied disunity, which had many facets, that caused the incipient division of Germany, not the other way round. But since the German Question was one that affected the victor powers' interests and emotions exceptionally strongly, and since it was in Germany that their armies faced each other directly, their conflicting aims there helped to drive them further apart.

Still, it is significant that when Churchill first spoke of the 'Iron Curtain' that had descended on Europe, he placed it 'from Stettin on the Baltic to Trieste on the Adriatic', that is, between the Soviet zone of Germany and Poland, not across Germany. That was in March 1946. Churchill's geography was soon out of date. In June the free movement of persons and goods between the Soviet and Western zones was halted, in response to Soviet alarm at the westward flight of property and people. Indeed it was economic policies, rather than strategic or ideological preconceptions, that first sent the zones on their different ways. Russia was naturally anxious to make good, as ruthlessly as possible, the damage and destruction that the Germans had inflicted, not least through the policy of 'scorched earth' in the wake of their retreat. America and Britain, on the other hand, after initially participating in the dismantling programme, soon gave higher priority to the economic revival of Germany, and the first step towards this was the fusion of their respective zones of occupation into the 'Bi-Zone' in 1947. Western unity was not complete, however: the French attitude towards reparations was closer to that of the Russians than of the 'Anglo-Saxons'. But France could not indefinitely pursue a German policy separate from those of both America and Russia; when, therefore, in order to stimulate the economy, a drastic currency reform was planned in the Bi-Zone, the French could not stand aloof. The reform, announced in June 1948, and covering all three Western zones, was the biggest step yet towards the division of Germany. The Soviets replied with a currency reform of their own, and a dispute followed on whether the Soviet move should apply to the whole of Berlin (which was geographically within the Soviet zone, but had a separate four-power occupation statute) or only to the Soviet sector of the capital, with the three Western sectors integrated with the economy of the Western zones. This led to the creation of two municipalities in Berlin, Eastern and Western, and to the Russian attempt to isolate West Berlin from the Western zones which became known as the Berlin Blockade, and which lasted seven months until Western determination to keep Berlin supplied by air was demonstrated. Spring 1948 also saw the last meeting of the Control Council, when the Russian representative walked out for good.

Gradually, over three years, the various moves in the contest over Germany had become regularized. The Western powers feared, especially after the Communist coup in Czechoslovakia in March 1948, a divided Europe subject to Russian expansion, and responded by dividing Germany as the lesser evil. The Russians, fearing a division of Germany that gave capitalist forces a predominant influence, put pressure on Berlin to secure Western concessions. In 1948 the first round went to the West; thereafter, with division a *fait accompli*, the roles were reversed. It was the Russians who now saw the division of

Germany as an earnest of their security, while the West, counting on the unpopularity of Russian occupation policies with the population, saw in reunification a possibility of extending Western influence. The second round, like the first, went to the power with the greatest stake in the *status quo*, this time Russia.

By 1948 the debate on the future of Germany was no longer restricted to the victor powers. Germans, both as politicians and as citizens, had once more begun to participate, and were lending increasing weight to decision-making. Even at the beginning of the occupation the Allies had needed the support of reliable civilian administrators, and their choice inevitably fell on men who were known to have been involved in anti-Nazi, or at least non-Nazi, public life – church dignitaries, labour leaders, office-holders in left-wing, Liberal or Catholic parties. Though some Nazis managed to insinuate themselves into responsible positions, the early years of the occupation were those of 'de-Nazification' – the painstaking inquiry into the political pasts of millions of people to test their fitness for public employment, or, where necessary, to put them on trial; and of re-education, a crash programme to train Germans in democratic civic virtues. The climax of this militant reckoning with National Socialism came with the War Crimes Tribunal at Nürnberg, where those major Nazi leaders who survived were put on trial for their crimes against humanity. (In addition to Hitler and Goebbels, those missing included Hitler's deputy, Bormann, and Himmler, who had swallowed poison when arrested by British troops.)

Since the victors could not in the long run deny democracy to the Germans, and since they were increasingly dependent on the goodwill of local functionaries, they decided early to encourage the formation of parties devoted to democratic principles, while reserving their right to veto suspect formations. The earliest parties to emerge from illegality were, understandably, the Social Democrats and Communists, whose organization had never been entirely smashed by the Third Reich and who could count on the greatest number of faithful supporters, reinforced by returning exiles. Among the 'bourgeois' politicians the problems were greater. With the exception of the Zentrum they had, before 1933, been notorious for their fragmentation, their poor discipline and weak organization. Partly to provide effective competition to the Left, partly in a genuine effort to learn from the mistakes of the past, the politicians of the Right and Centre came together in two major groupings – Catholics and some Protestant Conservatives in the Christian Democratic Union (CDU) and Liberals with some moderate

Nationalists in the Free Democratic Party (FDP, or LDP, Liberal Democratic Party, in the Soviet zone). In this course they were encouraged by the occupation powers, who were anxious to license as few parties as possible, partly for ease of control, but also because they saw in multi-partism a threat to effective democracy. From 1946 elections were once more held, at first only at the municipal levels, but by the end of the year for the constituent assemblies of the sixteen *Länder* into which the territory of Germany had been provisionally divided.

The elections further emphasized the growing divergence between the Soviet and Western zones. In their own zone the Russians enforced a fusion between the Communist and Social Democratic parties, on the pattern to be followed elsewhere in eastern Europe. Even so, the new Socialist Unity Party (SED) failed to win majorities in a part of the country with strong left-wing traditions, and after 1946 there were no further free elections in the Soviet zone. In the Western zones the Communists had much less support and the Social Democrats initially emerged as the strongest single party. Its impeccable anti-Nazi credentials and its superior organization helped, as did the economic misery in which the bulk of the population lived.

Whether these early party formations and elections would suffice to establish a viable democracy was an open question. The failure of Weimar had done nothing to encourage faith in parliamentary institutions, the experience of National Socialism had merely heightened disgust with all politics. Yet the Third Reich had also, unwittingly, brought about changes which might help, rather than hinder, democratic development. The exigencies of total war had forced the regime to turn German society in exactly the opposite direction from that which its leaders had originally wanted and its followers had expected. The peasant romanticism and anti-capitalist demagogy that constituted its social programme were incompatible with preparing for the war, let alone winning it. Industrialization, specialization, technological advance, promotion by merit were the measures that the regime was forced to adopt. The 'Americanization' of German society did not begin under Adenauer; ironically, it began under Hitler. It was a process that left a population less tradition-bound, less hierarchically minded, less steeped in nostalgia for a golden age than either under Weimar or under the Second Empire.

The political persecutions under Hitler also had their effect. Although his first victims were socialists and democrats, he later turned on precisely those forces who had given him their crucial support in the early thirties but who, one by one, saw him overstepping even the generous lines that they had been prepared to draw. All the pillars of the conservative order in Germany, the civil service and the judiciary, the schools and the Churches, but above all the army, felt his genius for destruction. The process which began in 1938, with the army purges and the displacement of career bureaucrats, culminated in his indiscriminate vengeance after the July Plot of 1944. Hitler certainly overthrew democracy and legality, but he also weakened the traditional opponents of liberalism and modernity. He destroyed Prussia more thoroughly than he destroyed German Marxism. True, Nazism made no positive contribution to Germany's political development, but its career and end ensured that the conservative coalition of industrial wealth and agrarian-military politics, which had dominated, with few breaks, since the 1870s, could never revive.

The dual reaction against Nazi tyranny and Prussian authoritarianism explain much in the political development of early post-war Germany. The first representative body to transcend the boundaries of the individual *Länder* was the *Wirtschaftlicher Rat* (Economic Council), representative of the *Länder* governments of the Bi-Zone in which the CDU and FDP between them had a small majority. Although the decision to regenerate the German economy through highly competitive private enterprise and the creation of a new currency, the *Deutschmark*, was that of the Western powers, it met with the approval of the Economic Council and of the Bi-Zonal economic director, Ludwig Erhard. Contrary to what the Social Democrats had assumed, most Germans did not think that the solution to their poverty lay in Socialism. Regimentation of the economy they associated with the ration queues and favouritism of the Third Reich and the incipient totalitarianism of the Soviet zone. Although the currency reform favoured those who possessed industrial capital or other real assets at the expense of those who had cash savings, and initially caused much hardship, it also ended overnight the black market and barter economy in goods and services. It was the beginning of the boom known rather misleadingly as the *Wirtschaftswunder*. The new economic competition, which was also identified ideologically with the 'free world', cushioned on Germany's well-established social security system, formed the basis of the *soziale Marktwirtschaft* (social market economy) over which Ludwig Erhard presided as Minister of Economics from 1949 to 1963. He may well claim to have been Germany's first successful Liberal statesman.

The same similarity of views between the Allied administration and the leading German politicians that had appeared over party formation and the currency reform appeared at the next, more ambitious step, the creation of a constituent Parliamentary Council for the three Western zones. This, too, consisted of representatives of the *Länder*, so that the CDU and FDP once more outnumbered the Left. The chairman of the British Zone CDU, Dr Konrad Adenauer, was elected president of the Council. Despite disagreements among the occupying powers them-selves, among the parties and, indeed, within them, and some disputes between the two sides, an acceptable constitution for a West German state, the *Grundgesetz* (Basic Law) was drawn up within eight months. The reason for this speed was that on aims, even if not on means, there was wide agreement. Even the SPD, traditionally the most centralizing of the German parties, conceded that a federal structure gave less opening to an abuse of power.

Remembering the Enabling Law of 1933, the constitution-makers gave considerable powers to the Bundesrat, or Upper House of the proposed parliament, the voice of the *Länder*. Remembering the use made of presidential decrees under Weimar, they weakened the powers of the Head of State. Remembering the effects of twelve years of single-party rule they voted for proportional representation, which would make inter-party co-operation almost inescapable, despite the odium that attached to Weimar multi-partism. There was no provision for plebiscite or referendum, but great emphasis on a constitutional court. The cynic might say that these were gimmicks for a retrospective prevention of the *Machtergreifung*. No doubt that is what attracted the Western powers to them; no doubt these cautious statesmen, who admired democracy but also distrusted it, acted as men do when they have been burned once. But there was a further reason for the shape of their proposals. These men from Baden and Bavaria, from Hanover and the Rhineland, spoke for non-Prussian Germany. Provincial, particularist, but also internationalist and European-minded, they saw a chance to undo the work of Bismarck, to revive the forces that had gone under in 1866. Half the population of the Western zones was Catholic, compared with one-third in the Reich.

On 1 September 1949 the German Federal Republic was established, with a provisional capital at Bonn. The elections in the same month confirmed the swing to the right that had accompanied the currency reform and the outbreak of the cold war: the CDU emerged as the strongest party and its leader, Konrad Adenauer, became the first Federal Chancellor, at the head of an anti-Socialist coalition.

Almost parallel developments had been taking place in the Soviet zone. A series of *Volkskongresse*, dominated by the SED and rather more pliable to the wishes of the occupying power than their Western counterparts, paved the way for the establishment of the German Democratic Republic on 7 October 1949. Its Prime Minister was an ex-Social Democrat, Otto Grotewohl, but real power rested on the First Secretary of the SED, Walter Ulbricht, a veteran Communist hatchet-man. In contrast with the Western zones the expropriation of private industry and large estates was well advanced, that of small-scale agriculture was to follow.

The two German states have lasted, in the way that the provisional often does. Neither, at the time of writing, recognizes the other; neither is a member of the United Nations. Berlin is still subject to Allied military government. The completeness of the physical barrier between them is more recent than 1949. Until the building of the Berlin Wall in 1961 travel was still possible via Berlin, and some two million East Germans settled in the West. Nor was 1949 the beginning of anything more than limited sovereignty. Not until 1954 did the Western powers abandon their occupation rights in the Federal Republic, as a prelude to West Germany's joining NATO. The Soviet Union did not follow suit until the German-Soviet treaty of 1970. Though the German Democratic Republic enjoys full sovereign rights *vis-à-vis* the Soviet Union and has been a member of the Warsaw Pact since 1954, these are presumably subject to the doctrine of 'limited sovereignty', promulgated by Mr Brezhnev in 1968 at the time of the invasion of Czechoslovakia.

Despite their prosperity, their stability, their economic power, their military significance and their diplomatic influence, both Germanies remain in their separate waiting-rooms, ritually reciting the promise of a peace treaty with a united Germany enshrined in the Potsdam document. The historian can safely conclude that the life of a German nation-state began in 1871 and ended in 1945. Whatever else, good and bad, has survived from that experience, the institutions of national unity have not.

Bibliography

* = a book originally published in German

GENERAL SURVEYS

BALFOUR, M. *West Germany*. Nations of the World. London, 1968.
DAHRENDORF, R. *Democracy and Society in Germany*.* London. 1967.

MANN, G. *A History of Germany since 1789.*★ London, 1968.
PASCAL, R. *Growth of Modern Germany.* London, 1946.
PINSON, K. S. *Modern Germany. Its History and Civilisation.* 2nd edn. New York, 1966.
STOLPER, G. *The German Economy, 1870 to the Present.* Rev. edn. London, 1967.

WORKS ON INDIVIDUAL TOPICS 1871–1918

ROSENBERG, A. *The Birth of the German Republic, 1871–1918.*★ London, 1931. (Also published as *Imperial Germany.* New York, 1970.)
EYCK, E. *Bismarck and the German Empire.* London, 1950.
BALFOUR, M. *The Kaiser and his Times.* London, 1964.
ROEHL, J. C. G. *Germany Without Bismarck.* London, 1964.
CRAIG, G. *The Politics of the Prussian Army.* Oxford, 1955.
STEINBERG, J. *Yesterday's Deterrent. Tirpitz and the Birth of the German Battle Fleet.* London, 1966.
DEHIO, L. *Germany and World Politics in the Twentieth Century.*★ London, 1959.
FISCHER, F. *Germany's Aims in the First World War.*★ London, 1967.
ROTH, G. *The Social Democrats in Imperial Germany.* Totowa, N.J., 1963.
PULZER, P. G. J. *The Rise of Political Anti-Semitism in Germany and Austria.* New York, 1964.
RYDER, A. J. *The German Revolution of 1918.* Cambridge, 1967.

WORKS ON INDIVIDUAL TOPICS 1919–1949

EYCK, E. *History of the Weimar Republic.*★ 2 vols. Oxford, 1962–3.
NICHOLLS, A. J. *Weimar and the Rise of Hitler.* London, 1968.
BULLOCK, A. *Hitler. A Study in Tyranny.* Rev. edn. London, 1964.
SONTHEIMER, K. *Antidemokratisches Denken in der Weimarer Republik.* Munich, 1962.
ESCHENBURG, T. (ed.) *The Path to Dictatorship.*★ New York, 1966.
SCHOENBAUM, D. L. *Hitler's Social Revolution. Class and Status in Nazi Germany.* New York, 1966.
BROSZAT, M. *Der Staat Hitlers.* Dtv-Weltgeschichte des 20. Jahrhunderts, Vol. IX. Munich, 1969.
TAYLOR, A. J. P. *The Origins of the Second World War.* 2nd edn. London, 1963.
ROTHFELS, H. *The German Opposition to Hitler.* London, 1961.
MERKL, P. *The Origins of the West German Republic.* Oxford, 1963.
GROSSER, A. *Germany in Our Time. A Political History of the Postwar Years.* London, 1971.

INTERESTING COLLECTIONS OF SHORT DOCUMENTS

BOEHME, H. (ed.) *Die Reichsgründung.* Dtv-dokumente 428.
RITTER, G. A. (ed.) *Historisches Lesebuch 2, 1871–1914.* Fischer-Bücherei 834.
KOTOWSKI, G. (ed.) *Historisches Lesebuch 3, 1914–1933.* Fischer-Bücherei 852.
HOFER, W. (ed.) *Der Nationalsozialismus 1933–1945.* Fischer-Bücherei 172.
ROEHL, J. C. G. (ed.) *From Bismarck to Hitler.* London, 1970.
REMAK, J. (ed.) *The Nazi Years. A Documentary History.* Englewood Cliffs, N.J., 1969.

6 The German Idealists and Their Successors

PATRICK GARDINER

Introductory

'Ours is a significant epoch, a time of ferment, when the spirit has made a jerk, transcended its previous form, and is gaining a new one. The whole mass of previous notions, concepts, the bonds of the world, have dissolved and collapsed like a dream image. A new emergence of the spirit is at hand.'

It was in these ringing terms that Hegel, lecturing at Jena in 1806, characterized the revolutionary temper of his age, going on to claim that philosophy must 'welcome its appearance and recognize it'. And it is certainly true that during the early part of the nineteenth century German philosophy took a new and arresting turn. Not only do the developments of that time constitute in themselves a curiously fascinating chapter in the history of ideas, but they also had far-reaching consequences, involving an intellectual upheaval whose repercussions are still discernible in our own period. It is not going too far to say that, had such developments not occurred, our present view of ourselves and of our place in the world would be importantly different from what in fact it is. The theories and conceptions forged by the German Idealists and those who immediately succeeded them have left an enduring mark on Western thought and consciousness.

This does not mean that the nature of their contribution is easy to describe. On the contrary, its interpretation and appraisal is an exceedingly complicated and many-sided affair. Some of the more specific problems and difficulties raised will emerge in what follows; at the outset, however, it will be useful to mention a few of the general and pervasive features of what was written that are liable to present obstacles to understanding. These derive in part from the novelty of what the theorists concerned were trying to communicate, but are also due to the manner in which they chose to express themselves.

It is notorious, for instance, that the Idealists tended to employ an exceptionally cumbrous and opaque mode of literary presentation. In this respect alone they differ from most of their great European predecessors. The elegance of Descartes, the methodical precision of Spinoza, the lucidity and respect for the vernacular typified by the British empiricists – such qualities are notably absent from the style of writers like Fichte, Schelling and Hegel. Admittedly, in some of their so-called 'popular' works they showed themselves capable of being reasonably clear and direct; their major treatises, on the other hand, are composed in a prose that is studded with obscure quasi-technical expressions and with sentences whose tortuous and barbarous complexity has proved the bane of their translators. In adopting this manner they seem to have been consciously following the example set by Kant, himself no master of lucid exposition; but, whatever the reason, the fact remains that they all too often appear needlessly to try the patience of their readers and even, at times, to invite Nietzsche's gibe that they regarded being boring as in some way morally meritorious.

Another difficulty, perhaps more fundamental from a modern point of view, concerns the kind of project upon which philosophers of the period conceived themselves to be engaged. It was characteristic of them to set out and formulate their ideas within the framework of comprehensive 'systems' in terms of which they apparently sought to provide an account or explanation of reality considered as a whole. Moreover, the type of account offered was not propounded as merely affording some sort of inclusive description of the universe as we ordinarily find it; nor, again, as if it were a form of very general scientific theory, inductively established and confirmed. Rather, the impression given is that the systems in question sprang from a profound philosophical reflection, an overall rational insight, which operated at a deeper level than the piecemeal procedures of everyday empirical inquiry and which issued, furthermore, in a conception of the world radically dissimilar to the familiar 'commonsense' picture. Because of this, it has become common to regard them as presupposing a view of the function and scope of philosophy that has for long been subject to the strictures of English-speaking philosophers. For, according to a line of British and (later) American critics stretching back to the seventeenth century, all attempts to understand and explain reality in terms that transcend the limits set by sense-perception and the resources of scientific inquiry are open to very serious objections. In general, these writers have contended that, so far as our knowledge of matters of fact is concerned, no proposition is acceptable unless it can be shown to rest securely upon the findings of observation and experiment, and they have strenuously resisted the notion that alternative methods are available – purely logical reasoning for instance, or an alleged suprasensuous intuition of the ultimate nature of things – for the discovery of informative truths about the world. More recently, such claims have been supplemented and reinforced by arguments deriving from the philosophical analysis of language, with the consequence that the very possibility of attaching any determinate sense to transcendental assertions and theories has been put in question. Inasmuch, therefore, as the products of German Idealism can be said to exemplify *a priori* metaphysical speculation of this kind, it is scarcely surprising that they should have acquired a somewhat suspect reputation in the Anglo-Saxon world.

It is difficult to deny that the German system-builders often spoke in a way that seems amply to justify the unsympathetic constructions placed upon their work by sceptical empiricists. For example, they undoubtedly wrote at times as if they were endowed with a mysterious capacity, the credentials of which they deemed it unnecessary to explain, for divining the innermost character of the universe. Nor, again, is it hard to deflate some of their more high-flown pronouncements by raising pointed questions concerning the actual significance, the precise conditions of application, of the misty abstractions they so freely used. And, with this in mind, it is tempting to move (as, indeed, some of their contemporary critics did move) to the conclusion that their pretentious terminology served merely to camouflage an underlying absence of meaningful thought or content. But though instances can certainly be cited in its support, as a general truth such a conclusion appears wide of the mark.

To understand why this should be so, it is important to realize that it is frequently both possible and illuminating to read a metaphysical system in more than one way. What from one point of view may seem an unplausible extravaganza, purporting to portray states of affairs inaccessible to ordinary or scientific modes of cognition, may present itself from another as constituting an attempt to formulate and develop a theoretical scheme whose principal concern is with the concrete facts of human life and experience. When looked at from the latter standpoint, the metaphysical enterprise may be seen as one of setting these already familiar facts in a different light, an unaccustomed perspective, rather than one of descrying recondite facts that elude discovery by normal means. Governed by some central vision of existence in general, or forcibly impressed by certain of its features which he feels to have been insufficiently recognized or understood, the speculative philosopher can frequently be regarded as seeking to construct a framework of categories and principles that entails sweeping revisions of accepted modes of approaching and representing empirical phenomena. The fact that, in the course of restructuring the scheme of ideas through which it has become habitual to look at and think about experience, he may at the same time appear to be delineating the features of some transcendent reality beyond the range of established forms of inquiry should not be allowed to obscure the double aspect which his procedure often displays.

The notion that metaphysical theories are intelligible at more than one level is not in itself new; as we shall see later on, some such thought underlies the method of 'transformational criticism' which Feuerbach and (above all) Marx were to apply to the Hegelian system in the 1840s. Nevertheless, it is unnecessary to take account of Marx's specific concerns and aims in order to appreciate, in a very general fashion, how points of the kind just mentioned bear upon the interpretation of early nineteenth-century German philosophy. Their relevance perhaps emerges most clearly from a consideration of the historical context within which Idealist doctrines initially took shape.

As some of the authors of these doctrines themselves explicitly recognized, they were in many ways consciously reacting against an intellectual trend which had prevailed in Europe during the previous century. One important key to the set of multifarious ideas and attitudes that has come to be known as 'the Enlightenment' lay in the overriding priority attached by its representatives to the progress of natural science. Theological notions and explanations were in general rigorously eschewed; not only were the tenets of religious orthodoxy regarded as having their roots in primitive superstition and ignorance, but they were also treated as affording one of the instruments by which the ruling classes of society kept the mass of the population in a condition of bemused and uncritical servitude. By contrast scientific discoveries, and in particular those of Newton, were held to have opened up possibilities of unlimited advance, not least in the sphere of human affairs; the belief that scientific conceptions and methods, analogous to those that had proved so fruitful in acquiring understanding and control of physical nature, could be extended to cover the domains of human life and behaviour attained in some quarters the status of an unchallengeable truism. Hence a great deal of eighteenth-century thought about man, whether considered individually or in a social setting, tended to exhibit a pervasively naturalistic or materialistic bias. This bias found most extreme expression in works like La Mettrie's *L'Homme machine* and Holbach's *Système de la nature*, but it was also shared, to a greater or lesser degree, by a host of other writers.

It was inevitable, in such a climate of opinion, that a variety of traditional and respected assumptions about human nature should suffer a fundamental reappraisal; amongst others, free-will doctrines that ascribed to men a causally undetermined power of choice, and affiliated conceptions that portrayed the human mind or 'soul' as an incorporeal entity whose operations were independent of physical factors or organic processes. Apart from their unwelcome religious associations, notions like these were felt to be alien to, and (unless radically reinterpreted) inconsistent with, the scientific approach which it was the aim of Enlightenment theorists to advocate and apply. In their place an attempt was made to substitute mechanistic models of human thought and activity, all of which presupposed some form of determinism, whether physiological, psychological, or a combination of the two. Thus the individual human mind tended to be pictured as a field of forces and elements which could be methodically listed and examined; these would then be found to be subject, like everything else in the universe, to determinate regularities and laws. It was argued, moreover, that a similar situation obtained at the stage of social life, even if the complexity of the phenomena involved made the detection of uniformities more difficult. It was essential, all the same, that their discovery should be undertaken; for only by taking account of the laws that necessarily govern human motivation and behaviour at all times and at all levels would it be possible to encompass a rational reorganization of society answering to the universal needs and interests of men. The scientific convictions integral to the Enlightenment outlook were inextricably bound up with an equally firm belief in the amelioration of the human condition through social and political reform.

In the course of developing their own theories the German Idealists, openly or by implication, questioned a great many of the cardinal assumptions and purposes that had inspired their eighteeth-century predecessors in France and England. This comes out in various ways; it can be seen, for example, in their manner of depicting certain aspects of the natural world, in the approach they adopted to religion, in their notions of historical evolution and change, in their political recommendations and ideals. It was, however, their refusal to accept the status typically accorded to man himself in the Enlightenment scheme of things that perhaps constituted the mainspring and centre of their most profound divergences. As has already been indicated, eighteenth-century thinkers tended to assume the adequacy of scientific concepts and modes of explanation to all departments of experience, the paradigm of this type of understanding being conceived to lie in the accounts offered by Newton and his followers of the character of physical reality. Hence there was a strong inclination to argue that what happened in the human sphere must be either directly explicable by, or reducible to, physical factors, or else that it must be such that laws similar in form and scope to those found applicable to the physical world could be formulated to cover specifically psychological or mental phenomena. A major, indeed a crucial, component of Idealist thinking consisted in its reversal of the priorities implied by these suggestions.

It was no accident, for instance, that the Idealists took as their point of departure what they were prone to call 'the subject', this term comprising such notions as those of rationality, purpose and will. In their opinion what was in question here was in an important sense original and underived, and there must therefore be a misconception involved in trying to explain and understand it by reference to the terms in which we find it convenient to classify and interpret events falling within such fields of inquiry as physics or chemistry. Rather than attempt to exhibit the phenomena of thought and intelligent behaviour as understandable in the light of inquiries like these, we should instead recognize that the rational subject is itself the source of the categories and schemes through which empirical science is able to comprehend the objective world. As such, it has to be investigated and discussed in ways appropriate to it, and not along lines suggested by scientifically inspired models which necessarily give rise to distortion and misrepresentation. Once this is acknowledged the way stands open to a fresh approach, not only to the problem of achieving a true insight into human nature and the life of the mind, but also to the larger question of how the philosophical enterprise should itself be conceived. For the German Idealists, indeed, the two were intimately fused, their more fruitful and influential philosophical ideas being integrally related, in one way or another, to the human studies.

What was involved in the change of outlook envisaged? It would not be correct to suppose that there existed for the thinkers concerned some monolithic body of doctrine to which they unanimously subscribed: there was perhaps more agreement in the rejection of previous standpoints than consonance in positive theory. It is possible, none the less, to identify certain, very general, common themes. The most convenient approach to these lies through a consideration of the Kantian philosophy.

The Kantian Background

At first sight it might seem surprising that the creators of the Idealist systems should be thought to owe much to Immanuel Kant (1724-1804). For, whatever his divergences from eighteenth-century empiricism in other respects, Kant at least shared with such philosophers as Hume the belief that our knowledge of the world is confined to what lies within the sphere of possible experience, and he expressly denied the validity of attempts by speculative metaphysicians to step outside that sphere in order to provide an all-embracing portrayal of ultimate reality. Moreover, he was at one with most Enlightenment thinkers in his profound regard for Newton and in his general acceptance of the prevailing scientific conception of the natural world. Even so, there were strands in Kant's thought which were taken up by his less cautious and scientifically minded successors in a manner that helps to explain the form their own doctrines finally assumed.

In the first place Kant developed an epistemology that represented a significant departure from earlier views. In previous theories of human knowledge it had been customary to picture the human intellect as confronting a ready-made world of physical objects and events, the cognitive function of the mind being regarded as one of recording what was presented to it in a passive, mirror-like fashion. By contrast, Kant treated the mind's role in knowledge as being, in a quite crucial sense, active or creative. For it is we (Kant claimed) who, as thinkers and observers, ourselves supply the basic structure or framework within which the raw material of sensory experience is organized so as to constitute an objective world – a world susceptible to rational investigation and concerning which we can make communicable judgements. It was with this in mind that he spoke of there being certain *a priori* 'forms of intuition' (space and time) and universal concepts or 'categories' (such as *cause* and *substance*) which the conscious subject imposes upon the presentations of sense. The fact that what we are aware of appears to us as spatio-temporal in form and as ordered in relations of causal dependence presupposes the operation of the intellect; it is this that, by ordering and synthesizing the sensory data, makes knowledge as we normally understand it possible.

This epistemological thesis, with its stress upon the creative function of the mind and its implication that the natural world as it presents itself to us has the status of being 'appearance' only, represented the essence of Kant's celebrated 'Copernican revolution' in philosophy. And it was connected with a further important conception, which was also influential in the development of subsequent Idealist thought. This was the doctrine of the *Ding an sich*, or 'thing in itself'. Kant was certainly insistent that the structural ideas and principles he had referred to in propounding his theory of knowledge were restricted in their valid employment to the empirical or phenomenal domain; there could thus be no question of using them to make justifiable cognitive claims about the nature and characteristics of what lay beyond that sphere. At the same time, he was far from wishing to maintain that phenomenal reality exhausted the field of what could be said to exist. In asserting that what was apprehended in perception ultimately amounted to no more than 'appearance', Kant nevertheless assumed that it must be possible to speak of there being something of which the appearances concerned were the phenomenal manifestation; he suggested, too, that whatever this something was 'affected' the conscious subject so as to give rise to the sensory data that formed an ineliminable component of all objective experience. Nor, incidentally, could the subject so affected be itself included among the phenomena of which it was, in a sense, the architect. Kant was therefore led to introduce the idea of what he called 'noumena' or 'things in themselves': these must be presupposed as, so to speak, a necessity of thought, even though – since they were *ex hypothesi* inexperienceable – there could be no knowledge, or indeed intelligible description, of their actual constitution and character. Hence, at the theoretical level, the notion of noumena essentially functioned in the Kantian scheme as a 'limiting concept' (*Grenzbegriff*) only; although indispensable, it could play no part in any positive characterization we might wish to make of reality.

This was not, however, the whole of the matter. For on the practical plane, and specifically in relation to our experience as moral agents, Kant implied that the conception of things in themselves could be employed in a fashion that would appear to lend it a more substantial significance. In a general way he argued that, where our moral convictions were in question, it was necessary to accept certain assumptions concerning the nature of things that transcended, and so could not be established within, the empirical sphere. These, while being in no sense cognitively demonstrable, were none the less requisite as 'postulates' – one might say 'articles of faith' – if moral thought and discourse were to be considered meaningful or applicable at all. Kant included amongst such postulates two which could be considered intrinsic to religious, or at least Christian, belief; thus, for reasons that he perhaps never made sufficiently clear, he regarded the claim that God exists and the claim that the soul is immortal as indispensable presuppositions of moral thought and action. Yet a third postulate, of more obvious intuitive relevance, concerned the reality of human freedom. It was a fundamental Kantian contention that in moral contexts men must regard themselves as capable of being practically determined by rational considerations; indeed, acting morally just consisted in acting in conformity with, and from respect for, the demands of reason as opposed to merely following the promptings of natural desire or inclination. In so far, however, as we are deemed to act rationally we cannot – as we can, for example, when we respond in a quasi-mechanical fashion to sensuous wants or subjective impulses – treat what we do as being no more than the causally conditioned consequence of certain prior factors. But this, according to Kant, involved embracing the view that we do not belong solely to the phenomenal domain, which was, on his own principles, of its essence a causally determined system. Instead, it was necessary that we should conceive ourselves to be members of what he called the 'intelligible' or noumenal world, the latter having already been proclaimed to lie beyond the scope of causal categories. Man, in other words, might be comprehended from two, quite distinct, standpoints. Under one aspect, he was a phenomenal being, subject like everything else in nature to scientifically ascertainable laws. Under the other, and viewed as belonging to the noumenal realm, he could be regarded as capable of determining himself to act in conformity with laws prescribed by reason, such laws being identified by Kant with those of morality; 'one might', he wrote at one point, 'define practical freedom as independence of the will on anything but the moral law alone.' Thus by distinguishing man as a creature of nature, subject to physiological and psychological laws, from man as a rational self-determining being, and by merging this distinction with that posited as holding between phenomena and things in themselves, Kant believed that he had afforded a means of escape from a dilemma which the spread of materialistic doctrines during the eighteenth century appeared to have rendered especially acute. Given the basic tenets of his philosophy, there need be no contradiction in principle between, on the one hand, accepting the claims of scientific determinism and, on the other, retaining the assumption of human 'free will' which deterministic doctrines were popularly supposed to undermine.

N

This conclusion, which preserves a circumspect balance between the requirements of science and morality while at the same time carefully avoiding the elevation of ethical presuppositions to the status of established truths, is typical of the general tenor of Kant's approach to the fundamental problems of philosophy. Moreover, it can also be said to provide a particular illustration of a certain dualistic tendency which manifested itself in much that he wrote and which was reflected in the imposing array of distinctions that found expression at various different levels of his thinking: the role of sensory intuition as against that of discursive understanding, the theoretical use of reason as against its practical use, the demands of duty as against the pressures of passion, the realizable ends of empirical investigation as against the unrealizable aspirations of transcendent speculation, the claims of cognitive science as against the tenets of religious faith. Such characteristic divisions did not go unnoticed by Kant's immediate followers. But, though recognized, they were not accepted as they stood; rather, they were treated as constituting a challenge. Instead of incorporating them uncriticized within their own systems, philosophers like Fichte and Hegel were inclined to regard the hard and fast dichotomies that figured so prominently in the Kantian scheme as being symptomatic of deep-lying tensions and inadequacies; they were a sign that Kant had not himself understood the full import of the innovations he had introduced, and it was therefore the task of future inquirers to show how the limitations inherent in his point of view could be overcome.

This was not to deny the magnitude of the Kantian achievement, which for the Idealists principally consisted in setting the relation of mind or consciousness to the natural order in a radically new and previously unsuspected perspective. Mental or cognitive processes were no longer conceived to be dependent upon, or derivative from, physical ones; the situation was, rather, the reverse, with the entire natural world being pictured in a way that exhibited it as owing its pervasive structure and character to the operations of the intellect. Furthermore, the comprehensive shift in point of view that Kant had initiated involved a drastic reappraisal of the whole manner in which the workings of the mind or psyche, in relation both to thinking and behaviour, had previously been described; in particular, it meant that it was no longer possible to accept the interpretative framework implicit in standard empiricist and sensationalist accounts. The reduction of all significant thought about ourselves and the world to a set of unitary ideas drawn or copied from the elementary data of experience, the panoply of associative mechanisms introduced to explain their various modes of combination and succession, the priority accorded to mere habit and conditioned response in the analysis of complex patterns of reasoning, emotion and conduct – these had ceased to carry conviction as devices for characterizing mental activity as it was actually undertaken and known. In their place Kant had proposed a model according to which the human intelligence was exhibited as being an essentially autonomous and constructive agency. Epistemologically considered, it was to be seen as originating the rules and procedures that enable us to make sense of what we apprehend and as supplying from its own resources the criteria and standards that are a prerequisite of all rational discourse about experience; in the last resort, reality is intelligible because we make it so. On the practical side, the mind was to be understood as capable of leading us to act in conformity to principles grounded in reason alone. Such principles could, moreover, exert an effective influence independently of, and even in direct opposition to, those 'natural' proclivities and forces upon which empiricist psychology had been so insistent, treating them as the ultimate determinants of all human action. Rationality was thus conceived as performing a creative or directive role in human life, and no excuse remained for viewing it as subordinate to the purely passive determinations of feeling or sensation, still less for resolving it into these.

Yet, despite the undoubted attractions of Kant's position when this was compared with the doctrines of his predecessors, the Idealists none the less felt that it was defective in important respects. Kant had spoken as if sensibility and understanding were separate faculties, while at the same time apparently finding nothing problematic in the suggestion that the material afforded by sense experience was wholly amenable to the processes of discursive thinking. What justification was there, however, for such confidence in the capacity of the postulated faculties to co-operate in the required manner? Moreover, this question was connected with wider ones concerning Kant's entire notion of there being things in themselves which, as the obverse of phenomena, affected the sensibility in determinate ways. On the one hand, the conception of noumena involved a radical limitation upon the power of human reason to penetrate and achieve understanding of reality; thus the position of eminence to which Kant seemed to have raised the thinking subject in his account of its relation to the world turned out to be of far less consequence than at first sight appeared. On the other, and notwithstanding the various and guarded formulations he himself gave of the doctrine, it lay exposed to serious objections arising internally from the side of Kant's own logical and epistemological presuppositions. For had he not gone to considerable lengths to argue that the application of the most general and fundamental concepts of thought was of necessity restricted to the phenomenal domain? And, if so, did not an insuperable problem emerge concerning the possibility of putting forward existential claims purporting to relate to what lay beyond that domain? With what right, for instance, did Kant speak of things in themselves 'affecting' the subject of knowledge, given his express stipulation that the legitimate use of the concept of *cause* was confined to empirical contexts alone?

To Fichte, and to Schelling and Hegel after him, it seemed in fact clear that one could not preserve what was valuable and suggestive in the Kantian philosophy and at the same time retain the idea of the inexperienceable *Ding an sich*: the conception of an external reality necessarily beyond the reach of mind was not only inconsistent with the principles that underlay Kant's thinking but was also inimical to the spirit that informed it. The conclusion was therefore drawn that the 'thing in itself' must be eliminated, thereby giving unrestricted rein to the idealistic implications inherent in the Kantian system. And it is precisely in their departure from Kant at this point, and in the consequences they believed to flow from it, that one can discern the germinating centre of the Idealists' own highly speculative ontological doctrines. For it appeared that, if noumena in the Kantian sense were to be rejected, the only intelligible alternative was a view of reality that represented it, in essence and as a whole, in mental or 'spiritual' terms: the world in its totality, and not merely in part or as seen from a certain limited standpoint, was to be regarded as the expression or manifestation of thought, of rational mind. But this clearly involved an extension and revision of the original Kantian programme so radical as to amount to its virtual transformation. The picture of human knowledge provided by Kant had still retained – in however altered or modified a form – the traditional assumption of an extra-mental reality which confronted the knowing subject as something irreducibly different from, and other than, itself. Believing this assumption to be in the final analysis unacceptable, the Idealists adopted the drastic expedient of widening the notion of the subject in such a fashion as to make it incorporate all that with which, on traditional theories, it had been customarily contrasted. What appeared to the conscious thinking individual to be *toto genere* distinct from himself was not so in fact, and the task of showing both how this 'untrue consciousness' (as Hegel was to call it) arose, and also how it could be dispelled, became a fundamental preoccupation of Idealist metaphysics in its subsequent development. The notion of a 'bifurcated reality' – the belief in the existence of an insuperable division fixed between mind and world – was deeply engrained in everyday thinking and experience; the function of future philosophy was not to sanctify this time-honoured preconception, but to disclose its true source and character. Moreover, if it were the case that the world, when correctly interpreted, revealed itself to be a manifestation of mind, this insight opened up at a single stroke possibilities that were specifically excluded by the Kantian theory. For in so far as philosophy constitutes a systematic reflection upon the categories and principles which govern mental activity, it could now be claimed that it was no longer justifiable – as Kant had maintained – to confine its scope to the examination of the manner in which the human mind structures and organizes its experience. Reality as a whole, and not merely the intellectual operations of the finite individual, could be said to fall within the province of legitimate philosophical investigation.

If one source of Idealist speculation may be located in the somewhat ambivalent reaction of Kant's immediate successors to his epistemological doctrines, another may be discerned in their no less equivocal response to the central tenets of his moral theory. Certainly the Kantian view that reason has an essentially practical or active function, capable of leading men to interpret and to act upon the world in such a way as to comply with its laws and commands, was not without influence in adding further important dimensions to Idealist thought. Thus it helped, in the first instance, to promote a conception of the individual human subject whereby he was envisaged as an agent rather than as a passive spectator, as a self-moving participant in the world whose very nature implied the positing and pursuit of practical ends. It was with this in mind that Fichte (in particular) insisted that the sense that a man has of himself as an active self-determining being constituted the primitive datum of all self-consciousness, expressly linking such a pervasive 'intuition of self-activity and freedom' with an awareness of the requirements of the moral law. And when, by a metaphysical extension, reality in general was regarded as sharing, at a fundamental level, characteristics that achieved determinate expression in the conscious life of the individual self, it too tended to be conceived along lines that exhibited it as a dynamic self-creating process, its development governed by principles that derived from its inherent essence as a rational autonomous system. The Idealist picture of the world was, in other words, permeated by ideas suggestive of agency and, indeed, of purpose. 'Spirit', Hegel declared, 'is alone reality'; the essence of spirit lay in self-expressive activity, and it was to be understood as continually striving towards what he termed 'the realization of its Ideal being'. In the light of such affirmations it is not perhaps altogether fanciful to see in the Idealist notion of a 'world-self', constantly seeking to realize itself in fresh and more adequate forms, a kind of gigantic projection on a cosmic scale of the original Kantian image of the moral nature of man.[1]

Nevertheless, Idealist thinkers tended at the same time to be profoundly critical of certain aspects of the theory of human nature Kant had propounded. Kant had represented man's condition as a moral agent in terms of ineradicable opposition and separation, the duality that haunted his treatment of human knowledge in relation to ultimate reality re-emerging in the account he offered of the human character itself. On the Kantian analysis of moral experience man was pictured as a divided personality. In part he was a creature activated by natural inclinations and desires, in part he was the embodiment of a superior consciousness that strove to subdue those propensities in an effort to make his behaviour conform to its dictates; only in so far as his actions were rationally determined in the latter sense could he properly be said to be free. It was true that Kant had ingeniously suggested that the distinction in question did not apply to human nature as such, being concerned rather with the different aspects – phenomenal and noumenal – under which human beings could be comprehended. To Kant's critics, however, this proposal appeared at best unconvincing, at worst actually incoherent; nor was it easy to reconcile with much that he has written in the course of his own frequent excursions into the field of moral psychology. For these, it was claimed, portrayed the psyche as a scene of bitter internecine war: man was to all intents and purposes split into two distinct selves, the higher of which despised and tried to subjugate its inferior rival. Kant implied, moreover, that there could be no final resolution of this conflict within the sphere of man's mortal existence, it being impossible for him to acquire complete mastery over those elements within himself which obstructed the fulfilment of his true or rational nature. How far, though, was this picture of our condition really acceptable?

[1] Cf. R. Tucker, *Philosophy and Myth in Karl Marx* (Cambridge, 1961), Part I.

Schiller

Kant's tendency to divide the human psyche into separate compartments had been attacked in a general way by his influential contemporary, J. G. Herder (1744–1803); in various works dealing with historical, anthropological and literary topics the latter had underlined the need to treat the human personality as a unitary whole and had gone out of his way to condemn the false abstractions and reifications of conventional faculty psychology. It was, however, the poet and dramatist, Friedrich Schiller (1759–1805), who was perhaps more directly responsible for drawing the attention of German readers to what he considered to be the basic inadequacies of Kant's account of human nature.

Schiller's *Letters on the Aesthetic Education of Man*, which was first published in the year 1795, can be seen, indeed, as a landmark. Apart from its interest as a contribution to the philosophy of art, it also served to adumbrate in embryonic form a theme that was obsessively to preoccupy German thinkers during the ensuing half-century under such labels as 'estrangement' and 'alienation'. Schiller had read Kant with admiration, referring to him in tones of great respect; and much in the *Letters* in fact echoes the account of aesthetic judgement and experience which Kant had offered in his last major work, the *Critique of Judgement*. Even so, he was forcibly struck by certain features of contemporary life and behaviour which he not only felt to be intrinsically undesirable but which also seemed to him to be reflected in a number of leading Kantian conceptions, being presented there as if they exemplified eternal and inescapable truths about the human condition. As Schiller put it in one place, 'with us . . . the various faculties appear as separate in practice as they are distinguished by the psychologist in theory';[1] he wrote, too, of how under the pressure of modern developments the 'inner unity of human nature' had been 'severed', and of how this manifested itself in – amongst other things – the discord which men feel between the 'sensuous' and the 'formal' (or rational) drives that inform their natures. One or other of these drives might gain an ascendancy in the personality of some particular individual; nevertheless, the result would not be harmony but a sort of armed peace precariously preserved by the tyranny of the stronger. Thus Schiller speaks of 'a master within, who not infrequently ends by suppressing the rest of our

[1] *On the Aesthetic Education of Man*, edited and translated by E. M. Wilkinson and L. A. Willoughby (Oxford, 1967), p. 33.

potentialities',[1] and elsewhere he refers to two ways in which man can be 'at odds with himself' – 'either as savage, when feeling predominates over principle; or as barbarian, when principle destroys feeling'.[2] Yet to assume that psychological descriptions of this kind, with their Kantian overtones, are universally applicable to men at all times and in all environments is (he implies) to believe something that historical experience alone is sufficient to belie: the state of man in contemporary society may, for instance, be contrasted with what it was in Greek times, when 'sense and reason' did not 'rule over strictly separate domains' and when 'no dissension had as yet provoked them into hostile partition and mutual demarcation of their frontiers'.[3] And it was in the light of such considerations that Schiller entertained the possibility that man might once more be restored to a condition of wholeness and inner concord through the reconciliation of those elements in his disposition that had become separated and set in conflict with one another. The *Letters* give eloquent and classic expression to the belief that artistic activity and experience – which for Schiller were associated with an ideal of freedom that, unlike the Kantian, implied the harmonious interplay of our sensuous and intellectual capacities – would perform an indispensable role in achieving this.

On its first appearance Hegel, in a letter to Schelling, described Schiller's essay as a masterpiece; and it was, in fact, largely through the medium of Hegel's own writings that some of Schiller's leading ideas passed into general philosophical currency. They admittedly underwent elaboration, even drastic transformation, in the process; yet the extent of the influence, which was especially evident in Hegel's first published book *The Phenomenology of Spirit* (1807), remains clear and undeniable. Such influence did not derive solely from Schiller's discussion of fragmentation at the level of personal psychology and his insistence upon the need to heal the divisions involved, though these were certainly important components; they were reflected, for instance, in the observations on the nature and function of philosophy contained in a lengthy pamphlet which Hegel wrote in 1801 and in which it was suggested that a role similar to that ascribed by Schiller to art might be attributed to philosophical thinking itself. The conception of restoring 'rent harmony' was, however, conceived by Hegel as having wider implications, particularly in relation to social and historical phenomena, and here again anticipations are discernible in Schiller's writings. For the latter had implied that it was impossible to treat individual psychology in

---

[1] *On the Aesthetic Education of Man*, pp. 33–5.   [2] Ibid., p. 21.   [3] Ibid., p. 31.

isolation from social conditions, tensions and discrepancies in the sphere of the personal conciousness being bound up with and accentuated by divisive tendencies in the sphere of society. The increasing specialization that was a feature of modern life, the separation of people into distinct 'ranks and occupations', brought in its train a progressive diminution of the capacity for individual self-expression; certain of men's aptitudes were developed to the total exclusion of others, with the result that a person was liable to become 'nothing more than the imprint of his occupation or his specialized knowledge',[1] his characteristic manner of thought and behaviour determined by forces over which he himself exercised no control. For the State had become, in Schiller's words, 'a stranger to its citizens'; the apparatus of government, the laws and the public authorities who promulgated and administered them, appeared in the eyes of the governed as something 'external', fundamentally indifferent or hostile to their interests as human beings. People lacked a sense of participating in the affairs of the community to which they nominally belonged, and they were hence for the most part conscious of leading an impoverished existence in which they felt excluded and deprived. Schiller's stress upon the intimate connections linking individual with social conflicts and frustrations was echoed in much Idealist and post-Idealist writing: so, too, was the underlying notion that an adequate understanding of man could not be attained without taking into account his evolution as a being who both creates and is at the same time formed by the complex of institutions and ideas that constitutes his environment at any given period. In giving prominence to such considerations the *Letters on the Aesthetic Education of Man* played a significant part in enlarging the perspective within which human development came to be viewed, while also helping to prepare the way for interpretations of man's nature whose emphatically social and historical orientation distinguished them, sharply and profoundly, from the models framed by earlier theorists.

Nevertheless, Schiller himself was neither by inclination nor training a philosopher in any strict sense. However much his individual insights may have incidentally contributed to the direction and content of subsequent Idealist thought, his own aims in writing the *Letters* were limited in scope and he certainly entertained no metaphysical ambitions of a general or systematic nature. The same can hardly be said of J. G. Fichte (1762–1814); and it is to him, rather than to Schiller, that we must look if we wish to identify the author who was in the first instance

[1] Ibid., p. 35.

responsible for the dramatic turn taken by German speculation at the opening of the nineteenth century.

Fichte

When, in 1792, Fichte's first book appeared he seemed firmly wedded to Kantian principles and methods of philosophy. So strong, indeed, were the marks of Kant's influence that the work, entitled *Essay towards a Critique of All Revelation* and published anonymously, was at first widely believed to have been written by Kant himself. Subsequent volumes made it clear, however, that Fichte was by no means content to follow tamely in the master's footsteps. From such writings as *Basis of the Entire Theory of Science* (1794), *The System of Ethics* (1798) and *The Vocation of Man* (1800), it transpired that for him Kant's philosophy represented not so much a complete and acceptable system in its own right as the propaedeutic to such a system. He envisaged his mission to be one of advancing to new positions rather than of simply consolidating the gains his predecessor had made, even if this meant – as in fact was to happen – reaching conclusions that incurred Kant's express disapproval.

In common with many of his contemporaries, Fichte accepted the Kantian view that the human mind was to be conceived as a creative agency rather than as a mere passive receptacle of sense-impressions. He was also profoundly struck by Kant's moral philosophy with its emphasis upon the primacy of practical reason, his own metaphysic, as it finally emerged, taking the form of a kind of moral teleology whose cornerstone was the idea of duty and the ethical will. On the other hand, he repudiated (as has already been seen) the doctrine of noumenal things in themselves, considering this to be an inconsistent regression to a philosophical position that had in effect been superseded by the innovations Kant himself had introduced. To avoid such a blind alley it was essential to return to what, for Fichte, constituted the true starting-point of Kant's 'critical' revolution. This was the notion of the self, or 'ego'.

What did Fichte understand by the ego, and in what sense was it of fundamental importance for the development of his conception of the world?

In the first place, he speaks of it as something of which we are directly and necessarily aware at every moment of our conscious lives: 'I cannot take a pace, I cannot move hand or foot, without the intellectual in-

tuition of my self-conciousness in these actions.' The manner in which
Fichte expresses this primitive intuition is significant. Thus he does not
wish to suggest that I am aware of myself in the form of some kind of
substantial entity or object; rather, I know myself, simply and solely,
as activity. Basically, the ego as it presents itself in self-conciousness is a
'doing', pure and unalloyed – 'one should not even call it an active
thing'. Nor (Fichte insists) is there anything especially mysterious or
recondite in the notion of self-conciousness so described; it refers only
to what may be confirmed by an appeal to the commonest experience,
representing the characteristic mode under which each one of us is
aware of his own existence all the time. He adds, moreover, that this
inner and pervasive sense of ourselves as centres of activity is accompanied by an equally unassailable conviction of freedom. Throughout our
ordinary daily lives we are continuously aware of an ability to do such
things as control our processes of thought or turn our attention from
one matter to another, although – he typically maintains – it is in moral
experience that the innate feeling of a capacity to choose between alternatives achieves most forceful expression. He also at times implies that
a deeper reflection upon the idea of human freedom may elicit the conclusion that we are ultimately responsible, not just for individual
thoughts or actions entertained or performed on particular occasions,
but for the entire framework of conceptions that governs our overall
outlook upon existence as well.

Taken by itself, and leaving aside its conceivable merits as a phenomenological account of certain aspects of human conciousness, what has
been said so far would appear to provide a somewhat fragile basis upon
which to erect a comprehensive metaphysic. Yet Fichte certainly
thought that it had far wider implications than might be at first sight
supposed, affording, when properly understood, the key to a fully
fledged idealist interpretation of reality as a whole. Why exactly he believed this to be so is not easy to determine; the various arguments he
put forward were complex and tortuous, and involved a number of
dubious steps. Even so, it is possible to unravel some of the main threads
of his reasoning.

Let us return to the notion of activity, in which the essence of selfhood
is held to reside. What does such activity imply? Fichte claims that it
requires us to accept the existence of what he terms a 'non-ego': in
other words, an externally conceived reality which is experienced as
subsisting over against the ego and which is presented to it objectively
in sense-perception. It can thus be affirmed that, in so far as I express and

am aware of myself as a being capable of thought and action, I am committed thereby to acknowledging the presence of a world beyond myself: this stands opposed to me, setting limits to my possible projects and operations. Fichte treats such reciprocal inter-dependence of ego and non-ego as a universal condition of the kind of conciousness that pertains to finite selves; and in so doing he may be interpreted as having been influenced by at least three important considerations.

To begin with, he was doubtless partly impressed by the important claim, advanced and developed by Kant in various sections of the *Critique of Pure Reason*, that the possibility of conceiving of myself as a particular conscious subject presupposes, as a necessary correlate, the con-ception of an empirically ascertainable world of objective phenomena. In the absence of an 'outer' spatio-temporally ordered realm of things and events it would be impossible for me to speak of myself as having experiences at all; for it is only by reference to, and in distinction from, such a realm that statements purporting to describe my subjective states of consciousness acquire a determinate meaning. Thus the supposition that I, *qua* solitary individual, might encompass within my own mind the whole of reality is an incoherent one: as Kant put it, 'the conscious-ness of my existence is at the same time an immediate consciousness of other things outside me'.[1] Yet though this purely theoretical argument is accorded attention in Fichte's own theory, more stress is placed upon further points that are closely related to the generally practical orientation of his thought. First, it seemed to him clear that the primal intuition which we have of ourselves as active striving beings was in-separable from an experienced resistance to our various impulses and drives. But such resistance in turn involves the conception of there being something, in the shape of an external force or obstacle, which opposes itself to us. Hence the sense of being in some way restricted or checked, which is a precondition of the consciousness of self-activity, at the same time provides us with what is in fact our most immediate criterion for asserting the presence of something other than ourselves. Secondly, Fichte considered it to be in any case obvious that we could not intelligibly conceive of ourselves as agents, and (more specifically) as moral agents, without assuming the existence of a world which presents us with a field for our activities and in which we can seek to realize our objectives. The existence of an objective reality was in this way a necessary postulate for human subjects in so far as they were

[1] *Critique of Pure Reason*, B 276.

regarded, and regarded themselves, as practical beings; their very nature as agents demanded that they should interpret the facts of experience in a manner that represented them as affording a concrete sphere for the fulfilment of practical ends. Thus Fichte could affirm that it was from the necessity of action that our consciousness of a real world, set over against ourselves, finally derived; 'we do not act because we know, but we know because we are called upon to act – the practical reason is the root of all reason.'[1]

This, though, brings us face to face with a crucial question: namely, what is the status of that perceptible and manipulable reality which, on the account just given, is treated as a prerequisite of human self-consciousness and activity as Fichte understands them? More specifically, how is what he says about it to be reconciled with his avowed purpose of affording a characterization of the world in purely 'ideal' terms, with the notion of things in themselves jettisoned and everything instead traced back to the fundamental conception of the conscious subject or ego? It is one thing to argue that the presence of a 'non-ego' in the Fichtean sense is a condition of any consciousness that can validly be imagined; it would appear to be quite another thing to maintain that the ego itself 'posits', or produces out of its own inner resources, that to which it necessarily finds itself opposed. Whereas the first claim may seem to have much in its favour, the other may strike us as being *prima facie* inherently implausible, even absurd. Yet Fichte himself habitually writes as if the two claims were integrally connected and as if both were evidently true. The difficulty here may be partially resolved if it is recognized that, in putting forward the second contention, he appears to have had in mind two separable theses, between which, however, he did not always clearly distinguish.

When Fichte is following one line of thought, his references to the ego as positing the non-ego may be regarded as a way of drawing attention to the point that our modes of interpreting and categorizing the empirical data are all in the end dependent upon our basic needs, interests and goals. The various discriminations we make and the types of classification we employ, the distinctions we draw between the 'real' and the 'illusory', the objective and the subjective – such things are rooted in our fundamental constitution as active beings with particular wants and purposes. It is in this spirit that he sometimes writes as if speculative questions about the actual existence of an independent

[1] *The Vocation of Man*, Book III, translation by W. Smith, in *Fichte's Popular Works* (London, 1889), Vol. I, p. 421.

external world were really idle and empty. For the character our experience has is ultimately determined by what we make of it, how we 'take it'; and the way in which we take it is in turn determined by what we seek. 'Not by mental ideas,' Fichte writes at one point, 'but by hunger, thirst and their satisfaction, does anything become for me food and drink . . . I do not hunger because food is before me, but a thing becomes food for me because I hunger.'[1] And if we move from the plane of appetite to that of moral motivation similar considerations apply. From an ethical standpoint the world is viewed as the medium of moral activity, as something to be worked upon or fashioned in such a way as to conform to the demands that are imposed upon us by conscience; so conceived, it can be said to represent 'the stuff, the material for our duty, made manifest to the senses'. But once again, the fact that it presents itself to us in this light and as having this specific character is a function of our practical projects and objectives: here, as elsewhere, the picture we form of reality is determined by, and bears the imprint of, our underlying intentions and aims.

There is nothing particularly mysterious or paradoxical about such suggestions; indeed, in some ways they may be regarded as anticipating the ideas of latter-day pragmatists who have expressly eschewed metaphysical ambitions or pretensions. Even so, it would be wrong to think that they constituted all, or even the most central part, of what Fichte wished to affirm concerning the dependence of the world upon the ego. For he also propounded a doctrine in which this dependence was asserted to hold in a far more full-blooded and thoroughgoing fashion. Admittedly, he was careful to point out that he never at any time intended to give the impression that the individual himself literally creates or constructs the world in which he finds himself, complaining that he had been persistently misrepresented on this score; people who had attributed to him this brand of subjective idealism had been 'completely mistaken'. What, on the other hand, he did quite explicitly maintain, particularly in his later writings, was the thesis that the world of everyday experience is the expression of an 'absolute' ego, or (as he put it elsewhere) of an infinite mind or will; furthermore, we ourselves, as finite conscious beings, were likewise to be regarded as manifestations of the same all-encompassing mind or spirit. On this view, therefore, it was not a question of the objective world – the 'non-ego' – being posited 'through the individual as such'. Rather was it a matter of a postulated absolute subject establishing, on

[1] *The Vocation of Man*, loc. cit.

the one hand, the perceived world of common experience and, on the other, the finite centres of human consciousness to which that world presented itself as an objectively given reality.

In putting forward such a theory Fichte might well have thought, with some justification, that he had successfully obviated a standard type of objection to his philosophy. Yet he can only be said to have done so at a certain cost in consistency. For one of the chief considerations upon which he based his original rejection of noumenal things in themselves had been the contention that nothing could be conceived of as existing outside the sphere of human consciousness. And it is not easy to square this claim with his subsequent references to absolute spirit and to the natural world of which it is held to be, in some sense, the ground. But however this may be, the system he was led to expound certainly embodied conceptions that played a crucial role in the general development of German Idealism. The notion that familiar commonsense and philosophical dichotomies must be subordinated to a monistic picture of the universe that portrayed it as constituting a single spiritual whole; the suggestion that what appears to the individual mind as something external to itself in fact derives from the selfsame ultimate principle to which it, too, owes its existence; the accompanying thought that, in so far as men strive to impress their wills upon the world, moulding it to their purposes, they can thereby be said to affirm their identity with a reality which, though seemingly resistant and 'other', is at a deeper level one with themselves: these were all highly influential themes that recurred, though with numerous and important variations, in the works of later thinkers. What was preeminently distinctive in Fichte's own manner of interpreting them stemmed from his profound concern with morality. In his eyes man was of his essence a moral being: he did not recognize – as Kant had done – a clear-cut division between the natural and the ethical propensities of men; instead he regarded the latter as continuous with, and as developing out of, the former. Likewise, the sense of the world in general for him lay in its significance as an ethical totality: if from one point of view it was to be seen as representing a sphere within which each person was called upon to fulfil the moral potentialities of his nature, from another it was to be comprehended as providing, in the form of challenges to be met and obstacles to be overcome, the prerequisites for such fulfilment. Thus Fichte's metaphysic, as it finally emerged, was inextricably bound up with the ideas of conscience and duty. 'The kind of philosophy one adopts', he once proclaimed, 'depends upon the sort of man one is.' As a vivid illustration of this dictum he might have cited his own writings.

Absolute Idealism: Schelling and Hegel

If we follow Fichte through the many tortuous convolutions of his thinking we may feel that, when all has been said, he never really succeeded in emancipating himself from his Kantian origins. To the end he gives the impression of trying to superimpose upon the epistemological structure he inherited from his great predecessor a speculative ontology it was never designed to bear; hence flaws and cracks are apt to make their appearance at crucial points of his system. In the works of F. W. J. Schelling (1775–1854) and of G. W. F. Hegel (1770–1831), on the other hand, such tensions are less pronounced, this being perhaps partly due to their having evolved their theories at a further remove from the Kantian source. To Hegel, for instance, the Fichtean claim that reality as a whole was interpretable in ideal or spiritual terms seems to have presented itself more as a fundamental philosophical insight standing in need of detailed application and elaboration at the level of historical and social analysis than as a conclusion somewhat precariously derived from an abstract consideration of what is involved in the notion of individual self-consciousness. Moreover, neither he nor Schelling gave much evidence in their writings of the solipsistic tendencies which critics, understandably if erroneously, were prone to attribute to Fichte himself. While postulating an ultimate identity between subject and object, mind and world, the ideal and the real, both thinkers made it reasonably plain that they had no wish to be taken as implying that the universe was in any sense a mere projection of the individual ego.

So far as Schelling was concerned, it remains none the less true that the debt he owed to Fichte was considerable, at any rate in the initial stages of his rather variegated intellectual career. Thus, to give only one example, in the *System of Transcendental Idealism*, which was published in 1800, he offered an account of the conditions and development of consciousness that in a general way clearly reflected the pattern of argument Fichte had deployed when discussing the same topic in his *Wissenschaftslehre* of 1794. Yet even here – as subsequently emerged in an extremely acrimonious exchange of letters between the two – there were significant differences of emphasis. And further volumes produced by Schelling at this period, which succeeded one another with bewildering rapidity, served to underline more profound divergences of interest and outlook.

Schelling's name is commonly associated with the development of German Romanticism, and rightly so. Not only did he number amongst his most intimate friends such outstanding representatives of the movement as Novalis, Tieck and the Schlegels; he also, in his own work, gave eloquent philosophical expression to dominant Romantic themes, above all the notion of there being deep and pervasive affinities between man and a vitalistically conceived natural order. Thus, although he accepted Fichte's portrayal of reality as a spiritual whole of which human consciousness and nature were complementary manifestations, the attitude he adopted to the natural realm was markedly dissimilar. Where Fichte had pictured it as being – in Josiah Royce's phrase – 'duty solidified to the senses' and as affording the means and material for moral self-realization, Schelling by contrast stressed its claims to be respected in its own right as a worthy and inspiring object of curiosity and contemplation. A metaphysical justification, founded upon the notion of 'absolute spirit' but curiously intermixed with elements drawn from the observational sciences, underlay this different approach. Nature, regarded as the product of an active 'organizing principle' or 'world-soul' (*Weltseele*) which externalized itself in the sphere of objective phenomena, formed an animated unity that was ultimately intelligible in evolutionary and teleological terms; it represented, in other words, something that was involved in a continual process of creation and re-creation, the various levels of its development being related to one another in a purposive or functional manner. These stages might be the subject of different branches of scientific investigation – such as physics or biology – but they were none the less interdependent and could not be truly comprehended in isolation. For example, the inorganic sphere, governed by the laws of mechanics, was a precondition of the possibility of an organic order of living things, and this in turn was required for the actualization of consciousness as we find it exemplified at the level of human life. The development of such consciousness was, indeed, regarded by Schelling as the culmination and goal of the entire process. Spirit, having objectified itself outwardly in the natural world, now returned to itself under the aspect of human subjectivity or mind. It was therefore illegitimate to speak, as dualists had done, as if the physical and the psychical were separated from one another by a great divide. If from one standpoint (which could almost be said to be that of a form of evolutionary naturalism) consciousness was described as presupposing an objective realm of matter out of which it developed in determinate stages, from another – the 'transcendental' – point of view the natural sphere was for its part to be seen as 'slumbering spirit', finally awakening to consciousness at the level of human experience and knowledge. It was precisely the task of philosophical reflection to make the import of the latter claim clear: the apparent opposition and division between nature and mind, in terms of which theorists had traditionally characterized the perceptual and cognitive situation, disappeared with the realization that this situation, correctly interpreted, was ultimately one of spirit's apprehension of itself. If looking for analogies, we might partially illustrate what Schelling had in mind by comparing what he called the *Weltseele* to an artist who, having finished a work, subsequently looks back upon his creation, recognizing it to be the expression of his own inward nature.

The relevance of artistic experience to his overall conception of reality was, in fact, something with which Schelling himself became increasingly preoccupied as he continued to follow out the implications of that conception. He referred, for instance, to the objective world as the 'unconscious poetry of the spirit', and went on to affirm that the same creative force that operates unconsciously in nature also manifests itself – though here in consciousness and freedom – in the production of human works of art. With this in mind, he was led to assign a profound metaphysical significance to artistic activity, devoting a series of lectures to the subject in the years 1802–3. The lectures in question contained material that was, in its way, both illuminating and suggestive; Schelling possessed an acute feeling for poetry and he managed to define in a memorable form much that was characteristic of the Romantic approach to literature. Moreover, many of the ideas put forward on the topic of genius and on the role of imagination in the arts could be understood and appreciated without accepting the more questionable tenets of the philosophy he wished to expound. As such, they constituted an interesting contribution to aesthetic theory in their own right, and one that proved to be of lasting historical importance and influence.

The same was hardly true, however, of Schelling's so-called 'system of absolute identity'. He first alluded to this obscure doctrine in a book entitled *Exposition of my System of Philosophy* (1801), discussing it further in *Bruno* (1802) and in *Philosophy and Religion* (1804). It purported to deal with something presupposed by his earlier doctrines of nature and consciousness which was now referred to as 'absolute reason', this being the primal source both of the natural world and of the centres of mental activity to which that world manifested itself; thus he was prepared to characterize it as 'the ground of existence, the primeval night, the mother of all things'.[1] At the same time, he insisted that it was on no account to be treated as the 'cause' of the existing universe, and was to be conceived rather as that in which all finite things ultimately participated and had their being. The elucidation of such pronouncements was not assisted by Schelling's further qualification of absolute or infinite reason as 'pure identity', representing an undivided, simple and seamless whole; within it nothing was 'distinguishable from anything else', and for this reason it was not susceptible to discursive understanding but could be apprehended 'only through intuition'. He spent numerous pages elaborating these gnomic utterances, of which the somewhat disappointing upshot seems to be that concerning the absolute in itself nothing positive can be asserted; in any case, it would be unprofitable to pursue the ramifications of his thought on the subject. Here, as elsewhere, his reasoning was not conspicuous for economy or rigour, being flawed by much needless repetition and apparent inconsistency. It is true that what he wrote regarding the unity of man and nature often seems to contain perceptive intimations of later empirical theories of emergent evolution; even so, his attempt to compel everything to conform to the high-sounding interpretations he sought to impose upon reality all too often makes his philosophy appear the prototype of a certain kind of vapid speculation which still survives, in some quarters, to the present day. A number of his compatriots were, indeed, quick to draw attention to such features of his thinking; and it is noteworthy that Hegel himself, who was at one time very close to Schelling, exhibited a sharp awareness of his limitations. Thus, in the Preface of his *Phenomenology*, he condemned Schelling's habit of reducing diverse phenomena to one another by means of abstract schemata and suspect metaphors as being 'as insufferable as the repetition of a sleight of hand one sees through'. He also severely criticized the latter's 'identity system': 'to pass off one's absolute as the night in which, as one says, all cows are black – that is the naïveté of the emptiness of all knowledge.'[2]

Yet despite his caustic strictures upon the use Schelling had made of

---

[1] *Bruno*, p. 124.

[2] *The Phenomenology of Mind*, Preface; translation by Walter Kaufmann in *Hegel: Reinterpretation, Texts and Commentary* (London, 1966), pp. 386 and 430.

the idea, Hegel was far from abandoning the conception of absolute spirit or mind as such; on the contrary, he incorporated it, though in an altered form, within his own system. And the same holds good for his treatment of other notions that had figured prominently in Schelling's philosophy. The idea of cosmic development, for example, and the suggestion that through such development spirit arrives at an awareness of itself in human consciousness were also themes that Hegel emphasized, adapting them once again to his specific metaphysical purposes. Furthermore Schelling, like Fichte before him, had made considerable play with the conception of triadic movement, this being held to apply both to processes of thought and to things or forms of existence: in very crude terms, a given position (or 'thesis') was envisaged as giving rise to its opposite (the 'antithesis'), these in turn generating a mediating position which transcended each in the shape of a higher unity, or 'synthesis'. Hegel was not, as some have supposed, the inventor of this schematic device, whose origins may be traced back to the 'antinomies' discussed in the second part of Kant's *Critique of Pure Reason*, and he in fact made a far less rigid and extensive use of it than is often alleged. All the same, its outlines are visible in a number of his actual arguments and logical transitions, while in a more general fashion its influence is implicit in his 'dialectical' conception of the world as a dynamic process involving the continual emergence and resolution of contradictions. There were therefore more than superficial resemblances between the two main representatives of German Idealism, at any rate so far as the frameworks within which they formulated their respective philosophies were concerned.

The distinctiveness of Hegel's contribution, making him appear in retrospect a more significant and fertile figure than Schelling, lay in the manner in which he used and interpreted the basic Idealist scheme. For one thing, and notwithstanding the heavy abstract jargon in which he tended to clothe his ideas, he displayed in much of his writing an acute sensitivity to the intricate complexity, the rich diversity, of concrete thought and experience: behind his most extravagant speculative flights it is often possible to discern the presence of some quite specific conceptual or empirical consideration that lends force and substance to what is being asserted. For another, the general orientation of his philosophy was importantly different. If the emphasis in Schelling's thinking fell chiefly upon the relation between man and nature, Hegel's concern was rather with the relation between man and man.

Certainly a profound preoccupation with human existence was manifest from the beginning of Hegel's intellectual development. It will be remembered that as a young man he had been greatly struck by Schiller's critique of current psychological and social trends, with its stress upon tensions that existed, not only between the individual and society, but also within the confines of the individual's own mind and personality. Hegel's earliest manuscripts, written at a period when he was earning his living as a private tutor and before he had embarked upon his academic career, make this amply plain. While ostensibly concerned with the history and interpretation of religious belief, these at the same time show how he was also deeply taken up with questions centring upon human relations and man's status as a social and historical being: indeed, for him the two inquiries were closely intertwined. He was, as Schiller had been, impressed by the apparent contrast between modern societies and those of classical Greece, comparing the internal divisions and antagonisms of the former with the integration and harmony he attributed to the latter: he deplored, too, the anarchic individualism of contemporary European life, in which people had lost a sense of common purpose and dignity and were no longer able to identify themselves with a unitary community whose institutions and customs could be said to fulfil their innermost aspirations. Religion, and in particular Christianity, might have suggested a remedy; but here again Hegel encountered difficulties. For religion, at any rate in many typical forms, appeared in its turn to involve separation and disunity; God – the human ideal – was posited as distant and transcendent, and as subsisting in a realm eternally set apart from the one occupied by a suffering and fallen humanity. Thus in the religious sphere, as in the individual and the social, there was opposition and estrangement. How did such estrangement arise, and how might it be resolved and overcome?

When Hegel eventually came to construct his own philosophical system these problems were still very much at the forefront of his attention. Here, though, they were taken up and reformulated in the context of a vast synoptic vision wherein every facet of the world, every department of knowledge and existence, was assigned a determinate position and provided with its appropriate explanation and rationale. The twin conceptions that had played so obsessive a part in his early thought – division and unification, estrangement and reconciliation – returned to dominate this comprehensive picture, giving it its distinctive design and tone; they re-appeared, however, in a new and more majestic form. For whereas previously they had been treated as expressive only of partial aspects of human life and experience, they were now construed as representing the terms in which the totality of things, including man himself as situated within that totality, could be satisfactorily delineated and comprehended. The transformation in question was achieved through the categories of the Idealist metaphysic, and above all through the concept of absolute spirit or *Geist*.

Hegel characterized spirit as 'the process of its own becoming'; he said too that it became actual 'only by its development and through its end'. We have seen that he had no use for Schelling's portrayal of the absolute as consisting in its essence of a pure undifferentiated identity, this being thought of as in some way logically prior to the reality of which it was the 'ground'; the idea that spirit, so understood, could be validly considered and discussed in complete abstraction from its concrete and determinate manifestations in reality was, indeed, foreign to the whole tenor of Hegel's philosophical approach. For him spirit's essential nature precisely consisted in the multifarious ways in which it developed and revealed itself; and this might suggest that, in the last analysis, one could no more finally separate what it actually was from how it variously expressed itself than one could, for example, separate a man's character from the manner in which he typically thought and felt and behaved. Thus it might reasonably be maintained that the Hegelian philosophy was far from being the other-worldly fantasy it is sometimes made out to have been, and that on the contrary Hegel considered this world, rather than some mysterious 'beyond', to constitute the true subject and concern of philosophical investigation. Even so, and despite its plausibility, such an interpretation stands in need of an important qualification. For Hegel also undoubtedly wrote as if it were possible to give an account of the inner structure of reality which, so to speak, went behind the world of ordinary experience and expressed the truth of things 'as it is, without husk' – that was to say, in terms of the unfolding of logical categories within the medium of pure thought alone. The study of such categories in their dialectical relations and development was, in fact, the proper subject-matter of logical inquiry as he understood it.

Though notorious difficulties and obscurities surround this part of his doctrine, it at least serves to highlight a cardinal Hegelian theme. For Hegel would have insisted that the claim that the ultimate nature of the universe conforms to the above description only appears paradoxical in so far as the relation between subjective consciousness and objective existence is supposed to be one of irreducible duality and opposition; and this was a supposition he wished to challenge. He admitted that, from the standpoint of what he called 'understanding' (*Verstand*), such a division inevitably appeared permanent and insuperable; it was, indeed, intrinsic to our commonsense and scientific modes of comprehension that we should everywhere seek to impose clear-cut distinctions and sharply demarcated concepts. Yet it was the task of philosophical thinking to transcend this limited and practically orientated outlook and to demonstrate how, when subjected to analysis, the components of our familiar conceptual schemes dissolved, broke up and passed into one another in a fashion that made it no longer feasible to regard them as affording a finally acceptable representation of things. What emerged instead was a recognition that the duality of subjectivity and objectivity, thought and existence, along with other oppositions and polarities built into everyday interpretations of experience, must be taken up within, transcended by, a deeper and more comprehensive insight; the apparent 'otherness' of the world would then be seen in a different light, the division between the conscious subject and an objectively conceived 'external' reality being now apprehended as a division within spirit itself. The condition in question Hegel described as being one in which spirit was estranged from itself; it represented spirit's 'self-alienation'. What exactly did this amount to?

We saw how Hegel initially spoke of spirit as essentially involving active development towards an end in which it might be said to achieve confirmation of its own being; it was what it did, and in a sense created itself. In concrete terms this meant that the history of the world was to be understood as a teleological process, whereby spirit in the first instance externalized itself in the form of an outward reality that was expressive of its inner potentialities – in Hegel's terminology, it made itself 'its own deed, its own work' and thus became 'an object to itself'.[1] The process referred to was held to take place, in effect, at two distinct levels. At one level spirit was regarded as manifesting itself 'unconsciously' in the production and establishment of the realm of natural phenomena: here there were, of course, clear affinities with the doctrine already propounded by Schelling in his philosophy of nature. But Hegel further maintained that spirit was active at the human level as well, in the creation of societies and civilizations which both

[1] *Lectures on the Philosophy of History*, trans. J. Sibree (New York, 1944), pp. 73–4.

represented concrete expressions of its essential nature and at the same time exhibited stages of its evolution towards a progressively fuller consciousness and understanding of its own character. The conception of there being in this manner a double aspect under which human history could be viewed was, indeed, a crucial element in the specifically Hegelian interpretation of the Idealist *Weltanschauung*. On the one hand, Hegel emphasized – in a manner that went far beyond anything suggested by Schelling or Fichte – the need to envisage man as a developing being whose nature could only be grasped historically through its putting itself forth in the shape of successive patterns of life and culture; these were, metaphorically speaking, the mirror in which man, as the embodiment of spirit, could perceive his own image reflected. On the other hand, Hegel stressed the extent to which the outlooks men take up towards the world, and towards themselves as members of that world, were themselves historically conditioned and subject to continual change and displacement. How men see things, how they picture reality and their situation within it, what theoretical schemes they employ and what practical projects they adopt – these were not (as philosophers had traditionally assumed) something fixed and given to all eternity, but on the contrary were in a constant process of shift and revision; moreover, the alterations they underwent had to be understood in a social context and as conforming to a determinate historical order. It was Hegel's contention that, as this total process continued, involving on one side the emergence of distinct social forms and institutions and on the other the evolution of fresh and more adequate modes of interpreting experience, spirit gradually moved towards an ever deeper comprehension of its own nature. Its consummation was to be found in what he called 'absolute knowledge', this being a state of philosophical understanding in which spirit finally came to recognize that the entire world, in all its varied manifestations, was the product and articulation of itself as the ultimate metaphysical 'subject'. Such understanding could be characterized as the reappropriation of the world through the medium of thought, through the fully developed consciousness of individual finite minds. Thus the duality of subject and object, which – though taking a plurality of forms – was a common and recurrent feature of less developed conceptions of reality, was finally seen to be apparent only. The world, it might be suggested, was to be 'internalized' through philosophical knowledge, spirit as it exhibited itself at the level of the consciousness of the finite individual thereby coming to realize that the totality of things, previously taken to be external and 'foreign', was the projection of its own rational nature. In this manner spirit, by means of philosophical reflection, could be thought of as 'returning to itself' and the division between thought and reality, constituting the original condition of self-estrangement or self-alienation, considered to be healed or overcome. In Hegel's words, it was the aim of knowledge 'to divest the objective world that stands opposed to us of its strangeness, and, as the phrase is, to find ourselves at home in it; which means no more than to trace the objective world back to the notion – to our innermost self'.[1] And this task (he more than once implied) had been brought to a conclusion by his own philosophical system.

The religious overtones of the Hegelian theory have often been noted by interpreters and commentators, and Hegel himself drew attention to them, claiming that his philosophy gave rational formulation to insights that appeared in religious dogmas in a figurative, and sometimes misleading, guise. Thus the Christian doctrines of the fall and of subsequent atonement and reconciliation may be regarded as having an analogue in the Hegelian conception of spirit's self-alienation and ultimate return to itself; moreover, Hegel specifically implied that there was an underlying correspondence of content between the Christian idea of God and his own, purely philosophical conception of absolute spirit. Here, however, it is important to recognize that, in so far as his system involved an identification of spirit with the world as a whole, it contained no counterpart of God considered as a transcendent personality, existing over and above the universe and independent of it. In fact Hegel, on more than one occasion, went out of his way to treat the latter notion as a fundamental distortion of the truth, a distortion which, though prevalent at particular stages of human development, was dispelled when spirit attained the kind of total knowledge and understanding of its own nature that was envisaged in the Hegelian philosophy. Thus, in a famous section of his *Phenomenology of Spirit* entitled 'The Unhappy Consciousness', he treated human beliefs in a transcendent 'beyond' as symptomatic of a dissatisfaction springing from conditions of life in which men felt at odds both with their external social environment and also, inwardly, with themselves. In such circumstances man, conceived as a split personality or 'alienated soul', was aware of an acute disparity between his actual character and

---

[1] *The Logic of Hegel*, trans. from *The Encyclopaedia of the Philosophical Sciences* by William Wallace (London, 1950), p. 335.

situation, on the one hand, and his potentialities as a free and self-affirming social being, on the other; this sense of pervasive inner disharmony found outlet in the mythical notion of a nether realm and in the idea of a gulf separating God from man. Symbolically understood, such a vision – exemplified for Hegel *par excellence* by the Catholicism of medieval Europe – was valid, providing the key to the condition in which man, as the manifestation of spirit at a certain period of its development, found himself. But understood in literal terms it was untrue, since so interpreted it concealed the fact that it was the final destiny of spirit to realize its possibilities and satisfy its aspirations in this world, and not in some unearthly sphere projected by the imagination.

The story of the steps by which, at the level of human thought and action, spirit moved towards the fulfilment of this destiny was given by Hegel in two principal works: abstractly and schematically, as a sort of rational reconstruction of the evolution of consciousness, in the early *Phenomenology*; concretely and within an explicitly historical framework in his later, posthumously published *Lectures on the Philosophy of History*. Despite clear divergences of approach and point of view, both books aim to show how the various forms spirit assumes in the course of unfolding its nature on the human plane follow an intelligible order and progression. The pattern exhibited is not, however, portrayed as being one of smooth uninterrupted development, nor is it depicted as taking place in conformity with the conscious designs of individual historical agents. The social structures in which spirit successively embodies itself are not the intentional products of human thought and planning; on the contrary, Hegel never tires of pointing out that what primarily moves men to act are limited interests and personal passions, and that the larger outcomes to which their deeds give rise are seldom, if ever, anticipated by those who perform them; it is only subsequently, in the light of retrospective reflection, that their significance for world history becomes apparent. He argues, too, that the historical sequence of cultures and of the outlooks that inform them has its source in conflict and contradiction: spirit, in his picturesque phrase, is 'at war with itself', each phase of the historical process involving the transcendence of limitations that were inherent in its predecessor and at the same time incorporating, in its turn, deficiencies that must likewise be overcome. In practice this means that periods in which men find satisfaction in the societies they belong to, seeing in these the expression of their basic beliefs and ideals, alternate with others wherein they have, so to speak, outgrown the principles that originally endowed the established order with life and meaning; the institutions and cultural forms with which they previously identified themselves now strike them as being dead and cold, no longer related to their essential interests as human beings and representing barriers to further development rather than means to self-fulfilment. Some of Hegel's most brilliant characterizations occur in the sections in which – echoing Schiller – he delineates the sense men have of being 'outside' and estranged from their communities, paying lip-service to standards and outwardly conforming to practices that have lost all hold upon their inner minds and hearts: these are times when people feel driven back upon themselves and their own resources, and when what Hegel calls 'the soul of nobler natures' is impelled to 'seek refuge from the present in ideal regions – in order to find in them that harmony which it can no longer enjoy in this discordant real world'.[1]

According to Hegel, then, history exhibits a continual interplay between man's self-created social world and his evolving attitudes towards the environment he has produced. There is thus a repeated oscillation between the creative and the critical moments of the process: in Hegelian terminology, spirit seeks to express itself in ever new forms, each form constituting a transitional achievement that must make way for another as its inadequacies are revealed in the light of a larger understanding. In what, though, does such deepening insight consist? As in other areas of his thought, Hegel envisages it as comprising spirit's growing knowledge and awareness of its own ultimate nature. Here therefore, at the specifically human level of social and political change, it is to be construed as involving a developing comprehension of the fundamental essence of man, and this Hegel locates in the idea of freedom: freedom, he affirms, 'is the actuality of men – not something which they have, as men, but which they are'. Hence history, truly interpreted, is the story of the realization of this cardinal notion; externally and objectively it manifests itself in a series of civilizations which represent different degrees of its incarnation,[2] inwardly and subjectively it is enriched through an increasing consciousness of its implications as men acquire a fuller grasp of their own needs and a profounder recognition of the relations in which they stand to one another. The culmination of the process is reached when less developed

[1] *Lectures on the Philosophy of History*, p. 69.
[2] 'The East knew . . . that *One* is free; the Greek and Roman world that *some* are free; the German world knows that *All* are free.' Ibid., p. 104.

conceptions of liberty – such as those current in 'master–slave' societies in which the freedom of some members is maintained at the cost of the oppression of others, or in individualistic ones which issue in internal conflict and dissension – are displaced by the notion of a social order wherein mutual respect between persons supersedes antagonism and distrust, each feeling his self-identity to be confirmed through participation in a differentiated social whole that at once enhances and transcends his own individuality. In a society so conceived – the properly ordered and 'mature' State portrayed by Hegel in his *Philosophy of Right* (1821) – the will of the individual and the will of the community can be said to coincide. Every member comes to understand the rules and customs he is required to observe as embodying standards and norms which he himself inwardly accepts and desires to promote; they do not, in other words, present themselves to him as restrictions or fetters upon him, as arbitrary impositions deriving from some alien source, but instead strike him as according with, and giving articulate form to, aspirations that spring from the depths of his own rational and socially orientated nature. Thus he recognizes the tasks and duties he is asked to fulfil, the roles he is obliged to perform, as contributing to the interests and well-being of the community as a whole, a community whose values he shares and with whose aims he can unreservedly identify himself. An early intimation of this concept of the State appeared in Hegel's *Phenomenology*, when he spoke of a 'free unity' of persons in which 'the laws give expression to that which each individual is and does':[1] later he referred to the State as that in which the individual has his 'substantive freedom', its being his 'essence', 'the end and product' of his activity.[2] With its attainment history, Hegel suggested, would reach its consummation, at least at the level of social and political consciousness. Freedom in the fullest sense would be actualized, man seeing his inner potentialities carried out and his essence completed in a world which he had created and in which he found himself 'at home': the deforming psychological and social tensions that (as we saw) preoccupied Hegel from his earliest days as a thinker would have been finally overcome and abolished, and spirit, reflecting upon and restored to itself, would be satisfied.

Hegel's philosophy was nothing if not comprehensive, and was intended to cover every aspect of spirit and its development. Hence it

---

[1] *The Phenomenology of Mind*, trans. J. B. Baillie (London, 1931), pp. 377–8.
[2] *The Philosophy of Right*, trans. T. M. Knox (Oxford, 1942), p. 155.

would be incorrect to assume that he regarded his account of the manner in which the *Weltgeist* unfolded itself objectively in the sphere of politics and society as representing the whole, or even the most crucial part, of its progress towards a total realization and knowledge of its character. And he in fact passed on the examination of forms of thought and activity of which life in an organized society was certainly an indispensable condition but with which, equally clearly, it could not be identified; namely, the arts, religion as revealed in the figurative dogmas of Christianity, and – at the pinnacle – philosophy itself, the last-named constituting the supreme expression of absolute mind in its quest for complete self-consciousness. Nevertheless, it was in the fields of social and historical theory that the seminal influence of Hegelian conceptions made itself most directly and powerfully felt. These conceptions, moreover, took root amongst writers of a markedly radical persuasion, who turned out to have little use for metaphysical or theological speculation in the traditional sense and whose work ultimately led to a repudiation of the Idealist assumptions that lay at the basis of Hegel's own system.

The Hegelian Aftermath

Admittedly, the initial impact of the Hegelian philosophy upon the intellectual world of Germany during the 1820s provided few intimations of what was to come. From early on Hegel had spoken as if his metaphysic could be treated as elucidating rather than contradicting the tenets of established Christian teaching, while in his later writings it was noticeable that he tended to adopt an increasingly theological tone in putting forward his claims concerning the absolute and its workings. Hence it is scarcely surprising that his asseverations on this theme found a ready and receptive audience amongst many contemporary upholders of orthodoxy: where Kant had sharply and emphatically distinguished between the spheres respectively occupied by knowledge and faith, Hegel (it was quite commonly believed) had demonstrated how reason and religion might after all overlap and even coincide. In the secular domain, too, Hegel's position was considered to entail conservative rather than reformist consequences, requiring that men should conform to the institutions of society as they found them rather than seek to change or overthrow them in favour of something better; and this conclusion was seemingly corroborated by the suggestion, implicit in his political philosophy, that a form of constitutional monarchy closely approximating to the one exemplified by the Prussia of his time might best fulfil the conditions in which freedom as he understood it could be realized.

Yet, comforting though such interpretations might be in the eyes of defenders of the existing order, it was not long before views implying a quite different assessment of Hegel's historical significance found adherents. In the late thirties and early forties, a group of German intellectuals, who came to be known as the 'Young Hegelians', maintained that the inner meaning of the master's doctrines had either been overlooked or misconstrued, and that when their true implications were elicited and followed through they could be seen to lead to positions greatly at variance from those attributed to him by his conservative followers. It was not denied that there were pervasive ambiguities in his system, or that Hegel had sometimes concealed, both from others and himself, the real bearing and explosive import of a number of his central ideas. It was argued, however, that what he wrote had too often been accorded a merely superficial treatment. Thus it did not follow from the much-quoted dictum that 'the real is the rational' that whatever happened to exist at a given time and place was necessarily right or deserving of respect: this was to ignore the normative and teleological connotations inherent in the Hegelian concept of reality. Again, when some of Hegel's fundamental contentions – for example, the identification of absolute spirit with the world-process as a whole and the claim that spirit finally fulfils its nature in and through the consciousness of finite human individuals – were properly grasped, his philosophy assumed an aspect which, amongst other things, made its interpretation as a kind of sophisticated apologia for Christian orthodoxy appear somewhat implausible. Hence D. F. Strauss, whose *Life of Jesus* caused a furore when it first came out in 1835, was regarded as applying essentially Hegelian principles when he represented the Gospels as being mythological expressions of the human mind at a particular stage of its development; while Bruno Bauer, in a pamphlet published in 1841 and entitled *Trumpet of the Last Judgement over Hegel the Atheist and Antichrist*, fervently proclaimed that the logical outcome and extreme result of Hegelianism was the denial of God in any form. It was, though, in Ludwig Feuerbach (1804–72) that the line of thought that originally inspired the Young Hegelian radicals found its most persuasive advocate. At the same time it is true to say that through Feuerbach's numerous works, and initially through his widely read and admired *Essence of Christianity* (*Das Wesen des Christentums*) which was published in 1841, the Hegelian world-picture underwent a profound transformation.[1]

For Feuerbach was not content merely to offer a reappraisal of Hegel's system; he also subjected it to a severe and very wide-ranging critical analysis, this being in fact complementary to the positive interpretation he sought to provide. Although the system could be seen to yield important insights, the truths it contained were refracted through the distorting medium of an unacceptable metaphysics. The nature of the distortions involved had to be identified and exposed before its inward significance could be made plain.

According to the position developed by Feuerbach in his *Thesen* and elsewhere, Hegel's crucial error – one that he shared with many of his predecessors – lay in a failure to recognize the necessary priority of existence to thinking. Briefly, 'being is the subject, thought the predicate'. Thought presupposed, and was dependent upon, a sensuously apprehended natural world of objects and events; human beings belonged to that world, and it was by reference to it that the thoughts they entertained in the last analysis acquired meaning and content. It followed that there was no justification for a philosophical procedure which, starting at the opposite end and taking pure conceptions as its point of departure, went on to try to extract the whole of nature from these. Yet it was just such a procedure (Feuerbach claimed) that Hegel had in effect followed, his philosophy from one point of view taking the form of an elaborate metaphysical conjuring trick. Thus his arguments to show how, beginning with the notion of a self-generating series of high-level concepts, it was possible to arrive at the spatio-temporal universe familiar to ordinary experience owed whatever plausibility they might seem to possess to his having assumed from the outset the conclusions he eventually reached: the evolving sequence of Hegelian categories, supposedly subject to a remorseless dialectical logic, represented in essence no more than the reflection in thought of what Hegel already knew to be the case on the basis of independent observation. The entire speculative project, indeed, of trying to pass directly 'from the abstract to the concrete, from the ideal to the real' was misconceived in principle. Where Hegel had spoken of the fundamentally spiritual character of the world, it was necessary instead to treat it as being irreducibly concrete and material; where he had

[1] Also influential, especially so far as Marx was concerned, were Feuerbach's *Vorläüfige Thesen zur Reform der Philosophie* and his *Grundsätze der Philosophie der Zukunft*; both essays were published in 1843.

emphasized the inner rationality of things, their transparency to reason, it was necessary to stress their essentially contingent status; where he had exalted the claims of abstract thought and logical method as sources of knowledge, it was necessary to reassert the epistemological primacy of sensory experience and perception.

Feuerbach's line of attack, forceful though it was, partly depended upon assumptions concerning the relation of Hegel's logical doctrine to his philosophy of nature which – for reasons that cannot be entered upon here – have sometimes been disputed. But, in view of the sweeping character of his objections, it might in any case be inquired how it was that he still felt justified in ascribing value to a philosophy he had so destructively criticized. The solution lies in his conviction that Hegelianism, properly understood, was 'esoteric psychology' and that Hegel had expressed, albeit in the mystifying and 'inverted' manner of Idealist speculation, a revealing insight into a central area of human life and consciousness. The essence of this insight emerged when speculative philosophy was, as it were, set on its feet or (in Feuerbach's phrase) 'turned upside down'; by such 'transformational criticism', which involved stripping the Hegelian theory of its Idealist trappings and 'putting the predicate in the place of the subject everywhere', the truth it embodied would stand forth in its 'unconcealed, pure, manifest form'. What truth? And in what form?

In his *Essence of Christianity* Feuerbach sought to provide answers to these questions within the setting of a general account of the role and significance of religion. Unlike some of his radical contemporaries, he appeared to take seriously the thesis that Hegel's philosophy was basically consonant with Christian belief, merely articulating its underlying content in rational form; he maintained, for instance, that if Hegelian doctrine seemed to contradict religion, it did so in the sense that 'a developed, consequent process of thought contradicts an undeveloped, inconsequent, but nevertheless radically identical conception'. At the same time he admitted that there was much in traditional theology that ran counter to the Hegelian theory, since the former 'by means of the idea of personality . . . makes God and man independent existences'. Hegel, on the other hand, who had consistently treated such dualism as involving an illusion, implied that it was in man that the 'divine essence' or spirit finally realized and unfolded itself: for him, spirit (or God) and man were intrinsically connected with one another – '*man's* consciousness of God is the *self*-consciousness of God' and hence 'the human consciousness is, *per se*, the divine consciousness'.[1] And by in this fashion bringing together the two 'properly inseparable' ideas of God and man Hegel had (Feuerbach argued) taken a crucially important step towards reaching an adequate interpretation of the religious consciousness and of what lay behind it. He was, however, prevented from drawing the correct conclusions from the point he had implicitly understood. For, faithful to his Idealist preconceptions, he had treated what are in fact attributes of man – namely, thinking and reasoning – as if they constituted the essence of a self-subsistent, 'absolute', God-like subject to which concrete human existence stood as a mere manifestation and as something secondary or derived. But such hypostatization of abstractions was illegitimate, involving an 'alienation of man from himself': 'it is', Feuerbach wrote, '*man* who thinks, not the Self, not Reason.' Thus the 'departed spirit' of traditional theology could be said to have returned in the end to haunt Hegel's own system, leading a 'ghostly existence' therein. To arrive at the truth hidden beneath the original Hegelian characterization of the relation between God and man it was necessary to transpose the terms in which it had been stated. The assertion that God becomes conscious of himself in man must, in other words, be replaced by the assertion that man becomes conscious of himself in God. 'Man's knowledge of God is man's knowledge of himself, of his own nature.'[2]

The proposition just quoted represents the kernel of Feuerbach's developed theory of religion. According to him, religion implied the projection by man of his essential properties and powers into a transcendent sphere in such a way that they appeared before him in the shape of a divine being standing over and above himself. 'The divine thing', he proclaimed, 'is nothing else than the human being, or, rather, the human nature purified, freed from the limits of individual man, made objective – i.e. contemplated and revered as another, a distinct being.'[3] Hence in worshipping God man is in reality worshipping himself, though without realizing that this is what he is doing; he is the victim of a kind of illusion. It does not, however, follow that the illusion in question has not a significant role to play in human development. Historically considered, Feuerbach says, it served the vital function of bringing man to an objective understanding of himself and of his true potentialities: it is, indeed, man's earliest form of

[1] *The Essence of Christianity*, trans. M. Evans (London, 1881), pp. 226–31.
[2] Ibid., p. 230.   [3] Ibid., p. 14.

O

self-knowledge, making him aware – in however indirect and deceptive a manner – of what he has it within him to become. Even so, the positive contribution made by religion to the promotion of human self-consciousness and self-transcendence was, Feuerbach believed, counter-balanced by negative elements that necessitated its eventual supersession, and it was to the consideration of these latter factors that he chiefly addressed himself. Thus he pointed out that men tended to project into their idea of God only the highest characteristics and aspirations of the human species – 'as God is, so man *should* be and *desires* to be.' But by forming an idealized conception of the divine, by making God the external repository of all that was most worthy of respect and development in human nature, they were at the same time inevitably led to diminish their own status as empirical beings in the world: by comparison with the image of authority and nobility that had been conjured up they could not fail to be struck by their own weakness and inadequacy. In short, the enrichment of the heavenly sphere proceeded *pari passu* with the impoverishment of the earthly. On the one hand, man sought to submit his will to that of a mythical transcendent being, thereby relegating himself to a condition of self-imposed subservience and dependence in which he was unable to realize his latent capacities or satisfy his true needs. On the other, he tended to find compensation for the frustrations and renunciations of his earthly existence by participating vicariously in a fantasy world of his own making: real human passivity was matched by imagined divine activity, real human suffering by imagined celestial bliss. The removal of this state of affairs depended upon man's coming to a clear recognition of the illusions to which he was subject; only thus could he reappropriate to himself all that he had treated as extraneous and as belonging to a transcendent reality. He must see that the qualities and powers he had ascribed to God were in fact his own qualities, his own powers: the way would then be open for each individual to actualize his inner potentialities as a human being in a creative and fruitful fashion. Since, moreover, Feuerbach held that men were essentially social by nature, the individual's fulfilment would be achieved in a community of free persons like himself and united to one another by bonds of affection and sympathy.

Feuerbach's discussion of typical religious attitudes is often highly reminiscent of Hegelian disquisitions on the same theme, and particularly of that given in the section on the 'unhappy consciousness' in the *Phenomenology*; it was not for nothing that he had listened to Hegel's lectures when a student at Berlin, and despite his subsequent criticisms his debt remained a considerable one. It is understandable, all the same, that he should have regarded his 'transformation of theology into anthropology' as going far beyond anything actually envisaged by Hegel himself. It is understandable, too, that he should have been hailed by his young contemporaries in Germany as a 'liberator', who had demonstrated how central notions of the Hegelian system could be redeployed in a manner that implied a complete emancipation from Idealist mystification. Thus alienation was no longer to be understood as being a matter of spirit's estrangement from itself in nature or 'objectivity', but instead as being one of humanity's estrangement from itself in the God of religion. The destiny of the world was to be conceived, not in terms of the absolute's return to itself through self-knowledge, but in terms of man's return to himself through the recognition and realization of his own powers and possibilities. History as the story of the evolving *Weltgeist* became history as the story of man's evolution as an empirical being in the context of a natural environment. It was with proposals such as these in mind that many felt that Feuerbach had not merely set Hegel's philosophy within a radically new perspective; he had also propounded a methodological approach to the problems of human life in society which, properly developed and exploited, could be shown to have profound practical, as well as purely theoretical, consequences. Amongst those to whom it appealed was the somewhat eccentric anarchist, Max Stirner, who extended to contemporary ethical and humanistic ideals a treatment similar to that accorded by Feuerbach to religious modes of thought and who claimed that submission to abstractions like 'mankind', 'the State' and even Feuerbach's own much-vaunted 'human essence' signified the emergence in a fresh guise of the religious alienation of earlier times: the solution, he argued, consisted in each man's coming to understand that he was responsible to himself alone for what he thought and did, and that neither established social institutions nor falsely reified values had the slightest claim – moral or otherwise – upon his will. Stirner was, however, a rather peripheral figure in the intellectual history of the period. The same cannot be said of Karl Marx (1818–83), upon whom Feuerbach's ideas also produced a deep impression and in this case with results that proved momentous.

Marx is usually regarded as an economist and sociologist, and as the founder of a revolutionary creed, rather than as a philosopher in his own right; and it may be granted that his later writings, including the massive *Capital* of which the first volume appeared in 1867, contain little that is ostensibly related to matters of philosophical concern. It is also true that it was his reading of French and British works on political economy that in the first instance inspired a number of his leading ideas. Yet the fact remains that it was in terms of a scheme of thought owing much to current philosophical conceptions that he originally evolved his theories of society and of the nature of historical change. The influence in question was manifest in *The Holy Family* (1845) and *The German Ideology* (1846), and was perhaps most pronounced in what have come to be known as the 'Economic and Philosophical Manuscripts' which were written in 1844. Taken together, these various works clearly exhibit the major part played by Feuerbachian and Hegelian principles in helping to shape the framework in which he initially developed his doctrines.

Feuerbach's transformational method, by means of which it appeared that Hegelian metaphysics could at one and the same time be both 'overcome' and also shown to embody cardinal insights into the character of human thought and activity, came to Marx with the force of a revelation, leading him to describe Feuerbach as 'the only person who has a *serious* and *critical* relation to Hegel's dialectic, who has made real discoveries in this field, and above all, who has vanquished the old philosophy.'[1] Marx, in other words, accepted the contention that the mystical Hegelian world-spirit was a piece of philosophical mythology; though treated as the 'ultimate subject', it was in fact only the abstract reification of an attribute of the true subject, this being 'real corporeal *man*, with his feet firmly planted on the solid ground, inhaling and exhaling all the powers of nature'.[2] He accepted, too, the correlative claim that, once the 'inverted' nature of his thinking was grasped, much that Hegel had written could be 'translated' into a form that threw a penetrating light upon how things stood in the actual human world. Such an approach had, indeed, enabled Feuerbach to arrive at a new understanding of the meaning of religion. But this by no means exhausted its possibilities.

To understand what Marx conceived these to be, it is necessary to return to the Hegelian concept of alienation; in common with Feuerbach, he treated this as central to the entire programme of transformational criticism. The two thinkers diverged, however, in their respec-

[1] 'Critique of Hegel's Dialectic and General Philosophy', in *Karl Marx: Early Writings*, trans. and ed. T. B. Bottomore (London, 1963), p. 197.
[2] Ibid., p. 206.

tive interpretations of the ideas. Whereas Feuerbach, in conformity with his religious preoccupations, had presented it as essentially consisting in man's projection of his nature upon a purely mythical or fictitious being, Marx by contrast saw it as finding expression in a host of other ways, and above all in institutional and economic phenomena which, far from having a wholly notional existence, were palpably objective facts. Thus for Marx alienation was not confined to cases in which it involved a kind of communal illusion of the human mind, and neither therefore could its dissolution always be accomplished simply through removing the scales from men's eyes: inasmuch as the factors implicit in man's self-estrangement were objectively related to his concrete social situation, their destruction required practical as opposed to merely cognitive or theoretical activity. Such considerations, furthermore, pointed to inadequacies in Feuerbach's account of religious alienation itself. For this had left unanswered the question of why such alienation occurred in the first place, a question which (Marx maintained) could only be resolved by undertaking an analysis of the social conflicts that gave rise to the religious mode of consciousness. As he put it in a famous passage: 'The fact that the secular basis deserts its own sphere and establishes an independent realm in the clouds can only be explained by the cleavage and self-contradictions within this secular basis. The latter, therefore, must itself be both understood in its contradictions and revolutionized in practice.'[1]

In stressing the sociological aspects of human alienation in the manner he did, Marx can be regarded from one point of view as developing a line of thought which had been discernible at certain levels of Hegel's philosophy but which had tended to drop out of sight in Feuerbach's. For, as we saw, Hegel in his theory of history had suggested that man lives in a world that he has himself constructed, that the institutions and forms of life that surround him and provide the medium of his existence are the results of his own activity, and, moreover, that under certain historical conditions these institutions and the beliefs that inform them may be experienced as hindrances or obstacles to further advance. Admittedly, Hegel had expressed this in a way that implied that in the last analysis everything was to be ascribed to the agency of an absolute mind or spirit: the passions and deeds of

[1] *Theses on Feuerbach* (1845), trans. T. B. Bottomore, in *Karl Marx: Selected Writings in Sociology and Social Philosophy*, ed. T. B. Bottomore and M. Rubel (London, 1956).

individual human beings represented the means whereby what was called 'the cunning of Reason' realized its own exalted ends, and different historical periods were to be understood primarily as the incarnation of conceptions, these being distinct phases in the development of the rational Idea. It was with just such notions in mind that Marx criticized Hegel for having 'turned the world on its head', giving priority to ideas as against flesh-and-blood existence and depicting the history of humanity as the history of 'a spirit above and beyond real man'. Nevertheless, when the categories Hegel had introduced were taken out of their metaphysical setting and firmly placed in a sociological one, a very different picture emerged.

Marx's own theory of historical and social change was in fact shot through with Hegelian ideas. Like Hegel, he envisaged history as conforming to a 'dialectical' pattern, fresh social and cultural forms arising in consequence of the tensions that beset and finally destroyed old and out-dated ones. He saw it, too, as a progressive movement towards the realization of a rational society in which men would achieve fulfilment as free and creative beings; it is noteworthy that he spoke, as Hegel had done, of freedom as pertaining to man's essence, even if his vision of the kind of social order in which it would find expression was markedly dissimilar. And he was furthermore insistent upon the notion that, in the course of building the environments in which they live, men at the same time transform themselves, not merely in the sense of gaining new aptitudes and skills, but also in the sense of acquiring new needs, goals and interests; from this point of view he claimed that the conception, underlying Hegel's *Phenomenology*, of 'the self-creation of man as a process' embodied a profound insight into the fundamental nature and direction of historical development. Its true implications, however, only became plain when the Hegelian priorities were switched and when it was recognized that it was the forces of material – as opposed to what he termed 'abstractly spiritual' – production that really determined the course of human evolution. On the revised Marxian account man could indeed be said to create both himself and his world; but he did so in the first instance as a being who, through the invention and use of practical techniques, achieved a progressive mastery over nature with the object of making it conform to his purposes and provide the means of his material subsistence and satisfaction. It was this very capacity for productive and technological activity, expressing itself in what Marx called 'the practical construction of an objective world, the manipulation of inorganic nature',[1] that above all else distinguished men from other living creatures.

Such a view entailed a number of consequences. Marx accepted the Hegelian thesis that the various aspects of a social whole were closely interrelated with one another and could not properly be understood in isolation. He argued, though, that all the different manifestations of the life of a given society – in particular, its political and legal institutions and the valuational concepts that underlay these – were finally intelligible only by reference to the condition and state of development of its productive technology; this point could be put epigrammatically by saying that 'the windmill will give a society with the feudal lord, the steam mill a society with the industrial capitalist'. As basic methods of production change, new groups or classes rise to positions of dominance, challenging the old order and creating in their turn forms of social organization through which they can conserve and exploit the advantages that accrue to them in virtue of their possession or control of the productive forces. Thus the notion of progression through conflict, which figured in Hegel's philosophy of history, returned in the one put forward by Marx; here, however, it was presented in a form that postulated a recurrent struggle between economically determined classes, the oppressed of one age becoming the oppressors of the next. Society, in other words, was to be thought of as divided between opposed groups, one appropriating for its own use what had been produced by the labour of the other and legitimizing such appropriation by both institutional and ideological means. It was in terms of this theory that Marx developed his sociologically orientated interpretation of the doctrine of alienation.

What did this interpretation amount to? Despite the central position the concept of alienation occupied in his early thought, Marx did not in fact employ it in any very precise or systematic manner, the fundamental theme of man's estrangement from himself undergoing at his hands a somewhat bewildering series of variations and metaphorical extensions. At a general level he often uses it to refer to the way in which men are prone to treat as autonomous forces or agencies social procedures or systems of ideas that are in reality the expression of their own powers and activities. Again, he tries to show how institutions that originally served the historical function of ministering to or promoting the wants and needs of human beings become in the course of

[1] 'Alienated Labour', in *Karl Marx: Early Writings*, trans. and ed. T. B. Bottomore, pp. 127-8.

time bonds or fetters upon them, hindering the free development of their potentialities: as with Feuerbach, man is regarded as enslaving himself, though not in a fashion that can be spirited away by a mere change of intellectual outlook. But Marx also utilizes the concept in a more specific sense and in such a way that it is tied directly to the actual labour process itself, especially as he conceived this to operate in the context of nineteenth-century capitalist society. The latter interpretation, which is prominent in his 1844 manuscripts, is rooted in the view that man, so to speak, objectifies or externalizes himself in the artefacts he produces; thus Marx writes of 'everyday material industry' representing the 'essential human faculties transformed into objects'. Alienation occurs through the objects, in the production of which man has spent himself and his powers, being cut off or torn from him, with the result that 'the life which he has given to the object sets itself against him as an alien and hostile force':[1] he is dominated and impoverished by a world which he himself has made, so that it can be said that 'the more the worker expends himself in work the more powerful becomes the world of objects which he creates in face of himself, . . . and the less he belongs to himself'.[2] Marx suggests, too, that under capitalist society men are not only alienated from the products of their labour but also become estranged from their true nature as creative beings: far from being something in which men find satisfaction and self-fulfilment, work comes to be experienced as intensely disagreeable, acquiring a mechanical compulsive quality that is utterly opposed to the 'free conscious activity' which is the real 'species-character of human beings'. And Marx sees yet a further dimension of the meaning of alienation in the human relationships engendered by the type of society he has described. From this standpoint man can be portrayed as self-estranged in the sense that men are estranged from one another. For the 'alien being' who appropriates to his own advantage the worker's products is none other than man himself: it is through the activities of the capitalist 'or whatever one chooses to call the master of labour' that his fellow men are reduced to a condition of economic servitude and degraded to the status of mere commodities, to be bartered or exchanged in the labour market. 'Not the gods, nor nature, but only man himself can be this alien power over men.'[3]

As various commentators have noted, some of the ideas contained in

[1] 'Alienated Labour', in *Karl Marx: Early Writings*, trans. and ed. T. B. Bottomore, p. 123.
[2] Ibid., p. 122.   [3] Ibid., p. 130.

Marx's account of the alienation of labour were prefigured in the analysis of human domination and slavery which Hegel had given in a particular section of his *Phenomenology*;[1] it was perhaps partly with this in mind that Marx himself spoke on one occasion of the latter work as including 'elements of criticism' that went 'far beyond Hegel's own point of view'. Yet that point of view remained, when all was said, a metaphysical one, Hegel's particular empirical insights into the workings of human society being presented and absorbed within a theory that conceived alienation to be ultimately an affair of absolute spirit and its resolution to be a matter, in the end, of philosophical understanding alone. Marx took pride in having so transposed the Hegelian categories that it became clear that the true solution of the problem of alienation lay, not through theoretical knowledge of the world, but through practical intervention within it. For the alienation of which he spoke was not 'spiritual' but 'material', and as such it could not be overcome through 'a purely inward spiritual action'. Rather, it was to be resolved by the reappropriation by the proletarian class of the material world which it had itself created, which was in a sense its own, and of which it had been dispossessed. The tenets of Idealist speculation had been translated into a programme of revolutionary activity.

Schopenhauer

If the imprint of Hegelian preoccupations and modes of thought remained clearly visible in the work of the men discussed in the previous section, the same cannot be said of another thinker who none the less played a significant role in the evolution of German Idealism. This was Arthur Schopenhauer (1788–1860).

It was, indeed, no accident that Schopenhauer first began to achieve widespread prominence in Germany during the 1850s. For this was a time when the influence and prestige of Hegel in academic circles suffered a considerable decline: in consequence, the vituperative attacks upon Hegelianism contained in Schopenhauer's collection of essays, *Parerga and Paralipomena* (1851), met with a more sympathetic response than had greeted his earlier criticisms and were amongst the factors that initially led to his belated recognition as an important and original philosopher. Yet he had, from the start, advertised his opposition to Hegelian principles. The first edition of his chief meta-

[1] See J. B. Baillie, op. cit., pp. 229–40.

physical work, *The World as Will and Idea*, had been published in 1819, shortly after Hegel's appointment to the chair of philosophy in Berlin; he had, moreover, at the same period himself obtained a position at the latter university, deliberately timing his lectures to coincide with those given by the man he was later to accuse of having corrupted an entire generation of German intellectuals. But circumstances were against him, the alternative system he wished to propound awakening no interest. Accordingly, rather than try to trim his teaching to the prevalent climate of opinion, Schopenhauer chose instead to give up the prospect of following an academic career. He withdrew into private life where, in scornful defiance of contemporary trends and fashions, he proceeded henceforth to pursue and elaborate to his own satisfaction his highly individual conceptions and insights.

Many of Schopenhauer's explicit objections to the Hegelian style of philosophizing derived from his belief that Hegel and his followers had fatally obscured Kant's discoveries concerning the nature and possible extent of human knowledge. Employing a pretentious and mystifying jargon, they had made claims which were unwarranted by experience and which often overstepped the limits of intelligible discourse, resulting in sheer nonsense. He also represented Hegel as a servant of the establishment, disseminating doctrines that were nicely adapted to the interests of Church and State alike; his 'absolute' was a 'new-fangled title for God', while his political theory afforded a handy weapon with which to rebut the arguments of those hostile to the Prussian governmental system. To later commentators Schopenhauer's polemics, with their cynical imputations of dubious motives, have often seemed exaggerated and unjust, owing more to personal passion and resentment than to fair-minded judgement. But be this as it may, there can be no question that they also mirrored profound divergences of temperament and philosophical outlook. Schopenhauer, for instance, took little interest in political matters, and there was a conspicuous absence from his thought of the progressivist optimism, the acute sensitivity to social change and development, which figured so largely in Hegel's thought and which was transmitted to his more radically inclined successors. Likewise he was deeply antipathetic to the historicist tendencies of his age; human characteristics and perspectives did not, in his eyes, undergo fundamental alterations from one period to another, and he regarded history as forming a sequence in which what were at root the same basic human traits expressed themselves endlessly in continually repeated patterns. Nor did he share the view that salvation was to be found at the level of co-operative social endeavour, as Marx and Engels had implied. By contrast with such theorists he argued that the actions of men, together with the desires and projects that inspired them, were inherently suspect; for, when considered in the context of his metaphysics, these emerged as being mere manifestations of a non-rational cosmic force or agency that underlay all things, human and non-human alike. The force in question was referred to by Schopenhauer as the will, and it was in terms of this notion that he propounded his overall conception of the world. How did he arrive at such a position, apparently so far removed from those adopted by his Idealist compatriots?

Schopenhauer's starting-point was, as theirs had been, the Kantian philosophy. He claimed, however, that he had, unlike them, remained faithful to the essential tenets of the Kantian programme. And it is true that much that he had to say has a markedly Kantian flavour. Thus Kant's distinction between phenomenal appearance and noumenal reality was preserved in the theory of knowledge that Schopenhauer put forward, being reflected in the categories of 'idea' and 'will' that formed the framework of his own epistemology. The world of every-day perception, which afforded the subject-matter of both ordinary commonsense thinking and of scientific investigation, derived from the productive activity of the human mind, being in a sense its crea-tion: as with Kant, the intellect was to be understood as imposing a determinate structure upon the data of sensation and so presenting us with a law-governed universe of objective things and events. This phenomenal realm, which appeared at the level of the naïve conscious-ness to constitute 'reality' and which stood at the foundation of all everyday knowledge and language, was referred to by Schopenhauer as being ultimately no more than 'idea' or 'representation' (*Vorstellung*): by this he meant that its universal character as a spatio-temporal and causally ordered system was in the last analysis due to the contribution of the perceiving subject and could not validly be ascribed to the world in its innermost essence. The conceptions of space, time and causality were, in other words, applicable to the phenomenal sphere alone, attempts to employ them to interpret what lay beyond that sphere being illegitimate; herein, indeed, was a principal source of the errors that had traditionally beset metaphysical speculation. But he did not go on to argue that all knowledge of the noumenal sphere, of the world as it is in itself, was thereby rendered in principle unattainable. On the contrary: Schopenhauer's philosophy was based upon the conviction that an acquaintance with the underlying nature of existence was in fact open to us, emerging through our inward awareness of ourselves as active willing beings – the will 'reveals itself to everyone directly as the in-itself of his own phenomenal being'.[1] Thus we have (he claimed) a 'double knowledge' of ourselves: from one point of view we appear as 'objects among objects', perceivable embodied entities that conform to the same conditions and laws that hold for the rest of the phenomenal world; while from the other we stand revealed under a quite distinct aspect, an aspect that corresponds to our true nature and character.

Schopenhauer therefore departed from Kant in claiming, through his doctrine of self-knowledge, that noumenal reality fell within the range of human cognition. Yet, as he himself allowed, there were at the same time evident connections between that doctrine and the Kantian theory of moral experience wherein man was portrayed as belonging to two separate domains, one 'sensuous' and the other 'intelligible'. And it might also be said to owe more than its author cared to admit to the voluntaristic analysis of self-consciousness that had been provided by Fichte – a thinker he professed to despise. As developed by him, however, it gave rise to a comprehensive account of the world, and of man's place within the world, that was very much his own.

Schopenhauer laid great stress upon the point that his system was not a product of empty word-spinning, but was instead firmly based upon the direct intimations of inner experience. Here was the clue which, properly interpreted, showed the way to a solution of the riddle of existence as a whole. Yet it might seem at first glance hard to understand why he should have felt himself justified in treating the concept of will, which in its normal employment is largely restricted to the field of human activity, in so extensive a manner, using it to characterize and explain all things, animate and inanimate alike. The difficulty is perhaps somewhat reduced, though not altogether removed, when it is realized that he interpreted the notion in a sense very different from that given to it by most of his philosophical predecessors. He did not, for example, follow Descartes in regarding it as finally inseparable from the notion of rational mind or soul, nor did he conceive it, as Kant had done, as implying a capacity to act in accordance with self-imposed practical principles. All such traditional formulations,

[1] *The World as Will and Idea*, trans. R. B. Haldane and J. Kemp (London, 1883), Vol. II, p. 119.

which tended to depict the will in exclusively intellectualistic terms, were in his view the result of a deep-seated illusion that was in its turn partly born of human vanity: men liked to suppose that all that they did lay within the provenance of conscious thought and reason. Yet the truth was quite otherwise. The will was not a component of the intellect, set apart from the body and acting upon it; rather, it should be recognized that the body was no more than the will 'objectified', the various physical movements a man makes being merely the overt expression – in 'phenomenal' terms – of the inner workings of his will. So far as the intellect itself was concerned, it was not so much the master of the body as the servant or instrument of the will: its primary function (Schopenhauer repeatedly emphasized) was one of providing information that was of use to us in satisfying our wants and needs, our whole manner of viewing the world and of categorizing the material presented to us by our senses being determined by practical interest and adapted to the fulfilment of those drives and appetites that constituted our essential nature as will-governed individuals. Thus our ordinary modes of knowledge and understanding could in the end be traced back to the self-same all-encompassing principle which, at the level of action, informed every aspect of our be-haviour.

The picture of human nature that Schopenhauer drew was not, and was not meant to be, a flattering or reassuring one. In a fashion that often recalls Freud, he insists that men are largely unaware of the true motives that activate them, being frequently deceived into thinking that they are prompted by considerations which bear little or no resem-blance to those that actually move them. For human beings are skilled at inventing, consciously or unconsciously, comforting rationalizations of what really leads them to act; they are adept, too, in turning their gaze from the cruder features which a disinterested examination of their conduct would reveal. Much of Schopenhauer's most perceptive writing was devoted to this theme. In passages which are, in the light of subsequent developments, of great interest and which exhibit at times a psychological acumen equalled by few other philosophers, he offers examples designed to show how totally blind men can be to the true import of their actions and how little preconceived aims and resolutions (often quite sincerely entertained) may influence behaviour when these conflict with the primary urges by which people are driven. Foremost amongst the latter Schopenhauer placed the instincts of self-preservation and sexuality ('the focus of the will'): not only was it beyond the power of conscious deliberation to escape the sway of such forces; they also (he held) set men upon courses that could bring them no lasting peace or contentment, condemning them instead to an unending round of disappointment and to a mutual antagonism which inevitably brought suffering in its train. Human life, in other words, was enmeshed in illusion and sorrow; and it was in the light of this profoundly pessimistic vision of our condition, so harshly opposed to that of the eighteenth-century Enlightenment, that he delineated his metaphysical conception of the world as a whole. For the entire realm of nature, down to its most primitive elements, was to be understood as sharing the same essential character as man himself. All could be seen as an expression of the identical voracious will that exhibited itself so fearsomely in the human sphere: all participated in the same ceaseless struggle for existence; all was likewise doomed to eventual frustration and dissolution.

Given the disenchantment which pervaded his general view of the universe, it is not surprising that Schopenhauer should have reached conclusions widely at variance with those favoured by his more sanguine German contemporaries. Ultimate reality was not to be seen as a moral totality with which we should gladly seek to identify ourselves; nor (again) could it be envisaged as a dialectical progression leading inexorably towards some absolute reconciliation of thought with being. Schopenhauer might follow Hegel in questioning the validity of the framework of ideas with which we are accustomed to try to explain and cope with the world. He did not, however, do so on the ground that it failed to capture a rational order that somehow transcended commonsense or scientific notions and procedures, for he believed that in the final analysis there was no such order to be discerned; what lurked beneath the phenomenal surface of things was fundamentally antithetical to all value, devoid of any overall goal or purpose that could lend meaning and significance to the whole. The only appropriate reaction to the will and its workings was rejection, not respect or veneration; the sole proper response lay, not in affirming it, but in seeking liberation from its trammels. But how was such liberation possible? Did not the basic tenets of the theory propounded preclude it? Schopenauer did not think so. For an answer he turned to two areas of human consciousness to which he assigned supreme importance: the aesthetic and the ethical.

There was a sense in which these two departments of our experience stood in the closest connection with one another; for they both,

Schopenhauer maintained, involved some degree of release from the forms of knowledge which governed our everyday apprehension of the world. In aesthetic awareness we were, he held, no longer subject to the practically orientated mode of approaching things which constituted our normal condition and which consisted in looking at them solely with a view to their potential uses to us as active beings. As a result reality now appeared to us in a totally transformed perspective. For, in place of the plurality of particular objects and events that made up our everyday picture of the world, we instead became conscious of the 'permanent essential forms of the world and all its phenomena' which stood to the phenomena of ordinary sense perception as 'archetypes to their copies': with Plato in mind, Schopenhauer referred to these eternal forms as 'Ideas', treating them as the objective counterpart or correlate of the disinterested mode of contemplation that represented the distinctively aesthetic attitude. When the world was viewed from this standpoint we were – for a time at least – freed from the relentless pressures of the will, ceasing to concentrate upon 'the where, the when, the why, and the whither of things' and looking instead 'simply and solely at the *what*'.[1] It was to such a frame of mind and outlook that the initial conception, if not the detailed execution, of all genuine works of art belonged; artistic creations were the vehicles of profound intuitions and truths to which men, obsessed by the utilitarian preoccupations of their daily lives, remained for the most part blind and insensitive.

Considerations in some ways analogous applied in the interpretation of the ethical sphere, though at a deeper level and with different implications. Despite his generally bleak portrayal of human nature, Schopenhauer did not intend to deny that there existed men whose dispositions were good; this was a datum that had to be accepted, the problem for moral philosophy being the account that was to be given of it. Like the artist or aesthetic observer, the morally good individual could be said to apprehend the world in a light other than that in which it typically presented itself when regarded through the distorting lens of ordinary 'will-governed' cognition: what Schopenhauer called the 'principle of individuation' (*principium individuationis*), whereby reality appeared before us as fragmented into a host of phenomenal particulars with specific spatio-temporal locations, was here to some extent in abeyance, together with the pervasive consciousness of separation from

[1] *The World as Will and Idea*, trans. R. B. Haldane and J. Kemp (London, 1883), Vol. I, p. 231.

other living beings that was at once the prerequisite and the prime source of egoism. Thus the qualities characteristic of the good life sprang in the end from an insight which – penetrating to what lay beneath the phenomenal surface of the world and was beyond even the ideal forms that constituted the subject-matter of art – recognized the fundamental identity of all things and persons: each was ultimately no more than an expression of the underlying unitary will postulated by Schopenhauer's metaphysic. Such superior understanding exhibited itself in conduct of a compassionate and altruistic nature, showing that the agent drew 'less distinction between himself and others than is usually done'; although Schopenhauer was at the same time anxious to insist that the insight in question was not, or not necessarily, something of which its possessor had an articulate grasp. Rather it took the form of an intimate sense of belonging together with the rest of the world, an inward 'feeling' which – despite its force – tended to elude clear conceptualization.

Schopenhauer's treatment of ethics, his claim that the apparent divisions separating men from each other and from their environment are the product of a mode of consciousness which from a higher standpoint is seen to be illusory, may seem (somewhat ironically) to echo the theme of alienation and its resolution at the level of knowledge and understanding that was implicit in the writings of other thinkers of his time. But his particular conception of the world as will did not allow him to conclude his work at this point, and the morals he drew were quite different from theirs. Thus he went on to argue that a complete realization of the inner nature of things could only issue in a recognition of the ultimate worthlessness and vanity of all existence. With this in mind, and influenced by Buddhist texts which he freely cited, he suggested that final enlightenment only dawned when the condition exemplified by persons of good disposition was superseded by one that involved an absolute renunciation of the world and withdrawal from its concerns; in such a case one could speak of the will's 'turning and denying itself'. He admitted that, on his own principles, it might appear hard to envisage how this could possibly occur. For, according to those, everything a man willed and did was regarded as following inexorably from his character, this being itself fixed and given; the so-called 'turning of the will', on the other hand, was said to imply the complete abolition of his former personality. Schopenhauer maintained, however, that what he had in view was not something that could be produced by the individual of his own deliberate volition, and must be seen rather as a change that came to him as though 'from outside'; if comparisons were wanted, one could cite the phenomenon of religious conversion. In any case, he had no wish to deny that the sort of thing discussed was of its essence mysterious, implying a total negation of the conditions requisite to knowledge as we understand it and being therefore beyond the reach of rational discourse. For the will, and hence the entire realm of idea or representation that was its 'mirror', had been denied, the mystical illumination that accompanied such denial being itself necessarily inexpressible. To try, as some were tempted to do, to speak of what lay beyond the will and the world was in principle misconceived; it was 'to seek to make a vain show of positive knowledge of that which is forever inaccessible to all knowledge, or at the most can be indicated by means of a negation'.[1] Schopenhauer's final position can, indeed, be regarded as one that implied the ultimate transcendence of philosophy: in this respect, if in no other, he resembled Marx. Whereas, however, Marx had envisaged such transcendence in terms of active participation in the affairs of the world, Schopenhauer by contrast saw it as a matter of quietism and resignation, and of deliverance from the bondage of earthly existence.

Conclusion

In their different ways the works of Schopenhauer and Marx form a natural boundary to the period of thought with which we have been concerned. With these men – one rejecting the theoretical postulates and ambitions of Hegelianism, the other undertaking their radical transformation – the metaphysical impulse that inspired the great systems of the early nineteenth century may be said to have returned upon itself, encompassing its own dissolution. It is not without significance, for instance, that the most influential German thinker of the century's second half was Nietzsche, a writer hostile to speculative system-building in all its forms and profoundly contemptuous of the grandiose structures in which his predecessors had attempted to encase reality. Yet, as was indicated in the Introduction to the present survey, the products of German Idealism cannot be written off as being no more than obscurantist or arbitrary fantasies deriving from an over-stimulated philosophical imagination; looked at from another standpoint, some of them can be seen to embody revolutionary proposals that

[1] *The World as Will and Idea*, trans. R. B. Haldane and J. Kemp (London, 1883), Vol. III, p. 431.

involved a drastic revision of our picture of ourselves and our situation in the world. Hegel's approach to historical change and the suggestive models by which he sought to analyse the development of human consciousness in a social setting; Schopenhauer's conception of the will as an interpretative device pointing towards the exploration of strata of the mind that had never been charted before: these were amongst the important contributions made at this time towards enlarging man's understanding of himself. As such, they deeply influenced the lines taken by subsequent thought and empirical inquiry, particularly in the areas of social science, history and psychology: they helped, too, though less dramatically, to refashion opinion concerning the roles of art and religion in human life. And if one often discerns in what was written the intimations of a more sombre theme, seeming to presage later storms and conflicts, this is scarcely surprising. For the period was also one in which powerful ideologies that have come to dominate the political landscape of our own times first began to take shape. Here, as in other ways, it retains a peculiar and poignant relevance for the modern historian of ideas.

Bibliography

GENERAL SURVEYS

COPLESTON, F. C. *A History of Philosophy*, Vol. VII. London, 1963.
HOOK, S. *From Hegel to Marx*. New York, 1935.
LÖWITH, K. *From Hegel to Nietzsche*. Trans. D. E. Green. London, 1965.
MANDELBAUM, M. *History, Man and Reason*. Baltimore and London, 1971.
MCLENNAN, D. *The Young Hegelians and Karl Marx*. London, 1969.
MARCUSE, H. *Reason and Revolution*. London, 1941.
PLAMENATZ, J. P. *Man and Society*. Vol. II. London, 1963.
POPPER, K. R. *The Open Society and its Enemies*. Vol. II. London, 1945.
ROYCE, J. *The Spirit of Modern Philosophy*. Boston, 1892.
SCHACHT, R. *Alienation*. London, 1971.

WORKS ON INDIVIDUAL THINKERS

KÖRNER, S. *Kant*. London, 1955.
MILLER, R. D. *Schiller and the Ideal of Freedom*. Oxford, 1970.
ADAMSON, R. *Fichte*. Edinburgh, 1881.
CAIRD, E. *Hegel*. London, 1883.
FINDLAY, J. N. *Hegel: A Re-examination*. London, 1958.
KAUFMANN, W. *Hegel: Reinterpretation, Texts and Commentary*. London, 1966.
KAMENKA, E. *The Philosophy of Ludwig Feuerbach*. London, 1970.
BERLIN, I. *Karl Marx*. London, 1939; rev. edn. 1963.
LICHTHEIM, G. *Marxism: An Historical and Critical Study*. London, 1961.
TUCKER, R. C. *Philosophy and Myth in Karl Marx*. Cambridge, 1961.
GARDINER, P. L. *Schopenhauer*. London, 1963.

7 Modern German Thought

ALASDAIR MACINTYRE

There is no modern society of which it would be possible to write a true history of its thought in isolation from the history of its social order. But in the case of Germany there are special reasons why this is impossible. For the attitude of German society to its thinkers has been profoundly ambiguous since the middle of the nineteenth century. The revolutions of 1848 in Germany were the first and last occasion on which German intellectuals even approached the wielding of political power; and their failure of nerve upon that occasion, their self-abasement before the facts of power, anticipated their for the most part passive acceptance of first the imperial and later the Nazi social order. The institutionalization of learning in the unversities had provided a system in which the professor became a kind of only semi-independent functionary. It is 'the professor' so understood whom the Danish theologian, Sören Kierkegaard saw as a kind of intellectual parasite. Thus German intellectuals can be divided into those who accepted the professional function as officially defined and identified with it and those who stood outside this established order.

But the portrait of the German intellectual between 1890 and 1940 is a more difficult one to draw than this suggests. For as well as the official culture of Wilhelmine Germany there was the larger culture of the German-speaking world and more especially the metropolitan culture of Vienna. The mark of this latter culture was a degree of self-consciousness about the intellectual life which has rarely, if ever, been attained elsewhere in intellectual history. From this culture was born an intense preoccupation with language as the medium of all human culture and existence, and with the borderlines between the meaningful and the meaningless and between the conscious and the unconscious. Austrian Society or in its own smaller way German-Swiss society was in many ways as marked by the official culture of the universities as was Wilhelmine Germany. But it was open to penetration by this counter-culture of self-consciousness which was apt to reveal all too clearly how unstable the complexities of German society and culture were.

Yet the full extent of conflict and complexity has not been envisaged until a third element is added. In both Germany and Austria the working-class movement had brought into being in the last decades of the nineteenth century self-avowedly Marxist political parties which were engaged in deliberately creating as complete a cultural environment to rival the official one as was possible. These political parties had in some ways the aspect of churches; they were concerned with every part of life. They had their own newspapers, their leisure organizations and their own festival occasions through which they reinforced a perspective of immediate trade-union and parliamentary activity and of more ultimate revolution. These intellectuals too are part of the German cultural scene; and although the Marxist culture of the German social-democrats was believed both by those who accepted it and by almost all those who condemned it to stand in stark contrast to the established order, it did in fact reproduce many of the characteristic features of the established order at its bureaucratized, stylized, didactic worst. The Marxist movement too had its professors.

The contributions of individual thinkers must then be understood against this background, even though it is one of the marks of German thought in this period that the background was not itself clearly perceived. One reason for beginning a history of modern German thought with Nietzsche is that he does seem to have understood the German predicament more clearly than anyone else.

Nietzsche

Nietzsche saw the culture of the German Empire as an artificial creation, aesthetically vulgar in its symbols, and based on falsehood and self-deception. The sentimentality of the cult of Luther, the arrogant notion that the Germans are just by virtue of being Germans the bearers of certain pre-eminent values and the Pan-Germanism that was the political counterpart of this notion were all scourged by him. The anti-Semitism which in both Germany and Austria flourished in Pan-Germanic circles he peculiarly loathed. But his indictment of German official values was only part of his indictment of the values of the modern world. In Nietzsche's view all these values represent one more stage in a degeneration rooted in the influence of Christianity. The aristocratic values of the best men of the ancient world had been subverted by the slave morality of Judaic religion. In place of the exaltation of strength, of courage and of the values of self-assertion by those few who excel, Judaism puts the virtues of the weak and the slavish who continue together to subvert the strong by preaching humility and self-abasement. Christianity inherits this morality from Judaism, and modern liberalism, in such versions as Kant's invocation of duty for duty's sake, merely reinstates the same morality in a new secular guise. So does modern socialism in all its forms.

Against the false altruistic spirituality of the modern world, which is the counterpart of its political levelling and its bureaucratization of life, Nietzsche counterposed the emergence of a new set of values, the bearer of which will be an 'Übermensch', a superman (when Nietzsche first used this expression, it had none of the associations which it has since acquired). About the character of this superman Nietzsche is not very clear; in one striking phrase he speaks of him as a 'Roman Caesar with the soul of Christ', and he greatly admired Julius Caesar. But why does he think that the aristocratic values which the superman will represent are superior to the values of Christianity, liberalism and socialism?

For two main reasons. First the values which Nietzsche is attacking rest their claim to our allegiance upon a false claim to objectivity. They purport to be defensible by rational argument, but all such arguments are fallacious. What in fact they express is an unadmitted will to dominate. Nietzsche sees the fundamental drive in all human life, indeed in all life, as being the will to power. So the second reason which he has for thinking the aristocratic values which he defends to be superior to those which he rejects is that they are based on a conscious recognition of the will to power and thus avoid the self-deception and falsehood of the slave moralities. The Jew, the Christian, the liberal and the socialist who praise humility and poverty of spirit or fraternity and equality are in fact expressing a jealousy and a hatred of the strong and the excellent which they cannot bear to admit either to themselves or to others, but conceal behind the mask of their ideals. This meanness and envy Nietzsche sees both in St Paul and in Luther. He says that Luther's faith was 'only a cloak, a pretext, a *screen* behind which the instincts played their game – a shrewd blindness about the dominance of certain instincts.'

What then is the will to power which lies behind these disguises? By power Nietzsche does not seem to have meant primarily domination over others, although his ideal aristocratic men do dominate. He means primarily a quality of self-affirmation, of an assertion of all the excellences of which the personality is capable. The will to power, when it is repressed and unavowed, becomes rancour and envy; when avowed it is expressed as courage and doing. But most people are incapable of aristocratic excellence. 'Not to the people let Zarathustra speak . . .' he wrote in his imaginary portrayal of the prophet Zarathustra, and he refers to the mass of people as 'the herd'.

Nietzsche is of course an exceptional figure; he had abandoned a conventional academic career and viewed the conventional professor with scorn. In 1878 his publication of *Human, All Too Human* with its dedication to Voltaire marked his wish to break with the German culture of his own age. In 1879 he retired from his professorship and thereafter until his collapse into insanity lived in France and Italy rather than in Germany. Although acquainted with the natural science of his day, and even capable of using arguments drawn from that science occasionally, he believed that the theoretical constructions of science, indeed of all logically ordered thought, consisted of fictions, of fixed forms imposed upon and falsifying the flux of reality. The materialism and the utilitarianism of his age he abhorred: 'Man does not seek happiness; only the Englishman does that.'

In 1890 Nietzsche became insane. The causes of his insanity are not wholly clear. There is some none too decisive evidence that he suffered from syphilis. But the nature of his own vision of man has an importance quite independent of Nietzsche's personal history. For Nietzsche's view that every established, or apparently established, system of values reflects an unacknowledged will to power and self-assertion suggests that such systems of values could be impotent in the face of a sufficiently ruthless and open assertion of a will to power. This fragility of the values of German society became all too evident in the years from 1918 onwards.

The Marxists

About this fragility the Marxist intellectuals were not in doubt. The German Marxists of the 1890s saw themselves as the direct heirs of Marx and Engels, and as such exempt to some degree from the corruptions of the social order. Their own political programmes had been personally criticized by Marx and Engels and had been revised in the light of that criticism. One of their cleverest analysts, Eduard Bernstein, had learned much of his Marxism directly from Engels. The most important Marxist thinker in Germany was Karl Kautsky who was to edit the party newspaper until 1917. Kautsky had been influenced by evolutionary ideas springing from Darwinism before he had become a Marxist, and strong traces of these ideas remained in his own formulation of the Marxist position. On his interpretation of Marx's view all bourgeois society, and German society in particular, was predestined to move through a set of predetermined stages until capitalism had finally reached a point of crisis which would make a socialist revolution possible. The belief that capitalism would so progress to a point of crisis he derived entirely from the arguments of Marx's *Capital*. Capitalism would be unable to provide for the goods which it produced markets which would provide a return on investment sufficient to maintain the expansion of production. Consequent slumps would intensify and the problems of poverty and unemployment created for the working class thereby would radicalize that class. Tendencies towards monopoly and towards large-scale units of production would mark the development of capitalist organization; the concentration of workers in such units would facilitate their organization in trade unions and political parties.

The background to this view of capitalism was a belief in the theory of historical materialism according to which level of technology in a given social order plays the key part in determining the economic relationship, and the economic relationships in turn determine the character of the cultural, legal and political life of the social order. This view of the economic basis as cause and the cultural and political superstructure as effect (it being allowed that the superstructure might in turn affect the basis, but not in such a way as to alter its ultimately determining function) rested on Engels's interpretation of Marxism; for the German Marxists it became canonical. Since the economic was the determining factor and since the economic processes of capitalism had to move slowly onward towards capitalism's downfall, the political processes could not outpace them. The German Marxists represented their Social Democratic Party as a party of revolution, but the revolution was so far in the future that it could scarcely affect their day-to-day actions. These were restricted to modest parliamentary and trade-union activity.

It may therefore have seemed to Eduard Bernstein that very little would be altered in the immediate political activity of himself and his colleagues if the ultimate aim of revolution was renounced. That it ought to be renounced Bernstein came to conclude in the 1890s, because he decided that Marx's predictions about the course of capitalist development were not being borne out by the facts. Capitalism was not in fact failing to expand, it was coping more efficiently rather than less so with succeeding crises or threats of crisis, and it was providing a steadily rising standard of living for the working class. It did not follow, however, that there was nothing for socialists to do. Many kinds of injustice and inequality had to be remedied and could be remedied by the kind of reformist activities in which the German party was already engaged. But these activities must not now be envisaged as means to some more ultimate end; they must be carried through for their own sake. 'The movement is everything, the end nothing.' Yet hitherto the German Marxists had claimed that they engaged in these activities precisely because they were the means to the end of revolution. If this reason for activity was removed, what reason remained?

At this point in his argument Bernstein turned back to Kant. He accepted a Kantian distinction between our knowledge of the world and how it goes on the one hand and our moral beliefs on the other, such that we do not find in our knowledge of the world any support for our mutual beliefs. Morality is a matter of the categorical imperative of duty and men have a duty to try to remedy the miseries of their fellow-men whatever the facts about capitalism and its future development. The basis for socialism is purely moral. Kautsky at once stigmatized this attempt to revise Marxism and attacked both Bernstein's factual analysis and his arguments about the basis for socialism. He argued that Bernstein was being misled by short-term and transient phenomena; the long-term trends were still as Marx had described them. On the issue of the reasons that men might have for struggling for socialism, Kautsky fell back on a crude utilitarianism. Men do struggle and the mass of men will struggle for socialism because they can see that it is in their interests to do so, that they will be happier under socialism.

The ruling circles of the Social Democratic Party accepted what they took to be Kautsky's vindication of Marxism, although Bernstein remained in the party. Kautsky was greatly aided in his polemics with Bernstein by the contributions of the most brilliant Marxist writer of the period, Rosa Luxemburg. Her arguments against Bernstein were of a quite different order from Kautsky's. She argued that reform and revolution are neither alternative ends to which the same actions can be means nor alternative means to the more ultimate end of a socialist society. For the relationship of means and ends in political activity is such that even an ultimate aim of revolution will alter what means are appropriate now and the type of society created by a revolution must be utterly different from that created by reforms no matter how radical.

In any case capitalism sets important and narrow limits to the possibility of reform.

When Kautsky published Rosa Luxemburg's articles against Bernstein he seems to have supposed that her position and his own were identical and perhaps at the level of formulas this was correct. But Kautsky's deep and persistent weakness was that he combined revolutionary theory with reformist activity. He wrote like Rosa Luxemburg, but he acted like Bernstein. It is scarcely surprising that although he and Rosa Luxemburg had been close friends in private life, they were soon political antagonists. This antagonism reached its height when the German Social Democrats split over the question of what their attitude to the war of 1914–18 should be. In the nineteenth century Marx and Engels had believed that one could discriminate between more advanced and less advanced societies and had appeared willing in at least some circumstances to support in time of war the more advanced against the less advanced. So Germany, Bismarck's Germany, was superior to the barbarism of the Russian Tsardom. When the vast majority of the German Social Democrats supported the war effort in 1914, notably by voting for the war credits in the Reichstag, they believed themselves to be merely repeating this position of Marx and Engels. Rosa Luxemburg, however, argued that a Marxist was required to accept the resolution of the Second International – which the German Social Democrats themselves had supported – which had embodied her own and Lenin's view that a war between capitalist and imperialist powers was a war in which the working class could have no interest and could support no side. Instead the working class of each country must work in a spirit of revolutionary defeatism to overthrow its own government. In her opposition to the war she was at one with Karl Liebknecht, whose father had been the friend of Marx and Engels, and who was himself a Kantian, although a very different one from Bernstein. (Bernstein too opposed the war from his own non-revolutionary position.)

Rosa Luxemburg and Karl Liebknecht founded a new small revolutionary party, the Spartacists. She supported the Russian revolution of October 1917, but criticized the Bolsheviks fiercely for not recognizing that democracy, both as an end and, *so far as possible*, as a means, is an essential part of the content of socialism. Kautsky was predictably not just a critic, but a bitter opponent of the Bolshevik revolution, denouncing it for its violence. In the revolutionary uprising in Berlin in 1919 a group of soldiers acting under the orders of a Social

Democratic Minister of Defence, a colleague of Kautsky's, murdered Rosa Luxemburg and Karl Liebknecht. The choice, so it had turned out, had not in fact been between revolutionary violence and non-violence, but between revolutionary violence and counter-revolutionary violence, and the reformist Social Democrats ended, as they have so often done, by supporting the latter.

In their earlier period both Kautsky and Rosa Luxemburg wrote extensively on a variety of subjects and Marxism for a short time expressed itself in a rich intellectual culture. In the 1920s this culture had its heirs in a number of independent Marxist scholars, but within the new German Communist Party creative thought was soon the victim of a passive acceptance of a party line dictated from Moscow. The most important Marxist thinker of the age, Georg Lukács, wrote in German, like many Hungarian intellectuals, and was widely influential in Germany. He defended the Bolsheviks against Rosa Luxemburg's criticism, but his most radical work lay in attacking Kautsky's version of Marxism in an even more profound way than Rosa Luxemburg had done. In Lukács's view any version of historical materialism which made the economic factors the causes of social development and reduced politics and culture to mere effects was inadequate, both for understanding pre-capitalist societies, and for understanding the period in which the transition from capitalism to socialism had to be made. In this latter period the working class has become an agency for changing history such that it is in its power to produce immediate revolution. The economic development of capitalism does not have to be waited upon. Politics have been at least partially released from the constraints of economics.

Lukács's views were denounced by the leaders of the Communist International and as a loyal Communist Lukács renounced them, thus infecting his own work with a sterility and even with a dishonesty which have made his later writings a sad decline from his early creative originality. The same sterility infected the whole life of the German Communist Party and led it into a series of mindless manœuvres in the years before 1933 – attacking for example the Social Democrats instead of concentrating on the Nazi threat, making both it and its working-class supporters helpless and tragic victims of National Socialism.

Max Weber

If any one thinker represents the bourgeois culture of imperial Germany at its best, it is Max Weber. The young pre-Marxist Lukács had been his pupil; all subsequent sociologists were to be in some sense his pupils. Until 1918 Weber led an entirely academic career; no one has ever insisted more firmly on the independence of academic inquiry from direction by social and political considerations. His belief in this independence was grounded on that same distinction between the realm of value and the realm of fact which I have already noted in the thought of Eduard Bernstein. Weber quarrelled bitterly with those who thought that intellectual inquiry into the facts about society could never of itself reveal what we ought to do. But his distinction between 'is' and 'ought' was not drawn in the interests of any view of social science as socially useless. We must, according to Weber, keep our intellectual work untainted by our values, precisely so that it will be unbiased enough to be useful.

Weber's first sociological work in the 1890s exemplifies his point of view admirably. He was employed to examine the size and effects of the influx of Polish immigrant agricultural labour on to the landed estates of eastern Germany. It was increasingly profitable for landed proprietors to make use of such labour. Their needs for labour were seasonal and they did not have to pay wages to the immigrants when they did not need them. To their German workers they had stood in a more permanent and traditional relationship, master and servants having clearly defined rights and duties, duties which involved responsibility for workers throughout the year. Weber saw the replacement of these semi-feudal relationships by those of the cash nexus and the adoption of criteria of profitability by the landed proprietors as disintegrative of the German social order. Such disintegration he deplored as a citizen, not as a social scientist; the empirical work which showed the disintegrative effects of replacing German with Polish labour in itself was factual and neutral.

This factual, calculating, value-neutral work of the mind not only inspired Weber with an ideal for his own work; it represented also the outcome of a trend towards rationality in Western society, a trend some hundreds of years in the making whose representative in the economic order was capitalism. Weber posed two questions about the origin of capitalism. The first arose from his reading of Marx. Marx treated the origin and development of capitalism as a purely economic matter. Since economic relationships are the fundamental causes of change, Protestantism, for example, was treated by Marx, albeit only in passing, as a mere ideological effect of rising capitalism. But was this really so? Moreover, feudal societies had apparently existed in many parts of the world. But it was only in western Europe that capitalism had arisen out of a feudal society. Why was this so? What was different about western Europe? Later on in his career Weber did extensive work on the nature of Indian and of Chinese society which in his view re-inforced his conclusion that it was in its religion that western Europe differed from other societies and that the possession of certain particular religious beliefs and activities was a necessary element in the genesis of capitalism. Capitalism could not have flourished as an economic system, unless 'the spirit of capitalism' had moved men, a distinctive and new set of motives which set men both to the work of economic acquisition and also to that of saving and of investment. But the spirit of capitalism, according to Weber, required the prior existence of Protestantism. Protestantism turns out to be not effect, but cause. How is this so?

The particular form of capitalism with which Weber was concerned was Calvinism, and the notion that he took to be crucial in Calvinism was that of 'the calling'. A man could not be saved by good works, but was justified before God by faith alone; none the less the man chosen by God for salvation was called by him to a particular field of worldly activity, where he must work, not for the sake of material gain, but simply because called by God to do so. So Calvinism both provides an energy to inform work in the world and at the same time a will not to consume, not to waste in luxury what work produced. Hence accumu-lation and hence saving and investment proceed. Calvinist asceticism, its insistence on a disciplined way of life, its hostility to pleasure, provide just the motives for work that the development of capitalism required.

Was Weber right about this? The evidence he produces in *The Protestant Ethic and the Spirit of Capitalism*, which he wrote in 1904–5, is sketchy. He took Protestantism to be permanently associated with economic enterprise and quotes evidence about the differential effects of Catholic and Protestant education on economic motivation from the Baden of his own day as well as a variety of sources from the sixteenth, seventeenth and eighteenth centuries. But his use of evidence is selective. His contemporary, Werner Sombart, argued that it was the dispersed Sephardic Jews and not the Protestants who provided the generation of entrepreneurs that set capitalism going. Later historians have pointed out, as against both Sombart and Weber, that not only were Catholic entrepreneurs as involved as Protestants or Jews in the development of capitalism, but that Weber and Sombart were wrong in supposing that developed capitalism did not exist before the sixteenth century. What matters most however is that Weber laid bare the complexity of the relationship of economic to other factors, such as religious factors, in historical development. He insisted that he was not trying to replace the Marxist view of the economic as cause, the religious as effect, with an equally simple causal view of the religious as cause, the economic as effect. This sense of complexity informs all Weber's later work. So also does the attempt to work on the same large scale as Marx did.

Weber's method is to use large classificatory schemes. His classifications depend on the identification of 'ideal types', of paradigms of social behaviour to which in a given age the behaviour of a given group of men will approximate. There is, for example, the form of authority found in traditional societies, where the claim to authority rests upon established rules and customs. At the other extreme there is the charismatic authority of the leader who dominates by reason of the magnetic personal attraction that he exerts over his followers. But in modern society authority tends more and more to be exercised through bureaucratic hierarchies. The growth of bureaucracy in the modern world is associated with the extension of that technical, fact-finding rationality that Weber saw as extending its hold in association with Protestantism. For bureaucracy is rational in the sense that each task is broken up into its component parts, that specific responsibility for preparing a given set of tasks is assigned to a given functionary and that there is a superintendant hierarchy to make sure that the total task is carried out. But it is characteristic of bureaucracy understood in this way that it is means rather than ends which are rationalized. Ends are taken as given. For this very reason Weber holds that in the realm of values bureaucratic values must not be allowed to be ultimate.

If they did become ultimate, men would become the impotent creatures of the bureaucratic machine that they had created. How is this to be prevented? Weber has no general answer to this question, precisely because he has no simple view of there being any one overriding factor which controls social life. In his analysis of society he uses the notion of class in a way not unlike that in which Marx uses it; but he also introduces the notion of status. Men are importantly linked to other men not only by their relationship to the ownership of the means of production, but also by their relationships of mutual esteem. Class has to do with the way men are ranked in the eyes of others. Status and class stand in close relationship, but they are far from identical. Here as elsewhere Weber prevents us from having an over-simple picture of society.

So, as I have already noted, it is with the question of the relationship of religion to the rest of social life. What that relationship is varies both with the form of social life and with the type of religion involved. Weber's typology here is again threefold. There is the religion in which the sorcerer is the central figure. The sorcerer characteristically manipulates nature and society by means of magical formulas. The priest is the duly appointed and qualified officiant in a rite; worship not manipulation, and often sacrificial worship, is at the heart of priestly religion. The prophet is the religious innovator whose message has the authority and the attraction of his personal charisma. But these do not exhaust the religious possibilities; not only can we find societies whose religions are complex combinations of different elements, of the magical and the priestly, or of the priestly and the prophetic, but we can also find at least one society, our own, in which religion is no longer at home at all in the way that it was. We live, according to Weber, in a disenchanted world.

Weber was not concerned to classify and to construct typologies for their own sake. He did so in the hope of using them to formulate causal generalizations which would explain the dynamics of historical change. He also insisted that there was another prerequisite for formulating such explanations correctly, namely that we should understand what an action means to the agent who performs it, that the sociologist should be able to identify himself with the point of view of those whom he is studying. Sociology differs from the natural sciences in having this preliminary task of interpretation to carry through; it resembles them for the most part in the rest of its inquiries.

The value-free character of the social sciences is part of this resemblance. When Weber came to make his own value commitments as a citizen, he placed the highest value of all on the preservation of the German social order. For most of his life he saw the chief threat to that order coming, not from the masses, but from the heedless and self-interested policies of the upper classes. In 1918, however, he became a bitter opponent of any socialist revolution. It is paradoxical that Weber, the most sensitive of the founding fathers of sociology to the demands of complexity, should in the end have adopted a simple nationalist attitude of the kind adopted by thousands of unsophisticated, patriotic, bourgeois citizens. It almost seems as if the logical gulf which

Weber held to exist between the realm of fact and that of value led him to separate his beliefs as a sociologist from his choices as a citizen in a way which disastrously prevented the sophistication of the former from correcting the simplicity of the latter.

Husserl and Heidegger

Academic philosophy in German in the late nineteenth and early twentieth century was dominated by the followers of the neo-Kantian, Hermann Cohn, among whom Rickert and Natorp stand out. But such philosophizing was in a large degree a continuation of the past; a decisively new direction was given to German philosophy by Edmund Husserl who, after an academic training which included a doctoral thesis in mathematics and work in experimental psychology, became a professor of philosophy at Göttingen in 1900. There and at Freiburg im Breisgau he was a dominant influence until and after his retirement in 1928.

Husserl believed that in their examination of the natural sciences the neo-Kantians had not investigated the true and ultimate foundations of knowledge. Sometimes Husserl described his project as being an attempt to carry through successfully the task which Descartes had set himself, that of discovering a set of completely certain truths which are presupposed in all other knowledge, but which themselves rest on no further presuppositions. The first step in discovering such truths is to recognize the *intentional* character of mental activity; in his account of intentionality Husserl followed his own teacher in Vienna, Franz Brentano. What did Brentano and Husserl mean by 'intentionality'?

Every mental act has an object. If I want something or fear something or judge that something is the case, then what I want or fear or judge is an object to which my mind is directed. But that to which my mind is directed in wanting or fearing or judging is not an object outside the mind. If I fear the-war-that-I-believe-to-be-about-to-break-out, then my fear has an object whether such a war does or does not break out. These objects are themselves part of the furniture of the mind and to say that mental activity is intentional is just to say that all its acts are directed towards, in-tend towards these objects. Suppose then that we wish to examine the intentional activity of the mind, what should we do? How do we free ourselves from our everyday, commonsense assumptions in order that we may see things as they are? It was because Husserl asked this question systematically, because he insisted that his method would at last lay bare the phenomena of experience and mental activity as they really are, that he used the name 'phenomenology' for his philosophy. To penetrate to the deepest layers of our mental experience we have to pass from what we actually *do* experience to discover what we can experience. The limits which pure possibility sets to what we can perceive and know and will and feel are discovered by abstracting from experience all those elements which are accidental and contingent. We perform this abstraction, for example, in the case of the objects of perception, by starting from some arbitrarily chosen actual object of perception. We then, in an imaginative mental exercise, strip away from this object everything that can be changed in it without it ceasing to be the thing that it is. So we arrive at a form which is presented to us embodied in this particular object, which constitutes its essence or idea. The study of essences or ideas is the proper subject-matter of philosophy.

But the essences with which we are most concerned are not the essences of that which we perceive or want or judge but the essences of perceiving and wanting and judging and of other mental acts. To discover what these are we discard, in another act of the imagination, such beliefs as those in the existence of a spatio-temporal world, in one's own bodily existence and experience, in all the findings of science and about the structure of science, and are thus enabled to give a purified account of what underlies all these beliefs that we have. What do we discover if we do this? I take perception for an example. In a series of perceptions of a house, it is crucial that we perceive all these as perceptions of the *same* house. But the sameness is not given to us in our perceptual experience of the house in the same way that its red roof is. Equally I perceive in one sense only part of the house, its front, part of one side and part of the roof, say. But what I perceive directly I perceive precisely as a part of a whole that I am confronting. More is given to me in my experience than I directly perceive. Moreover, whatever I perceive I perceive against a background and in a context which are not themselves the object of my direct perception. So in these respects at least what we grasp in the act of perception goes beyond the bare, given sense-impressions that we receive. Why is it important whether Husserl is right or not in this phenomenological account of perception?

German philosophy ever since Kant had been concerned with the refutation of any empiricist philosophy that holds that knowledge consists of nothing but what is given immediately in sense-impressions. By holding this empiricists present an impoverished view of experience and a passive view of the mind. Husserl by contrast takes the mind to grasp a world constituted on principles that are not given in sense-impressions and so he takes, for instance, a quite different view of science from that taken by empiricists. But, it might be retorted, does not Husserl himself present us avowedly with a view of mental activity only in terms of its formal structures which we have abstracted from the concreteness of actual experience? Must we not return from the study of essences to the study of existence, of the mind as actually part of the real world which it grasps? In what manner does mind, do men, exist in this real world? These are the questions about the Husserlian method from which Martin Heidegger began, making the transition from phenomenology to existentialism.

Heidegger wished initially to use phenomenological methods to lay bare the structure of human existence (*Dasein*), and he contrasted his approach not only with that of Husserl but also with that of Descartes. Descartes supposed that we can begin from the situation of a mind conscious only of itself; but Heidegger retorts that we are never conscious of ourselves except as existing in a world, the experience of which is as much a basic datum as is the experience of self. *Dasein* is always structured by its relationship to certain universal and inescapable limiting and determining factors: care, anxiety, the relationship of being to death, alienation, guilt and decision. Experiencing himself as determined by these man experiences himself as radically finite.

This picture of man is sharply contrasted by Heidegger with the picture of man presented by traditional philosophy, whether Aristotelian or Kantian. Traditional philosophy, according to Heidegger, tries to understand man in terms of categories such as those of substance, quantity, quality, causality and the like, which are applicable to nature. When applied to man they obscure the difference between man and all other beings and man is reduced to the status of a thing. Human uniqueness is bound up with man's relationship to time; he has a remembered past and a projected future, as no non-human being has. Men have to rescue themselves from an inauthentic existence, dissipated from moment to moment, by choosing self-consciously to face up to their finitude in all its aspects. A man who lives with the thought of his finitude, and more particularly of the certainty of his death, constantly in mind has achieved an authentic existence.

Heidegger's *Sein und Zeit* was published in 1927. In 1928 he succeeded Husserl at Freiburg and in 1933 he became Rector Magnificus of the University of Freiburg. In his inaugural address he enthusiastically

P

welcomed the coming to power of National Socialism: 'Let not doctrines and "Ideas" be the rulers of your being. Today and in the future, only the Führer himself is German reality and its law.' The neo-Marxist philosopher, Herbert Marcuse, claimed that Heidegger's adherence to Nazism was the rational and logical outcome of his existentialism. Is this true? At the very least it has to be pointed out that Heidegger's views neither entail Nazi conclusions nor have such conclusions been reached by many whose philosophical position has been much the same as that of *Sein und Zeit*. But in Heidegger's abandonment of Husserl's insistence upon rigorous standards of argument and his obvious preference for the cryptic and the oracular we can see the first signs of the irrationalism that issued in Heidegger's Nazism.

The Theology of Karl Barth

Protestant theology in Germany before 1914 had responded to the intellectual and social movements of the nineteenth century in three ways. The historical criticism of the Bible had led theologians to minimize the miraculous and supernatural character of the biblical narrative. The philosophical climate had led theologians to present Christian belief as rationally justifiable to the mind of a modern man. The variety of liberal and socialist beliefs in social reform and social progress had led theologians to equate the coming of the Kingdom of God with the creation of a just society on earth. In its liberal Protestantism there was nothing unique about the German situation; but in the repudiation of that liberalism Germany was for over a decade unique. The agent of that repudiation was Karl Barth who published his commentary on St Paul's *Epistle to the Romans* in 1918. Barth was influenced not only by his own intellectual critique of the inadequacies of liberal theology, but also by his need as a minister to find a gospel he could preach cogently in the years of disaster for Germans, in the years during and after the war of 1914–18 when the mild optimism of liberal protestantism became tragically irrelevant.

Barth begins by insisting upon the uniqueness of the Christian gospel and the impossibility of building any intellectual or moral bridge between that gospel and any human philosophy or indeed any ordinary human belief. Certainly man does have natural tendencies to religious beliefs. But these tendencies are part of the corruption of his nature and what they issue in is not belief in the true God of the Christian revelation but a variety of forms of idolatry. God is a hidden God who reveals himself only as he chooses to do and his choice was to reveal himself in the history of Israel and in the apostolic testimony to Jesus Christ in whom he became incarnate. Man cannot of himself move towards God in any way. God has to reach out and save man. It follows that a belief in God arrived at by rational, philosophical argument or a belief in God based on the cultivation of religious experiences are both dangerous illusions. Man is wholly corrupt and wholly impotent before God. He can be saved by a divine intervention which he can only receive, and his response to which he also owes wholly to God.

In these doctrines Barth consciously revived the doctrines of Calvin and Luther. But he distinguished his position from that of classical Protestantism by insisting that the belief in the infallibility of the Bible was as much an idolatrous deification of something other than God as was the Roman Catholic belief in the infallibility of the Church. Certainly God speaks through the biblical narrative and certainly God speaks to the Church, but we must not absolutize what are mere instruments of the divine will. Barth restored the sermon to the place that it had in classical Protestant tradition, insisting yet again that the words of the minister about God must not be confused with the Word which God may choose to speak through the words of the minister. Christianity is thus simply to be proclaimed; it cannot be argued for God is wholly other.

Just as Christianity must not be confused with man's natural religious tendencies, so the Christian life must not be confused with the life of ordinary human morality. It was a commonplace of the nineteenth century to believe that one could discard Christian theology, but retain Christian morality. Barth insisted that, in an important sense, Christianity had no morality. For we cannot by reason of our sinful nature ever do what God commands; we cannot to any extent at all justify ourselves by doing what we take to be right. Before God we are always in need of justification by the saving work of Christ, we are always in the wrong. The Christian is thus liberated from the anxiety of trying to do what is right; he must set himself to whatever task God calls him and leave the question of the value of what he is doing and the outcome of what he is doing to God.

History is not, as liberals and socialist believe, a progress towards some earthly goal. It is what the Bible says it is, a movement from the Fall of Man to the Incarnation, and from the Incarnation to the Last Judgement. God will inaugurate the end of history as he wills. Barth sees in Marxism, as in other secular ideologies, human aspirations to self-deification. But it does not follow that God may not use such ideologies and movements to express his judgement upon the sins of contemporary civilization. God may indeed choose to speak to a man through anything that he wills to speak through.

Among Barth's earliest disciples was the Swiss theologian, Emil Brunner. Brunner however produced what he took to be Barth's doctrine in a version that evoked a fierce denunciation from Barth. According to Brunner, fallen man may be incapable by his own powers to respond to the divine saving initiative; but he does retain even in his fallen state certain rational capacities, such as the capacity for language, which he exercises in responding to God. The difference between Barth's doctrine and Brunner's, as stated, may appear to be trivial. But Barth saw in this difference the seed of a quite different and incompatible theology, and events proved Barth right. For Brunner's view of man's natural powers underlay his development of a view of human institutions such as the State and marriage as ordained by God for the preservation of man's natural life. Such institutions therefore have a basic claim on human loyalties. This view was also Luther's; and like Luther, Brunner has been a social and political conservative. The effect of Barth's doctrine has been by contrast socially and politically radical. For Barth holds that every human institution stands under judgement, that every social order has pretensions that must be denounced, that the Christian cannot identify himself wholeheartedly with any social order, but must always stand to what is established, whether ecclesiastical or political, as a protestant, as a dissenter.

When the Nazis came to power it was largely from Barth's disciples among the Evangelical pastors that the founders of the Confessional Church were drawn. It was within this group that were found the very few pastors who resisted and denounced the application of the Nazi anti-Jewish laws and the paganism and idolatry of the Nazi party; although in general their record of opposition to Hitler was feeble and pathetic. Barth himself had to leave Germany for Switzerland where he became Professor of Theology at Basle. German Christianity turned out to be as fragile and as vapid as Nietzsche had supposed.

Freud and Psychoanalysis

Sigmund Freud was born at Freiberg in Moravia (then in the Austrian Empire, now in Czechoslovakia) in 1856. His medical studies led him on from neurophysiology to study psychiatry with Breuer in Vienna and with Chaveat in Paris, and more particularly to inquire into the nature of hysteria. His realization that in hysterical paralyses the area paralysed is not that which one would expect on objective physiological grounds, but one which corresponds to the patient's beliefs about physiology (something of which the patient himself is quite unaware) and that hysteria can sometimes be cured by using hypnosis to revive memories of episodes about which the patient has forgotten played an important part in his formulation of a general explanation of neurotic disorders. Neurotic behaviour is informed on this view by unconscious purposes and motives. These purposes and motives have survived from early childhood and are now in adult life expressed in a form in which they are no longer recognizable either by the neurotic or by others as the manifestation of childish fears and anxieties which they are. How does this come about?

The infant is a bundle of instinctual drives and seeks for a satisfaction which is sexual in character. But these instinctual drives continually encounter frustration and checking by the parents and indeed by the whole social environment. The child moves from conflict to conflict, developing personal traits of one kind or another, and from time to time encountering episodes so painful that the memory of them is repressed into the unconscious. It is not only the actual episodes of childhood that are important in this respect; the child's fantasies are quite as important. What is repressed may then be reawakened in adult life and emerge in a number of disguises, in such occurrences of every-day life as dreams or slips of the tongue, as well as in neurotic symptoms.

This theory of the origin of neurotic symptoms suggests a therapy which is its counterpart. In psychoanalysis the patient, by using his own free associations and saying to the analyst whatever he will, and by responding to the analyst's interpretations of what he says, recovers the memories of the emotionally painful episodes which he has hitherto repressed. This enables him to work through the undischarged, infantile emotion and motives which have unconsciously informed his behaviour, and so he is able to free himself from their hold upon him. From 1897 onwards Freud conducted a self-analysis to the point at which he felt able to use psychoanalysis with his patients.

By 1908 psychoanalysis had established itself sufficiently well both as theory and therapy for the first International Psychoanalytical Congress to be held at Salzburg. Several of Freud's pupils were to develop doctrines of their own which led them to break with psychoanalysis. The most notable of these were Alfred Adler (also Austrian), who explained adult traits as the outcome of the individual's response to a universal childhood sense of inferiority, and the Swiss C. G. Jung, who saw the individual unconscious of the outcrop of a collective unconscious, a realm of universal symbols upon which the individual mind draws. But Freud and those of his followers who remained within the psychoanalytical movement gained steadily greater international recognition. Berlin very early became almost as much a home of psychoanalysis as Vienna had been.

It was in a paper presented there in 1922 that Freud developed his threefold scheme of the personality, id, superego and ego. The id is the biologically given, the instinctual. The superego is the internalized voice of the parental figures, demanding restraint and inhibition where the id seeks for the unlimited satisfaction of desire. The ego is the self which has the task of mediating not only between the demands of id and those of superego, but also between the claims of both and those of external reality. Psychological growth in general and psychoanalytic therapy in particular is a matter of strengthening the ego. 'Where id was, there ego shall be.' As the ego becomes less in the grip of id and superego, it acquires independent interests and concerns. In Freud's later thought this potential independence of the ego is given an importance which leads him to see the content of mature human cultural activity as much more than the expression of repressed and sublimated infantile drives. But it *is*, in Freud's view throughout his life, in such sublimation and repression that all culture has its roots.

Where morality is concerned the infantile is expressed in the arbitrary prohibitions imposed by the superego, which in adult life appears as the voice of conscience, which may be envisaged as the divine voice that was to be heard uttering divine commandments on Sinai, but which is in fact the remembered, but unrecognized parental voice. While morality remains superego morality, its injunctions are necessarily arbitrary and unjustifiable taboos. To recognize this infantile morality as what it is is to see the possibility of substituting instead a rational moral code through which ego can develop its mature interests. But when Freud pronounces on the content of such a rational morality, nothing that he has to say has any particular connections with psychoanalysis; Freud's own morality was a crude and commonplace version of liberal utilitarianism and his scattered utterances make it clear that he found such virtues as justice and reasonableness entirely unproblematic.

Freud also takes the falsity of religion for granted. Religious belief needs to be explained and Freud attempted to explain theistic religion by referring to the need to substitute an unfailing and omnipotent heavenly father for an earthly father with both failings and weaknesses. Some mystical experiences at least are to be explained as the survival from infancy of that 'oceanic feeling' which the child who still does not differentiate the self from its surroundings experiences. That religious belief is a species of wish-fulfilment based on human weakness does not of course guarantee that it will die out; men have so far always needed illusions to live by and to substitute reason for illusion is always difficult. Perhaps, in Freud's view, it is for the mass of mankind impossible. Freud takes civilization to be the work of an ascetic minority who renounced the indulgence of their instinctual drives, sublimated those drives and so made available the energy required for the tasks of high culture. But the masses are essentially governed by passions which are restrained only so long as they are ruled by a minority élite whose domination they accept on irrational grounds. Freud himself was a political conservative who feared what he took to be the irrationality of revolutionary movements and who believed in that old bogey-man of the Right, 'the mob'.

Before his death the threat of the Nazis in Austria made emigration necessary and Freud died in London in 1939. Psychoanalysis was denounced by the Nazis as Jewish in inspiration and the psychoanalytic movement became part of the German intellectual migration to the Anglo-Saxon world.

The Vienna Circle

The group of philosophers who formed the Vienna Circle in 1924 under the aegis of Moritz Schlick, the professor of philosophy at Vienna, had an already existing nucleus more than fifteen years before when a group of young physicists, mathematicians and social scientists met every Thursday in a Viennese coffee house to discuss issues in the philosophy of science. Out of these discussions, both before and after the formation of the Vienna Circle, there developed the attitude to philosophy which became known as logical positivism. The doctrines of logical positivism were strongly anti-metaphysical and opposed to the admission of the existence of anything beyond or outside the world of sense-perception. Their most important predecessors, the British empiricists of the seventeenth, eighteenth and nineteenth centuries, had always found it difficult to account for the truths of mathematics, if the only truths which we know are truths about the world of sense-perception. But Russell and Whitehead in *Principia Mathematica* had undertaken the project of showing how mathematical truths could be rigorously derived from the basic truths of logic and Ludwig Wittgenstein in his *Tractatus Logico-Philosophicus* had argued that the truths of logic were tautologies, true in virtue of the definitions of the symbols which compose them and devoid of factual content. Thus the truths of mathematics are not to be understood as examples of factual knowledge not derived from the senses; the only sources of knowledge are the factual observations of common sense and the discoveries of the sciences.

Statements which purport to refer to a reality other than that available for study by the sciences, theological or metaphysical statements are not false, but meaningless. They are not false, because it is not the case that they do not agree with the relevant facts; there are no relevant facts for them to either agree or disagree with and hence they are untestable. To be meaningful is to be testable, to be verifiable by sense-experience; to be unverifiable is to be meaningless. These negative doctrines are perhaps the most dramatic produced by members of the Vienna Circle; but they are not the most philosophically interesting or important. The members of the Circle were mostly primarily concerned with the nature of the sciences and especially of physics. The influence of the earlier Austrian philosopher and physicist Ernst Mach was strong and some of the central problems to which they addressed themselves had been posed by Mach.

Mach himself had believed that all mention of unobservable entities must be excluded from the sciences and he went so far as to include atoms among the items which he placed under this ban. But Mach's bizarre rejection of atomic theory – which none of his later followers shared – was bound up with a real problem. In physical theory mention is made of items that are not directly observable: Mach's unreal difficulty about atoms foreshadowed a very real difficulty about the later discovery of fundamental particles which – unlike atoms – are unobservable in principle and the existence of which, however, the physicist cannot avoid invoking if he is to explain the observed phenomena satisfactorily. If we rule out metaphysical and theological entities because they are unobservable, how can we admit the existence of electrons? The answer is that our statements about electrons stand in some precise logical relationship to statements the truth of which is confirmed directly by sense-experience in a way that statements about God or the absolute do not. But what is this logical relationship? The task of delineating it occupied especially Rudolf Carnap, who was also the author of the principle of testability discussed above.

If all knowledge is either purely formal or factual and scientific, it does not follow that the meaningless pseudo-statements of, for example, theology do not have a function. They express emotions and attitudes towards the world. So do moral judgements. Not all the logical positivists on this, or indeed on any other question, took precisely the same view. Schlick, for example, interprets certain moral judgements as factual statements about what modes of conduct will make men happy. But the consensus was to interpret moral judgements as expressions of attitude.

Two Viennese philosophers who were not members of the Vienna Circle and who were not positivists played an important part in their discussions. One of these was Ludwig Wittgenstein, who had studied with Russell in England before 1914, and who in 1929 returned to Cambridge where he became the single most influential philosopher in the Anglo-Saxon world. Wittgenstein's *Tractatus* had presented a view of language according to which behind the complexities of ordinary language could be discerned the form which propositions must have if they were to mirror the facts which they represented. This picture theory of language was to be criticized most radically by Wittgenstein himself in the interests of a view of language as essentially diverse, as having a wide diversity of forms and functions. This later view had the effect in the Anglo-Saxon world of undermining the logical positivist simple threefold classification of statements into the formal truths of logic and mathematics, the factual assertions of common sense and the sciences and the emotive utterances of theology and morality.

The other Viennese philosopher outside the Circle who influenced its members was Karl Popper, now Sir Karl Popper. Popper was concerned not to draw the line between the meaningful and the meaningless, as Carnap had been, but instead to demarcate the boundary between the scientific and the non-scientific. In Popper's view what makes a statement or a theory scientific is that it is refutable, that it is open to falsification. What cannot be falsified, what cannot be shown to be incompatible with some possible state of affairs is equally compatible with every possible state of affairs, that is, it has no special factual content at all. Science progresses by advancing hypotheses and trying to falsify them. Popper developed this and other views in his *Logic of Scientific Discovery*, published in German in Vienna in 1934.

The Vienna Circle by 1927, according to Herbert Feigl, one of its members who has also been its historian, felt itself to be a distinctive movement in philosophy. In 1929 Carnap and Hans Reichenbach started to edit the journal *Erkenntnis* which was the main forum for the expression of logical positivist views. Reichenbach had already founded in Berlin the Society for Scientific Philosophy which was a counterpart to the Vienna Circle. In Prague too the movement was influential and Carnap went to teach there. But once again the rise of Nazism led to emigration. Schlick was assassinated in 1936 by a student who was probably insane, rather than politically motivated. Carnap, Reichenbach and many others went to the United States during the thirties. Popper went to England.

The positivistic rationality of the Vienna Circle led them to be sharply critical not only of metaphysical positions, but also of those large portions of psychoanalytic theory which appeared to be – and indeed are – untestable. They produced what has been the most important philosophical alternative to phenomenology and a good deal of later philosophical history both in German- and in English-speaking countries has been taken up by controversy between these two movements.

Epilogue

On 19 May 1933 the *Manchester Guardian* listed 196 professors dismissed from their positions in German universities in the preceding few weeks as a result of the Nazi accession to power. The list was far from complete and we ought to note two things about it. The first is that it represented the effective end of intellectual life in Germany until the late 1940s. 'Thinking with the blood' took the place of thinking. There is no intellectual movement recorded in my chronicle so far which did not have either to find a new home or perish. To embrace Nazism, as a very few intellectuals such as Heidegger did (even if, as in his case, only for some months), was simply a degrading form of intellectual suicide. But, if few intellectuals actively joined the Nazi movement, it is also true that the list of those expelled from German universities represented only a tiny proportion of German academics. The vast majority had already allowed the universities to be centres of reactionary politics and of anti-Semitism. It was easy for them passively to tolerate and encourage Nazism.

Britain, to some extent, and the United States, to a very large extent, turned out to be the beneficiaries of German barbarism. The future history of sociology, of Barth's influence in theology, of Marxism, of phenomenology and of positivism was to lie in large part out-side Germany. The collapse of the German academic tradition in the face of Nazism is a fact so massive that post-war German culture has not yet been able to reckon with it adequately.

Bibliography

DANTO, A. *Nietzsche as Philosopher*. New York, 1967.

KAUFMANN, W. *Nietzsche: Philosopher, Psychologist, Antichrist*. New York, 1956.

GAY, P. J. *The Dilemma of Democratic Socialism: Eduard Bernstein's Challenge to Marx*. New York, 1952.

NETTL, J. P. *Rosa Luxemburg*. London, 1966.

BENDIX, R. *Max Weber: An Intellectual Portrait*. New York, 1960.

SPIEGELBERG, H. *The Phenomenological Movement*. The Hague, 1966.

MACKINTOSH, H. R. *Types of Modern Theology*. London, 1937.

JONES, E. *Sigmund Freud, Life and Work*. Abridged and edited by Steven Marcus and Lionel Trilling. New York, 1961.

RIEFF, P. *Freud: The Mind of the Moralist*. London, 1960.

AYER, A. J. (ed.). *Logical Positivism*. London, 1959.

EDWARDS, PAUL (ed.). *Encyclopaedia of Philosophy*. New York, 1966. Articles on 'Phenomenology' and 'Logical Positivism'.

8 German Literature in the Middle Ages

RONALD TAYLOR

Vernacular literature, in the conventional sense of a written record of creative artistic impulses, can be traced back in Germany only to the middle of the eighth century. At this time the Carolingian dynasty, officially established in 751 by the Frankish king Pepin, was taking root and beginning to exert its profound influence on the development of German culture. But this is not to say that no literature, whether recorded or not, existed before this time, nor that we have no knowledge of what made up this literature. The survival of written records is often due to historical chance, and the earlier the period with which we are concerned, the less complete will be the picture presented by the surviving material. Through other, circumstantial evidence, however, we can learn of the existence of whole genres of literature, no actual examples of which may have come down to us from the historical period in question. And however resolutely one must resist the temptation to dogmatize about works of art that do not exist, it is a very necessary exercise to assemble what knowledge one can about the antecedents of the works that happen to constitute the earliest written evidence.

Much of our knowledge of this 'pre-literary' period derives from Roman historians. It is, indeed, through their contact with the Roman armies that the Teutons, or Germanic peoples, first made their appearance in history. Caesar is the first to use the name 'Germani', in Book II of *De bello gallico* (52–50 B.C.), to designate certain tribes he encountered at that time who were trying to cross the Rhine into Gaul. Tacitus – who himself never left Rome but based his chronicles on reports brought back by homecoming legionaries – records in his *Germania* that the Germani had war-chants (*barditi*) and hymns (*carmina*) of a mythological-cum-historical nature, and in his *Annales* he states that heroic lays or ballads were sung in celebration of the deeds of such warriors as Arminius, famed for his victory over the Roman army of Varro in A.D. 9.

Of another branch of the Germanic peoples, the Goths, whose cultural empire stretched at one time from the Black Sea in the east to Spain in the west, the sixth-century historian Jordanes also reports that the heroic lay was widely cultivated, while it is to the Gothic communities which in the fourth century settled in what is today Bulgaria, that we owe the first literary monument in a Germanic tongue – the Bible translation, from the Greek, of the Arian Bishop Ulfilas (d. 383). Both from the linguistic and from the literary point of view this work – only fragments of which have survived, in manuscripts written between one and two centuries after Ulfilas's lifetime – is of immense interest and importance. One source of its importance is its age, for it is centuries older than any other extant literature in a Germanic tongue; added to this is the interest that attaches to the fact that Ulfilas had not only to determine the forms of the language into which he was translating but also to evolve an alphabet in which to present them. Looked at in this way, his achievement, whatever limitations it may seem to us today to have, is a quite remarkable one.

Like the Goths, the Franks also had their heroic lays which, according to the poet Venantius Fortunatus (530–600), they sang to the accompaniment of the harp at festive banquets. The chronicles of writers such as Gregory of Tours (540–94) and Paul the Deacon (*Historia Langobardorum*, c. 790) extend the range of literary forms to include songs of conviviality and friendship, dance-songs and laments for the dead, while from sermons and ecclesiastical edicts of the same period we learn of the existence of pagan charms, incantations and similar magic formulae which the Church was at pains to suppress.

This is only the first of many occasions on which the authorities – which, for practical purposes in our context, means the Church – unwittingly provide information about the activities of certain people, or the existence of certain practices, which were seen as inimical to the demands of Christian morality. We should know a great deal less about what went on in medieval life if we were not in possession of ordinances by which the Church sought to prohibit what was going on.

The cultivation of these forms of artistic expression lay to a considerable extent in the hands of a professional minstrel class, whose activities, as described in Anglo-Saxon literature, may be assumed to have followed the same pattern in the continental Germanic realm. This professional *scop*, as he was called, was poet, composer and singer in one, and enjoyed great esteem at court through his performance of songs and lays of the types mentioned above. Subsequently many a *scop* fell in social estimation and became one with the mimes and clowns and other itinerant circus-type entertainers familiar in Europe during the centuries of Roman decline. But others, like Volker in the *Nibelungenlied* and Horant in *Gudrun*, upheld the noble traditions of the class and also took their place as fighting men when circumstances required.

To the specific information about this 'pre-literary' period which can be gleaned from historical records, or from descriptions in the narrative literature of this or a somewhat later age, must be added the total literary evidence of the succeeding period itself. For although a manu-script from, say, the eighth century might happen to be the first known source of a particular literary genre, it would be quite mistaken to assume that this were in fact the first piece of literature ever written in that genre. Indeed, the more accomplished and sophisticated this piece of literature is, the greater is the probability of a substantial tradition within that genre, stretching back into the preceding centuries, a tradi-tion no less real and vigorous for being oral and undocumented.

The inferences one can make about the nature of this earlier literature concern both its subject-matter and its form. About the former, as has been mentioned above, we already have the scraps of more or less contemporary information embedded in such sources as historical chronicles and ecclesiastical decrees. But these cannot, in the nature of things, come as close to their subjects as do the descendants of these subjects themselves, and if this is true of the content – material, social, moral and spiritual – it is doubly true of the literary forms through which the content is expressed.

Thus a poem such as the early ninth-century *Hildebrandslied* (which is discussed in its appropriate place below) testifies in its own specific way to the tradition of Germanic heroic poetry which Jordanes, Paul the Deacon and other chroniclers describe. There is a backcloth of historical personages and events, a sequence of utterances and actions that reflect the values, the morality, the social conventions, the myth-ology and the religion of the society from which such literature has emerged. Equally, there is a formal poetic arrangement of the material in a manner directly dependent on the indwelling characteristics of the language itself. The most characteristic of the formal principles em-ployed is the use of alliteration to link together successive pairs of lines. Alliteration, which is directly expressive of the strong stress-accent system in the Germanic languages, was for Germanic verse what rhyme subsequently became for European poetry.

In the same way, the few remains of the popular genre of the charm (see the discussion of the *Merseburger Zaubersprüche* below) enable us to glimpse certain customs and beliefs that sustained German – or more properly, Germanic – civilization in this pre-literary period. And here, too, the poetic principle of alliteration holds sway.

In the sixth century Christianity was brought to Germany by monks from Ireland. The most famous among the early names are Columban and his disciple Gall; the latter, through founding a little missionary centre in Switzerland in the year 613, gave his name to what was to become one of the greatest of all medieval monasteries and seats of learning, St Gallen. In the following century further monasteries were established at Reichenau (on Lake Constance), Würzburg, Freising and Regensburg, and in 732 the most famous of the Christian missionaries, Winfrith Boniface of Devon, became Archbishop of Mainz. Boniface founded the monastery of Fulda, introduced the Order of St Benedict into all the monastic institutions within his see, and consolidated the authority of the Roman Church throughout Bavaria, Franconia and Middle Germany in general.

The historical climax of this early Christianization, and at the same time the codification of many of the conflicts latent in the civilization of medieval Germany, are reached with the ascendancy of Charlemagne, whose activities come within the purview of literary culture no less than that of history. For as in the ideal of the Holy Roman Empire he sought to reconcile the secular power of government with the spiritual claims of the Church, so in the realm of culture he strove for the education of his people through the application of the Christian message and the cultivation of classical Latin poetry.

Much has been written of this so-called Carolingian Renaissance, especially by sentimental and nationalistically inclined German scholars, that leaves the impression of a glorious age of enlightenment in which refined scholarship and inspired art permeated the whole of cultured society. The real situation was somewhat less romantic. Charlemagne himself, king of a barbarian tribe, could not read or write, and in the conduct of his own life, as Bertrand Russell icily put it, 'was not unduly burdened with personal piety'. But even after allowing for the exaggerations in an overly idealized picture, one is left with the undeniable reality that, through his own convictions and energies, Charles was personally responsible for the remarkable spread of learning that came to be given the name of a renaissance, and for inaugurating a policy of education, both for the clerics and for the laity, to promote the consolidation of Christianity in the Frankish kingdom.

The English influence that had already arrived with Boniface spread into this programme of education through the powerful figure of Alcuin of York. Charles engaged Alcuin both to teach at the royal court and to organize, through the founding of monastery schools, the teaching, not only of theology, but also of Latin grammar, rhetoric, dialectic and the other subjects that became codified in the system of the Seven Liberal Arts.

Aside from his educational programme and the Latino-Christian learning associated with it, Charles was concerned to promote the national interests of his people and it is here that his activities directly concern the literature of his time. His biographer Einhard (*Vita Caroli Magni*, written *c.* 820) tells us that the emperor ordered heroic lays current in his day to be recorded ('barbara et antiquissima carmina, quibus regum actus et bella canebantur'), and although his collection as such has not come down to us, it is possible, on the basis of what has survived – in the literature of somewhat later periods – of the legendary feats of Langobardic, Burgundian, Frankish and other Germanic heroes, to form a picture of the type of material it must have contained. In the field of music, too, he showed himself concerned that the practical and the theoretical sides of the art – that is to say, both the Gregorian chant sung in church and monastery, and the intellectual discipline of *musica* as one of the Seven Liberal Arts – should be intensively cultivated.

By his convictions and his demands, transmitted through poetic works such as the Latin hymns of the Roman Church, and through the prose of prayers, the Creed and the other items of the liturgy, Charles made himself the spiritual founder of religious literature in Germany. The monasteries became seats of learning, and throughout the ninth century scholars in Fulda, St Gallen and elsewhere became European authorities in theological and classical studies and consolidated the work which Charles had initiated.

It is from this Carolingian background of the spread of evangelical Christianity, the systematization of learning, and the lingering presence of the national Germanic tradition, that the first written literary records in Germany emerge – those works which mark the opening of what is called Old High German literature.

The term Old High German itself is in origin a linguistic one and has both geographical and chronological connotations. Historically it extends from the mid-eighth century, when the earliest documents appear, to the mid-eleventh century, the latter a time marked by a series of linguistic changes and also, more vital to our subject, by a shift in the social and political centre of gravity in Germany. This shift, which has been discussed in its historical place, put a virtual end to the impulses which had sustained vernacular literature throughout the preceding centuries.

Geographically High German denotes the dialects spoken south of the so-called Benrath Line, which extends east-north-east from near Aachen to Frankfurt a.d. Oder, passing near Düsseldorf, Cassel and Magdeburg. It is from these dialects that the modern standard language is descended, while the dialects to the north of the Benrath Line, in Low German territory, have retained their independent forms.

When one recalls the historical situation, it is not surprising to find that, with only three exceptions, all the surviving pieces of literature from the Old High German period are religious in subject-matter. And since the ability to read and write was the prerogative of the clerics – and, in fact, of only a very small proportion of them – it is a matter of remarkable good fortune that any literature at all from the pagan, pre-Christian tradition should have been committed to parchment and have survived down to our own day. Some of the more significant pieces of religious literature are discussed individually below, but there is inevitably a certain sameness about these works as a whole, since the purposes of the Christian missionaries forced them to concentrate on a limited range of activities and therefore to restrict their concern with the vernacular language to what would further these purposes and activities. One would willingly sacrifice a handful of the surviving prayers, confessions and other liturgical fragments for one more pagan charm, or a few more lines of Germanic heroic verse.

As it is, and apart from the lingering presence in other works of certain individual heathen attitudes and certain traditional Germanic characteristics of poetic form and manner, the only extant literary monuments which are sustained by the traditions of pre-Christian civilization in Germany are the two Merseburg Charms (*Merseburger Zaubersprüche*), from the ninth century, and the *Hildebrandslied*.

The charm, a short incantatory piece of prose or verse, designed to effect a protection against, or a deliverance from, sickness, suffering or other misfortunes, has deep roots in the primitive religion and mythology of the Germanic peoples. By invoking the aid of the deity or deities whose special powers were held to control the situation in which he found himself, the supplicator sought to bring about a miraculous cure of his affliction or a magical immunity against its attacks. The need for such divine intervention extended also to his property, so that he would call on the gods to heal a horse that had gone lame, or to protect his dogs from being attacked by wolves.

The first Merseburg Charm calls for the magical release of a prisoner from captivity; three alliterative lines describe his situation and the efforts of the Valkyries to help him, and the fourth line contains the charm formula itself: 'Escape from the fetters, flee from the foe!' The second charm, which is somewhat longer, similarly consists of a narrative section followed by the incantation:

> Phol ende Uuodan   vuorun zi holza.
> du uuart demo Balderes volon   sin vuoz birenkit.
> thu biguol en Sinthgunt   Sunna era suister;
> thu biguol en Friia,   Volla era suister;
> thu biguol en Uuodan,   so he uuola conda:
> sose benrenki,   sose bluotrenki,
>   sose lidirenki:
> ben zi bena,   bluot zi bluoda,
> lid zi geliden,   sose gelimida sin.

> (Phol and Wodan were riding into the forest.
> Then Balder's horse dislocated its fetlock.
> Then Sinthgunt spoke a charm over it, as did her sister Sunna;
> Then Freia spoke a charm over it, as did her sister Volla;
> Then Wodan spoke a charm over it, in the way he well knew:
> 'O broken bone, O wounded leg, O broken limb,
> Bone to bone, blood to blood,
> Limb to limb, as though they were joined together!')

In spite of certain difficulties of detail the general sense and purpose of the poem is clear, and by invoking the power of Wodan, a man whose horse met with a similar accident would seek to effect the magic act of healing which Wodan performed in the selfsame situation. The form presents typical features of Germanic verse: construction in pairs of short lines (*Halbzeilen*); the linking of each pair of lines by an alliterative element ('Phol . . . vuorun'; '. . . volon . . . vuoz'; '. . . Sinthgunt . . . Sunna . . . suister'); two main and two subsidiary beats in each short line; considerable freedom in the number of unaccented syllables between these beats, giving lines of irregular length.

Belief in pagan deities like those invoked in these two charms was one of the forces that the Christianizers of Germany had to counter. Since the attitudes that found expression in such forms were too firmly rooted to be destroyed by a radical, single-minded act of reform, the missionaries – and in this they acted as the proselytizers of all ages act – took the outer shell of such forms and filled it with a new content. The pattern of the familiar formulae was left undisturbed; but the formulae themselves now stated new propositions that derived from a totally new set of initial assumptions.

Thus the pagan charm, for instance, lived on into Christian times in its traditional epic-cum-incantatory form, but the Christian God takes the place of the heathen gods, and an appeal to the guardians of a pagan pantheistic mythology gives way to a supplication for the blessings of Jesus Christ and the Virgin Mary. From the monastery of Lorsch, for example, north of Mannheim, there is preserved a short double charm in rhymed verse, written in the tenth century. It relates to the care of bees, which, through the use of their wax in candles, and of their honey for sweetening – sugar was not known in Europe at this time – were of considerable economic importance in the Middle Ages, and required special laws for their protection. The first part of the charm beseeches the swarm, which has evidently broken out, to return to the hive and to God's care, because He so desires it; the second part enjoins the bees in the name of the Virgin Mary to stay peacefully in the hive and thereby act according to the will of the Lord. The need of the common people to appeal for supernatural aid and protection is preserved, but it is now the God of Christianity that has established himself in their consciousness.

The *Hildebrandslied*, the other surviving piece of literature that belongs in this pagan Germanic context, owes its importance to being the unique surviving piece of heroic poetry in the Old High German language. We do not know who wrote it, nor can we say anything more definite about the date of its composition than that it probably falls between 750 and 800. There are many linguistic and literary obscurities in the text, but they do not prevent us from following the course of the action. In this, the warrior Hildebrand, a comrade of the sixth-century Ostrogothic King Theodoric (i.e. the figure famed in Germanic legend as Dietrich von Bern) finds himself by a cruel stroke of destiny facing his long-lost son Hadubrand, now the representative of an enemy army, in single combat. Hadubrand does not believe that it is his father who confronts him, but once the challenge has been thrown down, there can be no turning back. The Germanic code of loyalty has no room for sentimentality, and honour demands that, whatever their personal relationship, those singled out for combat shall not flinch from it. So after the preliminary exchange of words father and son engage in the fight that for the one or the other can end only in death. The poem breaks off before the climax is reached, but from a twelfth-century Norse fragment of the same story – a story that has international currency from the literature of Persia, Greece and Rome to Old French, Danish, Russian and English – we know that the father kills the son. This is, indeed, what the tragic, fatalistic mood of Germanic poetry would lead us to expect.

The rugged – some might say primitive – alliterative verse-form in which the story is told, and the blunt economy of words in both narrative and dialogue, are the appropriate concomitants of the personal, social and ethical assumptions which underlie the action and constitute what can be called the philosophy of the world to whose conduct these assumptions are germane. It is a world of precise public values in which the proprieties, and the penalties for offending against them, are laid down; it is a stark world of black and white, and the demands of justice, however unreasonable, even cruel, the morality behind that justice may appear to us today, must be unquestioningly met.

Central to this morality are the virtue of loyalty and the courage to take up arms in its defence, whatever the consequences. Life itself has no unconditional value, and death is viewed with defiance and scorn. The most heinous of crimes is cowardice. But there is a divine concern to see that virtue and justice triumph, so that he whose courage wins the day must of necessity have justice on his side. The outcome of the fight between Hildebrand and Hadubrand will thus be an expression of the divine will, and, despite its efforts, the Christian Church took centuries to eradicate this fundamental fatalistic conception and the institution of the duel itself. As in the heathen charms, therefore, so also in the *Hildebrandslied* the Christian God infiltrates the pagan scene and presides over the fatalistic ritual, lending His authority to the tragic display of pride, defiance, blind loyalty and the other traditional values on which this society rested.

From the surviving religious writings of Old High German times, and including works written in the linguistic forms of Low German, one gains a more or less total view of the field of Christian activity in Germany during these centuries. At the most elementary level are the numerous glossaries, complete or fragmentary, from St Gallen, Reichenau, St Emmeram and other famous monasteries of the time, which give the German equivalents of the Latin terms which the introduction of Roman culture and of the Christian religion had made it necessary to learn. The earliest of these glossaries go back to about 750. The oldest poetic creations we possess, however, were recorded in the early ninth century, in Bavaria, and show a concern with ontological questions such as the origin of the world and the nature of the Last Judgement, often coupled with prayers for admission to a state of grace.

An interesting example is the incomplete alliterative poem, written in Bavaria in the ninth century, known as *Muspilli* ('End of the World'). It preaches the eschatology of Purgatory and the Last Judgement, holding up before men's eyes the rewards that await the righteous and the punishment that will befall the sinner. Drawing principally on the Book of Revelation, and with the combination of graphic narrative and minatory exhortation with which the missionaries had made the age familiar, the poet addresses himself to the task of revealing the relationship between man's conduct of life on earth and his fate in the life to come.

Much of the phraseology in this, as in all the works of the period, is so stylized that, apart from obvious biblical formulations, it is usually vain to try to trace individual sources from which a poet might have drawn his thoughts. Indeed, a great deal of misdirected zeal has been applied to the task of identifying the ultimate sources of individual motifs, thoughts and expressions in the vernacular literature of the Middle Ages in general. So many such motifs, thoughts and expressions were common property at the time that it is often idle to posit a single exclusive source for a certain idea in a certain writer, and still more idle to weave patterns of imputed influences over a framework of unproven and unprovable allegations about original sources. Moreover, the Middle Ages had an unquestioning respect for authority. Received knowledge was transmitted with awe and reverence, and the body of approved doctrine on which education in monastery schools was based, together with the conventional attitudes and formulae through which this doctrine was expressed, enjoyed common currency. The ultimate source of a particular concept or phrase may, for example, lie in one of the early Church Fathers: there is little to be gained from trying to identify the hands through which it has passed on its way to the written document with which one is at that moment concerned.

By far the most voluminous literary form of this period is the biography of Jesus, of which two striking examples, very different from each other, are extant: the Low German *Heliand* ('Saviour') and the *Evangelienbuch* ('Book of the Gospels') of Otfrid von Weissenburg.

The anonymous Old Saxon *Heliand* consists of almost 6,000 lines of alliterative verse. Through those of their tribe who had emigrated to Britain the Saxons, who resisted Christianization longer than the German tribes in the south and were only converted by Charlemagne himself in the ninth century, were particularly exposed to English influences. One such influence was the existence of an epic poetry on Christian subject-matter. The *Heliand* stands as the Old Saxon counterpart of this Anglo-Saxon epic poetry, and, as with the pattern of Christian teaching that followed in the wake of Boniface and his companions, testifies to the extent of Anglo-Saxon influence on German cultural life in these centuries. One of the fragmentary manuscripts of the *Heliand* even contains some three hundred lines of the story of Genesis in Old Saxon, the first twenty-six lines of which recur in an Anglo-Saxon version of the Genesis story, lines which have been shown to be an interpolation from the Old Saxon source. This is surely not the only occasion on which ideas, attitudes and practices passed between the Saxons who had gone to England and their kinsmen who had stayed on the Continent.

The *Heliand* itself draws its material mainly from the Gospel Harmony (*Diatessaron*) of Tatian, a Syrian Christian of the second century. It is planned as a popular epic in which the Christian message shall be communicated within the framework of the traditional Germanic partiality to the narration of glorious heroic deeds. The poet's ends therefore determine his choice of means, and whether one chooses to extol it for its vivid Germanic ruggedness or to berate it for its tedious and crude prolixity, one has to recall the purpose for which it was written, and judge it, in its historical context, against this purpose. The poet clearly saw himself as an artist, anxious to appeal to the tastes of his public and to employ to best advantage the familiar Germanic techniques of repetition and variation within the alliterative verse-pattern, while at the same time serving as the spokesman of the Christian message. Moreover, his work stands at the end of a literary movement, much of whose development had taken place in England during the preceding century.

Who the author of the *Heliand* was we do not know. With Otfrid von Weissenburg (Wissembourg, on the Alsatian-German frontier), however, we are in the presence of the first German poet known to us by name – although beyond the facts that he was a monk at the monastery of Weissenburg, and that he composed his so-called *Evangelienbuch* between 863 and 871 (this can be deduced from the careers of the dedicatees of the work, among whom is Louis the German, a grandson of Charlemagne), nothing is known of his life.

Like the *Heliand*, Otfrid's *Evangelienbuch*, which is arranged in five books and has a total of 7,000 lines, has for its subject the life of Christ, but there the resemblance ends. Where the author of the older work cast himself as a poet, Otfrid sees himself as an educator; where the *Heliand* set store by liveliness of narrative, Otfrid sets out to display his skill in exegesis and his expansiveness of learning, often seeing no reason to use ten words when fifty will do; where the *Heliand* still contained many of the gestures of the traditional Germanic epic, the *Evangelienbuch* has none. In the realm of form Otfrid introduced the revolutionary change from alliteration to rhyme, and from his time onwards all the surviving poetic monuments of Old High German literature, and on through the classical Middle High German period 400 years later, are cast in the rhyming four-bar couplets which he imported from the Latin Ambrosian hymns of the Church (the four-stress alliterative line of Germanic verse provided a not unhelpful starting-point for the change).

The *Petruslied* – the first German hymn (late ninth century) – to which the melody, unfortunately notated only in untranscribable neumes, is also preserved; the *Ludwigslied* – a historical ballad written in the year 881 in praise of the Frankish king Louis III; and the *Georgslied* – a religious ballad on the legend and martyrdom of St George, composed *c.* 900: works such as these owe their poetic form directly to Otfrid, and whatever criticisms of verbosity, monotony, line-padding and the like the *Evangelienbuch* attracts, its historical importance, like that of a German epic on the same subject written 900 years later, at which similar criticisms have been levelled – Klopstock's *Messias* – cannot be gainsaid.

To turn from the poetry of this period to the prose is virtually to pass from the world of free invention to the world of imitation, for with a very few exceptions the prose works of Old High German are translations from the Latin. This amounts to saying that their interest is linguistic rather than literary, for as the subject-matter is already known and given, the question of originality of thought does not arise, and what one witnesses is a technical exercise in the transference of this subject-matter from a language of established tradition and elegance to a language – or, more accurately, to a series of dialects, since there was no single, unified Old High German language – which had neither tradition nor elegance and was laboriously discovering its ethos through the practical disciplines of translation and conversion.

The work of translation rested, of course, in the hands of the clerics, of whom, however, only a very small proportion were equipped for the task of writing anything down. Glossaries and Latin/German inter-linear versions of hymns and liturgical texts mark the beginning of this activity. In the course of the ninth century, as a direct product of the authority of Charlemagne, the range widens to include sermons, catechisms and other branches of homiletic writing; in some cases the original Latin text is preserved alongside the German, while in others the German stands alone.

The highest achievements in the field of translation in the Old High German period are those of Notker III of St Gallen (known variously as Notker Labeo (i.e. 'thick-lipped') or Notker Teutonicus ('the German', from his activity as a translator)), the youngest of three famous monks of this name at one of the most famous of medieval schools. Notker died in 1022, and his work is usually seen as closing the Old High German period, both from the linguistic and the literary point of view. His translations from Latin into German, i.e. into the Alemannic dialect of his day, range from the Psalms and the Book of Job (both taken from the Vulgate) to Aristotle (a Latin version), and from Boethius's *De consolatione philosophiae* to Virgil and Terence, while for the educational programme of St Gallen he wrote original Latin treatises on grammar, rhetoric, music and the other disciplines of the Seven Liberal Arts. Not all his work survives, and much of what has survived is somewhat pedestrian, but when one bears in mind the undeveloped state of German culture at the time, one is bound to admire his industry and the breadth of his knowledge.

To complete the discussion of the literature of these centuries, mention should be made of certain original Latin poetic works that have survived, for these show how the experience of classical literature gained through study in the Seven Liberal Arts found its way into original composition. The fable, for instance, which was familiar to the Middle Ages through the Latin version of Aesop and widely cultivated as a vehicle for moral exhortation, is represented by a tenth-century epic poem in hexameters called *Ecbasis Captivi* ('Escape of the Prisoner'), in which a human message is conveyed allegorically through the behaviour of animals. A didactic purpose also underlies the dramas and verse legends of Roswitha von Gandersheim (*fl.* 960–1000), a nun whose work is prominent in the application of the newly rediscovered values of Latin culture in Germany during the reigns of the Saxon emperor Otto I and his successors. Two curious macaronic works, half in German, half in Latin, have also survived from this Ottonian period: one is an historical poem called *De Heinrico*, dealing with the reconciliation of one of the Ottos with the Duke Henry of the title; the other is *Ruodlieb*, a romance which, though written in Latin hexameters, treats German folk-tale motifs and contains an intriguing love-letter in a mixture of Latin and German.

German subject-matter also provides the substance of the last and most interesting of the works that belong in this context, the tenth-century Latin verse epic *Waltharius*. The story, part of the Germanic heroic tradition and set in the historical framework of that tradition, tells of Walther and Hildegunde and their adventurous journey from the court of Attila the Hun to Walther's home in Aquitaine. While the subject is Germanic, the style is Latin, modelled on Virgil and Statius; and, as the cap-stone, the ethic – vindication of virtue, humiliation of pride, punishment of avarice – is conventionally Christian.

Thus in the anonymous *Waltharius* we find once more the three elements which, combined in different proportions, constitute the cultural background against which German literature, from its beginnings until the millennium, has to be viewed. In the eleventh century, above all under the influence of the strict ascetic ideals that had emanated from the Burgundian monastery of Cluny in the tenth century and subsequently taken root in Germany, the thoughts of the Christian communities turned inwards and were directed towards the refinement of doctrine rather than to the continued propagation of the Word among the heathen. This meant that the monks left the vernacular language alone and addressed themselves to the cultivation of their Latin. When a strong, unimpeded current of significant literature in the German language reappears, the underlying presuppositions and attitudes of society have greatly changed.

The eleventh century was characterized by intense religious activity in Europe, by a dramatic increase in the power of the Papacy, and by a consequential aggravation of the corrosive conflict between Pope and Emperor which smouldered for two hundred years and ended by almost destroying the Holy Roman Empire itself. One of the most prominent forms taken by this religious activity was the cultivation of ideals of rigid asceticism and uncompromising adherence to doctrine. This movement, which had become particularly associated with the monastery of Cluny in the tenth century and had intensified with the approach of the year 1000 and the end of the world prophesied for that moment, was to reach a triple climax with the election of the firebrand monk Hildebrand as Pope Gregory VII (1073–85), the proclamation of the First Crusade (1095), and the foundation of the new, stricter monastic orders of the Carthusians and the Cistercians, as acts of reform in the face of alleged adulteration of the Benedictine rule. This spirit infuses German literary works such as the late eleventh-century poem known as *Memento mori*, a kind of homily in rhymed couplets, exhorting men to turn from the vanities of the world and think on their spiritual well-being.

Homiletic literature, in the form of sermons and prayers, is prominent throughout this century and well into the next. Of particular interest is the frequency with which invocations of the Virgin Mary appear, for this accompanies the rise of the ideal of the courtly lady and of chivalric virtue. Most of this literature is anonymous, but in the majority of cases we are able, sometimes on linguistic evidence, sometimes from allusions to patrons or other dignitaries, at least to identify the region and the approximate period to which a particular work belongs.

However, although it continues to be religious literature that dominates this century, the range and purpose of that literature are by no means restricted to those of prayer and sermon. And since more documents have survived from this period than from Old High German times, we can claim to have a reasonably comprehensive view of clerical literary activity.

A judgement on the quality of this literature, as on that of the religious works of the preceding centuries, has to be tempered by the realization that in this age the production of works of art springs from the service of a practical communal need, and not from a compulsive urge for self-expression on the part of an individual. Impersonality is a natural characteristic of such works, and the fact that the overwhelming majority of them are preserved anonymously is a logical corollary to this. We may therefore fairly say that their chief interest lies in their social and historical content and in the religious attitudes that stimulated their composition. Spiritually, intellectually, artistically and linguistically, the times do not yet allow the emergence of poetic personalities who can be approached with the techniques and expectations of modern literary criticism.

Much of the narrative literature of the eleventh century and the early twelfth century consists of versifications of individual books of the Bible (Genesis, Exodus, Song of Songs, Judith) or of particular stories and episodes from the Old and New Testaments (the story of John the Baptist, the Nativity, the Last Judgement); the subjects of such epics then extended to the lives of the saints and at the same time continued the tradition of the didactic exposition of Christian dogma.

One of the most interesting works of this latter type, and at the same time the first work to break the silence in the recorded tradition of German poetry which had set in almost 150 years before, is *Ezzos Gesang von den Wundern Christi* ('Ezzo's Song of the Miracles of Christ'), which consists of some 130 rhyming four-bar couplets in the style descended from Otfrid, and gives in blunt, straightforward style the history of mankind from Creation to Redemption. The poet was one Ezzo, a canon of Bamberg, and his poem was chanted on Bishop Gunther of Bamberg's pilgrimage to the Holy Land in 1064–5.

The many extant prayers, confession-formulae and exhortations to repentance have, by and large, little individuality and no more memorability. But there is one remarkable exception – the work of a Benedictine lay-brother at the Austrian monastery of Melk, an intolerant critic of contemporary society, a ruthless exposer of clerical immorality, and the first satirist in German literature: Heinrich von Melk (*fl.* 1150). Standing at the end of this transition period, a witness of the rise of the knightly class, which was on the threshold of its cultural supremacy, and himself probably descended from a noble line, Heinrich gave vent to his pitiless condemnation of human frailty in two poems, one known as *Von des todes gehugede* ('The Reminder of Death' – i.e. 'Memento mori'), the other as *Vom Priesterleben* ('The Life of the Clerics'). The poet's attitudes are in themselves revealing; even more so is the picture of the society of the day which emerges from the various attitudes and practices that he castigates, and which gives us social insights that we should not otherwise have.

Turning from the religious literature of the early twelfth century to the literature of secular subject-matter, whether written by clerics or by minstrels, one finds oneself in a very different atmosphere. The cultivation of the epic lay, traditional literary form of the Germanic peoples, and the province of the professional *scop*, had passed into the hands of the minstrels. It is through the literary activity of these men, in fact, most of it sustained, not by manuscript record but by oral tradition, that much of the subject-matter proper to the history and mythology of the Germans has survived. Throughout the centuries when religious concerns dominated the activities of those in control of the cultural destiny of the people – activities, one must remember, which start with the rare ability to read and write – the old secular, pagan subjects had been driven underground. But it would be very mistaken to assume that the absence of written documents means the non-existence of such subjects, and indeed, the survival from the early twelfth century of manuscripts of secular epics betokens the re-emergence in public, recorded form of what had of necessity been carried on beneath the surface up to that point.

We possess seven secular epics from this period, three written by named clerics, the others, of less certain origin, preserved anonymously. The oldest of them, composed 1130–40, and based on a French model, is the Lay of Alexander (*Alexanderlied*) by a priest from Trier called Lamprecht, the first extant translation into German of a work of French literature. Alexander the Great, the mightiest ruler of antiquity, was a magnetic figure to whom all manner of legendary adventures became attached, and who came to represent for the Middle Ages the ideal of a world-ruler. The French poetic source from which Lamprecht worked is itself derived from the Latin, medieval knowledge of Alexander being principally derived from Latin adaptations of the largely fictional biography ascribed to Callisthenes.

As Alexander stands for self-made, worldly success, so Charlemagne, *rex justus et pacificus*, stood for the Middle Ages as the greatest ruler in Christendom, the paragon of God-fearing virtue and the warrior chosen by the Lord to carry out His purposes on earth. Charles is the hero of a German version of the *Chanson de Roland* – the famous Old French strophic epic based on an episode in Charles's Spanish campaign in 788. The author of the 11,000-line German *Rolandslied* (*c.* 1130) is Konrad, a Bavarian priest from Regensburg, who has deliberately converted the strong national patriotic appeal of his French source into an exhortation to live by religious values, in particular those of the Crusades, and has thus turned a popular epic into a religious epic, and the praise of a nation into the praise of God.

This same Konrad is the author of the first real historical chronicle written in the German language – the so-called *Kaiserchronik*, a sequence of biographies of Roman and German kings and emperors from Romulus down to the poet's own day.

Of the four verse-epics of anonymous authorship – all of them written *c.* 1150–90 and in the dialect of the Rhine–Moselle area which formed the heart of the old Frankish kingdom – the oldest, longest and most interesting is *König Rother*, the familiar story of how a king set out to find a bride, how she was stolen from him, and how he then won her back again. The particular historical interest of this poem lies in the fact that it is the first surviving recorded work in the tradition of Germanic heroic poetry since the Old High German *Hildebrandslied* three centuries earlier.

This break in written tradition is due primarily to religious causes which have already been mentioned. During this time occurred the decisive development from epic lay to full-scale heroic epic, the radical change in prosody from the principle of irregular line-length governed by alliteration to that of regular couplets linked by rhyme, and the inheritance of the realm of the Germanic *scop* by the professional minstrel of the Middle Ages. The performers of *König Rother* and its companion-pieces were almost certainly such minstrels, but this does not entitle one to say that minstrels actually wrote them, since the minstrel class was largely illiterate and could in any case only have had access to costly parchment and writing implements under the patronage of a nobleman. It is more probable that educated laymen of the class, say, of *ministerialis* were concerned in the composing and recording of these epics, and also the *vagantes*, the wandering scholars, by whom many of the cultural and artistic values of the Middle Ages were transmitted.

The epic poems of the early twelfth century, the so-called Early Middle High German period, occupy a historical position which has the character in both linguistic and literary respects of a prelude to the period in which the real glories of medieval German literature emerge. For however much there may be that can fairly be called 'interesting' or 'revealing', in the sense that works of art, and above all works of literature, have an evident social content which, like any historical document, may reveal the conventions, assumptions and tensions of their age, few will wish to claim that Old High German or Early Middle High German literature has works to offer which are of substantial innate value. Indeed, the conditions of the emergence of German culture within the containing framework of the Holy Roman Empire make it wholly natural that this should be so. There is nothing to put alongside *Beowulf*, at the time of whose composition (*c.* 700), in fact, there seems to have been no written German literature at all, let alone a fully developed tradition of epic poetry. And there is nothing contemporary to put alongside the *Chanson de Roland* or the romances of Chrestien de Troyes, or the lyric verse of the early troubadours.

The foundations of the literary greatness that Germany was shortly to achieve lie in a revolution in society and in social attitudes, a revolution which spread to Germany from France and which became consolidated in the remarkable phenomenon known as courtly civilization, or the Age of Chivalry. The sources of the individual details of this phenomenon are often still a matter of dispute among scholars, but in so far as our concern here is rather with effects than causes, especially as Germany is the recipient at two removes of the influence in question, we may proceed from the observation that the birth of the courtly epic (*roman courtois*), the rise of troubadour poetry, and the eventual conversion of the whole of medieval Europe to the courtly mode of life and the ideals that it professed, were all closely connected with the rise of the Angevin empire and in particular with the person of Eleanor of Aquitaine, wife of King Henry II of England.

This extraordinary woman, granddaughter of the first troubadour known to us by name, William IX of Aquitaine, and mother of Richard Cœur de Lion, was probably the most powerful personality in the formulation and propagation of the ideals of chivalry. From about 1170, when she set up household in Poitiers, her court was the chief academy in western Europe for disseminating these ideals, and it was here that Andreas Cappelanus made his famous contribution to the doctrine of courtly love, in the form of the treatise *De arte honeste amandi*, the thirty-one articles of which rapidly attained the status of dogma in court circles throughout Europe.

Amor cortois set out to ennoble the all too earthly passions of the young nobleman by erecting an abstract ideal of womanhood and making the worship of this ideal, in the representative person of a chosen lady, both the spiritual goal and the emotional *raison d'être* of a man's life. The courtly epics of France and Germany, and the lyrical poetry of the troubadours, the trouvères and the Minnesinger owe their existence to the urge to express and to illustrate these values. Courtly love claims absolute power over mind and heart: it is both an end and the means to that end. As such, it stands in conflict with marriage, which is a restrictive legal covenant and thus inhibiting of natural self-expression. And as an immoral invitation to deny the sanctity of marriage, the code of courtly love inevitably drew upon itself the condemnation of the Church – though at the same time the rise of courtly love had undoubted associations with the cult of the Virgin Mary. Equally, as an ennobling but elusive ideal, it is unlikely to have had a great practical influence on actual conduct in given social contexts, and one need not take the professions and claims uttered in its name to reflect true patterns of behaviour. But the nature of the intention is clear, and it is with the expression and illustration of this intention that we are dealing in the literature to which it gave birth.

The cultivation of courtly literature lay in the hands of the knights – and also of their ladies. The prestige that the knights enjoyed within the feudal system, together with the twin concepts of service and loyalty which sustained that system, created the atmosphere in which they not only exercised their social power but also indulged the forces of their imagination and education. The age is one of expansion, of adventure, of enthusiasm, in the fields of ecclesiastical learning and artistic expression no less than of territorial conquest and material aggrandisement. It is the age of cathedral-building, of scholastic philosophy, of crusade. Perhaps the common denominator of these activities, the single powerful datum from which they can be seen to emerge, is curiosity about the world – the world of physical wonders, the world of the mind, the world of the spirit, the world of man, the world of God. In eager inquiry men look, wonder, worship, moralize. It is a time of discovery, of movement, of urges to understand and control.

The strength of the knights, together with the associated establishment of the orders of chivalry, stemmed from military considerations. The division, at one time irreconcilable, between free and bond knights became blurred, and common interests arose in groups formed of men of like-minded concerns, whether hereditary nobles or serving *ministeriales*. From this latter class, which reached the height of its power under the Hohenstaufen dynasty, came many of the greatest writers of the Golden Age of medieval German poetry, whose careers as professional poets were spent at whatever court or courts were indulgent of their particular gifts. Looked at in this way, their situation of dependence on the vagaries of patronage differs little from that of the minstrels and other wandering entertainers of humble origins, with whom, however disparate their cultural levels, they often found themselves classified. And from the internal evidence in the poetry of, say, Walther

von der Vogelweide we can readily see what uncertainties and dis-
appointments attended the itinerant Minnesinger – or, for that matter,
the epic poet – until he finally found the security he sought.

The literature of this 'classical' Middle High German period, whether
verse or prose, epic or lyric, exhibits a remarkable uniformity – or,
more accurately, near-uniformity – of language. This language has
come to be called the Middle High German *Dichtersprache* and it is just
that: a literary language, with a minimum of dialectal features, cultivated by poets for the embellishment of the motifs and attitudes of
courtly civilization. It was never a general language of communication,
and although its influence may well have come to be felt in the spoken
language of certain circles as a result of the oral transmission and public
performance of literature, it was in essence a written language, and died
with the chivalric ideals that sustained it. The modern German language, however, through words such as *Abenteuer, Harnisch, Lanze*
hübsch (from the same origin as *höfisch*), *fein* and *stolz*, still reveals many
of the concerns and values of the age.

The ideals of courtly love which inform the literary activity of the
Provençal troubadours and the French trouvères find parallel expression
in the lyric poetry of the Minnesinger. Strictly speaking, and in the
usage of the poets themselves, the term *Minnesang* denotes the songs of
love (*Minne*) written in the service of *amor cortois*, but for the purposes
of literary history it has come to be applied to all the lyric poetry of the
period, *Spruchdichtung* (political, moral and religious verse) as well as
Minnelyrik. And to complete the broad definition: the poetic text,
whatever the subject, is set to music, the melody being customarily,
though not invariably, composed by the poet, who would normally
perform his finished song before the court at which he was staying.

Yet the corpus of German lyric poetry is not to be characterized
simply as the German imitation of Romance originals – and one of the
most intriguing examples of its independence is the personality of the
very first Minnesinger known to us by name, the poet whom the manuscript calls simply 'Der von Kürenberg'. The Kürenberger, an Austrian
nobleman, was probably a knight of the family whose castle stood near
Linz on the Danube, and he appears to have been active in the 1160s.
The most interesting characteristic of his poetry, as of a few anonymous
lyric strophes from this earliest period, is that, far from being inspired
by the fashionable new ideal of courtly love, it represents a native
tradition of poetry sustained by quite different, realistic attitudes and
conventions: instead of the pained worship of a romantic ideal of

Q

womanhood, the Kürenberger depicts a proud, imperious knight with a woman pining for his love, a world controlled by masculine values, and in which the relationship between the sexes is as yet unaffected by the new Romance-inspired concepts.

The Kürenberger's basic form is a four-line strophe of rhyming couplets which later became (or had perhaps already by this time become) that of the *Nibelungenlied*. From this, as from other internal evidence, it is apparent that we are facing an accomplished poet who represents not the hesitant beginnings of a movement but the end of a cultured poetic tradition whose earlier course is lost to history.

One can only speculate about the origins of this pre-courtly secular love lyric. Tempting theories based on the assumption of a tradition of folk-poetry have to counter the difficulty that so few traces of such poetry remain that one cannot claim to recognize what motifs, attitudes and forms it exhibited, still less to identify any influence it might have had. Better documented is the tradition of *Vagantenlieder*, poems written by the wandering scholars, usually in Latin, but sometimes also in the vernacular. The largest Latin/German collection of such songs is the late thirteenth-century *Carmina Burana* (named after the monastery of Benediktbeuern in Upper Bavaria and now preserved in the Munich Staatsbibliothek). But the influence of this poetry on the Minnesang also seems to be marginal rather than central. One can, however, claim with reasonable certainty that it is in Austria that the main source of this early lyric poetry lies.

The poems attributed to 'Der von Kürenberg' are preserved in the largest and most sumptuous of Minnesang manuscripts, that commonly known as the *Manessische Liederhandschrift*, after the Swiss patrician Rüdiger Manesse (d. 1325), in whose commission it is supposed to have been compiled. Besides poems by some 140 Minnesinger of the twelfth and thirteenth centuries it contains formalized miniatures in brilliant colours of the individual poets and their armorial bearings, at their head the Emperor Henry VI. As Richard Cœur de Lion composed courtly lyrics in Provençal, so Henry VI, son of Frederick Barbarossa, wrote love-lyrics in the same vein, showing that the cultivation of the courtly manner occupied the minds of the highest in the land. Three further manuscripts, two from the fourteenth century, the other from the thirteenth, combine with the Manesse manuscript to provide the bulk of the poems known to us, many of them being preserved in more than one source. Unfortunately, however, only one of these large codices, the so-called *Jenaer Liederhandschrift*, contains the melodies that belong to the texts. Besides these principal sources we possess many incomplete manuscripts and isolated fragments, some of them giving valuable glimpses of aspects of the Minnesinger art not revealed by the large collections.

In the love-poems attributed to the Austrian nobleman Dietmar von Aist (d. *c.* 1170) – under whose name, however, the verses of more than one poet seem to have been gathered (the attributions in the manuscripts cannot always be taken at their face value, and different manuscripts sometimes ascribe one and the same poem to different authors) – Romance influence begins to make itself felt. The woman now becomes the centre of attraction, and the knight affirms his service and devotion to her.

But it is with the succeeding generation – the Flemish knight Heinrich von Veldeke (d. *c.* 1190), famed also as an epic poet, Friedrich von Hausen (d. 1190), a Palatinate knight in the entourage of the Emperor Frederick Barbarossa, and the Swiss count Rudolf von Fenis (d. *c.* 1195) – that the art of the troubadours and trouvères takes control of both the form and the content of the German love-lyric. The two last-named are among those who have been shown to have taken over from a troubadour or trouvère a particular strophic form (with, presumably, its melody) and re-expressed the thought-content in his own language – a procedure known as contrafacture.

The Romance influence brought with it, besides the motifs of courtly love-poetry, a new principle of poetic form which became the standard strophic pattern for the Minnesinger also – the tripartite pattern of two metrically similar sections (*Stollen*, or, in Dante's terminology, *pedes*: the two *Stollen* together = *Aufgesang* or *frons*) followed by an independent third section (*Abgesang* or *cauda*). The two *Stollen* (the terms are later coinages by the Meistersinger) are usually but not invariably set to the same group of melodic phrases, while the melody of the *Abgesang* is independent, though sometimes with echoes of the *Aufgesang*. Once established, a particular song-form (*Ton*) could be called into use again at any time by the poet – possibly even by another poet – and new strophes written to it. One can thus find, say, a love-song and/or a series of varied political and moral *Sprüche* all in the same strophic form. The nature of the subject-matter has little influence on the character of the melody. In form, the *Spruch* consists of a single strophe, whereas the love-song usually has more than one, but since the melody is repeated for each verse in turn, there is no formal problem.

Since within the artificial conventions of courtly love the choice of motifs for poetic treatment was very restricted, the originality of the individual poet found its chief expression in the field of technique – skill in strophic construction, subtlety of rhyme-scheme, interplay of words and music. This is not to say that there was no room at all for originality of expression; but since the conceptual data were given and defined, and since stock attitudes were required and stock reactions expected, the poet was forced to prove the original quality and sincerity of his professed emotions by giving individuality to the mode of his expression. And if there is no such strongly marked individuality, the result will be undistinguished and undistinguishable poetry. Indeed, so much medieval love-poetry, that of the troubadours and trouvères as well as of the Minnesinger, presents typical and generalized features, that one is not surprised to find that the manuscripts themselves often disagree over the ascription of particular poems and that scholars argue over the authorship of what strike many as singularly uninspired and unremarkable strophes.

Exceptionally, however, in the work of the Thuringian Minnesinger Heinrich von Morungen, who flourished from about 1190 to 1210, we find ourselves in the presence of a poet with an intensity of feeling, and a degree of personal moral involvement in his love-themes, which set him apart from his contemporaries. The Alsatian Reinmar von Hagenau (Reinmar der Alte), on the other hand (d. c. 1210), who spent most of his career at the Viennese court, brings to their consummation the formal and conceptual values of the courtly love-lyric in its strict, narrow sense and thus appears, as he did already to his own and to immediately succeeding generations, as the most representative poet of 'pure' Minnesang. We also possess lyrics by Hartmann von Aue and Wolfram von Eschenbach, but the importance of these two writers rests rather on their epic poetry, and they are discussed in that context below.

Parallel to the stream of love-poetry runs the cultivation of gnomic poetry (*Spruchdichtung*), first encountered in a poet called Spervogel, a wandering minstrel of humble origin who was active at the end of the twelfth century. Gnomic poetry is, of course, far older than this, but although early relics have survived from Scandinavia, there is no earlier written trace of it in Germany. In Middle High German times, however, the genre flourished, and from 1200 down to the end of the Meistersinger period there is an abundance of *Sprüche* – normally single strophes – on political, religious and general moral subjects, usually treated in an earnest, didactic tone. With the waning of courtly ideals, in fact, the later manuscripts of medieval lyric poetry tend to contain more and more didactic moral verse. Much of it is boring and repetitious, but some – one may mention Reinmar von Zweter (*fl. c.* 1230–60), Der Marner (*fl. c.* 1230–70) and Friedrich von Sonnenburg (*fl. c.* 1250–75) – is the work of more interesting and accomplished versifiers.

These and all other names, however, are overshadowed by that of Walther von der Vogelweide (*c.* 1170–*c.* 1230), the greatest lyric poet of the German Middle Ages. We do not know when or where he was born, but he belonged to the *ministerialis* class, learned his poetic craft in Vienna under Reinmar der Alte, and after a wandering, insecure existence for many years in the service of a succession of patrons both ecclesiastical and secular, was finally granted a fief near Würzburg by the emperor Frederick II in return for his support of the house of Hohenstaufen in its political struggles and its quarrels with the Papacy.

We possess some 200 poems by Walther which are generally acknowledged as authentic (the many spurious poems attributed to him in the manuscripts are an inevitable consequence of his fame and of the number of imitators he attracted): rather more than half of these are *Sprüche*; the remainder are love-lyrics, some, mostly from his early career, in the courtly tradition, others – like the famous *Under der linden* – in a fresh, uninhibited style in which the poses of court society give way before the forces of spontaneous emotion. The influence of the wandering scholars, whose Latin love-lyrics are equally free and un-restrained, and with whom Walther undoubtedly consorted during his itinerant years, may well be present here; so, too, may that of folk-poetry. This 'uncourtly' style, often referred to as *niedere Minne*, is one of the powerfully original traits in Walther, and leads directly to the realistic, sometimes vulgar *höfische Dorfpoesie* of Neidhart von Reuen-thal, Gottfried von Neifen and other 'naturalistic' poets of the later thirteenth century.

It is, however, in the realm of *Spruchdichtung* that Walther is at his most characteristic. An uncompromising religious moralist and idealist, a fierce patriot and opponent of clerical – including papal – interference in affairs properly secular, a zealous preacher of the values of an ordered, balanced, God-fearing life: such is the personality that emerges from the outspoken, often intolerant, even offensive tone of his verses. But the intolerance is part of his uncompromising view of right and wrong, and over all his utterances rules the unshakeable conviction that a man must be able to justify his every thought and deed before God, and make his peace with Him by going on pilgrimage to the Holy Land or by joining a crusade. Walther certainly experienced unpopularity in his lifetime, and his less admirable qualities are still evident to us today. But there is no other Minnesinger who can match his versatility, his intensity of feeling or his power of expression.

Walther von der Vogelweide's role in the development of the medieval German lyric, love-poetry and *Spruchdichtung* alike, was decisive. In one way or another, all the later poets of the thirteenth and fourteenth centuries stand in his debt, and few of them have more than a fraction of his talent. Outstanding among these few is Walther's younger contemporary Neidhart von Reuenthal (d. *c.* 1250), a Bavarian squire who later settled in Austria. Neidhart developed, in a way of which Walther himself disapproved, the anti-courtly trend associated with Walther's poems of *niedere Minne*, and evolved from the situation of the pastourelle (i.e. a knight wooing a village maiden) a genre that has come to be known as *höfische Dorfpoesie*. These poems were still written for performance in court circles, but their subject-matter consisted largely of lampoons of the peasants, with village situations into which Neidhart introduced himself by name as a knight from a superior background.

While some followed in Neidhart's wake, a few tried to salvage something from the disintegration of the courtly lyric, often exhibiting an extreme virtuosity of formal technique which came to be regarded as especially characteristic of the Meistersinger, who succeeded to the Minnesinger inheritance in the fourteenth century. Standing on the hazy border between Minnesang and Meistersang is the figure of Frauenlob (the pseudonym of Heinrich von Meissen, d. 1318), the legendary founder of the first Meistersinger school in Mainz. Like many thirteenth-century and early fourteenth-century Minnesinger, didactic *Spruchdichter* included, Frauenlob was particularly drawn to the poetic form of the *Leich*, or lyric lay, an aggregation of short strophic sections often arranged in an antiphonal pattern derived from the liturgical sequence, and often running to a length of several hundred lines. The challenge to formal ingenuity and the opportunities for structural sophistication in such an extended work are obvious. But all this, like the epics of the same period, is the work of *epigoni*, and the atmosphere of derivativeness and decadence contrasts starkly with the spirit of adventure and creativity that held sway a hundred years before.

As the conceptual ideals of chivalry and courtly culture found their most concentrated and most highly formalized expression in the lyric, so the pattern of this culture repeats itself, in discursive, illustrative form, in the other great literary vehicle of the time: the epic. As with the lyric, the subject-matter, the impulse and the form of the epic came to Germany from Romance literature, in this case not from Provence but from northern France, and above all through the work of the master of the *roman courtois*, Chrestien de Troyes, (*c.* 1135–90), whose Arthurian romances, entertaining in presentation but educative in purpose, became known in Germany in the late twelfth century.

Expansive in conception and in execution, the medieval narrative romance is the perfect vehicle for portraying the kaleidoscope of paradoxical elements which make up the civilization of the Middle Ages. Like the animated scenes in a great tapestry, wars and wooing, jousts and pageants, splendour and sordidness fill the thousands of lines to which, French and German alike, these poems run. And above all these adventures reigns the concept of the 'very perfect gentle knight', in whom is embodied the central ethic of all these epic romances: dedication to lofty ideals, and the achievement thereby, through the will of God, of a higher and fuller life.

The earliest German courtly epics, among them Eilhart von Oberge's *Tristrant und Isalde*, the first treatment in German literature of the Tristan legend, date from about 1170, and the *Eneit* (the story of Dido and Aeneas) of Heinrich von Veldeke, who was regarded by Middle High German poets themselves as the real founder of the German courtly epic, from about 1190. Both these poets, using the rhyming couplet of two four-bar lines, universal in both German and French courtly epics, worked from French sources.

But these and other early works recede into the background before those of the three great masters of the Middle High German courtly epic: Hartmann von Aue, Gottfried von Strassburg and Wolfram von Eschenbach.

Hartmann von Aue, the oldest of the three, was a Swabian *ministerialis* whose career lies between about 1190 and 1215 – although, as with all but a very few poets of the time, the only direct biographical information we have comes from what he says of himself in his works. From the inner evidence of his poetry, however, we can also draw conclusions as to the extent of his learning and the cast of his character. He wrote four epics. The first and the last (*Erec, c.* 1199 – the first known Arthurian romance in German – and *Iwein, c.* 1203) belong to the world of Arthurian legend and are based on the corresponding works by Chrestien de Troyes. The other two are moral-religious tales: *Gregorius*, a refurbishing of the Oedipan legend of Pope Gregory, and *Der arme Heinrich*, his most wholly successful work, a moral story of penitence and trust in God, told in a calm, direct and highly effective manner.

The essence of Hartmann's ethic lies in the concept of *mâze* – moderation, an ordered life in body, mind and spirit, free from extremes of emotion and from any excesses that would disturb that order. Thus in *Erec* the hero neglects the public duties of his knightly office out of excessive devotion to his wife; conversely, Iwein deserts his wife in order to indulge his immoderate desire to fight in tournaments. At the end both men are made to realize their faults and learn how to achieve the golden mean in the conduct of their lives. And once the acknowledgement of human shortcomings has been made, and the legitimate claims of human society have been recognized, the reconciliation can be sealed by God's grace, without which man's life can have neither purpose nor meaning.

Hartmann is a teacher, and saw himself as such. The modest artistic ability that he possessed was a means to an end, and his powers of imagination, never striking, were held subservient to his calculated moral purpose. His style is thus direct, his language simple: the self-consciousness and subtlety of a Gottfried von Strassburg are as foreign to him as the allusiveness and intensity of a Wolfram von Eschenbach. Yet, in a manner characteristic of the tradition-bound, paradox-ridden Middle Ages, his almost nondescript literary qualities could find themselves in the company of a remarkable power and single-mindedness of aim, and leave him, in the eyes of history, with the undeniable credit due to the innovator and pioneer.

In Gottfried von Strassburg (*fl.* 1210) we are confronted with a very different personality. From the fact that his title is not *her* but *meister* we can conclude that he was not a knight, but there is no documentary reference to indicate the particular circle to which he belonged. At all events he was a man of wide learning, familiar with contemporary theology, with the French language and with the classical literature then available in Latin. The only work by which he is known is his *Tristan*, an epic poem based on an Anglo-Norman version of the famous legend, and a work which, though incomplete, holds pride of place as the most accomplished, most subtle and psychologically most sophisticated of the medieval epics on the Tristan legend, French and German alike.

The tale of Tristan and Isolde – Celtic in its origins as legend, French in its emergence as literature – is one of world's great love-stories, and the classical legend of adultery. Since the very concept of courtly love itself, by virtue of its ideal and therefore supra-personal pretensions, presupposes an adulterous relationship, so the illicit but uncontrollable passion that binds Tristan to Isolde, his uncle's wife, presented an eminently acceptable subject to a courtly audience by reason of its spontaneity, its exclusiveness and its completeness. For such an audience this love did not raise issues of personal guilt or social responsibility but was an unconditional right which guaranteed the unrestricted fruition of the most ennobling, most absolute of human emotions.

Gottfried's moral purpose, as he states it in the prologue to his poem, is to offer to courtiers of fine feeling (*edeliu herzen*, literally 'noble hearts') an ideal presentation of the love relationship and with it the ethical canons which underline the morality of the situation. Love brooks no restraint, but there can be no love without suffering: he who does not suffer for his love is no true lover. To this Gottfried adds the virtues of education in the courtly accomplishments which he describes in detail in his poem, the total product to match the utopian chivalric principle of *got unde der werlde gevallen*, 'to be pleasing to God and to man'. Through their union, physical and spiritual, Tristan and Isolde symbolize the ideal relationship between man and woman, the one but a poor, incomplete creature without the other.

Gottfried is a conscious, not to say self-conscious, manipulator of the techniques of literary expression. The directness of his descriptive style ranges him alongside Hartmann von Aue and against Wolfram von Eschenbach, of whose involved and often obscure manner he disapproved, but his own linguistic facility sometimes brought with it an ill-controlled tendency to wordiness and empty virtuosity. At the same time one must grant him an articulacy of expression and an awareness of style that are quite remarkable in this age, and later epic poets are greatly in his debt for revealing the potentialities of a language which few could handle with fluency.

The greatest of these epic writers, however, and the profoundest of all medieval German poets, is Wolfram von Eschenbach. A Bavarian *ministerialis*, he spent part of his career at the court of the landgrave Hermann von Thüringen, an open-handed patron of men of letters, where Heinrich von Veldeke and Walther von der Vogelweide are also known to have stayed, and he died about 1225.

As it has come down to us, the corpus of Wolfram's literary work consists of eight lyric poems (five of them *Tagelieder*, dawn songs), the epics *Parzival* and *Willehalm* (the latter unfinished) and short fragments of a further epic known as *Titurel*. The last-named elaborates the story of Parzival and Sigune in Book III of *Parzival*, while *Willehalm* is a religious epic based on a French *chanson de geste* which tells the story of the famous crusader William of Toulouse. But his greatest work, and that which is to the forefront of one's mind when his name is mentioned, is *Parzival*, an epic of some 25,000 lines, probably written between 1200 and 1210, and one of the most considerable literary works of the Middle Ages, distinguished alike by elevation of purpose and moral tone, and by power of poetic inspiration.

Derived in the main from Chrestien de Troyes's epic *Perceval* or *Li contes del Graal* (*c.* 1180), Wolfram's *Parzival* introduces the legend of the Holy Grail into German literature. There are three focal points in the story. The first is the Grail itself, Christian in origin and ever-recurrent in Western literature, which embodies the highest expression of human aspiration. The Knights of the Grail, like the chivalric orders of Templars, Hospitallers and Teutonic Knights, are both knights and monks, symbolizing, albeit in a totally different spirit and manner, the chivalric ideal of *got unde der welt gevallen*, with which Gottfried von Strassburg's *Tristan* is also concerned.

The second is the story of the hero Parzival, the 'guileless fool', who through his innocence and artlessness reaches a goal denied to wiser men and becomes King of the Grail. This goes back to the popular fairy-tale motif of the simpleton who achieves success at the expense of his elders and betters.

These two themes are then set out into the framework of Arthurian legend, from which stem the ideals of knightly virtue that sustain the courtly literature of the period. The model Arthurian knight in the story is Arthur's nephew Gawein, whose adventures fill much of the middle section of the epic and whom Wolfram sets in contrast to Parzival.

In the *Bildungsroman* of Parzival's career, related in a sombre, often mysterious manner which alludes to rather than states, and conceals rather than exposes, Wolfram presents his religious picture of spiritual education and development. Where Hartmann von Aue praises the virtue of moderation in human conduct, and Gottfried von Strassburg the satisfaction of worldly happiness, Wolfram preaches the gospel of other-worldly values and directs attention away from the empirical and the temporal to the ideal and the divine. Through the sequence of Parzival's adventures, with their culmination in the temple of the Holy Grail, we are meant to see how the demands of the world and of God can be brought together in a single ethico-religious principle. In highly rhetorical and complex language, with mystical overtones that often render the opacity of meaning almost complete, Wolfram puts before us an allegory of the history of man – his innocent happiness as a child in God, his surrender to the enticements of the world, and his return to God after his reconciliation of the warring claims of the spirit and the flesh. Here, as in Gottfried's *Tristan* and in the *Nibelungenlied*, Wagner found starting-points for his own profound treatment of these perennial themes of human conflict, of love and of salvation.

Alongside the epic of chivalry and courtly values, which embodies the fashionable concepts of the society for which they were written, stands the heroic epic. This genre, the repository of traditional national interests, brings to the peak of their development principles evolved through centuries of epic lays and ballads whose origin goes back to the days of the Great Migrations of the fourth to the sixth centuries, and glimpses of which come with works like the Old High German *Hildebrandslied* and the tenth-century Latin *Waltharius*. Within the realm of Germanic legend there are some eight separate centres of attraction round which cycles of stories have collected, each cycle linked to events and personages in the history of the tribe in question – Bavarians, Saxons, Frisians, etc.

By far the most famous of these heroic epics is the *Nibelungenlied*, in which legends from the world of the Burgundians, the Franks, the Goths and the Huns are mingled. Composed of some 2,300 four-line strophes which divide to give thirty-nine different 'adventures', the poem as we have it, composed by an unknown Austrian poet at the turn of the twelfth century, tells first the story of Siegfried, culminating in his murder by Hagen, and then the story of the terrible vengeance wrought by Siegfried's wife, Kriemhild, which ends with her death and the defeat of the Burgundians, or Nibelungs.

The contrast between subject-matter of this kind and that of the Arthurian romances needs no labouring, and it is not surprising that courtly society in general tended to avert its gaze from the former. Pagan Germanic elements such as a belief in the inexorable course of fate – as revealed by the *Hildebrandslied* – and the relentless pursuit of guilt by punishment, together with an uncompromising commitment to the demands of loyalty, provide the motivation and the basic ethical framework of the poem. Yet at the same time the poet, preparing this traditional, very un-courtly material for the courtly audience of his day, has obviously been at pains to soften some of the harsher features of the story and introduce courtly motifs and modes of behaviour where he could. The limits to such attempts at adaptation are soon reached, and the total impression left by the work, particularly when one thinks of the blood-bath in which it ends, is hardly touched. But there remains an interest in the fact that the attempt should have been made at all.

The four-line strophic unit in which the *Nibelungenlied* is written distinguishes it at once from the continuous rhyming couplets of the courtly epic, and suggests that, unlike the latter, which was spoken or declaimed, the *Nibelungenlied*, together with its descendants like *Gudrun*, was sung to some repeated melodic formula, as were the strophes of the French *chansons de geste*.

In style and language the heroic epic is simpler and more direct than the courtly epic: actions count for more than thoughts, and the motivation of these actions is more instinctive and circumscribed, and less open to reflection and variation. Measured by criteria of poetic quality, the *Nibelungenlied*, blunt and unsophisticated in manner, can hardly be put alongside Wolfram's *Parzival* or Gottfried's *Tristan*. On the one hand the multiplicity and variety of the national legends from which the poem was drawn is too great to allow the formation of a balanced, unified work of art; on the other hand the strophic form itself hinders the development of sustained argument, since each strophe is, grammatically and constructionally, a self-contained unit of thought and action. But there is at the same time a stark, skilfully handled realism about the graphic descriptions of violence and destruction with which the poem abounds, and one cannot escape the fateful atmosphere of ultimate doom in which the poet has appropriately and effectively shrouded his narrative.

The classical age of Middle High German literature spans a mere eighty years or so, from about 1170 to 1250. Its rise and fall coincide with the ascendancy and decline of the courtly civilization whose aspirations it reflected and on whose patronage it depended. Attempts were made by latter-day knights like Ulrich von Lichtenstein in his *Frauendienst* (1255), an idealized autobiography in a kind of lyrical epic style, to keep the chivalric ideals alive, and even into the fifteenth century, with poets such as Hugo von Montfort (1357–1423) and the colourful personality Oswald von Wolkenstein (1377–1445), some of the old forms of the Minnesang managed to retain a certain hold on the imagination. But notwithstanding these rearguard actions, from the end of the thirteenth century the cultural initiative, along with social and political power, was passing from the castle to the town, from the *Ritter* to the *Bürger*, and with this shift came an inevitable change in the character and atmosphere of the literature.

This change shows itself at once in the linguistic field. The private, exclusive poetic language of courtly epic and lyric writers disappeared with their poetry, and the old dialects re-emerged. The gradual approximation of the more important of these dialects is the most important factor in the development of the German language in the course of the fourteenth and fifteenth centuries.

Coincident with this development is the rise of prose as a medium of literary expression. With the exception of a version of the story of Lancelot, there is virtually no prose writing in the classical Middle High German period. In France, too, prose versions of the Arthurian romances had only appeared after the poetic versions, while in Germany the combined forces of Latin prose and vernacular verse served to confine the development of vernacular prose within narrow, practical channels. The earliest German town charter, for example, dates from 1239; in this context belongs also the *Sachsenspiegel* of Eike von Repgow (*c.* 1220–30), a legal handbook for use by the Saxons, written first in Latin, then in the local Low German dialect. Another source of early prose writing is the religious sermon of the time, and in those of the Franciscan Berthold von Regensburg (d. 1272), the greatest German preacher of the thirteenth century, one can sense the urge towards an original prose style that is not held in the formal grip of Latin. With Geiler von Kaisersberg, 'the German Savonarola', the tradition of the sermon continues into the fourteenth and fifteenth centuries, in which religious literature is also represented by hymns, by allegorical and didactic works in both verse and prose, and by the first complete translations of the Bible.

Of incomparably wider imaginative power than any of these works, and at the summit of medieval German prose, stand the writings of the thirteenth- and fourteenth-century mystics, from the nun Mechthild von Magdeburg (*fl. c.* 1260) through the great Meister Eckhart (*c.* 1260–1328) to his two pupils Johannes Tauler (d. 1361) and Heinrich Suso (d. 1366). In their German works – they also wrote in Latin – the mystics can be seen grappling with the task of expressing their intense and highly personal visions of the nature of the Godhead and the Good Life in a language which had never before been made to bear such a weight of meaning and such a wealth of expressiveness. It is above all, perhaps, in the field of imagistic vocabulary, through their introduction or popularization of words like *Einfluß* and *einleuchten*, that their efforts towards the establishment of a sophisticated German prose style are most strikingly seen. On the other hand the works of the greatest German thinker of the fifteenth century, Cusanus (Nikolaus von Cues, 1401–64), whose thought is a blend of fourteenth-century mysticism and the new, Renaissance-inspired movement of humanism, are all in scholastic Latin.

The *Verbürgerlichung* of literature with the passing of the classical Middle High German era, the decline of the conceits of courtly society and the rise of 'realistic', town- and village-centred interests – these changes show themselves as much in the development of the traditional poetic forms, epic and lyric, as in the rise of prose. This is not to say that the values of the classical age vanished overnight: the impact of the three great epic poets alone was far too great for this to happen. The later thirteenth century brings us, for example, a considerable body of epic verse by men who saw themselves as continuators of the great tradition. Predominant among these are the knight Rudolf von Ems (*c.* 1200–60), who, in works of prodigious length on religious, secular and historical subjects, set himself up as the successor of Gottfried von Strassburg, and Konrad von Würzburg (d. 1287), a poet of humble birth who, from a markedly dualistic standpoint, wrote both epic and lyric works with a strong didactic content.

But efficient versifiers though they may be, these writers, both in their historical position and in their own view of their activity, are *epigoni*, men living on the intellectual and artistic capital of their predecessors, *laudatores temporis acti* rather than poets aware of the present needs, and concerned with the real future, of their art. The spirit of the age, and with it the concerns of literature – for the literature of the Middle Ages, like its cathedrals, its paintings and its tapestries, was 'applied' art, an act of service in response to the needs and pressures of society on whom its existence depended – was changing its character and giving to the backward-looking epics of men like Rudolf von Ems and Konrad von Würzburg a dated and slightly irrelevant quality which their purely literary excellencies were unable to conceal.

All the greater, therefore, is the contrast between such works and the satirical narrative poem known as *Meier Helmbrecht*, written by Wilhelm der Gärtner in the late thirteenth century. Its blunt, sometimes crude tone, and its mockery of both knights and peasants, put it in the

company of Neidhart von Reuenthal's *höfische Dorfpoesie*, and its confident, realistic presentation of an often grisly story heralds the style of
the earliest *Volksbücher* of the fifteenth century, as well as of that masterpiece of allegorical narrative, written around 1400 and standing Janus-
like on the frontier between the old world of the Middle Ages and the
new world of Humanism – *Der Ackermann aus Böhmen* by Johannes von
Tepl (sometimes known as Johannes von Saaz).

In the field of lyric poetry the process of *Verbürgerlichung* takes us
from the world of the courtly Minnesinger to that of the urban Meistersinger – although, as in epic poetry, there were still a few, like Oswald
von Wolkenstein, who sought to perpetuate the interests and attitudes
of an age gone by. The line between Minnesang and Meistersang is a
hazy one, but the concept of *Minne* is a spent force by the middle of the
thirteenth century, and one customarily regards Frauenlob (d. 1318) and
his younger contemporaries as marking the transition from the one to
the other. Tradition ascribes to Frauenlob the foundation of the first
Meistersinger *Singschule*, at Mainz, but it was not until the early fifteenth
century that these schools began to spread rapidly: early establishments
can be traced in Augsburg, Strasbourg, Worms, Nürnberg, Mem-
mingen and elsewhere in central and southern Germany, but not in the
north of the country.

To qualify for admission to the circle of 'master-singers' – the name
shows the association with the hierarchical organization of the medieval
craft guilds, a master-singer enjoying the same status as a master-cob-
bler or a master-butcher – a poet had to commit himself to the task of
writing verse according to strict strophic rules derived, in theory at
least, from the work of Walther von der Vogelweide, Reinmar von
Zweter, Frauenlob and the others who were venerated as the 'twelve
old masters' of the lyric art. Slavish imitation of these formal models
was the only course open until the late fifteenth century, when Hans
Folz of Nürnberg introduced the reform that also permitted the
composition of original strophic forms (*Töne*). The content remained
religious and predominantly didactic throughout the effective life of
the Meistersang, a situation which the impact of the Reformation only
served to confirm.

No doubt there was something to be said for learning to manipulate
language through these imitative exercises, but the pedantries associated
with them, the empty rituals and procedures, and the absence of a
figure of genius to shatter their restrictive hold, have left the Meistersinger in a position perilously close to ridicule. The climax of their

activity, together with the formation of the greatest number of *Singschulen* operating according to the rules of the craft, comes in the fifteenth century, and it is to this period that the only Meistersinger belongs whose name is known today outside the ranks of literary historians – Hans Sachs (1494–1576), the shoemaker of Nürnberg and the hero of Wagner's *Mastersingers*, who cobbled verses, lyric, epic and dramatic, with the fluency and matter-of-factness with which he presumably cobbled shoes.

As well as writing thousands of *Meisterlieder*, Hans Sachs was a prolific producer of verse dramas – tragedies and comedies based on Latin models, and Shrovetide Plays (*Fastnachtsspiele*). The latter were of popular origin, descended from village pageants and processions; in Sachs's hands they became an instrument for both the entertainment and the edification of the masses. Serious drama, on the other hand, had its origin in the Passion and Nativity stories, which were presented in church with the roles of the various characters assigned to different speakers.

In the field of intellectual Latin drama the tenth-century plays of Roswitha von Gandersheim stand in almost complete isolation in the German Middle Ages. There is also an interesting Antichrist Play from Tegernsee, written *c.* 1160 in Latin, and a few fragments of Passion Plays in German from the thirteenth century, but otherwise scarcely any dramatic literature has survived from the high Middle Ages. By the middle of the fifteenth century, however, and above all under the influence of humanism, drama, both in Latin and in German, was beginning to acquire something of the confidence which had long been enjoyed by epic and lyric poetry, and which was now being increasingly developed in the field of prose also.

The works of Latin humanist literature themselves hardly have a place, in spirit at least, in a discussion of the Middle Ages, but in point of time, in that confused hundred years or so of German cultural development from the early fifteenth century to the Reformation, they are in part contemporary with, and in part considerably older than, those of men such as Hans Sachs. The most outstanding work of German literature from the period of early humanism, a product of the wave of interest in the new learning that reached the imperial court of Charles IV in Prague in the wake of the activity of Petrarch, Boccaccio and Poggio, is *Der Ackermann aus Böhmen*. This takes the form of a prose dialogue between Death and a ploughman whose young wife has just died: in his grief, the ploughman bitterly challenges Death to justify his cruelty, and in the legal pattern of charge and counter-charge the exchanges between the two characters turn into a debate on the meaning of life and death, with God pronouncing the final judgement that neither life, i.e. the ploughman, nor death has autonomous power, but that both receive their meaning only from Him and are subject to His will. Humanistic in form and often in language, the *Ackermann* at the same time raises questions and adopts attitudes that are typical of the Middle Ages and express, moreover, the concerns of the common people. A great deal of the interest attaching to the work lies precisely in this dichotomy of origin and intention.

Much of the literary activity of later humanists takes the form of translation from Latin into German: tales by Boccaccio and Poggio, Aesop's *Fables* and the works of Aenea Silvio are among the most popular sources. At the same time others, like Konrad Celtis (1459–1508), who flourished as poet laureate at the Viennese court during the reign of the Emperor Maximilian I, and Willibald Pirkheimer of Nürnberg (1470–1530), wrote in Latin and were concerned rather with the propagation of classical values in their original linguistic setting.

Disparate and even mutually contradictory as the literary movements of the fifteenth and sixteenth century may appear – late courtly epic, realistic village poetry, Meistersang, Shrovetide Play, the prose of German mysticism and the prose of humanist translations – they are almost all characterized by an underlying didacticism. The proportion of purely didactic content, and the overt or covert manner of its introduction into the work, vary from genre to genre and from author to author, but the intent remains, and has led to the characterization of the sixteenth century as an age preoccupied with the intention 'die Menschen zu bessern und zu bekehren'.

This intention emerges in one of its most undisguised and most sustained forms in the satirical verse epic, the most familiar example of which is Sebastian Brant's *Narrenschiff* (1494), in which, in a dry, unsubtle tone, a succession of human follies is laboriously described and mocked. An idea of the range of tones and attitudes which, within the didactic framework, different poets could achieve, emerges from a comparison of a poem like Brant's *Narrenschiff* and the *Fastnachtsspiele* of Hans Sachs. Both are concerned to expose human weaknesses, to mock at pretension, dishonesty and immorality, and to educate men to better ways. But where Brant is strict and ascetic, Sachs is genial and relaxed; where Brant keeps his humourless gaze fixed on his moral message, Sachs has time to entertain as well as to instruct.

And it is in this context of didacticism, but on the highest plane that the age can offer, that the greatest German of the sixteenth century belongs, the man whose vision, determination, breadth of interest and force of personality dominate the scene from the moment of his intervention in the course of his people's history – Martin Luther (1483–1546). So profound was Luther's impact on the religious, intellectual and social life of Europe that his inclusion in a discussion of German literature, and above all of medieval German literature, might seem an irrelevancy, but the German literature of the sixteenth century cannot be properly understood if Luther is not brought into the picture.

On the one hand lies his work in the evolution of the German language through his translation of the Bible and through his hymns. In order to achieve his aim to make the Word of God accessible to the greatest possible number of his countrymen, so that each and every man could know for himself, without the interpretative intervention of the priest, what God would require of him at the day of reckoning, Luther was forced to bring the Bible into every home, and in a language which every home could understand. And that the appearance of Luther's Bible (first complete edition 1522) coincided with the spread of printing is a remarkable quirk of fortune.

At the same time Luther's Bible translation is a work of true scholarship, based not on the Vulgate, like earlier translations, but drawn from the Hebrew for the Old Testament and from the Greek for the New Testament. When one realizes the primitive state of the German language in the sixteenth century, probably the greatest tribute to Luther's achievement is that, although he had to carve out his language sentence by sentence, no modern translation, of whatever confession, has ever even threatened to displace his. Certain of the more archaic turns of phrase may have been modified, the orthography modernized and regularized, declensions and conjugations made uniform, but beyond such peripheral concessions to modern taste hardly anything has been changed.

By philological convention the language of sixteenth-century German literature bears the progressive appellation of Early New High German. And Luther's Reformation, like the contemporary but so different Renaissance, is often regarded as marking the frontier between medieval and modern times. Indeed, many of the most interesting figures in sixteenth-century Germany, like Ulrich von Hutten, leader of the Knights' Revolt, and Philipp Melanchthon, 'Praeceptor Germaniae', the humanist who gave his life to the service of the Lutheran cause, are those who attempt to blend the noblest elements of humanism and Reformation.

But whatever may be claimed for the Reformation – and there is a distinction to be drawn between the movement and its originator – there is in attitude and in mode of thought, as well as in form of language and expression, still much of the Middle Ages in Luther himself. 'Luther no longer believed in the miracles of the Catholic Church', said Heine, 'but he still believed in devils'. When one recalls the frequent appearances of witches, and of the Devil himself, in the *Fastnachtsspiele* of that staunch supporter of the Reformation, Hans Sachs, which are very close to the beliefs and reactions of the common people; and when one turns to the famous Reformation-inspired chap-book of the Faust legend (1587) and other *Volksbücher*, like that of *Till Eulenspiegel*: then one can see how real a figure the Devil continued to be in the sixteenth century. Features like these, together with a characteristic belief in witchcraft and magic, show how closely the literature and culture of sixteenth-century Germany, whatever seeds of modern attitudes may have been sown, remain linked to the Middle Ages.

Bibliography

GENERAL SURVEYS

BÄUML, F. H. *Civilization in Medieval Germany*. London, 1969.

EHRISMANN, G. *Geschichte der deutschen Literatur bis zum Ausgang des Mittelalters*. 4 vols. Munich, 1922–35.

HUIZINGA, J. *The Waning of the Middle Ages*. London, 1924.

SALMON, P. *Literature in Medieval Germany*. London, 1967. Contains a long, annotated bibliography on all aspects of the period.

WALSHE, M. O'C. *Medieval German Literature*. London, 1962.

INDIVIDUAL PERIODS AND AUTHORS

Old High German and earlier

BOSTOCK, J. K. *A Handbook of Old High German Literature*. Oxford, 1955.

High Middle Ages

BROGSITTER, K. O. *Artusepik*. Stuttgart, 1965.

BUMKE, J. *Wolfram von Eschenbach*. Stuttgart, 1964.

HALBACH, K. *Walther von der Vogelweide*. Stuttgart, 1965.

HATTO, A. T. *The Nibelungenlied*. Penguin, 1965.

— *Gottfried von Strassburg's Tristan*. Penguin, 1960.

NAGEL, B. *Meistersang*. Stuttgart, 1962.

TAYLOR, R. J. *The Art of the Minnesinger.* 2 vols. Cardiff, 1968.

WAPNEWSKI, P. *Hartmann von Aue.* Stuttgart, 1962.

WEBER, G., and HOFFMANN, W. *Gottfried von Strassburg.* 2nd edn. Stuttgart, 1964.

— *Das Nibelungenlied.* 2nd edn. Stuttgart, 1964.

WECHSSLER, E. *Das Kulturproblem des Minnesangs.* Halle, 1909.

Late Middle Ages

CATHOLY, E. *Das Fastnachtsspiel des Spätmittelalters.* Tübingen, 1961.

WENTZLAFF-EGGEBERT, F. W. *Deutsche Mystik zwischen Mitterlalter und Neuzeit.* 3rd edn. Berlin, 1969.

9 The *Goethezeit* and its *Aftermath*

T. J. REED

As a literature worthy of consideration alongside those of other European cultures, German literature re-emerges in the later eighteenth century. This is not to say that in the intervening centuries literature had ceased altogether, since literary activity of sorts is inseparable from even rudimentary civilization; nor that individual works were not written which are worth reading – an outstanding example would be Grimmelshausen's novel of the Thirty Years War, *Simplicissimus*. But no amount of concentration on such single works, or of antiquarian interest in the growth surrounding them, can argue away a remarkable hiatus between medieval Germany's rich poetic culture and the belated eighteenth-century rebirth. What remains striking is the fall from standards once achieved: from the psychological and spiritual refinements of *Tristan* and *Parzival* to the rough and ready romances of the sixteenth century; from the austere drama of the *Nibelungenlied* to the crude compilations of the *Volksbücher*; from primal poetic power to the merely primitive; from a coherent literature to a scattering of broken threads. Germany thus lacked a literature of which she could be proud (just as she lacked unified nationhood – the two things are not wholly unconnected) at a time when other countries could already show not just single major works but thriving literary traditions. At least from the seventeenth century, Germans are acutely conscious of their lack, and develop a kind of inferiority complex which explains much of the later course of German literary history.

Missing the benefits of a national tradition – something which is most beneficial when it can be taken for granted and scarcely needs to be thought of consciously – they repeatedly treat the problem of making a new start, making a literature. We find, not only in the prolonged post-medieval doldrums, a casting about for ways to make good their loss. Their position of weakness compels them to emulate and imitate foreign literatures, first one, then by sharp reaction a different one. Then eventually, by an impulse which only appears to be of a different kind, there is an insistence on original German-ness; but, as the aphorist Lichtenberg pointed out, Germans were never so much imitators as when seeking to 'be original' because other nations were.

How did the break in continuity occur in the first place? In his essay on German poetry of 1624, Martin Opitz quoted from the greatest of the medieval German lyric poets, Walther von der Vogelweide, and ruefully observed: 'Das nun von langer zeit her dergleichen zue vben in vergessen gestellt ist worden, ist leichtlicher zue beklagen, als die vrsache hiervon zue geben.' ('That people have long since forgotten to practise that sort of thing is easier to lament than to account for.') A full analysis would indeed tax a historian with unlimited space at his disposal. Social and political factors are certainly relevant, central among them the devastation and disruption caused by the Thirty Years War. Yet if literature is a superstructure resting on social foundations, it is also a separate entity with an internal development of its own. Writing around 1800, Friedrich Schlegel conceded that medieval poetry had to decline with the society which supported it, but insisted that literature could still have been preserved if the poetic flowering had been followed by an effective age of criticism – that is, of close attention to the masterpieces, consolidation and codification of their achievements. This, after all, was how the achievement of the Greeks had been made permanent. Schlegel puts his finger on the most important single factor in Germany's loss.

Even where a traditional continuity was claimed, it was tenuous and ineffectual. The rich skills of Minnesang hardly live on in the pedantries of the Meistersinger, who kept their poetry pure of any fresh impulse from experience. Humanist verse of the sixteenth century scarcely seeks such continuity at all: the greater part of it is in Latin, and it is the rhetorical canons of this alien literature, revived at the Renaissance, that establish themselves in the absence of a strong native competitor. This situation remains largely unaltered into the seventeenth century. Opitz in 1624 has to cajole would-be poets to write German, not just Latin. Clearly, one cannot speak of a national literature at all.

The question of language itself as a medium is here important. National consciousness and culture are strengthened by community of language, and literature only becomes possible through a flexible, resourceful language. Germany, politically fragmented, lacking major administrative and cultural centres, was slow to develop a unified language, even for simple communicative purposes, from its wealth of dialects. For long Latin was used in administration, and when it yielded place it was to a form of German made in its own rebarbative image and unusable for literary purposes. At this point, cause and effect become interchangeable in a vicious circle: there is no tradition to further vernacular writing, and little work is produced capable of founding or furthering such a tradition. For the educated, literary Latin is more polished and more convenient – just as later French will be.

Latin is also the language of much of the religious controversy which sprang from the Reformation. Such of it as was written in German only underlines how rough a medium German then was. But other factors than language help to dictate a general crudity. Luther's Bible translation (1522–45) did much to create a single German language, one essential precondition of a national literature. But in general the issues raised by the Reformation were not conducive to the rise of literature as such, in any language. *Odium theologicum* produces by its nature no generous visions and spurs no pure poetic enterprises. Harnessing literature to religious propaganda may at best produce satire. Even this, in the Reformation period, easily slips via polemic into abuse. Ire and narrow conviction eschew subtlety and reach for the club. Even beyond the period of hottest Catholic–Protestant confrontation, religion in other ways still dictates the uses and content of literature (the spiritual trials of baroque drama, the sublime world-renouncing rhetoric of baroque lyric) to just as great an extent as the feudal structure still determines the personal fate of the as yet wholly dependent writer. Literature is not as yet a realm with its own inner laws and freedoms, nor a self-sufficient profession for the dedicated man. Only gradually does the seventeenth century evolve poetry and poets who are anything like free from the peremptory demands of feudal or religious allegiance.

The seventeenth-century baroque poets and dramatists do produce an impressive body of work, for the most part massively reiterating a narrow range of doctrinally predetermined themes. Their forms, once more, largely derive from foreign models, their poetics from Latin or Renaissance rhetoric. Native forms take second place. Opitz insists that even the best natural talent must also be versed in 'the Greek and Latin books', or the poet will be wasting his time. While appealing for help in giving German poetry 'den glantz, welchen sie lengst hette kriegen sollen' ('the splendour she should long ago have got'), he defers to French literature as at least the equal of Latin and Greek. (It is heartening, but exceptional, when in 1645 the verbal virtuoso Johann Klaj praises German for its unspoilt purity – 'noch eine unbeflekte Jungfrau' ('still an immaculate virgin') – and makes of this a potential advantage for German poetry. Such a shrewd re-emphasis is rare between Tacitus' *Germania* and Madame de Staël's *De l'Allemagne*.) The habit of looking back to the classics and sideways to other European literatures stays with Germans, perforce, well into the eighteenth century. But then, at last, the dialectic between the conflicting programmes it inspires does begin to shape a new literature. After oscillating between self-abasement and compensating self-assertion, German literature achieves a balance and can have the courage of its own nationality, but without feeling the need to impose a ban on all themes, ideals and inspirations borrowed from abroad which are part of the normal traffic of culture. In establishing this confidence, the most important factor is the belated appearance of home-grown genius. The production of canonical literary works, what Leibniz had called *Kernschriften*, makes deference to other countries' achievements unnecessary. Goethe, in particular, turns dearth into superfluity (and incidentally, by so fulfilling the norm of genius, creates a new problem). His personal achievement is not an event which can be analysed into social, historical, or cultural causes. But it can be seen as the fortunate culmination of a lengthy process in which, throughout the eighteenth century, language and poetic technique were being exercised and enriched in preparation for just such a 'golden touch'.

The basic problem of language was how to make German a more supple medium than the complex latinate *Kanzleistil*, and a more subtle and sophisticated one than the basic alternative of crude popular language, still not wholly emerged from the stage of warring dialects. In literature there was the added problem of evolving forms which suited the language, the national temperament, and also certain new ideals of expression better than imposed foreign forms. In literary content, there was the equally hard task of challenging accepted 'cultural' subject-matter (the crew of tragic figures and themes derived from antiquity via France) with subjects more immediately appealing to Germans, nearer home in time, place and social level.

These developments take place against the pressure of French eighteenth-century cultural hegemony. Though ultimate authority still lay with the classics, especially Aristotle and Horace, it had devolved hardly diminished on the French, who were deemed to be their essential continuators. The hegemony is social as much as abstractly cultural. The numerous small German courts spoke French and considered German a barbarous tongue. Frederick the Great spoke German badly and advised those who knew none to safeguard their ignorance. The attitude was no less effective for being based on prejudice and contempt. Both are plain in Frederick's essay *De la littérature allemande* (written 1780, probably conceived thirty years earlier). The king sees clearly some of the reasons why German literature lags – the fragmented language, the long dominance of Latin, the devastations of the Thirty Years War. He knows some of the mechanisms of remedy – that great writers should influence the language, that princes should foster their work by patronage. Yet he is defeatist and fatalistic: it does not occur to him that he might himself have been such a patron; German culture will flourish – one day. He is also mesmerized by alien authority. He can only conceive of German literature developing by leaning on the crutch of the classics. He proposes massive translations from classical and French literature, to form the taste of the writers who are in turn to form the language. No native development is conceived, no spontaneous alternative. He thunders disapproval at the signs of new life – the interest in Shakespeare's plays ('worthy of a Canadian savage'), Goethe's *Götz von Berlichingen*. They disobey the rules. ('The rules of the theatre are not arbitrary. They are in Aristotle's *Poetics*.') Frederick's one positive ideal, in good eighteenth-century French-oriented fashion, is clarity. When he came to write his essay, his position had already been overtaken by the times, but it is more than a mere curiosity. It is a paradigm of the attitudes which denied German writers one main source of furtherance.

A similar pressure – indeed, almost the identical programme – comes from the equally absolute arbiter in the world of letters itself, Gottsched. Questioning neither the authority of the classics, nor how truly the French had interpreted them, he set up French tragedy as a model for the German stage, and produced translations and imitations of it. It is for this that he is usually cast as the villain in literary histories; but even in the field of language, where he had a beneficial influence as a critical grammarian, his highest ideal, like Frederick's, was clarity. This is admirable for practical but insufficient for poetic purposes. In so far as pursuing clarity meant excluding the metaphorical and suggestive power of language, Gottsched's position was negative.

One may say in defence that he was requiring the language to walk before it ran, to emerge from its disorganization before plunging into expressive aberration; but if this was his actual achievement, the second stage was not one he envisaged. Poetic richness, as against mere prosaic clarity, was championed by Gottsched's first major opponents, the Swiss critics Bodmer and Breitinger, who in the 1740s argued for metaphor and a freely creative use of language in poetry. True, when Breitinger extols *das Wunderbare*, he intends no such abandonment of the rational as the Romantics later did, but only a kind of disguise, a 'making strange' of the ultimately explicable by means of rich and unfamiliar imagery. Poetic language is still the clothing, not the flesh of thought. But Gottsched's constricting influence was countered and a new direction taken – not least in the examples Bodmer chose to support his arguments: an English poet, Milton, and the poetic language of Middle High German.

But the decisive stroke against Gottsched was Lessing's. Lessing is Germany's greatest man of letters for his unique combination of learning, vision, integrity, courage, penetration, lucidity, logic, debating skill, and wit – all subservient to a monumental rationality, which in him has the warmth of a passion. All these qualities appear in his stand against Gottsched. (Seventeenth *Literaturbrief*, 1759.) In two pages, Lessing destroys Gottsched's claims as a reformer of the theatre, and shows that his policy was arbitrary and inappropriate. German drama needed reforming – anyone could see that. Gottsched however has not reformed, he has replaced it. With what? A Frenchifying theatre, irrelevant to Germans' real temperament or needs. Against this blunder, Lessing sets the rich potential of English literature, Shakespeare against Corneille and Racine, not as a mere counter-proposal, assertion against assertion, but argued out point by point as fitting German character and taste. True, it is yet another foreign inspiration – but one at least which will help the Germans to find themselves, not keep them dependent. Shakespeare's genius, he says, is calculated to awaken native German genius. This is prophetic. So is Lessing's choice of a sample of German work: he appends to letter 17 prose scenes from an 'old drama' (actually his own) – *Faust*.

From now for twenty years, for better and for worse, Shakespeare dominates literary discussion and production. As misrepresented by Wieland's translation of the 1760s (twenty-two of the plays, all but *Midsummer Night's Dream* in prose) he had to serve the polemical purposes of a new generation, who bludgeoned down tiresome rules using his name and example. In his *Hamburgische Dramaturgie*, Lessing had sought to discredit the French classicistic drama by showing that it was Shakespeare's practice that agreed essentially with the spirit of Aristotle's *Poetics*. To this bold, rational reconciliation, Lessing's more simple-minded successors preferred conflict, setting Shakespeare on to Aristotle as Aristotle had formerly been set upon Shakespeare.

If Lessing's rationality is attractive (whatever he deals with he enlivens, down to the abstrusest point in a technical treatise), he also made it productive artistically, deploying his enormous reading and great critical acumen. His plays are sometimes dismissed patronizingly – in no small measure because of his own humility in disclaiming the title 'poet'. Yet even when Lessing used drama to present theological positions, being forbidden to engage in further public controversy (*Nathan der Weise*, 1778), he created a core of theatrical excellence. His resolution may be far-fetched: to symbolize human brotherhood, a final 'recognition' scene incredibly reveals nearly all the characters as related, across the bounds of race and religion. But comic tradition has always winked at preposterous dénouements, and Lessing more than makes amends with his deft organization of movement in a plot almost devoid of outer action and with masterly comedy of character, by turns satirical and mellow. His dialogue too has a unique quality, informally conversational in its blank verse framework, almost imperceptibly overlaying philosophical disputation with natural talk. This is intellectual high comedy. We are never far from the most serious issues of religious understanding and toleration; probably no comic work ever rested on such (for its time) advanced views of these matters, nor so skilfully constructed from them a human parable.

Lessing's other two mature plays stand unprejudiced examination as at very least the masterpieces of a great craftsman and, historically, an advance over all his predecessors in realistic psychology and nuance of character. In *Minna von Barnhelm* (1767) he first abandoned stock types and drew comedy from differentiated individuals, which is why his plot stays so close to serious, even tragic, ethical problems. *Emilia Galotti* (1772) brilliantly develops the genre of *bürgerliches Trauerspiel* which Lessing had transplanted to Germany to compete with classicistic high tragedy. It is a model of exposition and dramatic tension. The dexterously laid plot seems to work itself out with hardly a nudge from the dramatist, who prepares even an eleventh-hour 'surprise' (the decisive arrival of the mad Countess Orsina) with a perfect and unobtrusive touch at the very outset. The play weakens only in its final catastrophe, where the heroine's tragic decision falls into unconvincing rhetoric. Significantly, Lessing's fidelity to his long-cherished classical source is to blame, an episode from Livy which proves harder to motivate in the modern setting.

It seems clear that Lessing wrote plays to add example to precept. Yet in doing so he was not doctrinaire. Thus *Emilia* maintains the unity of time, even approaching Gottsched's extreme preference for an action which only takes three or four hours. Lessing had campaigned against the unities – but only as arbitrary impositions, arguing that what were taken to be 'rules' were only consequences of a feeling for the first dramatic *law*: unity of action (*Hamburgische Dramaturgie*, 46. Stück). In *Emilia Galotti*, it is haste that generates events – the villains' hurried machinations against Emilia, her father's rush to the rescue. The resulting compression is already an organic form, not subservience to a rule. The case supports Lessing's arguments infinitely better than a deliberate defiance of authority. As Lichtenberg remarked, to do the very opposite is only another form of imitation. Lessing is too mature to avoid unity of time just because it had been a dogma. Freedom means not *having* to do things, neither the things others demand, nor those which flaunt one's 'independence'.

True independence is Lessing's ideal and his achievement. It breathes in everything he wrote – literary criticism, theological controversy, aesthetic theory. (His *Laokoon* is the first of the great eighteenth-century German aesthetic inquiries, rough-hewing a basic distinction between the arts which others would later refine, and cutting away the ground from under the aberrant school of 'pictorial' poetry.) Lessing's prose style is also his independent creation, directly moulded by his cogent thought and without further adornment. Heine aptly wrote that, as the stones of Roman buildings rest on each other with no mortar but gravity, so Lessing's sentences were joined only by the invisible force of logic.

In campaigning against Gottsched, Lessing's principle was not narrowly national, though it is often so presented. He was a rational eclectic, seeking possibilities of growth where they could be found, and could even use French example (Diderot's *drames bourgeois*, which he translated) to help oust Gottschedian elevated tragedy. But French influence in the eighteenth century generally remains problematic. It is true that the French language helped lighten German as a literary instrument. Like the informal syntax of English which filtered into Germany through translations and imitations of novels and journals

(Defoe, *The Spectator*) it offered much-needed models of simplicity, and this was surely some gain by the criterion of the seventeenth *Literaturbrief*: a development, not a mere overlaying, of native materials. But there remained the danger of a too easy stylishness, a purely formal facility. This applies to the shallow-rooted culture Goethe found as a student in 'Little Paris' (Leipzig) in the 1760s. Gellert, whom even the French translated, was its doyen then. But the best example of polished writing is Wieland, who came nearest to being a major writer.

Where Lessing was eclectic as a national policy, Wieland's eclecticism is personal, an equable response to all influences – English (Shakespeare, Sterne) and Spanish (Cervantes) as well as the obligatory French and Greek. From his cultivation there sprang prose and verse of great charm and grace, all lightness and readability, and this was itself an achievement in the period. What he ultimately lacks is substance for his accomplishments and all compulsion to concentrate them. His work often reads like amiable, slightly diffuse pastiche. His Greek settings, inspired by the already parodistic Lucian more than by classical literature, recall Offenbach's *Belle Hélène*. His ironic play with narrative conventions is superficial where Sterne's is intricate and disturbing. His satire on human folly (*Die Abderiten*) lacks the punch of Voltaire, who made similar and more vital points in a fraction the length. Wieland's mellowness seems a touch complacent and premature. True, his broad culture did not make him wholly conservative. Though he defended a humane cosmopolitanism against would-be 'national bards' of Ossianic ambition, and acutely saw the cultural and political dangers of this trend, he also came to see how people prefer national subjects after spending their sympathies for decades on heroes from alien mythology. He appreciated equally the Greeks, the French, Shakespeare, even Goethe's *Götz*, for their intrinsic value, without feeling bound to approve their sundry imitators, who preserved externals but lacked the essentials. His comments (e.g. the third of the *Briefe an einen jungen Dichter*, 1784) put these literary controversies admirably into perspective. Indeed, Wieland was almost too reasonable to affect developments decisively himself. A more single-minded dynamism is what fathers new things.

The ideal of the Germanic bard was lived out only by Klopstock. Lifelong support from the Danish court let him treat poetry as a religious calling; he duly became something of a poetic Messiah in the eyes of his admirers. The Messiah, appropriately, was his consuming epic subject. *Der Messias*, conceived when he was fifteen, extended to twenty cantos (published 1748–73). Classical epics suggested the hexameter form – a momentous innovation for German literature – but it was Milton, as translated by Bodmer, who inspired him. His aesthetic too is a development from the Swiss critics' positions. Klopstock thought poetic language must be strikingly distinct from prose norms; the great poetry of all nations illustrated this. The Greeks were his prime example (not surprisingly, the French came nearest to being the exception) and he perceived structural affinities of German to Greek which promised creative scope. The strength and even proverbial roughness of German could be harnessed to his purpose. This was to move the reader's soul and intensify his impressions by violent departures from the expected: 'Unvermutetes, scheinbare Unordnung, schnelles Abbrechen des Gedankens, erregte Erwartung'. He duly forms bold new compounds and breaks down old ones, his transitive verbs usurp a direct object; especially in his 'lyrical' work, the odes, which use ancient Greek metres and his own variations on them, sentences are stretched on the rack of a complex form and split by long interpolations. Instead of being eased into a smooth flow of sense or sound (as in Wieland's treatment of the selfsame metres), words regain a rock-like separateness in their unfamiliar and deliberately unharmonious patterns. Klopstock *could* achieve a softer music when he wished, as in 'Die frühen Gräber'. But he aspired beyond smoothness, which risked appearing trivial, to a sustained sublimity and power in the treatment of grandiose subjects. 'Lyrical' in Klopstock can only refer to his intensity of feeling, which is why *Der Messias* is commonly called lyrical. Certainly it is unlike ancient epic in drawing in little of the real world. Sometimes the effect is positively dramatic (Jesus' trial in canto 7), but here too the reality of the actors is as little evoked as their surroundings. Jesus himself is unrealizable, a still centre of restrained divine power: 'So viel unerschütterte Stille' (7.558). Whether in ode or epic, the concrete phenomena recede. Intense feeling fuses with non-visual subjects in a poetry of abstraction, and the main achievement is the intricate ordering of language which grows increasingly compressed and self-sufficient with the years. Yet Klopstock's work left major gains even when its extreme positions were relinquished. His experiments with words and metre, including the 'free' verse which so easily grew out of hexameter rhythms, were a quarry of means for the young Goethe and even more so for Hölderlin, and they founded the tradition of a form and diction which can sustain high solemnity almost out of reach of scepticism and the ordinary.

The stage is now set for Goethe. He enters, oddly accompanied: by a mentor who was to refashion the European concepts of history and culture, and by a crew of young men confident they are geniuses but barely possessing talent. Herder, Goethe under his stimulus, and the *Stürmer und Dränger* following Goethe's lead: between them they subvert and supersede the *Aufklärung* outlook. They break bounds as a protest against its incompleteness and lack of imagination: its rationalism which ignored intuition and reduced feeling to a lower faculty; its subjection of nature to society; its preoccupation with analysing into parts instead of grasping wholes; its art, which was either the orderly imitation of a world believed orderly, or a means of education for rational conduct in such a world. *The Odyssey*, Gottsched thought, taught the harmful consequences of a father and ruler's absence. This is a caricature, but also a symptom. Wieland spoke of Shakespeare's moral qualities and made much of his moral *sententiae*. Even Lessing turned Aristotle's doctrine of pity and fear into a socially useful training in virtue.

Herder's own odyssey, a sea-journey in 1769, symbolically loosens set ways of thinking: 'Wo ist das feste Land, auf dem ich so feste stand?' In the movement of an unstable element, the very concept of virtue is shaken: 'jedes Datum ist Handlung; alles übrige ist Schatten, ist Raisonnement'. Art and thought are now launched on a rising flood which spills over the established categories. There are no rational safeguards, only the felt analogy between the creative individual and the ultimate Creator. Lessing too believed in creative genius – but as something which coincided eventually with reason, as analysis would and in the case of Shakespeare did show. Now there is no such implied reservation, genius is just untrammelled *expression* of the individual's uniqueness. (If of anything else, then of his similarly unique nation, or period. The new feeling for these particularities, *Einfühlung* in his own word, is Herder's revolutionizing gift to historical studies.)

The revolution is fundamental, and neither Lessing's relativizing of 'the rules' nor Klopstock's special kind of emotion does more than vaguely foreshadow it. But what is the result in literature? What quality of uniqueness is offered to fulfil this ambitious theory? Goethe excepted, it is unimpressive. It is the old question: freedom to, or merely freedom from? Moreover, in no time the *Sturm und Drang* had created a new convention (every bit as tedious) of flouting old conventions. It was easy to caricature and almost caricatures itself. Violence of language – anything to avoid decorum; violence of action, compounding sin, crime, misfortune – anything to avoid the humdrum; diffuseness of form – anything to avoid the unities and cock a snook at Aristotle and co. *Sturm und Drang* is a historical phase which cannot be ignored. It broke some ice. Some of its works have social interest. But as *art* it is hard to defend. Goethe used his freedom; the others merely took liberties. Excess became a norm, shouting became inaudible in general tumult.

A thin but clear line divides Goethe's early work from his friends' antics. In *Götz von Berlichingen* (1771), his language is fresh and frank, where situation demands, but it can also be soft. It makes characters, it responds to events without being programmatically 'wild'. His form is free, even undramatic, but it subserves a chronicle-action; we are not dragged headlong from one place to another merely to show the author dares. For Goethe as much as the *Stürmer und Dränger*, Shakespeare meant liberation. But there is again a difference. All of them – 'die wir von Jugend auf alles geschnürt und geziert an uns fühlen und an andern sehen' – found *nature* for the first time in Shakespeare's *art*. The danger was, Shakespeare might be taken as nature untouched by art (especially in Wieland's translation, which jettisoned his verse) and hence as an invitation to put nature unformed on the stage. Much *Sturm und Drang* zeal and fiasco originates here. Herder said chasteningly of *Götz* that Shakespeare had 'ruined' Goethe. It was truer of the others, for whom Shakespeare was an alibi; for Goethe he was a revelation. His first reading left him feeling like a blind man miraculously given sight.

Götz does not now seem revolutionary, simply because its principles have since become unquestioned. But appreciating novelty is an essential part of literary history, if not of literary enjoyment. Elisabeth's plain words of fidelity to Götz – 'bis in den Tod' – moved Wieland to tears, far more than the longest tirade of French eloquence could. The characters' speech altogether was – astoundingly – that of their epoch. It had occurred to nobody in Europe to do this before. These are the artistic applications of the vision Goethe shared with Herder: nature brought close, history made real. Though he was to change his position later, he had laid 'the foundation of modern realism' (Auerbach).

Something else is new. Character is grasped and rendered whole. Treachery (Weislingen) is not now constructed out of its notional conflicting elements: puzzled critics missed those scenes of 'inner' (i.e. spoken) struggle between passion and obligation which are typical of Corneille and the baroque. Yet Weislingen, finally unfathomable, convinces. Perhaps he has some of his creator's substance. At any rate, genius which models human nature in the piece makes the older tools for its analysis obsolete. The crucial change is that expression replaces construction, both as a technique and, even deeper, as the motive for writing. This makes distinctions of genre secondary, a matter of how things develop, not of different basic conceptions. Lyric, when it borrows a mask to talk through (Prometheus, Ganymed, Mahomet, Faust), easily flows over into drama, monologue splits into dialogue, situation engenders action. The material is penetrated and appropriated by *Einfühlung*. Treatment of a subject and self-expression through a subject are hard to separate.

Formally there is little sense of construction in Goethe's best early poems, as there is so acutely in Klopstock, but only of growth with its own inner shaping force. Form is not a receptacle for statement, but the bodily shape which statement takes on spontaneously. This is true of the early *Hymnen*, where 'free' verse is in fact a minute response to the pressures and particularities of an experience. But it is also true of entirely regular poems – 'Willkommen und Abschied', 'Auf dem See'. This last was written almost certainly in the situation it describes, in one piece. Only when revising it ten years later did Goethe himself notice the way its formal phases corresponded to the phases of emotional experience, and he brought this out by a slight typographical change. The perfection of form had been organic, not a calculated arrangement.

Herder had bewailed the death of poetry through dry intellect: 'wir sehen und fühlen kaum mehr, sondern denken und grübeln nur, wir dichten nicht über und in lebendiger Welt.' The influx of fresh experience in Goethe's poetry answered his implied appeal, just as the freshness of its language met Herder's ideal of a folklike *Kinderton*. (In 'Heidenröslein', Goethe matched a folk-refrain with three narrative strophes of his own which Herder took as genuine.) Experience and its freshness is present in all Goethe's poetry. He was the great transmutor of the particular into spontaneous forms. Yet what matters is not the virtuoso immediacy of response but the resulting perfection of the poems by objective standards. Increasingly, in the European Romantic age, self-expression and genuine experience came to be thought sufficient guarantees of literary value. With Goethe, one need not appeal to these as *criteria*. They are *characteristics* of his poetry, and of nobody's earlier or in greater measure; but the poems validate themselves. The fascination of his biography (a study over-cautious critics

R

discourage) is not to authenticate the poems, much less explain them away, but to watch and wonder at a uniquely powerful creative force in operation.

If experience and expression determine form in this organic way, certain things follow. Any traditional genre the poet uses will be deeply affected. The more fixed its forms (in the external sense), the more marked the effect will be. The result will be mixed and may require appreciation by an uneasy mixture of traditional standards and criteria tailored to its peculiar nature. Lyrical poetry does not raise these problems: provided it achieves beauty and control in a coherent pattern, creativity is there at its freest – and Goethe's consequently at its greatest. But drama lays down more specific conditions that cannot be ignored, involving the concentration of action into patterns of development and climax. It was an exaggeration when contemporary critics complained that *Götz* could not be staged – production is quite feasible; but the work is certainly less a drama than an epic, a dramatized chronicle which is the German ancestor of Brecht's epic theatre. The dramatic sub-form of tragedy arouses further expectations of its own, which are not merely a matter of cultural fashion. When Goethe wrote the word 'tragedy' into the title of *Faust*, he duly aroused them, but did not go on to fulfil them because his outlook was untragic. Against the grain of the legend he was exploiting, which was Christian, moral and deeply sin-conscious, he affirmed and celebrated earthly experience and human activity, overriding the single catastrophe and swallowing up tragedy more boldly than any rational theodicy or Christian apologia ever had. Tragic episodes can be found in *Faust*, but it is not a tragedy.

Faust most completely illustrates the problem which the new relationship of form to experience raises for category-based criticism. As the central figure accumulates experiences, so the overall structure accumulates and imperiously subordinates widely differing literary elements. Yet it does not even tie up all the threads, fill in all the gaps, reconcile the changing conceptions which fed its sixty-year-long gestation. To approach this monument to growth and change using ideas like 'dramatic unity' or 'internal consistency' as anything more than timidly provisional working hypotheses is to bring on disillusionment or the need for acutely sophistical explanations. *Faust* torments formalists, though it delights any lover of forms. It must be taken on its own terms because there is no term of comparison available for its totality and few peers for its finest parts. But in this it is only the extreme case which illuminates the general lesson: the counterpoint, sometimes conflict, between expression and the outward conventions and traditions it works through. This is implied by Goethe's famous saying that his works were all fragments of a single great confession, which clearly states that all means were subject to a paramount end.

And this same fundamental condition of all his work made difficulties for Goethe. He frequently began works, then abandoned them, then had to resume them in cooler, perhaps reluctant mood. Was it caprice? or loss of inspiration? In large part it was the problem of carrying through the prime impulse – lyrical in the broadest sense – when it came up against 'objective' requirements, such as the conditions which drama lays down.

Thus, Faust's opening monologues penetrate and render a mood and situation – the legendary figure's, the young Goethe's. But they will not alone make a Faust *drama*. Again, Goethe hardly needs a Mephistopheles to add the metaphysics – his Faust applies first to a quite different power, the *Erdgeist*, to which Mephisto is an eventual second-best. But given a Faust, a Mephistopheles can hardly be omitted. A low instrumentality is all Goethe allows him to be. But even this function bulks larger than the technicality of motivating his presence on the scene. His first appearance and the traditional pact are still not composed long after he has served his major turn in *Faust I* – bringing Faust to Gretchen, and the young Goethe to a fresh area where the expressive impulse can resume command, even though the Gretchen action is not very specifically part of a Faust play.

Action itself, here and in Goethe's other plays, is rarely impressive as such and he does not stylize it into climaxes with a theatrical hand like Schiller's. It pales altogether beside the almost self-sufficient life of the characters. Thus in *Torquato Tasso* (1790) events are only outward symptoms of incompatibilities and mutual incomprehension between characters in a closed society. Schiller's characters are rarely so at cross-purposes with each other, and at least they are linked from the outset by the mechanism of an action from which they are not conceived as separate. As action, only *Iphigenie auf Tauris* (completed 1787) is nearly orthodox, and here the outward course was prescribed by a Greek original, which left Goethe only to humanize the motivation of primitive characters and oracles. That he did this successfully (more so than is commonly allowed) shows that an intellectual idea marries better with a dramatic action than does the lyrical impulse.

For the objective requirements of a genre to accommodate Goethe's expressive impulse fully from the outset is rare, but the effect can be striking. For example, the epistolary novel requires deft technical management only when the plot is complex (as in, say, *Les Liaisons dangereuses*). The complexities of *Die Leiden des jungen Werthers* (1774) are not external but psychological and emotional. Goethe's own emotional entanglements took him empathetically into the far direr crisis of the young suicide Jerusalem, and he writes expressively from within it. Each letter can be self-contained, its length and movement dictated by a phase of feeling. This is next door to pure lyrical writing – and indeed, Goethe's earliest full self-expression had been in his letters, whose language and movement were already a revolution in embryo at a time when his poems were still mere exercises in Leipzig modishness.

Werther, then, is all expression: not in the popularly assumed sense that it 'is' the raw emotion of Goethe's Wetzlar romance, but in the sense that feeling, not action, is what it poetically formulates, and from within; the plot is there to ensure that feeling does not flag, and has little of fictional invention about it. No later novel project gave Goethe such advantages. *Wilhelm Meisters Lehrjahre* (1795/6) came nearest in that it took up the novel of individual education which makes the ideal of personal improvement a pretext for intense self-concern. But in this revision of an early subjective sketch, Meister has become much more an object of interest than a mask for subjective statement. Even more so in the *Wanderjahre* (completed 1829) where the genre is adapted to carry Goethe's mature wisdom. The framework narrative is heavy with it: static doctrine rather than the live insight which shapes Goethe's best philosophical poems. Nevertheless, the stories subtly inset in this bizarre work are the very finest of his narrative prose, delightful decoration on an edifice which commands respect rather than enthusiasm. Goethe's other substantial narrative, *Die Wahlverwandtschaften* (1809) is outwardly the one most like a conventional novel, but for once convention (here that of pure objective recounting) is used defensively, producing opacity in place of Goethe's usual confessional transparency.

These examples illustrate the effects on particular works of that primacy of experience and expression which Goethe established: it creates new forms when free (lyric), and when less free (drama, novel) it meets or reshapes, more or less harmoniously, external conventions. But it also affects the whole course of literature. Eighteenth-century controversies had turned, precisely, on externals: their imposition

(Gottsched), their rejection (Lessing), the adoption – though this was not how they saw it – of new ones (*Sturm und Drang*). A major creativity puts externals in their place. The question becomes: what externals will *result* from spontaneous creation? or, at most, how well will particular externals *serve* expressive purposes? This at last is the proper perspective and priority. The wildly swinging pendulum of controversy between alien and national products can be left to run down. The issue is out of date. True, the *Sturm und Drang* made *Götz* a weapon for national propaganda, and 'imitated' it as crudely as they 'imitated' Shakespeare. Yet Goethe himself even while composing *Götz* wrote to Herder that his sole study was – the Greeks. *Götz* is hardly even Shakespearian in any specific sense. Shakespeare had simply inspired (much as Lessing hoped) a self-fulfilment. This then constituted a position of strength from which to ignore old schisms. There need no longer be any compulsion to be narrowly national.

This opens German literature wide to fruitful outside stimulus, it lifts the veto on participating in the cross-fertilizations of world literature. (The very word *Weltliteratur* in German is Goethe's coining.) Much of Weimar classicism is duly Greek-inspired; the poem-cycles of Goethe's *West-Östlicher Divan* (1819) play with Persian forms and motifs. This is not a betrayal of the 'poetry of experience' but simply appropriates new means and ideals. And things appropriated by the German imagination – this applies especially to Greece – become thereby uniquely German, in a way the Gottschedian classicistic regulations never had. The difference between that earlier subjugation of German culture and these later raids on other cultures was hit off by Goethe's first English biographer: 'abundant fuel stifles miserable fires, it makes the great one blaze'. The 'great fire' also solves other problems which seemed ineradicably part of the national culture. It attracts a patron – Duke Karl August; it creates a centre – Weimar. When Goethe complains in his essay *Literarischer Sansculottismus* (1795) of the lack of these things, and of all the difficulties his literary generation laboured under, he is looking back. By now a new literary tradition is in the making, he and Schiller have entered on their fruitful alliance, and in fifteen years time Madame de Staël will be extolling German literature (extreme reversal!) as a model for the flagging French.

In these fifteen years, the culture of Weimar becomes Germany's classicism; this is the accepted description. But the things it describes are at odds with the term, if 'classicism' has any essential meaning.

Explaining why will bring out Goethe's and Schiller's achievement and touch on problems they left unmastered.

Two associations of the word 'classicism' seem to justify its use here. Firstly the classics of German literature are produced now, especially in the decade (1794–1805) of Goethe and Schiller's most intensive and mutually stimulating creation. Secondly, more important, the forms and ideals of the classical (Graeco-Roman) world enormously influence both poets. One might half-seriously date German classicism from 3 a.m. on 3 September 1786 when Goethe slipped away from Carlsbad to spend two years in Italy. But neither canonical greatness nor Graeco-Roman influence is the core of classicism, even though 'classicisms' in Europe have always drawn on Greece and Rome for their forms. Essentially, classicism consists in the balance and control which are fruits of stability and maturity. An ethos firmly founded beyond the reach of disturbing inquiry goes with a technical mastery which is beyond the need for impulsive experiment. Such qualities are not just personal. In seventeenth-century French and in English Augustan literature, they spring from advantages of the age – its social stability, its accepted religious and philosophical beliefs, its agreement about the forms and purposes of literature. In such conditions, the author-reader relationship can be – despite stylistic formality – one of intimacy, even identification. The classical writer is the voice of a mature society, confident of its place in the world. His is the talent, but he derives his assurance from outside himself.

Weimar classicism reverses this model. As *Literarischer Sansculottismus* makes clear, Goethe found no such ideal conditions – no mature society, not even a unified nation, no national culture or literary tradition to ease his apprenticeship, no public of taste. He had to work to create these things, after first developing alone. His classicism was first personal, then didactic. Both appear contradictions in terms. What do they mean?

In 1775 Goethe went to Weimar, undisciplined, emotionally volatile, but with an intuitive grasp of nature and a thirst for reality. For a decade he acquired realities – the ballast of administrative work (he was never a 'statesman) and scientific study. Meanwhile Charlotte von Stein charmed his emotions into uneasy subjection (and his poetry, not coincidentally, into a decently unvital pallor). Overwork, fragmentation of his time which prevented literary concentration, and emotional frustration drove him to the Hegira of 1786, to Italy. There, through landscape, architecture, art, climate and people, warmth and delight were restored to reality, which Goethe had tended increasingly to approach with sober analysis and solid knowledge. He now grasped the essential principles of natural growth and great art. They were the same: a force forming from within, an irresistible law. 'Was nicht eine wahre innere Existenz hat, hat kein Leben und kann nicht lebendig gemacht werden und nicht groß sein und nicht groß werden.' An ancient ruined temple is 'so natürlich und so groß im Natürlichen'. Such identifying of art with nature points now not to formlessness (as with the *Sturm und Drang*) but to the most organically intricate and least arbitrary of forms. It puts a finger on the governing principle of Goethe's own best poetry. But the personal is now reinforced by a sense of the laws – formal and natural – which underlie all particular phenomena. Italy was a revelation, wholly of this world. In classical surroundings, Goethe believed he touched the ancient way of life (it was certainly the Mediterranean way of life). When he returned to the northern gloom of Weimar and burst into classical metres – hexameter and elegiac couplet – he was not writing pastiche but reliving an ideal: 'die Schule der Griechen / Blieb noch offen, das Tor schlossen die Jahre nicht zu' (*Römische Elegien* xiii).

Goethe's revelation proved hard to convey, especially its frank sensualism and contempt for all 'spiritual' pretensions which timorously shut out certain areas of experience. Frau von Stein said of the *Roman Elegies* (or *Erotica Romana*): 'Ich habe für diese Art Gedichte keinen Sinn.' Significant wording! Goethe, with one regained sense more than his neighbours, was further isolated in the isolated culture of Weimar. In such conditions, his rebirth could quickly have changed to sullen withdrawal. The *Venetian Epigrams* of 1790 speak the bitter accents of discouragement at a Herculean task – bitter although (or precisely because) Goethe is so certain of his truths: 'Ist's den so großes Geheimnis, was Gott und der Mensch und die Welt sei? / Nein! Doch keiner mag's gern hören; da bleibt es geheim.' The poise, control, certainty of classicism have been achieved, but there is no community. The poet voices not the values of his society but timeless ones, rediscovered in nature and the past. This is what the paradox of a 'personal classicism' means.

What encouragement Goethe did enjoy came from friends who were specialists, Meyer in art, Knebel in the classical literatures. But successful preaching to converted antiquarians was small consolation. He desperately needed someone who could go to the core of his endeavours, who could grasp the full human meaning of his new work and see how inseparable it was from the new serene mastery of form. But who could do this without having shared Goethe's long development and liberating experience? Only a truly great critic. That this critic should appear; that he should have long been a passionate, because envious, analyst of Goethe's very fibre as a man and poet; that he should have arrived at something like Goethe's positions on nature and art by the alternative route of abstract speculation, stimulated by painful trial and error in his own poetic work and nagged by doubt over his own apparently failed creativity; that he should be, despite all this, himself a major poet, about to come out of the wood and resume an intense production; all this could scarcely be expected. But it was provided: 'Mehr als ich ahndete schön, das Glück, es ist mir geworden . . .' Goethe's lines on his mistress and wife Christiane Vulpius could as well apply to Schiller.

Not that Schiller was immediately welcomed with open arms. To Goethe's classical eye he seemed suspect, for literary sins akin to those of his own wilder youth. Schiller's works of the early 1780s – *Die Räuber, Kabale und Liebe* – were a remarkable after-explosion of *Sturm und Drang*, ten years behind the times yet far outdoing his forerunners. The schoolboy's reading – Rousseau and Plutarch besides the *Stürmer und Dränger* – brought on his talent, providing imaginative models on which to shape his resentments against the tyrannical order in Württemberg. Even if largely literature-induced, these plays are impressive still as a born dramatist's first structuring of the split universe his imagination inhabits and strives to mend: nature and convention, virtue and villainy, idealism and injustice, vengeance and regeneration. Wildness in the first *Sturm und Drang* was rarely matched by such power, or ranting raised to such brilliant rhetoric.

But the torrents on the page never flowed easily from the pen, even less so when the pen was all Schiller had to live by after escaping from Duke Karl Eugen's territory. The long genesis of *Don Carlos* shows a flagging impulse and uneasily shifting intentions. It ends as a flawed if grandiose construction (1787). But the switch to blank verse form and elevated diction hints at a changing approach. Abandoning drama for several years, Schiller worked at a systematic aesthetics which would solve his difficulties once for all. His speculative bent took fuel from a detailed study of Kant. The two main results were a theory of tragedy and an even more fundamental theory of art. This latter, despite its abstract origins, is what prepares his accord with Goethe. For Schiller, art springs from the interplay of man's sensuous and rational constituents, his two distinct and in practice conflicting modes of experience. By distracting each from the exclusive pursuit of its characteristic practical aims and uniting both in the common purpose of pure play, art can create a balance beneficial to man. This is its restorative function. Its visible product, the artistic form itself, ideally achieves an interpenetration of sensuous and rational, and this fusion of abstract and concrete is a symbol and expression of man's totality as a composite being. It is not far from such results to Goethe's new-found equilibrium of mind and body, his understanding of inherent laws shaping phenomena, his vision of the *Urpflanze*, the one basic form underlying all plant-life. In 1794, with Schiller on the verge of these formulations, and also of a typology which would explain the divergent approaches but ultimate common aims of the 'intuitive' Goethe and his 'speculative' self, their first real meeting occurred. Their talk – appropriately, on the *Urpflanze* – skirted discord, their essential agreement just perceptible enough to save the situation. Then a masterly letter from Schiller fully and lovingly analysed Goethe's creative constitution for him. Schiller was released from quarantine, classicism became a two-man alliance.

This did not alter the unfavourable conditions, but it improved Goethe's morale. Not only did Schiller's appreciation stimulate his work (Schiller blithely accepted the *Römische Elegien* for his journal *Die Horen*, wrote exhaustive letters on *Wilhelm Meister* as each section was completed, and sent Goethe back to the abandoned *Faust*); Schiller also put Goethe's situation and difficulties as a modern and a German into theoretical perspective. Goethe's specific genius and task and their historical context were made clear to him. But Schiller's support was not just from the sidelines. He joined Goethe in polemic and in the creation of exemplary works. War was the relationship he advocated with a public such as Germany had. In the joint *Xenien* epigrams the two poets attacked practically everything that moved on the then literary scene. Praise and honour were rarely bestowed (Lessing, Kant, Wieland) because rarely deserved. Then to follow up negation, they produced: Goethe his finest elegies, scientific poems, ballads, the 'epic' idyll *Hermann und Dorothea*, new scenes for *Faust*; Schiller, besides ballads and his finest philosophical poetry, the imposing series of his mature dramas, roughly one a year from 1800 to his death. The years spent mastering the *Wallenstein* trilogy (1794–9) had completed his apprenticeship and established a total technical command. There, if anywhere, diffuseness had threatened – as

Grillparzer later noted, the very use of a trilogy tends towards the epic. But while *Wallenstein* is broad enough to encompass the reality of the Thirty Years War, Schiller applies the controlled masses of historical material at precise points to create a concentrated, wholly dramatic action. Historical junctures are scaled down unforcedly into personal dilemmas, the historical and the individual do not merely run parallel, throwing up tragic episode, as in Brecht's *Mutter Courage*. It is this combination of mass and elegant precision that makes *Wallenstein* the greatest of German dramas. Even more formally perfect is *Maria Stuart* (1800) which turns the problem of making drama from the limited situation of a captive into a means of focusing attention on the heroine's spiritual struggle. The materials of history (a counterweight Schiller's imagination needed) here nicely balance his theatricality. His major 'unhistorical' scene is a meeting between Mary and Elizabeth. It may be high drama, but it also epitomizes the motivation of the two queens which he made the foundation of the play. The wilder departures from history of *Die Jungfrau von Orleans* (1801) and even the idealizations of *Wilhelm Tell* (1804) ring less true. *Die Braut von Messina* (1803) emulates Greek fate-tragedy, but the fateful secrets, unlike those in *Oedipus*, need too much authorial help in staying hidden. But the fragment Schiller left at his death in 1805, *Demetrius*, would at least have rivalled *Wallenstein*. Its executed scenes again embody the plastic skill Schiller had developed in emulation of Goethe; and the dilemma which his scenarios sketch – the sincere impostor Dmitri discovers in the moment of success that his claims to the Russian throne are false – would have been the most acute of all those inner divisions that provided Schiller's dramatic impulse.

This was Schiller's powerful contribution to the classical partnership. Add his sympathetic criticism of Goethe's works, and the conceptual framework for their efforts which his essays and their correspondence established, and it is clear why Goethe wrote in 1798 that Schiller had given him a second poetic youth. Take the work of both men in this short span, and it stands unequalled in volume and quality by the productions of any comparable period or school. Equally impressive is the variety its root-principles allowed. It was not a classicism restrictive of genre or form – its ideas of form were too internal, essential; nor of subject – what mattered was the way material was treated. Instead of being an outward conformity, form and treatment were a means of achieving aesthetic freedom. The artist's own aesthetic freedom lay, for example, in the way using verse mysteriously helped him to dispose recalcitrant material (*Don Carlos*, *Wallenstein*), or in the way it purified stark naturalistic effects (the revised final scene of *Faust I*). For the audience, aesthetic freedom meant that receptive state in which the content of experience could be contemplated with what Kant had termed 'interesseloses Wohlgefallen', i.e. apart from all practical relations and immediate moral purposes.

This was far from meaning that art had no social or moral function. But it was not a direct one. It is true that Schiller's plays have moral dilemmas as their material, and his essays define tragic enjoyment itself by reference to moral concepts. Schiller was an intensely moral being, and the ubiquity of his moral interests makes it easy to misunderstand or misrepresent him. But his figures remain tragic exempla, not mouth-pieces of morality, and his essays insist that art has no place for direct moral instruction. Even the lapidary utterances from his plays which are so often quoted as moral *sententiae* are rooted in character and action, and the stylistic quality which invites quotation is part of a characteristic search for exhaustive formulation, not a by-product of preaching. For Schiller, art at most offers analogues of truth and morality. The claims of morality begin only with the restored human wholeness which is the gift of art. Though the distinction is a fine one, too fine for later unsympathetic ages, it was a great advance on the eighteenth century's simple equation of 'art' and 'moral improvement'. Together with classicism's deepened conception of form, it made for a truly liberal aesthetic.

Yet in the event it could be illiberal, even dogmatic, in response to new kinds of poetry. Weimar classicism had its problematic side which shows up in the nineteenth century, equally in writers who emulated and who rejected its forms and ethos. Many factors – its swift and forced growth, its small nucleus, its didactic and even polemic nature, its sources in ancient rather than native culture, and not least its avoidance of direct involvement in society and politics (underlined by the fact that its most fruitful period came in precisely the years when Weimar was temporarily disengaged from the surrounding upheaval of the Napoleonic Wars) – were to provoke opposition and reproach. Its very breadth and maturity themselves soon defined opposition in the first group of what came to be the Romantic movement. The way the achievement of classicism is so immediately followed by its ques-tioning – indeed, the two overlap – gives German literature a pattern once again radically different from its neighbours. Where other Romanticisms were a true liberation from worn or shallow conventions of long standing, German Romanticism leaves us with a sense of loss. For all its own literary achievements, it seems a premature under-mining of great gains, an unnecessary reversion to immaturity, revolu-tion by retrogression. This charge can be made specific in relation to its aesthetic, philosophical, religious, social and political tendencies.

Goethe and Schiller in their poetry had felt for the reality that resided *in* things, they saw both the particular and in it those general laws which they knew governed it. Style itself, in Goethe's definition, rested on the deepest foundations of knowledge, on the nature of things as far as man could grasp it through visible and tangible forms. It was pre-cisely such knowledge of objective reality that Goethe and Schiller pursued in science and philosophy, just as a painter probes for the true form he is to paint by anatomical studies. This impulse made their work in the deepest sense realistic, even if they had by now retreated from (or passed beyond) the obvious realism of their early works. The Romantics broke with realism far more radically. In their theory and all too often in their practice, external reality is at best a mask for mystical ultimates, at worst a potential receptacle for their own 'higher' meanings. Thus where Goethe and Schiller tried to fuse phenomenon and meaning in the fulfilment of a symbol, the characteristic mode of Romantic writing is the allegory, which locked the one up in the other and frequently withheld the key. Philosophy provided, surprisingly, a basis for such an approach. Paradoxical developments from Kant's thesis on the inaccessibility of ultimate reality seemed to give the mind a sovereign right over the phenomenal world; such 'Idealism' became the foundation of a 'boundless Realism' – by which was meant the manipulative use of what is real, not its lovingly obedient penetration and rendering.

Thus even the impulses Romantic writers received from con-temporary natural science were adapted to a mysticizing vision of the world. Geology, for example, opened up the dark and wonderful inner core of the earth, the earth's unconscious, as it were, where mysterious powers resided. The miner duly became a poetic figure, moving daily in these thrilling regions, perhaps even catching sight of Nature herself as a woman of enthralling and dangerously seductive beauty. But symptomatically his significance obscures his reality. Even though Novalis, who made much of these motifs, was a pro-fessional mine administrator, it is not till much later, in Heine's *Harz-reise* (1826), that we get the description of a real mine. This tends to cut its mystical appeal considerably. Dirt-caked rungs lead down into a darkness of purely material danger. By then we are on the threshold of a new realism.

The release from an allegiance to reality is the central feature and the central problem of Romanticism. It has in itself no fixed value, the reader must discriminate between a confusing variety of imaginative gifts and literary motivations which manifest it in different ways and degrees. An early sample is Wackenroder's *Herzensergießungen eines kunstliebenden Klosterbruders* (1797), a rhapsody on painting whose over-rich emotionalism reduces pictures to carriers of religious messages in happy emulation of the religion-dominated Middle Ages, and replaces the idea of workmanship, the artist's skilled grasping of his subject, by a vague hope for the solve-all of divine inspiration. There is a similar vagueness, a sense of floating high above particular realities, in Friedrich Schlegel's grandiose plans for giving fresh impetus to literature by the invention of a new mythology. Both these examples are of writings *about* art: German Romanticism began with doctrine rather than new poetic creation, with (as Heine said) the judgement of past works of art and the recipe for future ones. But the same distance or even escape from reality shows in Romantic creative work. Its typical form is the *Märchen*, which in the hands of the Romantics becomes a strange mixture of the primitive and the sophisticated. The fairy-tale world is at once a release, the willing return of modern intellect to the non- or pre-rational, *das Wunderbare*; and also the source of motifs and arabesques through which deeper meanings can be cryptically implied. In other words, primitive *Märchen* will accommodate cerebral allegory. It is a mixture of extremes, and it is not surprising if they frequently fail to harmonize. The failure itself epitomizes the Romantics' dilemma. They were intellectuals to the point of ironic self-consciousness, yet they disapproved of intellect because it smacked of *Aufklärung*, of imaginative impoverishment, of what Novalis called the cold dead Spitzbergen of reason which had denied the richly adorned Indies of poetry. Accordingly they cast about for means to absorb intellect and achieve a state of mind such as simpler epochs enjoyed (which is why they were so fascinated by the Middle Ages). Yet intellect, certainly among the first Romantic group led by the Schlegels, remained their principal instrument to encompass this. Their efforts are thus like those of a man trying to jump over his own shadow. Only in such a context could the paradoxical proposal arise to *create* a new mythology. In particular works of art, like the comedies of Tieck, intellect is all too evident, playing with the conventions of a genre for ironic effect. This may appear a sovereign superiority of the mind; but it remains intellectual, not artistic. The play *with* form is a poor stop-gap for the strong forming impulse which is missing.

Of the early Berlin–Jena group, Novalis is the only impressive creative writer. He is as intellectually sophisticated as the Schlegels, perhaps even more deeply versed in philosophy, and yet his language has an apparently unstaged simplicity and naïve directness. The mysticism of his autobiographical novel *Heinrich von Ofterdingen* (1802) is fundamental to the whole conception, not mere allegorical arabesque. Even when, within the story, the poet-hero comes upon a book in which his adventures and fate are already recorded, this is not so much an instance of the infinite regressions of Romantic irony, whereby a work discusses itself. Rather it expresses Novalis's own conviction about the poet's – his own – life. If the novel is in parts obscure, with an allegorical fairy-tale inset in it that outdoes all its kind, still it is as a whole exploratory and expressive, not a mere clever construct. Similarly, Novalis's religious poetry stands out through its power and tautness of expression, which are kept up by the pressure of unironized feeling; for religion in Novalis was not (as it was in so many other Romantics) the deliberate adoption of belief so as to steady the mind in the midst of modern relativism. His *Geistliche Lieder* (1802) take up the form and rival the strength of Luther's hymns. The more personally coloured *Hymnen an die Nacht* of two years earlier make some use of the hymn, but are mostly freer effusions which can be considered either highly poetic prose (their first published form) or free verse (their form in Novalis's manuscript). His choice of the prose arrangement perhaps recognized the tentativeness and incomplete accomplishment of the form: it lacks the minute correspondence of the movement to each phase of the subject which would make it inescapably verse (as in Goethe's early rhapsodies, 'Ganymed', 'Prometheus', of which there are occasional echoes). The subject is yearning for night and death and ecstatic expectation of a reunion beyond the grave with the poet's dead love. Large sweeps of feeling result, a swelling rhetoric of emotion whose rhythms are affected adversely by the division into line-sections. It is perhaps not coincidental that good 'free' verse is rarely far from concrete particulars around which to take firm shape, whereas rhapsodic feeling with little admixture creates looser structures.

These part-religious, part-erotic themes, which are also the core of *Ofterdingen*, complete a picture of Novalis as the epitome of Romanticism: his passion for night and death, however personally motivated, is only an extreme form of a general Romantic predilection for life's *Nachtseite* – for the rationally inexplicable, the magical, the mystical, or – as in E. T. A. Hoffmann's tales – the sinister. Novalis's own conversion to night and death occurred through a vision at the grave of his fiancée in 1797, and it was the resulting hope of a supreme fulfilment in the 'bridal night' of death that made him write of light and the coloured things of the daylit world as poor and childish. The repercussions of this personal experience are momentous. It engendered a hostility to light in any form, and especially to light as the ideal and instrument of the *Aufklärung*, whose very name is a metaphor derived from light. Novalis attacked it in his essay *Die Christenheit oder Europa* (1799), and wished its impertinent rays might be kept from intruding into anything potentially poetic. 'Poetry', in this fragile conception, means an aura about things which has to be treated carefully lest it be destroyed. Such an anxious preservation of the 'poetic' may clearly entail obscurantism. Not surprisingly, the ideal society for poetry turns out to be precisely that medieval society in which religion (which has a vital interest, in every sense, in the miraculous) was a unifying and as yet unquestioned force. Novalis's ideal is mystery, preserved or restored. He even upbraids Protestantism because it made the Bible the cornerstone of Christianity, and thus laid religion itself open to textual and other critical inquiry. For the poet cloudiness is next to godliness. This is all very well if he feels that such are the preconditions his poetry needs. But quite apart from our doubts about the value of anything so delicate that it must assiduously seek the shade, what are the social effects of such an ideal? Poetic expedience may involve disaster in other spheres. Novalis's suggested restoration of a Europe unified in faith (with the aid of the Jesuits' return, for they are the 'model of a society') is an early but important sample of a recurrent German phenomenon: cultural exhortation which has practical consequences neither looked for nor cared about. And he was not alone, either in his ideals or his hostility to reason. Many Romantics shared his programmatic irrationalism and his enthusiastic if imprecise medievalism; they could hardly fail to exert an influence, in other fields besides literature, and they thus became (as their acutest critic was to point out) a retrogressive, even reactionary force.

Medievalism is equally central to the second Romantic group, at Heidelberg, but at first sight more as a source of motifs and materials than as an ideal of culture. The great and lasting achievement here was a lyrical poetry which sprang from the revivified native model of the *Volkslied*. For centuries the folk-poem had existed parallel with attempts, mostly unsuccessful, to establish a literary tradition. Now it became a literary tradition itself. Herder had extolled folk-poetry, Goethe had derived inspiration from it as one of many outside stimuli. Between 1804 and 1808 Arnim and Brentano compiled their massive anthology *Des Knaben Wunderhorn*, three centuries of German poetry from printed and oral sources in which 'die frische Morgenluft alt-deutschen Wandels' could be breathed. Like all Romantic undertakings, it is full of paradoxes. Its tone and forms were meant as a native counter-weight to foreign models, perhaps especially to the many Romance forms avidly appropriated by the Schlegels as translators and critics – yet there was a kind of exoticism in this stock-piling of past simplicity by literary sophisticates. The claims of old folk-poetry on the allegiance of moderns were its freshness and life – yet the editors themselves saw that these qualities were precarious, that they were trying to make fast what was on the point of final disappearance: a last hive of bees about to swarm away. The credentials of folk-poetry as a source of new poetic vigour lay in its authenticity – yet Arnim and Brentano freely adapted, polished, archaized, rewrote, and even slipped in poems of their own with faked 'sources' (all to the deep chagrin of the Grimm brothers who were simultaneously collecting German folk-tale and legend and laying the foundation of meticulous historical scholar-ship). As elsewhere in Romanticism, the most seemingly natural hides a calculated restoration. Yet this time restoration is triumphant. The *Volkslied* becomes the one wholly successful means for the Romantics to earth their literary sophistication in an apparently unselfconscious form, the simplicity of the models they learned from dissolves their dilemma by imposing simplicity. Brentano and Eichendorff, especially, achieve a *Volkslied* purity of tone which is not mere pastiche and a formal delicacy which goes far beyond most of the originals. They have clearly not just acquired a technique, they have learned a new way of seeing, of reconciling depth and simplicity. As Goethe wrote, reviewing the *Wunderhorn*: 'Der Drang einer tiefen Anschauung fordert Lakonis-mus.' Intensity of feeling gently suggested; a sense of identification with landscape and the varying moods of time and season which approaches the religious yet does not heavily allegorize; a plain diction with rich natural associations; an extreme musicality supporting the sense or, as often, catching the reader in an enchantment of sound above the logic of statement – all these things make the finest Romantic poems, within their narrower range, a rival in quality to Goethe's.

What were the practical relations like between the Romantics and the poets of Weimar? Despite their differences – in a sense, precisely because of them – the Romantics admired, even at times idolized Goethe as the one example of a modern poet in whose work consciousness was perfectly integrated with sensuous experience, balanced by formative power. Those disharmonies they were aware of in themselves and as a wider cultural problem were seen as resolved in him. They paid due court to him. Arnim and Brentano dedicated the *Wunderhorn* to Goethe, and Friedrich Schlegel made him the central norm of his critical essays. Goethe's attitude in response was diplomatic rather than cordial. He could not but see that the praise of his work was in part an attempt to drive a wedge between himself and Schiller, to appropriate him for purposes not necessarily his own. He could also see in the hyperconscious concern with literature an expression of literary weakness, not the sign of a growing vigour. The gulf between Romantic ambition and achievement, between knowing what is excellent in poetry and producing it, the problems of the 'Weg vom Subjekt zum Objekt' had been pointed out in a letter of Schiller's in 1801. In 1812 Goethe is summing up the contemporary scene along very much these lines as an 'epoch of forced talents', and finding shortcomings in the means by which writers tried to give substance to the thin combination of a consciously chosen idea and a consciously elaborated technique. For Goethe to the very end of his life substance meant experience ('poetischer Gehalt . . . ist Gehalt des eigenen Lebens; den kann uns niemand geben'). He saw this being replaced by religious attitudes and motifs from art in such a way that poetry and visual art were ruining each other. These charges are general, their reference in their cryptic context is uncertain, yet it seems most likely that he had the Romantics in mind; for when his onslaught does come, it is aimed at these targets. Certainly, the Romantics' orientation was profoundly alien to him. His vision was not drily rational (as one can see from the *Wahlverwandtschaften*, which probes the obscurer regions of natural forces and telepathic sympathies); but neither was it inclined to mystical or fantastic imagining. The central experience of Goethe's life had been Italy, and the hold it gave him on real phenomena remained his touchstone. Judged by this, Romanticism was an aberration.

Matters came to a head over Romantic painting: aptly so, because visual art, with its concreteness and its prerequisite of a technical mastery based on knowledge, was a constant analogy for the classical literary aesthetic and it had been, in the works Goethe observed in Italy, one generous source of that aesthetic. By contrast, one of the earliest Romantic writings was (we saw) a rhapsody which made of art a quasi-religious cult where both appreciation and creation itself depended on the gift of grace. Art for Wackenroder was 'above man', pictures were not to be described concretely, much less criticized (a 'foolish enterprise of man's vain pride'); final absurdity, they were not even there for the eye to *see* them at all! In 1805 Friedrich Schlegel declared that paintings should be hieroglyphs, their real purpose to hint at divine mysteries, all else subordinate to that end. Something very like this approach flourished in the 'Nazarene' school of German painters which had its headquarters (ironically) in Rome. Goethe and his ally Meyer published a sharp attack on their religiosity, medievalism, narrow patriotism and allegorizing, and in the same year (1816) Goethe at last brought out, as a far more positive counterblast, the first two parts of his *Italienische Reise*. This is far more than a fine travel book, compiled from the letters and diaries he wrote during his Italian journey. By reconstructing the genesis of his mature outlook, capturing the fresh impact of rich new experience and tracing the patterns of thought as they arise from it, the book is also a complete and vital statement of all that classicism meant: a comprehensive vision of nature, culture, society and the place of the individual in them all. It shows how broad and strong were the foundations for the single activity of poetry: Goethe's classical literary works were only the island peaks of this hidden range. In comparison with such a total grasp, Romantic thought looks slight and whimsical.

Yet, as has been hinted, classicism had its drawbacks, its inescapable limitations. It could be illiberal, complacent, conservative. Any form of classicism, being and knowing itself to be a fulfilment and a balancing of forces, will resist change because change must mean a disturbing of the balance. The manifestations of this attitude are various. There is the loss of the spirit for the sake of the letter, as in the sheer antiquarianism of Goethe's Homerizing epic *Achilleis*, authentic in every detailed allusion, hexametric, dead. (The flagging of impulse and Schiller's tactful hints kept it a fragment.) Or in those prize competitions Goethe and Meyer set for painters, imposing classical story-subjects and thus reviving, for the sake of 'classical' externals, the confusions Lessing had combated in *Laokoon*. These aberrations were admittedly few. More unfortunate were the critical negations of major talents: Hölderlin and Kleist were rejected because of a failure – temperamental or technical – to fit the patterns Goethe and Schiller had evolved through their own experience. Hölderlin's case shows up the problematic side of that established literary tradition which Germany now at last possessed. We see the difficult responsibility of accepted masters to foster new talent without forcing it into their own mould; we see the young writer's difficulties in reconciling a respect for others' achievements (Hölderlin's early admiration for Schiller was extreme) with the promptings of his talent to cut loose and rival them. A veil of wrong assumption impedes Goethe's and Schiller's view when they are faced with two poems of the transitional phase in Hölderlin's work. Schiller interprets the visionary intensity in the light of his own youth, as an excess of subjectivity. Hölderlin, he thought, should stay closer to the world of the senses and not get carried away by enthusiasm. Yet this was already the serener enthusiasm of sustained elevation, not the facile enthusiasm of immaturity. Goethe, more aptly, was reminded by the ode 'An den Äther' of paintings in which the animals are grouped about Adam in paradise. Yet despite this feeling for the metaphysical locus, the God's-eye-view of Hölderlin's poetry, Goethe's advice was to 'write little poems, choosing for each a subject of human interest'. Neither reader saw the new poetic dimension, the ease with which Klopstock's solemn heights were attained and yet at the same time the effect mellowed by a warmth of emotion which is both personal to the 'I' of the poem and generalized into anthropological statement. This is Hölderlin's keynote in his maturity: the transmutation of emotional experience, or rather its direct transference into a pattern which is at once unforcedly visionary, religious in the broadest sense. Every phenomenon and particular experience in life – bread, wine, air, separation, homecoming, childhood – goes to build up an elemental theology, is compulsively seen in the context of a whole life, of human life in general. For Hölderlin, this capacity seems given in the very act of writing poetry. He is not a nature poet in any ordinary sense, but Goethe was wrong to think his evocation of natural scenes conventional rather than 'seen'. This is like demanding Flemish exactitude of a Renaissance landscape, it fails to distinguish sight and vision. The harmony of nature is one pillar of all Hölderlin's thought and feeling. For this very reason, his depiction of a natural scene or process at once becomes a primal idyll or a symbolic ideal.

Hölderlin's immediate access to synoptic vision was not a comfortable gift. Goethe's advice might be read as an attempt to earth a dangerously high current. But the dangers were part of Hölderlin's avowed vocation: the poet stands exposed to the storms of historical crisis and the divine purpose; as the only possible mediator he receives the lightnings and passes them on to his fellow men, 'ins Lied gehüllt'. He is a prophet in both senses, accusing the ignoble present and announcing a coming fulfilment. Like so many other eighteenth-century Germans, Hölderlin drew from Greece the ideals in whose light modern life appeared fit only for lament. But in his later, fully prophetic phase, accusation and sorrow over reality (which had been strongest in his novel *Hyperion*, 1797–9) yield to the anticipation of a realized ideal. Ancient and Christian motifs and figures mingle with contemporary events, a divine return, a festival of peace and perfection is foretold for the poet's native land. This is a religious rather than a narrowly nationalistic theme, so personal in its symbolism and idiosyncratic in its conceptions that it is often obscure. Obscurity being grist to the modern mill, this late poetry now commands most attention. One may say of it that at least its difficulty springs from the complex nature of what Hölderlin was attempting (and to some extent from the incipient break-up of his mental powers), not from the mannered adoption of externals of which there are such obvious elements in modern 'prophetic' poetry like Rilke's. After the strain had finally become too great for his 'unselig feine geistige Organisation', Hölderlin still occasionally wrote poems in the long years to his death. In these, naïveté and awkwardness of language and movement can suddenly give way to the strange spasmodic wisdom of a released mind, creating beautiful and deeply suggestive phrases and fragments of visions. Nevertheless, Hölderlin's major poetic achievement must be the body of odes and elegies in Greek metres which preceded the formal, and eventually intellectual, dissolution of his prophetic works. German has never been so powerful and flexible at once, so completely fused with the intricate Greek forms and yet so unimpeded in expression, so complex and so controlled. And aside from all his staple forms, Hölderlin also created in 'Hälfte des Lebens' one of the most poignant short poems in German, a brooding, distraught reversal of Goethe's 'Auf dem See'.

Goethe and Schiller's judgement of Hölderlin was a failure of literary flair, not consciously a reaction of classical principle against the pathological. Indeed, of his later development and collapse they knew nothing. But with Kleist there is a direct clash. The pathological traits in his work and personality revolted Goethe like (as he put it) a body intended by nature to be beautiful but incurably diseased. This is usually presented as a failure of Goethe's humanity, and certainly for the already unhappy Kleist Goethe's rejection was a further blow. Yet, to be fair, it was a compulsive reaction, not a despotic whim. If classicism meant anything, it could not stomach Kleist. The very basis of Goethe's mature work and outlook is challenged by Kleist's authentic (i.e. not merely effect-seeking) statement of the baselessness of existence. This is a symbolic meeting of two ages. However personal and hard-won, Goethe's positive ethos and cautiously optimistic hold on life, his feeling as poet and scientist for the unity and harmony of the world, were fed from eighteenth-century sources (and, further back, Spinoza). In his science, even in the revolutionary new morphological approach to natural forms which he initiated, there are remnants of a teleology underwritten by nature's guiding agency; there is not yet the random, open-ended factor of nineteenth-century evolutionary theory. Goethe's is a world whose order is essential; Kleist's a world where order is chance and precarious, threatened by violence in man and around him – by natural catastrophe, by the possible malevolence of such higher powers as may govern the world, and by naked evil in individuals and reversions to barbarism in social groups. He was the first to sketch this darker vision, variants of which dominate the nineteenth century in literature and thought; and his forms remain some of the most powerful and artistically perfect. For technique his dramas rival Schiller's and his mature dramatic poetry is deeply original, even in the orthodox blank verse form which for ever after Goethe and Schiller one expects to find bedevilled by their echoes; while the prose style of his stories beggars comparison by the amazing perspicuity of its long, involved sentences. In them, syntax is transmuted from a grammarian's concept into a refined graphic instrument. The bald facts of subordination or co-ordination, of main clause and multiple but infinitely graded relative clauses, acquire more power than any image in exactly transmitting a situation or a sequence. Every detail of relationship and priority is duly grasped and rendered; what seemed at first glance a hopelessly cluttered maze turns out to be lucidly pre-organized for the reader's mind. At any given moment, the smallest structure reflects the point of the whole story with unerring calculation or instinct. In *Michael Kohlhaas*, for instance, the single-minded pursuit of vengeance stands out in the account of Kohlhaas's surprise attack on the Tronkenburg – from which the bird has flown. Amid a welter of gruesome sub-events like the murder of henchmen, all duly subordinated in their clauses, his colourless asking where his enemy is pins the complex sentence together and our attention on what really matters. The sensational is not important.

Such formal achievement has clear consequences. First, it underlines the non-artistic nature of the classical Goethe's instinctive objection to this alarming writer. Secondly, it warns us not to romanticize Kleist, because of his unhappy life and suicide, into a representative of total loss of control. The suicide cannot be argued away, nor the probability that too much of his dark vision at least joined with outward failure in bringing him to it. But the works, however terrible their content and theme, are as fully formed in their way as anything of Goethe's or Schiller's. And they also defy, through purely literary qualities, one other cliché picture of Kleist, this time as the despairing epistemologist. True, a recurrent theme is human error and the deceitfulness of appearances, and it is known that a reading of Kant upset the applecart of his youthful *Aufklärung* optimism. True, in his first play, the rather clumsily contrived *Familie Schroffenstein*, he consciously aimed to show fate as a trickster, heaven a deceiver, and man a prey to error. But the theme once set, it is treated thereafter in many tones – ironic (*Amphifryon*), broadly comic (*Der zerbrochene Krug*, the classic German comedy), dispassionately objective (the stories). Epistemological doubt was the lens through which Kleist looked, not the whole of what he saw. It was his angle on situations, not an exclusive obsession. Even in *Schroffenstein* it is human passion, especially the twisted mind of Rupert, that does as much as the twists of deceitful fate to determine the action: the radical evil in man, not just his melodramatic misunderstandings.

In Kleist's work, certain claims, both about man and his capacities and about the nature of the world, are abandoned. Man now has to live with the random and unguaranteed, and Kleist's deepest theme is the impact of this discovery on individuals, and their reactions. Because extreme situations show these best, the extreme becomes his normal material. What may result – moral or immoral, tragic or triumphal – is not governed by any ultimate commitment or security such as Schiller and Goethe had. The issues remain open, these are impartial studies in human potential. Kleist's protagonists may match terror from without by an answering violence: an old man murders the adopted son who has brought death and ruin on his family, and then refuses absolution before hanging so as to pursue his revenge anew in hell (*Der Findling*). Michael Kohlhaas, to avenge a minor wrong which corrupt society will not set right, spreads death and destruction wholesale. The paradox of his simultaneous guilt and righteousness, plus Kleist's masterly laying bare of every social, legal and psychological lever determining a complex action, makes this the greatest of German stories, despite the jarring aberration into a supernatural sub-plot at the eleventh hour. But equally, the reaction may be moral heroism, and the more impressive for depending on no such fixed code as Schiller's. There, heroism meant moral resolve and self-conquest – difficult enough; but in Kleist it means an emergency withdrawal into self-discovery, a desperate ingenuity which has to evolve a means of rescue from the resources of the inner self when the abyss suddenly opens. There are several victories on these lines in the plays and stories, of which the famous reconciliation with Prussian military justice in his last work, *Der Prinz von Homburg*, is only the most orthodox, almost Schillerian. For all the depths this play has, it has found the banal, if firm, foothold of patriotism. Some of the other works (*Die Marquise von O . . ., Der Zweikampf*) offer hints of a less limited existential humanism. *Penthesilea*, the play Goethe took exception to, is the most empty of even these mitigations, and Goethe's abhorrence is not hard to understand. In his own work he does not avoid tragedy, he skirmishes with it, often winning very satisfying tactical successes (*Iphigenie*) and resting with these limited gains. Kleist's insistent posing of the extreme case, and especially his acute intuition of the violence, sexual and other, lurking skin-deep in man, *could* only appear pathological. But they were arguably (to a far greater degree than anything in Romantic writing) the first thrusts of dionysian forces through the uneasy calm of society and culture.

The power in Hölderlin and Kleist shows the limitation of classicism and the impossibility of conserving it for long. It is true that Kleist had killed himself (1811) and Hölderlin was deranged (1806) long before Goethe ceased to write, before even classicism was reasserted in the *Italienische Reise* of 1816. Yet the *Italienische Reise*, besides recreating the birth of classicism, marks its end. Its dominance had already slackened with Schiller's death in 1805. Goethe's remaining years (to 1832) were taken up with completing *Wilhelm Meisters Wanderjahre* and *Faust II*, whose virtuosity and inner variety make it hard to label them anything but 'unique'. The classical ethos may be inherent in the philosophies they present and the solutions they reach, but they are not otherwise limited, not even excluding Romantic decorative elements. These late works, like the still unceasing flow of lyrical and philosophical poems, are the final alchemies of a supremely gifted individual who is once again essentially alone. Goethe is like a monument on the literary scene which stands in the way of a general reconstruction.

This effect continues after his death. He remains for the following decades a point of reference and a problem. Writers may try to maintain classical ideals or may react against them. Either way, Goethe's achievement impinges on them, inhibiting, overshadowing. He had transformed the relationship of literature to experience and given rich substance to the resulting new aesthetic. Formally he had been exhaustive. The available means of expression in lyric poetry in the mid-nineteenth century were those he had used. Most of them he had created or been the first to appropriate fully for German poetry. For other poets to find their own voice and present a substance which could even begin to compare was a severe problem. To do these things without being constantly aware of Goethe was impossible. Some fine poets sought refuge in restriction. Eduard Mörike made some perfect poems out of the simple materials of a Swabian country pastor's existence – superficially idyllic and often delightfully humorous, but shot through with unexpected hints of the demonic and tragic. Annette von Droste Hülshoff's poems seem wholly saturated with minute observation of nature, yet they also powerfully communicate unspoken emotions – unhappy love, religious feeling. Her outward forms are limited, her literary selfconsciousness slight. Both these poets show what can be made of the everyday object, the permanencies of nature, and the character of a small locality, if they are deeply enough known. Their achievements are made possible by willing acceptance of such limitation. Limitation in many forms is a characteristic of their period.

In drama too Goethe (and Schiller) had set norms of theme, treatment and ethos, even of tone, cadence, phrasing. At least until 1880, dramatists were driven into acquiescence or revolt. Acquiescence, willing or reluctant, could mean unoriginality, or at best a continuation of accepted modes which was consciously 'literary' while at the same time the writer uneasily sensed a discrepancy between what he had taken over and the changing infrastructure of his age. This is especially true of Grillparzer, whose devotion to the values of Weimar was absolute.

Similarly again with the novel. Goethe had made it a means to trace that, for him, most important thing in life, the individual's attainment of a mature and comprehensive practical philosophy. Under his influence, efforts at large-scale fiction continue to be canalized towards the *Bildungsroman* which, as a peculiarly German form, takes on a ritual prestige. Whereas the French and English novel of this period is firmly rooted in society, the *Bildungsroman* seems wholly unsocial. In *Wilhelm Meister*, the reality the hero knows is made up of a travelling theatre troupe, a mysterious beneficent masonic society, rich noblemen's estates and a utopian educational province located nowhere – all these are primarily catalysts to provoke his or others' personal development.

Now in Goethe's time this unsocial quality was a socially accurate statement. The sense of fragmentariness he transmits corresponds to the fragmentariness of German society. And *Bildung* in such a situation was a reasonable ideal, a positive response (limited though it may seem) to the problem of creating a society. Not that the *Wanderjahre* is in any sense a blueprint for a German social order. But the pursuit of personal maturity had social implications because, for Goethe and Schiller and friends of theirs like Wilhelm von Humboldt, the quality of the individual was the only guarantee of the quality of any social structure to come. Schiller's *Ästhetische Briefe* make this fully explicit. Unfortunately, the course of German history could not wait for the long-term social programme this view implied to take effect. The impact of Weimar classicism on German life was doubtful from the start. Its only direct influence on social policy was through the person of Humboldt, who was in charge of education during the brief period of liberal reform in Prussia which followed the traumatic defeats of 1806.

Yet the prestige which Goethe gave to the form-cum-ideal of the *Bildungsroman* perpetuated it as a literary tradition into later phases of social development. Its patterns go on recurring as deliberate preoccupations at times and in places where society could and should have been approached differently, most notably in Adalbert Stifter's *Der Nachsommer*. Even in the twentieth century it is revived in Thomas Mann's *Zauberberg*. Created before the rise of industrialism, nationalism and mass-politics, it seems dwarfed by these forces. Its underlying ideal seems increasingly an evasion, its formal conventions point to solipsism, as the sanatorium isolation of Mann's setting makes painfully clear.

Such maintenance of inherited forms and values into an age which is turning to other gods is the central issue of the post-classical phase. It creates the conflict which underlies Grillparzer's plays and Stifter's fiction. In both, the unease in face of change often comes over more strongly than the positive commitments. The ideals they preach or imply – the need to be content with what one has, simplicity of life, reverence for nature, restraint in human dealings – can also be seen as a series of withdrawals from the more dangerous areas of life (activity, ambition, the passions) and as an anxious defence of an ever-narrowing range of human possibilities.

For Grillparzer's essentially elegiac nature, the major tragic form seems too large. He does not embrace the tragic fact so much as turn it to yield the lesson: that man should withhold himself from those areas of life that threaten tragic consequences. Life itself is a threat for a poetess (Sappho), a priestess (Hero); action is repugnant to an emperor (Rudolf II) in whom the refusal to engage himself is most clearly pathological. Yet these forbidden areas also contain life's most desirable things – love, achievement, the resolution of conflict. Tragedy is the risk man runs, and the great tragic poets recognize this. The recognition makes their characters so absolute and makes possible that strange final harmony in tragedy which is not just the admission that to risk was wrong. Antony and Cleopatra do not die sadly and do not disown their past actions. But for Grillparzer it is better not to have loved at all than to have loved and lost. No other dramatist ever wrote so much 'tragedy' out of a *regret* that the world holds tragic potential. Regret and remorse would, if they could, retract the very action itself and quietism would reign. Meanwhile, a moral conclusion reminiscent of baroque drama may palliate, somewhat wordily, the final blow. Whatever the truth of Grillparzer's insights, they limit the stature of tragedy. Not surprisingly, the forms which the classical tradition prescribed are not filled out by his slenderer impulse. *Sappho* (1818), clearly meant as a tragic restatement of Goethe's *Tasso* theme, has contingent elements which blur the art–life antithesis; it becomes a psychological study of characters a little too small for their verbal gestures. A mythological drama, *Das goldene Vlies* (1821), yields similar results, unintentionally modernizing the Medea–Jason–Creusa triangle into squabblings which fall short of tragic myth. Medea starts as an embodiment of barbaric mentality, but declines in power to the point where her act of revenge seems only an obedience to the myth she inhabits. 'Ja, wär ich noch Medea, doch ich bin's nicht mehr,' as she says. Grillparzer's historical plays, too, emulate an established type, and the cultural echoes (Shakespeare, Schiller) are strong. The Austrian Habsburg themes (e.g. in *König Ottokars Glück und Ende*) are new, but the characters speak all too obviously the standard language of historical drama. Even more than in the tragedies, verse is a duty rather than a necessity, workmanlike but rarely taking fire, often slow, wooden, unurgent. It had risen to poetry in parts of the Hero and Leander treatment, *Des Meeres und der Liebe Wellen* (1831); and in *Ein Bruderzwist in Habsburg* (completed 1848) its brooding, halting movement is ideally suited to the undramatic meditations of the in-active emperor, whose voice is Grillparzer's own just as his thoughts on political order and the coming chaos of the Thirty Years War mask Grillparzer's own reaction to the revolution of 1848. But in general, Grillparzer's use of the classical heritage is a tribute to the past, and the past in return limited him, dictating structures, themes, language. How closely these three are connected, in success or failure, appears at once from those occasions when he did use an alternative. As an Austrian linked with the other Habsburg culture, he was drawn to the totally different dramatic style of Lope de Vega and the Spanish Golden Age. In a sense, one side of the *poeta doctus* here rescued the other. The Spanish four-beat trochaic lines allow no ruminative movement, no ponderousness, none of the rhetorical decoration which the iambic pentameter accommodates (or needs filling out with). The dramatic atmosphere changes with the altered stress and speed. What seemed wholly a characteristic of Grillparzer turns out to have been in good measure due to his forms. It was in fact the Spanish style which gave him his first public success, *Die Ahnfrau* (1817), where he freely used unclassical ghosts and robbers to make a splendid melo-dramatic entertainment of great verve. It is 'serious' literature (*pace* the analysts who probe it for philosophical implications) only in the sense that the brilliant, exhaustive use of any genre can claim to be so. It is a pity Grillparzer took up the Spanish form so rarely. In his *Jüdin von Toledo*, the two forms are juxtaposed, with the opening scenes in Spanish trochees (*c.* 1825) yielding to the iambic pentameters of the much later continuation. This seems symbolic: trochees to introduce the Jewess Rahel, Grillparzer's most vivacious, sensually fascinating creation, a woman for whom the King of Castile is to neg-lect wife and policy; iambics for the pale, formal, hesitant king and the court party who will kill her for it. Trochees for the poetic vivacity Grillparzer could attain, iambics for the more measured speech to which Weimar tradition drew him.

Fortunately he wrote one other 'Spanish' play, his clearest success. *Der Traum ein Leben* (1834) inverts Calderón's conception (*La vida es sueño*) to make a strength out of Grillparzer's weakness. The hero acts

out in dream the adventures he is restless for, experiencing entangle-
ment in evil and guilt – and can still wake, wiser, to make another
choice. Thus for once tragic action *can* be undone, yet without undoing
the formal structure. In the combination of dream and framework,
Grillparzer's always considerable craftsmanship finds a perfect embodiment for his theme of withdrawal. Once more, the form is symbolic
of the writer's relation to tradition, as he sensed himself. Dedicating
a copy to the new Duke of Weimar, he plays on his title-words: in
Weimar, art was a real life, for us it is at most a dream.

Grillparzer's was thus a problematic, not a facile traditionalism. He
was bitterly aware that he himself fell short of his predecessors (he
contemplated at one time an autobiographical novel on the life of a
'half-genius') and even more bitterly aware that the values he cherished
were becoming unreal and precarious in changing conditions. The
value (and the motives) of democratic politics seemed to him suspect,
'progress' a question-begging cry. It is an epigram against 'progress'
that contains his much-quoted, but sometimes incompletely quoted,
statement of allegiance to Weimar: 'Ich möchte, *wär's möglich*, stehen
bleiben, / Wo Schiller und Goethe stand' (my italics). Even while
determining the writer's attitudes, the ideal is balanced by its impossibility.

Weimar ideals themselves have new implications in changed circumstances. They were formulated in an oasis surrounded by war, from
which individual culture might appear a distant but hopeful prospect
for reconstruction, and its pursuit not narrowly political. But in the
age of European restoration after 1815, neither culture itself nor an
insistence on its primacy could be so neutral. A writer who in the name
of cultural ideals attacked new political movements and the politi-
cizing of literature was aligning himself, even if unwittingly or unintentionally, with reaction. As so often in later German history, a
subjectively non-political attitude was a real political factor.

Stifter, whose allegiances were similar to Grillparzer's, illustrates
this even more clearly. Two things stand out from the first in his
writing: a gift for natural description, and an interest in individual
education which is clearly linked with the *Bildungsroman* tradition.
This last is not accompanied by any move to analyse character, and his
early ventures into treating human relations directly show a clumsy
hand. At his best, he makes his characters objects in a landscape, understandable through it, participating ideally in its processes (e.g. *Das
Haidedorf*). His early stories, the *Studien* of 1843, are slow and undramatic,

but capable of the gentle moral influence which was all he claimed for them. But the uneasy times, and finally the revolutions of 1848, made his purposes more of a programme, his methods more heavily deliberate. His language becomes even simpler, his pace slower, his appeal to the guardians of order – tradition, the forces of nature – more explicit. As Grillparzer equated the political status quo with the eternal order (*Bruderzwist*), so Stifter appropriates nature itself for the cause of social stability – only with partial success. Criticized for the ordinariness of his characters and the uneventfulness of his stories, he invoked as a parallel nature's gentle processes (the growing of the corn, the wafting of the breeze) which are greater than her more violent manifestations (volcano, storm, earthquake). Such special cases are ephemeral, and so (Stifter implies) are the showier extremes of passion which his critic, the dramatist Hebbel, was in the habit of creating for the stage. It is not always realized that this accepts rather than refutes Hebbel's charge. In so far as Stifter's concern was with the permanent in life – not the bloodshed history records, but the love it leaves out – it is an escape from the historical. His decision to ignore an area of experience is as clear in the metaphors he uses as it was in Hebbel's allegation. Storm and earthquake may be infrequent, but they are events which articulate time. Hebbel was interested in them because he thought they were symptoms of radical change in humanity and society; exaggerated though his presentation often was, he did attempt to grasp complex processes and clarify them for the understanding. He was right to say that Stifter's art avoided this.

But it did more. Under an apolitical banner, in practice it took sides. The defender of 'timeless' values is in practice hostile to democratic stirrings. The ancient country nobility in *Der Kuß von Sentze* (1866) react unequivocally to social unrest. Those who are eminent in society through property or culture must be pillars of the legal order. Their power rests on a social contract and this basis is shaken if anybody may take what he needs. These falsisms of conservative argument are to be expected in such a context. What is more striking is the way classical Weimar thinking has been petrified into dogma. The 1848 situation is interpreted on the model of the French Revolution, with the help of Schiller's analysis from the *Ästhetische Briefe*. There political improvement was seen as dependent on individual character – which was therefore to be worked on through art. Here personal freedom through culture is made a precondition of political freedom so specifically as to exclude those who are now clamouring for freedom as unworthy of it. Schiller had made the point that *a* form of state must continue while improvement is sought through the separate agency of art; here we read that the Reich must be maintained first, then the 'right men' may find the path to freedom. Literary tradition has become the ally of reaction.

But Stifter's most elaborate 'answer' to the challenges of his time was *Der Nachsommer* (1857), a statement of the ideal development toward that requisite personal culture. Its elevatedness, but also its limitations, are suggested in a later letter. Stifter writes that, revolted by the crudely material aims and pleasures of the age, he has invented conditions of a totally different nature. Happy communal life for harmonious personalities with independent means had been an ideal in the very early *Feldblumen*. Now it is restated at enormous length and with emphasis. Stifter's renowned gentleness is the keynote. The gentle hero intersperses periods of diligent study at home and in the field with long visits to his elderly mentor's bucolic retreat. The meticulously cultivated roses bud; bloom; and fade. Another season comes, Heinrich returns, the roses bud; bloom; and fade. A young woman enters the picture. Surely Heinrich will eventually win her. He does, obedient to the patterns of fiction rather than to any depicted impulse: almost total silence is kept about the growth of their feelings. (This is again the limitation found from Stifter's earliest work, though his admirers claim it as a strength – reverence for human integrity prohibits psychological prying. Does this concede that the roots of ideal processes might belie them?) His characters likewise refrain from prying; they learn each other's names only very late in their acquaintance. Their actions are slow, ordinary, repetitive, a sublime monotony ('erhabenes Einerlei'). More important, so is the generalized colourless language in which they are just as repetitively described. By enumerating thus every insignificant phase of insignificant activity, Stifter is attempting a stylization towards ceremonial significance. But unlike the ceremonial features of early epic, his is never more than empty ceremony because it consistently avoids the problematic. Heinrich is gently led along a worthy path with never an impulse which would raise problems. The great teacher in the *Bildungsroman* tradition, error, is excluded; so is its mainspring, passion. All lessons have been learnt in advance by the older Risach. Nor is the outside world a source of difficulty. The characters are insulated from it by their position, we by the author's tunnel-vision. Yet the very pressure of its absence builds up. The worthy occupations seem brittle, their motives anxiety rather than harmony. Stifter's unruffled repetitions start to seem a slow-motion hysteria. Old objects are assiduously collected, restored, preserved. A model son is given a set of Goethe, but some works are forbidden him. We are not told which, but we do know the first work prescribed: *Hermann und Dorothea*, Goethe's heroic attempt at a modern idyll. This suggests a measure for Stifter's obvious emulation. As an idyll, *Nachsommer* will not stand comparison with *Hermann und Dorothea*, any more than it will as a *Bildungsroman* with *Wilhelm Meister*. Goethe's idyll took on the passions and the knotty resistant peculiarities of human individuals. Stifter's – and the very generality of his language reveals this – has ironed them out. But an idyll at no expense is a Utopia. Moreover as a Utopia it is too narrowly conceived, too escapist to have general validity. Its very setting, Risach's gently feudal estate, is a late Rousseauistic gesture, recalling Oscar Wilde's 'Anybody can be good in the country'. It lacks roots. Other nineteenth-century writers opposed to modern developments fought their rearguard actions from real bases, and their work records real voices from the dialogue of social evolution. The Swiss pastor Gotthelf could draw on and descriptively realize a peasant life of great character and inner strength. His *Schwarze Spinne* (1842), one of the great works of German fiction, starts with an evocation of authentic ceremony – a Swiss country christening – and then shows, in a chilling story of evil, how all achieved culture rests on knowing and engaging the forces which threaten it.

It is not wholly Stifter's fault and certainly not his gain that a modern vogue has made *Der Nachsommer* into a sacral object, a little candle in a naughty world, and has compared Stifter with Goethe as if the imposition of calm were the same as the growth of control. It is far from clear that we should open our hearts to his precarious ideal; by keeping our heads, we can see its limitations and its typicality as one product of the revolutionary tremors which crystallized conservative attitudes in so many artists and philosophers in the nineteenth century; as a not-so-distant relation of Hegel's theory of the State. Stifter's particular crystal shows the structure of *Biedermeier* thinking, and especially the way alarm at change grows, and swings from neutral quietism to positive conservatism, even reaction. In his early stories he had been able to see just such principles as *Nachsommer* preaches more critically. *Die drei Schmiede ihres Schicksals* (1844) ironized rigid devotion to past ideals. Elsewhere complacency is shown in all its precariousness. Guests at a party discuss whether it is the age itself or something deep in man that produces terrible events; the almost Kleistian anecdote is told of a father and son who meet in tragic combat in the revolutionary wars. When the guests depart, 'sagten sie sich schöne Dinge, gingen nach Hause, lagen in ihren Betten und waren froh, daß sie keine schweren Sünden auf dem Gewissen hatten'. This story is called *Zuversicht* – confidence. In its small way, it has a perspective which Stifter's later didacticism lacks.

If one decides Stifter is not a realist, this is a matter less of the increasingly stylized surface of his work than of his deeper escapism, his shying away from the realities of a new age. 'Realism' in this sense was requisite if his aims and solutions were to have value. But 'realism' is not in general a criterion of value by itself, nor even a term of fixed meaning. If it is nevertheless indispensable in discussing nineteenth-century literature, this is because it labels a very general new orientation, leaving the nature of particular cases, their rights and wrongs and their literary techniques still to be gone into. We have used 'realistic' to sum up Goethe and Schiller's aim of basing their work on objective realities as they conceived them. But those realities when investigated seemed to compose an order with which man could harmonize, in which he had a central place. Accepting them was compatible with a belief in the ultimate beneficence of nature, or in man's ultimate moral supremacy. Indeed such things were for Goethe and Schiller *part of* the objective order. Hence Goethe, though no Christian, could put his major statement on man into the metaphysical framework of the Faust legend without falling into empty parody; and Schiller needed to conceive of no circumstances, however dire, which man could not overcome by a rational morality, and this too was no empty formalism. All the time man could see himself thus as part of a system with meaning, his position could not be wholly tragic. The roots of this ultimate optimism reach into the subsoil of earlier ages of faith hardly less directly than does Lessing's tragic theory, which is a rational Christian theodicy.

In the nineteenth century, such reassurances are missing, 'things as they are' in a more purely material sense acquire unquestioned authority and uncompensated influence. Historical change seems to have a momentum, perhaps even laws and purposes, of its own; scientific analysis shows ever more of the complex interlocking of causes which underlies man's apparent freedom. Such forces, operating at the most general and the most detailed level, leave little room for human autonomy and cannot be guaranteed benevolent. Man is simply their object, a central point at which they can be thought of as concentrating, not the essential centre of an order. However one sees this new orientation – as a lamentable abdication or a laudable sobriety of spirit, as a 'disinheriting' of the mind or as its entry into a less extravagantly conceived inheritance – the nineteenth century is certainly, in Thomas Mann's phrase, 'vor der Wirklichkeit unterwürfiger', more prepared to submit to reality. What must be distinguished from case to case is the nature of the submission. A pair of dramatists, Hebbel and Büchner, provide contrasting examples here. They also illustrate further reactions to Weimar – assimilation, adaptation, rejection.

Friedrich Hebbel was a dramatist of considerable gifts, with a peculiarly acute sense of psychological conflict, especially between the sexes, which makes him a forerunner of Ibsen and even Strindberg. His dramatic verse is competent in the established pentameter form, and interspersed with violent, macabre images to match his often over-lifesize characters. Many of these are drawn from history and myth – Herod, Holofernes, Kriemhild and Hagen – and are thus adequately grandiose to fit into the classical grand tradition; but what fulfils the expectations their names create is the uncompromising intensity of their passions as conceived by a modern psychological extremism. Hebbel takes a gloomy delight in constructing situations without issue and often pathological responses. Far from the drawing-back typical of Grillparzer, there is almost a revelling in grimness. Yet construction is what we sense, not expression, the plays seem to spring from a pessimistic programme rather than a tragic vision. Though Hebbel sets out to portray the primitive power of emotion, an intellectual clarity is rarely far below the surface: the characters can be relied on to state their own motives and frequently the central issue of the play. This impression of an intellectual preponderance is there in the dramas themselves. Hebbel's voluminous diaries and essays in dramatic theory only intensify it. The latter especially carry reflection much further, interpreting the individual life and the tragic situations it throws up as a necessary part of a historical process man must accept. Hints at this historical process are built into some of Hebbel's plays, not always to their artistic advantage; the acceptance certain characters manage is Hebbel's form of tragic reconciliation.

Thus at least a higher order is re-established and a place in it assigned to suffering man. Is this so far from the satisfactions offered by Schiller, whose plays so impressed the young Hebbel? The similarity proves on examination to be purely formal. In Schiller's tragic dénouements, the character accepts his fate for moral reasons. That they *are* moral is

s

clear equally to author, character and audience; all three shift to the higher plane of moral necessity which makes physical necessity (relatively speaking) pale away. But in Hebbel the shift to a higher plane is not usually enjoyed by the suffering character but only by the audience or perhaps other characters. Thus *Agnes Bernauer* (1852), which has a similar theme to Grillparzer's *Jüdin von Toledo*, closes with a positive apologia for *raison d'état*: the audience is to recognize, as even Agnes's husband does, the necessity of her murder in the historical and social context. To make clear this higher necessity, the dramatist is prepared to break off the sympathy for the tragic sufferer which is vital in tragedy. Moreover, the necessity itself is not now moral in any sense Schiller would have recognized, it is (as one of the characters with typical Hebbelian explicitness states) a matter of cause and effect. And the 'higher plane' is merely the view of the individual's place in history – which is cold comfort unless we are sure that the historical process really is moral. How moral is it for Hebbel? As far as can be made out through the ponderous style and accumulated abstractions of his essays, Hebbel, from accepting the *fact* of historical process gradually slipped into accepting its *rightness*. This prejudges all issues of morality. Physical and moral necessity become one, where for Schiller they were sharply distinguished. 'Morality' for him was a criterion independent of actions and events; Hebbel's is determined by them. Hence when conflict occurs between individuals and 'higher' forces, the individuals tend to be abandoned. Hebbel is right to say that blamelessness like Agnes Bernauer's makes tragedy the more shattering – but it also makes his attempt at 'reconciliation' more disturbing.

The formal similarity of Hebbel's position to Schiller's at first glance obscures the crucial difference. This is a good example of a traditional pattern being adapted to a radically changed content. But Hebbel was not wholly responsible for the adaptation. His over-ready submission to real forces, to the extent of renouncing any standpoint outside them, calls to mind the 'realism' of Hegel's philosophy of history. There too, by the use of traditional concepts like reason and freedom from which the content has been hollowed out, an acceptance of the course of history is demanded. This is a caricature of theodicy. Hegel takes what occurs, hypostatizes it as a spirit, dubs its consummation 'rational', and rejects the claims of individual morality which chances to conflict with it as a purely 'formal' right, forsaken by God and the 'living spirit'. His premises, as the historian Jakob

Burckhardt later forcefully pointed out, were the very assumptions
that may not be made about history. Sensible contemporaries of Hegel,
like Grillparzer and Schopenhauer, saw at once the verbal sleight-of-
hand, the disguised medievalism of Hegel's thought. This did not
prevent it from dominating several decades; Hebbel, by more and less
direct intermediaries, sucked in this influence. Perhaps as an autodidact
he appreciated the imposing façade Hegelian terminology offered, and
as a tragic dramatist the added sense of inexorability in the idea of a
historical juggernaut.

Georg Büchner is at least as realistic as Hebbel in recognizing the
larger forces that act on man, but his reaction is different. Certainly
history seems a supra-personal force in his *Dantons Tod* (1835), but
it is called concretely 'das Muß' rather than being elevated into greater
abstraction, and it is seen unequivocally as man's curse. It is not his
only one: he is equally the victim of all the other conditions of nature
and society. Existence is tragic as such. Beside this fact, particular incident counts for little. That is why the historical 'plot' – Danton's downfall at the hands of Robespierre – is not screwed up into tension by
dramatic means. The outcome is preordained by Danton's inactivity.
This has its roots in his disillusionment with all action and his obsession
with the meaninglessness of life, and these are the play's main burden.
'Drama' intrudes only in the tribunal scenes which are transcripts
from the historical record – introduced on Büchner's principle of
objective accuracy, but rather belying his conception of a nihilistic
Danton by the energy the hero at last shows in his own defence. In so
far as one may speak of dramatic form at all, Büchner's is the loose,
epic kind, with scenes juxtaposed rather than inherently connected:
something akin to the technique the *Stürmer und Dränger* evolved in
the belief it was Shakespeare's and in defiance of Aristotle. One of them,
Lenz, certainly caught Büchner's imagination so much that he evoked
his later days in a brilliant short story which draws the reader into the
bewildering unstable moods and perceptions of mental breakdown.
Büchner also speaks his artistic credo through Lenz's mouth. But
the formal patterns of his drama derive less from passive acceptance
of a prepared technique than from the nature of his own thought. For
where there is no meaning, there is no tension. If life has no point, it
can have no highpoint. Dramatic-cum-moral climaxes are inconceivable
because there are no moral issues. Even death is merely a physical
fact, a final release from other physical facts. All the doomed Danton
desires is nothingness, and he fears that death itself may not be

able to give it to him. Dramatic tautness here would be a formal pretence.

Thirty years from Schiller's death, we are already an infinity from his view of man. For Büchner the idea of a moral will seems totally unreal, and Schiller's heroes accordingly mere idealistic marionettes. Where Schiller had insisted that helpless suffering without any moral resistance was not human and could only inspire revulsion, Büchner sees, and portrays, man precisely as helpless within the interlocking causalities of history, society and physical nature. Unlike Hebbel he declines to botch a pseudo-theodicy out of these. Brute facts remain brute facts. Büchner's response – clear-sighted, outraged, compassionate – remains at their immediate level. But it also changes and matures. In *Dantons Tod* he is still a little enamoured of the rhetorical gestures of unbelief and the freedom to be sardonic about a bitter existence. The characters are articulate and at least have clarity as a compensation. Similar cultured musings recur, in comic-lugubrious key, in the comedy *Leonce und Lena*. But in *Woyzeck* we are on tragic bed-rock. Woyzeck's existence in poverty of body and mind is just bearable until his mistress, the mother of his child, is seduced. Always obsessive, now deranged, he murders her, then either kills himself or is tried and condemned – the fragmentary text Büchner left at his death is undecided, and it hardly matters. A rounding-off would not have materially altered things – neither the empathy and pity with which Woyzeck's situation is made real, nor the bite of the spare, compressed dialogue. 'Artistic economy' never meant anything quite like this: language pared down to semi-articulate brevity yet poetically intense just below the surface of its low-life realism; action sketched in a scatter of compelling, but barely connected scenes. A few touches flay Woyzeck's tormentors (the officer, the doctor, caricatures of social man, hiding their hollowness behind pompous, complacent phrases), a few touches realize Marie – frivolous, loving, sensual, amoral, remorseful, terrified. Pathetic broken rhythms pulsing under his scarcely coherent words render Woyzeck's suffering deranged mind and avenging urge. The play can be analysed into causes, but within its bounds all is concrete. Author and audience have no energies to spare, emotional or intellectual, for higher concluding. In the real-life Woyzeck's case, Büchner found a wholly objective correlative for his thought and feeling: the residually self-conscious nihilism of *Dantons Tod* gives way to sheer compassion and human solidarity. It is hard to find anywhere an equal for this play.

Büchner, plainly, is a radically new kind of artist and thinker. His dramatic originality was not recognized till decades later, but then had enormous impact. Hauptmann, the Expressionists, Brecht, all owe much to Büchner and said so. Similarly with his intellectual position. This is far beyond the mere *Weltschmerz* of his period, and critics who attribute it to his youth (he died at twenty-four) are confusing age and maturity. It has firm foundations and must be argued with, not patronized. Büchner's philosophical reading was exhaustive. He was already a brilliant scientist and had seized the vital principle of evolution which was to invert the notions of teleology and 'design' in nature. (We do not have hands to grasp with, we grasp because we have developed hands.) If this anticipates Darwin, Büchner's politics anticipate Marx, concentrating on the material levers of revolution while ever-hopeful liberals were still pamphleteering for the constitutions which had been dangled before the Germans in 1813. (Büchner's own single pamphlet expounded hard economic fact.) The people, he wrote in a letter, were patiently dragging the cart on which liberals and princes played out their grotesque comedy. Only violence would serve, only misery produce it; let us hope for failed crops. There is nothing callow about this view of the human condition.

Realism to such a degree and in such disparate fields was rare in Büchner's day. He had a unique capacity for rejecting traditions and making a fresh start unencumbered. Others had to fight their way clear of traditional entanglements slowly and painfully. The classic case is Heinrich Heine's. Heine grew up with Romanticism and on a superficial reading there is nothing more typically Romantic than the poetry he was writing in the 1820s – mostly in ballad and *Volkslied* form. Yet in all but his most dazzlingly perfect samples, an incomplete absorption can often be plotted, a cool intellectuality observed manipulating theme, motif and artifice. This never lets him stray into the lyrical mysticism of Eichendorff or Brentano. What (for his critics) is worse, he shows increasingly an ironic detachment from the forms and materials of his inheritance, and this becomes a deliberate destruction within the poem. Romantic contexts are established, Romantic effects promised – and the structure demolished by a stroke of disillusioning wit from outside the convention. This is not however just a satire on Romanticism, since a satirist stands *wholly* outside what he attacks. Heine did not. He remained a Romantic with part of himself, and this makes his work complex, his effects far from facile. His ironic destruction of feeling is justified and itself poetically expressive because the feeling was his own. He presents the full situation of a Romantic latecomer, not just part of it. With his gift for assimilating and adapting, he could have romanticized on for years, had he not had the honesty to admit that his own literary means did not wholly convince himself. This honesty and the intelligence that served it are Heine's sin against the poetic spirit, in the eyes of his critics. They cannot forgive him for ill-treating poetry. But they fail to see that this sprang from a respect for poetry. Heine was not wilfully parodistic – he used the Romantic mode because as yet he had no other. He undermined it because it no longer matched the full reality of modern experience. (Perhaps it never had.) To pretend full absorption in it would actually have widened the gap between an increasingly empty 'poetic' convention and intellectual and imaginative reality. Such hypocrisy could hardly have done poetry a service in the long run.

Finding his poetic tools breaking in his hands, Heine sought substitutes: irregular verse in place of the repetitious jingling of little *Volkslied* strophes, North Sea seascapes in place of the stock image-concepts of romanticized 'nature'. The vein was short-lived. He also turned early to prose. Other pressures were moving him that way. Heine was a social and political animal – another reason for the disharmonies in his poetry, where 'Romantic' situations clash with bourgeois norms, yielding bitter indirect portrayals of contemporary society – and in a carefree account of a walking tour in the Harz mountains he discovered, half by accident, an ideal means to slip topical comment past the ubiquitous Restoration censorship. The traveller wandered, his thoughts wandered as freely; now he is describing landscape, now flirting à la Laurence Sterne, now a soft aside, a symbolic caricature, a subtle *double entendre* forks off into politics. Thus: a still twilight scene, melancholy ringing of bells, the sheep tripping home to their fold – the people into their church. The juxtaposition 'sheep–people' is nothing – and everything. 1815 restored religion as well as monarchy. Religion has helped underpin order, successfully so far. Heine modulates from a Gray's Elegy mood into the Marxian *aperçu* that religion is the opium of the people. New ideological wine in old poetic bottles is a recurrent trick of Heine's.

His *Reisebilder* made his first reputation, as an *enfant terrible*. Their formal flexibility, with lyricism, satire, wit and reportage unified only by the constant narrative voice, also seemed a solution to his creative dilemma. Prose, he said, had welcomed him into its broad embrace. Yet he went on writing poetry, and despite his ever more open and intense political involvement and exile in Paris from 1831, it remained the old sweet–bitter mixture. 'Reality' could undermine Romantic illusion, but not apparently replace it. Heine's residual attachment to 'pure' poetry kept out of his empty verse the real interests that could have filled it. A seam of sub-Baudelairean sensualism soon petered out. Heine was a superb poetic technique with nothing to do. For a decade, his only real poetry grew out of this dilemma itself: he was Tann-häuser in the Venusberg, or a knight kept from battle by emotional trivia, or a legendary warrior imprisoned by water-sprites.

Meanwhile he wrote journalism which is literature, on conditions in France for German readers, on German philosophy and the newest German literary movement for the French. As a cultural critic he is magnificent. There is no more brilliantly entertaining book on Romanticism (or any other literary phenomenon) than his *Romantische Schule* (1833). But his spring-heeled prose, his wit and humour serve a fundamental seriousness. He sketches historical developments with masterly foreshortening, he hits off the essence of men, ideas, works, with apt anecdotes, illuminating similes, satirical thrusts – and final fairness. No polemicist ever gave his enemies less quarter, or their qualities such exactly measured credit. Even the polemic is not basically personal. Heine judges Romanticism from a standpoint not 'purely' literary, versed though he is in all the tricks of the Romantic trade. It cannot be discussed, he says, without going deep into politics; the widespread influence of the Romantics had endangered the happiness and freedom of Germany. This seems a staggering charge. What Heine means is the effect of the Romantics' taste for things medieval, their religiosity, their flight into the past as a failure (or refusal) to come to terms with the present. Unlike France, where medievalism was only a harmless fashion, Germany had scarcely cast off feudalism: to worship the Middle Ages was to revitalize the worst features of German life. Intensified by the war against Napoleon, the preoccupation with the Germanic past had also fathered a narrow, belligerent nationalism. Again, the idealized image of a Middle Ages firm in one belief, together with the crisis of cultural pluralism the Romantics suffered, had driven many back into Catholicism. Heine draws a typical verbal cartoon of this generation queueing to throng back into the old prison of the spirit which it had cost their forefathers such efforts to get out of. In Heine's scheme, the Reformation had been at least a step towards freedom of thought. But religion as such still meant obscurantism and excessive spiritualization; it was at the root of Europe's social ills. His own faith, call it hedonism, pantheism, or socialism, was in an earthly fulfilment, the balancing of spiritual and physical. Like Nietzsche after him (so many of whose doctrines he anticipates) he championed health because he knew the sickness from intimate experience.

Heine was perhaps the first to judge literature so concretely by social criteria, outdoing Madame de Staël and foreshadowing Marx. His castigation of the Romantics for evading modern realities seems to link him with 'Jung Deutschland', a loose grouping of opposition littérateurs of diverse political shades. But he was not wholeheartedly with them, though he praised them in *Die Romantische Schule*. Reservations remained. He would relate literature and social effect, but not equate them. Hence his praise of individual Romantic works despite Romanticism's social implications. Conversely he later spurned right-minded 'jungdeutsch' writings for purely literary shortcomings. These men had harnessed their insufficient talents too crudely to their worthy aims. Only half of Heine was their ally; political commitment and poetic standards were divergent allegiances.

Symptom and symbol of this ambivalence is his attitude to Goethe: admiration and reverence for the poet and his achievement, but rejection of the pure aestheticism of the Weimar *Kunstperiode* which now demands to be superseded. Yet the strength of this tradition is what made Heine struggle so long before reaching the solution to his own problems which our hindsight so easily perceives: that he should let the modern social world fully into his verses, but create out of it poetry which would satisfy the highest standards. Even when he had done this, he still confessed to remorse at his desecration of the 'poetic' realm.

From *Atta Troll* (1841), a mock-epic of rich humour and fantasy satirizing the 'jungdeutsch' poets in the figure of an escaped dancing bear, Heine slips into political poetry. *Deutschland, ein Wintermärchen* (1844) is a verse travelogue where Romantic visions and effects are used to new purpose. Polished verse and barbed rhyme capture and transfix target upon target. Heine here aimed to supersede all bombastic *Tendenzpoesie* and render the political ferment of the day, but also to create a classic poem. He did. Aside from the great set-pieces – Cologne Cathedral, Barbarossa, the forest wolves, the Hamburg vision – even in the simplest canto-openings which sketch landscape and travel minutiae before devastation recommences, there is a terse plasticity and the purposeful movement of a splendid mechanism settled in to a major task.

Heine's satire has its crudities (not stylistic). As Saint-Just said, social ills are not cured with rose-water. Thus, monarchy rests on a superstitious respect. Heine accordingly in his shorter poems turns a precisely aimed extreme scurrility on the vices, public and private, of the German princes. The German people are lazy, servile, complacent, philistine: Heine tries with urbane but savage irony to sting them into action. He thought it on the whole unlikely, as Büchner did. They were right, but the failure of 1848 was a blow for Heine. At the same time spinal disease struck him down. Bedridden till his death (1856), he largely withdrew from engagement into a final great poetic phase. Besides personal poems, protesting, sardonic, 'blasphemously religious', unfailingly humorous, never quite despairing – sometimes even totally serious – he also wrote long poetic narratives where all his experience past and present was metamorphosed into a grim vision of Right defeated and Wrong brutally triumphant. The only justice left was poetic justice, his. The subjects are historical, but embody what Nietzsche called 'das Überhistorische' – insight into the essential sameness of phenomena, the everpresence of the typical. Involvement in his times had lifted Heine above them. Embracing the complexities of nineteenth-century existence which others evaded had matured him finally, as a poet.

It was a triumph that Heine remained a poet though a realist, preventing the two terms from becoming a contradiction. Having sieved experience through a modern critical and social awareness, he could still produce poetry – for which the modern imagination need not 'make allowances'. He is a *modern* poet much as Baudelaire is (who admired him) or Brecht (whose aims and effects often recall his). But the precondition for this preservation of poetry in modern conditions was to recognize the problem. Poetic wholeness, Heine wrote in 1828, was a thing of the past, of antiquity or the Middle Ages. It could be honoured, but to imitate it was a lie, since the modern poet was split (*zerrissen*) – necessarily so, because the modern world was split, and the poet's heart is the centrepoint of the world. Whoever claimed his heart was whole, thereby admitted it was a prosaic provincial hideaway heart ('ein prosaisches weitabgelegenes Winkelherz').

This diagnosis provides a perspective for viewing much of nineteenth-century literature. Alongside Heine's 'passionate titanic effort to swim in the mainstream of modern literature', by which Matthew Arnold did not mean mere opportunism, we do indeed find a widespread and resolute provincialism. True, Germany before 1871 *was* provincial, in its politico-geographical fragmentation, whereas Heine lived his mature years in a great capital and centre of change. But provincialism was also a mentality, an acceptance of literary limitation. Of course beauty and poetry do not depend on political institutions, social complexity or 'progress'. Some forms of 'progressive' society might even, as another piece of Heine's complex mind realized, declare poets redundant.) Fine poetry can be written in a narrow range and a limited setting – above all lyrical poetry. Thus Mörike's is exquisite, and not as limited by its overt subject-matter as at first sight appears. So when the Marxist critic Lukács calls Mörike a 'dainty dwarf' in comparison with Heine, one feels he is unjust. Yet he has a point. Part of our framework for judging poetic works is a sense of their implied comprehensiveness – not their monumentality or the amount they pack in, but their openness to the full range of experience their world offers. Even in the inherently limited genre of lyric, the poet can convey a sense of being alive at a given point in time and space on which particular complexities bear, and of having taken them into account. He can choose, alternatively, to retreat into areas where poetry seems more possible, less problematic. But the more he does so, the more likely his work is to be, not second-*rate* (since its quality lies in the relation between the form he finds and the task he set himself) but of the second order. Mörike is a great minor poet. Heine, as even his most adverse critic must admit, was attempting a project of another order of complexity. Limitation and smallness of project is the characteristic of that body of mid-century writing loosely labelled 'poetic realism'. Its formal unambitiousness, if not decisive evidence, is a pointer: the *Novelle* is its commonest medium, and only rarely is the effect one of great things masterfully compressed. Workmanlike miniatures predominate. The cliché that at this period the *Novelle* replaces tragedy is true only mechanically: tragedy stops and the *Novelle* starts, but it is no commensurate substitute. The subjects it treats show similar restrictions. Each writer limits himself to the people, customs, scenery of a region – Stifter Bohemia, Storm Schleswig-Holstein, Droste-Hülshoff Westphalia, Keller and Gotthelf different Swiss communities. (Meyer withdraws totally into a reconstructed historical – mostly Renaissance – décor.) One term will not do for all these depictions, and 'poetic realism' blurs rather than defines the issue; but they do all evoke a quiet, often idyllic way of life still untouched by industrialization and urbanization. They are concrete and precise. Nature and setting are not reduced to Romanticism's suggestive general

concepts – forest, flower, village, house – but specified with the par-
ticularity of a local naturalist or antiquarian. Hence the term 'realism'.
Yet it needs scaling down to fit the case, it refers to realia rather than
an embracing reality. There is no glance beyond the immediate circle
of vision. Droste-Hülshoff's physical short-sightedness seems symbolic.
Against these local backgrounds, odd-men-out are often portrayed –
misfits, occasionally an outstanding man or even a criminal. But the
normality of the background relativizes, sometimes even corrects,
human peculiarity. Hence what we see seems odd rather than tragic.
Keller's story of a village Romeo and Juliet is an exceptional attempt,
claiming full tragic typicality for the humblest figures. Yet even here
the lovers' final fate lies in the insurmountable bourgeois principles in
themselves, a pathetic inner defeat rather than the battle of star-crossed
lovers with hard circumstance. But the attempt itself is significant.
Keller is the one 'poetic realist' who does transcend limitations of
subject and form in a major work.

In his novel *Der grüne Heinrich* (1854–5, totally recast version 1879–80)
the humorous writer of neat moral fables and gentle satires based on
solid Swiss citizenly values is hardly recognizable. Working on autobiographical material, an altogether more complex realism encompasses the full development of an individual. It is a classic *Bildungsroman*: no other draws in so much external reality of place and period,
or shows its hero so deeply involved in error and failure. It is in fact a
novel of *unsuccessful* education, in that Heinrich finally abandons (as
Keller did) his attempt to be a painter. Not only is such failure a recognizable human reality, gratefully tempering the weakness of the
Bildungsroman for optimistic, even utopian solutions; the particular
vocation is itself significant. 'The artist' no longer has the almost
mystical fascination he had as the hero of Romantic novels, which
were Keller's initial model; nor is he, as so often in twentieth-century
writing, simply the one subject left to the artistic imagination that can
get no purchase on anything outside itself. For Keller, the artist's
training is both a real and a symbolic extension of man's wish and
duty of seeing true and acting right. Heinrich's results are as indifferent
in the art of life as they are in art. He exploits his impoverished widowed
mother without thinking or caring. Her death just as he returns home
forestalls any amends. He has failed to know her value in time. More
forgivably, his immature emotions confuse a real and an illusory
romantic love, and the real one is lost to him. Life is trial and error, but
the errors are not reparable. The presentation of action and moral is a

tour de force. The first-person narrator has just enough retrospective distance subtly to imply the standards his acting self fell short of. Judgement and remorse colour the account of his actions and feelings without openly moralizing. An integrated dual perspective does justice to major issues – love, loyalty, integrity – without losing sympathy for Heinrich. Equal narrative justice is done to the characters, especially women: Heinrich's mother, selflessly devoted and ill rewarded, is a superb portrait; and Judith, a passionate, mature woman of character and sensibility, is the first fully and sensuously live heroine to occur in a *Bildungsroman*, where female figures tend to a pale ideality. The powerful forces Judith embodies are a further guarantee of the completeness and reality of Keller's world. The Swiss background too can be evoked exhaustively in the novel's broader scope, no longer with the half-caricatural, half fairytale quality of his *Novellen*. The country scenes are saturated visions, set off by contrast with Heinrich's Zürich home; they are also, to his town present, the long family past. For unlike Wilhelm Meister and Stifter's hero, he has deep peasant roots set as his opening chapter tells in the mould of generations. Continuity is thus unbroken, for Heinrich's childhood is also fully narrated. (Meister's was only recalled in manhood, Stifter significantly leaves problematic childhood untouched.) We thus know Heinrich literally as a grown man, his nature is a living product of many forces.

Aside from a thinnish late episode in a nobleman's castle, there are few superficial reminders of Goethe; but he is more deeply present than in Stifter, who even names his ideal heroine after Meister's ideal bride. In *Nachsommer*, the young might read some of Goethe; Keller's Heinrich devours the complete works in forty days. His sense of Goethe's love for grown things and their history, for the self-sufficient right and significance each has, his recognition of Goethe's grasp on a world of wholeness and reality – these become a touchstone for him, a curb on the irresponsibility of imagination. This is an inheriting of the spirit rather than an appropriation of externals. Keller was aware that true inheriting and continuing was a delicate task. He wrote in 1851 that the classical texts would not do for modern needs, that art must now necessarily exclude materials and methods familiar to the classical age and include others it never knew. Ultimate aims were all that could be taken over, the essential core inside changed externals. As Goethe wrote in the *Wanderjahre*: 'Das Leben gehört den Lebendigen an, und wer lebt, muß auf Wechsel gefaßt sein.'

Keller's realism is a mature fulfilment. If it has limitations from a

German point of view, they are not literary. They lie in his foreignness. His achievement, like his liberal-democratic optimism, rests on his Swiss traditions and conditions. As a social foundation, these are adequate – that much *Der grüne Heinrich* proves – to support a major novel. This relationship between society and the novel as cause and effect is hard to measure but difficult to ignore. If the absence of great German novels to match nineteenth-century English, French and Russian work is not related to the nature (or virtual absence) of a German society in the national sense, then it is a very strange coincidence. And equally strange, then, is the coincidence that Germany's first social realist who stands comparison with writers of the European mainstream, Theodor Fontane, wrote precisely in the decades following Germany's unification, when along with the social substructure German attitudes had begun to change profoundly.

And yet Fontane hardly wrote a novel which did not concentrate on one intimately known area of geography and humanity – Prussia, the Mark Brandenburg and Berlin. This might seem as circumscribed as any 'poetic realist' subject-matter. But it proves not. First of all, Berlin (which Heine thought hardly a place) is now a great city with the social complexity to challenge and nourish a novelist. More important, Prussia is now not just another region, but the major force in the new Germany. If Germany is 'in the saddle' as Bismarck said, it is Prussia holds the reins. This gives Fontane's novels an added dimension – in our perspective, but also in his own. He could not but be conscious that the ethos he analysed and the people he drew were actors on a broader stage than his. The landscapes of Goethe's novels are unidentifiable, the noblemen's estates disconnected from the wider world. The old Junkers Fontane so richly portrays are Prussians to their fingerends, their sons officers who served at Königgrätz or Sedan. Even if no such mention is made, resonances from a larger world cannot be silenced – much as the small, peaceful societies of Jane Austen hint at the stability of a great European power, whose soldiers and sailors appear (apart from the Portsmouth episode of *Mansfield Park*) only as romantic leads.

But Fontane was not Prussia's eulogist or apologist. Even when lovingly recalling the past in his delightful *Wanderungen durch die Mark Brandenburg*, he speaks of Prussia as equally deserving of love and hate. And his attitudes in the novels (which he began writing, incidentally, only late in life) are just as complex; not surprisingly, since 'Prussia' could mean humanely traditional old Junkers in their country retreats

(*Der Stechlin*, 1897), officers of the smart regiments in their Berlin clubs (*Irrungen Wirrungen*, 1887), the higher administration (*Effi Briest*, 1894), the simple artisan people in their suburbs (*Irrungen Wirrungen*, *Stine*, 1890) or the rising bourgeois vulgar (*Frau Jenny Treibel*, 1892). On the whole Fontane is critical, but hardly in a way that makes it easy for readers or critics eagerly oriented towards 'social criticism' to extract a clear, emphatic message. Life has too many shades of grey between black and white for that, and no partisan truth is certain enough to be allowed to shout down art, which lives by complexity. At root, Fontane appreciates Prussian qualities but mistrusts Prussian pretensions. Prussia is playing a dubious role, which he watches with mixed fascination and misgiving. Victory and power do not in themselves convince him. Like Nietzsche, whose violent criticisms of the Reich he echoes with more delicate instrumentation, Fontane doubted whether military superiority proved cultural worth, and wondered if the real Germany had not lain elsewhere – in the freedom of the Hansa towns and independent *Reichsstädte*, in German culture, perhaps even now in the humane character of ordinary people, untouched by hard *Realpolitik*. His first mature novel, *Schach von Wuthenow* (1882), even tried to link by as direct an innuendo as a novelist dare use the Prussian defeat in 1806 and the human failings of the Prussian code. But this correspondence was too simple. How could history be thus the Last Judgement on ethics, when Prussia, with its rigid code unchanged, was now in the ascendant? A more complex task waited: to analyse, lay bare, criticize, unobtrusively but in the end unequivocally. The demands of this task, the responsibility – artistic as much as social – which it imposed, are what separate Fontane from his predecessors and make a major achievement possible.

They do not automatically make it actual. But for this the means were forthcoming, vastly more sophisticated than any the German nineteenth century had yet seen. Fontane's immediate realism bears comparison with the French: Maupassant, Flaubert, the Goncourts. In particular, no novelist ever wrote more perfect dialogue. But a bit below the seemingly casual surface, trivial actions and snippets of talk, plausible in themselves, make a weave of allusion and precise reference – to literature, to popular saying or song. The touch is of the lightest, never heavily 'symbolic' or a coy demonstration of culture, as later in Thomas Mann. But if the point is taken, it vastly enriches our understanding of character and situation. These at a deeper level Fontane subtly disposes so as to create from the impulses and failings of fully realized individuals a pattern of social constants. These are his major themes: society's self-preservation and the tyranny of its conventions; the naturalness of feeling and the rightness of what is natural. Even deeper yet, purely formal patterns show through, the artist's matrix in which 'issues' are set. The opposing forces in an action may appear in a single episode at the novel's centre (*Irrungen Wirrungen*), scaled down to the concretely natural, yet deftly grasping the general in the particular. This is near to Goethe's ideal of the symbol as something which conveys a larger meaning yet remains wholly itself. As Fontane himself wrote of Gerhart Hauptmann's scandalous first play: what the layman takes for a straightforward copying of life conceals an extreme degree of art.

As a critic, Fontane seems gentle, his tone seldom sharp. It is sometimes said he should not have been so tolerant of the Prussia he saw; sometimes (consolingly) that he became less so with time, or that his letters are more explicit than his fiction. But is explicitness a value? It does not necessarily enhance novels, and criticism may actually lose by being vehement. It is precisely the calm, mature tone of a tolerant man that guarantees the truth of what he paints and makes it strike home more effectively than rage and rhetoric. His very tolerance can be withering. Ironically, it is often Fontane's own picture of Prussia that provokes the outcry against it and against his gentleness. This is a tribute both to his humanity and to his tactics.

Fontane's perceptive tolerance even extended (something uncommon among writers) to the rising literary generation. He punningly acclaimed the 'Hauptmann der schwarzen Realistenbande' and cautiously prophesied a future for this uncompromising new approach when most critics were mocking or outraged. But this time the advent of a new phase, programmatic naturalism, was also the advent of a distinctively modern literary age. The tempo of cultural life changes, centred as it is increasingly on cities and affected by the problems (not to mention the techniques) of mass industrial society. 'Movements' differ more radically from each other and succeed each other faster as writers seek ways of expressing or even just asserting themselves in a world where literature, as process and as product, seems more and more problematic. Something Hugo von Hoftmannsthal said in 1923 exactly sums up this feverish pursuit of novelty and uneasy relationship with modern life: 'Die Epochen werden immer kürzer, die Zeit ist reißend geworden. Einst schufen die Dichter das Lebensgefühl ganzer Zeitalter, heute erhascht die Generation nur noch Fragmente.' His words return us to the themes of tradition and continuity with which, beneath the discussion of individual works and writers, this chapter has been concerned.

Bibliography

The following are suggested as further reading because they offer (i) perspective, (ii) stimulus, (iii) an English text.

Two kinds of general survey are an invaluable basis for understanding the eighteenth-century phase of German literature. W. H. Bruford's *Germany in the Eighteenth Century: the Social Background of the Literary Revival* (Cambridge, 1935, and frequent reprints), and its essential continuation *Culture and Society in Classical Weimar 1775–1806* (Cambridge, 1962) amply document and analyse the relationship of literature to social and political realities; while E. A. Blackall's *The Emergence of German as a Literary Language 1700–1775* (Cambridge, 1959) is a fruitful attempt to study together the developments of the German language in the eighteenth century and the growth of expressive power in literature which they made possible.

The achievements and shortcomings of the resultant new literature, and of its later nineteenth-century developments, are shown in a different light in chapter 17 of Erich Auerbach's masterly *Mimesis: the Representation of Reality in Western Literature* (transl. Princeton, 1953). Auerbach's concise argument, which outweighs many more massive discussions, places German work in its European context and assesses the nature of its response to modern, especially social, reality. The approach stops well short of dissolving literature into socio-political considerations, as is the practice of the Marxist critic Georg Lukács, whose works are wide-ranging and forceful, but subordinate accuracy of interpretation and documentation to the demands of unbudgeable dogmatic presuppositions. Nevertheless, there is much of interest in his *The Historical Novel* (transl. London, 1962) and *Goethe and his Age* (transl. London, 1968). Even more interesting on the political repercussions of cultural developments is Hans Kohn's *The Mind of Germany* (London, 1961) which does not purport to be literary criticism but relates literary evidence to other materials on German attitudes, establishing a coherent and convincingly documented picture.

A different borderland of literature, that with ideas and existential attitudes, is inhabited by Erich Heller's essays on the period from Goethe to modern times, collected in *The Disinherited Mind* (Cambridge, 1952) and *The Artist's Journey into the Interior* (London, 1966). These have their mannerisms but are always stimulating. The same writer has attempted a synthesis of modern European developments in the chapter on 'Imaginative Literature 1830–1870' of the *Cambridge Modern History*, Vol. X, 1960. A perceptive account of this period in German literature, which has many felicities in the treatment of individual writers, is Norbert Fuerst's *The Victorian Age in German Literature* (London, 1966).

There are not many outstanding monographs in English on authors of the period. For Goethe and Schiller, one can do worse than start with the Victorian biographers. Carlyle's *Life of Schiller* and George Henry Lewes's *Life and Works of Goethe* (the latter still in print in the Everyman Library) may be superseded in detail, but they do at least have and convey a feeling for the sheer stature of their subjects which has sometimes eluded later critics. Of modern work, Barker Fairley's *A Study of Goethe* (Oxford, 1947) most adequately grasps Goethe's spiritual complexities; and E. L. Stahl's *Friedrich Schiller, Dramatic Theory and Practice* (Oxford, 1954) is a lucid account. Of nineteenth-century writers, Heine has captured most English attention, beginning with Matthew Arnold and George Eliot, whose essays on him are still well worth reading. William Rose, E. M. Butler, Barker Fairley and S. S. Prawer have all made valuable contributions. Brief accounts of several of the authors discussed can be found in Michael Hamburger, *Reason and Energy* (London, 1957) and in J. P. Stern, *Reinterpretations* (London, 1964).

10 Modern German Literature

MALCOLM PASLEY

The beginnings of modern literature in Germany can be understood as a multiple hostile response to the booming, expansionist Second Empire under William II (emperor 1888–1918). Some writers were chiefly offended by the brashness and materialism of the epoch, others by the ugliness or distress attendant on the rapid growth of industry and towns. But all were agreed in condemning the hollow cultural ideals and moral values of the established order. German literature of the Wilhelmine period, by contrast to the literature of the preceding decades, displays vigorous opposition to the social and cultural *status quo*.

The most radical and influential assault on existing German culture was made by Friedrich Nietzsche, who styled himself 'the first immoralist' and undertook a 'transvaluation of all values' ('Umwertung aller Werte'). His life as a thinker presents a grandiose and disturbing drama, in which ruthless intellectual honesty struggled with the deepest emotional, religious and poetic needs. At great cost to himself he stripped away the supposedly false casing of accepted ideals and beliefs, in order to lay bare the hard and distasteful facts of existence. And he considered that these hard facts, unblinkingly confronted, offered the greatest challenge to man's will or vital energy and the greatest spur to a heroic affirmation of life. Nietzsche's mode of thought was dialectic: man could only ascend to the heights of 'yea-saying' if he had first plumbed the depths of nihilism; he could achieve the highest form of health only by assimilating the maximum of poison, sickness, decadence; not until he had 'swallowed' the fact that life and the world had no objective meaning or value was he truly free to attach his own meanings and values, and to exult in them. The greater the intellectual and emotional obstacles which the individual had to surmount, the more was his sense of power and freedom enhanced; by such means he could surpass or 'overcome' himself ('Selbstüberwindung') and become the prototype of a higher kind of man ('Übermensch'). For German writers after 1885

Nietzsche was 'das Erdbeben unserer Epoche' (Gottfried Benn). The whole course of modern German literature was profoundly affected by his aristocratic individualism, by his critique of 'decadent' Romantic idealism, by his attempt to 'overcome' morality and go 'beyond good and evil' with the aid of aesthetic and biological concepts, and by his preaching of the gospel of strength and self-enhancement to replace Christ's Gospel of compassion and selflessness. All those authors who assaulted the false moral façade of Wilhelm's Germany could call on Nietzsche's name – even the naturalists, whose social conscience and scientific pretensions he would have so greatly despised.

Naturalism 1885–1895

The chief slogan of the new movement was 'Naturalismus', following Zola's use of the term 'naturalisme'. In this so-called *Revolution der Litteratur* (title of a book by Carl Bleibtreu, 1886) many grand programmes for a more 'modern' and more 'realistic' literature were produced, but few works of lasting merit to match them.

The theorists of naturalism observed correctly that German literature had failed, by comparison with that of France, Norway and Russia, to keep pace with the great mid-nineteenth-century changes in both thought and society, and they called on German writers to treat contemporary subject-matter in an open and fearless way. In conformity with Nietzsche and Ibsen they wanted literature to be straight and tough, puncturing illusory values, and refusing to blink the unpalatable truths which the natural sciences were then delivering, especially in the biological field. A work was deemed meritorious in the measure that it faced the gloomier and seamier sides of life, which had become more obvious as a result of the rapid industrialization of society. Zola's chronicle of a family's decay (in the cycle of novels *Les Rougon-Macquart*) was a favoured model in this respect.

German naturalist theory was propounded in Munich and Berlin. In Munich M. G. Conrad founded the periodical *Die Gesellschaft* (1885–1902), as 'ein Organ . . . der resolut realistischen Weltauffassung'. It propagated ideas for social reform generally (e.g. emancipation of women), but reform of literature took chief place. It was common ground that the poet's first task was to reproduce contemporary social reality (understood as the product of the operation of determinable laws) as faithfully as possible. But there was dispute as to whether literature itself could properly be regarded as a form of scientific investigation, and – if so – whether it did not betray its own principles if it inspected man too exclusively from a physiological point of view. A related point of argument was whether Zola and his imitators had gone too far in selecting ugly and swinish aspects of human life for their reproductions, and hence failed to render a truthful picture. At the bottom of these often arid debates lay the central issue of naturalist literature: should the literary artist merely report social fact, or should he positively encourage social change? In the latter case he plainly required, whether or not he acknowledged the fact, a moral and political philosophy. There was one current assumption which exposed naturalist doctrine to justified ridicule: it was that all personal value-judgements had been somehow rendered obsolete by advances in scientific knowledge. The post-naturalist generation, affected by the aristocratic individualism of the late Nietzsche, was to challenge this assumption with the greatest fervour.

In Berlin, an important organ of naturalist theory was the periodical *Freie Bühne für modernes Leben* (founded in 1890). While sympathizing with naturalism it refused to tie itself down to an exclusively naturalist aesthetic programme; hence it remained adaptable to new developments, and still survives as *Die Neue Rundschau*. More international and less doctrinaire in its attitudes than *Die Gesellschaft*, it praised the modern Scandinavian authors (Ibsen, Björnsen, Strindberg) to the neglect of the Munich naturalists (Bleibtreu, Alberti, Conrad). Its special preoccupation was drama, as the art-form best suited to create a powerful illusion of objective reality, and its first editor – Otto Brahm – was an outstanding theatrical director. In 1889 he had founded with others the theatre club of the same name (Freie Bühne), which put on for its members private productions of naturalist plays, beginning with Ibsen's *Ghosts*. The Berlin theorist Arno Holz called for a type of naturalism ('konsequenter Naturalismus') more rigorous and more consistent than Zola's; he believed that this could only be achieved by adopting a doggedly chronological technique of reproduction ('Sekundenstil'). In practice this meant trying to imitate as accurately as possible the flow of ordinary talk, with no triviality spared. Examples of this technique furnished by Holz himself, in collaboration with Johannes Schlaf, remain mere curiosities (*Papa Hamlet*, 1889; *Die Familie Selicke*, 1890), but they encouraged Gerhart Hauptmann to use the new style effectively.

Hauptmann's *Vor Sonnenaufgang* (1889), sub-titled 'Soziales Drama', had a highly topical theme: the moral disruption caused by rapid economic change. The play presents a dismal picture of moral decay in a farming family, as a direct result of the sudden exploitation of coal deposits on their land. To this was added another fashionable theme, that of the hereditary 'curse' (here, the tendency to alcoholism), the transmission of the effects of depravity to innocent offspring. But the play deals primarily with an entirely traditional private dilemma: the central figure, a social reformer, has to choose between the claims of utopian idealism and the claims of personal affection (cf. Schiller's *Don Carlos*). Against this *Die Weber* (1892), a dramatization of the Silesian weavers' revolt of 1844, was a genuinely 'social drama': it took the suffering and fate of a whole social group, not an individual, as its subject. As an experiment in bringing social and political issues before an audience without recourse to a personal hero as intermediary, it is certainly a landmark in the history of modern drama. More importantly it showed – and this was something which despite the plays of Lenz, the young Schiller and Büchner had not been clearly apparent in Germany before – that the theatre could be an effective instrument of social and political change. The political impact of the play can be gauged from the debate of 21 February 1895 in the Prussian parliament. *Die Weber* achieved this impact precisely because it followed the naturalist recipe of apparent objectivity, and was not an overtly tendentious work. It was probably also an advantage that Hauptmann himself was not deeply interested in the reform of society, as his subsequent career made plain.

Evidently the cruder versions of naturalist mimetic theory (e.g. Holz's dictum 'die Kunst hat die Tendenz, wieder die Natur zu sein') betray a total misunderstanding of art. But it is too easy to dismiss the whole movement on this account. For it performed a most valuable function in helping to anchor imaginative literature in the carefully observed detail of the physical world; it sharpened the eyes of poets to the characteristic features of men and things. Hofmannsthal praised the work of Holz in 1893 by saying: 'jeder Strich charakterisiert, begrenzt, schafft plastische, springende Gestalt'.

Non-Naturalistic Literature 1890–1914: Aestheticist and Neo-Romantic Trends

Despite the noise and heat generated by the theorists of naturalism, German literature took a course very different from the one they proposed. The turn of the century is marked by a strong upsurge of artistic and religious impulses. The influence of positivist, scientific thinking proved short-lived, giving way to a variety of idealist and irrationalist creeds. Generally speaking, social and political realities dropped from view and writers turned their attention to exploring the creative resources of the human personality.

In a few cases, notably that of Frank Wedekind, it is proper to speak of a deliberate reaction against the naturalists' literary assumptions and techniques. In his early comedy *Die junge Welt* (first entitled *Kinder und Narren*, 1891) Wedekind mocks their so-called 'Notizbuchmethode', the mechanical imitation of external detail: the heroine declares that when the vogue for this kind of realism is over its practitioners will be able to earn their living in the secret police. His own technique was by contrast one of grotesque exaggeration and caricature, as can be seen in his satirical portraits of the schoolmasters in his most famous play, *Frühlings Erwachen* (1891). This is a tragedy of puberty, which romanticizes natural instinct and assaults the blindness and hypocrisy of the bourgeoisie in the matter of sex education. A schoolboy commits suicide; a schoolgirl dies of an abortion, and her death is politely ascribed to anaemia. (The theme of 'unnatural' education is the only predominantly social theme which receives regular literary treatment during these years.) Formally, *Frühlings Erwachen* is an illogical scene sequence, reminiscent of Lenz and Büchner, which reveals the action in an episodic and piecemeal way: the most striking affront to mimetic drama is the final scene, in which the suicide appears with his head underneath his arm and the hero is led out of the graveyard by a symbolic figure representing life. The language is a curious mixture of lyricism, brutality and philosophical rhetoric. It is mainly on the strength of this play, and of the Grand Guignol horror-plays *Erdgeist* (1895) and *Die Büchse der Pandora* (1904), that Wedekind is regarded as a precursor of expressionist drama.

The driving force behind Wedekind's work was certainly his hatred of conventional bourgeois attitudes. His sympathies lay not with the proletariat, but with bohemian types and robust scoundrels on the borders of society who were not ashamed of their natural instincts. Some of his work seems mere cynical clowning (e.g. the 'sick' ballad 'Ich hab meine Tante geschlachtet'), but at bottom his 'immoralism' was – like Nietzsche's – his way of expressing a profoundly moral distaste for sham ideals. In this respect, as in his choice of underworld characters and the aggressive toughness of his poetic style, he has much in common with the early Brecht. Wedekind was the great theatrical figure of his day in Munich, and he evidently made a powerful impression when performing his own work as actor and cabaret-singer. But without the support of his live personality most of his writing, which is above all declamatory, seems painfully crude and strained on the printed page. Wedekind was an embattled advocate of the socially nonconformist 'artistic' mode of life. Thomas Mann, who had one foot in the artistic world and the other foot in the *Bürgertum*, made the relation between the two his special theme, and he explored this over a long period in his carefully wrought ironical prose. One might think that the artist–society relationship was pre-eminently a social or even an economic question, but that was not how Thomas Mann saw it. He saw it as a philosophical question, which involved wide-ranging metaphysical speculations about life and spirit, health and sickness. For this reason alone his work must be considered under the heading of 'non-naturalistic literature', despite its obviously mimetic quality and its apparent social concerns, and despite the fact that he himself described *Buddenbrooks* (1901) as a 'naturalistic novel'. 'Das Sozialkritische gehört durchaus nicht zu meinen Passionen,' he declared in 1923.

Buddenbrooks traces the decay of a Lübeck patrician family in the latter part of the nineteenth century, and it draws extensively on Mann's own family history. It can certainly be enjoyed simply as a realistic novel of manners, but its true *raison d'être* lies in its grand philosophical thesis that art and knowledge are the enemies of morality and life. Both the vital energy and the solid practical morality of the Buddenbrooks are progressively eaten away from within by artistic and reflective impulses. The last but one in the line, Thomas Buddenbrook, struggles manfully to resist this inner decay and put a bold front on it, while his frail son Hanno – a mere vessel of artistic sensitivity – quite lacks the will to live. The manner of their respective deaths is symbolic: Thomas fails to survive the extraction of his rotten teeth and Hanno is swept away unresistingly by a wasting fever. Mann's careful insistence on significant physical details, until they become transparent indicators of inner states and processes, is his most striking and consistent literary device. He belongs here squarely in the nineteenth-century tradition of imaginative German prose writing (Goethe's *Die Wahlverwandtschaften*, Storm, Keller), to which he adds his personal note by concentrating on the processes of decay and dissolution (e.g. *Tristan*, 1903; *Der Tod in Venedig*, 1912; *Der Zauberberg*, 1924; *Die Betrogene*, 1953).

It can be argued against Thomas Mann that much of his work (in particular the later novels *Der Zauberberg*, *Joseph und seine Brüder*,

1933–43, and *Doktor Faustus*, 1947) is overweighted with philosophy and with the ballast of intellectual and cultural history, that his mental play with antithetical pairs of abstractions ('Geist' and 'Leben', 'Künstler' and 'Bürger', 'Kultur' and 'Zivilisation', etc.) led him too far away from the observable facts of the modern world, and that his attempt simultaneously to preserve and deflate the traditional form and style of narrative literature was ultimately self-defeating. But the lucid and intelligent power of his best stories is beyond dispute.

The underlying preoccupation of Thomas Mann's work, especially in the pre-1914 years, was the analysis – and the justification – of his own form of artistic talent, his own particular mode of artistic life. He located this not at the pole of 'pure art' or aestheticism, nor at the pole of unreflective life and solid burgher virtue, but midway between the two. In *Tristan* he caricatures the inhabitants of the two poles in the figures of Detlev Spinell and Herr Klöterjahn respectively, whilst in *Tonio Kröger* (1903) he presents a version of his own case: a young literary artist who is neither an aesthete nor a plain worthy citizen. 'Ich stehe zwischen zwei Welten, bin in keiner daheim und habe es infolge dessen ein wenig schwer. Ihr Künstler nennt mich einen Bürger, und die Bürger sind versucht, mich zu verhaften.' Mann came to believe that the apparent curse of his estrangement from both camps was really a disguised blessing, for it permitted him to practise an ironical and conservative kind of art which had an important mediating and humanizing function.

Thomas Mann's distrust of pure aestheticism, supposedly inherited from his father, was strengthened by Nietzsche's critique of the artist as a sly trickster, an empty and decadent showman (cf. *Bekenntnisse des Hochstaplers Felix Krull*, 1954, of which the first and best part appeared in 1922). However, Nietzsche the critic of bogus artists was much less generally influential than Nietzsche the champion of aesthetic against moral values. The many writers who glorified the aesthetic mode of living in the 1890s called readily on his name, often blurring the fundamental distinction he made between the 'healthy' and the 'decadent'. For Nietzsche could only approve that style of life and that kind of art which seemed to him to express a triumphant overflow of vital strength, or at least – in these poor modern times – a decisive surplus of life-affirming over life-denying impulses. Whoever cultivated the strong and the beautiful merely as a cloak or compensation for inner weakness remained for him, like the hero of Heinrich Mann's *Pippo Spano* (1905), a 'steckengebliebener Komödiant'.

The most uncompromising upholder of the primacy of aesthetic values was the poet Stefan George, who founded the periodical *Blätter für die Kunst* in 1892 as an organ of his cultural policy. In polemical opposition to naturalism ('das formlose plebejertum der wirklich-keitsapostel') the *Blätter* adopted a pose of haughty refinement, offering poetry of great technical perfection for the benefit of the cultivated few. The lyric poem was held to be the highest form of literary art; narrative writing was suspect because it had become confused with mere reporting on reality, dramatic writing because it was inclined to cater for the vulgar herd. According to the doctrine of the *Blätter* the true poet stood above morality, giving beautiful expression to his moods, and evoking spiritual reality by means of suggestive images and sound-effects. George, an admirer of Mallarmé, declared that art must be approached 'mit ernst und heiligkeit': the tone of sacerdotal solemnity which he set in the *Blätter* informed his own books of poetry as well (e.g. *Hymnen, Pilgerfahrten, Algabal*, 1890–2, *Das Jahr der Seele*, 1897). His rigorous pursuit of formal beauty extended to matters of typography and book production, and the aestheticist movement in Germany, as in England, gave great impetus to bibliophile publishing and elegant book-design.

Inspired by French symbolist example, George produced an entirely new kind of German lyric poetry which kept its distance from personal experience and helped to discredit the popular and sentimental imitations of Romantic song. But the extreme self-importance and self-regard which informs his poems makes them harder to appreciate than, say, the poems of Baudelaire or Verlaine. In his case the style is very much the man, and the man – though greatly venerated – is not easy to like. His early collection *Hymnen* (1890) goes out of its way to rebuff the reader who is looking for the easily likeable. These poems are not really 'about' anything except the poetic activity itself, which is represented as sacred: strict in form, deliberately dense and difficult in their vocabulary and syntax, they challenge us to admire them as a triumph of pure artistry. *Algabal* (1892), a masterpiece of German aestheticism, celebrates sumptuous artificiality and evil, and draws on the stock-in-trade of the French 'decadents' (an underground palace, metallic gardens, suave ruthlessness, and the cultivation of a black flower). By glorifying the self-indulgence of a ruler of the decaying Roman Empire George was delivering a calculated affront to the ethos and culture of Wilhelmine Germany, which as a disciple of Nietzsche he found lumpish and plebeian. This was not 'art for art's sake' so much as art for the sake of its own supremacy over the materialism and rationalism of modern civilization. That is to say, even the early collections, which seem to congratulate themselves on their beautiful purposelessness, contain an implicit doctrine, and this doctrine becomes increasingly explicit in the later work as George turns to poetry of a more didactic and prophetic character (*Der siebente Ring, Der Stern des Bundes, Das neue Reich*). Only through attachment to aesthetic values could Europe (and Germany in particular) be saved and regenerated, only by this means could man recover his lost dignity and reassure himself of his undying grandeur as a spiritual being.

George was convinced that he had a mission to usher in a new 'spiritual empire' ('geistiges Reich'). His method was to gather round him a circle of disciples, mould them to his taste by the example of his own style of life and poetry, indoctrinate them and chastise them where necessary, until they were fit to leaven the great lump of the German people. The 'George-Kreis' had something in common with a secret society and something in common with a monastic order, though it was never a formally constituted community nor even a very coherent one from the doctrinal point of view. George was at pains to guard against the profanation of his ideal of 'the beautiful life' ('das schöne Leben'), and a strong thread of the esoteric and the clandestine runs through his work. In his youth he had invented a private language; the structure of many of his collections and of their individual parts has hidden significance (magic numbers, acrostics, etc.); his later poems, one of which is entitled 'Geheimes Deutschland', are full of secret allusions.

The members of George's Circle did not achieve great distinction as poets, but certain of them disseminated the philosophy of the group by writing books about great figures of the past. Friedrich Gundolf's *Goethe*, Ernst Bertram's *Nietzsche*, Max Kommerell's *Der Dichter als Führer in der deutschen Klassik*, Ernst Kantorowicz's *Friedrich II* reached a wide public. These books exemplified the belief that all preoccupation with the past is sterile unless it brings home to us the values incarnate in the life and work of superior personalities. According to the doctrine of the Circle both criticism and historicism were pernicious; the only valuable kind of history was what Nietzsche called 'monumentalizing' history, the raising of history to the plane of myth. George's disciples declared open war on the whole late nineteenth-century tradition of historical–critical scholarship, and their mythologizing method set a dangerous precedent.

The greatest literary figure among George's adherents, Hugo von

Hofmannsthal, parted company with the 'Master' in 1906 and was never properly speaking a member of the Circle. George sought him out in Vienna in 1891 (when he was eighteen) and encouraged him in his belief that a renewal of German poetry was possible – that it was possible to achieve something in German comparable with the work of 'the great Englishmen from Keats onwards' and at the same time related to the 'great forms of Romance poetry' (as he explains in a letter written shortly before his death in 1929). In other words he felt a certain initial kinship of poetic sensibility and ambition with the older man. But he soon came to find George's habits too autocratic and his attitudes too exclusive and pretentious. Deeply immersed in poetry as he was, Hofmannsthal still recognized that one could be a civilized man without attaching prime importance to it. For George such an opinion was serious heresy. From the moment when Hofmannsthal introduced a friend of his to George (in 1896) with the remark: 'Er gehört völlig dem Leben an, keiner Kunst', it was plain that their views of the relationship of life and art could not be reconciled. But it was in their attitudes towards literary and cultural tradition that they diverged most sharply. While George wished to found a new 'empire', merely drawing inspiration from the great figures of the past, Hofmannsthal considered himself rather as a guardian and gentle transformer of Europe's spiritual and artistic heritage. This fundamental divergence was not simply a matter of temperament but also a matter of geographical origin. Hofmannsthal's work is rooted in Vienna and it belongs essentially to the declining Austrian Empire.

In opening this survey I pointed out that the beginnings of modern literature in Germany were marked by a belligerent disapproval of culture and society in the newly founded Reich. This aggressive hostility to the *status quo* was displayed by almost all the writers who were the subjects of Kaiser Wilhelm, whether they belonged to the naturalist or to the aestheticist camp. However strong their mutual dislikes and however irreconcilable their programmes they were united by their combative tone. But this fierceness of tone was not shared by the Austrian writers of the nineties. The cliché of an elegant, sceptical, frivolous, world-weary, at once gay and melanchony Vienna at that time contains much truth. The mood of the old and over-ripe Empire was quite different from that of the young and ambitious one. The tensions created for writers and artists by industrial expansion, and by the take-over bid of the natural sciences in all spheres of human activity, were far less strong in Austria than they were in Germany. The conditions for a naturalist literary movement barely existed there: equally there was no need for Austrian writers to proclaim the importance of aesthetic values with the desperate insistence of Stefan George. Being less preoccupied with waging war on the philistines, they could turn their attention to capturing the mood of the time in an impressionistic manner, or to the refined exploration of their own sentiments (pursuing what Hofmannsthal called 'the bacteriology of the soul').

For Hofmannsthal the aesthetic mode of life was not an ideal to be defiantly propagated as it was for George, but rather an inherited reality. It was to be savoured fully – but also increasingly to be deplored, in its extremer forms, from the standpoint of morality. When George chose to glorify the aesthetic flowering of the decadent Roman Empire in *Algabal* he was choosing a stock to lambast the German bourgeoisie. Hofmannsthal, on the other hand, felt a natural affinity with the world of Walter Pater's *Marius The Epicurean,* and yet that book merely confirmed his growing conviction that a purely aesthetic philosophy was not enough to build one's life upon. He is, in his early works, the most graceful exponent of aestheticism in German literature, but he is also – with Thomas Mann – one of its sharpest moral critics. In a letter of 1894 he speaks of his attempt 'von dem etwas leeren Ästhetizismus ins Menschlich-Sittliche hinüberzulenken', and his critique of the sterile self-absorption associated with an exclusively aesthetic mode of life is implicit in his earliest lyrical dramas (*Gestern,* 1890; *Der Tor und der Tod,* 1892).

For a long time Hofmannsthal was admired or condemned on the strength of his youthful work, the verses and poetic prose which reflect so perfectly the refined sensitivity of the *fin de siècle.* There is indeed something cloying about many of these products: in an essay on one of George's early collections he writes, 'Wir sind in einem Hain, den wie eine Insel die kühlen Abgründe ungeheueren Schweigens von den Wegen der Menschen abtrennen ... Hier nun redet die hochgezogene Seele eines Dichters.' This is the choice and fruity tone of aestheticism, which stern critics find positively repellent. On the other hand the best of his poems and poetic playlets are beyond criticism in their kind; they seem to show an instinctive mastery of poetic forms and of all the evocative resources of the German language. Hofmannsthal himself attributed his 'magical' power over words to a sense of mystical union between the self and the world, a childlike feeling of identification with all things. He called this dreamy condition, which was for him the fount of all lyrical expression, the state of 'pre-existence' and he soon came to recognize that it was both impossible and undesirable to prolong it far into adult life. The passing of this 'pre-existent' stage, and of the command of poetic language it assured, provoked a crisis in his life at the turn of the century. He felt like a magician who had lost his touch. No longer sure of his poetic control over reality he felt incompetent to assess it by using language in an evaluative manner. He became obsessed by the fear that he had no right 'überhaupt die Worte mit denen wir Werte bezeichnen, in den Mund zu nehmen' (letter to George in 1896). The crisis was overcome by his renouncing purely lyrical expression altogether and devoting himself, after 1900, to works of more popular, theatrical appeal and instructional character (*Der Rosenkavalier*, 1911; *Jedermann*, 1911). His turning to theatrical forms, especially to opera in collaboration with Richard Strauss, followed logically from his new conviction that the poetic word required external support if it was to succeed in its serious task of enhancing the quality of life and sustaining what was best in European culture. But he did not find popularization easy. Strauss was at first quite befogged by the libretto *Ariadne auf Naxos* (1912), with its ironic mixture of the comic and the heroic style, and there was something forced and stagey about the Salzburg Festivals which Hofmannsthal helped to found in 1919. In the fine comedy *Der Schwierige* (1921) he treats again the difficulty which chiefly beset him: the difficulty of social communication and involvement for a man who has been granted the doubtful gift of insight through introversion.

In the Austria of the 1890s, for the subjects of the ageing emperor Franz Josef, a major theme was the weight of the past: the burden of personal memories, or that of an over-long and over-rich tradition. In Arthur Schnitzler's *Anatol* (1891) the weak and self-indulgent hero is oppressed by a heavy load of 'undigested past' ('unverarbeitete Vergangenheit'). Exploring this theme as a medical scientist Sigmund Freud showed how such burdens, carried at an unconscious level of the mind, could lead to neurosis. Hofmannsthal himself, who was strongly aware of being a 'Spätgeborener', returns constantly to the idea that the stored material of the past requires digestion or 'transformation' ('Verwandlung') if one is to enter fully into the life of the present. Indeed his leading preoccupation was how to reconcile that proper allegiance to the past on which all morality rests with that self-surrender to the present which life demands.

Both in Austria and in Germany (as in Europe generally) the writers of the nineties dealt frequently with the aesthetic personality itself.

A central issue, as already indicated, was the compatibility of the moral and the aesthetic ways of life (Kierkegaard's 'either–or'), and the work and career of Oscar Wilde attracted the greatest interest in this connection. But at least equally important was the Nietzschean question of how the aesthetic personality stood in relation to the supposed values of 'life itself' (what Nietzsche called 'das Leben', implying unbroken vitality, creative power and amorality without shame). In the gallery of aesthetic figures presented in the German literature of this time we may distinguish the type of the sensitive and melancholic youth, who plays with life because he lacks the strength to enter it (e.g. Claudio in Hofmannsthal's *Der Tor und der Tod*), and the type of the robust hedonist whose playfulness is the direct expression of unreflective vitality (Hofmannsthal's Casanova-figures). The decade was marked by the self-inspection and self-portrayal of aesthetic man, and few writers – apart perhaps from Stefan George – were wholly satisfied with their own reflected image.

As far as literary form is concerned, a small scale was preferred. The short lyric poem, the prose poem, the prose sketch, the short story, the aphorism, the anecdote, the one-act play or single dramatic scene: such were the forms favoured as suitable vehicles for the expression of finely nuanced moods or insights, and for the rendering of piquant sensations and episodes. The term 'literary impressionism' (by analogy with impressionist painting and drawing) is often applied to such work, in so far as it sought to convey a uniquely personal view of some interesting corner of nature or elegant society. The prose sketches of the Viennese Peter Altenberg provide a good example of 'impressionist' writing in this sense (*Wie ich es sehe*, 1896; *Was der Tag mir zuträgt*, 1901): he wished to portray 'einen Menschen mit *einem* Satze, ein Erlebnis der Seele auf *einer* Seite, eine Landschaft in *einem* Worte'. Those authors who belonged to what we may broadly call the aestheticist movement looked on literature itself as a fine art, and they were much interested in the contemporary arts of design with which their work has obvious connections. However, in the case of George and Hofmannsthal at least, the closest parallels lie not so much with impressionist as with post-impressionist painting, and above all with the pictorial designs of *Jugendstil* (or *art nouveau*) which appear to celebrate the mysterious interconnection or interweaving of all earthly phenomena (cf. the title of George's book of poems, *Der Teppich des Lebens*). The theme of the hidden unity of all things, an eminently Romantic theme, leads us to a consideration of the neo-Romantic trends in German literature, which overlap with – and in some respects emerge from – the aestheticist movement.

In its narrower sense neo-Romanticism meant the revival of the literary themes and subjects of the German Romantics, the revival of legend, *Märchen* and myth. The term is most often applied to works of lyrical inspiration and style which depict wonderful and dream-like adventures of the soul, mystical yearnings of a mingled erotic and religious character, in vaguely medieval or Renaissance settings. Many of these works were 'lyrical dramas', and Maurice Maeterlinck was an acknowledged influence. Their authors were for the most part second-rate (e.g. Ernst Hardt, Karl Vollmoeller), but they clearly met the requirements of public taste for colourful legendary fare. Max Reinhardt, the Austrian theatrical director who took over the Deutsches Theater in Berlin in 1905, displayed his brilliant talent in preparing such dishes for the stage: his production of Vollmoeller's *Das Mirakel* in 1912, which was something of a European cultural event, brought this kind of empty make-believe to a lavish and spectacular climax.

Gerhart Hauptmann cashed in on the vogue for debased fairy-tale with his 'deutsches Märchendrama' *Die versunkene Glocke* (1896), a highly characteristic work of the period. The bell-founder Heinrich, a misunderstood genius, deserts his family in the 'valley' (i.e. the philistine world of established Christianity and morality) and aspires to the 'mountains' (i.e. the heights of personal liberation and creative achievement), drawn up by the golden-haired mountain-nymph Rautendelein and by a vague enthusiasm for sun-worship. Hofmannsthal's *Das Bergwerk zu Falun* (written 1899) is another eminently neo-Romantic drama, which uses the image of the mine to explore the lures and dangers of mystical absorption. Hofmannsthal said of Ricarda Huch's influential book *Blütezeit der Romantik* (1899) that it had unlocked for him more 'subterranean chambers' than he could number. But of course his deeply felt affinity with the Romantics, which expressed itself so plainly at the turn of the century, was merely one important factor in his literary career.

The same is true of Rainer Maria Rilke, whose work may be considered in this context. His strictly neo-Romantic works were, like Hauptmann's, his most popular: notably the sentimental prose-poem *Die Weise von Liebe und Tod des Cornets Christoph Rilke* (1899), copies of which could still be found in German knapsacks during the Second World War. *Das Stundenbuch* (written 1899–1903) is a long symphonic poem in which the author, speaking through the mouth of an imaginary Russian artist-monk, meditates in verse of rich imagery and rhyme on the subjects of God, art, death and poverty. In the last section, 'Das Buch von der Armut und vom Tode', there are signs of the firmer style of the later poetry which gained Rilke an international reputation.

Rilke is the veritable prototype of the fanatical literary artist, and most of his work is only accessible to those who can in some measure sympathize with his high estimate of art's importance. To his mind the objects of experience were simply material for aesthetic transformation, and the artist was the appointed saviour of this transitory world. His work is prolific and very uneven, in such a way that the bad reads like a pastiche of the good. In the early poetry he indulged freely and uncritically his command of the evocative resources of the language. From the time of his move to Paris in 1902, partly under the influence of Rodin and Cézanne (he acted for a period as Rodin's private secretary), he adopted a more objective style and a more disciplined craftsmanship in his verse. The famous poem 'Der Panther' (1902 or 1903) marks the beginning of his great achievements. It was the first of the *Neue Gedichte* (published in two parts, 1907 and 1908), his so-called 'Dinggedichte', which devote themselves to single objects and attempt to distil their essence in the process of poetic re-creation. Some of these poems, such as 'Spanische Tänzerin', are perfect in their kind.

As the poem 'Wendung' (1914) indicates, the years 1902–14 (during which he was based in Paris, but travelled very widely) were years of deliberate training for the fulfilment of his poetic mission. He devoted himself to what he called the 'work of seeing' ('Werk des Gesichts'), attempting to capture and assimilate the significant shapes, patterns and rhythms of the external world. Once he had thus acquired by hard labour a stock of images which no longer seemed merely private and random, he was able to use them as his natural and characteristic vocabulary in poetry of a more meditative and philosophical variety. The cycles *Duineser Elegien* (written 1912–22) and *Sonette an Orpheus* (written 1922) are the outstanding examples of his later style.

The *Elegien*, written in a very free version of the classical elegiac metre, explore the Romantic theme of man's nostalgic estrangement from the great cosmic rhythm: unlike children and animals man does not feel 'dependably at home in the interpreted world' (First Elegy). Lament over the transience of the things of this world and the apparent purposelessness of human existence is balanced by the joyful assertion that man has, after all, a uniquely important task of an aesthetic nature,

T

namely to 'rescue' earthly reality into the sanctum of his consciousness and so bestow on it a kind of permanence. Man is conceived as a sort of bee (the image is used by Rilke in one of his innumerable letters), transporting the nectar culled from mortal flowers into invisible and immortal hives. The *Sonette* are informed by this hard-won conviction that human life finds its justification in the power to experience intensely and to transform poetically: 'Einzig das Lied überm Land / heiligt und feiert.' Whatever our judgement of Rilke's view of life may be (and few are likely to agree with his doctrine that it is destructive to make another human being the object of one's love), the force and skill of these later poems is undeniable: they adapt the traditional forms and tones of German lyric poetry to achieve a wide range of expression, making subtle and original play with verbal and pictorial associations.

Hermann Hesse belongs, like Rilke, in the general context of neo-Romanticism. This 'letzter Ritter aus dem glanzvollen Zuge der Romantik' (Hugo Ball), who began with *Romantische Lieder* (1899), achieved some fame as a gentle continuer of the nineteenth-century German tradition of story-telling. He traces the difficult development of sensitive and educable heroes through worlds which are recognizable but whose contours have been simplified and softened. *Peter Camenzind* (1904) tells the story of a Swiss farmer's son who breaks away from home to indulge his *wanderlust* and literary ambitions; after some fairly harmless aberrations he finds the way to his 'true self' and returns, morally improved, to take his useful place in society. Hesse's heroes reflect his own amiable and generous personality, at once excited and repelled by the dark world of adult sexuality, and seeking a variety of exits (psychoanalysis, Buddhism) from unnaturally prolonged youthful tensions, or – to express it more positively – looking for a spiritual path to replace the pietistic Christianity which had moulded him. His most successful works are those in which his personal difficulties are handled most transparently: *Unterm Rad* (1906), on the theme of painful schooling which preoccupied so many writers of that time; *Demian* (1919). *Der Steppenwolf* (1927) gives an impresson of novelty in that the traditional story-line is largely dissolved, but the underlying pattern is familiar enough: Harry Haller is another emotionally disturbed artist-figure who is brought out of his alienated state to insight and personal salvation. The later novels, notably the utopian novel *Das Glasperlen-spiel* (1943), confirm the fact that Hesse was too preoccupied with his soul to take much account of the public realities of the twentieth century. The title of a collection of his stories published in 1931 – *Weg nach Innen* (after Novalis: 'nach innen geht der geheimnisvolle Weg') – marks the chief limit of his appeal as a narrative writer.

As already indicated, 'neo-Romanticism' is normally taken by literary historians to designate those works, popular at the turn of the century, which resuscitated Romantic themes and handled them with a certain lassitude and studied refinement, often indeed with marked preciosity or sentimentality (cf. the paintings of Arnold Böcklin). But it is permissible to apply the term also, more widely, to a whole movement of thought and feeling between 1895 and 1914 whose different strands were held together by a profound hostility to the rational organization of life and society. When Eugen Diederichs described himself in 1900 as the leading publisher of the neo-Romantic movement he was using the term in this wide sense: for him neo-Romanticism was the 'neue Geistesrichtung' which enrolled man's intuitive powers and religious impulses in the struggle against shallow materialism. In his emphasis on the creative powers of the individual and his consequent desire to reform the German educational system, just as in his objection to positivist science, Diederichs was a true disciple of Nietzsche. But he blended Nietzsche with his national and mystical enthusiasms to produce an ominous mixture.

Diederichs began with new editions of the Romantics (e.g. Novalis, 1898) and the mystics (e.g. Meister Eckhart, 1903), and with such foreign authors as Maeterlinck, J. P. Jacobsen and Tolstoy. He went on to devote his energies increasingly to the cultivation of the German national heritage ('deutsches Volkstum') and the fostering of what he called 'the religious renewal outside the Church'. It is instructive to follow his publishing career because it shows how inextricably, during these years, the urgent wish for spiritual and cultural renewal in Germany was bound up with the love of folk-tale, folk-book, folk-song and all the trappings of the German past. Diederichs was actively associated with the German Youth Movement (*Jugendbewegung*), and he propagated the reactionary doctrines of Paul de Lagarde's *Deutsche Schriften*. Two of the editors he chose in his early days were Adolf Bartels (who became the chief anti-Semitic historian of German literature) and the even more notorious Houston Stewart Chamberlain (author of *Die Grundlagen des 19. Jahrhunderts*). These connections are pointed out, not in order to damn Diederichs, whose work was in some respects admirable, but as a reminder that the Romantic revival in Germany – in so far as it combined the search for a new religion with the cult of 'deutsches Volkstum' – turned out in the end to be anything but harmless.

The Romantic revival over which Diederichs presided was linked at one extreme with the conservative and earthy literature known as *Heimatdichtung* or *Heimatkunst*. While the writers normally called 'neo-Romantic', in the narrower sense defined above, combined their taste for mystic lore and folkishness with dreamy introspection and the cult of a self-consciously 'modern' poetic sensibility, the *Heimatkünstler* were determined to make no concessions to the modern age. They saw no reason why they should not go on writing as if the social and cultural changes of the latter nineteenth century had never occurred. Fritz Lienhard was the leading propagandist of the *Heimatkunst* movement, *Deutsche Heimat* (1900–4) its leading periodical. Lienhard's rallying cry was 'Los von Berlin!' – he regarded Berlin, the centre of naturalism and subsequent modern 'isms', as a great wen infecting German culture, a breeding-ground for all kinds of cosmopolitan decadence. What he demanded was a healthy and uncomplicated literature on the lines of mid-nineteenth-century realism, morally inspiring for the young and calculated to strengthen family, local and national bonds.

Heimatdichtung meant in practice realistic provincial novels (*Heimatsromane*) which demonstrated the value of traditional native customs and morals. Set usually in the past, they were staunchly conservative and conformist in their assumptions. Most of this honest story-telling was undistinguished, but it formed the solid popular background of literature against which the achievements of modernism must be seen. Among the better examples of this kind of conservative writing are the novels of Clara Viebig (e.g. *Die Wacht am Rhein*, 1902) and the tales and anecdotes of Wilhelm Schäfer.

Lienhard's assault on the literary business of Berlin – its international orientation, its refinement, its psychological preoccupations, its experimentalism and its supposed moral decay – was merely the most striking sign of a widespread reaction against cultural centralism during the first decade of the century. Wilhelm Schäfer founded the periodical *Die Rheinlande* (1900–22) to provide an organ for the culture of the Rhine area; Hermann Hesse (himself a major contributor to *Die Rheinlande*) joined with the Bavarian Ludwig Thoma to found *März* (1907–17), a periodical with a South German base. In Austria there was a similar regionalist reaction at this time against the literary hegemony of Vienna.

The Period of Expressionism and Related Styles, 1910–1920

Naturalism was a European movement to which Germany made a modest contribution; the aestheticist and neo-Romantic trends in German art and literature had their obvious foreign counterparts; but expressionism was a peculiarly German phenomenon, comparable to the 'Storm and Stress' movement a century and a half earlier. It embraced the pictorial as well as the literary arts, and a number of artists (e.g. Oskar Kokoschka, Ludwig Meidner, Ernst Barlach) practised an expressionist style in both media. Indeed it is hard to think of expressionist writing at all without its pictorial accompaniment, in particular those chunky and fiercely distorted woodcuts which correspond so closely to the verbal slabs and crushed syntax of the poetry.

The guiding principle of expressionism was that art, of whatever kind, should not imitate or represent the forms of the external world but on the contrary express the inner being, spirit, soul or essence ('Wesen') of the artist. 'The inner element, created by the vibration of the soul, is the content of the work' (Wassily Kandinsky, 1914). The artist's soul was thought of as intensely dynamic and the creative process as a violent discharge of energy. Even volcanic eruption was considered a suitable image in this connection. But in so far as such imagery is appropriate, the furnace within the expressionist poet was likely to leave nothing but lumps of glittering slag behind: Rilke complains of the 'schlackenhafte Wort-Monstren' produced by Theodor Däubler.

Certainly extreme condensation or coagulation was the most striking feature of the expressionist style, the so-called 'geballte Sprache' (compressed or 'clenched' language). In the hope of achieving a maximum of expressive power functional words were omitted and words of significant content strung together or compounded. These devices were not new in German literature (cf. Klopstock, Goethe's early poems) but they were taken further than ever before. The lyric poetry of August Stramm, and Walter Hasenclever's play *Die Menschen* (1918), mark the self-defeating limit of such literary compression. Attempts were even made to tell stories in this style (e.g. Carl Sternheim's *Ulrike*, 1917; Kasimir Edschmid's collections *Die sechs Mündungen* and *Das rasende Leben*, 1915) but the constant hammer-beat of the substantives and the short sentences is merely wearisome.

The idea that the shape of a work should be determined exclusively by its 'inner' (dynamic) content led the expressionists to reject, at least in theory, not only the classical conventions but all conventional form in art. 'Form will mich verschnüren und verengen, / Doch ich will mein Sein in alle Weiten drängen,' writes Ernst Stadler (using, however, a well-worn metrical scheme). 'Every conventional form is a scaffolding for a collapsing building or a corset for a decaying body,' announces Herwarth Walden in 1913, in the hectoring manner that was fashionable. For all that, few of the poems in *Menschheitsdämmerung* (1919) – the first major anthology of expressionist verse – are unconventional in their form, though the poem in free rhythms was naturally favoured. Their novelty lies rather in their style: their syntax, their use of imagery and their 'tone of voice'.

The expressionists did not merely wish to express their vibrating souls; they were also determined to communicate their vibrations. To this end they employed a mode of direct appeal to the public, speaking in tones of high excitement and impassioned exhortation. The warm address 'O Mensch' was rightly recognized as typical – as in Franz Werfel's poem 'An den Leser' which begins: 'Mein einziger Wunsch ist dir, O Mensch, verwandt zu sein!' The poet, says Stefan Zweig in 1909, must emerge from his isolation and kindle the holy fire of spiritual energy in mankind; his work must express and convey what he calls 'das neue Pathos' (the new fervour). He holds up as models the poetry of the young Schiller, of Nietzsche's *Zarathustra*, of Walt Whitman. In the following year a so-called 'neopathetisches Cabaret' was founded in Berlin, where the new poets could fling their fervour straight at the audience. Public poetry readings, at which this high tone prevailed, became the order of the day; they were based on the rather suspect theory of immediate intoxication through literature. However, not all the writers laid such passionate emphasis as Werfel upon activating the spiritual resources of their fellow men: the rhetorical aspect of expressionist writing is matched by its visionary aspect. Where rhetoric prevailed, as in the case of Werfel, Albert Ehrenstein or Johannes R. Becher, the poetry was constantly dissolving into hot air. It was where the shaping of powerfully expressive images took precedence over the rage to communicate that the movement achieved its real triumphs: in the macabre and intensely felt visions of Georg Heym and Georg Trakl and – on the borders of expressionism – in the work of Franz Kafka and Gottfried Benn.

The expressionists employed the lyric poem as the obvious vehicle for intense feeling, often giving it the character of an emphatic proclamation; but at the same time they also turned to the theatre in order to make visible their tribulations and longings, and experimented with new methods of projecting states of mind on the stage. They drew support from the example of Goethe's *Faust*, Büchner's *Woyzeck* and the later plays of Strindberg. The stage is no longer a 'set', imitating a place where persons really meet and actions really occur, but it stands rather for the human soul itself where the interior drama of life is played out. The expressionist play unfolds in a sequence of loosely connected scenes (sometimes called *Bilder* to emphasize their dream-like quality), which denote the stages (*Stationen*) of the inner development of the central figure. And this central figure is always closely allied to his author. Normally the hero is engaged on a grandiose quest for his own salvation and/or the salvation of the world, and the stages of his development are shown as stages of progressive enlightenment through suffering. Reinhard Sorge's *Der Bettler* (1912), Walter Hasenclever's *Der Sohn* (1914) and Ernst Toller's *Die Wandlung* (1919) are characteristic examples of expressionist drama in the above respects. All three plays draw on external autobiographical fact, but they use this material in an unrealistic, distorted fashion which makes clear that we are witnessing the story of an inner life. But whose inner life? That of the author himself, no doubt; and yet these authors were firmly convinced of the representative nature of their experiences and unusually determined to present them as typical of their generation, if not of mankind as a whole. Thus it is that the hero of expressionist drama – thanks to the high degree of abstraction employed – is at once the projection of the author's own subjectivity and a kind of Everyman. Spurning all psychological analysis and all description, indeed all reference to the particular, these dramatists show us a gallery of well-intentioned but largely anonymous and interchangeable spooks. Bert Brecht sums up his criticism of such plays by calling them 'Proklamationen des Menschen ohne Menschen' ('proclamations of humanity in the absence of human beings').

Most expressionist literature was urgently committed literature, literature with a cause. Stated in the most general and abstract terms (as it usually was) that cause was the wholesale moral and spiritual regeneration of mankind. By proclaiming the renewal of man ('die Erneuerung des Menschen', 'der neue Mensch') they hoped to usher in, immediately, a Utopia or paradise on earth. 'Wir wollen', declares Kurt Hiller, 'bei lebendigem Leibe ins Paradies.' The agent of the desired transformation of the heart was the word, charged with moral or spiritual energy (*Geist*), and many believed that the necessary social and political changes would occur automatically and peacefully as a result of man's inner change or rebirth. Thus the literary men of the expressionist decade saddled themselves with a Messianic task. Brecht refers to them disparagingly as the 'Heiländchen' ('little saviours'). Certainly the hope that the New Man could be born of the word alone was doomed to disappointment: it was killed by the confrontation with reality, in the shape of the 1914–18 war and the Bolshevik revolutions. Armed solely with their faith in immediate verbal power these writers were as incompetent to perform their appointed salvatory mission as the country doctor in Franz Kafka's story *Ein Landarzt*, and in due course most of them came to recognize the fact.

One of the most striking features of the literature of this decade is the theme of the father–son conflict. Freud's theory of the 'Oedipus complex' was elaborated during these years: he believed that every son harboured an unconscious murderous hostility towards his father, which had affected the whole history of human culture. But it seems more likely that he was merely diagnosing a mood of the time. Certainly the younger generation of writers felt themselves united in violent revolt against the 'world of the fathers' (*Welt der Väter*), i.e. all those in authority who exercised social, cultural, economic and military power. The 'father' was found a convenient and natural symbol for all the distasteful aspects of the old order, and 'paternal' (*väterlich*) became a term of opprobrium. Rigidity and oppression in the school system, capitalist exploitation in industry, ruthlessness in the pursuit of technological advance: all these were readily associated with the hated father-figure, the sadistic tyrant of the family circle. Patricidal fantasies made common literary stuff (cf. Arnolt Bronnen's *Vatermord*, written 1915): in two of the plays mentioned above, *Der Bettler* and *Der Sohn*, the son steps to freedom over his father's corpse. In Sorge's play the father is not an object of hatred, simply the manic embodiment of technological enthusiasm; but in Hasenclever's *Der Sohn* the father really does stand for the odious *ancien régime* whose overthrow is necessary. And yet today *Der Sohn* strikes us as unintentionally comic: the attempt to present the struggle between good and evil in the world as a crude struggle between 'fathers' and 'sons' could hardly succeed. Even Franz Kafka, who was very much at odds with his real father, came to the conclusion that the father–son conflict was best treated as a comic theme in literature: he refers us to J. M. Synge's *Playboy of the Western World*.

Politically, expressionism belonged well to the Left. The periodical

Die Aktion, the most important of the many periodicals which gave the movement a sense of identity, was launched in 1911 by Franz Pfemfert as a platform for 'die große deutsche Linke'. The propagation of a revolution in the arts went hand in hand with the propagation of political revolution. Pfemfert's own targets were relatively clear: he hated Kaiser Wilhelm's Germany; he was opposed to nationalism, militarism, capitalism and the parliamentary system. But the pre-1914 revolutionary fervour was expressed so hectically and turbulently by literary men that it is impossible to discern any definite programme. In the first number of the periodical *Revolution* (1913) the poet Erich Mühsam set the tone as follows:

> Alle Revolution ist aktiv, singulär, plötzlich und ihre Ursachen entwurzelnd . . .

> Einige Formen der Revolution: Tyrannenmord, Absetzung einer Herrschergestalt, Etablierung einer Religion, Zerbrechen alter Tafeln (in Konvention und Kunst), Schaffen eines Kunstwerks, der Geschlechtsakt.

> Einige Synonyma für Revolution: Gott, Leben, Brunst, Rausch, Chaos.

> Laßt uns chaotisch sein!

It is difficult to take this kind of thing seriously. And yet the contributors to this short-lived journal included Max Brod, Walter Hasenclever, Kurt Hiller, Jakob van Hoddis, Else Lasker-Schüler and Robert Musil, besides those who later made their names in the Dadaist movement: Hugo Ball, Emmy Hennings and Richard Huelsenbeck.

The outbreak of the Great War in 1914 merely confirmed the expressionists in their belief that the old order in Europe was rotten and ripe for self-destruction. Some of them had forecast such a holocaust with a mixture of horror and hope, assuming that nationalism, militarism, imperialism, capitalism and the whole authoritarian structure of the State were doomed to encompass their own ruin, and thus pave the way for international socialist brotherhood and perpetual peace. The idea was widespread that a great purging fire, a fearful visitation, was the necessary prelude to mankind's salvation, and this major theme of Old Testament prophecy is particularly noticeable in the work of Jewish writers (e.g. Alfred Wolfenstein's poem 'Die Friedensstadt').

Certainly war was an abomination to the expressionists, who were nothing if not humane idealists, but many of them were inclined to regard this particular war – initially anyhow – as the appointed destroyer of a bad old world. But whether they subscribed to what may be called the 'holocaust theory', or whether they were (like René Schickele or Franz Werfel) outright pacifists from the start, their hostility to the cause of the Fatherland was plain enough. For obvious reasons they could not express this hostility openly in wartime. Hence expressionism, in so far as it was a movement of political opposition in the widest sense, went underground during the war years. On 5 August 1914 Franz Pfemfert explained that *Die Aktion*, the most politically engaged of the pre-war expressionist periodicals, would in future be devoted simply to 'Literatur und Kunst'. René Schickele, editor of the outstanding periodical *Die Weißen Blätter*, moved its base in 1916 to neutral Switzerland, where it could fulfil its original promise to be 'nicht nur der künstlerische Ausdruck der neuen Generation, sondern auch ihr sittlicher und politischer'.

In 1915 Heinrich Mann (elder brother of Thomas) published in *Die weißen Blätter* his famous essay entitled 'Zola', which was a powerful indirect assault on the official doctrines and policies of Kaiser Wilhelm's Germany. 'Ein Reich,' he wrote, 'in dem nur befohlen und gehorcht, verdient und ausgebeutet, des Menschen aber nie geachtet ward, kann nicht siegen, und zöge es aus mit übermenschlicher Macht.' He was acknowledged as a leader by the more politically orientated expressionists (the so-called 'Activists') and his works enjoyed a reputation among progressive writers generally – which is difficult to understand outside the context of the time.

Heinrich Mann reacted against the ethos of late nineteenth-century German *Bürgertum* more radically than Thomas Mann, taking strong exception to that mixture of soulfulness (*Innerlichkeit*) and ruthlessness so well depicted by Theodor Fontane. In his early work he was, like his brother, much concerned with the psychology of artists and pleasure-seekers, but after 1900 he turned to the wider social implications of his psychological findings. He wrote satirical novels and stories (notably *Professor Unrat oder das Ende eines Tyrannen*, 1905; *Der Untertan*, 1918), embodying the kind of social criticism which his brother still fiercely deplored. A major link between his earlier and later work is his interest in the psychology of power, and he owed much to Nietzsche's speculations on this matter. As a literary artist he looked abroad for inspiration, particularly to France (e.g. Balzac), and during the 1914–18 war he was regarded as a kind of Trojan horse carrying the civilization of France in his belly. He was duly castigated by his brother (Thomas Mann: *Betrachtungen eines Unpolitischen*, 1918), who argued that the Germans should be permitted to cultivate their musical souls undisturbed by politics and rational thought.

Der Untertan, parts of which were published between 1911 and 1914, is one of the few German works conceived during the first decade of the century which deal in a lively, intelligent and critical manner with the realities of contemporary public life. Set in Prussia around 1900 it depicts the slimy road to success of Diederich Hessling, a paper manufacturer, who has all the most distasteful characteristics of the Wilhelmine bourgeoisie. He is an abject worshipper of authority, and by the same token a ruthless bully. *Der Untertan* (sub-titled 'Roman des Bürgertums') was supplemented by *Die Armen* (1918, sub-titled 'Roman des Proletariers') and *Der Kopf* (1925, sub-titled 'Roman der Führer') to form the trilogy *Das Kaiserreich: Die Romane der Deutschen Gesellschaft im Zeitalter Wilhelms II*. Heinrich Mann recognized the importance of the role played by French literature in 'nurturing democracy', and he wished to emulate the great nineteenth-century French novels by painting a grand critical picture of contemporary German conditions. But the *Kaiserreich* novels hardly transcend their intended social function (their 'Tendenz') and they cannot sustain the comparisons with Balzac and Zola drawn by his admirers at the time. All the same, his work stands as a major effort to deflect German literature from excessive inwardness and from silent acceptance of prevailing political assumptions.

'Expressionism' is an over-stretched and tattered label which has to do service for a variety of anti-traditionalist and opposition-minded literature during the decade under review. Whether we want to attach this label to a particular author or work depends on the importance we allow to the following: (i) the use of various anti-naturalistic or 'abstracting' devices, such as syntactical compression or symbolic picture-sequences, (ii) the assault on the sacred cows of the Wilhelmine bourgeoisie from a left-wing internationalist position, (iii) the choice of the theme of spiritual regeneration or renewal and (iv) the adoption of a fervent declamatory tone.

Now it plainly makes no sense to call Heinrich Mann an expressionist unless we attach exclusive importance to the second point. On the other hand Ernst Toller's play *Die Wandlung* satisfies all the above requirements and may be taken as an undisputed example of expressionistic writing. The 'Wandlung' of the title refers to the hero's change of heart, which is at once a political reorientation and a spiritual rebirth. The chief agent of his change is the experience of the inhumanity of war and capitalist exploitation. Once he has been himself enlightened he can inspire, by his rhetoric, a change of heart in the people at large: in the final scene he stands on the steps of a church and preaches with instantaneous effect the gospel of the fundamental brotherliness and decency of all mankind. But Toller's generous and humane sentiments (which can certainly move us in his autobiographical *Eine Jugend in Deutschland*, 1933) were not matched by constructive poetic ability; his plays dated rapidly and are today, together with the bulk of expressionist drama, of historical interest only.

Of greater artistic merit are the plays of Georg Kaiser written during these years (e.g. *Die Bürger von Calais*, 1914; *Von Morgens bis Mitternachts*, 1916). Their grand theme is once again the regeneration of man; in an essay of 1918 (*Vision und Figur*) Kaiser declares that the artist's sole task is to project his vision of the 'Erneuerung des Menschen', but he also stresses the importance of 'kühle Rede' if the projection is to be successful. In theory Kaiser might have achieved in the theatre something like what Kafka achieved in narrative prose; in practice, the content of his visions seems often inauthentic and the form of presentation too rationally contrived. But with *Die Bürger von Calais*, where he took a dramatic fable that was historically given, he achieved an exceptional success. Based on Froissart's account of the siege of Paris by the English in 1346–7, and probably inspired by Rodin's sculpture of the six burghers who volunteered their lives to spare the city, the play aims to bring out the superiority of pacific over military virtues. Kaiser heightened the dramatic nature of his subject-matter by a brilliant invention: while only six hostages are demanded by the English king, seven volunteer. In order to preserve the firmness and purity of their joint will to self-sacrifice Eustache de Saint-Pierre, their leading spirit, commits suicide. We are shown that exceptional case where deliberate self-destruction may be viewed as an act of exemplary moral heroism.

Die Bürger von Calais deserves attention on a number of counts. First of all it exhibits that dramatic quality which most expressionist plays lack: conflict and tension within a clearly delimited situation. On the other hand the characters are essentially spokesmen of ideas, and thus 'abstract' in a typically expressionist way: we are not interested in Eustache de Saint-Pierre as an individual, only in what he stands for. Next we may observe that in this work Kaiser can use the rhetorical speech-style of expressionism semi-realistically, since much of it consists of impassioned public addresses. Finally, he makes his play heavily dependent on non-literary devices such as expressive gesture, silence, non-verbal sound, lighting effects and pictorial symbolism – in short, on the artistic techniques of the silent film. Brecht noted (1921) in connection with a production of *Von Morgens bis Mitternachts*: 'Kaiser macht eine Filmaufnahme!'

It is worth noticing at this point that it was precisely during these years 1910–25 that the film began to develop as an artistic medium. In 1913 Kurt Pinthus edited a *Kinobuch* containing film-scenarios by Hasenclever, Else Lasker-Schüler, Max Brod, Albert Ehrenstein, Ludwig Rubiner, Paul Zech and other expressionist writers. Film techniques influenced the dramatic literature of the period (Toller, Kaiser), and probably the narrative literature too (Kafka, Döblin).

Franz Kafka (1883–1924) was the greatest literary artist writing during these years. It is worth keeping in mind the expressionist background against which he worked, but to label him an expressionist is unhelpful. He regarded the 'new fervour' ('das neue Pathos') as self-defeating and was the enemy of all noisy and violent literary effects. His achievement is independent and personal to an unusual degree.

The theme of his work (short stories and three unfinished novels) was also the theme of his life: the condition of solitary estrangement in a puzzling and threatening world. All his work is *Erlebnisdichtung*, i.e. based on his deepest personal experience (though it is not just veiled autobiography). By elaborating his poetic visions he sought to clarify his own existential difficulties, and at the same time to communicate – in the indirect way which alone seemed possible – a core of inner truth. The stories deal regularly with isolation and impotence, misunderstandings and defeats, and they certainly embody no ready-made answers to the problems of life. But it is quite wrong to dismiss them as merely 'negative' on that account, for the explorations of darkness are guided and sustained by an indestructible positive urge. Kafka's experience of estrangement and separation, so intensely rendered in his writing, can only be described as a religious experience: it seemed to him, as he once put it, that he could understand the Fall of Man (*Sündenfall*) better than anyone else.

The early works draw directly on his most oppressive private difficulty, the feeling of inadequacy and guilt *vis-à-vis* his overpowering father. For a long time his choice seemed to lie between irremediable self-banishment (which he associated with devotion to his lonely literary task) and the necessarily devious struggle to assert himself on his father's home ground (the ground of marriage and vital success). In his first great story *Das Urteil* (written 1912) the latter possibility is represented by the hero Georg Bendemann, and the former by Georg's 'friend in St Petersburg'. When Georg's father sees through his son's false life and condemns him, the judgement is irresistible. In *Der Prozess* (written 1914) the theme of the guilty life is treated in a more imaginative way. Josef K's existence is called in question and condemned, not by paternal authority this time but by a strange and complex judicial power whose highest organs remain inaccessible. He makes extended efforts to assert himself and to seek out the ground of his lurking guiltiness, but without success; in the end he acquiesces, like Georg Bendemann, in the judgement that he is unfit to live. The powerful and hypnotic effect of these early stories derives in part from Kafka's technique of telling them from the hero's own limited viewpoint. The narrator claims no superior knowledge and provides us with no reassuring signposts; he simply confronts us with the happenings as they swim into the hero's ken and forces us to respond, immediately and unaided, to the enigmatic face of reality.

The heroes of Kafka's early works are preoccupied with the need to justify their own lives; after 1916 the emphasis changes, and his heroes set their eyes, for the most part, on a grander and less selfish goal (*Ein Landarzt, Das Schloß*). The theme of the great spiritual mission, the great saving task, is what links Kafka's later work to that of his expressionist contemporaries. 'Nun plötzlich ist dir so,' he writes in 1920, 'als seiest du einberufen zu dem großen welterlösenden Kampf.' But it is essential, in reading the later works, to recognize Kafka's dialectical method, his mode of indicating the positive by presenting the negative. For his questing heroes are normally presented as incompetent, or Quixotic, or self-absorbed, or self-deceiving, or as devious *Realpolitiker*, quite apart from the fact that they are always unsuccessful in achieving their end. The inadequacy of Kafka's heroes is not supposed to disvalue the task with which they find themselves saddled; quite the contrary.

The most original and striking feature of his literary method is his choice of certain controlling images which are poetically (and often playfully) developed in terms of an apparently realistic narrative. Such images are those of a man imprisoned in his room in the shape of an insect (*Die Verwandlung*), a man spanning a river in the shape of a bridge (*Die Brücke*), a man in a village trying to find access to a castle on a hill (*Das Schloß*). These images are calculated to give shape to an inner reality; they are systems of signs which express, first of all, Kafka's own complex sense of estrangement, his deepest anxieties and longings. His works do not refer us to the external public world, e.g. the bureaucratic institutions of the Austro-Hungarian Empire, except in so far as we may regard bureaucracy – with Kafka – as a symbolic expression of man's fallen spiritual state. He regarded (to take another example) his own tuberculosis as the outward sign of an inner trouble ('die geistige Wunde') and in conformity with this way of looking at the world his stories are neither realistic nor allegorical, but symbolic. They refer neither to the realities of social, political and economic life, nor to any abstract concepts or theories, but are designed to make us aware of the hidden spiritual significance of our ordinary experience. Two of his own statements may guide us in understanding his works: first, his roundly idealistic assertion that the only real world is the world of the spirit ('es gibt nichts anderes als eine geistige Welt'), and secondly his declaration that language, having been developed as a tool for our material and practical use, can never make us aware of spiritual truths by means of direct equivalents and comparisons, but only by means of hinting and symbolic signs.

Kafka devoted his energies with exceptional rigour to the exposing of what seemed false in himself. He lent his heroes every kind of inauthenticity which he detected in his own life. And in the process of self-criticism he found himself involved, like Nietzsche, in some most uncomfortable exposing of man in general; works like *In der Strafkolonie* and *Das Schloß* show up by implication the inauthentic features of established habits of thought and belief, established ideologies, customs and institutions. With his quiet, unpolitical pen and his wistful brand of humour Kafka has done more than all the satirists and polemicists together to put fear in the hearts of false authorities.

Kafka was never sure enough of his own ground to indulge in pure satire, however much the society around him may have called for it. This call had to be answered by authors who felt more firmly anchored in the world they disapproved, e.g. Heinrich Mann (see above) and Carl Sternheim, who produced a series of comedies ironically entitled *Aus dem bürgerlichen Heldenleben* (1911–15). German literature, which had not been rich in satire for the previous 150 years, enjoyed a resurgence of this type of writing in the final years of the Wilhelmine and Austrian Empires. The great satirist of the age was Karl Kraus (1874–1936).

Like Kafka, Kraus was an uncompromising moralist, but unlike Kafka he elected to wage his battle against falsehood by assaulting specific evils in the world about him. This was the world of Vienna immediately before and after the collapse of the Austrian Empire. Kraus believed that the best way of setting the world to rights was to rub the noses of wrongdoers in their own misdeeds. His convictions were in the best sense humane and liberal, and almost all his targets were worthy of attack, but if he had (*per impossibile*) succeeded in his great satirical enterprise he would have become as superfluous as a schoolmaster who had set his heart solely on the eradication of error and achieved it.

The targets of Karl Kraus lay in the literature and society (in that order) of Austria and Germany. The use of language was for him the great shibboleth by which good and evil could be distinguished: a badly constructed sentence, a false concord, a loose metaphor, a jargon phrase, were infallible indicators of moral turpitude. He was unable to recognize that some bad writing is due simply to incompetence or stupidity. But he was on strong ground in his unflagging solitary campaign against the Viennese press, which he regarded as the chief purveyor of corrupt German, the clearest involuntary mirror of social abuses, and his most immediate enemy.

The form of Kraus's work makes access and judgement difficult. It appeared in his own periodical *Die Fackel* (1899–1936), which was written entirely by himself after 1910. It contained critical essays, glosses or commentaries on texts, aphorisms in prose and verse, lyric poems, and even (in three special numbers) the vast drama *Die letzten Tage der Menschheit*. Fortunately he published separate collections in book form (e.g. *Pro Domo et Mundo*, 1912; *Untergang der Welt durch schwarze Magie*, 1922) which present his output more coherently and give a good idea of his slant and his methods. As far as literary criticism is concerned the only steady criterion he applied, apart from good workmanship, was the notoriously tricky criterion of 'sincerity' and moral uprightness. He approved of Shakespeare, Nestroy, Goethe, Jean Paul, Liliencron, Wedekind, Ibsen, Strindberg, Heinrich Mann, Brecht; he disapproved of everybody who could remotely be accused of intellectual dishonesty or the prostitution of literature for gain. The same kind of sternness informed his social and political critique. He fought good battles against politically inspired justice, against oppression of minority rights, against militarism and against economic exploitation, but his moral puritanism led him to make enemies of some of his best friends on the Left.

His most important single work was *Die letzten Tage der Menschheit* (1919), a ruthless exposure of the vileness of the Great War on the Austrian and German side. The background of the 'heroic struggle' is laid bare as a pattern of empty phrases, vanity, greed, cynicism and petit-bourgeois prejudices. The work is based, in montage-style, on real incidents and on the documents of the time (cf. *Oh What A Lovely War!*), and where appropriate historical figures speak their own recorded words. Kraus incorporates in the play his own philosophical commentary, through the figure of 'Der Nörgler' (the grouser), whose dialogue-partner ('Der Optimist') is a cheerful supporter of official and accepted views. This gigantic work was not intended for the stage, and is indeed unstageable as it stands, though its techniques have proved influential. It is noteworthy that Kraus tried to provide Brecht with a stageable version, having earlier refused production rights to both Reinhardt and Piscator.

Kraus's work made its main impact during the years 1910–25 – through *Die Fackel* and through his hundreds of public readings or recitations – but he was not associated with the expressionist movement. Kraus was a 'movement' in himself. It is true that he numbered among his friends Herwarth Walden (editor of the periodical *Der Sturm*) and the publisher Kurt Wolff, true that he admired the painting of Kokoschka (his best-known portraitist) and the poetry of Lasker-Schüler and Trakl; but he was very much alert to the bogus and synthetic element in the work of the run-of-the-mill expressionists, whom he called the 'Neutöner'. While praising Else Lasker-Schüler he said: 'Ich halte alles, was um sie herum neugetönt wird, für eine Frechheit.' Particularly instructive are his attacks on Franz Werfel (see his satirical 'magic operetta' *Literatur*, 1921). Kraus, like Kafka, had been impressed by the intensity of Werfel's pre-war poems (*Der Weltfreund*, 1911; *Wir sind*, 1913) but turned against him once he recognized that the pursuit of fashionable literary success was more important to him than ethical and artistic probity. Kraus reserved his bitterest invective for those who stood close to him (cf. his essay *Heine und die Folgen*, 1910), especially for those German-Jewish writers who shared his liberal principles but who seemed on closer inspection to fall short of his severe standards of writing and conduct.

The most radical breaks with tradition – the most extreme 'modernist' experiments – were made not in Vienna or Prague but in Berlin. Both *Die Aktion* and *Der Sturm* were published there, and it was the chief centre of the literary and artistic avant-garde during these years. It was in Berlin that the expressionist literary revolution took its most iconoclastic forms. Pure negation and destruction, which superficial readers claim to find in Kafka and Kraus, really does mark some of this

Berlin literature. That hatred of the bourgeois and his smug assumptions which had fired Wedekind in the 1890s was strongly active among the early Berlin expressionists. Ferdinand Hardekopf, for instance, writes in 1916:

> Hier wird, auf einem Kap, Extremes geformt. Unsere Bücher werden euch unfaßlich sein, Bürger. Nicht fur euch haben wir Alpen durchfressen von Monstruosität Delicatesse Neurose Luxus Orgie ... Lustig zu Hause sind wir auf macabren Redouten und bei scabreusen Dérouten, in geschminkten Katakomben und clair-obscuren Cafés, in subcutanen Bars und auf ogivalen Stil-Spitzen ...

The expression of these anti-bourgeois resentments was no mere jovial fun-poking, either here or in the work of the Berlin Dadaists a few years later. The resentments were understandable enough, even if they could not by themselves produce great literature. But this smashing up of the German *gutbürgerliche Stube* became more sinister when it was extended, by students of Nietzsche and admirers of the Italian Futurist poet Marinetti, to a general denigration of all civilized and humane values. At this end of the expressionist spectrum – at the furthest remove from Ernst Toller – we come to Gottfried Benn.

The reputation of Benn, a doctor who practised in Berlin, rests chiefly on his lyric poetry. His early collections (*Morgue*, 1912; *Söhne*, 1913; *Fleisch*, 1917) dwell on the more repellent physical aspects of life. It is hard to detect, behind the overt cynicism and the macabre effects of these verses, much of that 'strong compassionate feeling' which Ernst Stadler generously ascribed to them. They express the poet's sense of nausea in contemplating a world bereft of meaning and value. In their form and style they are for the most part harsh and recognizably expressionistic: the syntax is chopped and compressed; striking and often brutal noun-compounds predominate; both rhyme and flowing rhythm are rare.

He found his most authentic personal style in the poems of the twenties, e.g. those collected in *Spaltung* (1925). Here the more violent mannerisms of expressionist diction are dropped. Powerful evocative effects are achieved by the incantatory three-beat rhythm of the rhymed octets, coupled with the images of lotus-eating and lovely extinction (cf. Stefan George's poem 'Da auf dem seidenen lager . . .' from *Algabal*). But what gives these poems their special character is the jazzy admixture of up-to-date cosmopolitan vocabulary and topical reference, the way in which Benn makes the world of the twenties dance to his beguiling and deeply melancholic tune.

Benn was a highly intellectual poet who found, like Nietzsche, that his own tendency to intellectual anatomizing made him extremely uncomfortable. He speaks often of the 'progressive cerebralization' of man and makes this the leading theme of his writing. His entire work may be read as the record of his attempts to overcome a pervasive sense of futility and emptiness, which in his view flowed necessarily from the over-development of man's analytical mental powers. In Benn's own language, an excess of brains (*Gehirn*) had led man inevitably to a total devaluation of his existence (*Nihilismus*). He felt sure (cf. Nietzsche again) that his own difficulties were peculiarly representative, that his own predicament was the Predicament of Modern Man, and that his own efforts to overcome nihilism had an important bearing on the future of the human race. The early poetry traces a number of familiar escape routes (e.g. cocaine) and conjures up a number of familiar artificial paradises; it expresses homesickness for a primeval state before evolution had moved far along its path to awareness of pain: 'O daß wir unsere Ururahnen wären. / Ein Klümpchen Schleim in einem warmen Moor.' (The poem 'Gesänge I' of 1913.) Benn's Garden of Eden is more radically regressive than that of the Romantics or even the poets of the 1890s. But his recipe for unhappy modern humanity is firmly an aesthetic recipe, amoral or 'post-moral' ('Beyond Good and Evil'). The sole significant activity left to man is the stern and unnatural activity called art, the transforming of life's disgusting futility into unchanging shapes which are deathly and therefore immortal – pure beauty, pure expression, pure style.

He expounded his version of the 'art for art's sake' doctrine with increasing insistence. What he advocated and pursued was *artistische Kunst* or *Artistik*, the 'pure' or 'absolute' poem, defined as 'the poem without faith, the poem without hope, the poem addressed to no one, the poem made of words which you assemble in a fascinating way'. This kind of aestheticism, which reminds us of the early Stefan George, derives from a profound distaste for biological processes as well as for the whole spectacle of change in human history. In Benn's own words it is the 'attempt of art to experience itself as a meaning within the general decay of all meaning, and to form a new style out of this experience' (*Probleme der Lyrik*, 1951). Art has the task of waging war on the meaningless dynamic of life in order to achieve *Stil*, that is to say, forms of static perfection: *Statische Gedichte* is the title of his most famous late collection (1949). In a note of 1950 Benn writes: 'Platen meint: die Schönheit – das ist Gorgo, das todbringende Haupt. Aber wir haben nur die Wahl: Gorgo oder das Nichts, Gorgo oder das Banale . . .' He suggests that unless we wish to drown in banality or abandon ourselves to nihilistic despair our sole course is to create or contemplate objects of deathly perfection.

But there is an inherent contradition in Benn's work. According to his theory he should have written only self-enclosed literature addressed to no one, *monologische Kunst*. In practice he was much concerned to communicate his theory, particularly in his many flashy and deliberately 'fascinating' essays. Even many of his poems preach the doctrine of extreme aestheticism, and by doing so refute the doctrine. What he produced was not so much 'art for art's sake' as art for the sake of his own desperately aestheticist philosophy – works designed to persuade us of the fact that art is 'die eigentliche Aufgabe des Lebens, die letzte Transzendenz innerhalb des großen europäischen Nichts' (*Rede auf Heinrich Mann*, 1931).

The Twenties

German literature during the 1920s displays no single dominating style comparable to naturalism from 1885 to 1895, neo-Romanticism at the turn of the century, or expressionism during the decade just reviewed. The term *die neue Sachlichkeit* (the new matter-of-factness) was applied in the mid-twenties both to literature and to the visual arts, but it hardly designates a consistent style. It rather indicates the prevailing temper of the time, which was hostile to sentiment and soulful enthusiasm, disenchanted with big ideas, and preoccupied in a somewhat hard-boiled way with facts. 'Kunst langweilt,' writes Alfred Döblin, 'man will Fakta und Fakta.' The post-war mood of disillusion was not conducive to new literary movements or groupings, which were in any case inhibited by economic hardship, political bitterness and a pervasive sense of social disintegration. In the literary field the attempts to regain touch with observable fact were highly diverse (e.g. Bert Brecht and Ernst Jünger). The non-literary arts, particularly the arts of design, were better placed to give coherent expression to the more sober and practical outlook, and by comparison with the achievements of the Bauhaus the literature of these years seems disoriented and scrappy.

Prose writing of a non-fictional or allegedly non-fictional character was chiefly in vogue: autobiographies, diaries and documentaries, besides essays, novels and plays dealing with contemporary or historically attested events. The many accounts of the 1914–18 war included Ernst Jünger's *In Stahlgewittern* (1920) and Ludwig Renn's *Der Krieg* (1928), the one glorifying the heightened experience and heroism of battle, the other implicitly condemning its cruelty, misery and waste. Both are tough and unblinking accounts, and yet they seem hardly to refer to the same war. As in the period of naturalism the professed respect for facts brought an increase rather than a decrease of political tendentiousness. The original, silent pre-selection of the facts was what mattered, particularly in the many *Zeitstücke* of the period, plays dealing with events of recent or topical interest (e.g. Friedrich Wolf's *Die Matrosen von Cattaro*, 1930; Carl Zuckmayer's *Der Hauptmann von Köpenick*, 1931). But the works which have lasted are not those which use simple imitation and reportage for political aims. The great names appear in retrospect to be those of Bertolt Brecht, Alfred Döblin and Robert Musil.

The Austrian Robert Musil, an engineer by training who was also well versed in philosophy and experimental psychology, devoted his life during the twenties and thirties to the grandiose project of his novel *Der Mann ohne Eigenschaften*, of which the first two parts appeared in 1930 and 1932. Like other experiments in the modern novel this work is not so much a story as an odyssey of the mind, a kind of open-ended programme of research. The hero Ulrich is plainly not fitted to be the central figure of a traditional narrative. He takes 'a year's leave from his life [it is the year before the outbreak of the 1914–18 war] in order to seek an appropriate use for his abilities'. His search is a purely mental one and his reflections make up the main content of the book. But it is not as abstract and bloodless as this may suggest. Ulrich is no boring cipher for Modern Man but is conceived in the image of a particular and recognizable brand of Austrian intellectual in the early part of this century. He is not so much a 'man without qualities' (he has been an officer, an engineer, and a successful mathematician) as one who has become thoroughly sceptical about the world for which accepted qualifications qualify: he examines the patterns and possibilities of life from an uncommitted, outside position. The novel relates him ironically to the world of pre-war Austria from which he has become disengaged. We are shown him acting as secretary to a particularly pointless public enterprise, the so-called *Parallelaktion* designed to prepare the Austrian emperor's seventieth jubilee celebrations as a parallel to the thirtieth jubilee of Kaiser Wilhelm. Thus Ulrich is anchored in a clearly and wittily delineated social context to which he outwardly belongs but from which he is inwardly estranged. His portrayal as a sceptical Austrian within the decadent empire, which allows full room for satire, is powerful and amusing, but his portrayal as a floating modern intellectual, who meditates at length on mystical experience ('der andere Zustand'), is less obviously persuasive. There are points at which we may ask whether such a weight of reflection can be effectively carried by a work of art, and indeed the author himself encourages us to do so (e.g. in Chapter 28 of Book One).

In *Der Mann ohne Eigenschaften* Musil adopts a detached, scientific viewpoint akin to that of his hero. He shares with Ulrich the melancholy awareness that it is extremely difficult to give any firm account of reality. As he says in a letter of 1930 their common problem is: 'wie komme ich zum Erzählen?' Ulrich reflects on this in Chapter 122 of Book One. Most men, he considers, are basically story-tellers in relation to themselves: they range their experience in a comforting chronological sequence without bothering too much about the whys and the wherefores. But Ulrich has lost the power to deal with his life as if it were a simple and orderly progression of events. He has forfeited 'dieses primitiv Epische, woran das private Leben noch festhält, obgleich öffentlich alles schon unerzählerisch geworden ist und nicht einem "Faden" mehr folgt.' In so far as the novel is about the difficulty of grasping reality it is also about the impossibility of old-fashioned story-telling – what some journalists still like to call 'the crisis of the modern novel'.

The dissolving or swamping of the narrative line was obviously a main feature of the more interesting novels of the time, and not only in Germany (cf. Proust and Joyce). Thomas Mann's *Der Zauberberg* (1924), Kafka's *Das Schloß* (1926) and Hesse's *Der Steppenwolf* (1927) have already been mentioned. Musil's novel is perhaps the most ambitious attempt to render the intellectual and spiritual adventures of a modern consciousness, to follow the fumbling search of an alert but disoriented mind. But his recourse to reflection and commentary, to the tracing of analytical and speculative thought processes, was merely one method of getting away from the naïve realism which no longer seemed adequate. Another method of 'modernizing' imaginative prose, best represented by Alfred Döblin, might be called the 'objective' method, since the emphasis lies rather on the complexity of an experienced world than on the corresponding bewilderment of a questing mind. No reflection or commentary on the author's part, no irony;

everything solidly and concretely presented; a coherent vision effectively designed to persuade us and carry us along; everything incontrovertibly 'real' in its fictional context.

Döblin first achieved fame by his novel *Die drei Sprünge des Wang-lun* (1915). It concerns the vicissitudes of a popular heretical sect, the 'Bund der Wahrhaft Schwachen', of which Wang-lun becomes leader, and its final crushing by the Chinese Imperial troops. The choice of subject was no doubt partly determined by Döblin's hostility to the Wilhelmine Empire and his (unsentimental) feeling of solidarity with social underdogs, partly also by his wish to break with the traditional artistic and intellectual assumptions of the West. The novel's main theme is the difficult choice confronting the opponents of an established power structure – active rebellion or the cult of pious non-violence – and it ends with the unanswered question: 'Stille sein, nicht widerstreben, kann ich es denn?' It may be noted that Taoist and Buddhist doctrines enjoyed a considerable vogue during the closing years of the Second Empire.

The chequered career of Wang-lun, the thieving son of a fisherman, serves to hold the novel together but his personal story is subsidiary to the great sweep of events in which he is set. Döblin took pains to give the book a genuinely Chinese flavour, but he had no wish to paint a historically accurate picture. Though based on authenticated detail and crammed with local colour his China is an autonomous product of the imagination (cf. the novel *Wallenstein*, 1920). Like Kafka, whom he admired, Döblin manages to convey the impression that the imagined worlds of his novels are intensely real for the figures who move in them, and hence for the reader also. He scored his greatest success with *Berlin Alexanderplatz* (1929), which unlike the earlier novels is set in a world of which he had first-hand knowledge – the tough and criminal underworld of the East End in contemporary Berlin.

Berlin Alexanderplatz tells how a rather pig-headed furniture-remover, Franz Biberkopf, tries to start a new life after coming out of prison. His story is presented in the manner of an eighteenth-century moral tale, with interspersed comments and admonishments by the narrator. But 'die Geschichte von Franz Biberkopf' is only the sub-title of the novel. Its aim is to convey a densely packed unit of collective reality, to which Biberkopf belongs as if he were merely one cell in a large and complex organism. Döblin uses the techniques of literary *montage* and *collage* to emphasize the inextricable interconnection of all the elements of this dynamic and fluid world in which his hero is embedded. The telling of his story is accompanied by excerpts from newspapers, official statistics, weather reports, stock market reports, police reports, etc., and the author deliberately foils our efforts to distinguish clearly between this patchwork and the contents of Biberkopf's personal consciousness. And indeed, in so far as the novel is a moral tale, this is what he learns: he comes to accept the fact that his obstinate attempts to assert himself as an independent individual are misguided and futile.

Döblin insists, in his many essays about modern epic writing, on the artistic virtue of *Sachlichkeit* as opposed to the portrayal of man's inner life; he recommends the novelist to render what is public rather than private, the collective in preference to the personal. 'Ich bin ein Feind des Persönlichen,' he declares. 'Es ist nichts als Schwindel und Lyrik damit. Zum Epischen taugen Einzelpersonen und ihre sogenannten Schicksale nicht.' Like Brecht, Döblin regarded the literature of soulful inwardness as inappropriate to the modern world.

Despite its 'moral tale' framework *Berlin Alexanderplatz* stands as the most radically modernist novel of the twenties. It offends all the classical prescriptions, such as regularity of form, unity of tone, linguistic decorum, a neatly resolved conclusion. It submits itself to both the disorderliness and the grand underlying rhythms of the physical world. The story is so soaked in reality, so full of the stuff of life, that the storyteller can go off on the most wayward and baroque excursions without fear of breaking the spell (cf. *Moby Dick*); he can lace his narrative with mythical reference and literary quotation without giving the impression of intellectual construction or private whimsy.

In his essay *Der Bau des epischen Werkes* (1929) Döblin declares that it is not enough for the epic writer to press his nose close against public reality; he must break through its surface to find the 'einfachen großen elementaren Grundsituationen und Figuren des menschlichen Daseins'. He regarded himself as a neo-Naturalist; he preached and practised a toughly realistic form of art which was, however, no longer hamstrung by crude mimetic doctrine, by the slavish imitation of externals. Unlike the naturalists he believed that if the writer was to produce a living work he must allow full rein to his imaginative story-building powers ('die springende Fabulierkunst des Autors'). On the other hand he was fully in sympathy with the naturalists' desire to get away from the refinements and artificialities of a purely literary language: in the good tradition of Luther he maintained that the writer should 'follow the stream of the living [i.e. the spoken] language'. In all the above respects, particularly in the last, Döblin's position is close to that of Brecht. What Döblin attempted during the twenties for the novel, Brecht attempted for lyric poetry and the theatre. In a letter to Döblin of 1928 Brecht speaks of the need to find a form of theatre 'die für die Bühne dasselbe möglich macht, was den Unterschied zwischen Ihren und Manns [i.e. Thomas Mann's] Romanen bildet', an epic form of theatre which could cope with the kind of material embodied in *Wang-lun* or *Wallenstein*. Döblin for his part declared in 1929: 'Ich sehe . . . keinen deutlichen Weg für den heutigen Epiker, es sei denn der Weg zu einer – neuen Bühne.'

Bertolt Brecht first achieved fame in the twenties, and all his later works and theories have their roots in that decade. Like Wedekind he was fired by a strong distaste for the bourgeoisie from which he sprang, and his early works celebrate the amorality and earthy vitality of social outcasts and outlaws (e.g. his first play *Baal*, 1922). He was fascinated by the images of jungle and ocean, tiger and shark, and many of his poems affirm with fatalistic delight the fierce self-seeking of natural life. (For Brecht the basic drive of the human animal was the pleasure-drive, not as for Nietzsche the power-drive.) His intense sympathy with man's natural hungers, which he always retained, came into conflict with his awakening concern for social justice. This is the main reason, apart from his intellectually demanding artistic techniques, why it is often so difficult to know how to take those of his works which are not overtly propagandist. His usual answer, namely that he just wants to puncture our preconceptions and set us thinking, is not always adequate. A case in point is *Die Dreigroschenoper* (première 1928).

Die Dreigroschenoper, based on John Gay's *Beggar's Opera* (1728), was Brecht's most popular work, but it owed its popularity more to its sheer entertainment value as a witty and novel kind of theatrical show than to the serious social implications by which the author set such great store. He over-estimated, not for the last time, the critical agility of his audience and the amount of intellectual work that can be expected of a man watching a show (even if he is allowed to smoke, as Brecht thought he should be). He took over most of Gay's characters and the outline of his plot. Macheath (Mackie Messer) secretly marries Polly Peachum, the daughter of another crook, and Peachum then plans his arrest. Through the treachery of a prostitute, Jenny, Macheath is captured, but he escapes again with the help of another of his women, Lucy (in Brecht's version she is the daughter of the police chief). He is recaptured and taken to the gallows, then reprieved at the last moment in order to satisfy operatic conventions ('Damit ihr wenigstens in der Oper seht / Wie einmal Gnade vor Recht ergeht'). While Gay's satire was intended to assault the supposedly remediable banditry of a given aristocratic group, Brecht wished to expose the built-in banditry of the bourgeoisie and to liken the workings of capitalist society, based on expropriation and exploitation, to organized crime. This works well enough with Peachum, who in Brecht's version regards misery as a commodity and is in trade as a fitter-out of bogus beggars. As a bourgeois type of criminal Peachum can duly indicate the criminality of the bourgeoisie. But it was not so easy to deny to Macheath all the characteristics which belong to the sympathetic criminal of literary tradition – boldness, quick-wittedness, zest for life, etc. Brecht had more than a sneaking admiration for the ruthless materialism and hungry vitality of the genuine criminal underworld, and he had to struggle to prevent his Mackie Messer from approximating to one of Wedekind's robust and aesthetically appealing scoundrels. In his 'Notes for Actors' he finds it necessary to insist that when Macheath visits the whores of Turnbridge he should be shown less as a pleasure-seeker than as a prisoner of middle-class routine.

The songs of *Die Dreigroschenoper* (set to music by Kurt Weill, see p. 650) are separate 'numbers' which interrupt the action and comment on its implications. The organ is illuminated, a placard giving the song-title is lowered, and the characters step out of their roles to perform their vocal number. 'Nothing is more revolting', says Brecht, 'than when the actor pretends not to notice that he has left the level of plain speech and started to sing.' Such songs, which are also introduced into most of the plays, provide a good illustration of the main principles of his work for the theatre. He required the various elements composing a theatrical work to remain clearly distinct, by contrast to the Wagnerian *Gesamtkunstwerk* in which text, music, gesture and visual effects are 'cooked' into a unified 'mush'. Instead of involving the audience emotionally in the events depicted on the stage, instead of giving them 'an experience' through the creation of powerful illusion, he wanted to ensure that they remained in a detached and critically alert frame of mind. Both in the construction of his works and in the manner of their presentation he tried every trick to keep the spectator on his toes and prevent him from falling into a state of bemused enchantment. Brecht's disenchanting, disillusioning or 'alienating' techniques (*Verfremdungseffekte*) – above all the abrupt breaks of tone and temporal sequence, and the switchings of perspective – were designed first of all to jolt the conventional aesthetic expectations of the bourgeoisie and the social attitudes underlying them. In a note of 1920 he declares that if he could get a theatre of his own he would engage a couple of clowns to shift scenes openly in tragedies and exchange vulgar comments about the action, the actors and the audience. Later on, after he had become fully committed to Marxist Communism in the late twenties, he found that his alienating devices were well fitted to expose the inherent 'contradictions' of capitalist society.

Brecht's major plays were written during his fifteen years of exile from Germany (1933–48). They all belong to what he called the 'non-Aristotelian' or 'epic' kind of drama, but they were highly diverse. *Der gute Mensch von Sezuan* (written 1938–41) and *Der kaukasische Kreidekreis* (1943–5) are parables; *Mutter Courage und ihre Kinder* (1938–9) is a historical chronicle; *Leben des Galilei* (1937–9) a dramatic biography. Whether or not they take the form of the parable they remain essentially instructional in character; they are educational exercises designed to open the eyes and sharpen the analytical wits of all who take part in them, including the audience. The instructor remains a convinced Marxist, and the truths that we are cunningly encouraged to perceive are Marxist truths, but these later pieces are no longer simple illustrations of socio-political theorems like the *Lehrstücke* of the early thirties (e.g. *Die Maßnahme*, première 1930). They are much richer than that. Characters like Galileo and Mutter Courage are no mere demonstration models used to bring out 'social contradictions'; they embody something of the living complexity and contradictoriness of real human beings. And they therefore engage our sympathy, as we observe them caught up in moral dilemmas and tragic or potentially tragic situations. Certainly our emotional involvement is constantly broken or neutralized, according to the general principle of the *V-Effekt*, but it looms larger than Brecht allowed for in theory. Indeed it is precisely the fruitful tension between moral/emotional engagement and scientific detachment which makes these plays so effective.

Brecht's major achievements lie in his work for the stage and in his verse. Just as one hesitates to call him a dramatist (he preferred to call himself a *Stückschreiber*) so there is some awkwardness in speaking of him as a 'lyric' poet. For he broke radically with what lyric poetry was commonly supposed to be, 'the expression by the poet of his own feelings' (Ruskin). His own poems are essentially communications, and they are written primarily with oral communiction to an audience in mind, rather than as private reading matter. Thus he tries to give them something of the 'gestural' (*gestisch*) quality of speech. His overriding aim was to break down the barriers that had come to separate poetry from the practical life of man in society, to write poems which 'need not fear the real world' (Max Frisch).

In terms of classical genre-theory Brecht wanted to approximate 'lyric' as well as 'dramatic' to 'epic', to infiltrate poetry as well as the theatre with elements of narrative and critical comment. In the field of the lyric this meant above all balladic writing: ballads or poems of that type bulk large in his verse, especially in his most famous collection *Bertolt Brechts Hauspostille* (1927). Here Rudyard Kipling, Frank Wedekind, and François Villon were his chief models. After the *Hauspostille*, under the pressure of rising Fascism, his poetry became either more coolly and rationally didactic or filled with political rage and scorn. The best of his later poems, however, transcend by their humanity both his justified but disfiguring hatred of the Third Reich and the arid dialectics of Marxist theory. His poem 'An die Nachgeborenen' (1938) ends thus:

> Auch der Haß gegen die Niedrigkeit
> Verzerrt die Züge.
> Auch der Zorn über das Unrecht
> macht die Stimme heiser. Ach, wir
> Die wir den Boden bereiten wollten für Freundlichkeit
> Konnten selber nicht freundlich sein.

> Ihr aber, wenn es so weit sein wird
> Daß der Mensch dem Menschen ein Helfer ist
> Gedenkt unsrer
> Mit Nachsicht.

Brecht regarded literature – and the other arts – as tools of social change, and many writers of the twenties shared this view. The polarization of art and letters according to the political allegiance of the author became more and more apparent, and at the extremes (particularly at the left extreme) they shaded over, through satire and 'documentary', into straight political journalism (Tucholsky) or into public political lessons and demonstrations (Piscator). The ablest of the left-wing satirists was Kurt Tucholsky (1890–1935), who also wrote under the pseudonyms of Peter Panter, Ignaz Wrobel, Theobald Tiger and Kaspar Hauser. He attacked with wit and passion the military, the nationalists, the stock exchange, the Church, the snobs and the

Korpsstudenten. Like his friend George Grosz, the great satirical draughts-man, he managed to discomfit his adversaries precisely because he rarely overstepped the thin border between politically engaged art and artless political engagement. Tucholsky was a major contributor to the periodical *Die Weltbühne*, which during the twenties was the most important organ of the intellectual Left.

Erwin Piscator's work as a theatrical director also deserves mention here: he gave an account of it in his book *Das politische Theater* (1929). According to Piscator, who was a revolutionary Marxist, the 1914–18 war had finally buried 'bourgeois individualism'. He took it as a fact that man had so far forfeited his autonomy in the modern world that he could no longer claim our interest save as a representative of his class and in relation to society as a whole. He quotes with approval Brecht's remark: 'Jeder chinesische Kuli ist, um sein Mittagbrot zu verdienen, gezwungen, Weltpolitik zu treiben.' Since there were, objectively speaking, no longer any private individuals or personal problems it could no longer be the task of art to deal with them. As far as the theatre was concerned, said Piscator, private scenes must be 'raised to the plane of history' ('ins Historische gesteigert'), by which he meant that their 'true' political, economic and social significance should be brought out and made plain.

In order to achieve this 'Steigerung der privaten Szenen ins Politische, Ökonomische, Soziale' Piscator used a variety of devices to supplement and elucidate the stage action. What the actors were capable of repre-senting had to be set, by montage, in its wider context. Mechanical recordings were pressed into service and the most striking device was the projection of documentary film. Here were the facts, here was the 'große Welt', in which all the incidents of the 'kleine Welt' were willy-nilly embedded. The film was used thus in Piscator's production (1927) of Ernst Toller's play *Hoppla, wir leben*, in which the audience was informed, by seven minutes of documentary film, about the nine years of history which had passed the hero by. The introduction of filmed pictures on to the stage, whether as background commentary or as a more closely integrated element of the action, was a main feature of Piscator's 'political theatre', which from the formal point of view was 'epic theatre'. His productions deserve that title with more justifica-tion than Brecht's associated experiments as a dramatic writer. He helped to set Brecht on his way, and his complaint in the twenties was the lack of scripts or scenarios suitable for his purposes. He used the *Zeitstücke* of Alfons Paquet (*Sturmflut*, 1926) and Ehm Welk (*Gewitter über Gotland,* 1927), turned Schiller's *Die Räuber* to account, and concentrated otherwise on adapting purely epic material (e.g. Jaroslav Hašek's *Die Abenteuer des braven Soldaten Schwejk,* première 1927).

Piscator was one of those who thought that life had become so permeated with politics that man was no longer artistically interesting save as a political object ('Der Mensch auf der Bühne hat für uns die Bedeutung einer gesellschaftlichen Funktion'). The extreme opposite view is represented by Gottfried Benn, who regarded mankind as essentially incorrigible and poured scorn on the idea of political literature. In a radio dialogue of 1930 with the poet Oskar Loerke he declared that works of art were great precisely because they had no historical effect and were of no practical consequence. Benn was a 'non-political' artist in the special sense that he abhorred the ideas of 1789 (cf. Thomas Mann's *Betrachtungen eines Unpolitischen*): his desire to preserve art in a sphere 'above' the vulgar issues of the day proved quite compatible with his support for the main features of the Nazi ideology (see below).

In this brief survey of the twenties stress has been laid on the 'modernist' writers who sought new forms of literary expression specifically appropriate to the time. But there were others who conceived it their task to build literary bulwarks against the time. These also deserve mention; they include especially those whose faith in Christianity, or whose reverence for the ideals of German classicism, was still intact. Hans Carossa wrote poetic autobiography (*Eine Kindheit,* 1922; *Rumänisches Tagebuch,* 1924) and stories (*Der Arzt Gion,* 1931) which lean heavily on Goethe. In lyric poetry there was a minor neoclassical revival: Rudolf Borchardt's *Vermischte Gedichte* (1924), Rudolf Alexander Schröder's collection *Mitte des Lebens* (1930), Friedrich Georg Jünger's *Gedichte* (1934). Such poems, self-consciously traditional in theme and form, belong at the opposite extreme to Brecht's *Hauspostille*. In the traditionalist camp there was talk of a 'creative restoration' ('Schöpferische Restauration', title of a speech by Rudolf Borchardt in 1927), and of a 'conservative revolution' (Hofmannsthal). In his essay 'Das Schrifttum als geistiger Raum der Nation' (1927) Hofmannsthal defines the goal of the conservative revolution thus: 'Ihr Ziel ist Form, eine neue deutsche Wirklichkeit, an der die ganze Nation teilnehmen könne.' The phrase has an unhappy ring and the humane conservatives who spoke in this manner soon found themselves at the mercy of the right-wing barbarians. An organ of the 'conservative revolution' in literature was the periodical *Corona,* founded in

1930 after Hofmannsthal's death and very much in his spirit. Between 1930 and 1933 the contributors included Rudolf Borchardt, Hans Carossa, Hermann Hesse, Ricarda Huch, Thomas Mann, R. A. Schröder and the Romance scholar Karl Vossler. But *Corona* also found room for authors of a very different character and outlook: the popular story-teller Rudolf Binding (*Opfergang*, 1912), the political novelist Hans Grimm (*Volk ohne Raum*, 1926) and the literary historian Josef Nadler (*Literaturgeschichte der deutschen Stämme und Landschaften*), none of whom found difficulty in accommodating himself to the Third Reich.

The Third Reich

The Nazis made use of their unchecked power to paralyse German literature as a civilized and civilizing force. Only those writers who were deemed racially and ideologically sound ('deutschblütig und im Sinne des neuen Staates einwandfrei') were permitted to remain active; the rest were silenced or driven from the country. Brecht and Döblin, Thomas and Heinrich Mann, Toller and Schickele, Werfel and Zuckmayer were among the hundreds who sought refuge abroad. Initially the exiles formed groups in Amsterdam and Vienna, Paris and Prague, Basle and Zürich, but as the German power spread over Europe they were pushed further afield: an account of one dramatic escape from France in 1940 is given in Döblin's *Schicksalsreise* (1949). Those who stayed behind were forced, if they wanted to preserve their integrity, into an 'internal emigration' (*innere Emigration*) which was often painful enough. Hitler's regime had to depend in the literary sphere on hacks and nonentities, for no writer of worth was willing to support it for long.

The case of Gottfried Benn is exceptional. He greeted the new state with fervour, writing gleefully of the 'Verlust des Ich an das Totale, den Staat, die Rasse, das Immanente', of the 'Wendung vom ökonomischen zum mythischen Kollektiv' (*Der neue Staat und die Intellektuellen*, 1933). History had spoken, he declared in the same essay, and had sent the 'new biological type' ahead; the time had come for each individual to fall silently into line and join the march. But he made it plain that 'history' needed some assistance from genetic engineers in breeding the new German type: 'Die Ergänzung dieses auszuscheidenden minderwertigen Volksteils [he refers to simple-minded children] soll durch qualitativ hochwertiges Menschenmaterial erfolgen' (*Geist und Seele künftiger Geschlechter*, 1933). The sentence may be analysed as a prime example of Nazi prose. Benn had indeed never made any secret of his contempt for liberal, humanitarian and democratic principles; what is disturbing from the literary point of view is that he could accommodate himself to crude jargon with such ease, and that later he showed no sign of grasping his own contribution to the pollution of letters.

In Benn the new masters of Germany had the sole poet of standing who supported their ideology. On the other hand the poetry that had made him famous was precisely the kind of modernistic and anti-naturalistic poetry that the official cultural policy deplored. Here was a famous poet who seemed to have the right ideas, but what he had actually produced was decadent ('entartete Kunst'). In order to maintain cordiality between Benn and the regime much shuffling was necessary on both sides. Benn for his part tried to make expressionism respectable in retrospect ('eine große geschlossene Front von Künstlern ausschließlich europäischer Erbmasse'); he also insisted on the connection between the cult of formal perfection in art and the imposition of the new political order (e.g. by likening the discipline of Stefan George's poetry to the 'Kolonnenschritt der braunen Bataillone'). As far as the regime was concerned, Himmler wrote in 1937 that he considered it pointless to hound Benn for his previous artistic misdemeanours since he had behaved 'absolutely impeccably' from a political point of view after 1933. But even Himmler could not shield him from the extremists: in 1938 he was excluded from the *Reichsschrifttumskammer* and forbidden to write.

Within Germany, meditative poetry of a private kind was best placed to escape damage. The nature-lyrics of Wilhelm Lehmann (*Antwort des Schweigens*, 1935; *Der grüne Gott*, 1942) are marked by great clarity and by severity of form; their emotional restraint was admired and imitated in the immediate post-war years. Another outstanding poet working within the framework of the traditional German lyric was Gertrud Kolmar (*Das lyrische Werk*, 1960). Not even a Nazi could describe her poetry as 'decadent'; nevertheless, being a Jewess, she met her death in an extermination camp in 1943. Apart from lyric poetry it was only the novel and the short story that offered serious writers some chance of continuing to speak with their own voice, provided always that they were not too experimental in their literary habits. The Christian faith afforded strength to many of them, and a measure – though a decreasing measure – of protection, e.g. Gertrud von Le Fort (*Die Magdeburgische Hochzeit*, 1936), Werner Bergengruen (*Der Großtyrann und das Gericht*, 1935). At its logical extreme 'internal emigration' meant writing books, while in constant danger of arrest by the Gestapo, that could only reach print if and when the Third Reich was overthrown. The most impressive of such books was the *Tag- und Nachtbücher*, *1939–1945* by Theodor Haecker, published posthumously in 1947. Haecker was a prolific Christian writer who had translated Kierkegaard and Newman into German; his wartime reflections and aphorisms show the resistance of a strong mind to totalitarian power. Among those who preferred to express their opposition to the regime publicly, in whatever muffled ways they could, there were some who had held pronouncedly nationalist views, like Ernst Jünger (*Auf den Marmorklippen*, 1939) and Rudolf Pechel, the editor of the *Deutsche Rundschau* during the early Nazi years. It is a mistake to suppose that the opposition to Nazism came solely from the Left. But the fact remains that little of merit was published in Germany during the Third Reich, and that the younger generation was totally inhibited from developing its powers freely. Having no literary past they were neither driven into freedom abroad nor sheltered by their reputation at home.

On 10 May 1933 'poisonous literature' ('das zersetzende Schrifttum') was consigned to the flames at all German universities in a symbolic act of purification. Three days later Oskar Maria Graf complained that his own books had not received the honour of destruction, and he added: 'Das Dritte Reich hat fast das ganze Schrifttum von Bedeutung ausgestossen, hat sich losgesagt von der wirklichen deutschen Dichtung, hat die größte Zahl ihrer wesentlichsten Schriftsteller ins Exil gejagt und das Erscheinen ihrer Werke in Deutschland unmöglich gemacht.' The literature thus dispersed in exile (*Emigrantenliteratur*) met grave difficulties, and it bears damaging marks of bitterness or despair. The suicide of such authors as Toller, Tucholsky, and Stefan Zweig seemed even to confirm Goebbels' barbaric judgement on the exiles of 1933: 'Ihr Lebensfaden ist abgeschnitten, sie sind Kadaver auf Urlaub.' Fortunately that is not the whole story.

The periodicals *Die Sammlung* (1933–5, published in Amsterdam), *Maß und Wert* (1937–40, published in Zürich), and *Das Wort* (1936–9, published in Moscow) showed that the literature in exile was a force to be reckoned with, despite all the political dissensions among Hitler's opponents and victims. In the field of drama the plays of Brecht stand out (see above); Carl Zuckmayer's *Des Teufels General* (1946) is a drama in realistic style which treats the theme of revulsion against the

U

Nazi regime with insight and understanding. Anna Seghers's story of escape from a concentration camp (*Das siebte Kreuz*, 1942) and Theodor Plievier's *Stalingrad* (1945), based on documentary evidence and the interrogation of German prisoners after the battle, are good examples of 'socialist realism' in the novel. In the United States the sentimental novels of Franz Werfel gained popularity (e.g. *Das Lied von Bernadette*, 1941). Among the novels with greater artistic and philosophical pretensions Thomas Mann's *Doktor Faustus* (1947) and Hermann Broch's *Der Tod des Vergil* (1945) deserve fuller mention.

In *Doktor Faustus* Mann reverts (as he explains in his long essay *Die Entstehung des Doktor Faustus*, 1949) to a main theme of his early work, namely the pathological and inhumane aspects of art. And he links this theme to another of his major concerns, the moral and spiritual health of Germany. The 'Faust' of the novel, Adrian Leverkühn, is a musician. He had to be so, Mann decided, if he was to symbolize the German artistic spirit at its most adventurous and dazzling, at its most exposed to the seduction of evil, and indeed if he was to symbolize all the most abstract and mystical leanings of the German mind. The tendency of this novel in general is to warn the Germans against the dangers of excessive *Innerlichkeit*. The life-story of the composer Leverkühn (1885–1940) is narrated by a pedantic schoolmaster, Serenus Zeitblom, and it is through the narrator that the history of the 'Faust' figure is connected with contemporary events: Nazism, the 1939–45 war and Germany's collapse. The symbolic figure of Leverkühn, who is modelled in many ways on Nietzsche, thus stands behind the foreground of the disastrous Third Reich and illuminates it. In addition to all this Mann uses the story of Leverkühn as a vehicle for exploring the development of modern music, drawing especially on the theories of Schoenberg, and he 'composes' imaginary musical works in descriptive prose of great virtuosity. But in the end *Doktor Faustus* tells us more about Mann's self-enclosed system of thought than about anything else.

The same applies even more strongly to Broch's *Der Tod des Vergil*. The book recounts the last hours of Virgil, mostly from within, as a kind of interior monologue; we are given the dying poet's memories, sensations and lyrical meditations, besides his weighty conversations with the Emperor Augustus. The chief theme is the Platonic question of the legitimacy of art, which had been so popular at the beginning of the century: how does art stand in relation to morality, to the powers of love and death, to knowledge of Truth or spiritual reality? The surface issue is whether Virgil should or should not destroy his *Aeneid*.

Der Tod des Vergil is an impressive literary experiment but it is extremely mannered and verbose, and it rebuffs many readers by proclaiming its own profundity with such solemn insistence.

It appears that exile was a tolerable condition only for the more introspective and reflective German authors, and that it had the effect of driving them deeper into their private labyrinths (cf. Musil's *Der Mann ohne Eigenschaften*, Hans Henny Jahnn's *Fluß ohne Ufer*, 1949ff.). Even Brecht, who may be regarded as the great exception, was forced to some extent into a world of private theory. So it happened that the Third Reich, by pressing German literature into 'internal' or into literal emigration, succeeded in prolonging and intensifying its most characteristic habit, that of self-isolation from public reality. The enforced emigrations of all kinds served to encourage the ancient tendency of German literature to form an archipelago of separate islands rather than a coherent landscape.

After 1945

Ferocious warfare and great devastation, followed by defeat and occupation, left Germany temporarily numb in 1945. It was the 'year zero' (*das Jahr Null*), when everything had to be rebuilt from scratch, and the task of remaking German literature was particularly daunting. There was first the matter of getting the machinery of literary life going again: book publishing, literary journals, literary societies, theatres. It was a slow job, and for a few years the most effective medium for writers and critics was the radio. It was by radio that an early post-war success, Wolfgang Borchert's play *Draußen vor der Tür* (written 1946), made its impact, and the radio play (*Hörspiel*) soon came into prominence as an independent literary form.

Apart from the practical difficulties of publication and communication, writers had to cope with the deepest spiritual gloom and intellectual confusion. And they had to handle a language that had been systematically perverted for a long time: 'nicht einmal die Sprache war mehr zu gebrauchen,' complains Wolfdietrich Schnurre; 'die Nazijahre und die Kriegspropaganda hatten sie unrein gemacht.' Moreover, during the years of proud self-isolation under Hitler, Germany had allowed a whole period of European and American literature to pass it by. Post-war authors were confronted and often bewildered by the need to catch up. Who were Joyce and Sartre? Who were Thornton Wilder, Faulkner and Hemingway? Indeed who were Kafka, Döblin and Brecht? After the sudden opening of the literary frontiers this need to catch up (*Nachholbedarf*) led to a good deal of indigestion and pastiche writing. Kafka and Hemingway in particular were much imitated.

In the Soviet occupation zone, later the German Democratic Republic, the opening of frontiers was of course selective. Writers in the eastern part of Germany merely received a new set of political leading-strings, and they soon found that they were required to toe the line of official cultural policy in the way to which they had become accustomed under Nazism. For example, a resolution of the SED (the ruling, Communist-dominated party) declared in January 1949: 'The contribution of artists and writers to the two-year national plan consists in the development of a "realistic" art.' This was an order and a threat, not a piece of avuncular advice. Since 1945 the division between an 'open' West German literature (that of the Federal Republic, allied to that of Austria and German-speaking Switzerland) and a 'closed' East German literature under direction from Moscow has become wide and painful.

A major feature of post-war German literature, at least until 1960, has been the preoccupation with the theme of moral responsibility and guilt in relation to Germany's immediate national past. As the scale of Nazi atrocities became known, in particular the murder of millions of innocent people on the grounds that they were racially undesirable, the weight of conscious or unconscious guilt-feelings made itself felt even where complicity in evil deeds was not the overt issue of the work. No writer of the late forties and the fifties could quite avoid a reckoning with the past (*Bewältigung der Vergangenheit*), even if he chose, like Ernst von Salomon (*Der Fragebogen*, 1951), to shunt the burden of guilt on to others. On the other hand there was a tendency among *bona fide* opponents of Nazism – particularly in East Germany – to get stuck in the barren rehearsal of vengeful and vindictive sentiments.

In 1947 Hans Werner Richter founded with some friends the 'Gruppe 47', a loose association of 'politically engaged publicists with literary ambitions'. This phrase of Richter's was carefully chosen; it indicates that the group, which had a decisive influence, was firmly opposed to any kind of aestheticism, to any cult of formal values. Writers whose aim was still to write 'beautiful prose' were despised as 'Kalligraphen'; words like 'Dichtung' and 'Poesie' were at a discount, while 'Aussage' ('personal statement') and 'Wahrheitsgehalt' ('truth content') stood at a premium. The members of Gruppe 47 were agreed that the social and political function of imaginative literature was of the first importance. They wished to write 'politically engaged' literature, without, however, betraying art to politics by becoming mere partisans. Their political position is best defined as belief in a genuinely democratic form of socialism. They had been opponents of Nazism and were opponents of Stalinism for similar reasons, but they also opposed the restoration of the capitalist system and of bourgeois habits and institutions in Germany. They were committed Europeans, distrustful of nationalism; anti-authoritarian, and for the most part anti-clerical. Generally speaking, they took up again – with far more success than the writers of the twenties – those *Aufklärung* ideals which Germany had so repeatedly rejected.

The Gruppe 47 has gradually ceased to emphasize its political stance, and during the late fifties and the sixties it has become more like a guild of literary craftsmen. Its enemies have accused it of becoming authoritarian itself and of trying to dictate the course of German literature; the truth is that it needed to exert no pressure to make itself the rallying point of what was best in post-war writing. The authors who have read their works at meetings of Gruppe 47 are not held together by any political or religious orthodoxy; what binds them is a shared sense of their moral responsibility as writers, coupled with a common willingness to renounce the vanities and pomposities to which successful literary men in Germany have been prone. They include Ingeborg Bachmann, Johannes Bobrowski, Heinrich Böll, Paul Celan, Günther Eich, Hans Magnus Enzensberger, Erich Fried, Günther Grass, Uwe Johnson, Siegfried Lenz, Christa Reinig, Martin Walser and Peter Weiss. With the addition of only a few names – the East German poet Peter Huchel, the Swiss authors Friedrich Dürrenmatt and Max Frisch, the Austrian novelist Heimito von Doderer – the above list probably contains the best authors writing in German since 1945.

For some years after the war German literature was governed by the need to effect a *Kahlschlag* (clear-felling) of the entrancing forest of German Romanticism, in whose shade the demons had thrived. This metaphor was not coined until 1949, but it fits the early post-war literature which is marked by severe linguistic circumspection, modesty of theme, restriction to personal experience and a tone of sober understatement. Writers were wary of rhetorical effects and emotional self-indulgence, wary of music and metaphysics and of all ideological systems. The short story was the most popular literary form, indeed it was the obvious literary form in which to state facts and record situations that were too appalling to require explicit comment. Each story was a modest item in the inventory (*Bestandsaufnahme*) of ruin. Lament and protest wore the mask of gruff objectivity, as in the stories of Wolfdietrich Schnurre (*Man sollte dagegen sein*, 1960, written 1945–7). The outstanding author of the *Kahlschlag* period was Heinrich Böll. Böll's war novel *Wo warst du, Adam?* (1951) is made up of nine loosely connected episodes. War is depicted in realistic detail, and without special emphasis on blood and torture, as the great meaningless pastime that calls man away from his humanity. Unlike Hans Werner Richter (*Die Geschlagenen*, 1949; *Sie fielen aus Gottes Hand*, 1951) Böll presents nothing to alleviate the gloomy picture; what is positive about the book, the sympathy and faith of the author, has to make itself felt indirectly by the manner of narration (cf. Kafka). As the title *Wo warst du, Adam?* implies (see the entry of 31 March 1940 in Theodor Haecker's *Tag- und Nachtbücher*), the novel is more than merely an indictment of war; its theme is basically man's willingness to accept an alibi, his readiness to acquiesce in whatever may relieve him of personal moral responsibility. This is a theme to which Böll frequently returns in his later novels depicting life in post-war Germany (e.g. *Und sagte kein einziges Wort*, 1953; *Haus ohne Hüter*, 1954). *Billard um halbzehn* (1959) is a more ambitious work than its predecessors and attempts to throw light on fifty years of German history, using techniques of flashback and reminiscent interior monologue. In some ways – the use of insistent leitmotifs and the preoccupation with family and national tradition – this novel harks back to the grand narrative patterns of Thomas Mann. But Böll's true talent lies elsewhere, in the imaginative (and often humorous) development of acutely observed detail. This comes out best in the early novels, in his radio plays and in his masterly short stories (*Wanderer, kommst du nach Spa . . .*, 1950; *Doktor Murkes gesammeltes Schweigen*, 1958).

Other prose works of the fifties include Ilse Aichinger's *Der Gefesselte* (1953; short stories), Hans Erich Nossak's *Spätestens im November* (1955; novel), Martin Walser's *Ein Flugzeug über dem Haus* (1955; short stories), Alfred Andersch's *Sansibar oder der letzte Grund* (1957; novel), Siegfried Lenz's *Jäger des Spotts* (1958; short stories). None of these works has the originality and vigour of *Die Blechtrommel* (1959), the novel that made Günther Grass famous.

Die Blechtrommel is a landmark because in it the whole wary, guilt-ridden *Kahlschlag* mentality is overcome and an ebullient artist displays his powers without inhibition. Here Grass is still writing, like the others, about the recent German past (the best part of the novel is set in Danzig during the Hitler period), but he treats it in a fanciful and humoristic manner. His chief device is to invent a gnome-like hero – Oskar – who has chosen to remain arrested at an infantile, pre-moral stage, and who can thus permit his author the luxury of exploring the world from a wholly irreverent and irresponsible viewpoint. With his magic weapons, a tin drum and a supersonic voice that cuts holes in plate-glass windows, Oskar can express his protest against established patterns of thought and behaviour. The novel gives us a scurrilous view of the world seen 'from below', with plenty of ruthlessly observed physical detail (cf. Swift). In his second novel, *Hundejahre* (1963), which is a more explicit reckoning with Germany's national past, Grass harnesses his visual imagination more firmly to the sober political convictions that underlie his work. But like most members of the Gruppe 47 he is acutely sensitive to the dangers of falling into dogmatizing and mere propaganda; by constantly asserting the autonomy of his inventive powers he makes it impossible for us to construe his novels as pamphlets. On the other hand, while emphasizing the 'artistic' nature of his writing, he takes good care to defend himself (e.g. by his obscenities) against any charge of haughty aestheticism.

By contrast to Grass's rather loose and free-wheeling novels, those of Uwe Johnson (*Mutmassungen über Jakob*, 1959; *Das dritte Buch über Achim*, 1961) are most carefully constructed. They are designed to bring out the difficulty of establishing the truth about human actions, about character and motive. This is done largely by confronting the reader with a confusing patchwork of evidence, which makes the novels hard to read (in *Mutmassungen*, for instance, there are long anonymous dialogue sections in which the speakers have to be identified). The context is Germany recently divided, with prejudice and cliché hardening on both sides of the internal border, and the strategic aim of Johnson's writing is to work against facile interpretations of events and crude political judgements. He was most anxious not to be 'used' politically when he came across from East Germany to the West in 1959.

While the post-war novelists within Germany, like Böll, Grass and Johnson, have been profoundly involved in the specific problems of their own country, the Swiss novelist Max Frisch could allow himself a more detached and philosophical view of modern difficulties. His novels (*Stiller*, 1954; *Homo faber*, 1957; *Mein Name sei Gantenbein*, 1964) turn on questions of personal identity and what the existentialists called an 'authentic' mode of life. Am I running away from my true self instead of accepting it? But how can I be sure what my true self is? Et cetera. Frisch tells his stories with persuasive realistic detail, but they remain subject to their rather bloodless conceptual scheme. The problem of self-identification has preoccupied a number of post-war German writers, and has often been treated as a matter of social psychology, with emphasis on the conflicting roles imposed on the individual by a complex social and cultural environment.

Post-war dramatic and lyrical work must be noticed more briefly. For some ten years the German stage was dominated by foreign plays in translation (American, French, English) and by the Swiss authors Friedrich Dürrenmatt and Max Frisch. Dürrenmatt considered that comedy, of a more or less grotesque kind, was alone appropriate to the modern world (see his essay *Theaterprobleme* of 1955). He went in for dramatic parables, with an admixture of parody and farce, and his best work is highly effective theatrically. The most successful of his 'serious comedies' was *Der Besuch der alten Dame* (1956); in some of his plays, e.g. *Romulus der Große* (1958), *Die Physiker* (1962), the positive characters put on the mask of clowns or madmen in order to preserve their integrity within a perverted world. The best dramatic parables of Frisch are *Biedermann und die Brandstifter* (1958) and *Andorra* (1961). A typical moral fable for the theatre in realistic style is Siegfried Lenz's *Zeit der Schuldlosen* (1961).

Since 1960 dramatists have tended to treat the pervasive theme of the individual's moral-political responsibility in the context of specific historical cases, and there has been a revival of a form popular in the twenties – the topical political play based on documentary evidence (Rolf Hochhuth's *Der Stellvertreter*, 1963; Heinar Kipphardt's *In der Sache J. Robert Oppenheimer*, 1964; Peter Weiss's *Die Ermittlung*, 1965). The anchor of historical fact, which had been almost obligatory in East Germany (e.g. Peter Hacks, *Die Schlacht bei Lobositz*, 1956), was now often freely chosen in the West. Günter Grass's *Die Plebejer proben den Aufstand* (1966), a personal attack on Brecht's attitude to the workers' rising of 1953 in East Berlin, is a case in point.

The lyric poem has flourished since the war, as the form most appropriate to the expression of an independent personal view. If in free societies it can be a lure to self-indulgence, in totalitarian states like East Germany it may be the literary artist's last resort. In the East, Johannes Bobrowski (*Sarmatische Zeit*, 1961), Peter Huchel (*Chausseen, Chausseen*, 1963) and Christa Reinig produced impressive collections, while Wolf Biermann (*Die Drahtharfe*, 1965) sang his lively and risky cabaret songs. Whatever of merit still appears there has to be assessed against the background of political dictation. In the West, where such considerations have not applied, the natural variety of lyrical expression is hard to classify. One might distinguish the neo-Brechtian 'committed' poets (e.g. Hans Magnus Enzensberger) from poets like Helmut Heissenbüttel who appear more interested in the formal effects to be derived from the manipulation of language. But, as the work of Erich Fried – for example – shows, grammatical games can themselves be a form of political criticism. Of the older-style 'lyrical' lyric poets, who express more private feelings in a more meditative and evocative way, Paul Celan (*Mohn und Gedächtnis*, 1952; *Sprachgitter*, 1959) and Ingeborg Bachmann (*Die gestundete Zeit*, 1953) have attracted the greatest attention.

Bibliography

The fullest information on this period in German is given by Albert Soergel and Curt Hohoff, *Dichtung und Dichter der Zeit*, 2 vols (Düsseldorf, 1961 and 1963). There are stimulating essays in German by Walter Muschg (*Die Zerstörung der deutschen Literatur*, 3rd enl. edn., Berne, 1958; *Von Trakl zu Brecht*, Munich, 1961), Wolfdietrich Rasch (*Zur deutschen Literatur seit der Jahrhundertwende*, Stuttgart, 1967), Walter Jens (*Statt einer Literaturgeschichte*, 5th enl. edn., Pfullingen, 1962) and Hans Mayer (*Zur deutschen Literatur der Zeit*, Reinbek bei Hamburg, 1967). As far as work in English is concerned, all the following have something to offer:

BITHELL, J. *Modern German Literature 1880–1950*. 3rd edn. London, 1959.
GARTEN, H. F. *Modern German Drama*. London, 1959.
GRAY, R. *The German Tradition in Literature 1871–1945*. Cambridge, 1965.
HAMBURGER, M. *From Prophecy to Exorcism. The Premisses of Modern German Literature*. London, 1965.
HELLER, E. *The Ironic German. A Study of Thomas Mann*. London, 1958.
MASON, E. C. *Rilke*. Edinburgh, 1963.
OSBORNE, J. *The Naturalist Drama in Germany*. Manchester, 1971.
SOKEL, W. H. *The Writer in Extremis. Expressionism in Twentieth Century German Literature*. Stanford, 1959.
SWALES, M. *Arthur Schnitzler*. Oxford, 1971.
THOMAS, R. H., and VAN DER WILL, W. *The German Novel and the Affluent Society*. Manchester, 1968.
VAN ABBÉ, D. M. *Image of a People. The Germans and Their Creative Writing under and since Bismarck*. London, 1964.
WAIDSON, H. M. *The Modern German Novel*. London, 1959.
— *The Modern German Novel 1945–1965*. London, 1971.
WILLETT, J. *The Theatre of Bertolt Brecht*. London, 1959.
— *Expressionism*. London, 1970.

11 German Music

RONALD TAYLOR

The starting-point for a survey of German music lies in the hazy realm of pre-history before there was any geographical, ethnic or other entity to which the word German can be given. That the tribes of pagan Germania sang ballads and heroic lays is reported by Tacitus in the first century A.D., while various chroniclers and contemporary observers also tell of vocal and instrumental music among the Goths, Franks, and other Germanic peoples in the succeeding centuries. The harp and the rotte – the latter akin to the Greek lyre – were used to accompany vocal performance; the earliest preserved relic of such an instrument is a six-string rotte which was discovered near Tuttlingen, in Swabia, in an Alemannic burial mound whose contents date from the fourth to the seventh centuries. Wind and brass instruments are also known to have been in use during these times; from the age of Roman rule we possess *inter alia* a *tibia* and a *fistula*, both discovered in Carinthia, and a mosaic of an hydraulic organ preserved in a Roman villa at Nennig, near Trier.

As to what this music, vocal or instrumental, could have sounded like, we have no idea. Furthermore, although on the basis of old illustrations or fragmentary remains one can often make a reasonable guess about the capabilities of these ancient instruments, or can even manufacture tolerable reproductions of some of them, we cannot know how they were actually played. The fact that it is possible to produce certain sounds on old instruments today does not mean that these sounds were in fact produced on them in former times – and this is true of any period in historical time remote from our own.

The coming of Christianity brought Gregorian chant to Germany, a music as different in style and ethos from indigenous musical tradition as were the concerns of Christian literature from those of Germanic paganism. As the chant established itself in the newly founded church and monastery, so the theoretical discipline of *musica* took its place as one of the Seven Liberal Arts which made up the curriculum of education in monastery schools. These centres of learning were attended not only by those destined for a clerical career but also by those sons of the nobility whose concerns were to be anything but ecclesiastical, so that eventually the Gregorian music which accompanied the liturgical offices could not but have made its influence felt in secular contexts also. Equally, as we know from various minatory decrees issued by the ecclesiastical authorities, certain monastic communities had a disturbing familiarity with music of secular provenance. These two traditions of music-making, the one ecclesiastical, the other secular, each discrete in origin yet far from isolated in development, give a framework within which much of the broad history of medieval music can be viewed.

In the realm of church music, the earliest school of composition and theoretical study to achieve importance on German-speaking soil was that at the Benedictine monastery of St Gallen, in Switzerland. This great centre of learning, which developed from the cell established in 614 by the Irish monk Gall, reached the peak of its power in the early tenth century, and its eminence in the field of music rests on a generation of teachers who bent their particular efforts to the cultivation of the liturgical sequence. The best known of these teachers was Notker, dubbed Balbulus ('The Stammerer', d. 912), the eldest of three famous brethren of this name (the second was a physician, the third an important translator of Latin works into German). Some fifty sequence-melodies attributed to Notker are extant.

Of the secular music of this period nothing, not surprisingly, has survived in written form. For one thing, access to precious parchment and writing materials was confined to monastic *scriptoria*; for another, even fewer scribes could record music than could record words. In these circumstances one would hardly expect to encounter either an opportunity, or an inclination on the part of a scribe, to copy, say, songs which were at best non-religious, and at worst inimical to the values which Christianity was at pains to inculcate. Furthermore, the transmission of folk-music has always rested on an oral rather than a written tradition. However, the literature of the time contains a fair number of descriptions of music-making in secular contexts, so that, although we have no actual music, we do at least have some knowledge of the social situations in which, for example, heroic lays were sung to the accompaniment of a harp, or instruments accompanied the singing and dancing that took place at weddings and other festivities.

The worlds of secular and religious music meet in the first substantial body of non-church music that has survived in Germany: the songs of the Minnesinger. Some of aristocratic descent, some – most of the greatest – of the class of *ministerialis*, un-free nobility, others of humble minstrel origin, these poet-musicians set their poems of courtly love (*Minne*) and their moral, religious and political verse to music, and performed the finished songs at the courts of their patrons. Their activity stretches from about the middle of the twelfth century to about the middle of the fourteenth century, but the 'classical' period of Minnesang lies between about 1180 and 1250. From the early and central periods, which include the greatest names, such as Heinrich von Morungen, Reinmar der Alte and Walther von der Vogelweide, we have only a handful of tunes, but from the generation of Neidhart von Reuenthal onwards (*fl.* 1220–50) the picture is much more complete – although here, too, the manuscripts contain far fewer poems with melodies than without.

There are upwards of 500 Minnesinger melodies extant. By far the greatest number belong to multi-strophe poems, but there are also single-strophe songs and, at the other extreme, *Leiche* – extended lyric lays composed of a large number of heterogeneous strophic sections and often running into hundreds of lines. The manuscripts which contain these melodies give us only a single melodic line, without accompaniment. We know, however, both from literary and pictorial sources, that solo songs could be accompanied on the harp or on the fiddle, and that dance-songs performed by a group of people could involve whatever string, wind or percussion instruments happened to be on hand. But since none of these accompaniments was written down, we cannot know what they consisted of. Certain later Minnesinger, however, the best known being the Austrian knight Oswald von Wolkenstein (*c.* 1337–1445), also wrote polyphonic songs, a fair number of which have been handed down to us alongside his monophonic melodies.

Many of the Minnesinger were educated in a monastery school, and in this environment they would necessarily have encountered the music of Gregorian chant. It is therefore not surprising that a large number of their songs should be cast in one or other of the melodic church modes – the Dorian is by far the commonest – and should show motifs and figurations of melodic line that are derived from plainchant.

At the same time, however, there are melodies in what we would call a 'modern' major key, melodies quite different in style and 'atmosphere' from those in the church modes, and stemming from a secular, not an ecclesiastical tradition. This secular tradition is also linked with the tradition of instrumental playing, and thus with that group in medieval society of whose *métier* performance on musical instruments was an integral part, namely the minstrels. Like the minstrels, and also like the wandering scholars, with whom they often found themselves thrown together, most professional Minnesinger led an itinerant life, roving from court to court and offering their artistic talents to whichever patron would pay for them.

It is in settings of this kind that the idioms of secular music would have passed into the musical vocabulary of the Minnesinger. It would seem probable also that folk-song formed part of this influence, but we cannot tell what the folk-music of the time was actually like, since none of it was written down; the recorded tradition of German folk-song only starts in the mid-fifteenth century.

The Minnesinger possessed a highly developed sense of musical and poetic form, and here too religious and secular sources of influence exist side by side. Certain songs, for example, derive from the antiphonal pattern of the church sequence, while others, such as dance-songs, are drawn from the forms of popular festivities and celebrations.

From the musical point of view, in contrast to the texts of the poems, there is little of a fundamental nature to distinguish the melodies of the Minnesinger from those of their successors in time, the Meistersinger, who continued to flourish down to the end of the sixteenth century and later. More stylized in approach, and with the emphasis on song-writing as a craft to be learned, as one learns any practical trade and becomes a master in it, the Meistersinger took over the principle of strophic and melodic construction which had guided the Minnesinger, but fell into slavish imitation which, as the parodistic but by no means entirely unhistorical presentation in Wagner's *Mastersingers* conveys, made their activity a lifeless art and brought them near to ridicule. As with the songs of the Minnesinger, there are Meistersinger melodies drawn both from the world of plainchant and from the world of secular song; secular instrumental pieces, too, sometimes provided a melody for a song.

An interesting wider aspect of Meistergesang is its relationship to the Reformation. In a famous poem, Hans Sachs (1494–1576), the best known of the Meistersinger, called Luther 'the nightingale of Wittenberg', and the texts of Meistersinger songs were based in large measure on the Lutheran Bible. This is why the cultivation of Meistergesang from the mid-sixteenth century onwards centres in Protestant rather than Catholic towns. Liturgical plays (mysteries) on the other hand, with their accompanying music, appear to have flourished chiefly in Catholic areas, while further elements of popular music found their way into the Protestant chorales.

Of the musical abilities and attitudes of Luther himself we are reasonably well informed through his *Tischreden* and his letters, as well as through the testimony of contemporaries. He had a hearty singing voice, and could play the lute and the recorder; and as a theorist, unlike many theorists of his own and later times, he was primarily concerned with the *effect* of music on the listener, for music was one of the forces which he harnessed to his reformatory purpose, to the pursuit of which everything was subjected. The firm, rugged nature of his melodies, reflective of the spirit of the times and close to the world of folk-song, is revealed in 'Ein feste Burg', 'Aus tiefer Not schrei ich zu dir' and his other famous tunes in the hymn-book which he was instrumental in compiling. This is a communal art, an art in which the participation of the congregation has replaced the dominance of the choir. And a straight line leads from the Lutheran chorale to J. S. Bach.

Meistergesang, mystery play and Protestant hymn, however much the one differs from the other, combine to make the point that in Germany, as in the other European countries with a traceable musical tradition, vocal music has pride of place over instrumental music until well into the sixteenth century. Such recorded instrumental music as exists in Germany before 1500 has an unindividualized, almost abstract character which does not distinguish between styles for string, wind and keyboard instruments, and since most of this instrumental playing appears to have been carried on for personal pleasure in the home, the choice of instruments, even as an accompaniment to the voice, will have depended on what was available, and what the performer wished, or was able, to play. The sixteenth century sees the development of differentiated instrumental styles, but the exclusive association of specific musical material with specific instruments – something still unknown to Bach, be it noted – is a much more modern phenomenon.

In so far as German music in the fifteenth and sixteenth centuries, whatever its intrinsic interest, appears in historical perspective as a transitional period preceding the age of Bach, we need to observe that to the Protestant chorale was added the exercise of contrapuntal techniques, partly Flemish, partly Italian in origin, which led in both vocal and instrumental music to the supreme achievements of polyphony. On the one hand the Flemish school, from Dufay (*c.* 1400–74) to Josquin des Près (*c.* 1445–1521) – the latter was particularly admired by Luther – introduced the canon, which is of secular origin, into the part-writing of their liturgical pieces and thus opened the path to the invention and exploitation of all manner of contrapuntal devices.

On the other hand there arose in Italy in the early sixteenth century the first great European organ school. Political and commercial links between Venice and the Netherlands had been close for some centuries, and when Adrian Willaert was appointed *maestro di cappella* at St Mark's in 1527, he would have taken with him many features of the polyphonic art of his Flemish homeland. But music in Venice does not start with Willaert, and whatever the Flemish influences that he brought to bear, the historical situation is that of a powerful Venetian school of organ-playing and contrapuntal keyboard composition to which many Germans came to study in the sixteenth century, taking back with them new techniques of performance, new possibilities of polyphonic writing and above all a new expansiveness and confidence in the exercise of their musical inventiveness. For this activity chorale melodies, firm in line and familiar in idiom, were an ideal foundation.

It is against the background dominated by these twin forces that the signs of a distinctive German school of composers appear. By the close of the sixteenth century Europe had seen the rise to glory of national schools in the Netherlands, in Italy, in England, in France and in Spain; alone among the great people of Europe, Germany, with an exception here and there, had made no memorable contribution to music as she had to lyric and epic poetry, to painting, philosophy, or to theology. In the first decades of the seventeenth century the foundations of a national tradition were truly laid, and the characteristics of an unmistakably German style became ever more apparent.

The first great figure in this tradition is Heinrich Schütz (1585–1672). Like many of his contemporaries he went to Venice to study with Giovanni Gabrieli, who, from his appointment as organist at St Mark's in 1585 until his death in 1612, attracted pupils to Venice from all over Europe. Italian influence is still strong in the madrigals and other choral works which Schütz wrote in his early career: these were the years of the ascendency of Monteverdi (*Orfeo*, 1607), whose church music, madrigals and early operas also formed part of Schütz's formative musical experience and who was himself appointed master of music to the Venetian republic in 1613. But in his mature compositions, written after his return to Germany, Schütz reveals an individual German musical personality, intense in power of experience and rich in expressiveness, a personality of seriousness and of devotion to the message of his art. His four settings of the Passion story, *Historia des Leidens und Sterbens unseres Herrn und Heylandes Jesu Christi* (*c.* 1665–72), following each of the four Gospel stories in turn, are the direct ancestors of Bach's Passion music, with the recitative for the role of the Evangelist and a three-part instrumental accompaniment for the words of Christ.

As Schütz worked his way through Italian influences to found a German style in the realm of vocal and choral music, so Johann Jacob Froberger (*c.* 1617–67), like Schütz a native of Saxony, went to Rome to study organ with the great Girolamo Frescobaldi (1583–1643) and returned to establish himself as the first important German composer of keyboard music. Building on the contrapuntal skills of his teacher and of the Dutch organist Jan Sweelinck (1562–1621), Froberger composed many pieces for organ and harpsichord, the most important and original among them being his harpsichord suites in which the constituent dance-movements – *allemande, courante, sarabande* and *gigue* – are given a musical content of a seriousness far exceeding that hitherto found in this form.

The German organ tradition leads from Froberger to Johann Pachelbel (1653–1706) – important above all for his cultivation of the chorale prelude, that ideal blend of strong tune and contrapuntal refinement – and hence to the greatest of Bach's predecessors, Dietrich Buxtehude (1637–1707). Swedish by birth, Buxtehude became organist at the Marienkirche in Lübeck in 1668, composing there cantatas and organ pieces which on occasion reach a level both of technical mastery and of expressive beauty equal to that of Bach himself.

But it is in the qualification 'on occasion' that the crux of the matter lies, for composers like Pachelbel and Buxtehude appear, in the wider historical context, as pioneers and prospectors in a territory where the odd nugget might be found, but whose real wealth had yet to be uncovered. The same is true of contemporaries of Bach such as Georg Philipp Telemann (1681–1767) and Johann Adolf Hasse (1699–1783). Both these men were prodigiously active in the field of Italianate opera as well as of keyboard and chamber music and ecclesiastical choral music, and enjoyed a greater fame in their day than Bach. But although they achieved isolated moments of true power and beauty, the measure of their inferiority to Bach is their inability to sustain and develop these moments. Most of the elements in the vocabulary of the musical language of the seventeenth century are common property: the difference between greatness and mediocrity lies in the quality of the thought that the language is used to communicate.

The aspirations and tendencies of German music from the late sixteenth century and throughout the seventeenth culminate in the two composers whose names are inseparably linked to produce what histories of music, with a good deal more justification than that which attends some of their other schematic compartmentalizations, call 'The Age of Bach and Handel'. For these two men, born in the same year in towns only eighty miles apart, heirs to a common tradition, yet who never met, not only brought to their highest peak of perfection the technical skills which the preceding century had been progressively developing, but between them shared dominion over the entire range of musical forms known at the time. As there were fields in which they were both active, such as keyboard music, so there were others which remained an individual prerogative – opera for Handel, for instance, and Passion music for Bach.

Where Handel is the worldly composer, an international figure at his ease in the environment of popular success, Bach is the religious musician, composing quietly *ad majorem dei gloriam* in a provincial context outside whose bounds he had hardly been heard of. The one is the spokesman of a broad, accessible and extrovert humanism, the other of an intense, personal, inward-looking pietism. It is the difference, sensed by any listener and not needing to be laboured by description, between the appeal of Handel's *Messiah* and that of Bach's *Christmas Oratorio* and Passion music – a difference paralleled by that between Beethoven's *Missa Solemnis* and a mass by Palestrina or Byrd. The amalgam of the activities of Bach and Handel, indeed, amounts to a comprehensive statement of the range, formal and spiritual, of eighteenth-century German music.

Older than Bach by one month, Georg Friedrich Händel (1685–1759; after settling in England he wrote his name as George Frideric Handel) was preoccupied in his early career with opera. The fashion of Italianate opera had already been current in Germany for some time, but Handel went to Italy himself in 1706 and composed a number of operas during the years he spent there. In 1712 he settled in England, became a naturalized subject in 1726, and, except for occasional visits to the Continent, remained in England for the rest of his life. His operatic ventures in London made him bankrupt more than once but he continued to compose and to produce operas into the 1730s, together with a mass of church music, instrumental and chamber music, secular cantatas, odes and a host of other occasional pieces. In 1739 came the first of his famous oratorios, *Saul*; *Messiah* was written in 1741 and was followed in the next ten years by *Samson, Judas Maccabeus* and many others. In 1751 his eyesight began to fail and for the last six years of his life he was almost totally blind.

Handel is probably the greatest assimilator of pre-existing material in the history of music. From Caldara, Johann Kerl, Porpora and many other, predominantly Italian, composers whose names survive only in the history books, Handel drew – some might prefer to say stole – theme after theme, and even whole movements, adapting and reworking them to the purpose of the moment. The best-known example of his voracious capacity for assimilation is in the oratorio *Israel in Egypt*, of whose 39 numbers 16 either use in their original form, or are based on, themes and movements by other composers. A certain naïve indignation has sometimes accompanied the latter-day discovery of such states of affairs. But what matters is surely the finished work of art for which Handel, whatever the source of his material, is alone responsible. Many of the tunes he took from his contemporaries only revealed their potentialities under the pressure of his own genius, and by raising the power of what he used, he became the most complete spokesman of his age.

This is inevitably a statement both of strength and of limitation, for while no artist can be free from, or be understood without reference to, the characteristics of his age, an artist's greatness rests on the extent to which his genius surpasses these characteristics. Handel not so much surpasses as codifies and perfects them. He brings substance to the grace and bravura of Italian, particularly Neapolitan, operatic melody; he brings to their culmination the formal instrumental and orchestral values of the Italian *concerto grosso* of Corelli and Geminiani; he breathes dramatic life into the presentation of Old Testament history and tragedy, making his oratorios into religious operas with a power overshadowing that achieved by Carissimi and Alessandro Scarlatti. His fluency; the ease – and the not infrequent carelessness – with which he recorded his musical thoughts; the juxtaposition of profound and almost commonplace moments; perhaps, too, a playing-down of intellectual intensity in favour of immediate sensuous beauty, a feeling for Italian melody rather than for German counterpoint: these are among the evident characteristics of his musical personality. The history of English music, paradoxically, needs him more than does the history of German music; while it is Italian music that can probably make the largest claim to his spiritual allegiance.

Johann Sebastian Bach (1685–1750), on the other hand, one of the greatest composers – many, particularly musicians, would say *the* greatest – the world has seen, stands at the summit of a German – indeed, a specifically North German, Protestant – tradition, while holding, in his Olympian stature, a position so much more than that of just the consummator of a tradition.

Apart from the occasional incidents, a chronicle of the external events of Bach's life amounts to little more than a list of his employers. He never left Germany, and the farthest he ever travelled from his native Thuringia was Lübeck – and that only for a brief period as a chorister and organ scholar. From 1723 onwards he was cantor at St Thomas's Church in Leipzig in succession to Johann Kuhnau (1660–1722), the interesting composer of a set of so-called 'Biblical Sonatas' for harpsichord, one of the earliest-known examples of extended programme music. Very little of Bach's music was published during his lifetime, and what reputation he had was as an organist and as an improvisor at the keyboard. It was for his fame in the latter capacity that Frederick the Great invited him to Potsdam in 1747, setting him themes on which to exercise his skill in canon, fugue and other contrapuntal techniques. On one such theme of the king's invention Bach built the work – one of his last, and one of the very few to be published in his lifetime – known as *The Musical Offering*.

Although Bach's work is properly seen as the culmination of the historical line that stretches back through Buxtehude, Pachelbel and Froberger to Schütz and Sweelinck, he also had an extensive knowledge of French and especially Italian music. Vivaldi in particular provided him with many starting-points for his own compositions, and certain of Bach's instrumental works are straight recastings, for different combinations of instruments, of pieces by Vivaldi. But, unlike Handel, these cases are not numerous, and the influence is peripheral. The great works with which the name of Bach is synonymous – the *Mass in B minor*, the *St Matthew Passion*, the *Brandenburg Concertos*, the organ preludes and fugues, *The Well-Tempered Clavier*, *The Art of Fugue* and the rest – present a massive, monolithic personality whose power to command emotional and intellectual reverence, to inspire the mind and to enrich the spirit, is as individual as it is irresistible.

Yet alongside the lofty language that seems appropriate to the description of such lofty works of art must be ranged the sober realization that Bach was a practical musician. He was not given to theorizing about his own or anyone else's music, and his only surviving theoretical works consist of two sets of thorough-bass rules, based on a current textbook, which he used for teaching his pupils. Also, he had the practitioner's view of what constituted good organ design, and had his intruments modified to meet his requirements. This is the great age of baroque organ builders, paramount among them Arp Schnitger (1648–1718) and the various members of the Silbermann family: Andreas Silbermann, with whom the family tradition started, built the Strasbourg Cathedral organ (1714–16), while his brother Gottfried built that at the cathedral of Freiberg in Saxony in 1714; Gottfried Silbermann was also the first in Germany to manufacture a pianoforte after the model of Cristofori, the Florentine inventor of this instrument.

Throughout his career, Bach was required by his various employers to produce works, religious and secular, to order, and his view of music as a craft as much as an art lay very much in the tradition of the whole Bach family. Of his 200 or so church cantatas, for example, the majority owe their existence to the blunt necessity of providing music for Sunday worship, and one would not expect the level of inspiration behind them to remain constant. The miracle is that so many of such occasional pieces, vocal, choral and instrumental, should occupy unassailable positions in the ranks of the world's greatest music.

Our modern, 'moral' distinction between secular and religious in music has no relevance to the world of Bach. That Bach himself was a deeply religious person is apparent from the spirit of his music alone, but this is not contradicted by such knowledge as that seventeen numbers of the *Christmas Oratorio* are borrowings from secular cantatas written by Bach for earlier and entirely worldly occasions. Bach himself would not have understood the suggestion that there could be an issue of 'propriety' at stake in the use of a secular melody for a Passion chorale. The moral, associative distinction between religious and secular is a phenomenon of the nineteenth and twentieth centuries.

Via-à-vis the works of his predecessors and older contemporaries, and in so far as one can put one's finger on the elusive constituents of greatness, Bach's compositions stand out above all in two respects: in their sheer size and the sustained intensity that justifies their size; and in their complexity.

The question of size is not merely academic. The contrapuntal techniques used by Bach are not his invention: there are many examples of canon, double counterpoint and fugue, many suites, chorale preludes and ricercars among the works of his predecessors. What Bach alone achieves is the sustained development of material and style, the full exploitation of stated ideas, the power to lead the mind from one peak of emotion to another within the confines of a single work.

This leads into the second, related field, that of the intensification of expression, the achievement of a complexity of organization that had been beyond the vision – and, be it added, the powers – of his ancestors. This intensification is at its most tangible in the combining of contrasting themes, the simultaneous development of thesis and antithesis, which represents a culmination of the fugal principle of the sixteenth and seventeenth centuries, and is at its purest and most original in the sonatas for unaccompanied violin and the partitas for unaccompanied cello, the *ne plus ultra* of the figured-bass tradition of chamber music. No earlier composer had composed for unaccompanied instruments on such a scale as Bach. Similarly, he raised the status of the harpsichord from that of an accompanimental to that of a solo instrument, even writing concertos for two, three and four harpsichords.

Beyond the adduction of such more or less superficial historical and descriptive observations, the act of criticism has little to offer in the presence of the gigantic phenomenon that is Bach. With Beethoven we can feel our way to a sensible extent into a physical and artistic presence, for Beethoven is a man, fallible within his greatness. But Bach is a god, cool, self-sufficient, inscrutable in his aloofness. The language of earth has little relevance to gods.

The name Bach enjoyed wide fame in Germany in the mid- and late eighteenth century, but it was not Johann Sebastian that people had in mind: it was Carl Philipp Emanuel (1714–88), one of a number of sons – among them Wilhelm Friedmann (1710–84), the eldest, writer of church cantatas and keyboard concertos, and Johann Christian (1735–82), the 'London' Bach, who lived the last twenty years of his life in London, a prolific composer of Italian operas, concertos, vocal and instrumental music – who made their own contributions to musical life in the eighteenth century.

For us today C. P. E. Bach is remembered more for his position in musical history than for the intrinsic value of his music, but enlightened opinion of the day accorded him high esteem, rating him far higher than his father, whose contrapuntal style was regarded as out of date, and whose apparently cerebral approach was felt to be uninspiring. Dr Burney, for example, author of a famous eighteenth-century history of music, wrote in 1771 that C. P. E. Bach's sonatas far excelled his father's fugues, while Haydn bluntly asserted: 'All that I know I have learned from Emanuel Bach.' The rococo spirit of the late eighteenth century was indeed inimical to what J. S. Bach stood for, and turned eagerly to the looser, more monodic and seemingly more expressive 'empfindsamer Stil', with which the immediate feelings of the composer and his audience could more readily be identified.

From 1740 to 1767 C. P. E. Bach served as domestic musician at the court of Frederick the Great in Potsdam, and, apart from a great deal of chamber and, above all, keyboard music, he produced during this time the first comprehensive textbook on the art of keyboard-playing. In his harpsichord sonatas he developed in particular the principle of contrasted, yet related harmonic sections, evolving thereby a form of instrumental movement which presages the full-scale sonata form of the classical period.

Contemporary with C. P. E. Bach, and also concerned with the evolution of the formal principles which underlie what is known as classical sonata form, whether in an instrumental or an orchestral context, is a group of composers who played in the orchestra of the Elector Karl Theodor (1743–99) at Mannheim, and who have come to be known as the Mannheim School. The conductor of this orchestra was Johann Stamitz (1717–57), who, together with his sons Karl and Anton and three or four others who had come to Mannheim from elsewhere, has left a number of orchestral symphonies and other works which, melodic, non-contrapuntal, emotionally varied and outgoing in style, are interesting forerunners of the classical repertoire.

The greatest interest of the Mannheim School, however, lies in the innovations it made in orchestral scoring and playing. The elder Stamitz, for example, himself a string player, began in his symphonies to emancipate the violas from their role of doubling the bass an octave higher; he also developed the woodwind chorus as an independent expressive ensemble, and appears to have been the first to introduce the clarinet – which had only been evolved from the old chalumeau at the beginning of the century – into the ranks of orchestral instruments. Mozart, who visited Mannheim in 1778, was enthusiastic about these clarinets, as he was also about the novel dynamic effects such as unexpected sforzandos, interpolated 'general pauses' and the famous 'Mannheim crescendo' which he heard the orchestra employ in their performances. The figured bass of baroque days had now virtually disappeared, and full orchestral scores, with parts written out and therefore individually developed and exploited, became the order of the day, heralding the modern era of orchestral music, with individual identities and autonomies accorded to each department and each instrument.

While, in the historical conspectus, the developments in orchestral and chamber music – the line between the two is often hazy until well beyond the middle of the century – particularly associated with C. P. E. Bach and the Mannheim School were leading towards the classicism of Haydn, Mozart and Beethoven, the 'exotic and irrational entertainment' of opera, as Dr Johnson called it, was undergoing not development but revolution. In Germany, as in England and in France, Italian opera dominated the scene throughout the first half of the eighteenth century: libretti were in Italian, Italian singers, however bad, were imported to sing the principal roles, and native singers were expected to adopt Italian mannerisms. Two forces brought this state of affairs to an end in the latter half of the century: one was the gradual spread of the comic opera with spoken dialogue and interpolated set songs, the genre known as the *Singspiel*, which in its pure form reaches its height in Mozart's *Seraglio* (1782); the other was the frontal assault on the whole Italian concept of opera by Christoph Willibald Gluck (1714–98).

Whether the new principles of opera enunciated by Gluck are original, and to what extent they may amount to a codification of ideas already held by the more progressive Italian composers of the day, may be debatable. It remains true, however, that it is he, and no one else, who had the force of personality both to propound a set of intellectual principles on which a reform of opera should be based, and to compose dramatic works whose powerful music compelled the acceptance of these principles. Not surprisingly, there was no lack of opposition to him. The defenders of musical orthodoxy in important centres such as Vienna opposed him from the beginning; so, too, did the French Academy of Music in Paris. Yet here, despite this opposition, he was later to write a number of his greatest works, to French libretti, among them *Iphigénie en Aulide* (1774) and *Armide* (1777).

His first 'reform' work, however, i.e. that which broke with the undramatic, exhibitionist conventions of Italian opera, was in Italian – *Orfeo ed Euridice*, produced in Vienna in 1762, which was followed five years later by another Italian opera on a classical subject, *Alceste*. In a famous preface to this latter work Gluck set out his philosophy of opera, demanding that the singers should not be at liberty to indulge in flamboyant vocal displays to the detriment of the dramatic interest; that the forms of the individual numbers in the work should be determined by the needs of the dramatic action; that the overture should be a proper emotional preparation for the drama that is to follow, and not just pleasant background music while the audience settle in their seats; and above all that the music should be subservient to, and have no existence independent of, the text.

These demands may not seem particularly revolutionary to us today, and the emphasis of the text – that is on the ideas, and thus on the dramatic content – has since received powerful reiteration from Richard Wagner. Yet in its day this manifesto met with great indignation and opposition. Its vindication came, not through force of theoretical argument, but with the sheer power of Gluck's own operatic practice. No composer before him had achieved such dramatic intensity. Leaving aside a few isolated masterpieces like Monteverdi's *Incoronazione di Poppea* and Purcell's *Dido and Aeneas*, one can reasonably claim that the tradition of grand opera in the modern theatre begins with Gluck.

A brief historical survey, of whatever subject, can hardly avoid giving the impression of proceeding from one crest of achievement to the next, leaving the intervening years as troughs in which little of value is to be found. *Mutatis mutandis* to dwell on what intrinsic interest resides in works which lead up to, or down from, the summits of greatness, might imply a detraction from the intensity or originality of this greatness. But when, in German music, one comes to the last twenty-five years or so of the eighteenth century, one is confronted with a series of giants whose pre-eminence lies beyond dispute – though not beyond sympathetic analysis – and who stand at the opening of the great century of German music, the century, indeed, in which Germany made her most characteristic contribution to European culture.

The first of these giants is Franz Joseph Haydn (1732–1800). Born in

Lower Austria of the humblest of families, a choir boy at St Stephan's Cathedral in Vienna until the age of seventeen, and a run-of-the-mill music teacher until his middle twenties, he had his great moment in 1761, when he entered the service of Prince Paul Anton von Esterházy. He remained resident Kapellmeister at Esterháza till 1790, producing under the patronage of this most enlightened of families symphonic and chamber music which gained him an international reputation, and making the court orchestra one of the best in Europe. In the second half of his mature creative life he lived more in the public gaze, although, having taken up residence in Vienna in 1795, he re-entered the service of the Esterházys and retained his position with them until his death. For his two visits to London in the 1790s he wrote twelve of his finest symphonies, and from his last years in Vienna come the great string quartets Op. 76 and Op. 77, and the two oratorios *The Creation* and *The Seasons*. His total output includes over a hundred symphonies, about 50 concertos, divertimenti and the like for various solo instruments, 84 string quartets, and some hundred other chamber works for various combinations of instruments, 42 pianoforte sonatas, masses, operas, incidental music for plays and a host of smaller occasional pieces.

Of the great German classical composers Haydn is the homeliest, the most accessible. The paternal geniality of the man, his closeness to the soil – which finds specific, tangible expression in his use of Croatian folk-melodies – communicate themselves through his music. So also do his spontaneity, his directness and his precise attention to the details of his craft. Of the maturation of his genius during his years at Esterháza he wrote, in completely unposed, unaffected manner: 'I was cut off from the world; and since there was no one to confuse or trouble me, I was forced to become original.'

Apart from the two late oratorios, *The Creation* (to a text translated from the English, based on the Book of Genesis and Milton's *Paradise Lost*) and *The Seasons* (to a German version of parts of Thomson's poem), Haydn's strength and originality reside almost entirely in his orchestral and instrumental music. With a firmer grasp of his material than C. P. E. Bach or the composers of the Mannheim School, he consolidated the form of the four-movement symphony and greatly increased the range and subtlety of the scoring.

But perhaps the most striking measure of his superiority to his predecessors is the degree of extended development to which, in the middle section of the symphonic or quartet movement, he subjects his themes. There is no shortage of pleasant tunes in the symphonies of the early eighteenth century, but as in the early evolution of any new principle, powers of inventiveness were short-winded, and whatever modest development these themes underwent was not attended by a build-up of tension or dramatic interest. Haydn, however, initially in the realm of the string quartet, had discovered a new expansiveness in the 'working out' of his themes, and subsequently gave the most splendid expression to his discovery in the two sets of symphonies, six in each set, that he wrote for his two visits to London (1791 and 1794) arranged by the impressario Johann Salomon.

For all that one dwells, inevitably and rightly, on Haydn the orchestral composer, it is ironical to recall that Haydn himself cherished hopes of success in that genre with which he is least associated, namely opera. The Italian operas that he wrote give no hint of a greatness that was not allowed to come to fruition; yet there are in *The Creation* dramatic moments which make it not impossible to think in terms of operatic grandeur, moments in which he achieves a vividness that is almost visual. As it is, however, greatness in opera is not his, but Mozart's.

Haydn and Mozart met on occasion between 1781 and 1791, the year of Mozart's death, and it is clear from their music that each learned something from the other. Yet although the public has yoked them together, like Bach and Handel, or Bruckner and Mahler, and although it is true that run-of-the-mill Haydn is barely distinguishable from run-of-the-mill Mozart, and both barely detectable alongside the best works of their contemporaries, the characteristic utterances of the two men at their greatest are unmistakable, those of the one complementary to those of the other.

Wolfgang Amadeus Mozart's short life (1756–91) was the life of a practical genius, a life packed with public activity. Unlike Haydn, he came of a cultured musical family, his father Leopold – some of whose compositions are still occasionally performed today – being an accomplished musician at the court of the Archbishop of Salzburg. The young Mozart was an infant prodigy: he could play the pianoforte at three and invent little pieces at five. At seven he could play the violin as well and, together with his sister, was taken by his father on a sensational series of triumphant tours of European cities between the ages of eight and eleven. He wrote his first opera, *La finta semplice*, at twelve, but over the following four years his father, an indefatigable family impressario, again took him on extensive tours, restricting his opportunities for composition to the intervals between concert appearances.

Subsequently he took a post as court musician at Salzburg and later at Vienna, where most of his great operas received their definitive productions, but right up to his death he still paid frequent visits to other cities for performances of his works.

Like Haydn, though perhaps less exclusively, Mozart lived his career within the framework of patronage, and from this circumstance spring his numerous occasional pieces for solo voices, for vocal groups, and for a variety of combinations of chamber-music instruments. Many of these works – the same is true of his serenades, divertimenti, cassations, dances and other occasional orchestral pieces – were composed for a particular court function or to a specific commission. The three great string quartets K. 575, K. 589 and K. 590, for example, belong to a set of six requested by King Frederick Wilhelm II of Prussia (the remaining three were never written). Other pieces owe their existence to the presence of an outstanding performer: thus both the clarinet quintet and the clarinet concerto were written for the Viennese virtuoso Anton Stadler, the leading contemporary performer on this still comparatively new instrument. And most of his piano concertos, indeed, he wrote for his own use on his European concert tours.

It is, in fact, in the field of the solo concerto, above all in the treatment of the solo part, that from the historical, evolutionary point of view Mozart's most distinctive contribution to orchestral music lies. In the solo concertos of the early eighteenth century the material of the solo part is derived from that of the orchestral ritornello: the form is thus unitary in conception, the statements of the musical argument being passed from the soloist to the orchestra and vice versa. This principle is inherited by the solo concerto from its predecessor, the concerto grosso, in which not one but a group of soloists is set against the orchestra, as in Handel's Concerti Grossi for strings, or Bach's Brandenburg Concertos. The unitary principle also prevails in Bach's solo concertos, and Haydn, too, was content to maintain a basic similarity between the substance of the solo parts in his concertos and that of the orchestral accompaniment. It is hardly a coincidence that Haydn's concertos are not staple elements in the modern repertory, or that the average concert-goer would be hard pressed even to say what instruments he wrote concertos for.

Mozart, however, developed on the one hand the independence of the solo instrument, and on the other the virtuosity that was required to handle it. The three-movement concerto became with him the standard pattern, the first movement, the most substantial, being an allegro, sometimes with a slow introduction, the second a slow movement, and the last a lively rondo. Although it is not hard to find exceptions, this structure remains the basic pattern throughout the nineteenth century.

Above all in his last piano concertos (he wrote twenty-five in all) and in the last three great symphonies – No. 39 in E flat major (K. 543), No. 40 in G minor (K. 550) and No. 41 in C major (the 'Jupiter', K. 551), which are among the most priceless treasures of symphonic music that the world has to offer – Mozart has left music of unsurpassed beauty. Yet viewing his achievement as a whole, and notwithstanding these glories of orchestral and instrumental music, one is drawn to the conclusion that it is not here but in opera that he is at his greatest. And in opera he had – many would say has – no equal.

From the beginning Mozart's view of opera, unlike Gluck's, was of an art form in which not the text but the music must be predominant. On the surface this sounds like a return to the bad old days of pre-Gluck Italian opera, when serious dramatic purpose was lost sight of in a flurry of empty vocal brilliance. But in reality Mozart so filled his works with vivid musical characters, depicted with a psychological depth unknown to earlier composers, a depth from which conflicts, the true stuff of drama, emerge directly and urgently, that music became the principal vehicle of the dramatic action, the means by which both motivation and characterization were most powerfully conveyed.

The measure of this can be gauged by taking the libretti – all by Lorenzo da Ponte – of his three great Italian operas (*The Marriage of Figaro*, 1786; *Don Giovanni*, 1787; and *Così fan tutte*, 1790) and reading them as dramatic texts: drama is just not there – which, for a Mozart, is as it should be, since the tensions and personalities of the dramatic action are to be literally 'realized' in the music. The same is true, though in a different way and for different reasons, of the greatest of his German operas, *The Magic Flute*, composed and first produced in the last year of his life. In instrumental music Mozart could be rivalled, sometimes perhaps equalled, by Haydn, and later ceded the profoundest expression of human emotions in this realm to Beethoven. But neither of these is his equal in the field of opera.

As for Haydn and Mozart, so also for Ludwig van Beethoven (1770–1827) Vienna was the spiritual centre of gravity, and all three died there. This led earlier, tidy-minded historians of music to call them, together with Schubert, The Viennese School, but in no meaningful sense do they form a school, with common aims and common

methods. Indeed, apart from the sheer futility of such classifying enterprises, there is something particularly comic in the thought that a
titanic figure like Beethoven could be contained within the confines of
a school or any such common enterprise.

Beethoven was born in Bonn, and both his father and his grandfather
had been professional musicians there at the court of the Elector of
Cologne. Having himself held a number of undistinguished musical
posts in the elector's entourage for some years, he went to Vienna at
the age of twenty-two to study with Haydn. Subsequently he made a
living by giving lessons in aristocratic families and began to gain fame
through his compositions, which were being increasingly performed
throughout Europe. His private life, however, was beset with un-
happiness, and during his last years he was completely deaf.

Confronted with an artist of the stature of Beethoven, one sometimes feels that it is pointless to do other than list his achievements and
leave the rest to personal experience. He needs no advocate, and whatever the legitimate scope may be for analysis and criticism of his
works, their total impact is such as to force one into silence. To be
sure, he has had his detractors; but when one hears the burden of their
song, one wishes that a famous remark by Goethe had been made, not
of Napoleon, but of Beethoven: 'You can rattle your chains as much as
you like, you will never break them: the man is too big for you.'

Perhaps one way of beginning to describe allusively, at least, something of what goes into Beethoven's greatness, is to point to the
human content of his art, that quality which communicates itself so
unmistakably to the ordinary listener that he knows at once that he is
being addressed in his own terms. This popularity – in the profoundest
sense – this closeness to common experience, is what gives his music
its power over men's minds and fills our concert halls for performances
of his symphonies, concertos, choral works and chamber music.

Expressed in this way, the nature of Beethoven's appeal is different
in kind from that of, say, Bach or Mozart. There is an aura of divine
infallibility about Bach, a communicable sense of being in the presence
of a mind whose mastery and perfection are inaccessible to explanation
in human terms. To Mozart, admittedly, there is human access, yet
not for nothing has he been called the darling of the gods; although
the situation is not as simple as it may look, to us his works seem to
appear from beneath his hand like a series of flawless polished gems and
to have, in their cool, classical beauty, an irreproachable, almost un-
canny inevitability and perfection that makes common mortals even

more aware of their inadequacies than they are already. But Beethoven emerges – like Haydn, with whom, among the classics, he has most in common – from among the ranks of mortal men themselves. The progress of his music is a passage to human greatness, a passage that human minds themselves can trace, and a musical achievement which stands unchallenged as a monument to the mind of man.

His output falls, broadly, into three periods. Down to 1800 his compositions stand to a greater or lesser extent in the shadow of Haydn and of the 'common' eighteenth century, the best known among them being the six string quartets, Op. 18, and the early pianoforte sonatas, including the 'Pathétique', Op. 13. It would not be true to call these works unoriginal, and there are moments in them which show the future iconoclast baring his claws, but taken as a whole they have the character of a continuation of the eighteenth-century tradition rather than the prelude to a new, radical development.

The year 1800 saw the appearance of the Piano Concerto No. 1 (Op. 15) and the First Symphony (Op. 21), and marks the emergence of the Beethoven of whom the average music-lover most immediately thinks. The very first chords of the first movement of this symphony show something of what is to come: the symphony is in C major, but Beethoven's opening chords consist of the dominant-seventh/tonic progression in F major, shaking at the very foundation of the pattern of key-relationships which constitutes the formal essence of the symphonic movement. He also converted the stately minuet, the standard third movement of the classical symphony of Haydn and Mozart, into a lively scherzo, a procedure which, with this scherzo followed by the final allegro, has the overall effect of quickening the pace and heightening the tension of the whole work. Although he returns to the minuet on a few later occasions, as in the Eighth Symphony, it is the scherzo that is now the regular third movement of symphony, quartet and sonata.

To this middle period of Beethoven's life belong the first eight symphonies, the five pianoforte concertos, the violin concerto, the opera Fidelio and the accompanying Leonore overtures, a substantial body of chamber music including the three Rasumovsky string quartets (Op. 59), and the fifteen or so 'central' piano sonatas, including the 'Appassionata' and the 'Waldstein'. It is not a coincidence that, with the exception of Fidelio, all these are instrumental works. Like Haydn, but unlike Mozart, and notwithstanding the Missa Solemnis and the finale of the Ninth Symphony – both works belonging to his final period – Beethoven was essentially an instrumental composer. 'I always hear my music on instruments, never on voices,' he once said. His vocal parts, like those of Bach, are instrumental in character and often lie uncomfortably for soloists and chorus alike, and although he did write a great number of songs, many of them in response to specific commissions, it is all too evident that he is not in his element in this form, and that there is a fundamental disharmony between the restlessness and intensity – or simply the sheer size – of his musical personality and the restricted form in which it is trying to express itself.

The final period of Beethoven's life contains his greatest music, which is at the same time some of the greatest music in the world: the Ninth Symphony, the *Missa Solemnis*, the last three piano sonatas and the Diabelli variations for piano, and the last five string quartets. If the works of his middle period, typified by, say, the Fifth Symphony, are the music of human commitment, symbols of a Faustian struggle for self-knowledge and self-fulfilment, then these last works, and above all the quartets, lead beyond the field of human striving into an otherworldly region where the known and the unknown, serenity attained in a sphere of mystery, a sense of personal achievement and an awareness of human transience, combine in a new paradoxical, divine-inspired dimension.

The slow movement of his Quartet in A minor, Op. 132, written two years before he died, is inscribed 'A song of thanksgiving offered to the Almighty by one recovering from sickness'. It is written in the Lydian mode, whose ethereal, unworldly quality, issuing from the tension-less idiom where the 'modern' concepts of keys and chords, and the relationships between them, do not apply, creates an atmosphere of timelessness, of eternal peace and repose. There is no music that can better symbolize both the spiritual victory to which Beethoven attained and the transcendental meaning of the works in which his victory is enshrined.

As the genius of Beethoven finds its most powerful, most complete expression in instrumental and orchestral music, so the genius of Schubert, the last of these four great Viennese masters, is at its most perfect in the realm of the solo song – a form rarely turned to by Haydn and Mozart, and one conspicuously absent from the company of forms in which the greatness of Beethoven himself is manifest.

Franz Schubert (1797–1828), who was born in Vienna, lived all his life there and died there at the age of thirty-one, was one of the most prolific of all the great composers. He never held any official musical post and lived solely from casual sources of income. He started composing music at an early age and showed signs of a precocity that rivalled that of Mozart, but his fame remained local. Indeed, until a group of his friends published twenty of his songs at their own expense in 1821, by which time he had already written seven of his nine symphonies, much chamber music, including the string trio and the 'Trout' quintet, operas, masses and piano music, as well as a quantity of songs, the musical world at large had hardly heard of him. Many of his works were never performed in his lifetime, and many were published posthumously. His fecundity can be gauged by his total output of songs alone, which stands at over six hundred, including seventy-one settings of poems by Goethe and forty-two of poems by Schiller.

There is splendid music to be found in Schubert's symphonies, in chamber works like the String Quartet in D minor ('Death and the Maiden') and in the posthumous piano sonatas, but both in their historical significance and in their intrinsic value these works are overshadowed by his songs. His facility in this direction was proverbial, and many of the most famous owe their existence to a flash of inspiration in the most unpredictable of circumstances.

The extent to which song-writing stands out as the field in which his creative gifts find their fullest and most natural expression – and the same is true of Hugo Wolf, though the musical result is very different – reveals the degree of his dependence on poetry for his inspiration. This need not be taken as a reproach, for, indeed, it lies at the root of all song-writing and also, though to a lesser extent, of opera. But it does mean that the music has a somewhat less than absolute quality, since its existence must initially be determined, and thus limited, by the poetic text which has liberated the composer's musical faculty. This is what led Liszt to call Schubert 'le musicien le plus poète que jamais'.

Schubert was, however, not particularly discerning in his 'poetic' judgement, for the texts of now almost forgotten poets were as welcome to him as those of Goethe, Schiller or Heine, and whereas 'Erlkönig' and 'Gretchen am Spinnrade' are fine poems, 'Liebesbotschaft' and 'Die Taubenpost', from the so-called *Schwanengesang*, his last song-cycle, are mediocre. This only shows what has long been observed, that a fine song can emerge from a poor text. Conversely, a beautiful poem is not bound to lead, even in the hands of a gifted composer, to a beautiful or successful song.

Expressed in this way, Schubert's power is seen to lie in his unequalled ability to produce a melody that is not just a 'setting to music'

x

of a verse of poetry but its musical equivalent – even its musical substitute. And to this melody he adds the perfect piano accompaniment. Indeed, he raises the accompaniment to a status which it had never before held, a status for which the term accompaniment is no longer adequate, for the essential 'meaning' of a Schubert song is as vitally conveyed through the piano part as it is through the melody. The melancholy drone of the hurdy-gurdy in 'Der Leiermann', the last song in the *Winterreise* cycle, or the relentless thudding of the horse's hoofs in 'Erlkönig', even simple nature-motifs in songs like 'Der Lindenbaum' and 'Auf dem Flusse' – both also from *Die Winterreise* – are not just naturalistic tone-painting but a vital element in the conception and expression of the song as a whole.

This, moreover, is as true of the songs he was writing in his teens as it is of those from the end of his life. One can fairly trace a line of development from the orchestral music of the early Schubert to that of the late Schubert; in his songs, however – apart from matters of technique and with the exception of a very few supreme moments like 'Der Doppelgänger', one of his last songs, whose dramatic power is probably unequalled in the world of song – no such simple linear development is present. Although virtually all the nineteenth-century German masters have each left a few beautiful vocal works, it is only at the very end of the century that we encounter a substantial corpus of songs that can be put alongside Schubert's, and only in the composer of this corpus of songs, Hugo Wolf, that we find a figure so completely identified with the art of song-writing as Schubert.

The combined careers of Haydn, Mozart, Beethoven and Schubert span a period of about sixty years, from the beginning of Haydn's maturity to the death of Schubert. In the concert-goer's mind these four, together with Bach and Handel, provide the consolidated foundation of the 'classics', an appellation whose validity is not limited to German music but which embodies a central concept in the history of European music as a whole. In fact, if one leaves aside Berlioz, Chopin and Verdi, the history of great European music in all but the last two decades or so of the nineteenth century coincides with the history of German music.

But classic is not a word with a single, unchanging meaning, and if, in the usage common in literary criticism and in the history of culture, it be set against the word Romantic – an even more volatile term, but having at its core the notion of subjectivity and free self-expression, unrestrained by formal conventions – then one realizes that, although Haydn and Mozart may with some reason be called classic, Beethoven certainly can not. Beethoven, the unrestrained human content and 'message' of whose music conveys itself to all who listen, is, in this aesthetic sense, the *fons et origo* of Romantic music. The nineteenth century is the age of Romantic music, and the great age of German music. Even expressed in such syllogistic form, and already at this historical moment, the inseparability of the three terms – German culture, Romanticism and music – is inescapable. The most powerful manifestation of this 'singularity', to use a mathematician's phrase, comes with Wagner, and a discussion of its deeper significance is more appropriately left until that point in our historical survey is reached.

The imaginative forces released by the Romanticism of the early nineteenth century manifested themselves in all forms of music. Response to the motifs and concerns of the new Romantic poetry gave an immediate stimulus to song-writing, and was later to inspire a virtually new musical form, the symphonic poem. Indeed, the presence of descriptive and pictorial elements in music generally, imported under the stimulus of literature and painting, where the new directions in art had first made themselves apparent, has come to be seen as a characteristic feature of Romantic music, and has led to the term 'programme music' being applied to works whose musical content acknowledgedly derives from a non-musical source.

Interesting early examples of such music have survived from the seventeenth and eighteenth centuries, among them the 'Biblical Tales' of Johann Kuhnau, Bach's predecessor as cantor at St Thomas's in Leipzig, but it is with Beethoven's Sixth Symphony ('The Pastoral'), published in 1809, that Romantic programme music is launched. This is great music in its own right, but the early nineteenth century also has a mass of fancy programmatic pieces to offer which retain – and probably only ever had – a quaint curiosity value. The *battaglia*, illustrating the sounds and events of battle, and traceable back to sixteenth-century France, was a particularly popular subject, and Beethoven made his contribution to it with his 'Battle Symphony' (*Wellingtons Sieg oder die Schlacht bei Vittoria*), composed in 1813. Schumann's *Carnaval* (1834) carries on the programmatic line in pianoforte music, but it is with Liszt, in the middle of the century, that the genre enters its richest period, reaching at the end of the century the outstanding German composer in this form, Richard Strauss.

It may be appropriate to recall at this point, since this is the historical moment at which the question becomes topical, that the conventional distinction drawn between 'programme music' and what is faintly comically called 'absolute music' has an irrelevance about it which conceals the real nature of the situation. For whatever one may be pleased to identify as the 'source of inspiration' of a work – a physical object or event, like a garden in the rain or a firework display (Debussy); a geographical locality, like the Bohemian countryside (Smetana) or the steppes of Central Asia (Borodin); a work of literature, like *Romeo and Juliet* (Tchaikovsky), Dante's *Divine Comedy* (Liszt) or *Don Quixote* (Richard Strauss); or simply an abstract musical idea *sui generis* – a piece of music has to stand in its own right *qua* music and make its claim on the listener in directly musical terms. A symphony is a symphony, a string quartet is a string quartet, and a sonata is a sonata. Whether a symphony be called 'Pastoral' (Beethoven), 'Fantastic' (Berlioz), 'Alpine' (Richard Strauss) or just 'in C minor', it will be understood and judged in the context of symphonic music, and its quality as symphonic music will be independent of the extra-musical experiences and stimuli that may have had a part in its genesis.

The question of the link between the literary and musical impulses, which was raised earlier in connection with the songs of Schubert, reappears in the subject of opera, and German Romantic opera, culminating in Wagner, reveals in their most highly developed form many of the deepest values of nineteenth-century German music.

The most important pioneer in this field, a composer whose large-scale works spend most of their time in the oblivion that befalls so many pioneers, is Carl Maria von Weber (1786–1826). One part of Weber's originality lies in his conception of opera as a more uniform, more closely knit structure than the eighteenth century had either attempted or achieved, and in his *Euryanthe* (1823) he began to achieve this greater homogeneity by moving away from the hitherto universally adopted division of an operatic work into set numbers, each self-contained and virtually detachable from its context. His most famous opera, *Der Freischütz* (1821), in which the musical continuum is broken by spoken dialogue, shows another side of his progressive talent, his handling of the orchestra, which, from providing accompaniments to the vocal items and adding certain atmospheric background effects, now assumes an individuality of its own. For example, he subdivides the strings for special coloristic effects, and exploits the qualities of eerieness and mystery that can be drawn from particular combinations of woodwind instruments.

Weber is not the only composer at this time, nor indeed the first, to be experimenting with new orchestral effects. One whose achievements in this direction Weber himself acknowledged was Ernst Theodor Amadeus Hoffmann (1770–1822). Today Hoffmann is first thought of as a literary figure, and is probably most widely known as the author of the stories on which Offenbach later based his French opera *The Tales of Hoffmann*. But his opera *Undine* (1813), in particular, based on Fouqué's fairy-tale of the water-sprite, met with considerable success on its production in Berlin. In it Hoffmann makes use of novel woodwind sonorities to underline the supernatural elements, and Weber, whose *Freischütz* also moves in the realm of the supernatural, sensed the potentialities of these new techniques. Hoffmann also wrote other operas, including a setting of Goethe's *Scherz, List und Rache*, as well as a considerable amount of orchestral, chamber and vocal music, but little of it has ever been published, and still less performed.

A contemporary of Weber's, and also a composer particularly associated with the achievement of theatrical effect in opera through the exploitation of orchestral colour, was Giacomo Meyerbeer (1791–1864), a native of Berlin who spent most of his creative life in Paris and built on the Italian tradition of Spontini, Auber and Rossini. Apart from a few excerpts, little is heard of his music today, but his operas *Robert le Diable* (1831) and the prodigious *Les Huguenots* (1836) made a sensational impact on the spectacle-loving Parisian audiences of the time, and led them to believe that the future of grand opera lay in his hands. In retrospect, however, his career appears as a fleeting moment when the Italian and German operatic traditions met, only to part again and move onwards to their respective climaxes in Verdi and Wagner.

While the fullest exploitation of the form of dramatic opera, or music drama, had yet to be reached, symphonic music in nineteenth-century Germany stands in the shadow of Beethoven. This is not to deny that there is a great deal of beautiful and effective music in this symphonic literature. But as it is virtually impossible to compose or listen to a fugue without the figure of J. S. Bach being present in one's conscious or unconscious mind, so the nineteenth-century symphonist could not but work in the knowledge of the unrivalled statements of symphonic thought that Beethoven had left. And with that awareness of history which no one can dissociate from his appreciation of music or any other art, the modern listener cannot but sense that the symphonies of the nineteenth century, and not only those by German composers, mark a choice of paths of descent from the summit.

In the four symphonies of Felix Mendelssohn (1809–47) the prevalent qualities are a felicity of melodic invention and a delicacy of scoring. Two of these symphonies, No. 3 in A minor ('The Scottish') and No. 4 in A major ('The Italian'), have become firmly established in the orchestral repertoire by virtue of their grace and their tunefulness, but Mendelssohn's lyrical musical nature does not find its natural expression in symphonic form. In such works as the overture to Shakespeare's *A Midsummer Night's Dream*, on the other hand, and in his string octet, both written when he was in his teens, he shows a limpidity of style and a refinement of orchestral technique that few composers of the early nineteenth century can match. If part of his individuality and popularity lies in his gift of lyrical melody and his directness of manner – witness the perennial appeal, in their different ways, of his violin concerto and of his oratorio *Elijah* – the other part, and the historically more distinctive, lies in his skill in painting sound-pictures of pictorial images. He was, indeed, responsive in an exceptional degree to external pictorial and situational impulses, and the titles of the works that reflect this – *Fingal's Cave, Calm Sea and Prosperous Voyage, Melusine, Ruy Blas*, together with *A Midsummer Night's Dream* and the other plays for which he wrote incidental music – show how considerable was his indebtedness to such stimuli.

To Mendelssohn's activities as a conductor we owe the revival of Bach's *St Matthew Passion*, which had lain in total oblivion since Bach's day and which Mendelssohn performed at a concert in Berlin in 1829.

Like Mendelssohn, Robert Schumann (1810–56) also drew many of his stimuli for musical composition from the other arts, particularly from literature, and like Mendelssohn, too, his gifts found their most natural outlet in the smaller lyrical forms. His songs – *Dichterliebe*, to poems by Heine; the *Liederkreis* (Op. 39), to poems by Eichendorff; and *Frauenliebe und -leben*, to poems by Chamisso, to quote the best-known cycles – are among the most beautiful in the whole repertoire. His range does not equal Schubert's, nor can he match the sheer dramatic power of works like Schubert's 'Erlkönig' and 'Der Doppelgänger'; but on the other hand he possesses a remarkable depth of psychological insight and a rare intensity of emotional sympathy with the situations of which his chosen poems speak.

In the larger forms Schumann, like Mendelssohn, was rarely at his ease. His Piano Concerto in A minor, like Mendelssohn's violin concerto, has a lyrical beauty that has made it one of the best-loved concertos in the repertoire, but his four symphonies, notwithstanding the occasional page of true symphonic writing, lack a sustained symphonic argument; they also have, in common with many of his piano works, a thickness of texture which, despite the harmonic interest, produces blurred outlines and a certain sameness of tone, both within one movement and from one movement to another.

There is an interesting historical link, as well as an inner musical affinity, between Schumann and Johannes Brahms (1833–97). In the year of Brahms's birth Schumann founded a musical journal called *Die neue Zeitschrift für Musik*. Twenty years later he wrote an article in this journal, hailing Brahms as the true heir to the tradition of Beethoven and as the composer for whom the world had been waiting. It is hard to see Brahms in this Messianic role today, and even harder, when one looks at the music that Brahms had produced up to that time, to see what could have induced Schumann to make such an awe-inspiring claim.

The spiritual *rapport* between Brahms and Schumann lies in the nature of their musical gifts and in the somewhat discrepant relationship between the character of these gifts and the character of the two men's aspirations. Brahms had met Schumann and his wife Clara in 1853 while on a concert tour as a pianist, and he became their intimate friend during the last unhappy days of Schumann's life. Whether or not this personal closeness is a source of the musical kinship between them, the kinship is there in musical terms.

Thus in his four symphonies, which contain some splendid, full-blooded Romantic music, Brahms is at his most natural, most individual – which is to say, his greatest – in the lyrical slow movements and in the graceful allegretto third movements which he fashioned out of the customary scherzo. The world of these movements is the world of the violin concerto, of the St Anthony variations, of the alto rhapsody, of the ballades, rhapsodies and intermezzi for piano, and of the songs (of which he wrote 190, most of them settings of German Romantic poets), and it is from this world that his most moving utterances come. Again, it is not that he has left no memorable music at all in a heroic vein: the Piano Concerto No. 1 in D minor and the piano Variations and Fugue on a theme of Handel stand as sufficient testimony to the contrary. But the real, inimitable Brahms, composer of an earnest lyrical beauty which belongs to the highest that German music has to offer, is elsewhere.

What seriousness and intensity are to Brahms, inventive daring and brilliance are to Franz Liszt (1811–86). Liszt's father was Hungarian, his mother Austrian, and a good deal of his early career was spent in Paris, but the activities of his maturity are centred in Germany. For a number of years he was conductor and music director at the court of Weimar, where he gave the first performance of many new operas, among them Berlioz's *Beatrice and Benedict* and Wagner's *Lohengrin*. Liszt's daughter Cosima, formerly married to the conductor Hans von Bülow, became Wagner's second wife in 1870 and managed the affairs of the Bayreuth Festival after Wagner's death in 1883.

Few are the artists around whom so much controversy has gathered. This stems partly, no doubt, from the much-publicized instability of his spectacular personal life and from the flamboyance of his career as a virtuoso pianist. But it is also connected with the cult of superficial brilliance, whether in his orchestral scoring or in his bravura piano-writing, which so often obtrudes in his works. His detractors can point fairly to a great deal of glittering but empty passage-work in his vast output of piano pieces, to the limitations of his formal sense, and to the not infrequent banality and vulgarity of his taste: in works like his two piano concertos and the twenty Hungarian Rhapsodies, it is not difficult to find evidence of all these traits.

Yet there are two directions in which Liszt's influence proved of decisive importance in the history of nineteenth-century music: one is the invention of the symphonic poem, the other is the extension of the harmonic vocabulary of music.

The emergence of programme music and its particular association with Romanticism have already been discussed. Suffice it to add here that the genre proper, a one-movement programmatic work for orchestra, was inaugurated by Liszt with works such as *Ce qu'on entend sur la montagne* (1848, after a poem by Victor Hugo), *Les Préludes* (1848, after the *Méditations poétiques* of Lamartine) and *Tasso* (1849, after Byron), and that the line of development leads directly from him both to nationalist composers of the descriptive, pictorial type of symphonic poem (Smetana, *Ma Vlast*; Sibelius, *Finlandia*; Respighi, *The Fountains of Rome*) and to those who concerned themselves with the presentation of portraits from literature (Tchaikovsky, *Romeo and Juliet* and *Hamlet*; Richard Strauss, *Don Quixote* and *Macbeth*; Elgar,

Falstaff). Liszt's two large-scale programme symphonies, *Dante* and *Faust*, are the successors of Berlioz's *Symphonie fantastique*.

The particular originality of Liszt's harmonic power – and this is a feature, not the only one, that gives him an affinity with Chopin – lies in his use of chromaticism. Together with Chopin and, to a lesser extent, Berlioz, he exercised an important influence on Wagner in the employment of chromatic melody and harmony, an influence which bore its fullest fruits in Wagner's *Tristan and Isolde* and *Parsifal*. Among Liszt's own compositions this harmonic power is particularly in evidence in three superb large-scale works for organ, possibly the greatest pieces of Romantic organ music in the repertoire: the Prelude and Fugue on BACH, the Variations on 'Weinen, Klagen', and the Fantasia and Fugue on 'Ad nos, ad salutarem undam'.

The development of this chromatic originality is directly linked to the programmatic extension of subject-matter which Liszt introduced, for with the depiction in music of scenes from nature, or of stages in the physical and spiritual life of a historical or fictional hero, came the stimulus to experimentation in technique. Novelty and subtlety of conception, especially in the portrayal of states of mind and stresses of emotion, to which the world of identified positions and straight antitheses is alien, lead away from the circumscribed forms of diatonic harmony and into the chromatic realm of fine distinctions, while the palette of orchestral tone-colour grows richer with the search for new scenes to paint and new experiences to reveal. In the context of European musical history as a whole many of Liszt's innovations in this field appear as directly anticipatory of techniques employed by Debussy and the impressionist composers in general.

Few would deny the appropriateness of the term Romantic to denote the basic musical nature and intentions of Schubert, Weber, Schumann, Mendelssohn, Brahms, Liszt and their many minor contemporaries. But the most complete embodiment of this term is the man who, having up till now hovered in the background of so much of this discussion of nineteenth-century music, now emerges as the figure destined to give the most powerful expression to the innate tendencies, both recognized and unconscious, of that music – Wagner.

The life of Richard Wagner (1813–83) was the turbulent counterpart to a turbulent personality. His education in music and the other arts was extensive, and his passion for opera can be traced back to his schooldays, but he was no child prodigy. Particularly interesting is that already for his very first opera, *Die Hochzeit,* begun when he was nineteen, he wrote his own libretto – a principle to which he adhered in all his subsequent works. He held a succession of posts as conductor and music director in theatres at Würzburg, Magdeburg and Königsberg, spent a penurious three years with his first wife in Paris, where he finished both *Rienzi* and *The Flying Dutchman,* then moved as second conductor to Dresden, where these two works, together with *Tannhäuser,* were first performed. In the revolution of 1848 he supported the liberal cause, as a result of which he was forced to flee to Zürich, where, under the inspiration of his love for Mathilde Wesendonck, wife of a friend and benefactor, he worked on his *Ring* cycle and *Tristan and Isolde.*

After brief stays in Venice, Lucerne, Paris and Vienna he received in 1864 an invitation from the 'mad' King Ludwig II of Bavaria to join his court at Munich. But as a result of his adulterous relationship there with Liszt's daughter Cosima, wife of the conductor Hans von Bülow, he was compelled to seek exile again in Switzerland, where Cosima later joined him, and where they were married in 1870. The years that followed saw the erection of the Festival Theatre at Bayreuth, where Wagner and his family settled, and where, in 1876, the first performance of the complete cycle of *Der Ring des Nibelungen* (*Das Rheingold*; *Die Walküre*; *Siegfried*; *Götterdämmerung*) was given. Deteriorating health drove him to pay frequent visits to Italy, and he died on one such visit to Venice. Cosima, mother of Siegfried Wagner (cf. Wagner's orchestral gem, the *Siegfried Idyll*) and grandmother of Wieland and Wolfgang – the latter the present director of the Bayreuth Festival – died in 1930, at the age of ninety-three.

In his theory of opera Wagner stated the need for a perfect synthesis of the arts – painting, through the visual impact of the setting; literature, through the libretto; and music – the whole to present a unified dramatic experience, a living proof of the axiom that the whole is greater than the sum of its parts. The union of the arts, the usurpation by Art of the throne of Religion, the equation of aesthetic experience with metaphysical knowledge – these ideals had been preached by the school of early German Romantic writers at the end of the eighteenth century, and had later acquired the status of philosophical doctrine in the hands of Schopenhauer. Allied with the aesthetic doctrines of the early Romantics were the solipsist philosophies of Fichte and Schelling, which provided a metaphysical framework for the exercise of unrestrained subjectivity in the forms of human expression. Schopenhauer, whose ideas made a deep impression on German artists and thinkers in the nineteenth and twentieth centuries, among them Wagner, went so far as to claim that it was through music, as the most abstract and therefore most perfect of the arts, that the purpose of the world was revealed.

This is the broad philosophical background against which one must view the claim that it is in music that the ideals of German Romanticism find their fullest expression, and that it is in Wagner that both the musical tendencies of nineteenth-century European music and the wider aesthetic aspirations of the Romantic movement reach their culmination. Of all the arts music is the farthest removed from material reality. It does not 'express' thoughts in the way that language expresses thoughts, or depict scenes in the way that painting depicts scenes. The power of its penetration of the human mind lies in its immediacy, the absoluteness and physical unrelatedness of its demands, and it is these qualities that make it the perfect medium for the communication of romantic yearning, romantic transcendence of temporal earthliness, and self-absorption into the infinite. 'While the other arts deal only with the shadow,' wrote Schopenhauer, 'music deals with the substance.'

It is probably the unconditional nature of these demands that has led to the intensity of the response, favourable or unfavourable, to Wagner's music. For whereas it would be ridiculous to call oneself anti-Bach or anti-Mozart or anti-Beethoven, it is somehow not incomprehensible that people should call themselves anti-Wagner. The unremitting intensity of the demands his music makes upon us; the ruthless exploration of the psychological implications and relationships in his works; the power to command utter surrender and thus to threaten the survival of one's own individuality – and an uneasy memory of the use to which Hitler was able to put this music in the Third Reich: these are some of the characteristics, sometimes firmly identifiable, sometimes vaguely sensed, that lie behind the controversy.

Yet controversial as it may be, the greatness of Wagner is undeniable – many would say irresistible. His theory of the *Gesamtkunstwerk* called for the union of the arts in the service of dramatic purpose, but his own music-dramas – a word of his own coinage, to symbolize his break with the conventions of 'traditional' opera – stand in fact as huge achievements in music. His libretti, apart from those of *The Flying Dutchman* and *The Mastersingers*, are almost unreadable, and no more able to exist as dramas than are the eighteenth-century libretti of Scribe and da Ponte. Whatever his far from consistent theories postulated (we may name *Das Kunstwerk der Zukunft*, 1849; *Oper und Drama*, 1851; *Beethoven*, 1870) about the multiple relationships between the visual element and the dramatic element, the poetic element and the musical element, in practice music has taken control of the *Gesamtkunstwerk*: the course of the dramatic action and the portrayal of psychological states and conflicts have become, at their most profound, the prerogative of the music.

Tristan and Isolde is, on one plane, a perfect example of this. An even purer case is Wagner's last music-drama, *Parsifal*, whose symbolic metaphysical meaning is dissolved, so to speak, in the ethereal quality of some of Wagner's most sublimely beautiful music, transmitting an experience which many would call religious. Not for nothing is a performance of *Parsifal* often received not by applause but by silence.

In the sober terms of the history of opera Wagner's greatest originality lies in his creation of 'endless melody' and in his fusion of voice and orchestra, the latter, indeed, frequently dominating the vocal parts and becoming the main vehicle of the dramatic action. This is the sense in which, with a view of his works in the totality of their intention and impact, one can see in Wagner, and not in any nineteenth-century symphonic composer, the true inheritor of the tradition of Beethoven. Whatever intrinsic beauty and interest may reside in the symphonies of Beethoven's successors, there is nowhere that intensity of experience and substantiality of thought-content which Beethoven achieved. It may be that the formal symphony had passed its apogee; but it is what might be called the true 'symphonic spirit' that sustains Wagner's music-dramas.

Wagner sums up an epoch. The power of his musical vocabulary, in particular his use of chromaticism; the sumptuousness of his orchestral texture – he even invented an instrument, the so-called 'Wagner tuba', to obtain a particular richness of timbre he required in the *Ring*; and more than anything else the building-up and sustaining of an unremitting emotional pressure, forcing, almost dragging, the listener along in its train: this is what he left to the generations that succeeded him. It is not surprising that so many composers should have eagerly claimed their share of this huge legacy, or that it should have been virtually forced into the hands of most of the rest. For Wagner, as Ernest Newman put it, 'was one of those dynamically charged personalities after whose passing the world can never be the same as it was before he came.'

One of those to put his share of the legacy to the achievement of a particularly original beauty was the Austrian Hugo Wolf (1860–1903), one of the greatest song-writers of all time. Speaking in only the most general of terms, one may distinguish two modes of song-writing: the one openly takes the text as a point of departure for independent musical creation, so that the words, though obviously part of the finished artistic product, come somehow to matter less than the music; the other sees the activity as the extension into musical terms of the conceptual meaning of the text, seeking to underline this meaning by the application of musical resources. The distinction is clearly only a rough-and-ready one, and qualities which might seem to derive properly from the former attitude are found in the work of composers whose general approach to song-writing is closer to the latter; but it does serve to illustrate the differences, both in approach and in musical practice, between, say, Brahms and Schumann on the one hand and Hugo Wolf on the other (in opera the same difference of approach distinguishes Mozart from Gluck and – in terms of theory at least – Verdi from Wagner).

Wolf's methods, which owed much to his declared idol, Wagner, led to the creation of songs of great dramatic and intellectual power, with shades of emotional intensity conveyed above all by harmonic subtlety and refinement of piano accompaniment. He wrote about 300 songs in all, including twenty to poems by Eichendorff, and fifty-one to poems by Goethe; his most intimate spiritual link, however, is with Mörike, an author who, though he also wrote in other forms, was by nature as completely a lyric poet as Wolf – who also wrote a few works in other forms, including two operas – was a song-writer. Wolf's fifty-three settings of Mörike contain some of the finest of all *Lieder*.

As in the field of song there is a line from Wagner to the Austrian Wolf, so in the symphony there is a line from Wagner to the Austrian Anton Bruckner (1824–96), whose nine symphonies carry into orchestral music the richness of harmonic vocabulary, the fullness of orchestral texture and, above all, the grandiosity of conception and design of Wagner's music-dramas. While it is difficult to avoid seeing in him one of the more distinguished victims of the cult of length for length's sake – a less fortunate aspect of the Wagnerian heritage – there remains much splendid music in his scores, more and more of which are establishing themselves in concert repertoires outside Germany and Austria. A slighter figure than Bruckner, one who in his choice of musical forms and his concern with counterpoint harks back to Bach, is Max Reger (1873–1916), who is known in this country chiefly for a few sets of orchestral variations and for an extensive collection of preludes and fugues, chorale preludes and other works for organ.

One of the most interesting non-operatic composers whose careers lie in the wake of Wagner, and also an Austrian, is Gustav Mahler (1860–1911), who, having had a steady but modest reputation in Germany over the last half-century, was suddenly 'discovered' in England after World War II and has come to figure regularly in the modern concert repertoire. There is in Mahler a strong, destructive dichotomy, or series of dichotomies, between his inner and outer life, between his true nature and the character of his aspirations. He sought in his music a universality of expression which his abilities would not allow him to attain, with the result that, for all the moments of individual beauty – and there are many – in his ten symphonies, there is a fatal disharmony between ambition and achievement, the outer form and the inner content. In the smaller forms, on the other hand, above all in the song-cycles *Lieder eines fahrenden Gesellen* and *Kindertotenlieder*, the lyrical nature of his gifts finds its natural outlet, and the result, despite – or perhaps partly because of – the *fin de siècle* melancholy characteristic of the artist at odds with the values of his age, is music of touching beauty.

In Richard Strauss (1864–1949), a contemporary of Mahler's, but who lived to experience the two world wars whose imminence Mahler's introspective gloom seemed to presage, we find the most extrovert and successful of the composers who in the realm of opera sought to extract the fullest possible value from the situation that Wagner had left. Although it is in opera that he is at his greatest, Strauss rose to fame on a series of symphonic poems in the Lisztian mould – *Don Juan* (1888), *Till Eulenspiegel* (1895), *Don Quixote* (1897) are probably the best known – to which he brought his own opulence of orchestral colour in techniques developed from Berlioz and Wagner. Like Mahler, he made his early career as a conductor of opera, and in 1891 was invited by Cosima Wagner to conduct *Tannhäuser* at the Bayreuth Festival.

Strauss's operas represent the last great flowering of the German Romantic genius. In the first half of the twentieth century Hans Pfitzner (1869–1949) was held in Germany and Austria to be comparable to Strauss, and his opera *Palestrina* (1915), in which the presence of Schumann as well as Wagner is clearly felt, still has a tenuous hold on German opera-houses, but elsewhere he is hardly remembered. In the same post-Wagnerian mould and Romantic temperament are

Engelbert Humperdinck (1854–1921), remembered for one work, the fairy-tale opera *Hänsel und Gretel* (1893), and the Austrian Franz Schreker (1878–1934), composer of *Der ferne Klang* (1912) and other Romantic operas.

But neither these nor any other works can be put alongside the operas of Strauss's maturity: *Salome* (1905), *Elektra* (1909), *Der Rosenkavalier* (1911) and *Ariadne auf Naxos* (1912), all to libretti by Hugo von Hofmannsthal. In the one-act works *Salome* and *Elektra* the weight of the psychological meaning is conveyed through the orchestral score on which the voices are superimposed; in the Romantic lyrical *Rosenkavalier* the voices reassert themselves as the principal carriers of emotional expression, and there is even a partial return to the set-number style of Italianate opera. But everywhere the music is continuous, in the Wagnerian mould, with a lavish intensity and an extravagant deployment of vocal and orchestral forces which leave no doubt as to the source of Strauss's spiritual allegiance.

Yet inseparable from the charms of these works is an air of *fin de siècle* decadence, an awareness of an insubstantiality of intellectual fibre. At its most genuine, as in the smaller-scale works written in the Indian summer of his seventies and eighties, like the *Metamorphosen* for strings and the *Four Last Songs*, Strauss's music conveys a sad, nostalgic quality which, for all its beauty, defines a cramped and limited world in which positive values are at a discount. Ironically, the works in which these values are present, like *Till Eulenspiegel* and *Don Juan*, have a programmatic purpose and an allied brilliance of surface presentation which set them from the beginning on a lower plane of aspiration. Strauss's world, like that of his English contemporary Delius, is one of precious beauty; but it is a very small world.

The composers described above, from Wolf to Strauss, all standing in the shadow of Wagner, are the last significant spokesmen of the diatonic tradition of the Romantic nineteenth century. We find in the early decades of the twentieth century a few intellectual attempts to break away from the played-out conventions of this tradition, such as that of Ferruccio Busoni (1866–1924), whose opera *Doktor Faust* (left unfinished and only produced after his death) contains some of the most striking music to be found in Europe at that time, and whose writings on musical aesthetics are of a rare sensitivity and perception. But it was clear that music had to be led into new channels, the relationship to the past restated, virtually a new rationale of composition evolved. This new rationale was embodied in the revolution in musical thought and composition proclaimed by Arnold Schoenberg (1874–1951).

Squarely confronting the distintegration of classical tonality and diatonic harmony, Schoenberg drew the logical conclusion: i.e. that musical composition based on relationship between keys – the formal principle underlying symphony, sonata, fugue, concerto and all classical music – was no longer possible and must be replaced by atonal (key-less) composition. The force of tonality had been undermined by the growing power of chromaticism in the music of Chopin, Liszt and, above all, Wagner: the removal of the relatedness of chromatic tones to a diatonic system – i.e. chromaticism made absolute – equals atonality.

However, Schoenberg did not launch his career on this revolutionary level, and his early pieces – the best-known are the string sextet *Verklärte Nacht* (1892) and the *Gurrelieder* (1901–10) – are exercises in the post-Wagnerian idiom. His first atonal works were the Three Piano Pieces, Op. 11 (1908), and for the succeeding twelve years or so most of his music was in this anarchic, negative vein. In the early 1920s, seeking for musical composition a recognizable unifying principle to replace that of key, he evolved the so-called twelve-tone technique which was to become such a force in twentieth-century music. Briefly, the technique requires that the twelve tones of the chromatic scale first be arranged in a chosen order – no note may appear twice until all the other eleven have each appeared once: this arrangement of the twelve notes is called the tone-row. From this basic form of the tone-row three other forms are then derived: (i) the inverted form, i.e. where the basic tone-row ascends, the inversion descends by the same intervals; (ii) the retrograde form, i.e. the notes of the basic tone-row played in reverse order; (iii) the retrograde inversion, i.e. the notes of the inverted form played in reverse order. From these four patterns, and possibly also from their transpositions (twelve-tone composers differ in their approach to this) is drawn the entire melodic and harmonic substance of each piece of music. The classical formal principle of harmony is thus replaced by the unifying discipline of fixed note-order.

Schoenberg's own compositions include operas, sundry orchestral works and a considerable variety of vocal and chamber music. But perhaps his most important role was as a teacher, and in Vienna and Berlin there collected round him a group of students from all over Europe. His two most famous pupils were Anton Webern (1883–1943), whose strict application of twelve-tone principles led to the composition of highly intellectual miniature pieces in which the thought is so concentrated and compressed as to be barely intelligible; and Alban Berg (1885–1935), the most accessible of the twelve-tone composers and virtually the only one to have contributed works to the standard modern repertoire.

Berg, the emotional and intellectual power of whose music derives from a remarkable blend of relived traditional values and the new range of expression opened up by twelve-tone techniques, left only a handful of compositions, but two of these are among the masterpieces of twentieth-century music: the opera *Wozzeck* and the violin concerto. *Wozzeck* (1925; the libretto from Büchner's drama *Woyzeck*), the most outstanding example of expressionism in music, is written largely in a free atonal style in which the union of words, music and dramatic action in a harrowing subject of human degradation and despair results in an almost unbearable intensity of expression. The same intensity fills the violin concerto (1935), in which, contrary to the spirit of twelve-tone theory and to Schoenberg's and most other twelve-tonalists' practice, the basic tone-row is arranged in a sequence of 'conventional' major and minor triads, plus a fragment of whole-tone scale. At the end of the work this original thematic material is blended with a Bach chorale to give music whose haunting beauty is almost without parallel in the twentieth century. His other opera, *Lulu* (the text drawn by Berg from two dramas by Wedekind), which was left unfinished at his death and is written in the twelve-tone style throughout, is far less convincing and powerful than *Wozzeck*.

The greatness of Alban Berg, like the greatness of Bela Bartók, has its roots in his acceptance of his links with the historical past, his will to relive and re-express in terms of contemporary experience the profound and inescapable values that underlie human existence. It is this that distinguishes him from those of his contemporaries who either turned away from the real challenge or contented themselves with intellectualizing the situation or imitating and embroidering the responses of others: the intellectualizers have severed the lifeline with the concept of 'art as communication', with the result that their music appears as an arid exercise from which warm human content has been excluded, while the imitators follow their derivative careers untouched by the real issues that confront their art.

Prominent in the intellectual pursuit of new styles was Paul Hindemith (1895–1963), who, like Schoenberg, exerted an influence as much through his teaching as through his compositions. Hindemith wrote an immense amount of music – operas and incidental music to plays, choral and orchestral works, a considerable quantity of chamber music, pieces for piano and organ – much of it under the slogan of *Gebrauchs-musik*, 'functional music'. These were pieces designed to meet the practical requirements of performers or the functional needs of particular occasions, in the manner – as Hindemith himself pointed out – in which most eighteenth-century music had come into existence. This is the point at which Hindemith's approach to his art – or rather, craft, since it is the technical skill that he emphasizes – makes contact with the neo-classical movement inaugurated by Stravinsky in the 1920s, and the desiccated cerebral manner affected by Stravinsky at this time left unmistakable marks on Hindemith's music.

Hindemith's technical mastery is well displayed in his *Ludus Tonalis* (1943) for piano, a sort of modern counterpart to Bach's *Well-Tempered Clavier*, consisting of twelve three-part fugues with linking interludes, in which all the classical features of counterpoint are displayed in a modern setting. And whatever aggressive modernity this music may seem to have, it is firmly anchored – witness the title – in tonality. In a warmer, less intellectual vein is the work of Hindemith's which has become most widely known, the symphony *Mathis der Maler*, derived from his opera of that name (1938) on the sixteenth-century German painter Matthias Grünewald, and containing some fine, virile music. His exuberant *Metamorphoses on Themes of Carl Maria von Weber* (1943) have also begun to find a place in concert programmes in recent years. Such works as the three sonatas for piano and the three sonatas for organ, on the other hand, like most of his chamber music, live in a colder, more rarefied atmosphere and may, like much of Hindemith's music, be for the pleasure rather of the performer than the listener.

An interesting contemporary of Hindemith's was Kurt Weill (1900–50), who, in collaboration with Bertolt Brecht, composed five *Singspiel*-type operas in a mordant, parodistic style, of which the best known is *Die Dreigroschenoper* (1928), a biting satirical version of John Gay's eighteenth-century *Beggar's Opera*, aimed at social iniquities and public corruption in contemporary Germany. Another musical collaborator in Brecht's bitter left-wing dramatic crusades against the evils of capitalist society was Hanns Eisler (1898–1962) who, like Weill, left Germany under Nazi persecution in the 1930s and settled in the USA. As one would expect, the music of these two composers, like that of any composers associated with Brecht, enjoys particular favour today in East Germany.

Present-day composers in Germany, as in any other country, tend to range themselves in two groups: those who still subscribe, in a broad sense, to what may loosely be described as the traditional belief in music as a means of communication, i.e. music that 'says something to us', and those for whom music is an arrangement *sui generis* of detached acoustical sense-impressions, to be judged – if it can be judged at all – by its novelty or by its qualities of 'pure' sound. Music of the former kind, however 'difficult' and intellectually abstruse it may be, still relies on the familiar contexts of orchestral and chamber music, and is still performed on familiar instruments played in more or less familiar ways. Composers in the latter style, on the other hand, often have recourse to synthetic, electronically produced sounds, to the treatment of familiar instruments in unconventional ways, e.g. by the use of a specially 'prepared' piano, and to the unplanned and unpredictable acoustical effects produced by performing from only partially completed scores which allow improvisatory freedom to the players or singers.

Among the composers of the former kind there are, as one would expect, a number still working with the techniques of twelve-tone composition. The allegiance, however, is often less to Schoenberg direct than to Webern, an allegiance that shows itself particularly in the fragmentation of the musical material – what has been called the 'disintegration of sounds into pinpoints of colour and silence'. At this stage in the development of twelve-tone composition, significantly and predictably, the problem of meaningful musical form reappears, one of the problems that has bedevilled serial composition from the beginning.

One of the most productive of contemporary German dodecaphonists is Hans Werner Henze (b. 1926), who, calling on techniques reminiscent of expressionism, has composed a number of extended works which have gained him an international following. Among these are six symphonies, ballet-music, and six operas, including *Der Prinz von Homburg* (1960; after the drama by Heinrich von Kleist). His radio cantata *Ein Landarzt* (1951), based on Kafka's story of that name, is a striking example of his bold, uncompromising style.

Of an older generation, and indebted rather to the diatonic-based avant-gardism of Stravinsky than to serialism, are Werner Egk (b. 1901) and Boris Blacher (b. 1903). Egk, who studied with Carl Orff (see below), composes primarily for the theatre. He has written a considerable quantity of ballet-music but, like Henze, has made his greatest impression in the field of opera. Among his works in this form are *Peer Gynt* (1938; after Ibsen); *Irische Legende* (after W. B. Yeats, first performed at the Salzburg Festival 1955); *Der Revisor* (1957; after the play by Gogol); and *Die Verlobung in San Domingo* (1963; after the story by Heinrich von Kleist).

Blacher, who has been director of the Staatliche Hochscule für Musik in Berlin since 1953, has also had a *penchant* for music in dramatic form. His *Abstract Opera No. 1* (1953) was something of a *succès de scandale* in its radical novelty, while at the other end of the scale, following in the wake of Stravinsky, he had earlier experimented in the idioms of jazz (*Jazz-Koloraturen* for saxophone and bassoon, 1929). Controversy also attended his *Zwischenfälle bei einer Notlandung* (1966), an avant-garde 'reportage' for singers, instruments and electronic devices. He also compiled the libretti for the operas *Dantons Tod* and *Der Prozeß* by his pupil Gottfried von Einem (see below).

Less intellectual than these, far directer and easier of access, is Carl Orff (b. 1895), a self-consciously homespun Bavarian who in his un-problematical Teutonic allegiances and his blunt extrovert manner would be a strong contender for the title of Grand Old Man of twentieth-century German music. He has written two operas on fairy-tales from the Grimms' collection (*Der Mond*, 1939, revised 1950; *Die Kluge*, 1943), together with a quantity of ballet-music and incidental music to plays, but he is best known, both inside and outside Germany, for his *Carmina Burana* (1937), the first of a trilogy of secular choral cantatas called *Trionfi*; the second part of the trilogy is *Catulli Carmina* (1943) and the third part *Trionfo di Afrodite* (1953). More experimental than these – rather self-consciously so – is his *Prometheus* (first performed 1968), half-opera, half-drama, the Greek text being spoken, intoned, chanted and declaimed.

Orff's style is monodic, his melodic motifs short, and his harmonic vocabulary basically traditional, but he adds a certain acidity of flavour through contrapuntal and rhythmical devices which serve to revamp the familiar material. The neo-classical strain in Stravinsky and Hindemith is very evident in his music: *Carmina Burana*, indeed, with its bitter-sweet blend of innocent folk-song heartiness and artful, mildly jarring modernity, is a kind of secular counterpart to Stravinsky's

Symphony of Psalms. A further link between Hindemith and Orff lies in their concern with musical education and with the stimulation of musical consciousness in children by performance rather than by precept. To this end, and principally with the cultivation of the sense of rhythm in mind, Orff has composed instructional material and published it under the collective title *Das Schulwerk* (1930–3). He has also edited versions of Monteverdi's operas *Orfeo* and *L'incoronazione di Poppea.*

The predilection for opera and stage-music in general, which characterizes Werner Egk and Boris Blacher, persists in the work of Blacher's Swiss pupil Gottfried von Einem (b. 1918), and again the word 'expressionist' comes to mind when one seeks to characterize the dynamic rhythmic effects and the stark unyielding harmonic idiom of Einem's operas and ballets. His eclecticism, however, tends to withhold from his music, effective though it usually is, the sense of self-sufficiency and self-justification that deep-felt art must command. His operas *Dantons Tod* (1947, after Büchner's drama) and *Der Prozeß* (1953, after the novel by Kafka), both of which received their premières at the Salzburg Festival, show *in extenso* the skills and the limitations of his eclectic method. It is clearly not by chance that Einem, like his compatriot Rolf Liebermann (b. 1910) – whose serial opera *Leonore 40/45* (1952), a recasting of the situation of Beethoven's *Fidelio* against the background of World War II, met with considerable success – and in common with Henze, Egk and other contemporary composers, should have turned for operatic material to subjects ruled by starkness and the violence of extremes. One particularly striking manifestation of this is the recourse for subject-matter to writers such as Kleist, Büchner and Kafka, depicters of extreme states of mind and extreme situations, authors whose power of personality dictates from the very beginning both the form of any operatic treatment of their works and the ultimate 'meaning' of the finished musico-dramatic opus. Works in this vein accord particularly well with the official cultural line prescribed in East Germany, and are regularly heard at opera-houses there as well as in the West.

Uncompromising and difficult of access as much of this music is – and this is probably even truer of the instrumental than of the vocal music – it is yet produced in more or less conventional contexts by 'normal' instruments played in more or less 'normal' ways. The difficulty of access, broadly speaking, derives from a change of attitude on the part of many young composers towards the function of musical composition – a movement away from music as communication and towards music as a self-sufficient arrangement of auditory sense-impressions. The aesthetic and philosophical issues that this raises cannot be discussed here, but many contemporary composers, with an urge to detailed self-explanation which would have astonished – and does astonish – older generations, have themselves been at pains to justify their approach in these detached, independent terms, so that we are bound to judge their actual music, at least in part, in the light of the theories that lie behind it. One of the quainter features of twentieth-century avant-garde music is the frequent provision by the composer of a substantial explanatory preface to a hearing of the music itself. The music is apparently somewhat less than self-sufficient, and the composer is afraid it might be misunderstood – or not understood at all.

These already considerable problems become greater when to the music of 'conventional' instruments are added synthetic sounds produced by electronic means. One of the foremost practitioners in this field is Karlheinz Stockhausen (b. 1928), who, under the stimulus of Olivier Messiaen and his pupil Pierre Boulez in Paris, the centre of *musique concrète*, took up the co-directorship of a centre established in 1953 by Cologne Radio for the exploration of electronically produced sounds.

The production of sound by wave-generators, photoelectric cells and the like is not the novelty that the contemporary vogue enjoyed by Stockhausen, the Italian Luciano Berio and others of their generation might suggest, but the isolated examples of electronic instruments invented in the early twentieth century, and in particular the attempts made in the 1930s by the Mexican composer Carlos Chavez to extend the range of musical expression by experimenting with such methods of tone-production, made little impression at the time.

The disintegration of the musical continuum which is characteristic of Webern is carried further by Stockhausen in non-electronic works such as *Zeitmasse* (1956) for oboe, flute, cor anglais, clarinet and bassoon, while in *Gruppen* (1960) in which three different orchestras are disposed at different points in the hall, he seeks to add a 'spatial' dimension to the temporal nature of music. In *Kontakte* (1960) he combines his electronic experiments with a penchant for coloristic percussive effects by taking a tape-recording of synthetic sounds and adding to it parts for piano and a fantastic array of percussion instruments, including African wood-drums, cow-bells and tom-toms. As co-editor of the journal *Die Reihe,* and in essays collected under the characteristic title of *Momente* (1963; it is also the title of a composition (1962) for soprano voice, four choruses and thirteen instrumentalists) he has expounded his views on developments in modern music and on the rationale of his own activities. One of his most extended exercises is *Stimmung für Sextête* (1968), a composition for six vocalists, who sit on six cushions among the audience, with a battery of electronic 'sound-spheres' controlled by one operator. Through the vocalizing of evocative names and words in a lengthy sequence of numerous gradations (the entire work lasts one and a half hours), the performers seek contact with the primeval forces of nature – a kind of self-obliterating musical meditation, and an expression, in part, of the contemporary cult of yoga, sitar music and other Oriental commodities.

Many of these developments, whether the product of human or mechanical agency, have gained popularity through festivals and through the activities of music academies, of which West Germany alone has fourteen of university status, quite apart from university faculties of music and private institutions. In recent years such annual events as the International Summer School at Darmstadt – where, incidentally, Stockhausen first met Messiaen and Boulez – and the festival at Donaueschingen have been particularly well-publicized fora for the presentation of avant-garde music, and attract a clientèle as international as that which attends the established festivals at Bayreuth, Salzburg, Munich and elsewhere.

An extension of the range of aural sensations, as one of the forms in which new philosophies of the art of musical expression have emerged, has been accompanied by new attitudes to the scope and purpose of musical education. One interesting result of these new attitudes has been to bring the worlds of art and science together at a number of points. The use of electronic means to produce acoustical phenomena that many would in any case be reluctant to call music may be little more than a passing pseudo-scientific-cum-artistic whim, though an increasing number of music academies are investing in such equipment. Of more demonstrable practical value is the move to provide for recording engineers both a musical and a scientific training to enable them to deal more satisfactorily with the problems of making gramophone records. The Staatliche Hochschule für Musik in Detmold was the first to provide a course of training of this kind, graduates in which are called *Tonmeister.*

However, the transmission of influences and stimuli in music, both in composition and in performance, has always been by personal, private contact rather than through the formal channels of institutionalized learning. Where an inspiring teacher happens to be – Nadia Boulanger and Messiaen in Paris, Schoenberg in Vienna, Matjas Seiber in London, Casals in Prades – there aspiring young musicians will collect, academy of music or no academy of music. And in this the present age is like any other.

Bibliography

GENERAL

MOSER, H. J. *Geschichte der deutschen Musik*. Berlin, 1920–4.
Individual entries in *Grove's Dictionary of Music and Musicians* for historical periods, genres, forms and composers: further bibliographies ibid.
The Pelican History of Music.

INDIVIDUAL PERIODS

REESE, G. *Music in the Middle Ages*. New York, 1941.
BUKOFZER, M. *Music in the Baroque Era*. London, 1948.
THOMAS, R. H. *Poetry and Song in the German Baroque*. Oxford, 1963.
EINSTEIN, A. *Music in the Romantic Era*. London, 1947.
RUFER, J. *Composition with Twelve Tones*. London, 1954.

INDIVIDUAL COMPOSERS

Concise accounts of the life and works of the major classical composers are to be found in the individual volumes of the 'Master Musicians' series (London, Dent), each of which has its own further bibliography. A few of the more important larger studies in English are listed below.

GEIRINGER, K. *Bach*. London, 1966.
— *Haydn*. London, 1964.
EINSTEIN, A. *Mozart*. London, 1946.
SULLIVAN, J. W. N. *Beethoven*. London, 1927.
SEARLE, H. *The Music of Liszt*. London, 1954.
NEWMAN, E. *Wagner as Man and Artist*. London, 1924.
GUTMAN, R. W. *Richard Wagner: The Man, His Mind and His Music*. London, 1968.
WALKER, F. *Hugo Wolf*. London, 1951.
MAR, N. DEL. *Richard Strauss*. 2 vols. London, 1962–9.
REDLICH, H. F. *Bruckner and Mahler*. London, 1955.
REICH, W. *Life and Work of Alban Berg*. London, 1965.
WELLESZ, E. *Arnold Schoenberg*. New York, 1969.

Index